SECOND BOOK

LATIN
FOR AMERICANS

B.L. ULLMAN
CHARLES HENDERSON, JR.
NORMAN E. HENRY

SEVENTH EDITION

GLENCOE
McGraw-Hill

New York, New York   Columbus, Ohio   Mission Hills, California   Peoria, Illinois

SECOND BOOK

LATIN

FOR AMERICANS

ABOUT THE AUTHORS:

B.L. ULLMAN enjoyed a distinguished career of teaching and scholarship at the Universities of Pittsburgh, Iowa, Chicago, and North Carolina. An authority on all aspects of the Roman world, ancient, medieval, and Renaissance, he was also a pioneer in modern methods of teaching elementary Latin.

CHARLES HENDERSON, Jr. collaborated with Professor Ullman in the previous revisions of this book. He has taught at New York University, the University of North Carolina, and at Smith College.

NORMAN E. HENRY, collaborator with Professor Ullman in earlier editions of the *Latin for Americans* series, taught for many years at the Peabody High School, Pittsburgh, and contributed material that had been tested in high-school classrooms.

A revision of *Latin for Americans, Second Book*, by B.L. Ullman, Charles Henderson, Jr. (1962, 1968, and 1981 editions), and Norman E. Henry, Copyright © 1942, 1950, 1956, 1959, 1962, 1968, and 1981 by Macmillan Publishing Co., Inc.

Send all inquiries to:
Glencoe
15319 Chatsworth Street
P.O. Box 9509
Mission Hills, CA 91395-9509

ISBN 0-02-646009-2

5 6 7 8 9   95

CONTENTS

v

INTRODUCTION

In content, theme, and organization, this edition of *Latin for Americans, Second Book* retains the emphasis earlier editions have placed upon American ideals and their classical background. The textbook makes comparisons between ancient and modern ways of life, upon English vocabulary-building through the study of Latin roots, and upon thorough and yet simple explanations of the similarities and differences between English and Latin grammar. The reading selections are often accompanied by exercises intended to help the student analyze the real sense of what is being said, to develop a feeling for the variety of meanings possible in many Latin words, depending upon the context, and to instill the confidence to use the full resources of his or her own English vocabulary.

It is not intended that all the Latin readings be completed by every class. The first three units present virtually all the essentials of second-year grammar, and the teacher should feel a certain freedom thereafter in matching the readings to the interests and abilities of the class. The wealth of material provides an ample choice for both regular classwork and for additional assignments to the better students. The reading in Caesar can well be postponed until the second semester, and there should be no need to feel that it must all be done. Numerous new color photos replace those found in earlier editions, providing visual appeal and reinforcement to the reading topics.

The *Workbook,* authored by Donald Peet and Marcia Stille, is a new ancillary component offering a wealth of supplemental practice. Both the Teacher's Manual and Key, and the Teacher's Key to the Progress Tests have been combined into one ancillary component, the *Teacher's Resource Guide*. The *Progress Tests* and a set of eight tapes are equally usable with this revision.

UNIT I

A ROMAN FAMILY

This study of a Roman temple is a watercolor by the French artist Georges Chedanne (1861–1940). In the background are typical battle scenes in honor of a Roman hero or deity. In the foreground, from left to right, we see the statues of Apollo, Mercury, and Diana. The Romans admired many aspects of Greek culture, and recognized numerous Greek gods, whom they knew by different names. Apollo had no Roman counterpart.

Lesson I

1. PŪBLIUS AND SECUNDA

SECUNDA: Ubi fuistī, Pūblī?

PŪBLIUS: In Forō Rōmānō fuī, Secunda.

SECUNDA: Quem ibi vīdistī, Pūblī?

PŪBLIUS: Patrem nostrum et Augustum, prīncipem cīvitātis, vīdī,
5 illum quī pācem cōnstituit. Nōnne dē hāc pāce audīvistī? "Pāx
Augusta" [1] ā populō grātō appellātur.

SECUNDA: Sī Augustus prīnceps cīvitātis est, estne pater noster, P.
Caecilius Rūfus, prīnceps familiae?

PŪBLIUS: Ita est; nōn autem prīnceps sed paterfamiliās [2] appel-
10 lātur. Māter nostra Fulvia māterfamiliās [2] est.

SECUNDA: Quid facit paterfamiliās?

PŪBLIUS: Ille tōtam familiam regit—et līberōs et servōs. Etiam
deōs familiae colit et sōlus omnia negōtia gerit. Auctōritās patris,
quae ā nōbīs Rōmānīs "patria [3] potestās" appellātur, maxima est.
15 Sī servum aut fīlium interficere cupit, potestātem habet. Sed nōn
timēre dēbēs, nam hōc tempore nūllī patrēs Rōmānī id cupiunt.
Pater noster bonus, nōn dūrus est. Nōs eum amāmus et omnēs servī
eum amant.

SECUNDA: Ubi nunc pater est?

20 PŪBLIUS: In Forō negōtia pūblica gerit; quondam mīles fuit.
Nōbilis et īnsignis est. Sed quid tū hodiē fēcistī, Secunda?

SECUNDA: Cum sorōre nostrā maiōre Caeciliā eram. Ea dē officiīs
mātris nostrae verba fēcit. Māter domina servārum est et labōrem
eārum regit. Ā patre nostrō semper cōnsulitur, nam docta ācrisque
25 est. Posteā māter mē docuit, nam puellae nōn in lūdum mittuntur.
Māter mē docuit dē factīs quae memoriā tenuit et dē hominibus
clārīs quōs ipsa nōvit et dē eīs dē quibus in librīs lēgit.

---

[1] So called after the emperor Augustus, who brought about a long period of
peace after many years of civil war.

[2] The second part of the word is an old genitive form; *paterfamilias* and
materfamilias are used in English.

[3] Adjective: *the father's power.*

2

Scala/Art Resource

The *ātrium* of the House of the Faun at Pompeii. Typically, the *ātrium* had a funnel-shaped roof designed so that rainwater would drain into the shallow pool called the *impluvium* (foreground), then to a cistern to be used for household purposes. In the distance, we can see the peristyle, or open area, at the rear of the house, where there was usually a garden and a fountain. The basic design of the Roman house can still be seen today in Italy and in other former Roman provinces in Europe.

Pūblius: Bene. Quid aliud māter docuit?

Secunda: Dē patre nostrō docuit. Pater "iūs trium līberōrum" [4] obtinuit, quod trēs līberōs habet, mē et tē et Caeciliam. Hoc iūs ab 30

---

[4] Fathers having three children were exempted from certain taxes and were given preference in official positions. Compare modern income tax exemptions for married men with children.

Augustō datum est quod in paucīs nōbilibus familiīs hōc tempore multī līberī sunt, et quod Augustus maiōrem esse numerum optimōrum cīvium Rōmānōrum cupit. Sed tū, Pūblī, quī iam vir es, quid nunc faciēs?

35 PŪBLIUS: Studia in lūdō nostrō perfēcī; iam in Graeciam, ubi clārae scholae sunt, nāvigāre parō.

SECUNDA: Ōh, fēlīx tū. Ego quoque in Graeciam nāvigāre cupiō.

PŪBLIUS: Hodiē alia in mente volvō, nam crās optimus diēs aderit.

SECUNDA: Quid est hoc?

40 PŪBLIUS: Sī bona puella eris, iam cognōscēs.

QUESTIONS

1. What legal right did a Roman father have?
2. What was the name of Secunda's father?
3. Whom did the Romans include under "family"?
4. Describe Fulvia's household duties.
5. Compare and contrast Roman and American family life.

2. Form Review

Nouns and adjectives of the first and second declensions (564, 565, 571).

Present, imperfect, and future indicative active of the first and second conjugations (585, 586).

Present, imperfect, and future indicative of sum (588).

Practice

1. Decline agricola līber, officium dūrum.
2. Tell the form of servō, paucīs, optimōrum, familiā, fīlī, fīliae, fīliī, virī, līberōs, negōtiīs.
3. Give the second person singular of obtineō and the third person plural of nāvigō in the present, imperfect, and future indicative active.

3. Syntax Review

Subject and predicate nominative (597).
Agreement of adjectives (596, 1).
Direct object (600, 1).
Ablative of "place where" (601, 14).
Ablative of "time when" (601, 15).
Apposition (596, 5).

4. Translation

1. The slaves at that time often had harsh masters.
2. Do you not wish to hear about Publius, son of Rufus?
3. The mother taught the daughters, and the father the sons.
4. Rufus consulted Fulvia about the duties of the children and slaves.
5. There were few children in many Roman families in the time of Augustus.

5. Vocabulary Review

appellō	habeō	obtineō	servus
doceō	līberī	officium	teneō
dūrus	nāvigō	paucī	timeō
fīlius	negōtium	populus	vir

The Vocabulary Review words in Unit I should already be familiar. If you have forgotten any, look them up in the Latin-English Vocabulary, memorizing the meanings and the *essential facts* about each word, i.e., if a noun, its nominative, genitive, and gender; if a verb, its principal parts; if a preposition, the case used with it, etc. Memorize the words above, enter them in your vocabulary notebook, and add English derivatives.

6. Word Study: Bases

Many English words in the singular retain the exact form of the Latin original, even though the meaning may have changed: *arena, radius, victor, impetus, species.* Many even retain the Latin ending in the plural.

Other English words preserve only the Latin base: *duct, legion, long, tend, timid.* Others preserve the Latin base plus silent –e; *mode, grave, produce, dire.* Still others show a minor change of spelling in the base: *boon* (**bonus**), *example* (**exemplum**), *pair* (**pār**), *obtain* (**obtineō**).

Give two more examples of each of the four types of derivatives presented above. The next stage will be to review the prefixes and suffixes commonly attached to the bases of Latin words.

7. READING IN THE LATIN WORD ORDER

When you read or listen to English you naturally take in the words as they come. So it is in Latin. When Romans were conversing they understood each other as the words were spoken. They did not stop to look first for the subject, then for the verb; that would have been impossible. In reading as in speaking they understood the meaning of the words in their Latin order. *And you should try to do the same.* The next page will show you how.

Pūblius, hīs rēbus impulsus, litterās longās prīmā nocte ad patrem amīcī mittit.

Just take the words *as they come; at the same time, try to see what words belong together in phrases:*

Pūblius: The ending shows that it is nominative singular—for this reason it is probably the subject. In English, it will probably come first.

hīs rēbus: These words seem to go together (demonstrative and noun) and are either dative or ablative plural. You have to wait until you read more of the sentence, however, before their meaning will be clear.

impulsus: This word, which is nominative singular masculine, looks like "impulse," which comes from the Latin verb meaning "impel." It must agree with **Pūblius,** since it has the same gender, number, and case. The punctuation shows that **hīs rēbus** depends upon it; the latter is therefore the ablative of means. The sentence so far reads: "Publius, impelled by these things (facts)."

litterās longās: These words clearly belong together, both being in the same case, number, and gender. They are in the accusative plural and must be the direct object of some verb or else the subject of an infinitive—we cannot tell which until we go on.

prīmā nocte: The quantity of the a in **prīmā** shows that it is ablative singular in agreement with **nocte.** The latter suggests "nocturnal" but is a noun. The phrase, therefore, probably means "on the first night"—or could it possibly mean "at the first (part of) the night"?

ad patrem amīcī: The sense seems clear as it stands: "to the father of (his) friend," for **ad** always is followed by the accusative and **patrem** must be its object; **amīcī** is genitive singular and evidently depends upon **patrem.**

mittit: At last the sense of the whole passage is clear! **Mittit** is the verb and it agrees with the first word, **Pūblius,** for it is third singular active. Now it is evident that **litterās longās** is the direct object of **mittit.** All the words seem to fall into line and make sense just as they stand.

We notice, as we go over the words with the thought of the whole sentence more or less clearly in mind, that the first meaning of a word is not always the best, and that the general sense of the passage (i.e., the "context") helps one decide the exact meaning to be given to each word. The complete sentence reads as follows:

Publius, urged by these considerations, sends a long letter at evening to the father of his friend.

The experience with **litterās** shows that we must not forget a word that has not been fully explained; this is like "carrying" a number in adding up a column of figures or in multiplying.

If you adopt the plan just described you will soon be able to grasp the thought naturally, and more or less automatically.

6

Augustus as shown on a cameo now in the British Museum. "He found the city (Rome) built of brick and left it built of marble."

Lesson II

8. A NEW COUSIN.[1]

Lūx erat: Pūblius praeceps ad patrem P. Caecilium cucurrit et eī
salūtem dīxit.

"Cūr properās?" pater rogāvit.

"Nōnne memoriā tenēs? Tempus adest quō Q. Fūrius erit noster."

Q. Fūrius amīcus firmus Pūblī erat. Familia Quīntī humilis fuit. 5
Pater eius sex līberōs sed pecūniam nōn magnam habuit. M. Caecilius,
frāter P. Caecilī, magnam pecūniam sed nūllōs līberōs habuit.

"Nōnne cupis fīlium adoptāre?" Pūblius Mārcō dīxerat.

"Certē," respondit Mārcus. Omnēs Rōmānī fīliōs habēre cupiēbant,
quod fīliī nōmen familiae servābant, deōs familiae colēbant, "patriam 10
potestātem" cōnfirmābant. Multae erant adoptiōnēs inter Rōmānōs.
Multī clārī Rōmānī adoptātī sunt. Fīlius minimus L. Aemilī Paulī ā
P. Cornēliō Scīpiōne, fīliō ducis clārī, adoptātus est, et posteā P.

---

[1] An amusing English play based on this story was made by the Roosevelt High
School, Honolulu. It is published as mimeograph No. 671 by the American
Classical League, Oxford, Ohio, under the title "Furianus Gets a Father."

Cornēlius Scīpiō Aemiliānus Āfricānus appellābātur. Augustus [2] ipse
15 ā C. Iūliō Caesare adoptātus erat, et nōmen tōtum quod sūmpsit erat
C. Iūlius Caesar Octāviānus Augustus.

Pūblius Q. Fūrium ad M. Caecilium dūxerat.

"Quīntus puer magnī animī est. Eum adoptāre cupiō," dīxit Mārcus.
"Cum meā familiā habitābit, sed saepe patrem, mātrem, frātrēs,
20 sorōrēs vidēbit."

Id grātum patrī Quīntī fuerat, et nunc tempus aderat. Multī
clientēs ad P. Caecilium iam veniēbant et salūtem dīcēbant. Cum
clientibus et fīliō Caecilius in Forum prōcessit et ad aedificium prae-
tōris accessit. Q. Fūrius, pater eius, M. Caecilius, amīcī iam aderant.
25 Q. Fūrius novam togam gerēbat.

Praetor condiciōnēs adoptiōnis prōposuit.

"Quīntum, fīlium meum, ā patriā potestāte meā līberō," pater
Quīntī ter dīxit.

Tum M. Caecilius dīxit, "Meus fīlius nunc est."

30 "Tuus fīlius nunc est," praetor dīxit. "In tuā potestāte nunc est.
Nōmen nōn iam Q. Fūrius est, sed M. Caecilius Fūriānus."

Omnēs Fūriānō novō et M. Caeciliō salūtem dīxērunt; tum discessērunt.

"Nunc noster Fūriānus es," Pūblius Fūriānō dīxit.

35 "Tibi grātiās agō," Fūriānus respondit, et cum patre novō discessit. Plūra dē Fūriānō et dē Pūbliō audiētis.

QUESTIONS

1. Who adopted Quintus and why?
2. Where did the adoption take place?
3. What was the name of Publius' uncle?

[2] An honorary surname (the "revered" or "reverend"), conferred by the Roman
Senate upon Octavian when he became emperor.

Furius. By mere chance this Roman sculpture bears the name of Furius, and therefore suitably illustrates our story.

Oxford University Press

9. Form Review

Nouns and adjectives of the third declension (**566–567, 572**).

Practice

1. Decline **frāter humilis, potestās nostra.**
2. Tell the form of **condiciōnēs, patrī, sorōrum, omnium, fīlium, salūte, togīs, nōminibus, mātrum, ducēs.**

10. Syntax Review

Ablative of accompaniment (**601,** 6).
Dative of indirect object (**599,** 1).

11. Translation

1. Who came to the Forum with Publius?
2. A new name is given to the humble boy.
3. I shall tell everything (*neut. plur.*) to my father and mother.
4. Publius proceeds to the praetor with his father and Marcus.

Italian stamp with picture of Augustus Caesar.

12. Vocabulary Review

condiciō	lūx	pater	salūs
dux	māter	potestās	servō
frāter	nōmen	respondeō	soror
humilis	omnis	rogō	toga

13. Word Study: Prefixes

Review the prefixes **ab–, dē–, ex–,** and **sē–** (**614**), noting that each has a basic "from" meaning.

Select the proper form of each prefix and define its English derivative:

(**ab**) *–rogate, –vert, –tain;*
(**dē**) *–duct, –cease, –scribe;*
(**ex**) *–tract, –vent;*
(**sē**) *–parate, –cede.*

14. New Words

Reading Latin as Latin of course implies acquaintance with a certain number of Latin words. We shall take it for granted that at the beginning of the second year you know all the ordinary prepositions and conjunctions and several hundred of the most common nouns, adjectives, adverbs, and verbs which occurred almost every day in your first-year work.

In your reading you will probably discover some new words. Your first impulse will be to turn at once to the Vocabulary at the end of the book for their meaning, but that always takes time and should be done only if other methods fail. There are three easier and better ways of getting at the meaning of a new word. Sometimes just one of them, more often a combination of two or of all three of them, makes it possible for you to get the meaning of the word. Try all three before you turn to the Vocabulary:

1. *Think of an English derivative from the Latin word* (about sixty per cent of our English words come from Latin). The English derivative, if the same part of speech as the Latin original, will serve as a stopgap until you can find a synonym which may suit the sense better.

2. If you can think of no related English word, try to *recall a related Latin word;* for example, **amīcitia** suggests **amīcus,** which you already know.

3. If no related English or Latin word suggests itself, *guess at the meaning from the context* and later check your guess by looking up the word in the Vocabulary.

A wall painting from an Etruscan tomb at Tarquinia, northwest of Rome, shows dancers performing to the accompaniment of lyres and flutes.

Photo Nimatallah/Art Resource

Lesson III

15. THE WOMEN HAVE THEIR SAY

Fulvia, māter Pūblī, cum sorōribus eius, Caeciliā et Secundā, Pūblium Rūfumque exspectābat.

"Dūrum est semper exspectāre," Secunda clāmāvit. "Virōs exspectāmus, nihil ipsae agimus. Vīta puerōrum et virōrum grātior est. In lūdum, in Forum, in loca pūblica prōcēdunt. Sed Rōma puellīs 5 inimīca est."

"Quid? Nōnne Rōma clārās mulierēs Rōmānās semper memoriā tenet?" rogāvit Caecilia.

"Vērum est," erant verba Fulviae. "Quis Veturiam, quae Rōmam servāvit, memoriā nōn tenet? Coriolānus, fīlius Veturiae, lēgem prō- 10 posuerat, quae cīvitātī nōn grāta erat. Itaque inimīcī Coriolānum in fugam dedērunt, et is ad Volscōs, hostēs Rōmānōrum, fūgit. Dux Volscōrum factus, ad portās Rōmae veniēbat et urbem occupāre parābat. Veturia cum aliīs ēgregiīs mulieribus Rōmānīs ad castra Coriolānī prōcessit pācemque petīvit. Coriolānus, verbīs mātris 15 affectus, dīxit, 'Māter, Rōmam servāvistī.' "

"Et quī Rōmānus factīs Cloeliae nōn permōtus est?" dīxit Caecilia. "Captīva, ex castrīs Etrūscōrum, hostium Rōmānōrum, fūgit et trāns flūmen trānāvit."

"Eīs temporibus facilius erat fāmam merēre quod Rōmānī bellum 20 gerēbant," dīxit Secunda. "Sed nunc pāx est. Quid mulierēs in pāce efficere possunt?"

"Multa!" respondit Caecilia. "Nōnne Virginēs Vestālēs officiīs sacrīs saepe Rōmam servāvērunt, deīs inimīcīs? [1] Et quis nōn Līviam [2] bonam memoriā tenēbit?" 25

"Sed in Forum nōn prōcēdunt."

"Nōnne Laelia ōrātiōnēs ēgregiās facere poterat?" Fulvia rogāvit. "Nōnne Hortēnsia causam Rōmānārum in Forō ēgit? In bellō cīvīlī triumvirī [3] mulierēs Rōmānās pecūniam dare iussērunt. Sed Hortēnsia in Forō dīxit: 'Cūr nōs pecūniam dare dēbēmus? Nūllam auctōritā- 30 tem in cīvitāte habēmus. Sī hostēs venient, pecūniam vōbīs dabimus,

---

[1] Ablative absolute: *when the gods were unfriendly.*   [2] *Livia,* wife of Augustus.
[3] *triumvirs,* a board of three officials.

11

sed numquam prō cīvīlī bellō auxilium dabimus.' Hīs verbīs triumvirī concēdere coāctī sunt.

"Puerī Rōmānī dē hīs et dē Cornēliā, Claudiā, Lucrētiā, Tucciā,
35 ipsā Caeciliā Metellā nostrā in lūdīs legunt audiuntque, et semper
legent audientque dum Rōma manēbit. Mulierēs Rōmānae bonae
cīvitātem mūniunt. Ubi perīcula venient, parātae semper erunt."

QUESTIONS

1. What did Cloelia do?
2. Who was Veturia's son?
3. Why did Coriolanus flee?
4. To what did Hortensia object?
5. What light does this story throw on the status of women in Rome?

16. Form Review

Present, imperfect, and future indicative active of the third and fourth conjugations (586).

Practice

1. Conjugate **fugiō** and **veniō** in the present, imperfect, and future indicative active.
2. Give the second singular of **gerō** and the first plural of **audiō** in the present, imperfect, and future indicative active.
3. Decline **magna cīvitās.**

An artist's restoration of the Forum, based on the remains shown on page 13. At the left, the Basilica Julia, Temple of Saturn, Temple of Jupiter (top); in the center, the Hall of Records; below, Arch of Septimius Severus.

James Sawders

The Forum as it now is, looking west, from about the same position as p. 12. The Temple of Saturn, the Hall of Records, and the Arch of Severus still stand.

17. Syntax Review

Ablative of means (**601**, 9).
Infinitive used as subject and object (**613**, 1–2).

18. Translation

1. Can girls in these times win fame by good deeds?
2. Coriolanus did not occupy the city with his troops.
3. It was not easy for many Roman women at that time to earn money.
4. Will the men order the women to give money or will Hortensia's words compel the men to yield?

19. Vocabulary Review

afficiō	dō	fuga	mūniō
agō	ēgregius	fugiō	occupō
cīvitās	facilis	gerō	pāx
cōgō	faciō	iubeō	veniō

20. Word Study: Prefixes

Review the prefixes **ad–, in–,** and **con– (614),** noting carefully that assimilation may take place, depending upon the initial sound of the base to which the prefix is attached.

Define: **admoveō, inveniō, confundō, commoveō;** *accede, impel, inquire, comprehend.*

Apply the proper form of the prefix and define the resulting English compound: **(ad)** *–similate, –gressive, –sent, –tribute;* **(in)** *–duce, –pede, –vert;* **(con)** *–fection, –lect, –mission, –rupt.*

13

This statue of the Emperor Augustus is now in the Vatican Museum. The name Augustus, meaning "revered," was a title of respect given by the Roman Senate. Augustus' long reign (31–14 A.D.) brought peace to Rome after a century of civil war. The month of August is named in his honor.

Scala/Art Resource

Lesson IV

21. DAYS WITH BOOKS AND WRITERS

In pulchrō templō Apollinis, quod Augustus in bellō vōverat et posteā in Palātīnō cōnfēcerat, erat bibliothēca pūblica ubi multī librī, et Graecī et Latīnī, continēbantur. Ibi Pūblius et Fūriānus saepe diū manēbant. Saepe per partem urbis in quā librāriōrum
5 tabernae erant ambulābant. Prō tabernīs pendēbant [1] librī ab auctōribus et novīs et nōtīs scrīptī. In tabernīs servī librāriōrum semper librōs dēscrībēbant. Magna taberna Sosiōrum grātissima Fūriānō Pūbliōque erat.

Quondam P. Ovidius Nāsō, poēta Rōmānīs eō tempore grātus,
10 carmina legere parāvit. P. Caecilius Rūfus, pater Pūblī, amīcum poētae nōverat; itaque Rūfus cum amīcō et cum fīliō Fūriānōque ad aedificium in quō Ovidius habitāvit prōcessit. Magnum erat studium Pūblī et Fūriānī; multa enim carmina Ovidī in tabernā Sosiōrum vīderant et explicāverant, et saepe Ovidium ipsum vidēre cupīverant.
15 In viā Rūfus amīcusque multa dē poētīs dīcēbant.

[1] *hung.*

14

"Ovidius poēta optimus est," amīcus clāmāvit. "Ubi hominēs nōmina omnium aliōrum poētārum quī nunc sunt ex memoriā dēposuerint, nōmen Ovidī remanēbit."

"Bonus est, sed nōn est melior quam Vergilius et Horātius, quōs puerī audiēbāmus. Meliōrēs quam illī erant Rōma neque vīdit neque 20 audīvit," dīxit Rūfus.

"Certē, certē, *Aeneidem*,[2] *Carmen Saeculāre*[3] nōn scrīpsit; *Amōrēs* et aliī librī eius grātī, nōn ēgregiī sunt. Sed multa dē novō librō eius, quī *Metamorphōsēs*[4] appellātur, audīvī."

"Augustusne eum librum vīdit?"   25

"Id nōn sciō. Ovidius autem Augustō nōn grātissimus esse vidētur. Augustus Horātium et Vergilium memoriā tenet."

Ad aedificium in quō Ovidius habitābat vēnerant, et Ovidius iam librum novum recitābat. Carmen dē Orpheō et uxōre eius lēgit.[5] Pūblius et Fūriānus cum magnō studiō audīvērunt. Carmine lēctō, 30 ex aedificiō tardē excessērunt.

"Poēta certē est!" erant verba Pūblī.

QUESTIONS

1. In what library did Publius read?
2. Where else did he see many books?
3. How did he come to appreciate Ovid's *Metamorphoses?*
4. Which poets did Augustus prefer?

22. Form Review

Perfect, past perfect, and future perfect indicative active of the four conjugations (585, 586).

Perfect, past perfect, and future perfect of sum (588).

Practice

1. Conjugate video and occupō in the perfect indicative active.
2. Give the third person singular of dīcō and the third plural of veniō in all tenses of the indicative active.

[2] *The Aeneid,* an epic poem by Virgil.
[3] *The Secular Hymn,* a poem by Horace written for the Secular (i.e., Century) Games.
[4] "Transformations," a long poem dealing with supernatural changes, or miracles, from the creation of the world out of chaos to the fabled transformation of Julius Caesar into a star.   [5] See 555.

23. Translation

1. Augustus had completed a beautiful temple of Apollo on the Palatine.
2. Publius had read many books written by Greek and Latin authors.
3. Publius had read many poems of Ovid but had not seen the poet himself.
4. "Ovid is certainly a good poet," said Publius to his father, "but Rome will always remember Virgil."

24. Vocabulary Review

amīcus	cōnficiō	grātus	novus
auctor	contineō	homō	pars
autem	cupiō	maneō	scrībō
clāmō	dīcō	nōscō	videō, videor

25. Word Study: Prefixes

Review the prefixes **re–, prō–, sub–** (614). Only **sub–** is assimilated. **Re–** adds a *d* before vowels and before forms of **dō**.

Define according to the prefix: **recēdō, redigō, reddō, redūcō, prōmoveō, prōpellō, succēdō, sustineō**; *recession, refer, proclaim, provide, subtract.*

Use the proper form of the prefix **sub–**: *–ficient, –ject, –cession, –gest, –port.*

Explain by derivation: *resurrection, cogent, remain, subvention, refugee, affection, repatriation, resumption.*

A few feet and 2000 years separate an ancient Roman tomb (popularly called the tomb of Virgil) on a hillside in Naples from the modern railroad tracks.

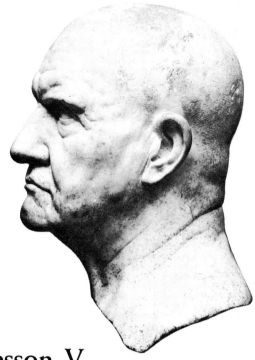

This Roman man looks stern enough to have been a senator. A statue in the Metropolitan Museum of Art.

Lesson V

26. THE LAWS OF THE TWELVE TABLES

Quondam haec verba ā Pūbliō recitābantur, Secundā, sorōre parvā, audiente: "Adversus hostem aeterna auctōritās."[1]

Dē hīs verbīs Secunda Pūblium rogātūra erat, sed hic in Forum excesserat. Itaque Rūfus pater ā Secundā petītus est. Rūfō inventō, Secunda rogāvit: 5

"Quid est 'Adversus hostem aeterna auctōritās'? Pūblium haec dīcentem audīvī."

Pater explicāvit: "Haec sunt verba dē Lēgibus Duodecim Tabulārum lēcta, quae ab omnibus puerīs Rōmānīs memoriae semper mandātae sunt, ab eō tempore quō scrīptae sunt." 10

"Quō tempore scrīptae sunt?"

"Prīmīs annīs cīvitātis, ubi Decemvirī potestātem habuērunt. Diū lēgēs Rōmānōrum, memoriā hominum retentae, nōn scrīptae erant. Sed ā populō Rōmānō scrīptae lēgēs petītae sunt, quod multae gravēs iniūriae ab hominibus verba lēgum nōn scientibus acceptae erant. 15 Cōnsiliō clārissimōrum hominum cīvitātis petītō, hic modus optimus

---

[1] *Against a foreigner the right (in property shall be) everlasting;* e.g., a Roman citizen could obtain legal possession of public land by settling on it, a foreigner could not.

inventus est: trēs virī clārī in Graeciam missī sunt, ubi lēgēs Graecōrum cognōvērunt. Aliī ad Hermodōrum, Graecum in Italiā habi-
tantem, missī sunt. Etiam nunc statua Hermodōrī, ā Rōmānīs posita,
20 in Comitiō stat. Tum summa potestās cīvitātis decem virīs data est,
quī iussī sunt lēgēs Rōmānās dēscrībere. Ubi hī virī, Appiō Claudiō
prīncipe, diū labōrāvērunt, magnum opus cōnfectum est. Lēgēs, in
tabulīs duodecim scrīptae, in Forō positae sunt. Ibi ab omnibus per
multōs annōs vīsae sunt, et ibi nunc videntur."
25   "Eās saepe vīdī. Sed quae sunt illae lēgēs?"
    "Multae sunt—dē poenīs, dē iniūriīs, dē familiīs, dē patriā po-
testāte, dē dēbitīs, dē viīs, dē sepulchrīs—dē iūre Rōmānō. Multae
aliae lēgēs posteā lātae [2] sunt, sed Lēgibus Duodecim Tabulārum
potestās Rōmāna cōnfirmāta est. Ubi illae lēgēs āmissae erunt, tum
30 potestās Rōmae āmissa erit; illīs manentibus, Rōma aeterna erit."

QUESTIONS

1. What were the Twelve Tables?
2. What is meant by "squatter's rights"?
3. Who was the most important of the Decemvirs?
4. Compare the origin of the Twelve Tables with that of the Constitution of the United States.

27. Form Review

Indicative passive of the four conjugations (585, 586).
Participles (585, 586).

Practice

1. Conjugate **āmittō** in the present passive, **inveniō** in the future
   passive, and **mandō** in the perfect passive.
2. Give the third singular of **āmittō** and the third plural of **cōnficiō**
   in the six passive tenses of the indicative.
3. Form and translate the participles of **pōnō, dō, videō.**
4. Give in Latin: *having been said* (acc. sing. neut.); *recognizing*
   (dat. plur.); *going to entrust* (gen. sing. fem.); *standing* (nom.
   plur. fem.); *having been sent* (abl. sing. neut.).

28. Syntax Review

Perfect participles used as adjectives and nouns (610, 2).
Ablative absolute (601, 8).
Participles used as clauses (610, 3).
Ablative of agent (601, 4).

----

[2] *proposed* (participle of **ferō**).

18

The Roman Forum: the rectangular building in the upper left is the Senate House. The columned building on the right is the Temple of the Emperor Antoninus and his wife Faustina.

29. Translation

1. Secunda heard Publius reciting strange words.
2. Having found her father, Secunda asked about the words (which she had) heard.
3. Her father said: "The words (which you have) heard were selected from the laws."
4. "These words were written on tablets under-the-direction-of [3] Appius Claudius."
5. "These laws, placed in the Forum, can be seen by all Romans. While they remain,[4] we shall be free."

30. Vocabulary Review

āmittō	cognōscō	iūs	modus	prīnceps
annus	gravis	lēx	opus	sciō
auctōritās	hostis	mandō	petō	stō
audiō	inveniō	mittō	pōnō	ubi

31. Word Study: Prefixes

Review the prefixes **in–** (*negative*), **dis–, per– (614).** All three may be assimilated. **Per–,** like **con–,** may have the intensive meaning "very," "thoroughly." Define according to the prefix: **inimīcus, impius, dispōnō, diffundō, perficiō, perlegō;** *inaudible, independent, disperse, permission.*

Select the proper form of each prefix: **(in)** *–legal, –proper, –responsible;* **(dis)** *–gest, –vert, –claim;* **(per)** *–manent, –turb, –lucid.* Explain by derivation: *imperfect, incognito, command, differ, invisible, ignoble.*

---

[3] Words connected with hyphens are to be expressed by one Latin word.
[4] Use ablative absolute.

An officer addresses the Roman senate. From the motion picture *Spartacus.*

Lesson VI

32. THE SENATE IN SESSION

Pūblius per iānuam vēnit, ad quam Fulvia māter diū exspec-
tāverat.

"Ubi fuistī?" Fulvia rogāvit. "Tardus es."

"Ad Cūriam Iūliam cum patre prōcessī," Pūblius respondit. "Putō
5 patrem iam ventūrum esse. In Comitiō, ad Cūriam, stābam. Iānuā
nōn clausā, multa audīvī et vīdī. Multī patrēs,[1] inter quōs clārissimōs
cīvitātis vīdī, per viās in Cūriam convēnērunt. Quibus [2] iam sedentibus, cōnsulēs accessērunt, tum Augustus ipse. Post sacrificium nūntiātum est ōmina bona esse. Tum Augustus litterās multās et longās
10 lēgit."

"Dē quō?"

"Audīre nōn poteram, quod multī puerī ad iānuam stābant, virōs
prementēs et clāmantēs. Quem putās eōs dīmīsisse? Fūriānus hoc
fēcit! Puerīs dīxit Augustum, prīncipem cīvitātis, patrēs dē gravibus
15 rēbus cōnsulere; deōs vocātōs esse et adesse; eōs puerōs clāmantēs deīs
iniūriam facere; eōs poenam datūrōs esse—haec et multa alia. Quō
modō, nōn vīdī; sed coēgit puerōs discēdere. Magnam vōcem habet;
puerōs eum timuisse putō. Augustus iam rogābat, 'Quās litterās

---

[1] *senators.*   [2] = **Hīs** (596, 4, *c*).

20

habētis?' et patrēs litterās legere iubēbat. Litterīs omnibus lēctīs, cōnsul verba fēcit: multōs Rōmānōs clārōs ā servīs oppressōs et 20 interfectōs esse; aliīs auxilium ā servīs nōn datum esse; hoc malum esse; servōs cīvis Rōmānī interfectī prehendī et torquērī dēbēre et tum interficī."

"Cuius modī erant sententiae?"

"Paene omnēs patrēs sēnsērunt cōnsilium cōnsulis bonum futū- 25 rum esse; paucī putāvērunt dūrum futūrum esse. Augustus nūntiāvit maiōrem partem patrum cōnsilium cōnsulis probāre."

"Quae erat sententia patris tuī?"

"Verba multa nōn fēcit, et ea audīre nōn poteram; sed putō eum in parte cōnsulis sēnsisse. Sententiīs datīs, Augustus dīxit: 'Nihil ³ vōs 30 teneō,' et omnēs patrēs ex Cūriā discessērunt."

QUESTIONS

1. What did Furianus do?
2. What was the consul's motion?
3. In what way was the meeting of the senate opened?
4. Compare the Roman senate with that of the United States.

33. Form Review

Infinitives of the four conjugations and of **sum (585, 586, 588).**
Quī and **quis (583).**

³ *not.*

A view from the air of the round tomb of Augustus, surrounded by modern buildings.

Fototeca

Practice

1. Give the present infinitive, active and passive, of **sentiō, cōgō,** and **appellō;** the future infinitive active of **accēdō, exspectō,** and **respondeō;** the perfect infinitive, active and passive, of **afficiō, nūntiō,** and **probō.**
2. Give the Latin for *whose* (plur.); *whom?* (fem. sing.); *to whom* (masc. sing.); *what?* (nom. sing.); *who?* (fem. sing.); *by whom* (plur.); *whose?* (masc. sing.); *to whom?* (plur.); *by whom* (fem. sing.); *what?* (acc. sing.).

34. Syntax Review

Tenses of the infinitive (**613,** 5).
Infinitive with a subject accusative (**600,** 4).
Infinitive in an indirect statement (**613,** 4).
Agreement of the relative pronoun (**596,** 4).

35. Translation

1. Publius had heard that the consuls would come to the Forum.
2. The consul reported that many Romans were being killed by slaves.
3. Fulvia asked: "Did your father feel that the consul's opinion was good?"
4. Fulvia did not know that Publius had been with her father in the Forum.

36. Vocabulary Review

accēdō	cōnsilium	interficiō	premō	sentiō
adsum	dēbeō	nūntiō	probō	tardus
auxilium	dīmittō	opprimō	putō	vocō
claudō	exspectō	poena	sententia	vōx

37. Word Study: Suffixes

The suffix **–ia** and its various combinations (**–cia, –tia, –antia, –entia**) form many nouns in Latin. Note the way they change in English.

LATIN	ENGLISH
–ia	*–y* (usually)
–tia (or **–cia**)	*–ce*
–antia	*–ance, –ancy*
–entia	*–ence, –ency*

Give the English forms of **glōria, prōvincia, iniūria, clēmentia, cōnstantia, Germānia, iūstitia.**

What must be the Latin words from which come *memory, providence, science, Thessaly, audience, instance?*

Seated at left, the goddess Vesta; behind her, four Vestal Virgins, in the ceremonial dress which only they and Roman brides wore. The Pontifex Maximus stands at the right. This relief is now in a Sicilian museum.

Palermo Museum

Lesson VII

38. HOLIDAYS

Mēnsis Mārtius iam aderat—ōlim prīmus novī annī inter Rōmānōs. Omnēs Caeciliī servīque eōrum vestibus novīs īnsignēs erant. Negōtium nūllī hominī mandābātur, quod mūnera tōtīus cīvitātis ob fēriās dēposita erant. Pūblius Fūriānusque per Forum prōcēdēbant inter multōs hominēs, aliōs ad templum properantēs, aliōs stantēs, 5 omnēs vestēs novās gerentēs. Pūbliō et Fūriānō [1] aedificia adōrnāta spectantibus,[1] per Forum nūntiātum est Vestālēs Virginēs ignem Vestae cum cūrā exstīnxisse māteriamque ad novum ignem iam collēgisse. Duo virī ad Pūblium stābant; alter alterī dīxit, "Bonum est. Illō igne semper manente, Rōma superārī nōn potest." 10

Nunc vōcēs audīrī poterant: "Saliī! Saliī veniunt!"

Illī per viās veniēbant, armātī et ancīlia ferentēs. Ūnum ex ancīlibus temporibus antīquīs dē caelō cecidisse dictum est. Rōmānī, nōn cupientēs hoc sacrum rapī, iusserant virum callidum alia huic similia facere. Itaque nēmō illud sacrum ancīle nunc cognōscere poterat. 15 Saliī currēbant, ancīlia quae ferēbant ostendentēs. Officium hōrum erat mala ē portīs Rōmānīs expellere.

[1] Ablative absolute.

Aliae antīquissimae fēriae erant multae numerō, variae nātūrā et auctōritāte: Cereālia et Parīlia (vel Palīlia), hae fēriae pāstōrum,
20 quōrum dea Palēs [2] erat, illae agricolārum, quī Cererem colēbant; fēriae Latīnae, ubi omnēs Latīnī Iovem in monte Albānō colēbant; Cōnsuālia, ubi equī pede celerēs in Circō currēbant; Lupercālia, ubi duo yirī per viās currēbant, rīdentēs et omnēs fēminās quās vidēbant verberantēs; Parentālia, ubi sepulchra tōtīus Rōmae adōrnābantur;
25 et aliae. Pontificēs sōlī illās omnēs memoriā tenēre potuērunt, sed Pūblius aliīque puerī Rōmānī multās memoriā tenuērunt, quod, studiīs intermissīs, lūdere potuērunt.

QUESTIONS

1. What did the Vestal Virgins do on March 1?
2. What three festivals had something to do with the food supply?
3. What method was adopted of preventing the theft of the sacred shield?

39. Form Review

Irregular adjectives (574).
Declension of hic and ille (582).
Conjugation of possum (589).

Practice

1. Decline hoc mūnus, alius nūntius, illa lēx.
2. Give the third singular of possum in all tenses of the indicative.
3. Give all the participles and infinitives of ostendō and exspectō.
4. Give the third plural of lūdō in all tenses of the indicative, active and passive.

40. Syntax Review

Ablative of respect (601, 16).

41. Translation

1. Roman holidays were strange in nature and many in number.
2. At these times the business of the entire people was always laid aside.
3. Some hastened to the Forum; others quickly proceeded to the temples.
4. The former looked-at the decorated buildings; the latter worshiped the gods.

[2] Pā'lēs.

The courtyard of the house of the Vestal Virgins, near the Temple of Vesta. The statues are those of some of the chief Vestals. The church in the background is built into the Temple of Venus and Rome.

42. Vocabulary Review

alius	currō	mūnus	pēs	semper
alter	expellō	nūllus	possum	similis
cadō	lūdō	numerus	properō	spectō
celer	mēnsis	ostendō	rapiō	tōtus

43. Word Study: Suffixes

Review the suffixes **–tās** (*–ty*), **–or** (*–or*), and **–iō** (*–ion*) **(615).**

Give the English forms of **nōbilitās, gravitās, condiciō, vocātiō.**

What must be the Latin words from which are derived *utility, facility, paucity, production, retention?*

Give and define according to their derivation four English words formed by adding the suffix *–or* to the present base of Latin verbs which you have studied, and four others formed by adding this suffix to the stem of the perfect participle.

Give five English words formed by adding the suffix *–ion* to Latin verbs and five formed by adding the suffix *–ty* to Latin adjectives.

Lesson VIII

44. SUPERSTITIONS

Quondam Rūfus, in Forum ad negōtium prōcēdēns, caelum spectāvit avēsque trēs in dextrā parte vīdit.

"Signum est!" dīxit. "Fortūna negōtiō meō amīca erit."

Ita accidit: negōtium bene ēvēnit; itaque Rūfus semper putāvit avēs
5 fortūnam bonam eī negōtiō dedisse.

Plūrimī Rōmānī signa et ōmina semper exspectābant—in caelō, in terrā, in flūminibus. Putābant deōs ipsōs ad hominēs somnō oppressōs saepe accēdere et eōs monēre. Multī Rōmānī in templīs cōnsilium ā deīs petēbant; etiam ibi somnum capiēbant. Eī quī nōn valēbant
10 Aesculāpium hōc modō cōnsulēbant; sed omnēs Apollinem hominibus ūtilissimum deōrum esse ob respōnsa eius putābant. Haec respōnsa plūrima, sed nōn saepe clārissima,[1] per pontificēs eius dabantur.

Rūfus, deōs familiae colēns, eadem verba semper dīcēbat, eadem mūnera sacra eōdem modō semper efficiēbat, familiā spectante. Putā-
15 bātur, deīs nōn ita vocātīs, familiam gravissimam poenam datūram esse.

Etiam mortuōs Rōmānī cum cūrā colēbant, quod putābant hōs facillimē et celerrimē ad amīcōs in terrā manentēs venīre posse et eōs terrēre; et mortuōs, sepultūrā nōn datā, per omnēs terrās iter dūrum
20 facientēs, multōs annōs in labōre gravī agere cōgī.

Tempore magnī perīculī deī et virī mortuī in viās ipsās vēnisse dictī sunt. Post pugnam Rēgillēnsem [2] Castor Polluxque in Forum vēnisse nūntiābantur. Caesare interfectō, virī mortuī et novissima animālia in viīs vidēbantur—ōmina gravissima, quae mōnstrāre putābantur fortūnam inimīcīs Caesaris dūram futūram esse.   25

Eō tempore fortūnam graviōrem et sacriōrem esse crēdēbant quam nunc. Virī quibus haec diū bona fuerat grātiōrēs deīs erant (ita putābant) quam eī quibus inimīca fuerat. Omnēs mīlitēs fortius et ācrius sub duce quī fortūnae grātus erat pugnābant—et ob eam causam saepius vincēbant.   30

Rōmānī, mala timentēs, stultī nōbīs videntur; sed nōnne ipsī multa eiusdem generis nunc facimus vel audīmus?

---

[1] The responses of the oracles were often so worded that they could be interpreted in two exactly opposite ways. So they were always right!

[2] The victory of the Romans *at Lake Regillus*, 498 B.C.

1. Compare belief in dreams among the Romans and among people today.
2. Compare belief in ghosts among the Romans and among people today.
3. Compare the belief among the Romans and among people today that some persons are naturally lucky.

45. Form Review

Declension of **is, īdem,** and **ipse (582).**

Comparison of regular adjectives and adverbs **(575).**

Remember that the comparative is sometimes best translated by *too* or *rather,* and the superlative by *very:* **difficilior,** *more difficult* or *too difficult;* **difficillimus,** *most difficult* or *very difficult.*

Practice

1. Decline **idem iter; ipsa lēx.**
2. Tell the forms of **ipsī, eius, illud, eundem, ipsō, eī, haec, id, hoc, ipsīus.**
3. Compare **ūtilis, celer, tardus, humilis, clārus; grātē, ācriter, amīcē, facile, graviter.**

Superstition.

46. Syntax Review

Dative with adjectives **(599, 5).**

47. Translation

1. The Romans consulted the gods themselves about signs.
2. They thought that Fortune was a goddess friendly to some, unfriendly to others.
3. Soldiers fought more bravely under a leader to whom fortune was most friendly.
4. When [3] Caesar was killed, very strange omens of the same kind were seen.

One of the temples to Apollo in Rome, vowed during a plague in the fifth century B.C. To the left are the remains of the Theater of Marcellus, first century B.C. Apollo, the god of prophecy and medicine, was important to both Greeks and Romans, especially to the Emperor Augustus, who built another temple to him on the Palatine.

Anthony Paccione

48. Vocabulary Review

accidō	efficiō	iter	terreō
ācer	flūmen	mīles	ūtilis
capiō	genus	moneō	valeō
cōnsulō	inimīcus	signum	vincō

49. Word Study: Prefixes

Review the prefixes **inter–, ob–, ante–, trāns– (614).**

Define according to the prefix: **intercipiō, occurrō, oppugnō, antecēdō, trānsmittō, trādūcō;** *intercede, interscholastic, opposition, antedate, transcription, transportation.*

Select the proper form of **ob–:** *–casion, –fer, –ject, –lige, –press.*

Explain by derivation *admonition, deterrent, invalid, public utility.*

³ Use ablative absolute.

Lesson IX

50. THE BIG SHOW

Ex extrēmīs viīs, ē Forō, dē summō monte Aventīnō et dē Caeliō, ex omnibus partibus Rōmae hominēs ad lūdōs gladiātōriōs [1] prōcēdēbant. Proximō diē Augustus maxima mūnera gladiātōria datūrus erat; nunc gladiātōribus cēna lībera in lūdīs dabātur, et multī Rōmānī, ad hōs properantēs, gladiātōrēs spectātūrī erant. Pūblius et 5 Fūriānus magnō studiō per viās cucurrērunt. Gladiātōribus prīmīs spectātīs, Pūblius clāmāvit, "Haec mūnera meliōra quam omnia alia erunt; hī sunt optimī gladiātōrēs quōs vīdī."

Nunc diēs mūnerum aderat. Amphitheātrum hominibus complētum est. In īnferiōre parte Pūblius cum Fūriānō sedēbat. Vir Pūbliō 10 proximus dīxit Augustum duo mīlia gladiātōrum ad haec mūnera parāvisse. Pūblius, coniūrātiōnem Spartacī memoriā tenēns, spērāvit nūllum perīculum Rōmae futūrum esse; sed Augustus ipse aderat, et Pūblius scīvit illīus potestātem maximam esse.

In arēnam prōcēdēbant plūrimī gladiātōrēs, armīs variīs īnsignēs. 15 Firmō pede inter clāmōrēs spectantium ad Augustum accessērunt et eī salūtem dīxērunt.

[1] *gladiatorial (training) schools.*

An emperor, probably Theodosius I (378–395 A.D.), holding a victory crown and flanked by two princes, presides over the games.

James Sawders

"Vidēsne illōs decem quī arma eiusdem generis gerunt?" rogāvit Fūriānus.

20 "Videō. Putō eōs esse captīvōs, ex ulteriōre Galliā missōs. Ācrēs videntur, sed nōnne putās illōs septem Aethiopēs melius pugnātūrōs esse? Sed quis est ille? Veturiumne, cīvem Rōmānum, in arēnā videō?"

"Ipse est. Pessimus ille homō damnātus est, quod patrem et amīcum 25 interfēcerat."

Prīmum octō paria servōrum eiusdem gentis, Hispānae, prōcessērunt; sed minus ācriter pugnāvērunt quam populus exspectābat et, omnibus irrīdentibus, ex arēnā discessērunt. Posteā decem Thrācēs cum decem Britannīs melius pugnāvērunt. Ūnus ē Britannīs,[2] quī 30 valēbat et optimē pugnābat, spectantibus grātus erat. Hic, ā Thrāce difficillimē superātus, nōn interfectus est et clāmōribus populī līberātus est. Tum hominēs cum animālibus, animālia cum animālibus pugnāvērunt. Tandem Veturiō sōlō adductō, leō ācer in arēnam missus est. Leō ā Veturiō vulnerātus est, sed hunc interfēcit.

35 Mūnera huius modī nunc crūdēlissima videntur; sed auctōritātem Augustī plūrimum cōnfirmāvērunt, quod populō Rōmānō maximē grāta erant.

QUESTIONS

1. Why did Veturius fight?
2. What three kinds of fights were there?
3. What six nationalities were represented among the gladiators?

51. Form Review

Comparison of irregular adjectives and adverbs (576–577).

Practice

1. Compare **multus, malus, dūrus, parvus, ācer.**
2. Compare **bene, magis, līberē, multum, celeriter.**
3. Give the positive of **optimus, minimus, humillimus;** the comparative of **minimē, bonus, ācerrimus;** the superlative of **magnus, facilius, graviter.**

52. Syntax Review

Uses of the ablative given in the preceding lessons.

[2] See **598,** 3, *b.*

53. Translation

1. Do you not think that these shows were very cruel?
2. Many prisoners and slaves were killed in the arena (while) Romans looked-on.
3. In the gladiatorial schools were very many men sent from the farthest parts of Gaul.
4. To these shows many thousands of the best citizens hurried with the greatest eagerness.
5. In those times condemned (men) often fought with the gladiators and were killed by them.

54. Vocabulary Review

ācriter	cōnfirmō	īnferior	proximus
addūcō	diēs	mōns	spērō
arma	extrēmus	pār	summus
cīvis	gēns	perīculum	ulterior

55. Word Study: Spelling

The spelling of English words is often made easier by considering the Latin words from which they come.

The Latin double consonant is usually kept in English, except at the end of a word: *expelled,* but *expel* (from **pellō**). Give five additional examples.

As assimilation of prefixes often caused a doubling of consonants, it is frequently possible to obtain help in spelling by analyzing the word. Compare *de–ference* and *dif–ference, ac–com–modate* and *re–com–mend.* Give five additional examples.

A modern bullfight in Beziers, southern France. Such fights are similar to those between gladiators and wild beasts in ancient Rome.

Standard Oil (N. J.)

UNIT II

TWO ROMAN STUDENTS IN ATHENS

The Acropolis, in Athens, is the ancient hill upon which the Greeks built their most famous monument to civilization, the Parthenon, which we see here. From this view, we can see the Propylaea, or entrance to the Acropolis, and at the far right the Temple of Victory.

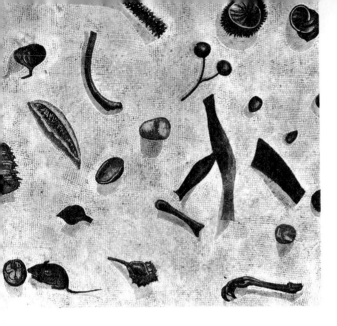

Mosaic floor of an ancient dining room, realistically showing fish and other bones, even a mouse nibbling at a nut.

Alinari-Anderson Photo

Lesson X

56. THE FAREWELL DINNER

Quondam domus nōbilis familiae Rōmānae, Caeciliae, maximē perturbābātur. Pūblius, fīlius P. Caecilī Rūfī, et Fūriānus, fīlius adoptātus M. Caecilī, diū in animō habuerant ad Graeciam nāvigāre et clārōs philosophōs Graecōs audīre; et nunc proximum diem exituī 5 cōnstituerant. Nōna hōra fuit—hōra cēnae. Cēna in ātriō domūs, nōn in trīclīniō,[1] parāta erat, quod adfutūrī erant paucī. In ātrium, in quō mulierēs exspectābant, ē balneīs vēnērunt virī.

Rūfus manibus signum dedit et clāmāvit: "Cēna pōnātur."

Virīs accumbentibus[2] et mulieribus sedentibus, soleae sunt 10 dēpositae, et mēnsa ā servīs in ātrium portāta est. Mēnsā positā, aqua et mappae[3] omnibus datae sunt.

Prīma pars cēnae, prōmulsis,[4] in ātrium allāta est—ōva et lactūca;[5] tum mulsum.[6] Aquā et mappīs iterum datīs, cēna ipsa allāta est. Cibus bonus erat, nostrō similis. Per cēnam multa dē Graeciā et 15 Graecīs dicta sunt.

Magnum erat studium Pūblī et Fūriānī, quod in Graeciam prōcessūrī erant et tempus exitūs aderat. Sed Rūfus verba gravia Mārcō dīxit: "In terram illīs novam prōcēdere cōnstituērunt. Cupiāmus eōs

---

[1] *dining room.* [2] The men *reclined* on couches, resting on their left elbows.
[3] *napkins.* [4] *first course.* [5] *eggs and lettuce.* [6] *grape juice.*

34

vītam dignam āctūrōs esse." "Semper memoriā teneant sē Rōmānōs esse," respondit Mārcus. "Nē iniūstē faciant—tum vītam dignam agent." [20]

"Servus Graecus audiātur," clāmāvit Pūblius.

"Et Graecum carmen canat," dīxit Fūriānus.

Postquam servus carmen cecinit, Rūfus dīxit: "Nunc linguīs faveāmus,[7] et deōs colāmus." [25]

Ubi Larēs in mēnsā positī sunt, Rūfus cibum et vīnum ad eōs posuit. Omnibus stantibus, silentium factum est. Tum, Laribus magnā cūrā remōtīs, secunda mēnsa [8] in ātrium portāta est—dulcia et frūctūs. Cēnā perfectā "ab ōvō usque ad māla," [9] Rūfus dīxit, "Servus Dāvus veniat." Ille in manibus, tum in capite stetit, et multa alia [30] fēcit.

Sed nunc erat tempus discēdere. Servī soleās parāre iussī sunt, et omnēs magnō silentiō discessērunt.

QUESTIONS

1. Where was the dinner?
2. Who stood on his head?
3. Who sang a Greek song?
4. What was the last course?
5. Who did not recline at table?

57. Review of the Fourth Declension

Study **568.** Most of the nouns of the fourth declension ending in —**us** are masculine; the chief exceptions are **manus** and **domus,** both of which are feminine. **Cornū** is the only fourth declension neuter noun used in this book.

Practice

Decline **exitus ipse, illa manus.**

[7] Literally, "let us favor with our tongues," i.e., by refraining from evil words; therefore, *let us keep silent.*

[8] As the dessert was brought in on a separate table, **secunda mēnsa** came to mean *dessert.*

[9] A proverbial expression which came to mean *from beginning to end* (cf. "from soup to nuts"), from the Roman practice of beginning a dinner with *eggs* and ending with *apples* or other fruits.

58. Subjunctive Mood

In English, various auxiliary verbs, such as *let, may, might, should,* are used to express certain ideas that are not presented as facts; sometimes, however, a separate verb form, the *subjunctive,* is used. We may say either, *If this be true* (subjunctive), or *If this should be true* (auxiliary).

In Latin, the subjunctive mood is often used to express such ideas and even to state facts. It has its own forms.

59. Present Subjunctive

The mood sign of the *present subjunctive* in the second, third, and fourth conjugations is **–ā–.** Added directly to the present stem, it causes the loss of the short stem vowel (**ĕ**) of the third conjugation (**pōnam**) and the shortening of the long stem vowels of the second and fourth (**doceam, mūniam**).[11]

	ACTIVE		PASSIVE
doceam	doceāmus	docear	doceāmur
doceās	doceātis	doceāris (–re)	doceāminī
doceat	doceant	doceātur	doceantur
	Similarly **pōnam, mūniam, capiam** (see **586**)		

Note the similarities and differences between the future indicative and the present subjunctive in the third and fourth conjugations.

Practice

Give the present subjunctive, active and passive, of **perficiō** in the first plural; of **colō** in the second singular; of **cōnstituō** in the second plural; of **teneō** in the third singular; and of **audiō** in the third plural.

[11] A vowel before another vowel is usually short.

Reclining at the dinner table was a city custom not always followed in the country and in the Roman provinces. A tombstone relief from Neumagen, Germany.

60. Volitive Subjunctive

Cēna pōnātur (line 8), *Let dinner be served.*
Nē iniūstē faciant (line 20), *Let them not act unjustly.*

Observe:

1. We translate the subjunctive in these sentences by *let*.
2. The mood idea is that of will; it is therefore called *volitive* (Latin **volō,** *I will*).
3. The subjunctive here is, in a way, a third-person imperative.
4. The negative is **nē.**

Find all the examples of the volitive subjunctive in the Latin passage of this lesson.

61. Translation

1. Let us hear about the departure of Publius and Furianus.
2. A great dinner was prepared, during which Publius' father spoke.
3. Then the father said, "Let my boy always remember that Romans are brave."
4. "Let him live a worthy life in Greece; let him remain dutiful and remember home and the gods."

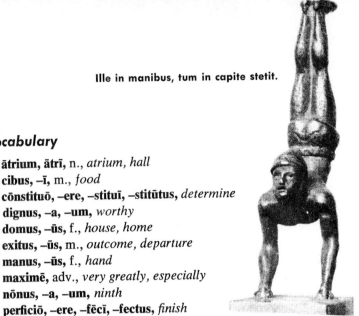

Ille in manibus, tum in capite stetit.

62. Vocabulary

ātrium, ātrī, n., *atrium, hall*
cibus, –ī, m., *food*
cōnstituō, –ere, –stituī, –stitūtus, *determine*
dignus, –a, –um, *worthy*
domus, –ūs, f., *house, home*
exitus, –ūs, m., *outcome, departure*
manus, –ūs, f., *hand*
maximē, adv., *very greatly, especially*
nōnus, –a, –um, *ninth*
perficiō, –ere, –fēcī, –fectus, *finish*
silentium, –tī, n., *silence*

The words in these vocabularies are basic words and should be thoroughly learned. Enter them in your vocabulary notebook and add English derivatives.

63. Word Study: Vowel Changes

In Latin, when a prefix is added to a word, as **in** to **capiō,** or **con** to **teneō,** the root vowel is often changed. This change is carried over into English.

1. Short –a– and short –e– before any single consonant except –r– usually become short –i–.

2. Short –a– before two consonants usually becomes short –e–.

3. The diphthong –ae– usually becomes long –ī–, and –au– becomes long –ū–.

Prefix	+	Word	=	New Word	(English)
in	+	**capiō**	=	**incipiō**	(incipient)
ex	+	**faciō**	=	**efficiō**	(efficient)
con	+	**teneō**	=	**contineō**	(continent)
in	+	**aequus**	=	**inīquus**	(iniquity)
ex	+	**claudō**	=	**exclūdō**	(exclude)

Give some additional examples of these rules by using different prefixes with the Latin words above; give also the English derivatives. Apply these rules to **agō, cadō, caedō, damnō, habeō,** and **statuō,** and give English derivatives. Not all the prefixes can be attached to each of these words.

Lesson XI

64. ON THE WAY

Nunc diēs aderat. Impedīmentīs et servīs parātīs, familia tōta
domum relīquit et ex urbe ad portam Capēnam pedibus prōcessit,
quod ob viās angustās nūllae raedae in urbe erant. Ad portam Pūblius
et Fūriānus et servī in raedam, quattuor equīs trāctam, ascendērunt,
mātre et sorōribus flentibus et omnibus "Valēte!"[1] clāmantibus.   5

Portā relīctā, in Appiā Viā prōcessērunt, quae iam ad flūmen
parvum dēscendēbat. Tum via plāna multa mīlia passuum per agrōs
tetendit. Pūblius Fūriānō dīxit, "Cōnsistāmus ut sepulchrum clārae
nostrae cognātae,[2] Caeciliae Metellae, videāmus." Multa alia sepulchra vīdērunt, inter quae īnsigne erat id Messālae Corvīnī.[3] Vīdērunt 10
Campum Sacrum Horātiōrum, ubi Horātiī cum Cūriātiīs temporibus
antīquīs pugnāverant.

Posteā ad palūdēs Pomptīnās vēnērunt, trāns quās nautae nāvigiō
parvō prīmīs hōrīs noctis multōs hominēs trānsportāre parābant.
15 "Properāre dēbēmus," Fūriānus dīxit, "ut in nāvigium ascendāmus,
nam multī aliī ascendere cupiunt." Ob numerum ascendentium
magnum perīculum erat. "Iam satis est!" eī clāmāvērunt quī in nāvigiō
locum invēnerant; "prōcēdāmus nē omnēs occīdāmur." Tandem

[1] *Farewell!*   [2] *relative.*   [3] *Messāʹla Corvīʹnus.*

Italian stamp showing the Appian
Way and the tomb of the noble
Roman lady Caecilia Metella. In the
Middle Ages the tomb was used
as a fortress.

nautae nāvigium solvunt et omnēs gaudent. Sed ob culicēs et rānās [4]
20 nēmō dormīre poterat. Praetereā nauta dē amīcā suā absentī cantābat.
Duōs hominēs īrātōs nautam in aquam ēicere cupientēs aliī nautae
retinuērunt. Tandem septimā hōrā noctis ad terram accessērunt sed
plūrimī in nāvigiō ad hōram octāvam vel decimam mānsērunt.

Tum Pūblius dīxit, "Celerius prōcēdāmus nē in hīs palūdibus
25 pessimīs vītam āmittāmus et ut noctem quārtam in vīllā hospitis
patris meī agāmus." Hōc factō, sextō diē in forum Capuae, ultimae
urbis Appiae Viae, pervēnērunt.

Quid in hāc urbe accidit? Aliō diē dē hōc legētis.

QUESTIONS

1. Where was the tomb of Caecilia Metella?
2. How many days did the boys take for this part of the journey?
3. Why did the two men want to throw the sailor into the water?
4. Compare traffic problems and restrictions in Rome and in our cities.

[4] *mosquitoes and frogs.*

Even today's traveler on the resurfaced Appian Way is impressed, as the ancient traveler was meant to be, by the tombs wealthy Romans built there long ago.

Anthony Paccione

65. Purpose Clauses with Ut and Nē

1. **Properāre dēbēmus ut nāvigium ascendāmus** (line 15), *We ought to hurry so that we may get on the ship,* or *We ought to hurry to get on the ship.*

2. **Prōcēdāmus nē omnēs occīdāmur** (line 18), *Let us go on so that we won't all be killed.*

3. **Celerius prōcēdāmus nē in hīs palūdibus pessimīs vītam āmittāmus** (line 24), *Let's go faster so as not to lose our lives in these wretched marshes.*

Observe:

1. In the subordinate clauses the verbs **ascendāmus, occīdāmur,** and **āmittāmus** express the purpose of the preceding acts.

2. The conjunction **ut** introduces the positive clause and **nē** the negative.

3. In English, the more common way of expressing purpose is by use of the infinitive (see "to get" in example 1 above, and example 3), which is never so used by Latin prose writers.

66. Translation

1. Is the sailor singing to scare the frogs?
2. Hurry, Furianus, in order not to be left behind.
3. Publius will hurry in order to proceed to Greece.
4. So as not to see Mother weeping, we will not wait.
5. Let us often stop to see famous places near the road.

67. Vocabulary

antīquus, –a, –um, *ancient*
decimus, –a, –um, *tenth*
dēscendō, –ere, dēscendī, dēscēnsus, *descend*
fleō, flēre, flēvī, flētus, *weep*
nē, conj., *(so) that . . . not*

octāvus, –a, –um, *eighth*
palūs, palūdis, f., *marsh*
quārtus, –a, –um, *fourth*
septimus, –a, –um, *seventh*
sextus, –a, –um, *sixth*
ut, conj., *(in order) that, so that*

68. Word Study

From the following English words derive the Latin ordinal numerals (*first,* etc.) and arrange them in the proper order: *tertiary, quintuplet, noon, quartet, secondary, octave, primary, decimal.*

Give the Latin cardinal numerals (*one,* etc.) for the following Spanish cardinal numerals: *tres, cinco, siete, dos, ciento, nueve, cuatro, ocho, seis, diez.*

Translate the following Spanish sentence:

En las (*the*) primeras horas de la (*of the*) noche muchos hombres fueron transportados por navío.

Lesson XII

69. AN ADVENTURE

Capua hōc tempore urbs amplissima atque pulcherrima erat,
maxima omnium in hāc parte Italiae. In plānissimō locō posita, viās
lātās optimāsque habuit. Ut urbem vidērent, Fūriānus Pūbliusque
ūnum diem manēre cōnstituērunt. Homō quīdam [1] eōs vidēns dīxit:
5 "Ut omnia bene hodiē videātis ducem habēre dēbētis. Ego vōbīs
omnia mōnstrābō; deinde vōbīs optimam cēnam dabō; meliōrem
enim cibum in nūllā urbe inveniētis." Puerī auxilium ducis accēpērunt. Sed paucīs aedificiīs mōnstrātīs, homō in viā angustā
pecūniam ex manū Pūblī rapuit et fūgit. Sed clāmōre puerōrum
10 audītō, duo mīlitēs hominem pessimum comprehendērunt.

Itaque puerī grātō animō Capuam relīquērunt. Iter nunc per
montēs et silvās faciēbant, .et via mala erat. Fūriānus Pūbliō dīxit,
"Raedae adhaereāmus, nē ēiciāmur." In hīs regiōnibus nūllī hospitēs
Rūfī habitāvērunt; itaque in caupōnam,[2] appellātam "Ad [3] Ele-
15 phantum," accēdere coāctī sunt, ut noctem ūnam agerent. Sed
caupōna sordida erat, neque dormīre facile erat. Proximō diē hominēs
armātōs in viā vīdērunt; sed servī arma cēpērunt, et hominēs fūgērunt.
Deinde maxima tempestās commōta est, et ad vīllam dēsertam pro-
perāvērunt nē tempestāte opprimerentur. Tandem, quārtō decimō diē,
20 ad portās Brundisī pervēnērunt. In hōc locō raedam relīquērunt
nāvemque celeriter petīvērunt, nē morā impedīrentur et ut quam [4]
mātūrissimē ad Graeciam veherentur. Sed gubernātor dīxit, "Magna
nunc tempestās in marī est. In hōc locō hodiē maneāmus, nē perīculum suscipiāmus." Itaque, litterīs ad familiam missīs, Pūblius et
25 Fūriānus apud [5] hospitem mānsērunt.

QUESTIONS

1. What happened to the boys in Capua?
2. How long did they stay in Capua? Why?
3. How many days did the whole journey take?

[1] *a.*   [2] *inn.*   [3] *At (the Sign of).*   [4] See final Vocabulary.
[5] *at (the house of).*

The Roman amphitheater in Capua, near Naples.

70. Imperfect Subjunctive

The imperfect subjunctive of verbs of all conjugations, regular and irregular, is formed by adding the personal endings to the present active infinitive, as **portāre–m**, etc.: [6]

ACTIVE		PASSIVE	
portārem	portārēmus	portārer	portārēmur
portārēs	portārētis	portārēris (–re)	portārēminī
portāret	portārent	portārētur	portārentur

Similarly **docērem, pōnerem, mūnīrem, caperem, essem** (see **586, 588**).

Practice

1. Conjugate **vehō** in the present and imperfect subjunctive active; **terreō** in the present and imperfect subjunctive passive.
2. Tell the forms of **flēmus, cōnstituātur, dēscenderētis, perficiēmus, sentīrētur, possētis, cōnfirmārēmur, accident, valētis, opprimātur.**

[6] The –e– before the ending is long except before final –m, –r, –t, –nt, and –ntur.

43

TAG DER BRIEFMARKE 1959

S 2.40 + 60g

REPUBLIK ÖSTERREICH

Publius and Furianus might have had an easier time if they had slept in this *carruca dormitoria,* a four-wheeled covered carriage. What are its modern counterparts? An Austrian stamp based upon a Roman relief.

71. Tense Sequence

In English and Latin, a subordinate verb that is in the indicative or subjunctive shifts its tense to match that of the main verb. Study the following examples:

*They **say** that he **is** at home.*
*They **said** that he **was** at home.*

He $\left\{ \begin{array}{l} \textit{studies} \\ \textit{will study} \end{array} \right\}$ *that he **may** learn.*

*He **studied** that he **might** learn.*

72. Tense Sequence in Purpose Clauses

The subjunctive has no future tense in Latin. In dependent purpose clauses the only tenses that can be used are the present and imperfect, as follows:

1. The *present* subjunctive is used when the main verb is *present* or *future.*

Venīmus ut videāmus, *We come that we may see.*

2. The *imperfect* subjunctive is used when the main verb is *past* (i.e., imperfect, perfect, or past perfect).

Vēnimus ut vidērēmus, *We came that we might see.*

73. Translation

1. They remained one day to see Capua.
2. So as not to lose their money, they left Capua.
3. They sought fresh horses so as not to be hindered by the bad roads.

4. They hurried (on) to spend the night in the villa of a guest-friend.
5. They hurried to the ship in order to sail to Greece and not spend another night in Italy.

74. Vocabulary

aedificium, –cī, n., *building*
amplus, –a, –um, *great, magnificent*
angustus, –a, –um, *narrow*
deinde, adv., *then*
enim, conj. (never first word), *for*
hodiē, adv., *today*

mātūrē, adv., *soon*
mora, –ae, f., *delay*
tempestās, –tātis, f., *storm*
vehō, –ere, vexī, vectus, *carry*
vīlla, –ae, f., *farmhouse, villa*

75. Word Study: Suffixes

The following suffixes have no sharply defined meanings, but if you know them you can recognize many English derivatives: **–ium** (English *–e* or *–y*), **–tium** (English *–ce*), **–men** (English *–men, –min, –me*), **–tūs** (English *–tue*).

Give the English form of **studium, officium, aedificium, sacrificium, spatium, volūmen, crīmen, virtūs.**

What must be the Latin words from which are derived *silence, commerce, remedy, prodigy, culmin(ate), lumin(ous), crimin(al)*?

Explain by derivation *amplifier, descendant, immature, manual, moratorium, vehicle.*

Originally the Appian Way went as far as Capua (see map, p. 153). Later it was extended to Brindisi. Along the early stretches leading out of Rome, we see the ancient tombs built by wealthy Romans long ago.

Albert Moldvay

Lesson XIII

76. SIGHT-SEEING AT BRUNDISIUM

Pūblius et Fūriānus Brundisī[1] diū mānsērunt ut sine perīculō trāns mare nāvigārent. Hōc tempore urbem explōrāvērunt. Namque in hāc urbe multa loca clāra erant. Multī ad hunc portum vēnērunt ut ad Graeciam Asiamque nāvigārent—mercātōrēs, imperātōrēs, exer-
5 citūs, nūntiī litterās ferentēs.

Fūriānus Pūbliō dīxit: "Haec urbs clāra est. Nōnne memoriā tenēs Cicerōnem in exsilium ēiectum ad hunc locum vēnisse ut nāvis eum ad Graeciam ferret? Ūnus amīcus eum dolentem excēpit, cui numquam satis grātiās agere poterat. Sed posteāquam Cicerō ex exsiliō
10 revocātus Brundisium[2] diē nātālī colōniae ipsīus vēnit, omnēs cīvēs cum maximō gaudiō eum excēpērunt."

Tum Pūblius dīxit: "Rēctē dīcis. Posteā in hōc oppidō Pompeius cōpiās collēgit ut trāns mare fugeret. Caesar ad oppidum properāvit ut eum interclūderet. Sed sine nāvibus eum retinēre nōn poterat.
15 Prōcēdāmus ad portum et propriīs oculīs spectēmus locum in quō Caesar exitūs portūs impedīre temptāvit." "Bene," respondit Fūriānus. Itaque duo amīcī prīmum ad locum ēditum prōcessērunt ut tōtam regiōnem vidērent. Deinde dē locō ēditō dēscendērunt et portum ipsum spectāvērunt. Quā parte[3] portus angustissimus erat
20 Caesar opera et ratēs collocāverat, sed Pompeius, nē interclūderētur, nāvibus opera rūperat et fūgerat.

"Certē haec urbs multa clāra facta vīdit et multōs et gravēs cāsūs tulit," inquit Pūblius.

QUESTIONS

1. Why did Caesar hurry to Brundisium?
2. What did Publius and Furianus see?
3. Why did many people go to Brundisium?

77. Conjugation of Ferō

The indicative of **ferō** is irregular in the present tense only; in all other tenses it is conjugated like a verb of the third conjugation:

[1] *at Brundisium.*   [2] *to Brundisium.*   [3] *where* (literally, *in which part*).

46

Philip Gendreau

Nashville, Tennessee, has this close copy of the Parthenon at Athens.

ACTIVE		PASSIVE	
ferō	ferimus	feror	ferimur
fers	fertis	ferris (–re)	feriminī
fert	ferunt	fertur	feruntur

The present active infinitive **ferre** is contracted from **ferĕre**, while the passive (**ferrī**) is formed by changing final **–e** to **–ī**, as in other verbs. The imperative is **fer.** The subjunctive is regular throughout; the imperfect is formed according to rule from the infinitive (see **70**).

Note in the vocabulary how different the stem is in the last two principal parts; but they are conjugated regularly (see **590**).

78. Present Subjunctive: First Conjugation

The mood sign of the present subjunctive in the first conjugation is **–ē–**, not **–ā–** as in the other conjugations.

ACTIVE		PASSIVE	
portem	portēmus	porter	portēmur
portēs	portētis	portēris (–re)	portēminī
portet	portent	portētur	portentur

Saul Weinberg

The facing page shows the Parthenon, the ancient Greek temple built between 447–432 B.C., in honor of the Goddess Athena. It represents the highest achievement of Greek architecture. Above: One of the beautifully fluted Doric columns of the Parthenon.

Practice

1. Give the third singular of **ferō** in all tenses of the indicative, active and passive, and in the present and imperfect subjunctive, active and passive.
2. Give all the infinitives and participles of **ferō.**
3. Conjugate in the present and imperfect subjunctive, active and passive: **colligō, cōnfirmō, dēbeō.**
4. Tell the form of **dolent, excipiāmur, nūntiētur, ferrētis, properent, rumperet, cōnstituantur, perficient, moneāminī, occupās.**

79. Translation

1. Publius and his friend proceeded toward the harbor to sail to Greece.
2. "Let us hurry (on) so that we shall not be left behind," said Publius.
3. His friend replied, "Let us proceed to an elevated place to see the whole region."
4. Caesar obstructed this harbor in order that Pompey's ships might not escape.

80. Vocabulary

colligō, –ere, –lēgī, –lēctus, *collect*

doleō, –ēre, doluī, dolitūrus, *grieve*

ēditus, –a, –um, *elevated*

excipiō –ere, excēpī, exceptus, *receive*

ferō, ferre, tulī, lātus, *bear, carry*

mercātor, –ōris, m., *merchant*

namque, conj., *for*

oculus, –ī, m., *eye*

portus, –ūs, m., *harbor*

posteāquam, conj., *after*

rumpō, –ere, rūpī, ruptus, *break*

81. Word Study: Latin in Medicine

Physicians make use of Latin words and phrases every day. The science of anatomy, with which all physicians must be familiar, uses a large number of Latin terms. In writing prescriptions, physicians use Latin constantly, and druggists must be able to understand it. The symbol ℞ at the top of a prescription stands for **recipe,** *take.*[4] Other examples are: **aq(ua) pur(a),** pure water; **aq(ua) dest(illata),** *distilled water;* **t(er) i(n) d(ie),** *three times a day;* **cap(iat),** *let him take;* **gtt.** (abbreviation of **guttae**), *drops;* **sig(na),** *write;* **stat(im),** *at once;* **a(nte) c(ibum),** *before meals;* **p(ost) c(ibum),** *after meals;* **det(ur),** *let it be given.*

Explain *ablative* (as applied to the nose-cone that is freed from a missile), *condolence, corruption, dilated, inoculate, oculist, rupture.*

---

[4] Other explanations given for this are incorrect. The stroke through the R is a sign of abbreviation, like our period.

49

Lesson XIV

82. A LETTER FROM ATHENS

Pūblius patrī et mātrī et sorōribus suīs s. p. d.[1] Sī valētis, bene est; valeō. Nunc valeō; sed nōn semper valuī. Namque Brundisiō post longam moram relīctō, posteāquam nāvis parva in mare lātum prōcessit, tanta tempestās commōta est ut putārem undās altās
5 nāvem frāctūrās esse. Fūriānus autem dīxit, "Nautae ita perītī sunt ut nāvem facile servent." Sed ego respondī: "Hoc nōn iam ferre possum. In īnferiōrem partem properēmus ut ibi somnum capiāmus et clārum caelum spērēmus."

Dēscendimus. Nāvis ita volvēbātur ut mors ab omnibus spērārētur;
10 sed post diem longum et noctem longiōrem ad urbem Graecam Dyrrachium pervēnimus. Viīs tam malīs iter per Graeciam fēcimus ut paene cōnficerēmur. Per oppida dēserta, per agrōs nōn cultōs, per urbēs bellīs cīvīlibus oppressās prōcessimus. Tandem ad clāram urbem Athēnās pervēnimus, quae urbs ita pulchra est ut omnia dē eā scrīpta
15 nōn satis dīcant. Agora, quae est forum Athēnārum, et Acropolis, Capitōliō Rōmānō similis, ita ēgregiae sunt ut nōn satis laudentur. Sed in proximīs litterīs plūs dē urbe scrībam. Nunc dē studiīs audīre cupitis.

Ubi ad portam Athēnārum accessimus,[2] vīdimus multōs vestem
20 scholasticam gerentēs et tantīs clāmōribus vocantēs ut cōnsisterēmus et cum silentiō eōs spectārēmus. "Nōnne petitis scholam Philippī?" "Nōnne petitis scholam Lycurgī?" et alia clāmābant. "Ad scholam Enchōriōnis rhētoris prōcēdimus," dīximus. Deinde ab aliīs relīctī sumus, ab aliīs prehēnsī. In aedificium parvum ductī sumus, et iānua
25 clausa est. Tam diū ibi mānsimus ut putārēmus illōs numquam reversūrōs esse. Tandem līberātī sumus nē perterrērēmur et ab illīs rīdentibus ad cēnam ductī sumus, post quam omnibus modīs lūdi-

---

[1] **salūtem plūrimam dīcit**, *sends heartiest greetings*. These words are regularly abbreviated.

[2] The following description of student life in Athens is based on that given by Libanius in the fourth century A.D., but it is not improbable that it is substantially correct for the age of Augustus.

ficātī sumus. Tum ad balnea ductī vestem scholasticam accēpimus. Posterō diē ad numerum scholasticōrum Enchōriōnis, quī grātus vidētur, ascrīptī sumus. Crās studia incipiēmus. Cum Graecā familiā 30 ad Agoram habitāmus.

Vidētis omnia bona esse. Saepe scrībēmus et saepe litterās exspectābimus. Valēte.

QUESTIONS

1. Why wasn't Publius well?
2. What was the Agora of Athens?
3. Where did Publius live in Athens?
4. What did Publius see on entering the city?

83. Result Clauses with Ut and Ut nōn

1. **Tanta tempestās commōta est ut putārem** . . . (line 4), *So great a storm was stirred up that I thought* . . .

2. **Viīs tam malīs iter per Graeciam fēcimus ut paene cōnficerēmur** (line 11), *We made our way through Greece by roads so bad that we were almost exhausted.*

3. **(Haec aedificia) ita ēgregia sunt ut nōn satis laudentur** (line 16), *These buildings are so remarkable that they are not praised enough* (i.e., *no praise is sufficient*).

Observe:

1. The verbs of the subordinate clauses are in the subjunctive and express the *result* of the state or act described in the main clause.

2. The negative is **nōn.**

3. The tense sequence is the same as in purpose clauses.

Such words as **ita** and **tantus,** used in main clauses to point to subordinate clauses of result, are like signboards which seem to say, "Stop, Look, Think! A Result Clause Is Coming!"

The Parthenon, the most famous of ancient monuments in Athens, was dedicated to Athena, the virgin goddess; its name is derived from *parthenos,* "virgin."

84. GRAMMAR SUMMARY

In Latin	*In English*

A. Purpose Clauses

1. Subjunctive.	1. a) Infinitive; b) indicative with auxiliaries *may* and *might.*
2. Introduced by **ut,** negative **nē.**	2. a) No introductory word; b) introduced by (*in order*) *that,* etc.

B. Result Clauses

1. Subjunctive	1. Indicative.
2. Usually prepared for by **ita, tam,** etc.	2. Usually prepared for by *so,* etc.
3. Introduced by **ut,** negative **ut nōn.**	3. Introduced by *that.*

85. Translation

1. We hurried into a building in order not to see the storm.
2. The storm on the sea was so great that all were frightened.
3. The waves were so high that the ship did not easily proceed.
4. Leaving the ship behind, we hurried toward the city (of) Athens.
5. This city is so adorned with beautiful buildings that it is praised by all.

86. Vocabulary

clāmor, –ōris, m., *shout*
forum, –ī, n., *market place, forum*
ita, adv., *so*
paene, adv., *almost*
perītus, –a, –um, *skilled*
perterreō, –ēre, –terruī, –territus, *scare thoroughly, alarm*

posterus, –a, –um, *following*
prehendō, –ere, –hendī, –hēnsus, *seize*
saepe, adv., *often*
tam, adv., *so* (with adjectives and adverbs)
tantus, –a, –um, *so great*
vestis, –is, f., *clothing*

87. Word Study: Spelling

Difficulties of English spelling due to silent or weakly sounded letters or to other causes are often cleared up by examination of the Latin. Give the Latin originals of the following words: *ascension, assign, comparative, conscience, consensus, debt, deficit, desperation, doubt, laboratory, receipt, reign, repetition, separate.*

Derivatives of compounds of **capiō** have *ei: receive, deceive, conceive, perceive.*

Explain by derivation *apprehension, penultimate, posterity, vestments.*

Fifteen states have towns named *Athens.*

The Porch of the Maidens of the Erechtheum, a temple near the Parthenon. These supporting statues, a substitute for columns, are called caryatids.

Gian Berto Vanni/Art Resource

Lesson XV

88. A GOSSIPY LETTER FROM ROME

M. Caecilius Fūriānō suō. Rogāvistī, "Quid agit rēs pūblica?"
Cōnsulēs proximī annī creātī sunt—Lepidus et Taurus. Ille Augustō
cārus est. Maiōrēs eius erant Sulla et Pompeius, Caesaris inimīcus,
sed Augustus tam concordiam cupit ut memoriam rērum eius modī
5 dēpōnere possit.

Hic nūntius multō gravior erit: Corellius, tribūnus, iam [1] decem
diēs mortuus est. Omnēs amīcī eius spem habuerant eum aegrum
paucīs diēbus diūtius vīctūrum [2] esse, ut frātrem, ex Galliā prope-
rantem, vidēre posset; sed hoc nōn permissum est. Fūnus īnsigne
10 erat—ōrātiō ante domum habita, pompa longa, cornicinēs,[3] plūrimae
imāginēs,[4] rogus [5] multōs pedēs altus (sed tot hominēs aderant ut
difficile esset rogum vidēre), sepulchrum ēgregium.

Ovidius poēta, ex urbe ad oppidum barbarum expulsus, iam paene
duōs annōs litterās supplicēs ad Augustum scrībit, sed hic nōn com-
15 movētur. Augustī autem silentium tantum est ut nēmō causam poenae
Ovidī cognōscere possit. Ovidius librum novum ēdidit, quem emam
et mittam ut legere possīs.

Nōvistīne Calpurnium, quī tantam pecūniam habet ut domus
ūna eam capere nōn possit—illum quī aedificia incēnsa celeriter
20 emit, tum, igne operā servōrum exercitōrum [6] exstīnctō, reficit?
Agrum magnum ēmit. Multōs diēs iam cupiō agrum parvum emere,
ut agricola in ōtiō sim. Pulchrum agrum in Sabīnīs, quī nōn multīs
mīlibus passuum ab eō Horātī poētae abest, invēnī. Quid dē hōc
putās?

25   Diēs omnēs paene similēs sunt. Surgō; clientibus audītīs, in Forum

---

[1] The present tense is used with **iam** where the English idiom calls for the present
perfect: *has now been dead.*   [2] From **vīvō.**   [3] *buglers,* i.e., a band.
[4] *wax masks* of ancestors who had held high public office. These were kept in
a special room in the house and served as a portrait gallery. At funerals they
were worn by hired mourners, so that it seemed as if all of a man's great
ancestors were at his funeral.   [5] *funeral pyre.*   [6] Not from **exercitus,** *army!*

54

prōcēdō, ut aut iūdicia audīre possim aut senātuī adsim; prandium [7] capiō; dormiō; exerceor; [8] in thermās Agrippae prōcēdō, et ibi amīcōs videō. Tum est cēna, tum quiēs. Haec cotīdiē agimus. Quid agit Fūriānus meus?

QUESTIONS

1. Where was Ovid?
2. Why was he punished?
3. Of whom was Augustus fond?
4. Where was Corellius' brother?

89. Review of Fifth Declension

The fifth declension includes comparatively few words. All are feminine except **diēs,** which is usually masculine. **Rēs** and **diēs** occur constantly and should be memorized **(569).** Other nouns of this declension usually have no plural.

90. Subjunctive of Sum and Possum

The present subjunctive of **sum** and **possum** has **–ī–** as its mood sign:

sim	sīmus	possim	possīmus
sīs	sītis	possīs	possītis
sit	sint	possit	possint

Practice

1. Decline **ipsa rēs pūblica, multī diēs.**
2. Give the second singular of **sum** and the second plural of **possum** in all tenses of the indicative and in the present and imperfect subjunctive.
3. Tell the forms of **sumus, erunt, potuistī, posset, fuērunt, possint, esset, poterō, posse, fuerāmus.**

91. Ablative of Measure of Difference

1. **Hic nūntius multō gravior erit** (line 6), *This news will be much more serious* (literally, *more serious by much*).
2. **(Ager) . . . nōn multīs mīlibus passuum . . . abest** (line 22), *The farm is not many miles distant* (literally, *distant by many miles*).

[7] *lunch.*   [8] *train myself, exercise.*

Observe:

The ablative is used without a preposition to express the measure of difference. Find all the examples of this construction in the story above.

Find all the examples of the accusative of extent in the story above.

92. Translation

1. Consuls were elected a few days before.
2. Ovid was banished to a town which was many miles away.
3. For two years Marcus had desired to buy a small farm so that he might be a farmer.
4. For many months Calpurnius had been setting buildings on fire so that he could buy them.

93. Vocabulary

aeger, aegra, aegrum, *sick*
cliēns, –entis, m., *client*
cōnsul, –ulis, m., *consul*
cotīdiē, adv., *daily*
ignis, –is, m., *fire*
incendō, –ere, incendī, incēnsus,
   set on fire, burn

maiōrēs, –um, m. pl., *ancestors*
opera, –ae, f., *work, effort*
quiēs, –ētis, f., *rest*
reficiō, –ere, refēcī, refectus, *repair*
tot, indeclinable adj., *so many*

94. Word Study: Prefixes

For meaning and use of **prae–** (*pre–*), **contrā–** (*contra–, counter–*), **bene–** (*bene–*), **male–** (*male–*), see **614.** Define according to the prefix: *prevent, premonition, predict, preclude, prerequisite, counterirritant, contradict, counterrevolutionary, benefactor, benediction, malefactor, malediction.*

What is the difference between a modern consul and an ancient Roman consul?

Explain *ignition, incendiary, refectory.*

Model of the Temple of the Emperor Trajan (98–117 A.D.) at Pergamum, in present-day Turkey. Under Trajan the territory of Rome reached its greatest extent.

The Temple of Victory is located on the Acropolis in Athens.

Erich Lessing/PhotoEdit

Lesson XVI

95. ALMA MATER

Cum Pūblius Fūriānusque Athēnās [1] iter facerent, multōs Rōmānōs in viā vīdērunt. Paucīs diēbus postquam Athēnās [1] pervēnērunt, multō plūrēs Rōmānōs vīdērunt. Namque plūrimī aliī Rōmānī eiusdem aetātis ad hanc urbem īnsignem vēnerant ut philosophōs rhētorēsque Graecōs audīrent. Tam clārī erant illī quī multōs annōs in hāc urbe 5 docuerant ut multī discipulī ad eōs ex omnibus terrīs venīrent.

Cum amīcī duo paucōs diēs in urbe fuissent et multōs magistrōs audīvissent, Fūriānus Pūbliō dīxit: "Nōnne exīstimās magistrum nostrum Enchōriōnem acūtum et optimum omnium esse?" "Rēctē dīcis," respondit amīcus. "Gaudeō quod patrēs nostrī eum ēlēgērunt. 10 Cēterōs quidem nōn contemnō, sed ille certē optimus est. Eō ōrātiōnem habente, mīrō modō affectus sum. Praetereā ea quae ille docet Rōmānīs ūtilissima sunt. Nam Rōmānī in forō senātūque ōrātiōnēs habent." Tum Fūriānus dīxit: "Etiam ea quae philosophī docent ūtilia sunt ut vītam bonam agāmus. Rōmānī quidem sumus, 15

[1] *to Athens.*

57

Model by Stevens of the Acropolis, showing Propylaea and Parthenon (right).

et Rōmānīs ūtilissimum est ōrātiōnēs habēre posse. Sed etiam hominēs sumus, et vīta bona ūtilior est quam ōrātiō bona."

Cum haec aliaque ab amīcīs duōbus nostrīs dē philosophīs rhētoribusque dicta essent, tandem Fūriānus dīxit: "Cōnsentīmus
20 Enchōriōnem optimum esse. Gaudeāmus igitur quod in eius scholā sumus. Vīvat [2] schola Enchōriōnis!"

QUESTIONS

1. Why was Publius glad?
2. What was useful to the Romans?
3. Why did many Romans go to Athens?
4. What is more useful than a good speech?

96. Past Perfect Subjunctive Active

The *past perfect subjunctive active* of any verb, regular or irregular, is formed by adding the active personal endings to the perfect active infinitive, as **portāvisse–m,** etc. (see **585, 586, 588, 589, 590).**

Practice

Conjugate the following verbs in the past perfect subjunctive active: **incendō, cōnsentiō, possum.**

97. Time Clauses: Ubi, Postquam, Cum

In secondary sequence (**604,** 5) the Romans regularly used **ubi** (*when*) and **postquam** (*after*) with the perfect indicative and **cum** (*when*) with the imperfect and past perfect subjunctive.[3]

1. **Cum Pūblius Fūriānusque Athēnās iter facerent, multōs Rōmānōs vīdērunt** (line 1), *When Publius and Furianus were on their way to Athens, they saw many Romans.*

2. **Cum iter fēcissent, multōs Rōmānōs vīdērunt,** *When they had finished their journey, they saw many Romans.*

---

[2] (*long*) *live.*   [3] Such **cum** clauses are sometimes called descriptive **cum** clauses.

58

3. **Postquam iter fēcērunt, multōs Rōmānōs vīdērunt,** *After they (had) finished their journey, they saw many Romans.*

Find other **cum** clauses in the story above.

98. Translation

1. When Publius was traveling with his friend, he saw many noted men.
2. A few days later the two friends arrived at **(ad)** the most beautiful city of Greece.
3. When they had seen and heard all the teachers, they said that their own teacher was the best.
4. After they had been [4] in the city for a long time, they agreed that their fathers had chosen most wisely.

99. Vocabulary

acūtus, –a, –um, *sharp*
cēterī, –ae, –a, *the others*
cōnsentiō, –īre, –sēnsī, –sēnsus, *agree*
contemnō, –ere, –tempsī, –temptus, *despise*

cum, conj., *when*
īnsignis, –e, *noted*
mīrus, –a, –um, *wonderful*
praetereā, adv., *besides*
quidem, adv. (follows emphasized word), *at least, to be sure*

100. Word Study: Musical Terms

Most of our musical terms come from Italian and thus ultimately from Latin. Explain the following, all derived from Latin words used in this book: *accelerando* **(celer),** *allegro* **(alacer),** *alto, cantabile, cantata, con amore, contralto, crescendo, da capo* **(dē capite),** *diminuendo* **(minuō),** *duet, finale, forte, fortissimo, libretto, mezzoforte* **(medius),** *octave, opus, piano, quintet, ritardando* **(tardus),** *sextet, solo, sonata, soprano* **(super),** *tempo, trio, vivace.*

[4] Use perfect indicative.

Model by Travlos of part of the Agora at Athens; Temple of Hephaestus at right.

From this angle, we see the Propylaea, or entrance to the Acropolis at Athens, and in the distance the Temple of Athena Nike.

Gian Berto Vanni/Art Resource

Lesson XVII

101. ATHENS THE BEAUTIFUL

Paulō post [1] Pūblius litterās ad patrem mātremque mīsit, in quibus multa mīra dē urbe Athēnīs nārrāta sunt.

"Cum ad hanc urbem accessissēmus," scrīpsit, "cupīvimus quam prīmum Parthenōnem, templum Minervae, vidēre. In monte stat quī
5 Acropolis appellātur. Huius montis portae, quārum nōmen est Propylaea, tam pulchrae sunt ut eō tempore diū spectantēs steterīmus. Ad Propylaea est templum parvum in quō est statua Victōriae sine ālīs facta. Cum dē hāc rogāvissēmus, respōnsum est: 'Dea Victōria ita facta est nē ab urbe discēderet.' Saepe dictum est Parthenōnem
10 pulcherrimum esse omnium aedificiōrum; cum per Propylaea prōcessissēmus et ad Parthenōnem ipsum vēnissēmus, hoc intellegere poterāmus. In eō est statua Athēnae, altior quam sex virī. Dea ipsa ex ebore [2] facta est, vestis et arma ex aurō. Ita īnsignis est ut nēmō eam nōn permōtus spectāre possit, nēmō memoriam eius dēpōnere
15 possit. Cum Parthenōnem vīdissēmus, ad aliud templum Athēnae prōcessimus, in porticū cuius sunt statuae virginum. Cum Acropolis relīcta esset, in Agoram dēscendimus. Ibi, inter alia, aedificium ā Caesare Augustōque factum vīdimus.

---

[1] Adverb.   [2] *ivory.*

"Cum in urbe multōs diēs fuissēmus, et cotīdiē multa alia clāra loca invenīre potuissēmus, haec optima vīsa sunt: Stadium; Olym- 20 pīeum, maximum templum Graeciae; Acadēmia, quae mīlle passibus ab urbe abest et in quā clārī philosophī docent. Tempus tam breve est et nōs tam dēfessī sumus ut lūdīs in theātrō habitīs nōndum adfuerīmus; theātrum autem vīdimus, et exīstimāmus id pulcher- rimum esse. 25

"Sed urbs tanta est ut nōndum omnia loca aedificiaque amplissima ā nōbīs inventa sint. Sed quam prīmum ea petēmus et dē eīs scrībēmus."

Cum litterae lēctae essent, Rūfus multa alia dē Athēnīs tam grāta nārrāvit ut tandem Secunda dīceret, "Ōh! Cūr puer nōn sum! Ad eam urbem pulchram statim prōcēdere cupiō!" 30

QUESTIONS

1. Of what materials was the statue of Athena made?
2. What other places did Publius see?
3. What did Publius want to see as soon as possible?
4. Why was the statue of Victory made without wings?

102. Subjunctive Perfect and Past Perfect

The *perfect subjunctive active* has the same forms as the future perfect active indicative with one exception. The first person singular, **portāverim,** ends in **–rim** instead of **–rō.** Unlike the future perfect indicative, the perfect subjunctive has long **–ī–** before the personal endings in the tense sign **–erī–,** except, of course, before final **–m, –t,** and **–nt.**

In forming the subjunctive perfect and past perfect passive, the present and imperfect subjunctive of **sum** are used with the perfect participle:

ACTIVE			
PERFECT			
portāve**rim**		portāve**rīmus**	
portāve**rīs**		portāve**rītis**	
portāve**rit**		portāve**rint**	

	PASSIVE				
	PERF.	PAST P.		PERF.	PAST P.
portātus (–a, –um)	sim	essem	portātī (–ae, –a)	sīmus	essēmus
	sīs	essēs		sītis	essētis
	sit	esset		sint	essent

Similarly **docuerim,** etc. (586, 588, 589, 590).

Alan Oddie/PhotoEdit

The Olympieum is an ancient temple in Athens, Greece.

Practice

1. Give the first singular of **intellegō,** the second singular of **ferō,** the third singular of **līberō,** and the third plural of **reficiō** in all tenses of the subjunctive, active and passive.
2. Tell the form of **prehendātur, cōnsēnsisset, contemnī, contempsī, potuerīs, incēnsus sit, dolērent, ruptī essent, vexissēmus, exīstimārem, sītis.**

The perfect subjunctive, like the perfect indicative, states an act as finished from the *present point of view;* while the past perfect subjunctive, like the past perfect indicative, represents an act as finished from the *past point of view.*

103. Summary of Sequence

Review **71, 72.**

1. **Primary tenses** (referring to the present or future)
   Indicative: Present, future, future perfect.
   Subjunctive: Present, perfect.
2. **Secondary tenses** (referring to the past)
   Indicative: Imperfect, perfect,[3] past perfect.
   Subjunctive: Imperfect, past perfect.

Primary tenses are followed by primary tenses, secondary by secondary.

---

[3] The perfect, even when translated with *has* or *have,* is generally regarded as secondary.

104. Translation

1. When Publius had been in the city a few days, he sent a letter to his father.
2. When Publius' sister had read his long letter, she asked many things about Athens.
3. The city was so large that he had not been able to see all the famous places.
4. A little later, when he stood before the Parthenon, he exclaimed, "This is the most beautiful of all temples!"

105. Vocabulary

dēfessus, –a, –um, *tired*
diū, adv., *long*
exīstimō, 1,[4] *think*
intellegō, –ere, –lēxī, –lēctus, *realize, understand*
nōndum, adv., *not yet*

passus, –ūs, m., *step, pace;*
  mīlle passūs, *mile*
quam prīmum, adv., *as soon as possible*
statim, adv., *at once*

Greek stamp with sculptured frieze of the Parthenon, showing a religious procession.

Greek stamp issued for the first modern Olympic Games (1896) shows Victory driving a chariot.

106. Word Study: Suffixes

For the meaning and use of **–ilis,** (*–ile, –il*), **–bilis** (*–ble, –able, –ible*), **–āris** (*–ar*), **–ārius** (*–ary*), see **615.** Give the English forms of **agilis, fertilis, memorābilis, possibilis, volūbilis, particulāris, necessārius.**

What must be the Latin words from which are derived *facile, docile, delectable, defensible, fragile, noble, popular, primary?* Find five other examples of each of the suffixes *–ble* (*–able, –ible*), *–ar,* and *–ary* in English words derived from Latin words already studied.

---

[4] From now on verbs of the first conjugation whose principal parts are regular (i.e., like **portō**) will be indicated by the figure 1.

A restoration of Delphi. The Temple of Apollo is the building with the long row of columns; below it are various treasuries (see p. 73); behind it, at left, is the theater.

The Metropolitan Museum of Art, Dodge Fund, 1930

Lesson XVIII

107. A REQUEST FOR FUNDS

Pūblius patrī et mātrī et sorōribus suīs s. p. d.[1] Sī valētis, bene est; valeō. Cum magnō gaudiō litterās vestrās hodiē accēpī, quās ante vīgintī quīnque diēs [2] scrīpsistis. Cum litterās lēgissem, Fūriānō eās dedī ut legeret. Cum dē Rōmā et amīcīs nostrīs locūtī essēmus,
5 Fūriānus dīxit Rōmam longē abesse. Sed fēlīcēs sumus, nam amīcōs hīc [3] habēmus, et urbs pulcherrima est.

Vīta nostra tam quiēta est ut paene nihil scrībere possim. Sed tamen ūna rēs est dē quā scrībere necesse est. Potesne, pater, sine morā pecūniam mittere? Doleō quod haec scrībere necesse est, sed
10 nōn est mea culpa. Omnia enim in hāc urbe tam cāra sunt ut paene tōta pecūnia mea cōnsūmpta sit. Enchōriō magister tam amīcus est ut multī mē fīlium, nōn discipulum eius esse arbitrentur. Sum tōtōs diēs cum eō et saepe noctis partem; nam mēcum [4] saepe cēnat. Hīs temporibus dē multīs rēbus ita bene loquitur ut multa ūtilia audiam.
15 Ob hanc causam eum saepe ad cēnam vocō. Hōc modō pecūnia celeriter cōnsūmitur.

[1] See **82**, n. 1.   [2] *Twenty-five days ago* (literally, *before twenty-five days*).
[3] *here.*   [4] *with me.*

Etiam ob aliam causam pecūniam habēre necesse est. Cum ab Enchōriōne multa dē partibus Graeciae dicta essent, dē Delphīs eum rogāvī. Ille respondit omnēs Delphōs propriīs oculīs vidēre dēbēre. Itaque quam celerrimē proficīscī cupimus ut illum locum 20 videāmus. Enchōriō pollicitus est nōbīscum [5] proficīscī et omnia mōnstrāre atque explicāre. Arbitror eum omnia scīre. Ita bene verba facit ut omnēs discipulōs mīrō modō affēcerit. Valēte.

QUESTIONS

1. Why was Publius happy?
2. What trip did he plan to take?
3. Whom did he often invite to dinner?
4. How long did it take his father's letter to reach Publius?

108. Deponent Verbs

Some Latin verbs are *active* in meaning but *passive* in form. They are called *deponents,* because they have *put away* (**dēpōnō**) their active forms: **arbitror,** *I think,* (not *I am thought*). Deponent verbs are conjugated throughout the indicative and subjunctive like the passive of regular verbs of the four conjugations (see **587**).[6]

109. Participles and Infinitives of Deponent Verbs

Note that some of the participles and infinitives of deponent verbs do not conform to the statement made in **108.** The present and future participles and the future infinitive (formed from the future participle) are active in both form and meaning. The perfect participle, while passive in form, is active in meaning.

PARTICIPLES	FORM	MEANING
Pres. **arbitrāns,** *thinking*	active	active
Perf. **arbitrātus,** *having thought*	passive	active
Fut. **arbitrātūrus,** *going to think*	active	active
INFINITIVES		
Pres. **arbitrārī,** *to think*	passive	active
Perf. **arbitrātus esse,** *to have thought*	passive	active
Fut. **arbitrātūrus esse,** *to be going to think*	active	active

[5] *with us.*

[6] In this book the principal parts of deponent verbs are given as present indicative, present infinitive, and perfect participle: **arbitror, arbitrārī, arbitrātus.** Regular deponent verbs of the first conjugation will be indicated by the figure 1 in the vocabularies.

Practice

1. Give and translate the third singular of **proficīscor** and the third plural of **polliceor** in all tenses of the indicative.
2. Give the second singular of **arbitror** and the second plural of **loquor** in all tenses of the subjunctive.
3. Give all the participles of **proficīscor** and the infinitives of **loquor.**

110. Translation

1. When Publius had spent all his money, he sent a letter to his father.
2. He said that his teacher spoke so well that he often invited him to dinner.
3. He wrote that his teacher had promised to set out with him (**sēcum**) to see Delphi.
4. Publius was with him almost night and day, and many thought that he was the teacher's son.

The Stadium and Acropolis of Athens as shown on a Greek stamp in honor of the Olympic Games of 1896.

111. Vocabulary

arbitror, arbitrārī, arbitrātus, *think*
cōnsūmō, –ere, –sūmpsī, –sūmptus, *use up, spend*
longē, adv., *far*
loquor, loquī, locūtus, *talk*
necesse, indeclinable adj., *necessary*

polliceor, pollicērī, pollicitus, *promise*
proficīscor, proficīscī, profectus, *set out, start*
quiētus, –a, –um, *quiet*
vīgintī, indeclinable, *twenty*

112. English Word Studies

Some "space" and "missile" terms derived from Latin were given in Book I. Here are a few more: *antenna* in Latin means "sail yard"; carbon is from **carbō,** "coal"; *detector* (**dē, tegō**);[7] *deterrent* (**dē, terreō**); *exhaust* (**ex, hauriō**); *flux* (**fluō**); *neutron* (**neuter**); *nucleus, nuclear, thermonuclear* (**nucleus, nux;** *thermo–* is from a Greek word meaning "heat") *operational* (**opus**); *radar, radiation, ray* (**radius,** "ray"); *rotate* (**rota,** "wheel"); *sensor* (**sentio**); *vehicle* (**vehō**).

---

[7] Latin words not explained will be found in the final vocabulary.

66

Lesson XIX

113. A WEDDING

Pūbliō in Graeciā studente, rēs grātissima Rōmae[1] agēbātur—
nūptiae Caeciliae, sorōris Pūblī, et M. Iūnī Vorēnī. Paucīs mēnsibus
ante Caeciliīs Iūniīsque in ātrium Rūfī cum amīcīs ingressīs, pater
Vorēnī cum fīliō prō Rūfō et Caeciliā cōnstiterat Rūfumque rogāverat:
"Spondēsne fīliam tuam fīliō meō uxōrem?"[2] Rūfus responderat: 5
"Spondeō." Tum Vorēnus Caeciliae ānulum,[3] Caecilia Vorēnō pul-
chrum servum dederat, et patrēs inter sē dē dōte[4] ēgerant—quantum
Rūfus in animō habēret dare, quō modō pecūnia parārī posset.

[1] *at Rome.*   [2] *(as) wife.*   [3] *ring.*   [4] *dowry.*

On an ancient cameo now in Boston, Cupids playfully stage a wedding. Over
the bridal couple (note their veils) one Cupid holds nuts or fruit, much as today
we throw rice. Another carries the wedding torch, and a third prepares the
wedding couch. This gem once belonged to the Duke of Marlborough.

Courtesy, Museum of Fine Arts, Boston, Pierce Fund

Anderson

This sarcophagus (stone coffin) shows the wedding of a man in the African grain trade. Note the lighthouse (far left), the oar, the cornucopia, and the grain baskets. At the far right is the goddess Africa, with a headdress of elephant tusks. The *pronuba* stands behind the wedding couple in the center.

Tandem diēs nūptiārum aderat. Prīdiē Caecilia mūnera Laribus
10 dederat; [5] nunc, sōle oriente, ōminibus optimīs nūntiātīs, ā mātre ad
nūptiās parābātur, et cum eā amīcae loquēbantur. Māter flammeum [6]
et deinde corōnam in caput Caeciliae posuit.

"Mīror quid frāter meus agat," dīxit Caecilia, "et quid arbitrātūrus
sit, nūntiō dē mē allātō."

15 Nunc Caecilia cum mātre amīcīsque in ātrium adōrnātum dēscendit,
ubi Rūfus et pontifex exspectābant. Cum Vorēnus et amīcī in ātrium
ingressī essent, prōnuba [7] manūs Caeciliae et Vorēnī iūnxit, et Caecilia
dīxit, "Ubi tū Gāius, ego Gāia." [8] Eīs nunc sedentibus, pontifex deōs
(maximē Iūnōnem) vocāvit. Deinde omnēs "Fēlīciter!" clāmāvērunt.
20 "Spērō vōbīs omnia bona futūra esse, vītam vestram longam!"

"Nōn iam nostra est," Rūfus Vorēnō dīxit, "sed tua."

Nōnā hōrā cēna maxima allāta est, et Rūfus nūntiāvit, "Nōs cibō
reficiāmus." Omnēs uxōrem pulchram mīrātī sunt.

Vesperī omnēs in viam sē recēpērunt. Ibi, mātre flente et Cae-
25 ciliam retinente, aliī pompam parāvērunt. Subitō Vorēnus Caeciliam
rapuit, et pompa profecta est, amīcīs canentibus, rīdentibus, "Talas-
siō!" [9] clāmantibus. Cum ad iānuam domūs Vorēnī accessissent,

[5] On the eve of her marriage the Roman girl dedicated her toys and childish
garments to the household gods.   [6] *bridal veil* (flame-colored).
[7] The *matron* who attended the bride.
[8] An old formula, equivalent to "Where you go, I will go."
[9] An ancient marriage cry, the meaning of which is unknown.

68

Caecilia eam adōrnāvit. Postquam Vorēnus uxōrem per iānuam portāvit,[10] Caecilia iterum dīxit, "Ubi tu Gāius, ego Gāia." In ātriō Vorēnus mātrōnae novae ignem aquamque dedit.[11] Posterō diē cēna 30 altera data est, ubi Caecilia deīs sacrificāvit. Familia eius nōn iam Caecilia, sed Iūnia erat.

QUESTIONS

1. What did the priest do?
2. What did the matron do?
3. By whom was a slave given?

114. Form Review

Personal and reflexive pronouns **(580, 581).**

Practice

1. Give and translate the dative singular and plural of **ego, tū, is, suī;** give the ablative singular and plural of the same.
2. Conjugate reflexively and translate the present and perfect tenses of **ego mē moneō, tū tē monēs,** etc.
3. Give the third singular of **sē contemnere** in all tenses of the indicative and subjunctive.

[10] So that she might not stumble on the threshold—an unlucky omen.
[11] With these gifts, symbols of the essentials of domestic life, the bride becomes the mistress of the house.

A Christian sarcophagus covered with Biblical scenes. Daniel in the Lions' Den is just below the central portraits of the married couple.

Anderson

115. Indirect Questions

1. **Quid frāter meus agit?** *What is my brother doing?*

2. **Mīror quid frāter meus agat** (line 13), *I wonder what my brother is doing.*

3. **Patrēs inter sē dē dōte ēgerant—quantum Rūfus in animō habēret dare** (line 7), *The fathers had discussed the dowry between themselves—how much Rufus intended to give.*

Observe:

1. Sentence 1 is a simple, *direct* question, and the Latin verb is in the indicative.

2. Sentence 2 is complex, containing the same question but in *indirect* form, reduced to a subordinate clause, and its verb in Latin is in the *subjunctive.*

3. The subordinate clause is the direct object of the main verb.

Indirect questions depend on verbs of *asking, learning, knowing, telling, wondering,* etc. (**rogō, cognōscō, sciō, dīcō, mīror,** etc.). The regular rules of sequence apply (**604, 5**):

I   Time: 3 P.M.   Place: Schoolroom   *you*

Rogō quid faciās,
I ask (now) what you are doing (now).

Rogō quid fēcerīs,
I ask (now) what you did (earlier).

Rogāvī quid facerēs,
I asked (then) what you were doing (then)

Rogāvī quid fēcissēs,
I asked (then) what you had done (earlier).

116. GRAMMAR SUMMARY

| *In Latin* | *In English* |

A. Indirect Statements

| 1. Infinitive. | 1. Indicative. |
| 2. No introductory word. | 2. Introduced by *that*. |

B. Indirect Questions

| 1. Subjunctive. | 1. Indicative. |
| 2. Introduced by an interrogative word. | 2. Introduced by an interrogative word. |

117. Translation

1. Caecilia wondered what Publius thought about the wedding.
2. Her (girl) friends asked her how much money was being given.
3. She kept-asking herself where Publius then was and what he was doing.
4. When the procession had started, the friends asked themselves how Vorenus and Caecilia would enter.

118. Vocabulary

ingredior, ingredī, ingressus, *step into, enter*
mīror, 1, *wonder, admire*
orior, orīrī, ortus, *rise*
prīdiē, adv., *on the day before*
quantus, –a, –um, *how great, how much*

sōl, sōlis, m., *sun*
studeō, –ēre, studuī, ——, *be eager (for), study*
subitō, adv., *suddenly*
uxor, –ōris, f., *wife*
vesper, –erī, m., *evening;* **vesperī,** *in the evening*

119. Word Study: Spelling

The base ending of the Latin present participle (**–ant, –ent, –ient,** according to conjugation) is used as a suffix in English. All English words derived from the first conjugation have *–ant;* most of those derived from the other conjugations have *–ent;* but some derived through the French have *–ant.* Give examples.

The addition of **–ia** to the base ending of the present participle gives a suffix **–antia, –entia** (*–ance, –ence, –ancy, –ency*). The same rule for spelling which was given above holds true. Give samples.

Explain *ingredient, loquacity, miracle, orient, quantity, soliloquy, solstice, uxoricide, vespers.*

Erich Lessing/PhotoEdit

Praeterea locus ipse pulcherrimus erat—et est. The great natural beauty of Delphi never fails to fill the visitor with a sense of wonder. In the foreground is a Greek theater which was restored by the Romans.

Lesson XX

120. THE TRIP TO DELPHI

Pater Pūbliō pecūniam praebuerat ut is et Fūriānus Delphōs [1] īrent. Cum diēs cōnstitūtus adesset, ad Enchōriōnem iērunt, quī pollicitus erat cum eīs īre. Itaque hī trēs cum servīs aliquibus ex urbe Athēnīs exiērunt.

5   Cūr cupīvērunt Delphōs vidēre? Quod hic locus erat, ut ita dīcam,[2] templum tōtīus Graeciae. In hōc locō erat īnsigne ōrāculum Apollinis. Multī ex omnibus partibus terrae vēnērunt ut ōrāculum cōnsulerent. Praetereā locus ipse pulcherrimus erat—et est.

Itaque amīcī nostrī duo per sacram viam eunt quae ad urbem 10 clāram Eleusim dūcit et ex illā urbe ad aliam urbem clāram, Thēbās, prōcēdunt. Cum post paucōs diēs ad fīnem itineris vēnissent, gaudiō et admīrātiōne complētī sunt. Namque urbs sub monte Parnassō posita pulcherrima erat. Fōrmam maximī theātrī habēbat. Ab [3] ūnā parte erant saxa alta; ab alterā, arborēs et flūmen et alter mōns.

---

[1] *to Delphi.*   [2] *so to speak;* literally, *to say* (*it*) *so.*   [3] *on.*

Haec omnia diū mīrātī ad fontem īnsignem Castalium vēnērunt. 15
Omnēs quī ōrāculum cōnsulēbant aquā huius fontis sē lavābant. Hic
fōns Apollinī Mūsīsque sacer erat.

Tum viātōrēs nostrī aedificia aliqua cōnspexērunt quae thēsaurī [4]
appellāta sunt. Haec cīvitātēs quaedam Graecae propter victōriam
aliquam aedificāvērunt. Auctor quīdam Graecus dīxit Cnidiōs nōn ob 20
rēs in proeliō bene gestās thēsaurum aedificāvisse sed ut opēs suās
ostenderent. In hīs aedificiīs et in aliīs partibus urbis erant tria mīlia
statuārum.

Hīs aedificiīs vīsīs, templum Apollinis ingressī statim sententiās [5]
septem sapientium Graecōrum [6] litterīs magnīs īnscrīptās cōnspexē- 25
runt: "Cognōsce tē ipsum," "nē quid nimis," [7] et cētera. Sed in
ōrāculum ipsum ingredī nōn potuērunt, quod ōrāculum tam sacrum
erat ut paucī ingrederentur.

Itaque ad fontem rediērunt et eum et saxa et arborēs et caelum
iterum mīrātī ad cēnam vesperī discessērunt.   30

[4] *treasuries.*   [5] *sayings.*   [6] For the "Seven Wise Men" see **126.**
[7] *nothing in excess.* What literally?

**The Treasury of the Athenians at Delphi (late sixth century B.C.). Here the
Athenians housed their trophies and offerings to Apollo.**

The Sphinx of the Naxians now guards a modern restoration of the Treasury of the Siphnians in the Delphi Museum. Note the two caryatids used as central columns. Out of respect for Apollo and in thanks for the oracle's good counsel, many Greek states built these miniature temples to house their records, trophies, and treasure on the sacred soil of Delphi.

Delphi Museum

QUESTIONS

1. What spring did the boys see?
2. What cities did they see after they left Athens?
3. Why did the Greek states erect buildings at Delphi?
4. What mottoes did the boys see in the temple of Apollo?

121. Indefinite Pronouns

Indefinite pronouns and adjectives refer to persons and objects in an indefinite way.

1. The most indefinite of all Latin pronouns is **quis** (declined like the interrogative **quis;** see **583**), *some, any,* used only after certain words (**sī, nisi,** and **nē** in this book): **sī quis,** *if anyone;* **nē quid,** *(that) not anything.*

2. **Aliquis,** a compound of **quis,** often means *"some one—I don't know who."* It is declined exactly like **quis,** except that it has **aliqua** in the nominative and accusative plural neuter.

3. **Quīdam,** *a certain one,* is less indefinite than **quis** and **aliquis.** It often means "some one whose name I can mention but won't"; sometimes it is almost like our indefinite article *a.* It is declined like **quī** [8]—the suffix **–dam** being indeclinable.

For full declension of **aliquis** and **quīdam** see **584**.

---

[8] Except in accusative singulár **quendam, quandam, quiddam,** genitive plural **quōrundam, quārundam, quōrundam.**

122. Conjugation of Eō

Eō is irregular in the present, future, and perfect tenses:

PRESENT		FUTURE		PERFECT	
eō	īmus	ībō	ībimus	iī	iimus
īs	ītis	ībis	ībitis	īstī	īstis
it	eunt	ībit	ībunt	iit	iērunt (–ēre)
		For full conjugation see **591.**			

Note that the stem vowel **ī–** is changed to **e–** before **a, o, u.** As **eō** is intransitive, passive forms are rare.

Practice

1. Decline **duo oculī, trēs arborēs, mīlle cōnsulēs, duo mīlia vīllārum.**
2. Give the third singular of **eō,** the first plural of **exeō,** and the third plural of **redeō** in all tenses of the active indicative and subjunctive.

123. Translation

1. Some often returned to see the place and to consult the oracle.
2. Delphi was so famous that many thousands of men went to see it.
3. This beautiful place was called by some the temple of entire Greece.
4. Publius got money from his father in order to go to the city (of) Delphi.
5. If any one desired to consult the oracle about a certain matter, do you know what he did first?

124. Vocabulary

aliquis, aliquid, *some (one), any*
arbor, –oris, f., *tree*
compleō, –ēre, –ēvī, –ētus, *fill*
eō, īre, iī, itūrus, *go*
ops, opis, f., *aid;* pl., *wealth*
praebeō, –ēre, –uī, –itus, *furnish*

propter, prep. w. acc., *on account of*
quīdam, quaedam, quiddam and (adj.) **quoddam,** *certain (one)*
redeō, –īre, rediī, reditūrus, *go back, return*
saxum, –ī, n., *rock*

125. Word Study

1. Legal phrases in English:

Supersedeas, (*I command that*) *you suspend* (*proceedings*).
Ne exeat, *Let him not go out* (*of the jurisdiction of the court*).
Caveat emptor, *Let the buyer beware* (*for he buys at his own risk*).
Scire facias, (*I demand that*) *you cause to know* (*why a certain court action should not be carried out*).

Habeas corpus, (*I command that*) *you have the body* (*of a certain person brought into court*), a writ issued by a judge to see whether a person is justly imprisoned.

Look up the meanings of **mandamus, nunc pro tunc, post mortem, prima facie, pro bono publico.**

2. Place names:

There are towns named *Delphi* in Indiana and Pennsylvania, and one named *Delphi Falls* in New York. Iowa, North Carolina, and Ohio have towns named *Castalia* and Tennessee has *Castalian Springs. Parnassus* is a town in Virginia and also in Pennsylvania.

126. THE SEVEN WISE MEN OF GREECE

A common practice of the scholars of antiquity was the drawing up of lists (called *canons*) of persons considered outstanding in their fields, as we have our Halls of Fame. Thus there have been preserved for us lists of "The Ten Attic Orators," "The Nine Lyric Poets," and "The Seven Wise Men." Here is one version of the names of the Seven Wise Men, with one of the sayings each is supposed to have made famous. Many of these men were politicians or poets, as well as philosophers; all them lived between 620 and 550 B.C.

Cleobulus of Rhodes	*"Moderation is the chief good"*
Periander of Corinth	*"Forethought in all things"*
Pittacus of Mytilene	*"Know your opportunity"*
Bias of Priene	*"Too many workers spoil the work"*
Thales of Miletus	*"To go bond brings ruin"*
Chilon of Sparta	*"Know thyself"*
Solon of Athens	*"Nothing in excess"*

The last three mottoes are said to have been inscribed on the temple of Apollo at Delphi. Give some modern counterparts of these sayings.

Delphi, the Castalian Spring. The spring was sacred to Apollo and the Muses and so came to represent poetic inspiration.

Erich Lessing/PhotoEdit

A bust of Pericles with his name on it, written in Greek letters and spelled Perikles.

Metropolitan Museum of Art

Lesson XXI

127. TOTALITARIANISM AND DEMOCRACY

Quōdam diē Pūblius Fūriānusque cum aliīs adulēscentibus dē Spartā Athēnīsque loquēbantur. "Certē omnibus concēdendum est Spartānōs antīquōs omnium fortissimōs fuisse," ūnus ē Graecīs dīxit; "nōnne Leōnidam memoriā tenēs, quī cum CCC cīvibus apud Thermopylās [1] tam fortiter pugnāvit? Alacrī animō suōs ad id proelium 5 hortātus est quō peritūrī erant."

"Ea quae dīcis nōn negō," alter dīxit, "sed Athēniēnsēs quoque fortēs fuērunt. Fortēs quidem Spartānī fuērunt sed aliās virtūtēs nōn habuērunt. Lycurgus,[2] dux ille antīquus, ob sevēritātem lēgum accūsandus est. 10

Deinde Fūriānus rogāvit quid Pūblius arbitrārētur. "Concēdō Athēniēnsēs meliōrēs esse," hic respondit. "Vīta dūra puerīs Spartānīs agenda erat. Septem annōs nātī [3] mātrēs relinquēbant ut ad bellum instituerentur. Cēnās ipsī parābant ex pessimīs cibīs, nam Spartānī crēdēbant famem optimum condīmentum cibī esse. Puerī flagellīs [4,15] caesī sunt, patribus ad patientiam hortantibus, ut dolōrem ferre discerent."

---

[1] *at Thermop'ylae*, a mountain pass in Greece.
[2] *Lycur'gus,* the king who was supposed to have originated the Spartan way of life.   [3] *at the age of seven* (literally, *born seven years*).   [4] *whips.*

"Etiam peior," quīdam adulēscēns Athēniēnsis dīxit, "erat vīta eōrum quōs Spartānī vīcērunt. Nōn sōlum servī factī sunt sed multae
20 iniūriae eīs ferendae erant. Ā quibusdam sēcrētō observābantur. Ille servus quī faciem hominis līberī habuit occīsus est. Vestis servīlis omnibus servīs gerenda erat. Cotīdiē caesī sunt ut memoriā tenērent sē servōs esse."

"Nōn negō vītam servōrum miserrimam esse," Fūriānus dīxit, "sed
25 pessima erat vīta Spartānōrum ipsōrum. Etiam in pāce semper in castrīs habitābant. Lībertās eīs nōn nōta fuit. Omnia prō patriā facienda erant; nihil tamen patria prō populō fēcit. 'Prō bonō pūblicō' significāvit 'prō bonō reī pūblicae,' nōn 'prō bonō cīvium.' "

"Vērum dīcis," Athēniēnsis dīxit. "Memoriā teneāmus verba nōbilis
30 Periclis, quī dīxit rem pūblicam Athēniēnsium in manibus plūrimōrum, nōn paucōrum, esse; cīvibus ēgregiīs omnium generum mūnera pūblica praemia esse; iūra paria omnibus esse. Athēniēnsibus lībertās cārissima fuit; itaque illī nōn īrātī fuērunt sī aliī fēcērunt id quod amāvērunt. Puerī eōrum in pāce vīxērunt nec ad bellum
35 semper īnstitūtī sunt. Alacrī tamen animō in bellō pugnāvērunt et periērunt. Artēs līberālēs coluērunt; itaque eōrum urbs schola Graeciae fuit."

"Vērum est," Pūblius dīxit; "etiam nunc haec urbs schola est, nōn sōlum Graeciae sed orbis terrārum. Athēnae statuās pulcherrimās,
40 aedificia ēgregia, librōs optimōs nōbīs dedērunt. Spērō omnēs gentēs semper Athēnīs, nōn Spartae, similēs futūrās esse."

QUESTIONS

1. Who died at Thermopylae?
2. In what way were Spartan slaves worse off than any others?
3. What did the Athenians consider to be of highest importance?

128. Future Passive Participle

The *future passive participle* (often called the *gerundive*) is formed by adding **–ndus, –a, –um** to the present stem of any verb: **porta–ndus, –a, –um,** *to be carried.* In the case of **–iō** verbs add **–endus: mūni–endus, capi–endus.** The stem vowel is shortened before **–nd–.**

Practice

Give the future passive participle of **caedō, negō, compleō,** and **excipiō.**

78

129. Use of the Future Passive Participle

1. **Omnibus concēdendum est Spartānōs . . . fortissimōs fuisse** (line 2), *It is to be granted by all that the Spartans were the bravest* (i.e., *it must* [or *ought* or *has to*] *be granted*).

2. **Vīta dūra puerīs Spartānīs agenda erat** (line 12), *A hard life had to be lived by Spartan boys.*

3. **Omnia prō patriā facienda erant** (line 26), *Everything had to be done for the fatherland.*

Observe:

1. When used with forms of **sum** as a predicate adjective, the future passive participle naturally expresses *obligation* or *necessity*.

2. The person upon whom the obligation rests is expressed by the dative, known as the dative of agent.[5]

130. Translation

1. Must boys always be trained for war?
2. What ought to be done by us for our country?
3. Publius asked why Lycurgus had to be blamed by us.
4. Why did dinner have to be prepared by the boys themselves?

131. Vocabulary

adulēscēns, –entis, m., *young man*
alacer, –cris, –cre, *eager*
caedō, –ere, cecīdī, caesus, *cut, beat, kill*
concēdō, –ere, –cessī, –cessūrus, *withdraw, grant*
famēs, –is, abl. **famē,** f., *hunger*
fortiter, adv., *bravely*

hortor, 1, *urge*
īnstituō, –ere, īnstituī, īnstitūtus, *establish, train*
negō, 1, *deny, say . . . not*
pereō, –īre, –iī, –itūrus, *perish*
quoque, adv. (follows the word it emphasizes), *too*
significō, 1, *mean*

---

[5] To be distinguished from the ablative of agent with **ā** or **ab,** regularly used with the passive voice of verbs.

Roman mosaic with a skeleton pointing to the Greek motto "gnothi sauton" (Latin "cognosce te ipsum," p. 73). The point is that life is short.

132. Word Study: Spanish

Spanish is so much like Latin that it is easy for those knowing Latin to recognize hundreds of Spanish words, especially if a few simple principles concerned with the loss or change of letters are known. Spanish nouns are usually not derived from the Latin nominative but from a common form made from the other cases.

Remembering that final letters and syllables often are lost in Spanish, give the Latin for *alto, ánimo, ceder, constituir, dar, fácil, gente, libro, orden, responder.*

Remembering that double consonants become single, give the Latin from which are derived *aceptar, común, difícil, efecto.*

Remembering that *e* often becomes *ie*, and *o* becomes *ue*, give the Latin for *bien, ciento, cierto, tierra; bueno, cuerpo, fuerte, muerte, nuestro, puerto.*

Since *c* and *q* sometimes become *g*, and *t* becomes *d*, what must be the Latin words from which are derived *agua, amigo; edad, libertad, madera, madre, padre, todo?*

Since *li* becomes *j*, and *ct* becomes *ch*, from what Latin words are the following derived: *ajeno, consejo, mejor; dicho, noche, ocho?*

133. THE ATHENIAN EPHEBIC OATH

Athenian boys who were sons of citizens were drafted into the army at thirteen. Known as *ephebi*, they were given military training for two years. The oath of allegiance which they took is a model for the citizens of any democracy:

I will not disgrace my holy weapons nor will I desert my comrade in arms. I will fight for our temples and our homes, by myself as well as with others. My country I will hand on to others not less but greater and better than I received it. I will respect those in authority and will obey the laws now in force and any others that may hereafter be put in force by the common will of the majority. If anyone shall try to destroy the laws or shall fail to obey them, I will not submit but will fight him by myself as well as with all my fellow citizens. I will honor the religion of my fathers. May the gods be my witnesses.

Compare this with the Boy Scout oath, the oath of allegiance of naturalized citizens, and the oath taken by those enlisting in the armed forces of the United States.[6]

[6] The first two of these are given in *The American Citizens Handbook* (Washington, D.C., National Education Association, 1941), pp. 42, 62. The ephebic oath is also given there.

Athens, Greece: The Stoa of Attalus, an open, porch-like structure, has been restored and is now used as a museum for objects found during excavations of the area. It was used as a market and to conduct other public business.

Tzovaras/Art Resource

134. ATHENIAN DEMOCRACY

The famous speech praising Athens which the Greek historian Thucydides ascribed to the great Athenian leader Pericles contains many passages which, although they are nearly 2500 years old, still represent the ideals and hopes of all democratic peoples today:

Since our state exists for the many, and not for the few, it is called a democracy. Before the law all share equal justice in their private disputes, and as for the status of the individual, if a man distinguishes himself in any way, he is advanced, not on the basis of his class, but of his merit; and not even a poor man, if he is able to serve the state, is hindered by the obscurity of his condition. We live in freedom, not only in our public affairs, but in our private lives as well, not putting on . . . sour . . . looks if our neighbor does as he pleases. Yet while we live without constraint as private citizens, a sense of reverence prevents us from breaking the public laws.

We are lovers of beauty, yet simple in our tastes, and we cultivate the mind without loss of manliness. We use our money not for talk or show, but when there is a real need for it. . . . It is a disgrace, not for a man to admit poverty, but to do nothing to avoid it.

We regard a person who takes no part in public affairs not just as an unambitious but rather as a useless person, and we are all, if not originators of state policy, at least sound judges of it.

To sum up: I say that Athens is the school of Greece, and that our individual citizen seems to adapt himself independently, and with the utmost versatility and grace, to the greatest variety of activities.

The ancient Stadium in Athens, restored in modern times for the revival of the Olympic Games. Olympia was the original site of the ancient games.

Lesson XXII

135. ATHLETICS AND PATRIOTISM

Quōdam diē Pūblius et Fūriānus ē scholā cum duōbus adulēscentibus Graecīs exiērunt. Accidit ut per viās gradientēs statuam
virī currentis, ā clārō Myrōne [1] factam, cōnspicerent. Itaque cōnstitērunt ut eam spectārent.

5 "Nōnne Graecī semper virōs currentēs amant?" Pūblius quaesīvit.

"Sī quis celerrimē currit," respondit ūnus ē Graecīs, "cārissimus
urbis suae est; et sī quis in lūdīs Olympicīs vincit, cārissimus est
tōtīus Graeciae. Illī lūdī, quī antīquī et īnsignēs sunt, Iovī in urbe
Olympiā hōc ipsō annō habentur et post quattuor annōs iterum habē-
10 buntur. Ad hanc urbem virī ex omnibus urbibus Graeciae eunt ut ibi
contendant. Virō sē nōn dignō modō gerentī, virō quī fraudem fēcit,
nōn permittitur ut contendat. Victōrēs corōnās, statuās, carmina
accipiunt."

"Nōnne audīvī dē quōdam virō quī tempore magnī perīculī longē
15 cucurrit?" Fūriānus quaesīvit.

"Philippidēs [2] erat," respondit alter ē Graecīs. "Nūntius eī por-
tandus erat. Ducēs Persārum, cum multīs mīlibus mīlitum in
Graeciam prōgressī, ad campum quī Marathōn appellātur dēscendērunt. Athēniēnsēs cōnstituērunt ut Philippidēs quīdam ad urbem
20 Spartānōrum īret ut auxilium peteret. Etsī haec urbs circiter centum
quīnquāgintā mīlia passuum aberat, ille secundō diē ad eam pervēnit

[1] *Myron,* a Greek sculptor.
[2] In Greek the name seems to have been Pheidippides.

et eōs hortātus est ut auxilium mitterent. Spartānī autem ob fēriās cōnstituērunt nē īrent. Itaque Athēniēnsibus sōlīs Persae dūrī expellendī erant, et Graecia servāta est. Post hoc proelium īdem nūntius Philippidēs ad urbem Athēnās celeriter cucurrit sed posteāquam in urbem pervēnit 'Victōria!' clāmāns subitō mortuus est." [3]

"Graecī fortēs sunt," dīxit Pūblius, amīcīs suīs Graecīs relīctīs. "Nōnne mīrāris quō modō accidat ut Rōmānōs nōn vīcerint?"

QUESTIONS

1. What did Philippides do?
2. What were the prizes for the winners at the Olympic Games?
3. Discuss the relation of physical training to national defense.

136. Noun Clauses

A. *Volitive*

Verbs expressing the will of the speaker, such as **cōgō** (*compel*), **imperō** (*command*), **petō** (*seek*), **cōnstituō** (*determine*), have as objects clauses in the subjunctive introduced by **ut** or **nē:**

1. **Athēniēnsēs cōnstituērunt ut Philippidēs quīdam ad urbem Spartānōrum īret** (line 19), *The Athenians decided that a certain Philippides should go to the city of the Spartans.*

2. **Spartānī autem ob fēriās cōnstituērunt nē īrent** (line 22), *But the Spartans decided not to go on account of the holidays.*

B. *Result*

The result clauses previously studied were adverbial. There are also clauses of result that are used as nouns. Verbs meaning to *hap-*

---

[3] The marathon race of today is so named because its length (about 26 miles) equals the distance which Philippides ran from Marathon to Athens.

The Olympic Games, seen here in the Los Angeles Coliseum have a long tradition.

Beatrice Hohenegger

pen (accidō) or *to cause* or *effect* (efficiō) require clauses of result in the subjunctive with **ut** or **ut nōn,** used as subject or object of the main verb:

1. **Accidit ut . . . statuam . . . cōnspicerent** (line 2), *It happened that they saw a statue.*

2. **Nōnne mīrāris quō modō accidat ut Rōmānōs nōn vīcerint?** (line 28), *Don't you wonder how it happens that they did not conquer the Romans?*

137. Translation

1. Did the messenger ask the Spartans [4] not to send aid?
2. By his speed he caused the Persians [4] to be defeated.
3. A messenger had to be sent to the city by the Greeks.
4. The Greeks determine that the defeated general should pay the penalty.

138. Vocabulary

campus, –ī, m., *plain*
circiter, adv., *about*
etsī, conj., *although*
exeō, exīre, exiī, exitūrus, *go out*
gradior, gradī, gressus, *walk*

itaque, adv., *and so, therefore*
prōgredior, prōgredī, prōgressus, *step forward, advance*
quaerō, –ere, quaesīvī, quaesītus, *seek, inquire*

139. Word Study: Suffixes

For the meaning and use of the suffixes **–ānus** (*–an, –ane, –ain*), **–ālis** (*–al*), **–icus** (*–ic*), **–īlis** (*–ile, –il*), **–īvus** (*–ive*), **–ōsus** (*–ous, –ose*), see **615.** Give the English forms of **hūmānus, urbānus, mortālis, cīvicus, virīlis, āctīvus, cūriōsus, bellicōsus.**

What must be the Latin words from which are derived *meridian, certain, liberal, classic, passive, morose?* Give three other examples of each of the above suffixes in English words.

Frequently several suffixes are used together in the same word. Sometimes these are joined together so closely that we think of them as one suffix. Particularly common is the attachment of noun suffixes to adjectives to form nouns, and vice versa: *simil–ari–ty, hum–ani–ty, fert–ili–ty, act–ivi–ty.* Sometimes several adjective suffixes are used together: *republ–ic–an.*

Out of the Latin participle **nātus** we make the noun *nat–ion,* then the adjective *nat–ion–al,* then the verb *nat–ion–al–ize,* then the noun *nat–ion–al–iza–tion.* Sometimes even more suffixes are used.

Do you know any towns named *Olympia, Marathon,* or *Sparta?*

---

[4] In Latin this will be the subject of the verb in the subordinate clause.

Bust of the blind Homer.

Alinari, National Museum, Rome

Lesson XXIII

140. NATIONAL HEROES

Dē virīs clārīs Pūblius et Fūriānus saepe cum adulēscentibus duōbus Graecīs loquēbantur. Pūbliō maximē grātum erat dē Graecō Dēmosthene audīre—quī puer vōcem pessimam habuerat, sed quī eam exercuerat loquendō ad lītus maris, clāmandō dum currit,[1] prōnūntiandō dum aliquid in ōre habet;[1] et quī tandem prīmum 5 locum inter omnēs ōrātōrēs attigerat. "Ille sōlus melior quam Cicerō erat et etiam Rōmānīs laudandus et in honōre habendus est," quondam dīxit Pūblius.

Fūriānus dē rēbus mīlitāribus locūtus est factaque Caesaris, Scīpiōnis, Pompeī, Marī nārrāvit. Sed ūnus ē Graecīs dīxit: "Mihi grātis- 10 simus imperātōrum Graecōrum est Themistoclēs. Tempore maximī perīculī, auctōritātem Athēnārum nāvibus summam fēcit, Athēnās optimē mūnīvit, Persārum exercitum tandem ē Graeciā expulit."

"Multī Rōmānī Graecīs similēs sunt," quōdam diē Pūblius dīxit. "Vergilius, clārissimus poēta Rōmānus, quī carmen dē Troiānīs et 15 dē Rōmā cōnstituendā scrīpsit, similis Homērō est, quī dē bellō Troiānō scrīpsit. Numa autem, quī temporibus antīquīs lēgēs quās ā deīs accēperat Rōmānīs dedit, similis Solōnī est, quī lēgēs fēcit ad Athēnās reficiendās."

"At quī Rōmānus philosophīs Graecīs pār est?" alter ē Graecīs 20 quaesīvit. "Cicerō, Lucrētius, quī dē atomīs et dē orīgine hominum rērumque scrīpsit, aliī philosophī Rōmānī—hī ad Graeciam audiendī

---

[1] In English the past tense is used.

et discendī causā vēnērunt. Quis Sōcratem memoriā nōn tenet, quī puerōs interrogandō docēbat et eōs ad bene vīvendum īnstituēbat; 25 quī malī [2] expellendī et bonī [2] mōnstrandī grātiā semper labōrābat; quī ob sententiās suās occīsus est?"

"At quī Graecus Augustō nostrō pār est?" respondit Fūriānus. "Periclēs quidem īnsignis erat—Athēnās adōrnāvit, auctōritātem urbis auxit, pāce regēbat. Augustus autem nōn sōlum Rōmam adōrnāvit 30 auxitque—urbem quam ex latere [3] factam accēpit nunc marmoream relinquit—sed nunc omnēs terrās pāce, sapientiā, iūstitiā regit."

Et duo Graecī concessērunt Augustum īnsignem esse.

QUESTIONS

1. Who beautified Rome?
2. What Greek was like Virgil?
3. What Roman was like Solon?
4. What was (and is) the Socratic method of teaching?

141. Gerund

The gerund corresponds to the English verbal noun in *–ing,* as in *We learn to do by doing.* It is formed by adding **–ndī, –ndō, –ndum, –ndō** to the present stem of any verb.[4] It is declined in the singular only, in all cases except the nominative. For the nominative constructions of the English verbal noun, Latin uses the present active infinitive: **Vidēre est crēdere,** *Seeing is believing.*

Note these differences between the gerund and the future passive participle:

GERUND	FUTURE PASSIVE PARTICIPLE
1. Is a *verbal noun.*	1. Is a *verbal adjective.*
2. Has only four endings (**–ī, –ō, –um, –ō**).	2. Has thirty forms (**–us, –a, –um,** etc.).
3. Is always *active* (translate "–ing").	3. Is always *passive* (translate "to be," "must be").
4. Never agrees with anything.	4. Always agrees with a noun or pronoun.

Practice

1. Learn the gerunds of the model verbs (585, 586).
2. Decline the gerunds of **nārrō** and **pōnō,** and the future passive participles of **capiō** and **exigō.**

---

[2] Neuter noun forms: *evil, good.*   [3] From **later,** *brick.*
[4] Add **–endī,** etc., in **–iō** verbs.

The Discus Thrower, or Discobolus, by the Greek sculptor Myron, noted for his ability to "stop" figures in action, almost as if with a high-speed camera. The original (fifth century B.C.) bronze statue does not survive; this copy is in New York.

Metropolitan Museum of Art

142. Uses of Gerund and Future Passive Participle

1. *The gerund, being a noun, may have noun constructions,* e.g., object of a preposition or ablative of means:

loquendō (line 4) *by talking.*

2. *The gerund usually does not have an object.* To avoid using the gerund with an object, the future passive participle is used instead, modifying the noun:

Carmen . . . dē Rōmā cōnstituendā scrīpsit (line 15), *He wrote a poem about founding Rome* (literally, *about Rome to be founded*).
dē cōnstituendō Rōmam (gerund) is not used.

3. *When the preposition used is* **ad,** *the phrase with gerund or future passive participle naturally expresses purpose:*

(Sōcratēs) puerōs . . . ad bene vīvendum īnstituēbat (line 24), *Socrates trained boys to live well* (literally, *for living well*).
Lēgēs fēcit ad Athēnās reficiendās (line 18), *He made laws to rebuild Athens* (literally, *for Athens to be rebuilt*).

4. *Purpose is also naturally expressed by* **causā** *or* **grātiā,** for the sake of, *with the gerund or future passive participle in the genitive:*

Malī expellendī . . . grātiā semper labōrābat (line 25), *He always worked for the sake of driving out evil.*

Is this a gerund or a future passive participle?

143. Translation

Translate the words in italics, using the gerund or future passive participle, as the case may be:

1. He sat down *to read.*
2. We felt the joy *of giving.*
3. I have come *to tell a story.*
4. This is no time *for talking.*
5. He gained fame *by writing.*
6. He sat down *to read a book.*
7. We felt the joy *of giving money.*
8. He gained fame *by writing books.*
9. He leaned forward *for-the-sake-of seeing.*
10. He leaned forward *for-the-sake-of seeing the man.*

144. Vocabulary

at, conj., *but*
attingō, –ere, attigī, attāctus, *touch, reach*
exercitus, –ūs, m., *army*
honor, –ōris, m., *honor*
imperātor, –ōris, m., *commander, general*

interrogō, 1, *ask, question*
lītus, lītoris, n., *shore*
occīdō, –ere, occīdī, occīsus, *kill*
prōnūntiō, 1, *recite*
sōlum, adv., *only*

Olympic runners as shown on a Greek stamp.

145. Word Study: Mottoes and Abbreviations

Animis opibusque parati, *Prepared in spirit and resources* (motto of the state of South Carolina).

Qui transtulit sustinet, *(God) who transported (us here) sustains (us)* (motto of the state of Connecticut).

Crescit eundo, *It grows by going (forward)* (motto of the state of New Mexico, from the Roman poet Lucretius).

Si quaeris peninsulam amoenam, circumspice, *If you are seeking a pleasant peninsula, look about you* (motto of the state of Michigan).

Find the Latin words for which the following abbreviations stand and their meanings: **etc., et al., s.v., ult., prox., e.g., A.B., A.M., S.B., LL.D.**

Servizio Editorio Fotografico/Art Resource

The Olympieum (see p. 62), one of the largest Greek temples known to us, was built by Hadrian in the Second century A.D.

Lesson XXIV

146. A VISIT TO THE ACADEMY

Saepe Pūbliō et Fūriānō grātum erat per urbem Athēnās ambulāre et virōs maximae auctōritātis causās ōrantēs audīre. Saepe autem grātius vidēbātur urbem relinquere sēque ad locum pulchrum et quiētum, Acadēmiam, legendī grātiā recipere.

Quōdam diē eō tardē prōcēdēbant, librōs carminum ferentēs. 5

"Quot Rōmānī dignī per hanc ipsam viam ambulāvērunt!—Rōmānī quī posteā clārissimī factī sunt," dīxit Pūblius. "Nōs quoque in studiīs dīligentēs sīmus ut clārī fīāmus—tū ut dux īnsignis fīās, ego ōrātor."

Nunc inter arborēs Acadēmiae stābant. Hae erant novae sed iam 10 altae.

"Quā magnitūdine arborēs fīunt!" Pūblius dīxit. "Audīvī quōsdam Athēniēnsēs dīcere hās paucīs annīs tam altās quam illās antīquās futūrās esse. Nam Sulla, quī illās cecīdit ut ē māteriā īnstrūmenta bellī fierent, rēs pulchrās contempsit. Statuās quidem ē Graeciā tulit; 15 hoc autem fēcit ut magnam praedam in urbem Rōmam referret."

Nunc sub arbore altā librōs quōs sēcum tulerant legunt. Tum Fūriānus dīxit, "Mihi grātissimum est ad hunc locum venīre carminum Horātī legendōrum causā, quod hīc Horātius ipse carmina legēbat et scrībēbat. Horātius, quī vir corpore parvō et rotundō erat, 20 bellō erat inimīcus—Sullae dissimillimus. Nūntiō bellī allātō, nōn

perturbātus est. Brūtus [1] sōlus eum permovēre potuit (saepe mīror quō modō) ut tribūnus mīlitāris fieret et ad bellum proficīscerētur. Brūtō et Cassiō ad urbem Philippōs victīs, Horātiō scūtum relinquen-
25 dum fuit (memoriāne tenēs?) ipseque fūgit. Posteā ab Augustō, contrā quem arma tulerat, amīcus dēlēctus est, et nōtissimus poēta factus est."

"Hīc saepe dē philosophīs admoneor," dīxit Pūblius; "de Platōne, quī prīmus hīc docuit; dē Aristotele, quī rēgem Alexandrum īnstituit;
30 dē Carneade, quī nunc prō iūstitiā, nunc contrā eam, verba īnsignia facere potuit."

Subitō accessērunt duo Graecī. Ab hīs certiōrēs factī rhētorem clārum causam in Agorā ōrātūrum esse et tempus adesse, Pūblius et Fūriānus librōs celeriter volvērunt et nōn iam morātī ex Acadēmiā
35 exiērunt.

[1] Brutus, together with Cassius and others, had killed Caesar and fled from Rome, pursued by Antony, Caesar's friend, and Octavian, Caesar's nephew, later called Augustus.

You can sense the exhaustion of these realistic bronze boxers now in a Roman museum. Note the detail of the facial expressions and the boxing gloves.

QUESTIONS
1. Against whom did Horace fight?
2. How was Horace different from Sulla?
3. What did Sulla do in the Academy?

147. Conjugation of Fīō

Faciō has no passive in the present, imperfect, or future tenses. To express *be made, be done, become* in these tenses, the Romans used an irregular verb, **fīō,** which, although it is for the most part active in form, has passive meanings:

	INDICATIVE		
PRESENT		IMPERFECT	FUTURE
fīō ——²		fīēbam, etc.	fīam, etc.
fīs ——			
fit fīunt			

SUBJUNCTIVE		IMPERATIVE		INFINITIVE
PRESENT	IMPERFECT	SING.	PLUR.	PRESENT
fīam, etc.	fierem, etc.	fī	fīte	fierī

Remember:

The stem vowel is long throughout, except before **- er** and final **–t.**

1. The perfect tenses of **faciō** are regular in the passive: **factus sum, factus eram,** etc.

2. The future passive participle and the gerund are also formed from **faciō: faciendus, –a, –um; faciendī.**

3. Compounds of **faciō,** such as **cōnficiō** and **efficiō,** form the passive regularly: **cōnficior, efficior,** etc.

148. Predicate Nouns and Adjectives

Fīō and such passive forms as **appellor** (*be called*) and **dēligor** (*be selected*) may be used with a predicate noun or adjective:

Dīligentēs sīmus ut clārī fīāmus (line 8), *Let us be diligent so that we may become famous.*

Find all the examples of this construction in the story above.

149. Translation

1. Horace, who had borne arms against Augustus, became a noted poet.
2. "Let us strive to become men of the greatest influence," said Publius to Furianus.

---

² This mark indicates that the form does not occur.

Model of the library built in Athens by the Roman Emperor Hadrian.

3. "Leaving the city behind, let us retire to the Academy, carrying our books with us."

4. Sulla, who had come to Greece for the sake of waging war, carried back many beautiful things.

150. Vocabulary

dēligō, –ere, dēlēgī, dēlēctus, *select*
dīligēns, gen. **–entis,** *careful*
eō, adv., *there*
fīō, fierī, (factus), *be made, become;*
   certior fīō, *be informed* (lit., *be*
   made more certain)
moror, 1, *delay*
ōrō, 1, *beg, plead*

perturbō, 1, *disturb*
quot, indeclinable adj.,
   how many; as (many as)
referō, referre, rettulī, relātus,
   bring back
scūtum, –ī, n., *shield*
tribūnus, –ī, m., *tribune*

151. Word Study

For the meaning and use of **circum–** (*circum–*) and **super–** (*super–*, *sur–*), see **614.** Define according to the prefix: *circumscribe, circumference, circuit, supervise, survive, supergovernment.*

Prefixes often have intensive force; this is especially true of **con–, ex–, ob–, per–: cōnficiō,** *"do up,"* do thoroughly; **efficiō,** *make out, complete;* **occīdō,** *cut up, kill;* **perficiō,** *do through and through, finish.* Define according to the intensive use of the prefix: *complement, commotion, conserve, experience, emotion, extensive, obtain, persist, permanent.*

Believe it or not, *squire* comes from **scūtiger,** *shield-bearer* of the medieval knight. A "blot on the scutcheon" is a blot on the *shield,* with its coat of arms.

Explain *fiat, gradual, inquisitive, interrogation, littoral, perturbation, progressive.*

Lesson XXV

152. ATHENS AND ROME

Fūriānus patrī s. p. d. Quaeris quibus modīs Rōma et Athēnae inter sē [1] differant et utram urbem magis amem. Mihi quidem respondēre difficile est. Rōma patria mea est et ob eam rem mihi cārissima est. Num [2] vīs mē Rōmam et Rōmānōs accūsāre? Iam dē aedificiīs amplissimīs quae hīc vīdimus scrīpsī. Sed Rōma quoque 5 aedificia pulchra habet. Viae Rōmānae certē meliōrēs sunt. Omnia sordidiōra hīc sunt—viae, aedificia prīvāta, hominēs. Nūllae cloācae [3] sunt. Aliquis Rōmānus hūc mittendus est ad cloācās faciendās. Aqua ita mala est ut multī pereant. Nōnne vult aliquis Rōmānus aquaeductum hīc facere? [4] Cum autem Acropolim cōnspiciō, tum haec 10 urbs pulcherrima omnium esse vidētur, neque iam [5] peiōra [6] memoriā teneō.

[1] *from each other.*
[2] Introduces a question expecting a negative answer: *you don't wish, do you?*
[3] *sewers.*   [4] This was actually done later at the Emperor Hadrian's expense.
[5] *longer.*   [6] *the more disagreeable things.*

A view of the Roman Emperor Hadrian's Villa near Rome. The Villa was built between 125–134 A.D. to remind Hadrian of his journeys in the east, including Greece.

Getty Center Photo Archive

Haec dē urbe ipsā; nunc dē populō quaedam dīcere volō. Concēdō Graecōs multās virtūtēs habēre, sed hae nōn sunt virtūtēs Rōmānae.
15 Nostrī sunt fortēs atque prūdentēs, maximē labōrant et optimē regunt. Graecī autem optimī philosophī, rhētorēs, poētae, medicī sunt et optima templa pulcherrimāsque statuās faciunt.

Multōs amīcōs Graecōs habeō; itaque nōlō omnēs Graecōs accūsāre. Sed Rōmānī mihi cāriōrēs sunt. Perfidia Graecōrum nōta est;
20 quamquam nōn negō Graecōs loquī dē perfidiā Rōmānā. Interest [7] utrum [8] Rōmānus an Graecus sīs.[9] Ita omnēs populī aliōs contemnunt. Nōnne nōs loquimur etiam dē Pūnicā perfidiā? Sed vērum est in tabernīs Graecīs fraudēs frequentiōrēs esse quam in Rōmānīs.

Etsī multī servī in Italiā sunt, numquam tot servōs vīdī quot in
25 hāc urbe. Omnia ā servīs fīunt; cīvēs enim ipsī nōn labōrant.

Maximē autem condiciō mulierum differt. Mulierēs Graecae nōn habent eandem lībertātem quam Rōmānae. Apud nōs mātrōnae in honōre sunt, sed nōn hīc. Virī volunt uxōrēs nihil vidēre, nihil audīre, nihil quaerere. Sed tamen puellae quās vīdī pulchrae fuērunt.

QUESTIONS

1. Did the Greeks or the Romans have better roads?
2. Did Rome or Athens have a better water supply?
3. Which city had better doctors? Which had more slaves?

153. Conjugation of Volō and Nōlō

The present indicative of both **volō** and **nōlō** is irregular. The present subjunctive has the tense sign **–ī–**, as in **sim.** The other tenses are regularly formed. There is no passive.

PRESENT INDICATIVE			
volō	volumus	nōlō	nōlumus
vīs	vultis	nōn vīs	nōn vultis
vult	volunt	nōn vult	nōlunt
PRESENT SUBJUNCTIVE			
velim	velīmus	nōlim	nōlīmus
velīs	velītis	nōlīs	nōlītis
velit	velint	nōlit	nōlint
IMPERATIVE	INFINITIVE	IMPERATIVE	INFINITIVE
—— ——	velle	nōlī nōlīte	nōlle
For full conjugation see **592.**			

---

[7] *it makes a difference.*   [8] *whether.*   [9] Double indirect question (**606,** 13, *Note*).

Observe:

1. The present stem is **vel–** in the subjunctive but **vol–** in the indicative.

2. The imperfect subjunctive of both **volō** and **nōlō** is formed regularly from the present infinitive **(velle, nōlle);** this explains why the **l** is doubled.

Practice

1. Give the second singular of **volō** and the third plural of **nōlō** in all tenses of the indicative and subjunctive.
2. Conjugate the following verbs in all tenses of the indicative and subjunctive, giving the first singular of the first verb, the second singular of the second verb, etc.: **prōgredior, sum, ferō, fīō, possum, eō.**

154. Translation

1. Do you wish to know which city (of the two) I like more?
2. It is very difficult for me to say, because they are so unlike.
3. I don't wish to criticize the Greeks, but they do not seem to be willing to work.
4. I have always been willing, however, to say that the Greeks excel us in all the arts.

155. Vocabulary

an, conj., *or*

differō, differre, distulī, dīlātus, *differ*

interest, *it makes a difference* (lit., *there is between*)

mulier, mulieris, f., *woman*

nōlō, nōlle, nōluī, ——, *not want*

num, adv., introduces question expecting negative answer; conj., *whether*

perfidia, –ae, f., *treachery*

prūdēns, gen. **–entis,** *sensible*

uter, utra, utrum, *which (of two)*

volō, velle, voluī, ——, *want*

156. Word Study: Latin Phrases

per se, *by itself.*

bona fide, *in good faith.*

in re, *in the matter (of).*

nolens volens, *willy-nilly.*

Deo volente, *God willing.*

me iudice, *in my judgment.*

Pax vobiscum, *Peace (be) with you!*

sui generis, *of its own kind,* i.e., *unique.*

sine die, *without a day (being set);* used of adjournment by a parliamentary body.

Fiat panis, *Let there be bread;* motto of the Food and Agriculture Organization of the United Nations.

These remains of the Roman Basilica in Pompeii show the typical rectangular area designed for conducting various types of public business, including legal matters and public trials. Archives of legal documents were kept at the far end of the two story tribunal. In the larger Roman cities, the basilica was also the banking and stock exchange center.

Lesson XXVI

157. THE HOME-COMING

Tandem diēs aderat quō, studiīs perfectīs, Athēnae Pūbliō Fūriānōque relinquendae erant.

"Illīs invideō quī nunc in Graeciā, nunc in Italiā habitant," dīxit
Fūriānus, volēns Rōmam vidēre, nōlēns tamen Athēnās dēserere.

Certiōrēs autem ā mercātōre factī viās bonās esse, sibi persuā- 5
sērunt ut sine morā proficīscerentur. Nūntiō allātō latrōnēs viātōribus
nocēre, servīs armātīs ut praesidiō impedīmentīs essent, per Graeciam
iter fēcērunt. Marī quiētō, in portum Brundisī sine cāsū nāvigāvē-
runt, et ibi duōs diēs mānsērunt, quod quaedam vidēre volēbant:
locum ubi Augustus nōmen Caesaris accēperat, et aedificium in quō 10
Vergilius mortuus erat postquam ē Graeciā rediit. Hoc tam grātum
Pūbliō erat ut discēdere nōllet. Fūriānus autem dīxit, "Nōnne dēsīderās
quam prīmum domum tuam vidēre?"

"Dēsīderō!" [1] respondit Pūblius. Itaque quam celerrimē profectī
sunt.   15

Magnum erat gaudium familiae Caeciliae, adulēscentibus duōbus
dēfessīs vesperī reversīs. Sōle oriente, clientēs vēnērunt, et paene tōtum
diem ātrium clientibus et amīcīs salūtem dīcentibus complētum est.
Posteā Caeciliī ad Campum Mārtium in pulchrās thermās Agrippae
iērunt. Ibi cum aliīs amīcīs locūtī, sē exercuērunt et lāvērunt.   20

Proximō diē, rogātus quid facere vellet, Pūblius dīxit sē velle in
Circum īre. Pater respondit nōn circēnsēs lūdōs, sed scaenicōs eō
diē darī; quendam poētam quoque carmina sua lēctūrum esse. Pūblius
dīxit sē nōlle istum poētam ignōtum audīre; lūdōs autem scaenicōs
sibi placēre et eōs vidēre velle.   25

Fābula, ā Plautō dē lārvīs scrīpta, grāta erat. Tum pantomīmus [2]
victōriās Augustī exprimēns tam bene saltāvit ut populus alacer
clāmāret, ad pantomīmum curreret, pecūniam iaceret. Etiam Augustus
eī corōnam dedit, quam accipere maximō honōrī pantomīmō erat.
Lūdīs perfectīs, omnēs per Forum reversī sunt.   30

---

[1] *Yes* was often expressed in conversation by repeating the verb.
[2] *pantomime, ballet dancer.*

Museo della Civiltà, Rome

Model of ancient Rome, seen from the Aventine Hill, with the Circus Maximus in the foreground, beyond it the Palatine Hill, then the Roman Forum.

Pūblius et Fūriānus nunc vītam cīvium Rōmānōrum iniērunt. Pūblius quaestor creātus est, perque tōtum cursum honōrum īre parāvit. Fūriānus, tribūnus mīlitum factus, auxiliō ducī ab hostibus circumventō missus est, sēque tam fortiter gessit ut lēgātus fieret. Itaque
35 et Pūblius et Fūriānus vītā suā magnam auctōritātem familiae Caeciliae et servāvērunt et auxērunt.

QUESTIONS

1. Whom did Furianus envy?
2. To whom did Augustus give a wreath?
3. What did Publius and Furianus do after their return to Rome?

158. The Dative with Special Verbs

With some verbs, such as **imperō, permittō,** and **persuādeō,** an indirect personal object is used in addition to a subordinate **ut** clause as direct object:

1. *Eī* **imperō ut . . .,** *I order him to . . .*
2. *Sibi* **persuāsērunt ut sine morā proficīscerentur** (line 5), *They persuaded themselves to depart without delay.*

With some other verbs, such as **invideō, noceō,** and **placeō** in the story above, the dative alone is used. For other such verbs see **599, 6.** It is best to learn them as they occur.

98

159. Datives of Reference and Purpose

Fūriānus . . . auxiliō ducī . . . missus est (line 33), *Furianus was sent to aid a general* (literally, *for an aid to a general*).

Observe:

1. The dative may be used to express purpose.
2. A second dative (of reference) is often used with the dative of purpose, especially when the verb is some form of **sum.** The dative of reference indicates the person concerned or referred to. It is often literally translated by "for."

Find other examples of these datives in the story above. Mention all the ways of expressing purpose in Latin that you know.

160. Translation

1. They were informed that bandits were molesting travelers.
2. Furianus, however, persuaded Publius to start as soon as possible.
3. They armed the slaves as a protection for themselves and the baggage.
4. It was pleasing to them to see home again, and they said that they wanted to make the journey as swiftly as possible.

Open-air opera in the ruins of the ancient Baths of Caracalla, Rome.

Life Magazine © *Time, Inc.*

20°   10°   0°   10°

MARE
GERMANICUM
(North Sea)

MARE SU
(Balt

HIBERNIA

BRITANNIA

Eboracum
(York)

Saxones

Albis

GERMANI

Londinium

Belgae GERMANIA

Remi
Lutetia
(Paris)

Matrona (Marne)

Sequana

Rhenus

(Elbe)

Liger (Loire)

(Seine)

Tibrus

GALLIA

Celtae (Galli)

Genua

RAETIA

NORICUM

PANNONIA

Lugdunum
(Lyons)

AQUITANIA

Garunna

Rhodanus (Rhone)

Helvetii

(Rhone)

ALPES

Mediolanum
(Milan)

ILLYRICU

Numantia

Narbo

Massilia
(Marseilles)

Genua

Padus (Po)

Rubico

Hiberus (Ebro)

HISPANIA

Tagus

PYRENAEI

Massilia
(Marseilles)

CORSICA

ITALIA

Dyrrach

LUSITANIA

Tarraco

Roma
Ostia

Cannae

Anas (Guadiana)

Saguntum

Neapolis
Pompeii

Tarent

Gades
(Cadiz)

Corduba

BALEARES

SARDINIA

MAURETANIA

Nova Carthago
(Cartagena)

MARE

SICILIA Aetna

Syracusae

ATLAS

NUMIDIA

Utica
Carthago

Zama

AFRICA

Thapsus

MELITA
(MALTA)

ME

Leptis Magna

Roman Walls

Roman Territory 264 B.C. *Before Punic Wars*

Added   "   238-201 B.C. *After First and Second Punic Wars*

"   "   133 B.C.

"   "   44 B.C. *Death of Caesar*

"   "   14 A.D. *Death of Augustus*

"   "   Second Century A.D.

30°

0°   10°   Longitude   East

IMPERIUM ROMANUM

30°   40°   50°   60°

50°

Tanais
(Don)

S A R M A T I A

S C Y T H I A

MARE CASPIUM

...ACIA

Danuvius

C A U C A S U S

40°

PONTUS EUXINUS
(Black Sea)

OESIA

THRACIA

Byzantium
(Constantinople)
Bosporus

BITHYNIA

PONTUS

A R M E N I A

...o.

Thessalonica

Phillipi

Troia

GALATIA

CAPPADOCIA

ASSYRIA

PARTHIA

...arsalus

Mare

ASIA

Aegaeum

Corinthus

...IA Athenae

PAMPHYLIA

CILICIA

LYCIA

RHODUS

Antiochia

MESOPOTAMIA

Euphrates

Tigris

PHOENICIA

Palmyra

SYRIA

Damascus

Babylon

30°

CYPRUS

CRETA

Tyrus

PALAESTINA

Hierosolyma
(Jerusalem)

E R R A N E U M

Alexandria

ARABIA

AEGYPTUS

Nilus
(Nile)

Scale of Miles

0   100   200   300   400   500

101

m   Greenwich   30°   40°

161. Developing "Word Sense"

You will remember that many fourth declension nouns are related to verbs, for example, **exercitus (exerceō)** and **exitus (exeō)**. The nominative singular of the noun regularly looks like the nominative singular masculine of the verb's perfect passive participle. Some of these verbal nouns are used only in the accusative or ablative singular. Generally they describe an action, and can often be translated by the English verbal noun in *–ing*: **vīsus (video)**, *seeing*, i.e., *sight* or *vision*.

Translate these sayings and identify the verbs related to the fourth declension nouns:

Labor sine *lūsū* **Jōhannem** (*Jack*) **brūtum** (*dull*) **facit.**
Fiat nōn *mandātū* **tuō, sed** *rogātū* (a rule of good manners).
Facile *dictū*, **difficile** *factū* (Tell this to a boaster!).
Plūrimum *sūmptūs*, **minimum** *quaestūs* (= **quaesītūs**; a shopkeeper's motto).
Facilis *dēscēnsus* **Avernō** (from Virgil; see section 560).

From your knowledge of the basic verbs, assign a meaning to these Latin nouns: **arbitrātus, cāsus, cōnsēnsus, cursus, flētus, gressus, habitus, impulsus, ingressus, intellectus, monitus, reditus, status.**

162. Vocabulary

cāsus, –ūs, m., *chance, misfortune*
circumveniō, –īre, –vēnī, –ventus, *surround*
dēsīderō, 1, *long for*
ineō, inīre, iniī, initūrus, *enter upon*
lēgātus, –ī, m., *envoy, general*
noceō, –ēre, nocuī, nocitūrus, *do harm to, injure*
persuādeō, –ēre, –suāsī, –suāsūrus, *persuade*

placeō, –ēre, placuī, placitūrus, *please*
poēta, –ae, m., *poet*
quaestor, –ōris, m., *quaestor* (a treasury official)
revertō, –ere, revertī, reversus (sometimes deponent), *turn back, return*

163. Word Study: Suffixes

For the meaning and use of **–tūdō** (*–tude*), **–mentum** (*–ment*), **–ūra** (*–ure*), **–faciō, –ficō** (*–fy*), see **615**. Give the English forms of **multitūdō, servitūdō, argūmentum, agricultūra, pictūra.**

What must be the Latin words from which are derived *altitude, solitude, instrument, moment, conjecture*?

Give three other examples of each of the above suffixes in English words.

Explain *casualty, circumvent, imprudence, initiative, innocent, legation.*

102

REVIEW OF UNIT II SYNTAX

164. Subjunctive Uses

I. INDEPENDENT: VOLITIVE

In Latin	*In English*
Present subjunctive. EXAMPLE: **Lūx fīat.**	*Let. . . .* *Let there be light.*

II. DEPENDENT

A. Purpose Clauses

1. Present or imperfect subjunctive. 2. Introduced by **ut,** negative **nē.** EXAMPLE: **Edimus ut vīvāmus.**	1. Infinitive. 2. No introductory word. *We eat to live.*	1. Indicative with auxiliaries *may* or *might.* 2. Introduced by (*in order*) *that*, etc. *We eat that we may live.*

B. Result Clauses

1. Subjunctive. 2. Usually prepared for by **ita, tam,** etc. 3. Introduced by **ut,** negative **ut nōn.** EXAMPLE: **Ita vīvāmus ut omnēs nōs laudent.**	1. Indicative. 2. Usually prepared for by *so,* etc. 3. Introduced by *that.* *Let us live in such a way that all will praise us.*

C. Noun Clauses: Volitive

1. Subjunctive; clause is object of such verbs as **cōgō, cōnstituō, imperō, petō,** etc. 2. Introduced by **ut,** negative **nē.** EXAMPLE: **Cōnstituimus nē ad lūdōs īrēmus.**	1. Indicative. 2. Introduced by *that.*	1. Infinitive. 2. No introductory word. *We decided not to go to the games.*

20th Century-Fox

A Roman library in the motion picture *Demetrius and the Gladiators*.

In Latin	*In English*

D. *Noun Clauses: Result*

1. Subjunctive; clause is object of such verbs as **accidō, efficiō,** etc.	1. Indicative.
2. Introduced by **ut,** negative **ut nōn.**	2. Introduced by *that.*
EXAMPLE: **Accidit ut caderem.**	*It happened that I fell.*

E. *Noun Clauses: Indirect Questions*

1. Subjunctive; clause is object of verbs of *asking,* etc.: **rogō, cognōscō,** etc.	1. Indicative
2. Introduced by an interrogative word: **quis, quid, cūr, ubi,** etc.	2. Introduced by an interrogative word: *who, what, why, where,* etc.
EXAMPLE: **Dīc mihi unde vēnerīs.**	*Tell me where you came from.*

F. *Time Clauses*

1. With **ubi** or **postquam,** always indicative.	1. With *when,* indicative.
2. With **cum** in secondary sequence, subjunctive.	2. With *when,* indicative.

104

165. Sequence of Tenses

1. **Primary tenses** (referring to the present or future).
   INDICATIVE: Present, future, future perfect.
   SUBJUNCTIVE: Present, perfect.
2. **Secondary tenses** (referring to the past).
   INDICATIVE: Imperfect, perfect, past perfect.
   SUBJUNCTIVE: Imperfect, past perfect.

Primary tenses are followed by primary tenses, secondary by secondary.

166. Summary of Purpose Constructions

1. **Ut** clause with subjunctive: **Venīmus ut Claudiam laudēmus,**
   We come to praise Claudia.
2. Dative: **Cui bonō est?**
   Whom does it benefit (literally, *To whom is it for a good*)?
3. **Ad** with gerund: **Ad laudandum venīmus,**
   We come to praise.
4. **Ad** with future passive participle: **Ad Claudiam laudandam venīmus,**
   We come to praise Claudia.
5. **Causā** or **grātiā** with gerund: **Laudandī grātiā venīmus,**
   We come for the sake of praising.
6. **Causā** or **grātiā** with future passive participle: **Claudiae laudandae grātiā venīmus,**
   We come for the sake of praising Claudia.

Silver service from a house in Pompeii, now in the Naples Museum. This beautiful set was found not many years ago. The scenes on the cups represent Cupids in a circus race.

Our Heritage

167. GREEKS AND ROMANS

Although we may sometimes think of the civilizations of the Greeks and Romans as identical, the Roman people differed in many respects from the Greeks. The languages of the two peoples were about as different as French and German today.

The Greek cities and states retained their independence for a long time and each contributed its bit to Greek civilization, although Athens played a more prominent part than the rest. The Greeks excelled in philosophy, science, mathematics, art, and literature.

The Greeks developed their civilization earlier than the Romans. The fifth and fourth centuries B.C. mark the high point of Athenian culture. At that time Rome was still a struggling small town, but

Restoration of the Roman library at Ephesus in Asia Minor.

Anderson

gradually it extended its influence, first over Italy, then over the rest of what was then the civilized world. The Romans were a practical people, with a genius for both law and government.

The earliest important contact of the Romans with Greek culture was an indirect one, through the Etruscans. This rather mysterious people who lived north of Rome borrowed a number of things from the Greeks, such as the alphabet, forms of architecture, and some religious practices, and transmitted them to the Romans. Later the Romans met Greek culture directly as they spread south to the Greek colonies in Italy and Sicily. In the second century B.C. Greece itself came under Roman rule. Then the influence of Greek culture and customs really began. The poet Horace says:

> **Graecia capta ferum victōrem cēpit et artēs**
> **Intulit agrestī Latiō, . . .**

Captured Greece took captive its fierce conqueror by bringing the arts to rustic Latium.

Though Greece was defeated by Roman arms, uncivilized Rome was conquered by Greek art. The Romans began to develop art and literature in imitation of the Greek but usually added the stamp of their own individuality. So Virgil, inspired by Homer, produced a masterpiece quite unlike Homer's. Greek architecture was imitated, but one can always tell a Roman building from a Greek. The Romans generally preferred the Corinthian style and, unlike the Greeks, often placed their temples and other buildings on a high base. The round temple with dome is distinctly Roman. Greek sculpture attained a beauty never since equaled, but the Romans excelled in making realistic portrait statues. The Greeks were superior in mathematics, especially geometry (the name of their greatest geometrician, Euclid, still is a synonym for geometry); the Romans developed applied mathematics, such as surveying and engineering.

For a thousand years after the downfall of the Roman Empire Greek thought and art were preserved in western Europe only through Latin literature and tradition. The civilization of western Europe, and therefore of America, was developed from this Roman tradition, with its Greek borrowings. Just as the Romans had been filled with Greek culture, so now the world was imbued with the Greco-Roman. Then, through the interest created by the praise of Greek literature found in Roman writers, Greek began to be studied again and the world supplemented its huge Roman inheritance by direct borrowing from the Greeks.

So it has come about that two such different peoples as the Greeks and Romans have, through Roman hospitality to Greek ideas, transmitted to us a joint Greco-Roman civilization. But it must be said that without Rome Greek culture might not have been preserved at all or at least the modern world would not have been prepared to appreciate and welcome it.

Virgil, the great poet who described Rome's ideals, stated that others (meaning the Greeks) were better sculptors, orators, astronomers, but:

> **Tū regere imperiō populōs, Rōmāne, mementō.**
> **(Hae tibi erunt artēs) pācīque impōnere mōrem,**
> **Parcere subiectīs et dēbellāre superbōs.**

Your mission, Romans, is to govern the peoples [of the Empire] (these will be your arts) and to make peace a habit. Treat subject peoples gently but be ruthless to the overbearing.

QUESTIONS

1. What do we owe to the Greeks? To the Romans?
2. Which modern nations are more like the Greeks than the Romans? Which are more like the Romans?

An Etruscan tomb painting at Tarquinia depicts a lyre player. Note the two birds in the tree at the left.

Photo Nimatallah/Art Resource

The Greek Temple of "Neptune" (really Hera) at Paestum, southern Italy. Best preserved and handsomest of Doric temples, it was built in the Fifth century B.C.

Photo Tomsich Rome/Photo Researchers, Inc.

A Latin Play
168. BULLA

Persōnae

Aelia, *parva puella Rōmāna*　　　**Damyx** ⎫
Lāneis, *serva*　　　　　　　　　　**Thoa** ⎬ *uxōrēs latrōnum*
Q. Aelius Frontō, *Rōmānus, pater Aeliae*　⎭

LOCUS: In oppidō Paestō, ante templum. (*Ē dextrā parte accēdunt Frontō, Aelia, Lāneis.*)

LĀNEIS: Aelia! Bulla tua aurea! Eam nōn videō. Estne āmissa?

AELIA: Ecce! Nōn āmissa est—sub tunicā est.

LĀNEIS: Quam[1] terrēbar! Necesse est tē eam semper dīligenter 5 servāre, quod tē ē malīs servābit.

FRONTŌ: Hoc est templum. Aelia, volō tē cum Lāneide hīc remanēre. Ego deōs ōrābō ut nōbīs iter fēlīx dent. Lāneis, manē cum Aeliā, quod magna perīcula adsunt.

LĀNEIS: Ita, ita. Manēbō. (*Frontō in templum it.*)　　　　　10

AELIA: Quandō domum[2] ībimus, Lāneis?

LĀNEIS: Quandō deī iter fēlīx nōbīs dare volent. Nōnne autem Paestum pulchrum oppidum est? Nōnne Titūrius, hospes patris tuī, nōbīs in hōc oppidō manentibus semper bonus est?

AELIA: Ita; et Titūrium maximē amō, sed—　　　　　　　　　15

LĀNEIS: Multōs servōs habet—labor meus hīc levis est. Nōnne vīs labōrem Lāneidis tuae levem esse?

---

[1] *how.*　　　　[2] *home.*

109

The Theater of Marcellus in Rome, built by Caesar and Augustus, was named after the latter's nephew. It could accommodate over 10,000 spectators.

AELIA: Sed mātrem vidēre volō. Iam diū eam nōn videō. (*Ante templum nunc cōnsīdunt.*)

20 LĀNEIS: Quam calidus est diēs! Cōnfecta sum.

AELIA: Lāneis, quandō pater sciet iter fēlīx futūrum esse?

LĀNEIS: Quandō ōmina bona erunt.

AELIA: Ōh! (*Lāneis dormīre parat.*) Lāneis, nōnne cupis Rōmam rūrsus vidēre?

25 LĀNEIS: Quid? Ita, ita.

AELIA: Multa agam. Prīmum mātrī salūtem dīcam. Tum omnibus amīcīs multa dē Paestō, dē Titūriō, dē itinere nārrābō. Nūlla ex amīcīs meīs iter tam longum fēcit. Quam mē mīrābuntur! (*Lāneis nunc dormit.*) Tum omnia illa dōna quae prō amīcīs ēmī eīs dabō—bene
30 erit. (*Ē sinistrā parte accēdunt Damyx et Thoa.*)

DAMYX: Vidēsne illam?

AELIA: Per viās ībō, et omnia aedificia nova spectābō.

THOA: Pulchra est. Et callida vidētur. Eam rapiāmus.

AELIA: Prō pūpīs[3] meīs novās vestēs faciam.—

35 DAMYX: Cum magnā autem cūrā agere dēbēmus. Serva adest.

THOA: Illa dormit. (*Aelia Thoam et Damycem videt. Prōcēdit ut eās spectet.*)

DAMYX: Puella pulchra es. Nōnne vīs nōbīscum ambulāre? Multa grātissima tibi mōnstrābimus.

40 AELIA: Nōlō. Pater iussit mē hīc remanēre.

THOA: Oho! Bona puella es. Nōs autem nōn longē prōcēdēmus. Brevī tempore revertēmur. Praetereā dōnum pulchrum dabimus.

AELIA: Nōn ībō.

[3] *dolls.*

DAMYX (*Thoae*): Quid faciēmus?

THOA (*Aeliae*): Sī nōbīscum veniēs, tē multa grāta docēbimus. 45

AELIA: Māter mē multa docet. Quid vōs mē docēre potestis?

THOA: Docēbimus quō modō magnam pecūniam sine labōre semper parāre possīs. Tum semper poteris emere omnia quae cupis.

AELIA: Vōbīscum nōn ībō. Fūrēs [4] estis.

DAMYX: Nōn fūrēs, sed Furiae sumus. Audīsne? Sī nōbīscum 50 libenter nōn ībis, tē īre cōgēmus.

THOA: Et sī clāmābis, tē interficiēmus.

AELIA: Vōs nōn timeō.

DAMYX: Quid?

AELIA: Furiae malae sunt, et malae rēs mihi nocēre nōn possunt. 55

THOA: Cūr?

AELIA: Ex omnibus malīs mē servat bulla. (*Bullam mōnstrat.*)

DAMYX: Ecce!

THOA: Aurea est. (*Eōdem tempore et Damyx et Thoa bullam rapere cōnantur; inter sē pugnant.*) 60

DAMYX ET THOA: Au—au! (*Lāneis sē movet.*)

THOA: S—st! Serva sē movet. Prehendēmur.

DAMYX. Fugiāmus. (*In sinistram partem celeriter exeunt.*)

LĀNEIS: Aelia!

AELIA: Adsum, Lāneis. 65

LĀNEIS: Paene dormiēbam. Calidissimus est diēs. (*Ē templō venit Frontō.*)

FRONTŌ: Aelia! Lāneis! Ōmina optima sunt. Deī nōbīs iter fēlīx dant. Hōc ipsō diē proficīscēmur.

AELIA: Bene, bene est. 70

FRONTŌ: Et quid agēbat Aelia mea?

AELIA: Duās Furiās vīdī.

FRONTŌ ET LĀNEIS: Quid?

AELIA: Ita. Mē sēcum īre cupiēbant. Cōnābantur mihi nocēre. Malae erant—sed bulla mea mē servāvit. 75

FRONTŌ (*parvā vōce*): Quid dīcit, Lāneis?

LĀNEIS (*parvā vōce*): Nihil est. Calidus diēs est, et puella cōnfecta dormiēbat. Haec in somnō vidēbat; nunc putat omnia vēra esse.

FRONTŌ: Intellegō. Prōcēdāmus, Aelia. Memoriam Furiārum dēpōnāmus, et nōs ad iter parēmus. 80

AELIA: Ita. Sed bullam meam semper amābō, quod haec mē ā Furiīs dēfendit.

LĀNEIS: Rēctē. (*Frontō et Lāneis rīdent. Exeunt omnēs in dextram partem.*)

[4] *thieves.*

111

UNIT III

LIVY

In this painting by Jacques-Louis David (1748–1825), we see the contest between the Horatii and the Curiatii that decided the outcome of the war between the Romans and the Albans (see page 115).

169. A GREAT HISTORIAN

Livy was one of Rome's most famous historians. Living nearly 2000 years ago in the time of Augustus, the most glorious period in Roman literature, he wrote a history of Rome from its beginnings to his own time. The purpose of the work was to give the Roman citizen a higher appreciation of the courageous acts and the moral integrity which had made his country great.

The work was divided into 142 books. Of these only thirty-five, including the first ten, are now in existence. On account of the very great importance of the work for the history of Rome, it has ever been the dream of historians to find the lost books.

The old Roman tales that Livy weaves into his early history of Rome may be mere legends, but they are, nonetheless, like the story of Washington and the cherry tree, of great importance and interest and give a good insight into Roman character and ideals. One historian says of them:

If now we take a general view of this wonderful collection of legends, caring little whether the details be wholly or in part imaginary, but regarding the heroes and heroines as at least a gallery of moral types, we may gain a fair notion of the kind of greatness that carried Rome, the city of the Tiber, to the headship of the ancient world. It is simple enough. There is a plain devotion to duty, a disregard of personal inclinations, a pride that disdains submission, a constancy of the finest temper. There is a clear grasp of the object of the hour and a willingness to take the necessary steps. . . . We are not dealing with a clever people, like the Greeks. Here there is no constellation of brilliant stars, but a succession of good citizens, able to coöperate and to obey, and preëminent among peoples ancient or modern in steadiness of nerve.

The stories in the following thirteen lessons are adapted chiefly from Livy.[1]

QUESTION

Can you name any prominent citizens of the world today with qualities similar to those mentioned in the quotation?

---

[1] Some parts are based on Eutropius, a writer of the fourth century A.D., who wrote a very brief history of Rome, in the early portion of which he used an abridged edition of Livy.

Lesson XXVII

170. EARLY KINGS OF ROME

Rōmānum imperium ā Rōmulō initium habet, quī urbem parvam
in Palātīnō cōnstituit. Cīvitāte conditā, quam ex nōmine suō Rōmam
vocāvit, haec ēgit: multitūdinem fīnitimōrum in cīvitātem recēpit et
centum ex seniōribus dēlēgit, quōs senātōrēs nōmināvit quod senēs
erant. Hōrum cōnsiliō omnia ēgit.   5

Post mortem Rōmulī Numa Pompilius rēx creātus est, quī nūllam
partem quidem Rōmae adiēcit, sed nōn minus cīvitātem quam Rōmulus iūvit; nam lēgēs mōrēsque Rōmānīs cōnstituit, quī cōnsuētūdine [1] proeliōrum ā fīnitimīs sēmibarbarī putābantur. Annum dīvīsit
in decem mēnsēs et multa sacra ac templa Rōmae [2] cōnstituit.   10

Huic successit Tullus Hostīlius. Hōc rēge, Rōmānī cum Albānīs
bellum gerēbant. Forte in duōbus exercitibus erant trigeminī [3] frātrēs
et aetāte et vīribus parēs. Horātiī erant Rōmānī; Cūriātiī, Albānī. Cum
hīs agunt [4] rēgēs, ut hī sōlī prō suā patriā exercitūque pugnent.

Tempore cōnstitūtō, arma capiunt. Duo Rōmānī, vulnerātīs tribus 15
Albānīs, interfectī sunt. Forte tertius Rōmānus integer fuit; tribus
Cūriātiīs sōlus nōn pār erat, sed contrā singulōs ferōx. Itaque, ut cum
singulīs pugnāret, fūgit. Tum respiciēns videt eōs magnīs intervāllīs
sequentēs; ūnus nōn multō [5] abest. In eum magnō impetū rediit; et
dum Albānus exercitus clāmat Cūriātiīs [6] ut opem ferant frātrī, iam 20
Horātius, caesō hoste, secundam pugnam petēbat et alterum Cūriā-
tium interficit. Iamque singulī supererant,[7] sed nec spē nec vīribus
parēs. Tertiō Cūriātiō quoque interfectō, Rōmānī cum gaudiō Horātium accipiunt.

Horātī soror spōnsa ūnī ex Cūriātiīs erat. Cum Horātius ad urbem 25
accēderet, soror eum vīdit gerentem palūdāmentum [8] Cūriātī quod
ipsa cōnfēcerat. Eam flentem [9] frāter interfēcit. "Abī [10] ad spōnsum,"
inquit, "oblīta [11] frātrum mortuōrum vīvīque,[12] oblīta patriae. Sīc eat
quaecumque Rōmāna [13] lūgēbit hostem."

---

[1] *because of their habit of (fighting) battles.*   [2] *at Rome.*   [3] *triplet.*   [4] *arrange.*
[5] *far.*   [6] Indirect object of **clāmat.**   [7] From **supersum.**   [8] *cloak.*
[9] *because she wept.*   [10] *go.*
[11] *having forgotten,* with genitive.   [12] Refers to himself: *your one living brother.*
[13] *So may every Roman woman go (to her death) who.*

115

1. Who was killed first in the battle of the Horatii?
2. Who was wounded first?
3. Under what king did the Horatii fight?
4. How would you apply the Latin motto "Dīvide et imperā" to the story of the Horatii?

171. The Dative with Compounds

Sometimes when certain prepositions are used as prefixes with intransitive verbs, the meanings of the verbs change in such a way as to require the dative. The English equivalent often calls for *to* or *for*. See **successit** in line 11. No general rule can be given. The dative regularly goes closely with the prefix. When the simple verb is transitive, the compound sometimes is used with both an accusative and a dative. See **adiēcit** in line 7.

172. Translation

1. Whom did Tullus Hostilius succeed?
2. After killing two Albans, Horatius approached the third.
3. Numa added no hill to Rome, but he gave the Roman laws.
4. Numa divided the year into months and established many customs.

173. Vocabulary

cōnsuētūdō, –dinis, f., *custom*	**sequor, sequī, secūtus,** *follow*
fors, fortis, f., *chance*	**succēdō, –ere, –cessī, –cessūrus,** *succeed*
initium, –tī, n., *beginning*	**vīvus, –a, –um,** *living*
intervāllum, –ī, n., *distance*	**vulnerō,** 1, *wound*
iuvō, iuvāre, iūvī, iūtus, *aid*	

The words in these vocabularies are basic words and should be thoroughly learned. Enter them in your vocabulary notebook and add English derivatives.

This famous Etruscan sculpture of the Apollo di Veio (c. 500 B.C.) was found in 1916. Veio was an important Etruscan city between the Eighth and Sixth centuries B.C. It was conquered by the Romans in 396 B.C.

174. Word Stories

There are many interesting derivatives of **sequor.** From it was derived **secundus,** English "second," whose chief meaning therefore is *following.* Its use as a measure of time arose thus: **hōra** means *hour;* **hōra minūta** means a *diminished hour,* or "minute" (from **minuō,** *make less,* which comes in turn from **minus**); **hōra minūta secunda** means a *second-degree minute,* or smaller division of a minute. The "sequence" of tenses refers to the way one verb *follows* another in the use of a tense. A "suit" of clothes is one in which the various pieces *follow* or match one another. A "suite" of rooms consists of several rooms *following* one another, i.e., one after the other. What is a "suitor"? An "executive"? A "prosecutor"?

Suitor.

Lesson XXVIII

175. OUT GO THE KINGS

Post Hostīlium Ancus Mārtius suscēpit imperium, tum Prīscus Tarquinius. Circum [1] Rōmae aedificāvit. Lūdōs Rōmānōs īnstituit. Vīcit īdem Sabīnōs. Mūrōs fēcit et cloācās. [2] Capitōlium aedificāvit.

Eō tempore rēs mīra accidit. Servius Tullius puer erat rēgis servus.
5 In capite huius puerī dormientis flamma appāruit multōrum in cōnspectū. Cum quīdam aquam ad exstinguendum ferret, ab rēgīnā retentus est, quae movērī vetuit puerum. Tum cum somnō etiam flamma abiit. Tum rēgīna rēgī sēcrētō "Vidēsne, Tarquinī," inquit, "hunc puerum tam humilem? Hic lūmen [3] rēgnō nostrō erit praesi-
10 diumque nōbīs; eī [4] amīcī sīmus et bonīs artibus īnstituāmus." [5] Hōc factō, puer fit vir īnsignis. Cum marītus quaererētur fīliae [4] Tarquinī, nēmō Rōmānus cum Tulliō cōnferrī potuit, rēxque eī sē fīliam suam spondēre mālle dīxit. Post mortem Tarquinī Servius, quī servus fuerat, rēx factus est.

---

[1] Noun.   [2] *sewers.*   [3] *glory.*   [4] Dative.   [5] *let us train (him) in good arts.*

Tullius montēs trēs, Quirīnālem, Vīminālem, Ēsquilīnum, urbī 15 adiūnxit; fossās circum mūrum dūxit. Prīmus [6] omnium cēnsum habuit, quī adhūc per orbem terrārum nōn cognitus erat. Sub eō Rōma, omnibus in cēnsum dēlātīs,[7] habuit LXXXIIII mīlia cīvium.

L. Tarquinius Superbus, fīlius Prīscī Tarquinī, Tullium occīdit et Rōmae rēgnāvit. Cum fīlius eius nōbilissimam mātrōnam Lucrētiam 20 iniūriā affēcisset, eaque dē iniūriā marītō et patrī et amīcīs dīxisset, in omnium cōnspectū Lucrētia sē occīdit. Propter quam causam L. Iūnius Brūtus populum contrā Tarquinium incitāvit. Posteā exercitus quoque eum relīquit. Cum imperāvisset annōs XXV, cum uxōre et līberīs suīs fūgit. Septem rēgēs CCXXXXIIII annōs rēgnā- 25 verant. Mors fortis mulieris cīvitātem līberāvit, nam post hoc duo cōnsulēs, quī singulōs annōs imperium habuērunt, ā populō creātī sunt.

QUESTIONS
1. Who was the fifth king?
2. How many kings did Rome have?
3. Who was the father of Tarquin the Proud?
4. Who was the son-in-law of Tarquin the Elder?

176. Conjugation of Mālō

Mālō (= **magis volō**) has the same irregularities as **volō**:

PRESENT INDICATIVE		PRESENT SUBJUNCTIVE	
mālō	mālumus	mālim	mālīmus
māvīs	māvultis	mālīs	mālītis
māvult	mālunt	mālit	mālint

The infinitive is **mālle**. For full conjugation see **592**.

177. Locative

As you know, the ablative with **in** is used to express "place where": **in Italiā,** *in Italy.* But names of towns, as well as **domus,** have a special case form, the *locative,* to express this idea. The ending of this case is the same as the genitive in the singular of nouns of the first and second declensions, and the same as the ablative elsewhere. No preposition is used: **Rōmae** (line 2), *at Rome;* **domī,** *at home;* **Athēnīs,** *at Athens;* **Carthāgine,** *at Carthage.*

178. Cum Clauses

Review **cum** clauses **(97)** and find those used in the story above.

___

[6] *He was the first of all to.*   [7] *enrolled.*

179. Translation

1. "Dear Servius," the queen said, "we prefer to be your friends."
2. The power of the state was given to the boy when the king died.
3. When the flame appeared on the boy's head, the king adopted him.
4. When he had ruled many years, he lost his power on account of his own son.

180. Vocabulary

adiungō, –ere, adiūnxī, adiūnctus, *join to*
cōnspectus, –ūs, m., *sight*
dēferō, dēferre, dētulī, dēlātus, *offer, enroll*

fossa, –ae, f., *trench*
inquit, *he said* (never first word)
mālō, mālle, māluī, ——, *prefer*
mūrus, –ī, m., *wall*

181. Word Study: Prefixes

The prefix **sēmi–** means *half* or *partly:* **sēmibarbarus,** *semibarbarous. Semiannual* means *occurring every half year.*

The prefix **bi–** or **bis–** means *twice* or *two:* **biennium,** *a period of two years* (from **annus**). Distinguish carefully *semiannual* and *biennial, semimonthly* and *bimonthly.* **Bi–** is often found in chemical terms: *bicarbonate, bichloride.*

The prefix **ūn–, ūni–** (from **ūnus**) means *one: uniform.*

The prefix **multi–** (from **multus**) means *much, many: multiform, multigraph, multimillionaire.*

Give three other examples of each of these prefixes.

Explain *adjutant, fortuitous, initiate, successor, vulnerable.*

This painting by Tiziano shows the noble matron Lucretia, and Tarquin.

Photo Nimatallah/Art Resource

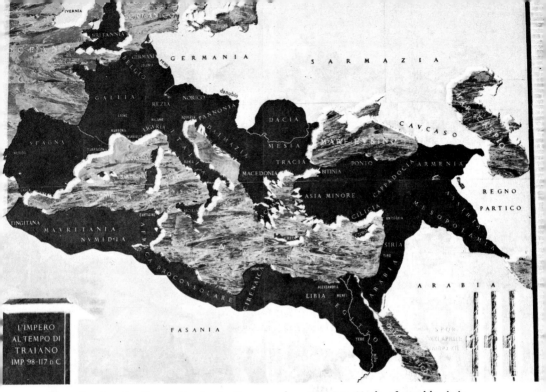

Map showing the Roman Empire in the second century A.D. Made of marble, it is fastened to the wall of the Basilica of Maxentius in Rome.

Lesson XXIX

182. HOW BRUTUS GOT HIS NAME

Altera fābula dē Brūtō nunc nārranda est. Dum Tarquinius, ultimus rēgum Rōmānōrum, Iovis templum Rōmae aedificat, ōmen terribile vīsum est: anguis [1] ex columnā ēlāpsus,[2] rēgis pectus anxiīs cūrīs implēvit. Itaque duōs fīliōs Delphōs [3] ad ōrāculum cōnsulendum mīsit. Comes eīs additus est L. Iūnius. Hic ex industriā [4] imitātus stultitiam, 5 cum sē suaque praedae esse rēgī sineret, Brūtī [5] quoque nōn recūsāvit cognōmen, ab Tarquiniō datum, ut sub eō cognōmine latēns, līberātor ille populī Rōmānī opperīrētur [6] tempora sua. Is tum ab Tarquiniīs, fīliīs rēgis, ductus est Delphōs,[3] lūdibrium [7] vērius quam comes. Quō postquam vēnērunt, perfectīs patris mandātīs, cupīdō incessit animōs 10

---

[1] snake.   [2] slipping.   [3] to Delphi.   [4] With ex: on purpose.
[5] The name means stupid.   [6] wait for, bide.   [7] laughingstock.

iuvenum rogandī ad quem eōrum rēgnum Rōmānum esset ventūrum. Ex īnfimō vōcem redditam audiunt: "Imperium summum Rōmae habēbit quī vestrum prīmus, ō iuvenēs, ōsculum mātrī dederit." Tarquiniī sortī [8] permittunt uter prior, cum ad patriam rediissent, mātrī

15 ōsculum daret. Brūtus aliō putāns spectāre [9] vōcem ōrāculī, velut sī prōlāpsus cecidisset, terram ōsculō contigit, quod ea commūnis māter omnium mortālium erat. Et sīc ēvēnit: post fugam Tarquinī et fīliōrum suōrum, Brūtus imperium Rōmae obtinuit.

QUESTIONS

1. What is the point of the story?
2. Who went to Delphi and why?
3. How did Junius get the name Brutus?

183. Future Passive Participle and Gerund

Review the future passive participle, the gerund, and the dative of agent (**611, 612, 599,** 9).

Find all the examples of these in the story above.

184. Translation

1. Who did Brutus think was the mother of all men?
2. A temple had-to-be-built at Rome by the citizens.
3. Brutus did not think that he had-to-fear [10] the king.
4. The two young men went to the oracle for the purpose of asking [11] which would be king.

185. Vocabulary

comes, comitis, m. and f., *companion*
contingō, –ere, –tigī, –tāctus, *touch*
impleō, –ēre, implēvī, implētus, *fill*
iuvenis, –is, m., *young man*

pectus, pectoris, n., *breast, heart*
sinō, –ere, sīvī, situs, *allow*
stultitia, –ae, f., *stupidity*

186. Word Study

Comes (cum, īre) is one who "goes with" you; a *companion* (**cum, pānis**) is one who shares "bread with" you.

Explain *additive, comity, contingency, elapse, juvenile, latent, narrative, osculatory, pectoral, ultimatum.*

---

[8] *to chance.*   [9] *had another meaning* (literally, *looked in another direction*).
[10] Use the passive.   [11] Use the gerund with **ad** or **causā.**

Left: A modern forgery but still a good portrait of an Etruscan soldier.
Below: Statue of an Etruscan soldier helping a wounded comrade.

Metropolitan Museum of Art

Lesson XXX

187. HOW "LEFTY" (SCAEVOLA) GOT HIS NAME

Tarquinius, ut reciperet rēgnum, bellum Rōmānīs intulit, Porsenā, rēge Etrūscōrum, auxilium ferente. Illō tempore Horātius Coclēs pontem dēfendit et Rōmam servāvit. Urbs tum obsidēbātur ā Porsenā, et frūmentī erat inopia. Sedendō [1] expugnātūrum sē urbem Porsena spērābat. Tum C. Mūcius in hostium castra īre cōnstituit. Nē forte 5 ā mīlitibus Rōmānīs retraherētur, senātum adiit. "Trānsīre Tiberim," inquit, "patrēs,[2] et in castra hostium īre volō. Deīs iuvantibus, magnum in animō factum fīxum habeō." Probant patrēs. Abditō intrā vestem gladiō, proficīscitur. Ubi eō vēnit, in multitūdine hostium ad rēgis tribūnal [3] cōnstitit. Ibi stīpendium mīlitibus forte dabātur, et 10 rēgis scrība,[4] quī rēgī simillimus ōrnātū [5] erat, multa agēbat. Mūcius Porsenam nōn cognōverat, neque rogāre volēbat, nē ipse aperīret quis esset; itaque scrībam, quem rēgem esse crēdidit, prō rēge occīdit. Deinde postquam per hostēs territōs gladiō viam sibi ipse fēcit, rēgis mīlitēs eum prehēnsum retrāxērunt. Ante tribūnal rēgis stāns, tum 15

---

[1] *by remaining encamped.* What literally? Cf. "sit-down strike."   [2] *senators.*
[3] *tribunal, platform.*   [4] *secretary.*   [5] *dress.*

Etruscan vase of the eighth century B.C. The design, cut into the clay, shows a dog with tongue hanging out.

Metropolitan Museum of Art,
Fletcher Fund, 1928

quoque in tantō perīculō timendus [6] magis quam timēns, "Rōmānus sum," inquit, "cīvis; C. Mūcium mē vocant. Hostem occīdere voluī, sed morī sciō. Nec ego sōlus in tē [7] hōs animōs habeō. Nūllus exercitus timendus tibi, nūllum proelium timendum est; ūnī tibi cum singulīs
20 rēs erit." [8] Tum rēx simul īrā commōtus perīculōque perterritus, ignem circumdarī iussit ut Mūcius īnsidiās statim explicāre cōgerētur. Mūcius autem, "Ēn tibi," [9] inquit, "ut sentiās quam [10] vīle corpus sit eīs quī magnam glōriam vident," dextramque manum ignī [11] ad sacrificium factō iniēcit. Rēx, tantam virtūtem mīrātus, Mūcium līberum dīmīsit.
25 Huic Mūciō posteā, quod dextram manum āmīserat, nōmen Scae-volae [12] datum est.

QUESTIONS

1. Why did Mucius kill Porsena's secretary?
2. How did Mucius get the same Scaevola?
3. Why did Mucius want to cross the Tiber?
4. Why was there a crowd at the king's tribunal?

188. Latin Sentence Structure

Mīlitēs eum prehēnsum retrāxērunt (line 15), *The soldiers seized him and pulled him back.*

Note the striking difference between English and Latin sentence structure.

[6] *to be feared.*   [7] *toward you.*
[8] *the decision will be between you and individual (enemies).*
[9] *Look you.*   [10] *how.*   [11] For the case see **599,** 7.
[12] *Left-handed ("Lefty"); pronounced Sev'ola.*

Latin prefers to vary the construction by use of participles (including the ablative absolute) and subordinate clauses of various sorts. English prefers coordinate constructions connected by *and*.

189. Translation

1. Mucius said that Rome was to be saved by him.
2. When Rome was being besieged, Mucius approached the senate.
3. He was to be feared by the enemy, for he had come to free Rome by fighting.
4. He set out for the enemy's camp for the purpose of killing the king.

190. Vocabulary

abdō, abdere, abdidī, abditus, *put away, hide*

aperiō, –īre, aperuī, apertus, *open, reveal*

circumdō, –dare, –dedī, –datus, *put around*

fīgō, –ere, fīxī, fīxus, *fix*

inopia, –ae, f., *lack*

īnsidiae, –ārum, f. pl., *plot, ambush*

intrā, prep. w. acc., *within*

obsideō, –ēre, obsēdī, obsessus, *besiege*

pōns, pontis, m., *bridge*

stīpendium, –dī, n., *pay*

191. Word Study: Spelling

We have many silent consonants in English words. They cause trouble in spelling. In some cases the difficulty is cleared up by taking thought of the Latin original, for Latin has no silent letters. Compare the following, often misspelled: *debt* (**dēbitus**), *honor* (**honor**), *assign* (**signum**), *mortgage* (**mortem**), *receipt* (**receptus**). Can you find other instances?

Roman relief sculpture, showing the Roman fondness for balanced arrangement.

Much of early Roman "history" is legend. This relief in the Forum marks the Lacus Curtius, where, according to one story, the Sabine Mettius Curtius fell off his horse into a swamp (*lacus*) while battling the Romans. Another version says that a young Roman knight plunged into a chasm at this spot as a self-sacrifice to save the state.

Anthony Paccione

Lesson XXXI

192. THE PLEBEIANS GO ON STRIKE [1]

Paulō post rēgēs exāctōs [2] bellum cīvīle propter aes aliēnum [3] inter senātōrēs et plēbem oritur. Hōrum [4] multī dīxērunt sē in fīnibus hostium prō lībertāte et imperiō pugnantēs ā cīvibus domī oppressōs esse, tūtiōremque in bellō inter hostēs lībertātem plēbis esse quam
5 in pāce inter cīvēs. Quīdam, quī Sabīnō bellō fortis mīles fuerat, "Mē absente," inquit, "ager vāstātus est, vīlla incēnsa, tribūtum imperātum. Aes aliēnum facere [5] mē oportēbat. Posteā agrum āmīsī et ā crēditōribus in vincula coniectus sum." Hōc audītō, multitūdō postulāvit ut senātus vocārētur. Senātū convocātō, nūntiātur Volscōs ad
10 urbem oppugnandam venīre. Omnēs, inimīcitiā dēpositā, pugnant, hostēsque vincuntur. Sed post bellum senātus nihil dē plēbe ēgit. Tum aliud bellum oritur. Cōnsulēs nōmina cīvium legunt. [6] Cum ad nōmen

---

[1] In early Rome there were two classes of citizens, the patricians (senators), who had all the power and privileges, and the plebeians, who had none. The explanation of the origin of this difference is uncertain.

[2] *after the expulsion of the kings.* What literally?

[3] *another's money,* i.e., *debt.* It is a wholesome thing for a debtor to think of a debt as someone else's money.

[4] i.e., the plebeians.

[5] *go into debt.*

[6] They called the roll in the draft.

nēmō respondēret; omnēs dīcunt lībertātem reddendam esse priusquam arma danda,[7] ut prō patriā cīvibusque, nōn prō dominīs pugnent. Dictātor plēbī meliōrem condiciōnem post bellum pollicitus est. Sed, 15 bellō cōnfectō, nihil āctum est.

Tum plēbs in Sacrum montem sēcessērunt.[8] Hic mōns trāns Aniēnem flūmen est tria ab urbe mīlia passuum. Patribus [9] placuit ad plēbem mittī Menēnium Agrippam. Is hoc nārrāvit:

"Ōlim reliquae partēs corporis hūmānī īrātae erant quod suā 20 cūrā, suō labōre ventrī [10] omnia quaerēbantur, quī ipse nihil agēbat. Coniūrāvērunt nē manūs [11] ad ōs cibum ferrent, nec ōs acciperet, nec dentēs cōnficerent.[12] Dum ventrem hōc modō vincere volunt, ipsa membra paene moriuntur. Inde appāret ventrem nōn magis alī quam alere." Cum Menēnius ostendisset quam [13] corporis discordia similis 25 esset īrae plēbis, pāx facta est hāc condiciōne, ut tribūnī plēbis creārentur neque ūllī patrī [14] licēret eum magistrātum capere. Tribūnī accēpērunt potestātem auxilī dandī [15] contrā cōnsulēs.

QUESTIONS

1. How did the civil war start?
2. Where was the Sacred Mount?
3. Who was permitted to be a tribune?
4. What power did the tribunes have?

193. Impersonal Verbs

Some verbs are at times used impersonally, either without an expressed subject or with a clause as subject. Compare **nūntiātur** in line 9 and **appāret** in line 24.

Other verbs are used only impersonally and therefore have no forms in the first and second persons. Note the differences in construction:

1. With **licet** the dative of the person is used: **Mihi hoc facere licet,** *It is permitted to me to do this; I may do this.*

---

[7] *before arms are given (to them).*

[8] 494 B.C. As **plēbs** is plural in thought, the plural verb is used. So in English we may say "The committee *is* meeting," when the committee is thought of as a whole, or "The committee *are* not agreed," when we think of the individual members.   [9] *senators.*   [10] *for the stomach.*

[11] Subject of **ferrent.** The parts of the body went on strike against the stomach.

[12] *"do up,"* i.e., *chew up.*   [13] *how.*   [14] *patrician.*

[15] i.e., to a citizen who appealed to them.

2. With **oportet** the accusative is used as subject of the infinitive: **Mē hoc facere oportet,** *It is necessary that I do this; I must (ought to) do this.* This may be expressed in two other ways: **Hoc facere dēbeō** and **hoc mihi faciendum est.**

3. With the impersonal form **placet** the dative is used and it generally has the idiomatic sense *it is decided by* (literally, *it is pleasing to*): **Mihi placet,** *It is decided by me; I have decided.*

194. Translation

1. No senator will be allowed to oppress the common people.
2. It will not be necessary (for) them to demand better conditions.[16]
3. The citizens ought not to be seized and thrown into chains by creditors.[16]
4. It has been decided by the senate to make peace by promising certain conditions.

195. Vocabulary

aes, aeris, n., *bronze, money*
alō, alere, aluī, alitus, *feed, nourish*
coniūrō, 1, *conspire*
licet, –ēre, licuit or **licitum est,** *it is permitted*
magistrātus, –ūs, m., *magistrate, office*

ōlim, adv., *once*
oportet, –ēre, oportuit, *it is necessary*
oppugnō, 1, *attack*
plēbs, plēbis, f., *common people*
postulō, 1, *demand*
tūtus, –a, –um, *safe*

196. Word Study: Terms Used in Geometry

acute **(acūtus)**
adjacent **(ad–, iaceō)**
circumscribe **(circum–, scrībō)**
coincide **(co–, incidō)**
complementary **(compleō)**
concurrent **(con–, currō)**
equidistant **(aequus, dis–, stō)**
equilateral **(aequus, latus)**
inscribe **(in–, scrībō)**

locus **(locus)**
median **(medius)**
plane **(plānus)**
quadrilateral **(quattuor, latus)**
Q.E.D. **(quod erat dēmōnstrandum)**
Q.E.F. **(quod erat faciendum)**
subtend **(sub–, tendō)**
tangent **(tangō)**
transversal **(trāns–, vertō)**

Define the preceding words and find other geometrical terms derived from Latin.

[16] Translate in two ways.

Italian stamp with a picture of Cicero for the two-thousandth anniversary of his death.

POSTE ITALIANE L.25

CICERONE
43 a.c.-1957

This Roman temple is a shrine of American democracy. The Jefferson Memorial in Washington imitates Monticello, Jefferson's Virginia home, which he designed.

197. CIVIL LIBERTY AND DEMOCRACY

As stated in the American Declaration of Independence, we believe that men have "certain unalienable rights," and "that to secure these rights Governments are instituted among Men, deriving their just powers from the consent of the governed."

But in ancient Rome, even after the expulsion of the kings, the common people had very little voice in the way in which they were governed by the senatorial and patrician oligarchy (*rule by the few*). They struggled for several hundred years for the right to hold certain political and military offices, for intermarriage among the classes, for fair taxes, and for adequate protection in the courts. Our word *plebiscite,* a vote of the people, is an inheritance from that struggle. The history of Rome shows that the fight for liberty and democracy is never completely won, that we must always be on the alert to defend both, that we must never take them for granted.

The new office of tribune, open only to plebeians, had the power of veto over the actions of the patrician consuls and senate. This led to a system of checks and balances which was adopted in the Constitution of the United States. We use the Roman tribune's word, **vetō,** *I forbid,* of the President's power to reject the acts passed by Congress. Compare too the veto power in the Security Council of the United Nations.

The settlement of the strike has a lesson for us. It was ended by mediation and through concessions by both sides. The plebeians did not strike in order to destroy their country but because they had just grievances, which they tried to settle by peaceful means.

129

Universal-International

Scene in the peristyle of a Roman house. From the film *Spartacus*.

198. LATĪNUM HODIERNUM

Pictūrae Mōbilēs

Amāsne tēlevīsiōnem? Habēsne domī māchinam ad tēlevīsiōnem accommodātam? An pictūrae mōbilēs quae in theātrīs videntur magis tibi placent? Vīdistīne tālēs pictūrās quae dē vītā antīquā agunt? Inter eās est *Iūlius Caesar,* illa fābula quam Pīlīvibrātor
5 (Anglicē Shakespeare) scrīpsit, et *Antōnius et Cleopātra.* Deinde sunt eae quae dē Rōmānīs et Christiānīs agunt, ut *Quō Vādis, Chlamys,*[17] *Dēmētrius et Gladiātōrēs, Ben Hur.* Hae omnēs nimis crūdēlitātem īnsāniamque imperātōrum, gladiātōrēs in arēnā pugnantēs, Christiānōs leōnibus aliīsque ferīs animālibus obiectōs dēscrībunt sed
10 tamen spectācula iūcunda praebent, quae mīlitēs, senātōrēs, virginēs Vestālēs, gladiātōrēs mōnstrant, nec nōn [18] amphitheātra, templa, aedificia antīqua. Similis est pictūra *Spartacus* appellāta, quae dē servīs ā Rōmānīs crūdēlibus oppressīs agit. Sed mihi maximē placent pictūrae mōbilēs quae quidem dē vītā hodiernā agunt, Rōmae tamen
15 factae, pulcherrimōs prōspectūs praebent, et ruīnās Rōmānās et aedificia moderna, nam antīqua et hodierna Rōmae ita cōnfūsa sunt ut ōva mixta vel carō modō Hamburgiēnsī cocta. Plūrēs pictūrās huius generis vīdimus; aliae certē prōdūcentur.

Quod tot pictūrae huius generis nunc in theātrīs nostrīs mōnstrantur
20 nōn sine ratiōne est: conicere possumus haec spectācula Americānīs grātissima esse, rēs Rōmānās nōbīs iūcundissimās, vītam antīquam et imperium Rōmānum populō nostrō magnae cūrae esse.

---

[17] *The Robe.*   [18] *and also.*

130

Lesson XXXII

199. EXTRA! ROME CAPTURED BY THE GAULS [1]

Gallī, Italiae dulcibus frūctibus maximēque vīnō captī, Alpēs trānsiērunt et contrā Rōmānōs prōcessērunt. Sed cum Rōmānī pugnantēs cum fīnitimīs populīs saepe dictātōrem creāvissent, eō tempore nihil extraōrdināriī [2] imperī aut auxilī quaesīvērunt. Plūrimum terrōris ad Rōmānōs celeritās hostium tulit. Ad flūmen Alliam Rōmānī 5 superātī sunt. Maxima pars eōrum ad urbem Veiōs fūgit; nihil praesidī Rōmam [3] mīsērunt. Aliī Rōmam petīvērunt et, nē clausīs quidem portīs urbis, in arcem fūgērunt. Tam facile Rōmānī victī erant ut Gallī mīrantēs prīmum stārent, īnsidiās veritī. Cum equitēs rettulissent nōn portās urbis clausās, nōn 10 mīlitēs in mūrīs esse, īnsidiās et noctem veritī, inter Rōmam atque flūmen Aniēnem castra posuērunt.

Cum spēs nūlla urbis dēfendendae esset, Rōmānī cōnstituērunt ut iuventūs mīlitāris [4] cum mulieribus ac līberīs in arcem Capitōliumque concēderet. Ibi, frūmentō collātō, deōs hominēsque et Rōmānum 15 nōmen dēfendere parant.

[1] 390 B.C. Rome was not again captured by a foreign foe for 800 years.
[2] The genitive of –ius adjectives is not contracted like that of nouns (564).
[3] *to Rome.* [4] *capable of bearing arms.*

These modern chairs take their design from the ancient *sella* used by the Romans, the stylish wallpaper from the coins of different Roman emperors.

Nancy McClelland　　　　　　　*Bassett & Vollum*

Senēs autem in aedibus [5] suīs adventum hostium obstinātō [6] ad mortem animō exspectāre māluērunt. Eī quī magistrātūs gesserant, augustissimā veste vestītī in mediō aedium in eburneīs sellīs [7] sēdērunt.

20 Posterō diē Gallī urbem ingressī ad praedam properant. Venerā-bundī [8] spectābant sedentēs virōs, quī ob vestem et maiestātem gravitātemque deīs simillimī vidēbantur. Cum Gallī, ad eōs sedentēs velut ad imāginēs versī, stārent, ūnus ē senibus Gallum barbam suam permulcentem [9] scīpiōne eburneō [10] percussit. Hoc initium caedis fuit.

25 Cēterī in aedibus suīs interfectī sunt. Post prīncipum caedem nēminī parcitur,[11] dīripiuntur aedificia, iniciuntur ignēs. Sed arcem capere Gallī nōndum cōnantur.

QUESTIONS

1. When did the Gauls enter Rome?
2. What did the old Roman men do?
3. Why did the Gauls come into Italy?
4. Why did the Gauls not enter Rome as soon as they arrived there?

Italian stamp with Roman ruins, issued in honor of the Olympic Games of 1960.

200. Genitive of the Whole

1. **nihil imperī** (line 4), *no power.*
2. **plūrimum terrōris** (line 4), *a great deal of terror.*

The genitive of the whole *represents the whole to which a part belongs.* It may depend on any noun, pronoun, adjective, or adverb which implies a part of the whole. Ordinarily the construction is the same as in English and causes no trouble (example 2). At times, where the genitive is used in Latin with such words as **nihil, satis, quid** (example 1), we prefer in English to use an adjective modifier. Still we sometimes use such expressions as *nothing of good.*

---

[5] *houses.*   [6] *resolved.*   [7] *ivory chairs.*   [8] *full of reverence.*
[9] *stroking his* (i.e., the old man's) *beard.*
[10] *ivory staff*—part of the insignia of a triumphing general. He was seated, as we might say, in full uniform, wearing all his medals, awaiting his doom.
[11] *No one is spared* (**599, 6, a**).

With cardinal numerals and **quīdam** the ablative with **dē** or **ex** is preferred to the genitive of the whole:

ūnus ē senibus (line 23), *one of the old men.*

201. More About Cum Clauses

Review **cum** clauses (**606,** 11). In some clauses **cum** (*when*) is best translated by *since,* in others by *although.* In such clauses the subjunctive is always used.

1. **Cum spēs nūlla urbis dēfendendae esset,** (line 13), *Since* (literally, *when*) *there was no hope of defending the city.*
2. **Sed cum Rōmānī . . . saepe dictātōrem creāvissent** (line 2), *But although the Romans had often appointed a dictator.*

Find one other example of each of these uses in the story above.

202. Translation

1. Nothing (of) good is inspired by a great deal of terror.
2. Of all the Romans the old men alone determined to die in the city.
3. Although the gates had not been closed, the rest withdrew to the citadel.
4. Since the Romans feared the approach of the enemy's horsemen, they fled and left no (nothing of a) guard.

203. Vocabulary

adventus, –ūs, m., *arrival*
caedēs, –is, f., *slaughter*
dīripiō, –ere, dīripuī, dīreptus,
   plunder
mīlitāris, –e, *military*

nē . . . quidem, adv., *not even*
parcō, –ere, pepercī, parsūrus,
   spare (w. dat.)
terror, –ōris, m., *terror*
vereor, verērī, veritus, *fear*

204. Word Study: Prefixes

Review the prefix **inter–** (**614**). The preposition **intrā** (*within, inside*) is also used as a prefix in English. The two must be carefully distinguished: an *intercollegiate* contest is one *between* two (or more) colleges, as Harvard and Yale; an *intracollegiate* contest is one *within* a single college, as when the freshmen and sophomores of Yale play a game. What is the difference between *interscholastic* and *intrascholastic, interstate* and *intrastate?*

Intrō– (*within*) is also used as a prefix: **introdūcō,** introduce, *introspection.*

Extrā– (*outside*) is found in *extraordinary* (from **ōrdō**).

Define *extralegal, intramural, extramural.*

Clangore ansarum excitatus est M. Manlius. A relief from Ostia shows the sacred geese giving the alarm. From these fragments scholars are able to form an idea of the Temple of Juno Moneta, where the geese were kept. The relief shows that the temple had Ionic columns.

Fototeca Unione

Lesson XXXIII

205. ROME SWEET HOME

Arx Capitōliumque in magnō perīculō fuērunt. Nam Gallī nocte tantō silentiō in summum ēvāsērunt ut nōn custōdēs sōlum fallerent sed nē canēs quidem excitārent. Ānserēs [1] nōn fefellērunt, quōs sacrōs [2] Iūnōnī in summā inopiā cibī [3] Rōmānī tamen nōn occīderant. Quae
5 rēs Rōmānīs salūtī fuit; nam clangōre [4] eōrum excitātus est M. Mānlius, quī, armīs raptīs, ad arma cēterōs vocāvit. Eī Gallōs facile dēiēcērunt.

Sed posteā nōn sōlum cibus sed etiam spēs dēfēcit. Tum tribūnīs mīlitum negōtium datum ut pācem facerent. Ācta rēs est, et mīlle
10 pondō [5] aurī pretium factum est. Pondera [6] ab Gallīs allāta inīqua et, tribūnō Rōmānō recūsante,[7] additus est ā Gallō ponderī gladius, audītaque vōx Rōmānīs nōn ferenda,[8] "Vae [9] victīs!"

Sed dī [10] et hominēs prohibuērunt esse redēmptōs Rōmānōs. Nam nōndum omnī aurō pēnsō, Camillus, quī absēns iterum dictātor creātus
15 erat, vēnit. Gallōs discēdere iubet et eīs imperat ut sē ad proelium

---

[1] *geese.*   [2] *(being) sacred.*   [3] *(although) in the greatest need of food.*
[4] *cackling.*   [5] Used as an indeclinable noun: *pounds.*
[6] *weights,* for weighing the gold. When the Romans complained that the weights were too heavy, the Gaul insolently threw in a sword as an additional weight.
[7] i.e., the weights.   [8] *intolerable to Romans.* What literally?   [9] *woe.*
[10] For **deī.**

expediant. Suōs ferrō, nōn aurō, recipere patriam iubet. Gallī in Rōmānōs currunt sed vincuntur; castra capiuntur; nē nūntius quidem proelī relīctus.

Sed nunc plēbs voluit ruīnās Rōmae relinquere et in urbem Veiōs migrāre. Camillus ōrātiōnem vehementem habuit et eōs mōvit: 20

"Nōnne tenet vōs haec terra quam mātrem appellāmus? Mihi quidem, cum patria in mentem venit, haec omnia occurrunt: collēs campīque et Tiberis et hoc caelum sub quō nātus ēducātusque sum. Nōn sine causā dī hominēsque hunc urbī cōnstituendae locum ēlēgērunt, marī propinquum, regiōnum Italiae medium. Argūmentō [11] 25 est ipsa magnitūdō tam novae urbis. Nōn singulae urbēs, nōn coniūnctī cum Aequīs Volscī, nōn tōta Etrūria bellō vōbīs pār est. Hīc Capitōlium est, quod ā deō respōnsum est caput imperī futūrum esse. Hīc Vestae ignēs, hīc ancīlia dē caelō dēmissa, hīc omnēs dī propitiī manentibus vōbīs." 30

QUESTIONS

1. How was the Capitol saved?
2. What river flows through Rome?
3. Why did the Romans want to make peace?
4. Why was the gold not given to the Gauls?

206. Datives of Purpose and Reference

Review the datives of purpose and reference (**599**, 2–3). Find all the examples of these constructions in the story above.

207. Omission of Sum

A form of **sum** is often omitted either when it might be used as a copula or in compound tenses of the indicative or infinitive of verbs. Can you find five examples in the story above?

208. Translation

1. What circumstance was a source-of-safety to the Romans?
2. "The gods," said he, "have chosen Rome as a home for themselves."
3. The Romans had made peace with the Gauls by paying (*fut. pass. part.*) money.
4. When the Gauls were already near the top (of the) hill, the Romans threw them down.

---

[11] (*serves as*) *proof.*

209. Vocabulary

collis, –is, m., *hill*

custōs, –ōdis, m., *guard*

dēficiō, –ere, dēfēcī, dēfectus, *fail*

dēiciō, –ere, dēiēcī, dēiectus,
throw down, dislodge

inīquus, –a, –um, *uneven, unjust*

mēns, mentis, f., *mind*

nāscor, nāscī, nātus, *be born*

occurrō, –ere, occurrī, occursūrus,
meet, occur

pendō, –ere, pependī, pēnsus,
hang, weigh, pay

propinquus, –a, –um, *near*

vehemēns, gen. –entis, *vigorous*

210. Word Study

Many English words containing *c, g,* or *s* sounds are often misspelled. When these are derived from Latin, it will be helpful to think of the Latin original: *circumstance, voice, concern, suggest, legislation, origin, cordial, graduate, presume, vision, decision.*

Explain *alimentary, custodian, deficient, dementia, expenditure, illicit, impend, iniquitous, nascent, nativity, occurrence, propinquity.* Explain the difference between *liberty* and *license.*

Illinois and New York have towns named *Manlius.*

Model of the western end of the Forum (cf. p. 13). In front, the rostra (speakers' platform); behind it, the temples of Vespasian and Concord. Beyond these, the Hall of Records. Top left, the Temple of Jupiter on the Capitoline Hill.

Statue of a dying Gaul, wearing a torque around his neck. Now in a Roman-museum.

Alinari Photo

Lesson XXXIV

211. TORQUATUS, OR COURAGE AND DISCIPLINE [1]

Gallī contrā Rōmānōs pugnābant. Quīdam. ex Gallīs quī et vīribus et magnitūdine et virtūte cēterīs praestābat prōcessit et vōce maximā clāmat: "Sī quis mēcum pugnāre vult, prōcēdat." Omnēs recūsant propter magnitūdinem eius atque immānem faciem. Deinde Gallus irrīdēre incipit atque linguam ēicere. Tum T. Mānlius, mīles Rō- 5 mānus, prōcessit et contrā Gallum cōnstitit. Gallus, quī duōs magnōs gladiōs habuit, scūtō prōiectō, exspectābat; Mānlius scūtō scūtum percussit [2] atque Gallum dē locō dēiēcit. Eō modō sub Gallī gladium successit atque parvō suō gladiō eum interfēcit. Torquem [3] eius dētrāxit eamque sibi in collum impōnit. Quō ex factō ipse posterīque 10 eius Torquātī sunt nōminātī.

Postquam Torquātus cōnsul factus est, bellum contrā Latīnōs susceptum est. [4] Latīnī Rōmānīs similēs erant linguā, mōribus, armō-rum genere, īnstitūtīs mīlitāribus. Itaque Torquātus et alter cōnsul cōnstituērunt cum maximā cūrā pugnāre et imperāvērunt nē quis extrā 15 ōrdinem in hostēs pugnāret.

Forte inter cēterōs quī ad explōrandum et pābulandum dīmissī

---

[1] From Aulus Gellius and Livy. The incident referred to took place in 361 B.C., on the occasion of the second invasion of the Gauls.
[2] *struck (the Gaul's) shield with his own.*
[3] *collar of gold,* worn by soldiers as a military decoration, like our medals.
[4] 340 B.C.

137

erant T. Mānlius, cōnsulis fīlius, ad castra hostium ēvāsit. Cum
equitem Latīnum vidēret, imperī patris oblītus [5] est et cum hoste
20 pugnāre coepit. Quod ubi audīvit cōnsul, statim mīlitēs convocārī
iussit. Tum fīliō, "quoniam tū," inquit, "neque imperium cōnsulis
neque maiestātem patris veritus, extrā ōrdinem cum hoste pugnā-
vistī et disciplīnam mīlitārem, quā stetit ad hanc diem Rōmāna rēs,[6]
solvistī, trīste exemplum [7] sed salūbre [8] posterīs nostrīs erō. Mē quidem
25 et amor līberōrum et virtūs tua movet; sed tū quoque, sī quid in tē
nostrī sanguinis est, volēs disciplīnam mīlitārem poenā tuā restituere."
Hōc dictō, imperāvit ut fīlius statim morte afficerētur.

Post hoc Latīnī magnā pugnā superātī sunt.

QUESTIONS

1. What happened to Torquatus?
2. How did Manlius get the name Torquatus?
3. Why was Manlius so cautious in his war against the Latins?

212. Volitive Clauses

Review volitive clauses (**606**, 5). Find examples of such clauses
in the story above.

213. Indefinites Quis, Aliquis, and Quīdam

After **sī, nisi,** and **nē, quis** is used as an indefinite pronoun (*some,
any*) in place of **aliquis** (cf. lines 3, 15, and 25). Review the declension of **quis, aliquis,** and **quīdam (583, 584).**

Practice

Tell the form of **quid, cuidam, aliqua, quoddam, quaedam, alicuius,
quōrundam, aliquī.**

214. Translation

1. The two consuls had warned their (men) to obey the order.
2. The consuls had asked that no one fight with the enemy unless
   ordered.[9]
3. So as to be a wholesome example to the rest the consul ordered
   his own son to be killed.
4. Certain of the soldiers were sent out to reconnoiter, and the
   consul's son too begged to go with them.

---

[5] *forgot;* with the genitive (**imperī**).
[6] = **rēs pūblica.**
[7] Predicate nominative: *I shall be an example.*
[8] *wholesome.*
[9] Use **iubeō.**

215. Vocabulary

coepī, coeptus (perfect tenses only),
  began
eques, equitis, m., *horseman*
extrā, prep. w. acc., *out of, outside of*
magnitūdō, –dinis, f., *greatness, size*
praestō, –āre, –stitī, –stitūrus,
  stand before, excel

prōiciō, –ere, –iēcī, –iectus,
  throw or *thrust (forward)*
quoniam, conj., *since*
restituō, –ere, restituī, restitūtus,
  restore

216. Aviation Terms from Latin

accelerometer **(ad–,**
  celer)
aileron **(āla)**
airplane **(āēr, plānus)**
altimeter **(altus)**
aviator **(avis)**

contact **(con–, tangō)**
interceptor **(inter–,**
  capiō)
jet **(iaciō)**
motor **(moveō)**
propeller **(prō–, pellō)**

retractable **(re–, trahō)**
stabilizer **(stō)**
supersonic **(super–, sonus)**
turbo-prop **(turbō, prō–,**
  pellō)
visibility **(videō)**

Find other aviation terms derived from Latin.

Left: The warrior of Capistrano, with a short sword and a big helmet.

E. Richter, Rome

A small terra-cotta figure of a war elephant and its driver. In the armored tower, much like the turret of a modern tank, up to fifteen soldiers could be stationed. At first, elephants panicked Roman infantry, but eventually the Romans learned to fight against them, and even used them occasionally.

National Museum, Naples

Lesson XXXV

217. THE PUNIC WARS [1]

Prīmō bellō Pūnicō Rōmānī prīmum in marī pugnāvērunt et hostēs vīcērunt. Neque ūlla victōria Rōmānīs grātior fuit, quod, invictī in terrā, iam etiam in marī plūrimum poterant. Postquam Sicilia capta est et Corsica Sardiniaque vāstātae sunt, bellum in Āfricam trānslātum
5 est. Victī Carthāginiēnsēs pācem ā Rōmānīs petīvērunt. Illō tempore Rēgulus, dux Rōmānōrum, senātuī persuāsit nē pācem cum Poenīs faceret. Tandem cōnsul Catulus profectus est cum CCC nāvibus in Siciliam; Poenī contrā ipsum CCCC nāvēs parāvērunt. Numquam in marī tantīs cōpiīs pugnātum est.[2] Carthāginiēnsēs superātī sunt.
10 Bellum Pūnicum secundum Rōmānīs ab Hannibale illātum est. Cum magnō exercitū Alpēs trānsiit. Post complūrēs parvās victōriās Hannibal Rōmānōs ad lacum Trasumennum gravissimē vīcit.

Rōmae ad prīmum nūntium proelī populus cum magnō terrōre in Forum concurrit. Mulierēs rogāvērunt omnēs quae fortūna exer-

---

[1] First Punic War, 264–241 B.C.; Second Punic War, 218–201 B.C. The word "Punic" is derived from **Poenī,** another name for the Carthaginians, who originally came from Phoenicia.   [2] *was (a battle) fought.*

citūs esset. Tandem praetor, "Pugnā," inquit, "magnā victī sumus." 15
Posterīs diēbus ad portās maior prope multitūdō mulierum quam
virōrum stetit, quae aut suōrum aliquem aut nūntiōs dē eīs exspectābat. Ūnam fēminam in ipsā portā incolumī fīliō [3] subitō occurrentem
in complexū [4] eius exspīrāvisse dīcunt; alteram, cui mors fīlī falsō
nūntiāta erat, sedentem domī ad prīmum cōnspectum redeuntis fīlī 20
gaudiō mortuam esse dīcunt.

Proximō annō Rōmānī ab Hannibale pulsī etiam maius dētrīmentum ad Cannās accēpērunt. Multae Italiae cīvitātēs ad Poenōs
dēfēcērunt. Quae tamen rēs Rōmānōs nōn mōvit ut pācis umquam
mentiō apud eōs fieret. Servōs mīlitēs [5] fēcērunt, quod [6] numquam 25
ante factum erat. Hannibal trēs modiōs [7] ānulōrum aureōrum Carthāginem mīsit, quōs ex manibus equitum Rōmānōrum mortuōrum
dētrāxerat.

Rōmānī tamen post multōs annōs Hannibalem vīcērunt.

QUESTIONS

1. What was the first war the Romans won on the sea?
2. Why did victory on the seas please the Romans so much?
3. What visible evidence did the people of Carthage have of the
   greatness of Hannibal's victory at Cannae?
4. What other great victory did Hannibal win?

218. The Relative as Connective

In Latin the relative pronoun or adjective is often used to connect
a sentence with a preceding sentence. In English a personal or
demonstrative pronoun with or without a conjunction (*and, but,* etc.)
is more common.

Quae tamen rēs Rōmānōs nōn mōvit (line 24), *This fact did not, however, induce the Romans.*

219. Place to Which

Carthāginem mīsit (line 26), *He sent to Carthage.*

Ordinarily "place to which" is expressed by the accusative with
the preposition **ad** or **in.** The preposition is omitted before names of
towns and a few other words, such as **domus.**

---

[3] Dative, depending on **occurrentem** (**599,** 7).   [4] *embrace, arms.*
[5] *They made soldiers (of) the slaves.*   [6] *(a thing) which.*   [7] *pecks of rings.*

141

220. Translation

1. You all know that the Romans received a great loss the next year.
2. Not moved by the words of women and friends, Regulus returned to Carthage.
3. Although terrified by reports of the defeat, nevertheless Rome did not make peace.
4. Regulus, when sent unharmed to Rome, persuaded his country to make war upon the enemy.

221. Vocabulary

complūrēs, –a or **–ia,** *several*
dētrīmentum, –ī, n., *loss*
fēmina, –ae, f., *woman*
incolumis, –e, *unharmed*

īnferō, īnferre, intulī, illātus, *bring*
multitūdō, –dinis, f., *(great) number*
nisi, conj., *unless, except*
prope, adv., *almost*

222. Word Study: Suffixes

The suffix **–idus** (English *–id*) is added chiefly to verb stems to form adjectives: **timidus,** *timid.* When the noun suffix **–tās** (English *–ty*) is added, **–idus** becomes **–idi–**: **timiditās,** *timidity.*

The suffix **–īnus** (English *–ine*) is added to noun and adjective stems to form adjectives: **equīnus,** *equine.* When the suffix **–tās** is added, **–īnus** becomes **–īni–**: **vīcīnitās,** *vicinity.*

Define the following and give the Latin words from which they are derived: *fluid, placid, rapid, valid, vivid, feminine, marine, submarine.* Give additional examples of these suffixes in English words.

Thirteen American states have towns named after *Carthage;* New York and Ohio have a *Sardinia;* Pennsylvania and South Dakota have a *Corsica.*

A Roman villa from the Third century A.D., at Carthage, near modern Tunis.

Gian Berto Vanni/Art Resource

Our Heritage

223. THE BATTLE OF CANNAE

The battle of Cannae was the greatest defeat the Romans suffered in their long history—and yet they won the war. The Romans had 50,000 to 80,000 men in this battle, the Carthaginians only 40,000, but Hannibal chose his own battlefield and used the plan of encirclement—closing in on the Romans on right and left while his center withdrew. This encircling movement of Cannae has been extensively imitated in modern warfare, on a much larger scale, of course. The Germans used it in Poland in 1939, in Belgium and France in 1940, in Russia in 1941. General Eisenhower won great success with it in capturing the Ruhr district of Germany in 1945.

Of the Romans at Cannae, only 10,000 escaped; most of the rest were killed.

The Carthaginian victory made necessary a strategy which one Roman general, Quintus Fabius Maximus, had advocated against the more aggressive policies of his colleagues: by constantly hounding Hannibal's forces but avoiding pitched battles, Fabius eventually wore down the Carthaginians' strength. This course of action won for him the cognomen *Cunctator* ("Delayer" or "Slowpoke"), which only later came to be used as a mark of respect. The poet Ennius wrote:

Ūnus homō nōbīs cūnctandō restituit rem, "One man, by delaying, saved our state for us."

But it was not only Fabius' very Roman qualities of caution and stubborn courage that saved Rome. Hannibal himself did not follow up his victories, and gradually he lost the support of the war party in Carthage. The morale of the Roman senators and of the ordinary Roman legionaries was unshakeable and cannot be praised too highly. Finally, in the last stages of the war, the boldness of the young Scipio and his military genius in reorganizing the army brought victory.

The outcome of this war determined the future of the world. It made certain that Rome, not Carthage, was to rule and to transmit its civilization to future generations. Life today would be vastly different if the Carthaginians had won the war—whether better or worse is something to argue about.

Alan Oddie/PhotoEdit

The Temple of Apollo at Corinth.

Lesson XXXVI

224. *THE ROMANS GIVE LIBERTY TO THE GREEKS*

Post Pūnicum bellum secūtum est Macedonicum,[1] quod cum
Philippō rēge Rōmānī gessērunt ut Graecās cīvitātēs līberārent. T.
Quīnctius Flāminīnus contrā Philippum missus rem bene gessit.
Corinthum prōcessit ut ibi in lūdīs Isthmiīs [2] condiciōnēs pācis dēferret.
5 Omnēs ad spectāculum cōnsēderant et praecō,[3] ut [4] mōs erat, in
medium prōcessit et, tubā silentiō factō, prōnūntiat senātum Rōmānum
et Quīnctium imperātōrem iubēre omnēs gentēs Graeciae līberās esse.
Audītā vōce praecōnis, vix satis crēdere potest sē quisque bene audī-
visse.[5] Tum tantus clāmor est ortus ut facile appārēret nihil omnium
10 bonōrum multitūdinī grātius quam lībertātem esse. Aliī aliīs dīcēbant [6]
esse gentem quae suā pecūniā, suō labōre ac perīculō bella gereret [7]
prō lībertāte aliōrum.

Duōbus annīs posteā Quīnctius in Italiam profectūrus Graecōs
hōc modō monet: "Concordiae cōnsulite. Contrā vōs cōnsentientēs [8]

[1] 200–197 B.C.

[2] *Isthmian;* similar to the Olympic games. They got their name from being
held on the Isthmus of Corinth. Eight American states have towns named
Corinth.   [3] Nominative: *announcer.*   [4] *as.*

[5] *no one could really believe that he had heard correctly.*   [6] *one said to another.*

[7] Subordinate clauses in indirect discourse are in the subjunctive.

[8] Conditional: *if you agree.*

nec rēx quisquam nec tyrannus satis valēbit.[9] Aliēnīs armīs redditam 15
lībertātem vestrā cūrā servāte, ut populus Rōmānus dignīs datam
esse lībertātem sciat." Hās velut parentis vōcēs cum audīrent, omnibus
mānāvērunt [10] gaudiō lacrimae, ita ut Quīnctium ipsum quoque cōn-
funderent dīcentem.[11]

QUESTIONS

1. Why did Flamininus go to Corinth?
2. What advice did he give the Greeks?
3. How did Flamininus' words affect the Greeks?
4. Why did the Romans start the war against Philip?

225. Imperative

The passive imperative has the same forms as the second person
present passive indicative, except that in the singular only the alternate
form ending in **–re** is used: **portāre, portāminī.** What other form of
the verb is like the singular passive imperative? Review all imperatives
(**585** ff.).

226. Quisque and Quisquam

Quisque as a pronoun is declined like **quis;** as an adjective, more
like **quī (584). Quisquam** (singular only) is like **quis,** except that
quicquam is usually used for **quidquam (584).**

Quisque is usually placed after a pronoun or a superlative adjective:
optimus quisque, *all the best men.*

Quisquam is stronger than **aliquis** and is usually found in sentences
containing or implying a negative. It is often best translated *any at
all:* **Estne quisquam fortior?** *Is anyone braver?*

Practice

Tell the form of **quōque, quendam, aliquod, quicquam, quaeque,
quid, cuiquam, quaedam, quidque, alicuius.**

227. Result Clauses

Review result clauses **(83).** Find two examples in the story above.

---

[9] Cf. "United we stand, divided we fall."

[10] *flowed for all* (i.e., *from the eyes of all*).

[11] Gen. Ridgway, commenting in *Life* on our treatment of Japan after World
War II, said: "One must go back to Flamininus' liberation and restoration of
sovereignty to the Greek cities to find in history a comparable act of
magnanimity in victory."

228. Translation

1. "Tell us what he said," each one asked.
2. All were so overcome that they could hardly speak.
3. "Agree among yourselves and no king will be so brave as to attack you."
4. The messenger had spoken, and not a single one could believe his words.

229. Vocabulary

cōnsīdō, –ere, –sēdī, –sessūrus, *sit down*

quisquam, quicquam, *anyone, anything, any*

quisque, quidque, *each*

tuba, –ae, f., *trumpet*

vix, adv., *scarcely*

230. Word Study: Spanish

We have already seen that a few simple principles will enable one to recognize the Latin origin of many Spanish words **(132)**. On the basis of these principles, explain Spanish *campo, útil, vivo; ocurrir; desierto, puente; vida, virtud; mujer.*

Since *d* is sometimes lost between vowels, what must be the Latin words from which Spanish *caer* and *juicio* are derived?

Since an *e* is added before *sc, sp,* and *st* at the beginning of a word, what must be the Latin words from which the following Spanish words are derived: *esperar, especie, escribir, estar, estudio?*

Since Latin *ex* sometimes becomes *ej* in Spanish, what is the Latin for *ejemplo, ejército?*

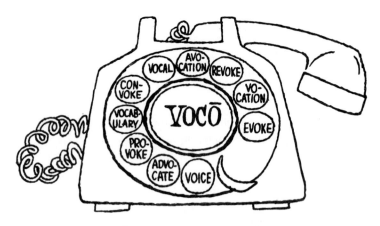

Quem numerum vocās?

Inspiration of Francis Blair,
High Point, N. C.

Lesson XXXVII

231. CIVIL WAR

M. Tulliō Cicerōne ōrātōre et C. Antōnio cōnsulibus,[1] L. Sergius
Catilīna, vir nōbilissimī generis, ad dēlendam patriam coniūrāvit cum
quibusdam clārīs quidem, sed audācibus virīs. Ā Cicerōne urbe expulsus est. Sociī eius comprehēnsī occīsī sunt. Catilīna ipse victus
proeliō est et interfectus.   5

Sed Cicerō Rōmānōs timōre bellī cīvīlis nōn līberāvit. C. Iūlius
Caesar, quī Catilīnam iūvisse ā quibusdam dīcitur, cōnsul est factus.
Dēcrēta est eī Gallia et Īllyricum cum legiōnibus decem. Annīs novem
in potestātem populī Rōmānī ferē omnem Galliam redēgit.[2] Britannīs
mox bellum intulit, quibus ante eum nē nōmen quidem Rōmānōrum 10
cognitum erat. Eōs victōs, obsidibus acceptīs, stīpendium pendere
coēgit. Germānōs trāns Rhēnum aggressus proeliīs vīcit.

Caesar rediēns ex Galliā victor coepit poscere alterum cōnsulātum. Senātū negante, contrā patriam cum exercitū prōcessit.

Deinde in Graeciam trānsiit et contrā Pompeium pugnāvit. Prīmō 15
proeliō victus est, ēvāsit tamen, quod, nocte intercēdente, Pompeius
sequī nōluit. Dīxit Caesar Pompeium nōn scīre[3] vincere et illō diē
tantum[4] sē potuisse superārī.[5]

Deinde in Thessaliā ad Pharsālum pugnāvērunt. Numquam ante
maiōrēs Rōmānae cōpiae in ūnum locum convēnerant neque meliōrēs 20
ducēs habuerant. Tandem Pompeius victus est et Alexandrīam petīvit ut ā rēge Aegyptī auxilia acciperet. Sed rēx occīdit Pompeium
et caput eius ad Caesarem mīsit. Caesar lacrimās fūdisse dīcitur,
tantī virī vidēns caput et generī[6] quondam suī.[6] Caesar rēgnum
Aegyptī Cleopātrae dedit.   25

Caesar, bellīs cīvīlibus in tōtō orbe terrārum perfectīs, Rōmam
rediit. Agere coepit contrā cōnsuētūdinem Rōmānae lībertātis. Cum

---

[1] Ablative absolute expressing time: *in the consulship of* (63 B.C.). The Romans
used the names of the consuls to date the year. Why did they not say 63 B.C.?
[2] 58–50 B.C. [3] *know how* (with infinitive). [4] *only*. [5] *could have been defeated*.
[6] *his former son-in-law* (genitive of **gener**); Pompey had married Caesar's
daughter Julia in 60 B.C. After her death in 54 B.C. Caesar and Pompey
drifted apart.

honōrēs [7] ex [8] suā voluntāte tribueret quī ā populō anteā dēferē-
bantur aliaque rēgia [9] faceret, coniūrātum est in eum ā LX vel amplius
30 senātōribus equitibusque Rōmānīs, quōrum prīncipēs fuērunt C.
Cassius et duo Brūtī. Itaque Caesar, cum Īdibus Mārtiīs [10] in senātum vēnisset, XXIII vulneribus acceptīs, mortuus est.

QUESTIONS

1. How did Catiline die?
2. Where was Pompey killed?
3. How many years did Caesar fight in Gaul?
4. Why was there a conspiracy against Caesar?
5. Why did Caesar fight against his own country?

232. Ablative of Separation

Urbe expulsus est (line 3), *He was driven out of the city.*
Timōre . . . līberāvit (line 6), *He freed from fear.*

Separation is usually expressed by the ablative with **ab, dē,** or
ex. But with some verbs, such as **excēdō** and **līberō,** the preposition
is regularly omitted; with other verbs it is occasionally omitted.

233. Translation

1. Cicero drove Catiline from Rome after seizing his accomplices.
2. You all read that civil war occurred between Caesar and Pompey.
3. Since Caesar had not driven his personal-enemies from the city sixty or more of them later killed him.
4. Having conquered Gaul, Caesar also attacked the Britons, who were much braver than the Gauls.

[7] *offices.*   [8] *in accordance with.*   [9] *regal (kinglike) things.*
[10] *the Ides of March* (March 15).

Coin issued by Brutus celebrating the assassination of Caesar. "EID MAR" stands for "Ides of March." The conical cap is a symbol of liberty, since it was usually worn by slaves who had won their freedom.

234. Vocabulary

aggredior, aggredī, aggressus, *attack*
amplius, adv., *more*
anteā, adv., *before*
audāx, gen. **–ācis,** *bold*
dēleō, –ēre, –ēvī, –ētus, *destroy*

fundō, –ere, fūdī, fūsus, *pour, shed*
legiō, –ōnis, f., *legion*
obses, obsidis, m., *hostage* [11]
timor, –ōris, m., *fear*
voluntās, –tātis, f., *wish*

235. Words Easily Confused

Look up and distinguish carefully the following sets of words
which are somewhat similar in pronunciation or spelling:

alius, alter, altus	eques, equus	nē, –ne
audeō, audiō	gēns, genus	post, posteā, postquam
cadō, caedō, cēdō	liber, līber, līberī	quīdam, quidem
cīvis, cīvitās	mora, mors, mōs	reddō, redeō
dīcō, dūcō	morior, moror	Rōma, Rōmānus

236. Word Study: Spelling

In English, after the prefix *ex–*, a root word beginning with *s* drops
the *s:* **ex–sequor,** *ex–ecute;* **ex–sistō,** *ex–ist;* **ex–spectō,** *ex–pect.*

Explain *aggression, audacity, confusion, delete, indelible, infusion,
legionary, projectile, timorous, voluntary.*

Virginia and twelve other American states, including New Hamp-
shire and Louisiana, have towns named *Alexandria.* Kentucky and
Michigan have towns named after *Brutus. Pompey* is in New York.

237. LATĪNUM HODIERNUM

Medīcina

Mīror cūr medicīna ferē semper amāra [12] necesse sit. Sīc et nunc
est et apud Rōmānōs fuit. Nunc quidem dulce quiddam in medicīnā
liquidā pōnimus vel pilulās dulcī tegimus. Rōmānī quoque hoc
fēcērunt. Saepe ōram pōculī [13] melle contingēbant ut puer innocēns
tōtum, dulce et amārum, biberet priusquam sentīret gustum maxi- 5
mae partis horribilem esse. Etiam crūstula [14] puerīs puellīsque dabant
ut medicīnam libenter sūmerent. Sed sī aeger es, medicīna sūmenda
est, cum crūstulīs vel sine crūstulīs. Posteā quandō valēbis banānam
fissam vel lac agitātum tibi habēre licēbit.

Fortasse putās hanc fābulam prō crūstulō esse ut Caesaris et 10
aliōrum rēs gestās libentius legās. Sī hoc putās, nōn errās.

---

[11] A hostage is a person of a conquered territory who is held by the conquering
nation as a pledge that no unfriendly act will be committed.
[12] *bitter.*   [13] *cup.*   [14] *cookies.*

Lesson XXXVIII

238. PĀX RŌMĀNA [1]

Octāviānus, nepōs Caesaris,[2] ā Caesare adoptātus, posteā Augustus est dictus. Iuvenis fōrmā praestantī et vultū tranquillō erat. Post mortem Caesaris Octāviānō, adulēscentī XX annōrum, cōnsulātus datur. Nōn multō post cum M. Antōniō contrā Brūtum et Cassium,
5 quī Caesarem interfēcerant, profectus est. Ad Philippōs, Macedoniae urbem, Brūtus et Cassius victī et interfectī sunt.

Antōnius, repudiātā[3] sorōre Caesaris Augustī, Cleopātram, rēgīnam Aegyptī, dūxit[4] uxōrem. Tum magnum bellum cīvīle commōvit, cōgente uxōre Cleopātrā, quae cupīvit in urbe[5] quoque rēgnāre.
10 Victus est ab Augustō nāvālī pugnā clārā apud Actium, quī locus in Ēpīrō est, ex quā fūgit in Aegyptum et, dēspērātīs suīs rēbus, ipse sē occīdit. Cleopātra sibi aspidem admīsit[6] et venēnō eius exstīncta est. Aegyptus ab Augustō imperiō Rōmānō adiecta est.

Pāce Rōmānā cōnstitūtā, Augustus Rōmānōs timōre bellī līberāvit.
15 Ex eō annō rem pūblicam per XLIIII annōs sōlus obtinuit. In campō

[1] Under Augustus (31 b.c.–14 a.d.) a long era of peace began.
[2] Actually Octavian was the grandson of Caesar's sister.   [3] *divorced.*
[4] *married* (with **uxōrem**). [5] i.e., Rome. [6] *let an asp* (a poisonous snake) *bite her.*

Cassius (standing) and Brutus discuss strategy before the battle of Philippi. From the motion picture of Shakespeare's *Julius Caesar*.

Metro-Goldwyn-Mayer

The vast palace of Diocletian (284–305 A.D.) at Split on the Yugoslavian coast. Surrounded by a sixty-foot wall, it covered eight acres. Since Diocletian came from this region, it was natural for him to have a retreat here.

Mārtiō sepultus est,[7] vir quī meritīs quidem deō similis est putātus. Neque enim quisquam aut in bellīs fēlīcior fuit aut in pāce moderātior. Scythae et Indī, quibus anteā Rōmānōrum nē nōmen quidem cognitum erat, mūnera et lēgātōs ad eum mīsērunt.

Pūblica opera plūrima Rōmae exstrūxit et cēterōs prīncipēs virōs 20 saepe hortātus est ut monumentīs vel novīs vel refectīs urbem adōrnārent. Spatium urbis in regiōnēs XIV dīvīsit. Contrā incendia vigiliās īnstituit. Viās et templa refēcit. Annum [8] ā Iūliō Caesare in ōrdinem redāctum, sed posteā neglēctum, rūrsus ad prīstinam ratiōnem redēgit. Sextīlem mēnsem ē suō nōmine Augustum nōmināvit. 25

QUESTIONS

1. Where was Cassius killed?
2. Where was Augustus buried?
3. Where and how was Antony killed?

[7] *was buried.* [8] i.e., the calendar, which was very inexact before Caesar's time.

239. Description and Measure of Difference

Review the genitive and ablative of description and the ablative of measure of difference (**598,** 2; **601,** 13; **601,** 12) and find one example of each in the above passage.

240. Translation

1. Cleopatra urged Antony to neglect his own interests ("things").
2. Antony was a man of the greatest courage; Augustus was a youth of twenty years.
3. Augustus erected monuments and temples of the greatest size in all parts of the Roman Empire.
4. Despairing of victory, Antony killed himself, and not much later all-other enemies were defeated.

241. Vocabulary

admittō, –ere, admīsī, admissus, *let to*

dēspērō, 1, *despair (of)*

exstruō, –ere, exstrūxī, exstrūctus, *build*

neglegō, –ere, –lēxī, –lēctus, *neglect*

rūrsus, adv., *again*

242. Etiam and Quoque; Quidem

Distinguish carefully the following words: **etiam** and **quoque** both mean *also,* but **etiam** generally precedes the word it emphasizes, **quoque** always follows. In the same way English *even* generally precedes, like **etiam,** while *too* follows, like **quoque. Quidem** means *certainly, to be sure,* and follows the word it emphasizes. **Nē . . . quidem** means *not even,* and the emphatic word is placed between **nē** and **quidem. Quidem** alone never means *even,* nor is **nē . . . etiam** ever used for *not even.*

243. Word Study: Suffixes

The suffix **–ārium** (English *–arium, –ary*) is added chiefly to noun stems. The suffix **–ōrium** (English *–orium, –ory, –or*) is added chiefly to participial stems and so is usually preceded by **–t–.** Both suffixes mean a *place where:* granary, a *place where grain* (**grānum**) is kept. The plurals of *–ary* and *–ory* are *–aries* and *–ories.*

Define the following words according to their derivation and give the Latin words from which they come: *aquarium, itinerary, library, laboratory, mirror* (**mīror**), *auditorium, factory, armory.*

Caution: Other Latin suffixes besides **–ārium** and **–ōrium** sometimes take on the English forms mentioned above; e.g., *primary* from **prīmārius,** *honor* from **honor,** *cursory* from **cursōrius.**

ITALIA

Scale of Miles

0   25   50   75   100

A   L   P   E   S

LIGURIA

ug. Taurinorum
(Turin)

Mediolanum
(Milan)

Verona
Mantua

Ticinus

G

Padus (Po)

Trebia

VENETIA

ILLYRICUM

Rubico

MARE HADRIATICUM

Genua

(Gulf of
Genoa)

Luca
Florentia
Arnus
Pisae

Ariminum

Sentinum
Metaurus

Aesis

Arretium
L. Trasumennus

Clusium
Volsinii

ETRURIA

CORSICA

Faleri
Narnia
Tarquinii Feronia
Veii
Caere

SABINI
Carsioli
Anio Tibur

Asculum

PAELIGNI

FRENTANI

Roma
Ostia
Tiberis
Tusculum
Ardea
Antium

LATIUM

Praeneste
Sora

Bovianum

Luceria

Fregellae
Circei

SAMNIUM

Beneventum

Benevenum
F. Caudinae

Aufidus

Cannae

Tarracina
Formiae
Cumae
Misenum

Capua

CAMPANIA

Venusia

Brundisium

CALABRIA

Neapolis
(Naples)
Pompeii

LUCANIA
Paestum

Tarentum
Heracles

SARDINIA

MARE
TYRRHENUM

(Gulf of
Tarentum)

MAGNA

BRUTTIUM

GRAECIA

Croton

Eryx M.

Erde M.

Messana

AEGATES
INS.

Panormus

Mylae

Locri
Rhegium

CALATHA I.

Lilybaeum
Drepana

SICILIA

Aetna M.

Catana

Hippo Zarytus

Agrigentum

Utica **Carthago** *Pr. Mercurii*

Ecnomus
Gela

Syracusae

Bagrada

COSSYRA

Pachynum Pr.

MIDIA   AFRICA

10°   12°   14°   16°   18°

This frivolous-looking portrait of Nero, now in the Capitoline Museum, seems to illustrate the stories about him. Although Nero did not start the great fire of 64 A.D., he did take advantage of the catastrophe to occupy about one square mile of the devastated land. On it he built his famous Golden House.

Photorapida—Tierni, Italy

Lesson XXXIX

244. ROMAN SCANDALS

Dē Nerōne[1] multa īnfāmia nārrābantur. Nerō erat prīnceps inūsitātae lūxuriae, adeō ut unguentīs lavāret et rētibus[2] aureīs piscārētur. Nūllam vestem bis gessit. Semper mīlle carrīs vel amplius fēcit iter. Soleae mūlārum eius ex argentō factae sunt. Domum ā Palātiō ad
5 Ēsquiliās exstrūxit, quam auream nōmināvit. In eius vēstibulō locāta est imāgō Nerōnis CXX pedēs alta. Erant lacūs, aedificia, agrī, silvae, cum multitūdine omnis generis animālium. In cēterīs partibus omnia aurō tēcta, ōrnāta gemmīs erant. Cum hanc domum dēdicāret, dīxit: "Tandem quasi homō habitāre coepī."
10 Etiam saltāvit et cantāvit in scaenā. In Graeciam profectus est ut ibi cantāret. Cantante eō, excēdere theātrō nēminī licitum est. Multī, dēfessī audiendō laudandōque, clausīs oppidōrum portīs, aut fūrtim dēsiluērunt dē mūrō aut, morte simulātā, fūnere ēlātī sunt. In Italiam reversus studium nōn remīsit. Cōnservandae vōcis grātiā
15 neque mīlitēs umquam appellāvit neque quicquam ēgit nisi prope stante phōnascō[3] quī monēret ut parceret sibi ac sūdārium[4] ad ōs applicāret.

Frātrem, uxōrem, sorōrem, mātrem interfēcit. Urbem Rōmam incendit[5] ut spectāculum simile incendiō Troiae antīquae cerneret.

---

[1] 54–68 A.D. [2] *nets.* [3] *singing teacher.* [4] *handkerchief.*
[5] This was a false charge, as Nero was not in Rome when the fire started, but at Antium. It burned six days and seven nights continuously and then started again.

Magnam senātūs partem interfēcisse dīcitur.

Tandem ā senātū hostis iūdicātus est. Cum quaererētur ad poenam, fūgit et sē interfēcit. In eō omnis Augustī familia cōnsūmpta est.

QUESTIONS

1. Who killed Nero?
2. Whom did Nero kill?
3. Where did Nero sing?
4. Where was Nero's statue?

245. Relative Purpose Clauses

prope stante phōnascō quī monēret (line 15), *a singing teacher standing near to warn* (literally, *who might warn*).

The relative pronoun may be used instead of **ut** to introduce a purpose clause in the subjunctive when there is an antecedent. The pronoun must of course agree with the antecedent.

246. Translation

1. Nero built a house covered with gold in which to live.
2. He summoned slaves who were to erect beautiful buildings.
3. He is said to have burned Rome to furnish a spectacle for himself.
4. He led a life of great luxury and cruelty and spent his time in singing.

247. Vocabulary

adeō, adv., *so, so much*
bis, adv., *twice*
efferō, efferre, extulī, ēlātus, *carry out*

locō, 1, *place*
simulō, 1, *pretend*
tegō, –ere, tēxī, tēctus, *cover*

248. Word Study: Prefixes

The prefix **sē–** means *apart from* in Latin and English: **sēparō,** *separate.* Define according to the prefix: *secret* **(cernō),** *secede, seclude, secure* **(cūra).**

The Latin adverb **nōn,** meaning *not,* is freely used as a prefix in English: *nonsense, nonpartisan.* Give three other examples.

The preposition **ultrā** (related to **ultimus**) is used as a prefix in English with the meaning *extremely: ultrafashionable.* Give two other examples.

Explain *admission, collocation, desperation, detective, negligence, simulated (pearls).*

249. SUMMARY OF PRONOUNS

A. Personal (for their declension see 580)

ego (*pl.* **nōs**)	I (we)
tū (*pl.* **vōs**)	you (you)
is, ea, id (*also* **hic** *and* **ille**; *see below*)	he, she, it

B. Reflexive (581)

meī (*gen.*)	(*pl.* **nostrī**)	of myself	(of ourselves)
tuī	(*pl.* **vestrī**)	of yourself	(of yourselves)
suī	(*pl.* **suī**)	of himself, herself, itself	(of themselves)

C. Demonstrative (582)

hic, haec, hoc	this (here), the latter, he, she, it
ille, illa, illud	that (there), the former, he, she, it
is, ea, id	this, that, he, she, it
iste, ista, istud	that (where you are)
īdem, eadem, idem	the same
ipse, ipsa, ipsum	–self, the very

The City of Rome as it was in ancient days.

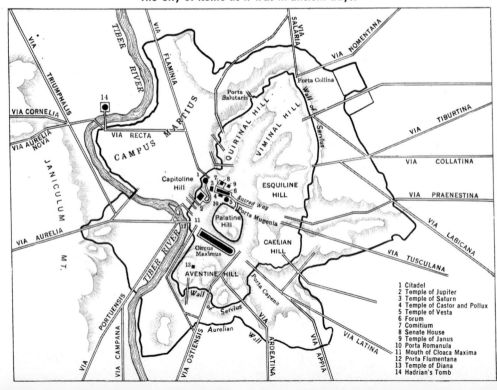

1 Citadel
2 Temple of Jupiter
3 Temple of Saturn
4 Temple of Castor and Pollux
5 Temple of Vesta
6 Forum
7 Comitium
8 Senate House
9 Temple of Janus
10 Porta Romanula
11 Mouth of Cloaca Maxima
12 Porta Flumentana
13 Temple of Diana
14 Hadrian's Tomb

Erich Lessing/PhotoEdit

The island in the Tiber at Rome, shaped like a ship. It has a hospital on it now as it did in antiquity. Note the bridges, which are in part ancient.

D. *Relative* (583)

quī, quae, quod (*pron. and adj.*)	who, which, what, that

E. *Interrogative* (583)

quis? quid? (*pron.*)	who? which? what?
quī? quae? quod? (*adj.*)	who? which? what?

F. *Indefinite* (584)

quis, quid (*pron.*) [1]	anyone, anything, someone, something
quī, quae (qua), quod [1] (*adj.*)	any, some
aliquis, aliquid (*pron.*)	someone, something, anyone, anything
aliquī, aliqua, aliquod (*adj.*)	some, any
quīdam, quaedam, quiddam (*pron.*)	a certain one (person or thing)
quīdam, quaedam, quoddam (*adj.*)	a certain, a, one, some
quisquam, quicquam (quidquam)	anyone, anything
quisque, quidque (*pron.*)	each one, each thing
quisque, quaeque, quodque (*adj.*)	each

G. *Indefinite relative*

quīcumque, quaecumque, quodcumque	whoever, whatever

[1] Indefinite after **sī, nisi,** and **nē.**

Our Heritage

250. THE ROMAN EMPIRE

The establishment of the extensive Roman Empire was a remarkable achievement at a time when communications were so slow and difficult. A glance at the map (pp. 100–101) will show that, during the second century A.D., the Roman Empire rimmed the Mediterranean and covered parts of three continents. Some of these territories have not yet recovered the prosperity they had in Roman times. Libya in northern Africa, for example, used to be a chief source of wheat for Italy, but today the United States is sending wheat to that country. While you are looking at the map, note that in World War II, which began in 1939, there was fighting in or over almost all the countries that once belonged to the Roman Empire.

The Empire brought not only prosperity but peace and security. Occasionally foreign wars were fought in remote parts which meant nothing to most citizens, and sometimes there was a flare-up of civil war.

Political liberty was of course diminished during the Empire, compared with the Republic, but for most citizens this meant merely that the emperor and his officials ran things instead of the nobility who composed the senate during the Republic. The government was an efficient bureaucracy, and the emperors were, by and large, very capable administrators. Personal liberty was not affected, nor even the self-rule of the many communities scattered throughout the Empire. In the East the emperors did not force the people to give up their Greek language. In the West the people of their own accord gradually abandoned their native languages in favor of Latin.

The greatest freedom was allowed the individual. The Romans did not look upon themselves as a superior race, although there was of course some race prejudice. There was occasional persecution of the Christians, it is true, but that was not due to a desire to suppress individual religious beliefs but chiefly to the unwillingness of Christians to conform to practices which were considered part of one's duty to the state.

Something is to be said for the claim that the Roman Empire was based on the Stoic doctrine that all men are equal.[1] Citizenship was granted to men of the most diverse origins. A real world state, a kind of United Nations, was achieved, in which the chief right relinquished by its members was that of making war on their neighbors. The Empire was not an utterly despotic government that aimed at dominating the private lives of its subjects.

Pliny the Elder remarks on the mighty majesty of the Roman peace **(immēnsae Rōmānae pācis maiestāte),** which made the people and places and products of the whole world known to everyone, and prays that this gift of the gods may last forever, for, he says, the Romans are a gift to humanity comparable only to the sun which shines over all the world. In 400 A.D. the poet Claudian praises Rome for being the only nation that ever welcomed to her arms those she conquered, treating the whole human race as sons, not slaves, giving citizenship to the vanquished and uniting the most remote regions by the bonds of loyalty.

Exaggeration? Without doubt. But the reference to Rome's treatment of human beings as sons, not slaves, is of particular significance in estimating the place of the Roman Empire among the empires of history.

[1] This was felt by some to be true of slaves too. Roman slavery is not to be confused with some modern forms of slavery, for many Roman slaves won or bought their freedom.

Model of the Temple of Augustus and Rome in Ankara, the capital of modern Turkey. The model is in a museum in Rome.

Anderson

UNIT IV

THE ARGONAUTS

Jason and the Argonauts is a famous story from Greek mythology. It was one of many Greek tales admired and preserved by the Romans. In this painting by Lorenzo Costa (c. 1460–1535), we see Jason and his friends sailing in search of the Golden Fleece.

251. THE STORY OF THE GOLDEN FLEECE

The story of the Trojan War, made famous by the Greek poet Homer, was but one of the many interesting tales, sometimes fact, sometimes fiction, often both, which the Greeks told and retold. Another was that of the Argonauts, those adventurers who sailed unknown seas in search of the Golden Fleece. The story runs as follows:

Aeson (Ēson), king of Thessaly, had a brother Pelias (Pe'lias) and a son Jason. Pelias drove out Aeson, seized the throne, and planned to kill Jason. But Jason escaped by the help of friends, who then told Pelias that his nephew had died.

An oracle told Pelias to beware of a man wearing only one shoe. Some years later Pelias announced a great festival, and crowds came

Map of the voyage of the Argonauts. According to the story, they sailed to Phasis, at the eastern end of the Black Sea. Here they found the Golden Fleece, near modern Batum, terminal of the pipe line which brings oil, "black gold," from the Baku oil fields.

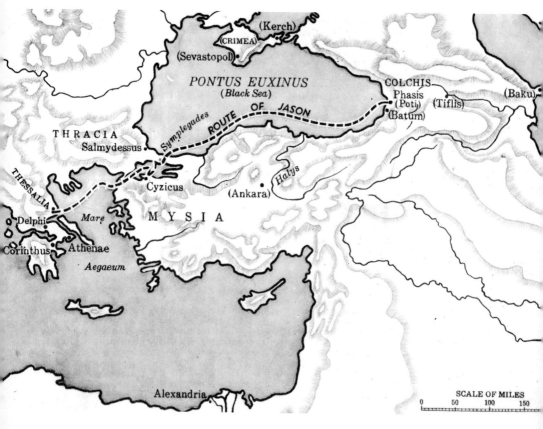

to the city. Among them was Jason, now grown to manhood. On the way he lost one shoe. When Pelias saw him, he recalled the oracle. To get rid of Jason, he gave him the seemingly impossible task of obtaining the Golden Fleece. Jason got Argus to build him a ship and gathered about him a group of brave friends. After many adventures they finally reached Colchis on the Black Sea.

From this point on the story becomes chiefly that of the witch Medea (Medē′a), daughter of Aeetes (Ēē′tēs), king of Colchis. She fell in love with Jason, and by her help he obtained the Golden Fleece. Jason and the Argonauts returned to Thessaly, taking Medea with them.

Medea now determined to get rid of Pelias so that Jason might be king. Pretending to make Pelias young again, she killed him. But the people were so incensed that they drove out Medea and Jason, who then went to Corinth. Here they quarreled, and Medea killed her own children. She fled to Athens, and Jason was killed in an accident.

252. The Argonauts and Latin Grammar

The story of the Argonauts as given in part in the following pages was published some years ago in a book by Ritchie called *Fabulae Faciles*. It is written in simple Latin and is intended to give intensive drill on the subjunctive and other constructions common in Caesar. In the lessons that follow, identify every subjunctive, giving its form and the construction, if it is one that has already been covered. Identify also all uses of the future passive participle and gerund and of the infinitive.

Remember that it is one thing to determine what a Latin sentence means, and another, often much more difficult, to put this meaning into good English. You should *understand* Latin as Latin, but *translate* it as English. Two hints for translation: if you can keep the natural English word order close to the Latin, so much the better; if you cannot, turn the whole Latin sentence upside down, if need be, to produce a smooth English version. Second, wherever you easily can, avoid the passive voice in English. The passive is very frequent in Latin, but its constant use in English makes the style flat, weak, and stilted.

Chiron, the wise and just centaur, on a black-figured Greek vase now in the British Museum. The man-horse Chiron was the teacher of many Greek heroes, including Jason.

British Museum

Lesson XL

253. THE WICKED UNCLE

Erant ōlim in Thessaliā duo frātrēs, quōrum alter Aesōn, alter Peliās appellābātur. Aesōn prīmō rēgnum obtinuerat; at post paucōs annōs Peliās rēgnī cupiditāte adductus nōn modo frātrem suum expulit, sed etiam in animō habēbat [1] Iāsonem, Aesonis fīlium, interficere.
5 Quīdam tamen amīcī Aesonis puerum ē tantō perīculō ēripere cōnstituērunt. Noctū igitur Iāsonem ex urbe abstulērunt, et cum posterō diē ad rēgem rediissent, eī renūntiāvērunt puerum mortuum esse. Peliās [2] cum hoc audīvisset, speciem dolōris praebuit et quae causa esset mortis quaesīvit. Illī autem cum bene intellegerent dolōrem eius 10 falsum esse, fābulam dē morte puerī fīnxērunt.

Post breve tempus Peliās, veritus [3] nē [4] rēgnum suum āmitteret, amīcum quendam Delphōs mīsit, quī ōrāculum cōnsuleret. Ille igitur

---

[1] *planned* (with **in animō**).
[2] Subject of **audīvisset** but placed outside the **cum** clause, because it is also the subject of the following verbs. This is common in Latin.
[3] *fearing.* The past participles of some deponent verbs have present force.
[4] *that.*

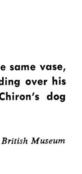
Here, on the other side of the same vase, we see Achilles' father handing over his small son for instruction. Chiron's dog greets the visitors.

British Museum

quam celerrimē Delphōs prōcessit et quam ob causam [5] vēnisset dēmōnstrāvit. Ōrāculum monuit Peliam ut, sī quis venīret [6] calceum ūnum gerēns, eum cavēret. Post paucōs annōs accidit ut Peliās mag- 15 num sacrificium factūrus esset. Diē cōnstitūtō magnus numerus hominum undique convēnit; inter aliōs vēnit etiam Iāsōn, quī ā pueritiā apud centaurum [7] quendam habitāverat. Dum tamen iter facit,[8] calceum alterum [9] in trānseundō flūmine āmīsit.

254. Vocabulary and Word Study

brevis, –e, *short*

cupiditās, –tātis, f., *desire*

morior, morī, mortuus, *die*

noctū, adv., *by night*

renūntiō, 1, *report*

undique, adv., *from all sides*

Review etsī, posterus, praebeō, quaerō, quīdam, redeō, tantus, vereor.

Explain *abbreviate, cupidity, fratricide, inquisition, mortuary, nocturne, posterity, reverend.*

---

[5] *for what reason.*   [6] Subjunctive by attraction (**606**, 15).

[7] *centaur,* a fabulous monster, half man, half horse.

[8] The present tense with **dum** has the force of the imperfect.   [9] *one.*

This Roman terra-cotta relief shows Athena comfortably seated, helping to rig the sails of the *Argo.* Although the story of the Argonauts is filled with myth and miracle, it probably records some dim memory of the Greeks' first exploration of the Black Sea.

Lesson XLI

255. THE GOLDEN FLEECE AND THE BUILDING OF THE ARGO

Iāsōn igitur, ūnō pede[1] nūdō, in rēgiam pervēnit; quem[2] cum Peliās vīdisset, subitō timōre affectus est; intellēxit enim hunc esse hominem quem ōrāculum dēmōnstrāvisset.[3] Hoc igitur iniit cōnsilium. Rēx erat quīdam nōmine Aeētēs, quī rēgnum Cholchidis illō tempore 5 obtinēbat. Huic commissum erat vellus[4] aureum quod Phrixus[5] ōlim

[1] Ablative absolute: *with one foot bare.*
[2] **Quem** is used for **eum** to connect closely with the preceding sentence; translate as if **cum eum.**
[3] The subjunctive is used in a subordinate clause in indirect discourse (**606,** 14).
[4] *fleece* (the woolly coat of a sheep).
[5] Phrixus and his sister Helle fled from a cruel stepmother on the back of a winged ram sent by Jupiter. On the way Helle fell into the sea which was from that time on named the Hellespont. Phrixus arrived in Colchis, on the Black Sea. He sacrificed the ram to Jupiter and gave its fleece, which was of gold, to Aeetes, king of Colchis.

166

ibi relīquerat. Cōnstituit igitur Peliās Iāsonī negōtium dare, ut hoc vellus obtinēret; [6] cum enim rēs esset magnī perīculī eum in itinere peritūrum esse spērābat. Iāsonem igitur ad sē arcessīvit et quid fierī vellet docuit. Iāsōn autem, etsī intellegēbat rem esse difficillimam, negōtium libenter suscēpit.   10

Cum Colchis multōrum diērum iter [7] ab eō locō abesset, nōluit Iāsōn sōlus proficīscī. Dīmīsit igitur nūntiōs in omnēs partēs, quī causam itineris docērent et diem certum conveniendī dīcerent. Intereā negōtium dedit Argō [8] ut nāvem aedificāret. In hīs rēbus circiter decem diēs cōnsūmptī sunt; Argus enim tantam dīligentiam praebēbat ut nē [15] noctū quidem labōrem intermitteret. Ad multitūdinem hominum trāns-portandam nāvis paulō erat lātior quam quibus [9] ūtī cōnsuēvimus.

256. Vocabulary and Word Study

cōnsuēscō, –ere, –suēvī, –suētus, *become accustomed;* in perf., *be accustomed*

intereā, adv., *meanwhile*
paulō, adv., *a little*
ūtor, ūtī, ūsus, *use* (with abl.)

Review **circiter, cōnsūmō, enim, ineō, pereō, proficīscor, subitō.**
Explain *consumer, corroborate, public utility, robust, solitary, usage.*

[6] The clause is in apposition with **negōtium.**
[7] Accusative of extent.   [8] From **Argus,** a man, not from **Argō.**
[9] Supply **eae:** *those which.*

Greek postage stamp with a picture of the ship *Argo* (spelled out in Greek letters in the upper left corner). The ship's magic eye helps it to see its way and protects it.

Gramstorff Bros.

Jason urges his friends to join the expedition. This painting by Walter McEwen in the Library of Congress, Washington, testifies to the universal appeal of the story of the Argonauts.

Lesson XLII

257. DINNER UNDER DIFFICULTIES

Intereā is diēs aderat quem Iāsōn per nūntiōs ēdīxerat, et ex omnibus regiōnibus Graeciae multī undique conveniēbant. Trāditum est autem in hōc numerō fuisse Herculem, Orpheum, Castorem, multōsque aliōs quōrum nōmina nōtissima sunt. Ex hīs Iāsōn, quōs [1] arbitrātus est ad
5 omnia subeunda perīcula parātissimōs esse, eōs ad [2] numerum quīn-quāgintā dēlēgit; tum paucōs diēs morātus ut ad omnēs cāsūs subsidia comparāret, nāvem dēdūxit, et tempestātem [3] ad nāvigandum idōneam nactus solvit.[4]

Post haec Argonautae ad Thrāciam cursum tenuērunt et ibi in
10 terram ēgressī sunt. Cum ab incolīs quaesīssent [5] quis rēgnum eius

---

[1] The antecedent is **eōs** below, which should therefore be translated first.
[2] *about.*   [3] *weather.*   [4] *set sail;* literally, *loosed (ship).*   [5] = **quaesīvissent.**

regiōnis obtinēret, certiōrēs factī sunt Phīneum quendam tum rēgem esse. Cognōvērunt hunc caecum [6] esse et suppliciō afficī, quod ōlim sē crūdēlissimum in fīliōs suōs praebuisset. Cuius [7] supplicī hoc erat genus. Missa erant ā Iove mōnstra quaedam speciē horribilī, quae capita virginum, corpora volucrum habēbant. Hae volucrēs, quae 15 Harpyiae appellābantur, Phīneō summam molestiam afferēbant; quotiēns enim ille accubuerat, veniēbant et cibum appositum statim auferēbant. Quae cum ita essent,[8] Phīneus famē paene mortuus est.

258. Vocabulary and Word Study

comparō, 1, *get ready*
cursus, –ūs, m., *course*
ēgredior, ēgredī, ēgressus,
  go out, land

idōneus, –a, –um, *suitable*
nancīscor, nancīscī, nactus, *meet with*
trādō, –ere, –didī, –ditus, *hand over, relate*

Review **arbitror, cāsus, famēs, moror, paene.**
Explain *convention, egress, moratorium, subsidy, tradition.*

[6] *blind.*   [7] *his.*   [8] *as a result.* What literally?

Caput virginis, corpus volucris habet. This terra-cotta Harpy once decorated the roof of an Etruscan building of the fifth or sixth century B.C. It is called an antefix.

Alinari—Art Reference Bureau

Lesson XLIII

259. TWO GOOD TURNS

Rēs igitur in hōc locō erant cum Argonautae nāvem appulērunt. Phīneus autem, simul atque audīvit eōs in suōs fīnēs ēgressōs esse, magnopere gāvīsus est. Nōn enim dubitābat quīn [1] Argonautae sibi auxilium ferrent. Nūntium igitur ad nāvem mīsit quī Iāsonem sociōsque 5 ad rēgiam vocāret. Eō cum vēnissent, Phīneus prōmīsit sē magna praemia datūrum esse sī illī remedium repperissent. Argonautae negō- tium libenter suscēpērunt et cum rēge accubuērunt; at simul ac cēna apposita est, Harpyiae cibum auferre cōnābantur. Argonautae prīmum gladiīs volucrēs petīvērunt; cum tamen vidērent hoc nihil prōdesse, 10 Zētēs et Calais, quī ālīs īnstrūctī sunt, in āera [2] sē sublevāvērunt ut dēsuper impetum facerent. Quod cum sēnsissent Harpyiae, perterritae statim fūgērunt neque posteā umquam rediērunt.

Hōc factō, Phīneus, ut prō tantō beneficiō grātiās referret, Iāsonī dēmōnstrāvit quā ratiōne Symplēgadēs vītāre posset. Symplēgadēs 15 autem duae erant rūpēs ingentī magnitūdine. Hae parvō intervāllō in marī natābant et sī quid in medium spatium vēnerat, incrēdibilī celeritāte concurrēbant. Iāsōn, sublātīs ancorīs, nāvem solvit et mox ad Symplēgadēs appropinquāvit. Tum in prōrā stāns columbam [3] ēmīsit. Illa rēctā viā per medium spatium volāvit et priusquam rūpēs 20 cōnflīxērunt, ēvāsit, caudā tantum āmissā. Tum rūpēs utrimque dis- cessērunt; antequam tamen rūrsus concurrerent,[4] Argonautae summā vī rēmīs contendērunt et nāvem perdūxērunt.

260. Vocabulary and Word Study

appropinquō, 1, *come near to*
cōnflīgō, –ere, –flīxī, –flīctus, *dash together*
cōnor, 1, *try*
impetus, –ūs, m., *attack*
magnopere, adv., *greatly*
ratiō, –ōnis, f., *manner, reason*

rēmus, –ī, m., *oar*
reperiō, –īre, repperī, repertus, *find*
simul, adv., *at the same time;*
  simul atque (ac), *as soon as*
sublevō, 1, *raise;* w. reflex., *rise*
tollō, –ere, sustulī, sublātus, *raise*
vītō, 1, *avoid*

Review eō (adv.), **intervāllum, rūrsus, statim.**
Explain *aerial, conflict, impetuous, repertory, simultaneous, volatile.*

[1] *that,* used after a negative expression of doubting to introduce a clause in the subjunctive (**ferrent**).   [2] Accusative singular of **āēr, āeris,** m., *air.*
[3] *dove.*   [4] For the mood see **606,** 12.

Lesson XLIV

261. A RISKY JOB

Brevī intermissō spatiō, Argonautae ad flūmen Phāsim vēnērunt, quod in fīnibus Colchōrum erat. Eō cum in terram ēgressī essent, statim ad rēgem Aeētem prōcessērunt et ab eō postulāvērunt ut vellus aureum sibi trāderētur. Ille īrā commōtus diū negābat sē vellus trāditūrum esse. Tandem tamen, quod sciēbat Iāsonem nōn sine auxiliō 5 deōrum hoc negōtium suscēpisse, prōmīsit sē vellus trāditūrum esse, sī Iāsōn labōrēs duōs difficillimōs perfēcisset; [1] et cum Iāsōn dīxisset sē ad omnia perīcula subeunda parātum esse, quid fierī vellet ostendit. Prīmum iungendī erant duo taurī speciē horribilī, quī flammās ex ōre ēdēbant; tum, hīs iūnctīs, ager arandus erat, et dentēs dracōnis serendī. 10 Hīs audītīs, Iāsōn, nē hanc occāsiōnem reī bene gerendae [2] āmitteret, negōtium suscēpit.

At Mēdēa, rēgis fīlia, Iāsonem amāvit, et ubi audīvit eum tantum perīculum subitūrum esse, rem aegrē ferēbat. Intellegēbat enim patrem suum hunc labōrem prōposuisse eō ipsō cōnsiliō, ut Iāsōn morerētur. 15 Quae cum ita essent, Mēdēa (quae summam scientiam medicīnae habēbat) hoc cōnsilium iniit. Mediā nocte clam ex urbe ēvāsit et herbās quāsdam carpsit; ex hīs unguentum parāvit quod vī suā corpus aleret [3] nervōsque [4] cōnfirmāret. Hōc factō, Iāsonī unguentum dedit; praecēpit autem ut eō diē quō istī [5] labōrēs cōnficiendī essent corpus 20 suum et arma oblineret. Iāsōn, etsī paene omnibus [6] magnitūdine et vīribus corporis praestābat, tamen hoc cōnsilium nōn neglegendum esse cēnsēbat.

262. Vocabulary and Word Study

aegrē, adv., *with difficulty*
cēnseō, –ēre, cēnsuī, cēnsus, *think*
clam, adv., *secretly*

iungō, –ere, iūnxī, iūnctus, *join, harness*
occāsiō, –ōnis, f., *opportunity*

Review **alō, diū, neglegō, postulō, praestō.**
Explain *dental, conjunction, liniment, moratorium, postulate, Unguentine.*

---

[1] *would perform.* In direct discourse the verb would have been in the future perfect indicative.   [2] *of accomplishing his mission.* What literally?
[3] Translate with "would." See **606,** 3.   [4] *muscles.*   [5] *the above-mentioned.*
[6] For the dative see **599,** 6.

Lesson XLV

263. SOWING THE DRAGON'S TEETH

Ubi is diēs vēnit quem rēx ad arandum agrum ēdīxerat, Iāsōn, ortā lūce,[1] cum sociīs ad locum cōnstitūtum prōcessit. Ibi stabulum ingēns repperit in quō taurī erant inclūsī; tum, portīs apertīs, taurōs in lūcem trāxit, et summā [2] cum difficultāte iugum imposuit. Tum Iāsōn, 5 omnibus aspicientibus, agrum arāre coepit; quā in rē tantam dīligentiam praebuit ut ante merīdiem tōtum opus cōnficeret. Hōc factō, ad locum ubi rēx sedēbat adiit et dentēs dracōnis postulāvit; quōs ubi accēpit, in agrum sparsit. Hōrum autem dentium nātūra erat tālis ut in eō locō ubi sparsī essent virī armātī mīrō modō gignerentur.

10 Postquam igitur omnēs dentēs in agrum sparsit, Iāsōn lassitūdine exanimātus quiētī sē trādidit, dum virī istī gignerentur. Paucās hōrās dormiēbat; sub [3] vesperum tamen ē somnō subitō excitātus rem ita ēvēnisse ut praedictum erat cognōvit; nam in omnibus agrī partibus virī ingentī magnitūdine gladiīs galeīsque armātī mīrō modō ē terrā 15 oriēbantur. Hōc cognitō, Iāsōn cōnsilium quod dedisset Mēdēa nōn omittendum esse putābat. Saxum igitur ingēns in mediōs virōs coniēcit. Illī undique ad locum concurrērunt, et cum sibi quisque id saxum habēre vellet, magna contrōversia orta est. Mox, strictīs gladiīs, inter sē [4] pugnāre coepērunt, et cum hōc modō plūrimī occīsī essent, reliquī 20 vulneribus cōnfectī ā Iāsone nūllō negōtiō [5] interfectī sunt.

264. Vocabulary and Word Study

aspiciō, –ere, aspexī, aspectus, *look on*
contrōversia, –ae, f., *dispute*
exanimō, 1, *exhaust, kill*

imperō, 1, *command, order*
iste, ista, istud, *that*
iugum, –ī, n., *yoke*
merīdiēs, –ēī, m., *midday, noon*

Review **aperiō, at, coepī, occīdō, orior, quiēs, saxum, vesper.**
Explain *aspect, disperse* (from **spargō**), *imperative, lassitude, quietus.*

---

[1] Ablative absolute: *at daybreak.* What literally?
[2] Modifies **difficultāte.** The order *adjective, preposition, noun,* is sometimes used when the adjective is emphatic.　　　[3] *toward.*
[4] *with one another.* What literally?　　　[5] *without trouble.* Why ablative?

172

Jason reaches up to steal the fleece, while Athena (center) looks on. At the right, one of the Argonauts holds the rail of the good ship *Argo*. We might expect the hero Jason to be a little bigger and less awkward than this. A red-figured Greek vase in New York.

173

Lesson XLVI

265. JASON GETS THE FLEECE

At rēx Aeētēs, ubi cognōvit Iāsonem labōrem prōpositum cōn-
fēcisse, īrā graviter commōtus est; intellegēbat enim Mēdēam auxilium
eī tulisse. Mēdēa autem, cum intellegeret sē in magnō esse perīculō,
fugā salūtem petere cōnstituit. Omnibus igitur rēbus ad fugam parātīs,
5 mediā nocte cum frātre Absyrtō ēvāsit et quam celerrimē ad locum ubi
Argō ¹ subducta erat prōcessit. Eō cum vēnisset, ad pedēs Iāsonis sē
prōiēcit et multīs cum lacrimīs eum ōrāvit nē in tantō perīculō sē ²
dēsereret. Ille libenter eam excēpit et hortātus est nē patris īram
timēret. Prōmīsit autem sē quam prīmum eam in nāvī suā āvectūrum.³
10 Postrīdiē Iāsōn cum sociīs suīs, ortā lūce, nāvem dēdūxit, et
tempestātem idōneam nactī ad eum locum rēmīs contendērunt quō
Mēdēa vellus cēlātum esse dēmōnstrāvit. Eō cum vēnissent, Iāsōn in
terram ēgressus, ipse cum Mēdēā in silvās contendit. Pauca mīlia passuum per silvam prōgressus vellus quod quaerēbat ex arbore sus-
15 pēnsum vīdit. Id tamen auferre rēs erat summae difficultātis: nōn modo
enim locus ipse ēgregiē et nātūrā et arte mūnītus erat, sed etiam dracō
speciē terribilī arborem custōdiēbat. Tum Mēdēa, quae, ut suprā
dēmōnstrāvimus, medicīnae summam scientiam habuit, rāmum quem
ex arbore proximā arripuerat venēnō īnfēcit.⁴ Hōc factō, ad locum
20 appropinquāvit et dracōnem, quī faucibus apertīs eius adventum
exspectābat, venēnō sparsit; deinde, dum dracō somnō oppressus
dormit, Iāsōn vellus aureum ex arbore arripuit et cum Mēdēā quam
celerrimē pedem rettulit.⁵

266. Vocabulary and Word Study

apertus, –a, –um, *open*
contendō, –ere, –tendī, –tentūrus,
   struggle, hasten
difficultās, –tātis, f., *difficulty*
postrīdiē, adv., *on the next day*

quam, adv. and conj., *how, as;*
   with comp., *than;* with
   superl., *as . . . as possible.*
suprā, adv., *above*

Review **arbor, excipiō, hortor, passus.**
Explain *contention, dragon, hortatory, infection, projectile, sus-
pension.*

¹ *Argo* (the ship). ² i.e., Medea. ³ *would carry away.*
⁴ Use the derivative. ⁵ *withdrew* (with **pedem**). What literally?

174

Lesson XLVII

267. ESCAPE THROUGH MURDER

Postquam Iāsōn et Mēdēa, vellus aureum ferentēs, ad nāvem per-
vēnissent, omnēs sine morā nāvem rūrsus cōnscendērunt et prīmā
vigiliā [1] solvērunt. At rēx Aeētēs, ubi cognōvit fīliam suam nōn modo
ad Argonautās sē recēpisse sed etiam ad vellus auferendum auxilium
tulisse, nāvem longam [2] quam celerrimē dēdūcī iussit et fugientēs [3]   5
īnsecūtus est. Argonautae omnibus vīribus rēmīs contendēbant; cum
tamen nāvis quā vehēbantur ingentī esset magnitūdine, nōn eādem
celeritāte quā [4] Colchī prōgredī poterant. Quae cum ita essent, ā
Colchīs sequentibus paene captī sunt. At Mēdēa, cum vīdīsset quō in
locō rēs essent, nefārium cōnsilium cēpit.   10

Erat in nāvī Argonautārum fīlius rēgis Aeētae, nōmine Absyrtus,
quem, ut suprā dēmōnstrāvimus, Mēdēa fugiēns sēcum abdūxerat.
Hunc puerum Mēdēa interficere cōnstituit ut, membrīs eius in mare
coniectīs, cursum Colchōrum impedīret; [5] sciēbat enim Aeētem, cum

---

[1] *watch.* The night was divided into four "watches."   [2] i.e., *a warship.*
[3] *the fugitives.* What literally?   [4] *as.*   [5] Understand Medea as the subject.

In this relief Medea poisons the dragon as Jason prepares to cut off the Fleece.

E. Richter, Rome

15 membra fīlī vīdisset, nōn longius prōsecūtūrum esse. Neque opīniō
eam fefellit.[6] Aeētēs, cum prīmum membra vīdit, ad ea colligenda
nāvem dētinērī iussit. Dum tamen ea geruntur, Argonautae mox
ex cōnspectū hostium remōtī sunt, neque prius [7] fugere dēstitērunt
quam ad flūmen Ēridanum [8] pervēnērunt.

20 Tandem post multa perīcula Iāsōn in eundem locum pervēnit unde
ōlim profectus erat. Tum ē nāvī ēgressus ad rēgem Peliam statim
prōcessit et, vellere aureō mōnstrātō, ab eō postulāvit ut rēgnum sibi
trāderētur. Peliās prīmum nihil respondit, sed diū in eādem trīstitiā
tacitus permānsit; tandem ita locūtus est: "Vidēs mē aetāte iam esse
25 cōnfectum; certē diēs suprēmus mihi adest. Liceat [9] igitur mihi, dum
vīvam, hoc rēgnum obtinēre; cum autem tandem dēcesserō, tū in
meum locum veniēs." Hāc ōrātiōne adductus Iāsōn respondit sē id
factūrum quod ille rogāvisset.

268. Vocabulary and Word Study

cum prīmum, *as soon as*
dēsistō, –ere, dēstitī, dēstitūrus,
cease
fallō, –ere, fefellī, falsus, *deceive*

īnsequor, īnsequī, īnsecūtus, *pursue*
opīniō, –ōnis, f., *opinion*
priusquam, conj., *before*
unde, adv., *from which* (*place*)

Review colligō, cōnficiō, cōnspectus, licet, loquor, mora, ōlim, prōgredior, sequor, vehō.

Explain *circumlocution, detention, fallacy, illicit, infallible, nefarious, opinionated, survivor, taciturn.*

[6] From fallō: *she was not mistaken.* What literally?
[7] To be taken with quam = priusquam.   [8] *the Po,* a river of northern Italy.
[9] *let it be permitted.*

Above: Postage stamps of France and
Uruguay showing centaurs (cf. p. 164).
Left: Turkish stamp with Roman column in
Istanbul, on the route of the Argonauts.

White-haired King Pelias watches Medea (center) perform her magic while the ram boils. At the right is one of Pelias' daughters. A slave, or perhaps Jason, tends the fire. Is this vase red-figured or black-figured?

Lesson XLVIII

269. BOILED MUTTON

Hīs rēbus cognitīs, Mēdēa rēgnī cupiditāte adducta mortem rēgī per dolum īnferre cōnstituit. Ad fīliās rēgis vēnit atque ita locūta est: "Vidētis patrem vestrum aetāte iam esse cōnfectum neque ad labōrem rēgnandī perferendum [1] satis valēre. Vultisne eum rūrsus iuvenem fierī?" Tum fīliae rēgis ita respondērunt: "Num [2] hoc fierī potest? Quis enim 5 umquam ē sene iuvenis factus est?" At Mēdēa respondit: "Scītis mē

[1] Which is the gerund—**rēgnandī** or **perferendum?** How are gerund and participle to be distinguished? See **611, 612.**

[2] Introduces a question implying a negative answer: *this can't be done, can it?*

177

Robert Whitehead and Oliver Rea

Medea (portrayed by Judith Anderson) and Jason at Corinth in Robinson Jeffers'
adaptation of Euripides' play *Medea*. Although generally unpopular during
Euripides' lifetime, his plays were acclaimed widely after his death.

medicīnae summam habēre scientiam. Nunc igitur vōbīs dēmōnstrābō
quō modō haec rēs fierī possit." Hīs dictīs, cum arietem aetāte iam
cōnfectum interfēcisset, membra eius in vāse aēneō [3] posuit et, ignī
10 suppositō,[4] in aquam herbās quāsdam īnfūdit. Tum carmen magicum
cantābat. Mox ariēs ē vāse exsiluit et, vīribus refectīs, per agrōs
currēbat.

Dum fīliae rēgis hoc mīrāculum stupentēs intuentur, Mēdēa ita
locūta est: "Vidētis quantum valeat medicīna. Vōs igitur, sī vultis
15 patrem vestrum in adulēscentiam redūcere, id quod fēcī ipsae faciētis.
Vōs patris membra in vās conicite; ego herbās magicās praebēbō."
Quod ubi audītum est, fīliae rēgis cōnsilium quod dedisset Mēdēa nōn
omittendum putāvērunt. Patrem igitur Peliam necāvērunt et membra
eius in vās coniēcērunt. At Mēdēa nōn eāsdem herbās dedit quibus [5]
20 ipsa ūsa erat. Itaque postquam diū frūstrā exspectāvērunt, patrem
suum rē vērā [6] mortuum esse intellēxērunt. Hīs rēbus gestīs, Mēdēa
spērābat sē cum coniuge suō rēgnum acceptūram esse; sed cīvēs cum
intellegerent quō modō Peliās periisset, Iāsone et Mēdēā ē rēgnō
expulsīs, Acastum rēgem creāvērunt.

270. Vocabulary and Word Study

aetās, –tātis, f., *age*
coniciō, –ere, –iēcī, –iectus, *throw*
frūstrā, adv., *in vain*
necō, 1, *kill*

satis, adv. and indeclinable adj.,
   enough
umquam, adv., *ever*

Review **ignis, ita, quantus, spērō.**
Explain *conjugal, dismember, frustrate, imperishable, infusion,
internecine, intuition, miraculous, rejuvenate.*

[3] *of bronze.*   [4] *placed under,* i.e., the pot.
[5] The ablative is used with **ūtor.**   [6] With **rē:** *in fact, really.*

178

Lesson XLIX

271. DEATH AND MORE DEATH

Post haec Iāsōn et Mēdēa ad urbem Corinthum vēnērunt, cuius
urbis Creōn rēgnum tum obtinēbat. Erat autem Creontī [1] fīlia ūna
nōmine Glaucē. Quam cum vīdisset, Iāsōn cōnstituit Mēdēam uxōrem
suam repudiāre, ut Glaucēn [2] in mātrimōnium dūceret. At Mēdēa, ubi
intellēxit quae ille in animō habēret, īrā graviter commōta iūre iūrandō 5
cōnfirmāvit sē tantam iniūriam ultūram. Hoc igitur cōnsilium cēpit.
Vestem parāvit summā arte contextam; hanc īnfēcit venēnō, cuius vīs
tālis erat ut, sī quis eam vestem induisset,[3] corpus eius quasi ignī
urerētur. Hōc factō, vestem ad Glaucēn mīsit. Illa autem nihil malī
suspicāns dōnum libenter accēpit, et vestem novam, mōre fēminārum, 10
sine morā induit.

Statim Glaucē dolōrem gravem per omnia membra sēnsit et post
paulum summō cruciātū affecta ē vītā excessit. Tum Mēdēa furōre
impulsa fīliōs suōs necāvit et ex eā regiōne fugere cōnstituit. Sōlem
ōrāvit ut in tantō perīculō auxilium sibi ferret. Sōl autem hīs precibus 15
commōtus currum mīsit cui dracōnēs ālīs īnstrūctī iūnctī erant. Mēdēa
currum cōnscendit, itaque per āera [4] vecta incolumis ad urbem
Athēnās pervēnit. Iāsōn autem post breve tempus mīrō modō occīsus
est. Ille enim sub umbrā nāvis suae, quae in lītus subducta erat, ōlim
dormiēbat. At nāvis in eam partem [5] ubi Iāsōn iacēbat subitō dēlāpsa 20
virum īnfēlīcem oppressit.

272. Vocabulary and Word Study

cruciātus, –ūs, m., *torture*	**prex, precis,** f., *prayer*
iūs iūrandum, iūris iūrandī, n., *oath*	**suspicor,** 1, *suspect*

Review **fēmina, incolumis, opprimō, sentiō, sōl, uxor, vestis.**
Explain *context, deprecate, excruciating, investiture, morale, moral-
ity, suspicion, tinge, uxoricide.*

> *Oh how I wish that an embargo*
> *Had kept in port the good ship Argo!*
> —Lord Byron

---

[1] Dative of possession (**599,** 8).
[2] Accusative (Greek form).
[3] Subjunctive by attraction.
[4] *air;* a Greek form of the accusative.
[5] To be taken with **dēlāpsa:** *falling towards that side.*

B R I T A N N I A

Cenimagni

Cassi   Trinovantes

Londinium

Tamesis (Thames)   (Dover)

Ancalites   CANTIUM
(Kent)

Segontiaci   Bibroci   *Fretum Gallicum*

Morini   Levaci
Portus Itius   (FLANDERS)   Gr
(Boulogne)   Atrebates   BELGIU   Nervii
(Arras)   Sabis (Samb

Samara   Ambiani   Viromandui
(Somme)

(Cherbourg)   Caleti   Samarobriva   Bellovaci
(Amiens)   (Oise)   Suessiones   Bibrax

Venelli   Bratuspantium   Noviodunum   Axona
(Breteuil)   *Isera*   (Soissons)   (Aisne

Essuvii   Vellocasses   Durocor
Lexovii   *Sequana*   Parisii   (Rei
(NORMANDY)   *(Seine)*   Lutecia   *Matrona*
(Brest)   A R E M O R I C   (Paris)   *(Marne)*
Osismi   Coriosolites   Diablintes   Metiosedum
(Melun)   Senones   *Sequana*
A   Redones   Aulerci   Agedincum
(BRITTANY)   Andes   Carnutes   (Sens)   *(Seine*
Veneti   Mandubii
Namnetes   *Liger*   Cenabum   Alesia
Ambiliati   (Tours)   (Orleans)   (Dijon)
C   Turoni   *(Loire)*   E   Bituriges   L   Noviodunum   T   I
Pictones   Avaricum   (Nevers)
(Bourges)   Boii   Bibracte
Lemovices   (Vichy)
Santoni   Gergovia   Segusiavi
Arverni   Vie
(Vi

(Bordeaux)   *Duranius*
Garunna
Sotiates   M. CEBENNA   *Rhodanus* (R)
AQUITANIA   Tolosates   PROVI
Tolosa   (Nîmes)
(Toulouse)   Arelate
Garunna   Volcae   (Arles)
Carcaso   Narbo
(Narbonne)

H I S P A N I A   P Y R E N A E I   M O N T E S   MAR
180

GALLIA

Roman Miles

0   25   50   100   150

English Miles

0   25   50   100

Usipetes

Tencteri

rones

Sugambri

oxii

Atuatuca

ondrusi

Caerosi

orum opp.

nur)

NA SILVA

Treveri
(Treves)

Mossella

VOSEGUS MONS

Latobrigi

Tulingi

sontio
sançon)

Rauraci

JURA MONS

quani

ubis

Tigurini

Helvetii

L. Lemannus

Verbigeni

ua

Veragri

Allobroges

Octodurus

Ceutrones

Graciceli

Ocelum

Caturiges

ntii

L I G U R I A

assilia
arseilles)

GER

M

A

N

I

A

Suebi

Ubii

Rhenus (Rhine)

HERCYNIA SILVA

Danuvius
(Danube)

Rhenus (Rhine)

Norici

Rhenus

E   S   S

Aquileia

Mediolanum
(Milan)

Ticinus

G A L L I A

Cremona

(Po)

Placentia

Padus

CISALPINA

APPENNINUS

Ravenna

Rubico

Ariminum

Genua

MONS

MARE HADRIATICUM

Luca

Pisae

Tiberis

Clusium

50°

45°

INTERNUM

CORSICA

10°

UNIT V

DĒ BELLŌ GALLICŌ I

The *curia* was the meeting place of the Roman Senate. It was the scene of all the major decisions which made Rome a great power, especially in the early days of the Republic. Theoretically the Senate could not legislate; however its resolutions were generally obeyed.

When Julius Caesar entered the political scene, about 78 B.C., he took up the cause of the general populace against the senatorial clique, made up of a small number of noble Roman families who had ruled Rome well but autocratically for centuries. Upon becoming Roman leader after the Gallic Wars (58–50 B.C.), Caesar had the Senate House rebuilt, and in the process he renamed it the *Curia Julia*. Caesar also raised senatorial membership from 600 to 900 in order to reward his supporters. From this time on however, the Senate changed its character completely. Although it continued to be a political institution, it lost its former power and influence in the governing of the Roman Empire.

The Temple of Venus and Rome, in the Roman Forum, was restored by the Emperor Maxentius in 307 A.D. It was dedicated to Venus (the supposed ancestress of Julius Caesar's family) and to all the local divinity of Rome.

Scala/Art Resource

Our Heritage

273. JULIUS CAESAR

No man is more immediately associated with Rome than is Julius Caesar. To most people the name Caesar symbolizes the dynamism and greatness of the republic which he did so much to turn into an empire. The word Caesar is preserved in the titles Kaiser and Czar, and has come so nearly to be a synonym for royal or dictatorial power that we speak of a minor autocrat as a "little Caesar." Few of us have not heard or used many of the phrases which have grown up around him—"crossing the Rubicon," "the Ides of March," "Et tu, Brute," "great Caesar's ghost." No other Roman has been the subject of so much later attention: we have a biography in Latin by Suetonius, one in Greek by Plutarch, plays by Shakespeare and George Bernard Shaw; and continually novels and motion pictures celebrate his life and character.

Gaius Julius Caesar was born in 100 B.C. to a patrician family whose members flattered themselves on being so ancient that they could trace their line all the way back to a divine ancestress—Venus, the mother of Aeneas. But, in spite of their aristocratic lineage, the Julians had, in the early first century B.C., been associated with the political program of the common people. Whether from these connections, or from personal conviction, or from shrewd political insight into the way his ambitions could most easily be realized, and probably from all three, Caesar early adopted the popular cause against the senatorial clique, made up of a small number of noble families who had ruled Rome well but autocratically for centuries. Caesar's stand alarmed the conservative dictator Sulla and nearly cost Caesar his life, but, by a combination of a gambler's daring, great acumen in wooing the favor of the people, and an almost irresistible personal magnetism, he steadily made his way up the political ladder. Somewhat before 60 B.C. he had allied himself with Crassus, a wealthy politician (who underwrote the enormous debts Caesar had contracted), and in that year he joined Pompey, the greatest military hero of the time, and Crassus in the coalition called the First Triumvirate ("Three-man Rule"). As a result, in 59 B.C., Caesar was elected to the consulship, the highest office in the Roman government, and so dominated his colleague Bibulus that the year was jestingly called, not "the consulship of Caesar and Bibulus," but "the consulship of Julius and Caesar." Many senators, realizing the danger that Caesar presented to their conservative position, tried to restrict the importance of the command he would hold as an ex-consul, but by political maneuvering Caesar won the proconsulship of Gaul and Illyricum. In all he spent nine years (58–50 B.C.) in subjugating and governing Gaul; in the following pages you will be reading his own account of that conquest, the *Commentaries on the Gallic Wars*. Caesar is remarkably tight-lipped about his own personal motives. It is apparent, however, that

The Roman theater at Orange, southern France, is once more used for stage plays.

Debra and Robert Bretzfelder/PhotoEdit

at the start of his command his attitude was a defensive one of simply protecting Italy and the Roman Province in southern France from the barbarian tribes. Then he shifted to an aggressive attitude aimed at the reduction of all Transalpine Gaul to the status of a Roman province. Possibly he realized that "a good offense is the best defense" (he often states that friendly Gallic tribes appealed to him for protection against their more aggressive neighbors); possibly he was driven farther and farther north by a consuming ambition for military power and glory. It is certain, however, that he used these years to develop his extraordinary military talents and to weld for himself a highly loyal and efficient fighting force. There is also much evidence to show that even while Caesar was away in Gaul he was using his prestige and captured gold to build a strong political party at Rome.

Unquestionably he was a great military commander; his absolute physical courage, his self-confidence, his iron will, his fairness, and his generosity with praise and rewards made him an unparalleled leader of men. He was a master tactician, relying on great mobility to surprise his enemies, quick to adapt his maneuvers to the terrain and to press every advantage in the field. He showed no less skill in dealing with the people of Gaul, capitalizing on their failure to unite and on their vacillation, trusting those who became his allies (some would say he trusted them too much), and employing harsh punishments only when the offenders' rebelliousness was incorrigible.

Caesar's successes in Gaul, Britain, and Germany and the growth of his party at Rome led inevitably to conflict with Pompey and the Senate, and in 49 B.C. to the Civil War, which started when Caesar crossed the Rubicon, the boundary between Cisalpine Gaul and Italy proper. The Senatorial army under Pompey's command abandoned Italy and was defeated near Pharsalus (in Greece) in 48 B.C. Within the next three years Caesar had overrun all opposition and become virtually master of the Western world. In the few years before his assassination in 44 B.C., he brought about many reforms in Roman political and economic life, and laid the basis upon which his grand-nephew and adopted son Octavian built the Roman Empire.

Caesar was most expert in "public relations." He wrote his *Commentaries* (or *Notes*) *on the Gallic Wars* not simply to provide a record of the campaigns for future historians, but principally to keep himself and his victories before the eyes of the Roman voters. Since he regularly refers to himself in the third person (only occasionally using the modest "we"), the work takes on a deceptively impersonal air, and the reader is inclined to forget that the image of this dynamic and unconquerable, yet understanding and merciful, general is being

The altar marks the spot where Caesar's body was burned. Above the site, a temple was built. At the right is the Temple of Vesta.

created by the "hero" himself. The style is likewise deceptively straight-forward and clear, and the facts apparently so complete that no ancient historian ever needed or dared to rewrite his story. His three-book account of the Civil War is a valuable document of that bloody period, but it is the earlier work which assures Caesar a place among the first rank of military historians.

It is, therefore, easy to see why so versatile a man was not only a great general, statesman, and writer, but also one of the best orators of his day, remarkable for the vigor of his speeches. But you might be surprised to know that he was something of a poet, and was seriously interested in Latin grammar.

As a military man, Caesar ranks with such geniuses as Alexander, Hannibal, and Napoleon. Like Pericles, Washington, and Churchill, he was a great statesman, one whose military triumphs and political activities profoundly affected the future of the world. Yet, with all we know about him, there remains some of the mystery and controversy which surround all great men. Naturally he had his faults. He was a bit vain about his personal appearance, and particularly sensitive about his baldness. Although not especially superstitious himself, he capitalized on the people's belief that Fortune favored him. Even though "Caesar's wife must be above suspicion," Caesar himself was not. But the gossip which attended his personal life served only to spread his reputation and to aid him at the polls. Much more serious is the charge that he was nothing more than a tyrant, bent on destroy-ing the Roman republican form of government to satisfy his own lust for power. This question is still hotly debated, and, as you read his own words in the pages that follow, you will have a chance to decide the answer for yourself.

274. CAESAR'S ARMY AND THE AMERICAN ARMY

Caesar's army (**exercitus,** literally, a body of "trained" men) was composed mainly of Roman citizens, who served as foot soldiers (**peditēs**), but it also contained a cavalry force (**equitēs**), which during the Gallic War averaged about 4,000 men. The cavalry were foreign mercenaries recruited in Spain, Germany, and Gaul. They were used mainly for scouting and surprise attacks, in preliminary skirmishing to test the enemy's strength, or in pursuit of a retreating foe.

In 1939 the United States Army returned to a system of drill movements very much like that of the Roman army. The advantages are simplicity and maneuverability. The Roman army unit corresponding to a modern company marched in eight ranks or rows; our platoons march in three or four ranks.

The Roman army was organized as follows:

I. Groupings

   A. Infantry (**peditēs**)

      1. **Legiō.** The average size of one of Caesar's legions during the Gallic War was probably about 3,200, though the full or "paper" strength was supposed to be 6,000. It is comparable to a *division* in the United States Army, for, like a division, it was a complete unit, consisting of various types of troops. The wartime strength of a division today is roughly 13,500 officers and men, including five infantry battle groups of about 1,300 men each and in addition the specialized troops that support them. In 1961 the Army announced plans to return to a division of three brigades, in place of five battle groups.

      2. **Cohortēs.** Each legion was divided into ten *cohorts* (**cohortēs**), averaging 360 men each. The similar grouping in the United States Army is the *battle group,* consisting of about 1,300 men in five companies. Since the possibility of nuclear warfare today requires that combat units be more mobile, more self-sustaining, and capable of wider dispersal than in the past, the latest reorganizations of the United States Army assign to battle groups the various types of troops needed to allow them to operate independently, at least for limited periods. Thus the

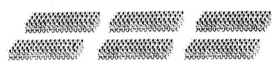

Legiō (Decem cohortēs).

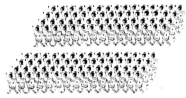

Manipulus (Duo ōrdinēs).

Cohors (Trēs manipulī).

Ōrdō (Centuria).

battle group also is in many respects comparable to the Roman legion. The specialized combat troops which support the infantry, such as combat engineers, field artillerymen, tank personnel, signal corps men, etc., are usually grouped into *battalions* ranging in size from 500 to 2,000 men.

3. **Manipulī.** Each cohort was divided into three *maniples* (**manipulī**) of 120 men each. This corresponds to our *company,* with nearly 200 men (four platoons).

4. **Ōrdinēs.** Each maniple was divided into two *centuries* (**ōrdinēs** [1]), originally of 100 men each but averaging 60 in Caesar's army. This corresponds to our *platoon,* with about 50 men.

B. Cavalry (**equitēs**)

1. **Ālae.** The **āla,** or *squadron,* consisted of 300 or 400 men commanded by a **praefectus equitum** (*cavalry prefect*).

2. **Turmae.** Each **āla** was divided into **turmae,** or *troops,* of about 30 men each.

3. **Decuriae.** Each **turma** was divided into **decuriae,** or *squads,* of 10 men each.

---

[1] This term is sometimes used in Caesar in the sense of line, position, or rank.

189

C. Auxiliaries **(auxilia)**

1. **Levis armātūrae peditēs.** *Light-armed troops* recruited from allied or dependent states. Their officers were Romans. Caesar did not depend upon his **auxilia** to win battles but used them mostly for raiding and foraging.
2. **Funditōrēs.** *Slingers,* principally from the Balearic Islands (Majorca, etc.), near the east coast of Spain.
3. **Sagittāriī.** *Bowmen,* or *archers,* from Crete in the eastern Mediterranean and Numidia in Africa.

D. Noncombatants

1. **Cālōnēs.** *Camp servants,* including slaves attached to the officers' quarters. Each legion had about 500.
2. **Mūliōnēs.** *Muledrivers* in charge of the heavy baggage of the army.
3. **Mercātōrēs.** *Traders* allowed to accompany the army and conduct canteens outside the camp.

II. Personnel

A. Enlisted Men

1. **Mīles legiōnārius.** A *legionary soldier* was usually a citizen volunteer who enlisted for the regular term of twenty years. Roman citizens between the ages of seventeen and forty-six were subject to military draft **(dīlēctus).**
2. **Ēvocātus.** A *volunteer* who had served his full time but had reënlisted. Such men were the flower of Caesar's army.
3. **Signifer.** *Standard bearer* of the maniple, resembling the modern color bearer.
4. **Aquilifer.** *Bearer of the eagle,* emblem of the legion.
5. **Centuriō, decuriō.** Each of the sixty centuries of the legion was in charge of a *centurion,* a noncommissioned officer appointed from the ranks in recognition of brave and efficient service. The centurions correspond in a general way to our sergeants, the first sergeant ("top sergeant") being called the *first centurion* **(prīmipīlus).** They were fearless officers who fought in the ranks, leading their men in person. Much of the success of an army depended on them. They maintained strict discipline, which they enforced with the **vītis,** similar to a policeman's club (see p. 230). The commander of a squad of cavalry was called a *decurion.*

B. Commissioned Officers

1. **Tribūnus mīlitum, praefectus equitum.** Each legion had six *military tribunes,* the lowest commissioned officers. They were usually young men, well educated and of good family, but

untrained, and were entrusted with duties of minor importance, such as the command of a legion in camp or on the march (the modern second lieutenant). These men usually were in the army to get the military experience which was prerequisite to a political career. A *cavalry prefect*, similar in rank to a military tribune, commanded an **āla**.

2. **Quaestor.** Like a *quartermaster*, the **quaestor** supervised the pay of the men and the purchase of supplies; in battle he sometimes commanded a legion.

3. **Lēgātus.** Caesar had a number of *staff officers* **(lēgātī)**, who were appointed by the Roman senate with the rank of a modern *lieutenant general* or *major general*. In battle each legion was usually commanded by a **lēgātus**, but the **lēgātī** did not hold permanent command.

4. **Dux, imperātor.** The *general* **(dux)** assumed the title **imperātor** after winning his first important victory. After defeating the Helvetians, Caesar was regularly addressed as **imperātor,** a title which corresponds to that of *commanding general* in a modern army. Any staff officer appointed by the **imperātor** to command a division of troops became temporarily **dux** of that division.

C. Specialists Attached to the General Staff

1. **Fabrī.** *Engineers* specially trained or detailed from the ranks to build ships, bridges, siege engines, and winter quarters. Such work was in charge of the chief of engineers **(praefectus fabrum).**

2. **Speculātōrēs.** *Spies* employed singly by the general to obtain news by going within the enemy's lines, often in disguise.

3. **Explōrātōrēs.** Mounted *scouts,* or *patrols,* who scoured the country for information. They usually went out in small parties.

Battle between Romans and Gauls as shown on a Roman Tomb.

Lesson L

275. A GEOGRAPHY LESSON

I, 1. Gallia est omnis [1] dīvīsa [2] in partēs trēs, quārum ūnam [3] incolunt Belgae,[4] aliam Aquītānī, tertiam eī quī ipsōrum linguā [5] Celtae, nostrā [6] Gallī appellantur. Hī omnēs linguā, īnstitūtīs, lēgibus inter sē [7] differunt. Gallōs [8] ab Aquītānīs Garunna [9] flūmen, ā Belgīs
5 Matrona [9] et Sēquana [9] dīvidit.[10]

Hōrum omnium fortissimī sunt Belgae, proptereā quod ā cultū atque hūmānitāte Prōvinciae [11] longissimē absunt, minimēque saepe mercātōrēs ad eōs veniunt atque ea quae ad effēminandōs animōs pertinent important. Proximī sunt Germānīs quī trāns Rhēnum in-
10 colunt, quibuscum semper bellum gerunt. Quā dē causā Helvētiī quoque reliquōs Gallōs virtūte superant, quod ferē cotīdiānīs proeliīs cum Germānīs contendunt, cum [12] aut suīs [13] fīnibus [14] eōs prohibent aut ipsī in eōrum [15] fīnibus bellum gerunt.

Eōrum [16] ūna pars, quam Gallī obtinent, initium capit ā flūmine
15 Rhodanō; continētur Garunnā flūmine, Ōceanō, fīnibus Belgārum; attingit etiam ab [17] Sēquanīs et Helvētiīs flūmen [18] Rhēnum; vergit ad septentriōnēs.[19] Belgae ab extrēmīs Galliae fīnibus oriuntur, pertinent

---

[1] *as a whole,* i.e., *Greater Gaul. All Gaul* would be **omnis Gallia.** See map of Gaul (pp. 180–181).　　　[2] Predicate adjective: *is divided.*
[3] Supply **partem.**　　　[4] Ancestors of the modern Belgians.
[5] *in their own language* (literally, *by*).
[6] Supply **linguā.** What language is meant?
[7] *from one another.* What literally?
[8] Caesar here limits the name *Gauls* to the natives of the central part, and this is the sense in which he usually employs the term.
[9] *Garonne, Marne, Seine.*
[10] Look at the map (pp. 180–181) and see whether you can tell why Caesar uses this verb in the singular.　　　[11] Southern France is still known as *Provence.*
[12] Conjunction.　　　[13] Note the emphasis on **suīs** and **eōrum.**
[14] Ablative of separation.　　　[15] i.e., **Germānōrum.**
[16] Some think that lines 14–21 were not written by Caesar but added later.
[17] *on the side of;* literally, *from* (*the direction of*).
[18] Accusative.
[19] From the point of view of the Romans in the Province.

Erich Lessing/PhotoEdit

Today this Roman statue looks out on what was formerly Gaul, now Orange, France.

ad īnferiōrem partem flūminis Rhēnī, spectant in septentriōnēs et orientem sōlem. Aquītānia ā Garunnā flūmine ad Pyrēnaeōs montēs et eam partem Ōceanī quae est ad [20] Hispāniam pertinet; spectat inter [20] occāsum sōlis et septentriōnēs.

[20] *near* what part of the Spanish coast? See map (pp. 180–181).

1. Why were the Helvetians brave?
2. What were three reasons for the bravery of the Belgians?
3. Find the three divisions of Gaul on the map (p. 180–181) and indicate their boundaries.

276. Grammar Review

Give the positive of **fortissimus, longissimē;** the comparative of **minimē, saepe;** the superlative of **īnferior, saepe.**

Ablative of respect (**601,** 16).

277. Translation

1. The rest-of-the Gauls were surpassed by the Belgians in courage.
2. In what respects ("things") did the Gauls differ from one another?

278. Vocabulary

cotīdiānus, –a, –um, *daily*
ferē, adv., *almost*
incolō, –ere, incoluī, ——, *inhabit, live*

propterea, adv., *on this account;* **proptereā quod,** *because*

Review **differō, initium, mercātor, occāsus, orior, saepe, sōl.**

279. Foreign Names

Add English endings to Latin proper nouns wherever possible, as in *Belgians, Aquitanians, Celts.* When the Latin form is kept, use the nominative case and pronounce the letters as in English but keep the Latin accent. Consult the Vocabulary. Always give the modern French forms of all Latin names of rivers, mountains, and lakes in Gaul. To find them see the Vocabulary.

280. Word Study

To what extent Spanish is like Latin may be seen from the following translation of the beginning and end of the first chapter of the *Gallic War:*

La Galia entera stá dividida en tres partes, de las cuales los belgas habitan una, otra los aquitanos, y la tercera los que se llaman celtas en su lengua, galos en la nuestra. Todos estos difieren entre sí en cuanto a lengua, instituciones y leyes. . . . Aquitania se extiende desde el río Garona hasta los montes Pirineos y aquella parte del océano que está cerca de España; mira hacia el ocaso y hacia el septentrión.

Explain *culture, differential, effeminate, humanities, mercantile, occident, verge.*

Restoration of the Roman town Aventicum in Switzerland.

Lesson LI

281. AN ENTIRE NATION EMIGRATES

I, 2. Apud Helvētiōs longē nōbilissimus fuit Orgetorīx. Is, M. Messālā M. Pīsōne cōnsulibus,[1] rēgnī cupiditāte inductus coniūrātiōnem nōbilitātis fēcit, et cīvibus persuāsit ut [2] dē fīnibus suīs cum omnibus cōpiīs exīrent.

Id [3] facilius eīs persuāsit, quod undique locī nātūrā Helvētiī continentur: ūnā [4] ex parte flūmine Rhēnō lātissimō atque altissimō, quī agrum Helvētium ā Germānīs dīvidit; alterā ex parte monte [5] Iūrā altissimō, quī est inter Sēquanōs et Helvētiōs; tertiā, lacū Lemannō et flūmine Rhodanō, qui prōvinciam nostram ab Helvētiīs dīvidit. 5

Hīs rēbus fīēbat [6] ut et minus lātē vagārentur et minus facile 10 fīnitimīs [7] bellum īnferre possent; quā dē causā hominēs bellandī [8] cupidī magnō dolōre afficiēbantur. Prō [9] multitūdine autem hominum et prō glōriā bellī angustōs sē fīnēs habēre arbitrābantur, quī in longitūdinem mīlia passuum CCXL, in lātitūdinem CLXXX patēbant.

---

[1] 61 B.C.; see **231**, n. 1.

[2] The clause is direct object of **persuāsit (599,** 6, *b;* **606,** 5).

[3] Direct object of **persuāsit.**

[4] The position of the adjective before the preposition emphasizes the adjective. Translate *on one side.*   [5] *mountain range.*   [6] *it happened.*

[7] Why dative? See **599,** 7.   [8] Gerund depending on **cupidī.**   [9] *in proportion to.*

15   3. Hīs rēbus adductī et auctōritāte Orgetorīgis permōtī cōnstituērunt ea quae ad proficīscendum pertinērent [10] comparāre, carrōrum
quam maximum numerum emere, frūmentum quam plūrimum serere,
ut in itinere cōpia frūmentī esset, cum proximīs cīvitātibus pācem et
amīcitiam cōnfirmāre. Ad eās rēs cōnficiendās biennium sibi satis esse
20 putāvērunt; in [11] tertium annum profectiōnem lēge cōnfirmant.

    Ad eās rēs cōnficiendās Orgetorīx dēligitur. Is sibi lēgātiōnem ad
cīvitātēs suscēpit. In eō itinere persuādet [12] Casticō Sēquanō ut
rēgnum in cīvitāte suā occupāret, quod pater ante habuerat; itemque
Dumnorīgī Haeduō, frātrī Dīviciācī, quī [13] eō tempore prīncipātum
25 in cīvitāte obtinēbat, ut idem cōnārētur persuādet, eīque fīliam suam
in mātrimōnium dat. Dīxit sē ipsum suae cīvitātis imperium obten-
tūrum esse.

QUESTIONS

1. Who was Orgetorix?
2. With whom did Orgetorix conspire?
3. Why did the Helvetians want to migrate?
4. How did the Helvetians prepare for migration?

282. Grammar Review

Conjugation of **fīō** (**593**).
Future passive participle with **ad** (**611**, 2, *Note*).

283. Translation

1. An embassy was sent to other states for-the-purpose-of encour-
aging their departure.
2. The Helvetians were always ready to carry on war with those
who inhabited that part of Gaul.

---

[10] Translate as if indicative (**606**, 15).   [11] *for.*
[12] For the sequence see **604**, 5, *Note a.*   [13] Dumnorix.

Swiss stamps always show the ancient Latin name of the country—
Helvetia or *Confoederatio Helvetica.*

M. Messager

The handsome Roman arch in Orange. Southern France (Provence, the ancient *Provincia*) has many notable Roman remains—temples, arches, theaters, tombs, etc.

284. Vocabulary

cupidus, –a, –um, *desirous*
dīvidō, –ere, dīvīsī, dīvīsus, *divide*
item, adv., *also*
lātitūdō, –dinis, f., *width*
lēgātiō, –ōnis, f., *embassy*
nōbilitās, –tātis, f., *nobility*

pateō, –ēre, patuī, ——, *stand open, extend*
prīncipātus, –ūs, m., *first place*
profectiō, –ōnis, f., *departure*
vagor, 1, *wander*

Idioms: **inter sē, quā dē causā.**
Review **angustus, arbitror, cōnor, dēligō, persuādeō, proficīscor, undique.**

285. Word Study

Item was once used in English as in Latin, to mean "also" in a list: "2 lbs. sugar, item 3 lbs. flour," etc. Then it came to be used wrongly for every article in the list, including the first. *Item* occurs fourteen times in George Washington's will.

Explain *biennial, cupidity, extravagant, itemize, latitude, patent, principate, vagabond, vagary, vagrant.*

197

A modern view of Geneva, Switzerland with Lake Geneva in the distance.

Servizio Editorio Fotografico/Art Resource

Lesson LII

286. A MYSTERIOUS DEATH AND A BONFIRE

I, 4. Ea rēs est Helvētiīs ēnūntiāta. Mōribus [1] suīs Orgetorīgem ex [2] vinculīs causam dīcere coēgērunt. Eum damnātum [3] oportēbat ignī cremārī.

Diē cōnstitūtā Orgetorīx ad iūdicium omnem suam familiam,[4] ad [5]
5 hominum mīlia decem, undique coēgit [6] et omnēs clientēs suōs, quōrum magnum numerum habēbat, eōdem condūxit; per eōs sē ēripuit neque causam dīxit.

Cum cīvitās ob eam rem incitāta armīs iūs suum exsequī cōnārētur, multitūdinemque hominum ex agrīs magistrātūs cōgerent, Orgetorīx
10 mortuus est. Helvētiī suspicantur ipsum sē interfēcisse.

5. Post eius mortem nihilō minus [7] Helvētiī id quod cōnstituerant facere cōnantur, ut [8] ē fīnibus suīs exeant. Ubi iam sē ad eam rem parātōs esse arbitrātī sunt, oppida sua omnia, numerō ad duodecim, vīcōs ad quadringentōs, reliqua prīvāta aedificia incendunt. Frū-
15 mentum omne, praeter quod sēcum portātūrī erant, combūrunt, ut, reditūs spē sublātā, parātiōrēs ad omnia perīcula subeunda essent.

Persuādent Rauracīs et Tulingīs et Latobrīgīs fīnitimīs utī, oppidīs

---

[1] *in accordance with* (**601**, 17).   [2] We say *in,* not *from.*
[3] Participle with conditonal force: *if condemned.*
[4] *household* (including all his slaves).
[5] *about;* **ad** is an adverb when used with numerals.
[6] Note the different meanings of the word here and in line 2.
[7] With **nihilō:** *nevertheless.*   [8] The clause is in apposition with **id** (**606**, 5).

198

suīs vīcīsque combustīs, ūnā cum eīs proficīscantur. Boiōs,[9] quī trāns Rhēnum incoluerant et in agrum Nōricum trānsierant Nōreiamque oppugnābant, ad sē sociōs [10] recipiunt. 20

6. Erant omnīnō itinera duo quibus domō [11] exīre possent: [12] ūnum per Sēquanōs, angustum et difficile, inter montem Iūram et flūmen Rhodanum, quā [13] vix singulī carrī dūcerentur; [14] mōns autem altissimus impendēbat, ut facile paucī prohibēre [15] possent; [16] alterum [17] per prōvinciam nostram, multō facilius atque expedītius proptereā 25 quod inter fīnēs Helvētiōrum et Allobrogum Rhodanus fluit, isque nōn nūllīs [18] locīs vadō trānsītur. Extrēmum oppidum Allobrogum est,[19] proximumque Helvētiōrum fīnibus, Genua.[20]

Ex eō oppidō pōns ad Helvētiōs pertinet.[21] Allobrogibus sēsē vel persuāsūrōs exīstimābant [22] vel vī coāctūrōs ut per suōs fīnēs eōs īre 30 paterentur. Omnibus rēbus ad profectiōnem comparātīs, diem dīcunt quā diē ad rīpam Rhodanī omnēs conveniant.[23] Is diēs erat a. d. V. Kal. Apr.,[24] L. Pīsōne A. Gabīniō cōnsulibus.[25]

QUESTIONS

1. Why was Orgetorix tried?
2. In what way did he escape?
3. How, apparently, did he die?
4. What was the effect of his death on the Helvetians?
5. What choice did the Helvetians have in leaving their country?

[9] The name of the Boii is preserved in the word "Bohemia."
[10] For construction see **596, 5,** *Note.*   [11] *from home* (**601, 2,** *Note*).
[12] See **606,** 10.   [13] *where.*
[14] *could be drawn* (**606,** 10). The Rhone valley for a distance of about 17 miles narrows down to a steep ravine with cliffs 1000 feet high, known as "Mill Race Gorge" (Pas de l'Écluse). One of the largest dams in Europe has been built there. The railway passes under the mountain through a tunnel over two miles long. Switzerland is at one end of the pass, France at the other.
[15] Supply **eōs.**   [16] A clause of result.   [17] Supply **iter.**
[18] Two negatives make an affirmative: *several.* Supply **in** (**601,** 14).
[19] In translating, put **est** after **fīnibus.**
[20] The spelling usually found is **Genava** but all the manuscripts have **Genua,** which is now accepted as the original form.
[21] Parts of this bridge have been found.   [22] i.e., the Helvetians.
[23] *on which all are to assemble* (**606,** 5). Note the variation in the gender of **diēs.**
[24] **Ante diem quīntum Kalendās Aprīlēs,** *the fifth day before the calends* (*first*) *of April;* i.e., *March 28.* In counting time the Romans included both ends.
[25] 58 B.C. Piso, a cruel and corrupt politician, was the father of Calpurnia, Caesar's last wife, whom he married one year before this. He had obtained the consulship through Caesar's influence. His colleague Gabinius owed his election to Pompey. In these two political maneuvers we see the activity of the First Triumvirate (Caesar, Pompey, Crassus), formed in 60 B.C.

287. Grammar Review

Indicative clauses with **ubi** and **postquam** (**605,** 2).
Subjunctive clauses with **cum** (**606,** 11).

288. Translation

1. After they saw that they could cross by a bridge, they were impelled to go with the Helvetians.
2. When this had been reported, the Helvetians suspected that he would bring-together all his clients.
3. When [26] they were ready to burn their buildings, they persuaded their neighbors to set out with [27] them.

289. Vocabulary

eōdem, adv., *to the same place*
expedītus, –a, –um, *unencumbered, easy*
fluō, –ere, flūxī, flūxus, *flow*
omnīnō, adv., *altogether*
praeter, prep. w. acc., *besides, except*
prīvātus, –a, –um, *private*
quā, adv., *where*

recipiō, –ere, recēpī, receptus, *take back, receive*
trānseō, –īre, –iī, –itūrus, *cross, pass*
ūnā, adv., *along*
utī = ut
vīcus, –ī, m., *village*

Review **aedificium, cliēns, incendō, magistrātus, suspicor, vix.**

290. Word Study

The legal phrase **a vinculo matrimonii** is used in English in divorce cases. Translate. Learn the phrase: **sic transit gloria mundi.**

Explain *flux, incendiary, recipient, riparian, transient, transitory.*

---

[26] Use **ubi.**   [27] See p. **601,** 6, *a.*

"Julius Caesar stopped here." A plaque at the Tour de l'Ile in Geneva commemorates Caesar's arrival in 58 B.C. Can you read the Latin?

Office du Tourisme, Geneva

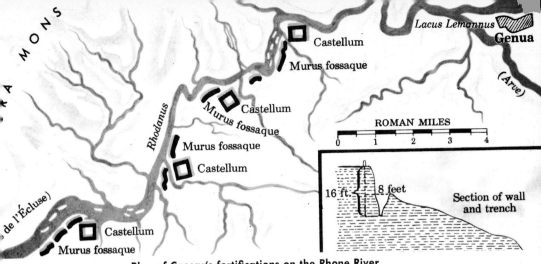

Plan of Caesar's fortifications on the Rhone River.

Lesson LIII

291. CAESAR SAYS: "YOU SHALL NOT PASS"

I,7. Caesarī cum id [1] nūntiātum esset, eōs per prōvinciam nostram iter facere cōnārī, mātūrat ab urbe [2] proficīscī et quam maximīs potest itineribus [3] in Galliam ulteriōrem [4] contendit et ad [5] Genuam pervenit. Prōvinciae tōtī quam maximum potest mīlitum numerum imperat [6] (erat omnīnō in Galliā ulteriōre legiō ūna [7]), pontem quī erat ad Genuam iubet rescindī. 5

Ubi dē eius adventū Helvētiī certiōrēs factī sunt,[8] lēgātōs ad eum mittunt nōbilissimōs cīvitātis. Hī rogāvērunt ut sibi licēret iter per Prōvinciam facere. Caesar lēgātīs respondit diem [9] sē ad dēlīberandum sūmptūrum. 10

8. Intereā ab lacū Lemannō, quī in flūmen Rhodanum īnfluit, ad montem Iūram, quī fīnēs Sēquanōrum ab Helvētiīs dīvidit, mīlia [10]

[1] Explained by the infinitive clause, **eōs . . . cōnārī.**
[2] *The* city is always Rome.
[3] *by as rapid marches as possible.* What literally? Plutarch says that Caesar covered the distance in seven days, an average of 90 miles a day. Of course he traveled on horseback and had no army with him.
[4] This term would ordinarily mean all of Gaul except the Roman Province. Here it includes the Province.   [5] *near;* see **600,** 3, *Note.*
[6] With dative and accusative: *he levies upon* (**599,** 6, *b*).
[7] This one was the famous Tenth, soon to become Caesar's favorite.
[8] *were informed.*
[9] *time;* clearly more than a single day (see line 16).
[10] With **perdūcit (600,** 2).

201

passuum XVIIII mūrum [11] in altitūdinem pedum XVI fossamque [11]
perdūcit. Eō opere perfectō, praesidia dispōnit,[12] castella mūnit, utī
15 eōs trānsīre cōnantēs prohibēre possit.

Ubi ea diēs quam cōnstituerat cum lēgātīs vēnit, et lēgātī ad eum
reverterunt, negat sē mōre [13] et exemplō populī Rōmānī posse iter [14]
ūllī per Prōvinciam dare; et, sī vim facere [15] cōnentur, sē eōs pro-
hibitūrum ostendit. Eā spē dēiectī,[16] aliī Helvētiōrum nāvibus rati-
20 busque complūribus, aliī vadīs Rhodanī, quā minima altitūdō flūminis
erat, nōn numquam interdiū,[17] saepius noctū perrumpere cōnātī sunt.
Sed operis mūnītiōne et mīlitum concursū et tēlīs repulsī, hōc cōnātū
dēstitērunt.

QUESTIONS

1. Where did Caesar hear about the Helvetians?
2. What was Caesar's answer and what did he do?
3. What did the Helvetians ask him to let them do?

[11] *rampart* (of earth) *and a trench.* Today the banks of the Rhone are high
and steep for the greater part of the distance, and so Napoleon III, whose map
is on page 201, thought that Caesar built the rampart at a few points only.
But recent excavations indicate that Caesar strengthened the natural defenses
most of the way, especially where the river could be forded.

[12] Note the force of the prefix: *he stations at intervals.*

[13] For the case see **601,** 17.　　　　　[14] (*right of*) *way.*　　　　[15] *use force.*

[16] *disappointed in this hope* (**601,** 1).　　　[17] *in the daytime.*

**Although the banks of the Rhone are naturally steep in the Mill Race Gorge,
Caesar built additional walls and forts for most of its distance. Roman soldiers
were experts at this sort of work.**

Office du Tourisme, Geneva

A storage jar (*dolium*) found in recent excavations at Ensérune, northeast of Narbonne, France. It is pre-Roman. Note the identifying mark.

292. Grammar Review

Indirect statements (**613,** 4).
Subordinate clauses in indirect discourse (**606,** 14).

293. Translation

1. Caesar thought that the Helvetians would not cross the river.
2. He said that, if they tried to cross, he would prevent them by defenses.
3. When they were not able to persuade Caesar, they said that they would send envoys to the Haeduans.

294. Vocabulary

altitūdō, –dinis, f., *height, depth*
castellum, –ī, n., *fort*
mūnītiō, –ōnis, f., *fortification*

nōn numquam, adv., *sometimes*
tēlum, –ī, n., *weapon*
vadum, –ī, n., *ford*

Idioms: **alter . . . alter, certiōrem faciō, certior fīō, quam** with superlative.
Review **complūrēs, dēsistō, fossa, intereā, negō, noctū, pōns, spēs.**

295. Word Study

From what Latin words are the following derived: **altitūdō, castellum, mūnītiō, noctū, quā?**
Explain *legionary, munitions, renegade.*

Arch of Tiberius and Germanicus at Saintes, which preserves the name of the Santoni, mentioned in the text below.

Lesson LIV

296. THE HARDER WAY

I,9. Relinquēbātur ūna per Sēquanōs via, quā, Sēquanīs[1] invītīs, propter angustiās[2] īre nōn poterant. Hīs cum suā sponte persuādēre nōn possent, lēgātōs ad Dumnorīgem Haeduum mittunt, ut hic ā Sēquanīs impetrāret. Dumnorīx grātiā et dōnīs apud Sēquanōs
5 plūrimum poterat et Helvētiīs erat amīcus, quod ex eā cīvitāte Orgetorīgis fīliam in mātrimōnium dūxerat; et cupiditāte rēgnī adductus novīs rēbus[3] studēbat et quam plūrimās cīvitātēs suō beneficiō habēre obstrictās[4] volēbat. Itaque rem suscipit et ā Sēquanīs impetrat ut per fīnēs suōs Helvētiōs īre patiantur, obsidēsque utī inter sē dent perficit:[5]
10 Sēquanī obsidēs dant[6] nē itinere[7] Helvētiōs prohibeant; Helvētiī, ut sine iniūriā trānseant.

10. Caesarī renūntiātur Helvētiīs esse in animō[8] per agrum Sēquanōrum et Haeduōrum iter in Santonōrum fīnēs facere, quī nōn longē ā Tolōsātium fīnibus absunt, quae cīvitās est in Prōvinciā. Caesar

[1] Conditional. [2] See 286, footnote 14.
[3] In politics "new things" are a revolution. For the case see 599, 6.
[4] *bound*. Modern politicians distribute favors for similar reasons.
[5] The English order would be **perficit utī dent obsidēs inter sē.**
[6] i.e., *they guarantee*. [7] For the case see 601, 1.
[8] *that the Helvetians have in mind*. **Helvētiīs** is dative of possession (599, 8).

intellegēbat magnō cum perīculō Prōvinciae [9] futūrum esse ut hominēs 15
bellicōsī, populī Rōmānī inimīcī, haec loca patentia maximēque frūmentāria occupārent.[10]

Ob eās causās eī mūnītiōnī [11] quam fēcerat T. Labiēnum [12] lēgātum
praefēcit. Ipse in Italiam magnīs itineribus contendit duāsque ibi
legiōnēs cōnscrībit, et trēs quae circum Aquileiam hiemābant ex 20
hībernīs ēdūcit, et proximō itinere in ulteriōrem Galliam per Alpēs
cum hīs quīnque legiōnibus īre contendit.

Summary of the End of Chapter 10. The Ceutrones try to block Caesar's
way but are defeated. From Ocelum (near modern Turin) he proceeds to
the Province, arriving on the seventh day, then to the Allobroges and
Segusiavi.

QUESTIONS

1. Why did Dumnorix help the Helvetians?
2. Why did Caesar object to the Helvetians' plan?
3. Why did he go to Italy at this critical moment?
4. Of what fortifications did Labienus have charge during Caesar's
   absence?

297. Grammar Review

Cum clauses (**606,** 11).

298. Translation

1. What will you do since you cannot influence him by kindness?
2. Although they sent envoys to him, they did not obtain-their-
   request.
3. Since the Gauls were-eager-for a revolution, Caesar placed a
   general in charge of the legions.

[9] *to the Province* (genitive modifying **perīculō**).
[10] *for men . . . to seize* (literally, *that men . . . should seize*).
[11] For the case see **599,** 7.
[12] One of the bravest and most trusted of Caesar's staff officers. But later, during
the Civil War, he fought against Caesar.

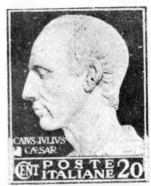

**Italian postage stamp with portrait of
Gaius Julius Caesar.**

299. Developing "Word Sense"

Did you understand the idiom **plurimum poterat** (*"was very power-ful"*) in the third sentence of section **296?** Here are some more sentences to extend your mastery of this use of the accusative as an adverb with **possum.** Translate:

1. **In omnibus rēbus hūmānīs cōnsuētūdō multum potest.**
2. **Multum terror mortis potest, plūs tamen cupiditās glōriae.**
3. **Dīviciācus grātiā plūrimum poterat, Dumnorīx propter adulēscentiam minimum poterat.**
4. **Quantum in bellō Fortūna potest!**
5. **Helvētiī equitātū nihil poterant.**
6. **Caesar intelleget quid invictī Germānī possint.**

300. Vocabulary

cōnscrībō –ere, –scrīpsī, –scrīptus,
  write, enlist
hīberna, –ōrum, n. pl., *winter quarters*
impetrō, 1, *gain one's request*
invītus, –a, –um, *unwilling*
patior, patī, passus, *permit*

praeficiō, –ere, –fēcī, –fectus,
  put in charge of
sponte, w. **suā,**
  of his (their) own accord, by this (their) own influence

Idioms: **alicui esse in animō, magnum iter, multum (plūs, plūrimum) posse, novae rēs.**

301. Word Study

Things are not always what they seem: *invite* has no connection with **invītus,** nor *Hibernian* with **hīberna.**

Hibernating Hibernian.

From what Latin words are the following derived: **angustiae, cōn-scrībō, hīberna, hiemō?**

Explain *conscription, hibernate, impatient, prefect, spontaneous.*

The praetorium (general's headquarters) of the permanent Roman camp at Lambèse, Algeria, built in the third century A.D.

Lesson LV

302. THE GAULS APPEAL TO CAESAR

I, 11. Helvētiī iam per angustiās [1] et fīnēs Sēquanōrum suās cōpiās trādūxerant et in Haeduōrum fīnēs pervēnerant eōrumque agrōs populābantur. Haeduī, cum sē suaque [2] ab eīs dēfendere nōn possent, lēgātōs ad Caesarem mīsērunt ut rogārent auxilium. Eōdem tempore Ambarrī, cōnsanguineī Haeduōrum, Caesarem certiōrem faciunt sēsē, 5 vāstātīs agrīs, nōn facile ab oppidīs vim hostium prohibēre posse. Item Allobrogēs, quī trāns Rhodanum vīcōs possessiōnēsque habēbant, fugā sē ad Caesarem recipiunt et dēmōnstrant sibi praeter agrī solum [3] nihil esse reliquī.[4] Quibus rēbus adductus Caesar nōn exspectandum esse sibi statuit dum, omnibus fortūnīs sociōrum cōnsūmptīs, in San-10 tonōs Helvētiī pervenīrent.

12. Flūmen est Arar, quod per fīnēs Haeduōrum et Sēquanōrum in Rhodanum īnfluit. Id Helvētiī ratibus ac nāvibus iūnctīs trānsībant. Per explōrātōrēs [5] Caesar certior factus est trēs iam partēs [6] cōpiārum Helvētiōs id flūmen trādūxisse, quārtam vērō partem citrā [7] flūmen 15

[1] Mill Race Gorge (Chaps. 6 and 9). [2] *their possessions.*
[3] *soil.* [4] With **nihil (598, 3).**
[5] Caesar owed much of his success to his efficient intelligence service.
[6] Object of **trādūxisse; flūmen** depends on **trā– (600, 5).**   [7] i.e., Caesar's side.

Ararim [8] reliquam esse. Itaque dē [9] tertiā vigiliā cum legiōnibus tribus ē castrīs profectus, ad eam partem pervēnit quae nōndum flūmen trānsierat.

Eōs impedītōs aggressus [10] magnam partem eōrum concīdit; reli-
20 quī sē fugae mandārunt [11] atque in [12] proximās silvās abdidērunt. Is pāgus appellābātur Tigurīnus; nam omnis cīvitās Helvētia in quattuor partēs vel pāgōs dīvīsa est. Hic pāgus ūnus, cum domō [13] exīsset, patrum nostrōrum memoriā [14] L. Cassium cōnsulem interfēcerat et eius exercitum sub iugum mīserat.[15]

25 Ita sīve cāsū sīve cōnsiliō deōrum immortālium, ea pars cīvitātis Helvētiae quae īnsignem calamitātem populō Rōmānō intulerat, prīnceps [16] poenam dedit. Quā in rē Caesar nōn sōlum pūblicās sed etiam prīvātās iniūriās ultus est; nam Tigurīnī L. Pīsōnem lēgātum, avum Caesaris socerī,[17] eōdem proeliō quō Cassium interfēcerant.

30 13. Hōc proeliō factō, reliquās cōpiās [18] Helvētiōrum ut cōnsequī posset, pontem in Ararī facit atque ita exercitum trādūcit. Helvētiī repentīnō eius adventū commōtī, cum id quod ipsī diēbus XX aeger-rimē cōnfēcerant, ut [19] flūmen trānsīrent, illum ūnō diē fēcisse intel-legerent, lēgātōs ad eum mittunt.

QUESTIONS

1. What reasons does Caesar give for attacking the Helvetians?
2. How long did it take Caesar to cross the Saône?
3. How many cantons of the Helvetians crossed the Saône safely?
4. Which canton did Caesar defeat and why did this particularly please him?

303. Grammar Review

Dative of possession (**599,** 8).
Subjunctive in anticipatory clauses (**606,** 12).

---

[8] Accusative form.

[9] *during.* The night (from sunset to sunrise) was divided into four **vigiliae,** or *watches,* varying in length with the time of the year.

[10] The perfect participle of a deponent verb is often best translated, as here, by the present active: *attacking.*   [11] For **mandā(vē)runt (595).**

[12] *in;* motion is implied in **abdidērunt.**   [13] *from home* (**601,** 2, *Note*).

[14] *within the memory of* (**601,** 15). The defeat of Cassius had occurred in 107 B.C., 49 years before this.

[15] *had sent under the yoke,* equivalent to unconditional surrender. Two spears were stuck into the ground and a third tied across the top, and the defeated army was forced to march through this arch of spears without arms. Cf. "sub-jug-ate."   [16] (*was the*) *first* (*to*); adjective used with adverbial force.

[17] *father-in-law.* See **286,** footnote 25.   [18] Object of **cōnsequī.**

[19] The **ut** clause is in apposition with **id.**

208

304. Translation

1. The enemy had many ships and men.
2. The Haeduans have many villages across that river.
3. They were unwilling to wait until Caesar should arrive.
4. Caesar hurried in order to arrive before they could cross.

305. Vocabulary

calamitās, –tātis, f., *disaster*
explōrātor, –ōris, m., *scout*
pāgus, –ī, m., *district, canton*
populor, 1, *destroy*

repentīnus, –a, –um, *sudden*
sīve (seu), conj., *or if;* **sīve . . . sīve,**
  whether . . . or
vel, conj., *or;* **vel . . . vel,** *either . . . or*

Idioms: **dē . . . vigiliā, fugae mē mandō, mē recipiō.**
Review **abdō, iugum, nōndum.**

306. Word Study

A "pagan" was really a person who lived in a *country district*
(**pāgus**). In the old days new things and ideas, such as Christianity,
came to the country districts last of all, and so there was a time when
the **pagānī** were pagans after the **urbānī** had become Christians.

From what Latin words are the following derived: **abdō, concīdō,
explōrātor, īnferō, nōndum?**

Explain *calamitous, concise, consanguinity, exploratory, inferential,
influence, influenza.*

Below: Model of Augustus'
arch at Susa, near Turin.
Right: The same arch as it
looks today.

*Metropolitan Museum of Art, Gift
of the Italian Government, 1939*

Roman helmet from Norfolk, England, showing picture of a dragon with three tails.

British Information Services

Our Heritage

307. ROMAN MILITARY ACCOMPLISHMENTS

F. E. Adcock ends his book [1] with these words:

"The art of war under the Roman Republic was something that belonged to Rome, a plant that grew in Roman soil, something which needed for its application talent, not genius, but in its culmination it did produce a soldier greater than itself, a soldier in whom there was that fusing together of intellect and will that marks off genius from talent."

An interesting manual on the art of war, written in the fourth century A.D. by Vegetius, contains this paragraph:

Nūllā enim aliā rē vidēmus populum Rōmānum orbem subēgisse terrārum nisi armōrum exercitiō,[2] disciplīnā castrōrum, ūsūque mīlitiae. Quid enim adversus [3] Gallōrum multitūdinem paucitās Rōmāna valuisset? [4] Quid adversus Germānōrum prōcēritātem [5] brevitās po-
5 tuisset audēre? Hispānōs quidem nōn tantum numerō sed et vīribus corporum nostrīs praestitisse manifēstum est; Āfrōrum dolīs atque dīvitiīs semper imparēs fuimus; Graecōrum artibus prūdentiāque nōs vincī nēmō dubitāvit. Sed adversus omnia prōfuit tīrōnem [6] sollerter [7] ēligere, cotīdiānō exercitiō rōborāre, quaecumque ēvenīre in aciē
10 atque proeliīs possunt, omnia in campestrī meditātiōne [8] praenōscere, sevērē in dēsidēs vindicāre.[9] Scientia enim reī bellicae dīmicandī nūtrit audāciam: nēmō facere metuit quod sē bene didicisse cōnfīdit. Etenim [10] in certāmine bellōrum exercitāta paucitās ad victōriam prōmptior est, rudis et indocta multitūdō exposita semper ad caedem.

---

[1] *The Roman Art of War under the Republic,* Cambridge, Harvard University Press, 1940, p. 124.
[2] from **exercitium,** *training.*
[3] Prep. w. acc.: *against.*
[4] *would have availed.*
[5] *tallness.*
[6] *recruit.*
[7] *skillfully.*
[8] *practice in the field.*
[9] *to punish the idle.*
[10] *For.*

Lesson LVI

Summary of Chapters 13–20. After crushing the rearguard of the Helvetians at the Saône, Caesar crosses in pursuit of the main body. The latter now send a deputation to Caesar. The parley fails, and the Helvetians resume their march. Caesar follows; his cavalry is defeated in a skirmish. Meanwhile his supplies give out because the Haeduans, his Gallic allies, fail to furnish grain any longer. Caesar complains to the Haeduan chiefs who are in his camp and is told secretly that Dumnorix, a rich and powerful noble, is responsible; that he has a Helvetian wife and therefore favors the Helvetians; furthermore, that Dumnorix alone is to blame for the recent defeat of the Roman cavalry, for he led the retreat in person. Caesar decides that Dumnorix must be punished but fears to offend his friend Diviciacus, chief magistrate of the Haeduans and brother of Dumnorix. He therefore urges Diviciacus himself to punish him. Diviciacus pleads so earnestly for his brother's life that Caesar pardons him.

308. A SURPRISE THAT FAILED

I, 21. Eōdem diē ab explōrātōribus certior factus hostēs sub monte cōnsēdisse mīlia passuum ab ipsīus castrīs octō, quālis esset [1] nātūra montis et quālis in circuitū [2] ascēnsus, explōrātōrēs quī cognōscerent mīsit. Renūntiātum est ascēnsum facilem esse. Dē tertiā vigiliā T. Labiēnum lēgātum cum duābus legiōnibus et eīs ducibus [3] quī iter 5

---

[1] Indirect question introduced by **quālis,** depending on **cognōscerent.**
[2] *on the other side;* literally, *in going around.*   [3] Appositive to **eīs:** (*as*) *guides.*

Le Morvan, a mountainous region in which Bibracte (Mont Beuvray) is situated.

French Embassy Press & Information Division

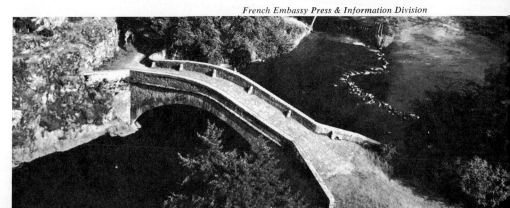

cognōverant, summum iugum montis ascendere iubet; suum cōnsilium ostendit. Ipse dē quārtā vigiliā eōdem itinere quō hostēs ierant ad eōs contendit, equitātumque omnem ante sē mittit. P. Cōnsidius, quī reī [4] mīlitāris perītissimus habēbātur [5] et in exercitū L. Sullae et posteā in 10 M. Crassī fuerat, cum explōrātōribus praemittitur.

22. Prīmā lūce, cum summus [6] mōns ā Labiēnō tenērētur et ipse ab hostium castrīs nōn longius MD passibus [7] abesset, neque (ut posteā ex captīvīs comperit) aut ipsīus adventus aut Labiēnī cognitus esset, Cōnsidius, equō admissō,[8] ad eum accurrit. Dīcit montem quem ab 15 Labiēnō occupārī voluerit [9] ab hostibus tenērī; id sē ā Gallicīs armīs atque īnsignibus cognōvisse. Caesar suās cōpiās in proximum collem subdūcit, aciem īnstruit. Labiēnō imperāverat nē proelium commit-teret, nisi ipsīus cōpiae prope hostium castra vīsae essent,[10] ut undique ūnō tempore in hostēs impetus fieret. Itaque Labiēnus, monte occu-20 pātō, nostrōs exspectābat proeliōque abstinēbat. Multō [11] dēnique [12] diē per explōrātōrēs Caesar cognōvit et montem ab suīs tenērī et Helvētiōs castra mōvisse et Cōnsidium timōre perterritum quod [13] nōn

[4] Depends on **perītissimus (598,** 4). Caesar takes special pains to state the military training and experience of Considius because the latter's later con-duct is all the more unaccountable.   [5] *was considered.*
[6] *top of the mountain.*   [7] For the case see **601,** 5.
[8] *with his horse at full speed* (literally, *with horse let go*).
[9] The subject is Caesar.
[10] The verb would be future perfect indicative in direct discourse.
[11] *late in the day.*   [12] *finally.*   [13] Supply **id** as antecedent.

Roads such as this one at Vienne, southern France, helped Roman civilization penetrate Gaul and the rest of the Roman Empire.

vīdisset prō [14] vīsō sibi renūntiāvisse. Eō diē, quō intervāllō [15] cōnsuēverat, hostēs sequitur et mīlia passuum tria ab eōrum castrīs castra
pōnit.   25

QUESTIONS

1. What did Caesar tell Labienus to do?
2. What did Caesar tell Considius to do?
3. What was the mistake that Considius made?
4. What was Caesar's purpose in giving these orders?

309. Grammar Review

Purpose constructions (**606,** 2, 3; **611,** 2, *Note;* **612**).

310. Translation

1. He ordered (**imperō**) them to wait until he should arrive.
2. He summoned the generals for the sake of showing his plan.
3. The Romans were accustomed to send ahead scouts who were
   to learn where the enemy were.

311. Vocabulary

aciēs, aciēī, f., *battle line*
ascendō, –ere, ascendī, ascēnsus, *climb*
comperiō, –īre, –perī, –pertus, *find out*

equitātus, –ūs, m., *cavalry*
īnsigne, –is, n., *ornament*

Idioms: **castra moveō, castra pōnō, prīmā lūce, rēs mīlitāris,
summus mōns.**
Review **cōnsīdō, cōnsuēscō, perītus.**

312. Word Study

From what Latin words are the following derived: **abstineō, equitātus, īnsigne, subdūcō?**
Explain *abstinence, ascension, circuitous, insignia.*

---

[14] *as seen.*
[15] For **eō intervāllō quō.** The antecedent is sometimes put in the subordinate
clause.

Abstinence.

213

Pre-Roman Gallic art, found at Entremont in the Roman Province.

Lesson LVII

313. THE FIGHT IS ON

I, 23. Postrīdiē eius diēī,[1] quod omnīnō bīduum supererat[2] cum exercituī frūmentum mētīrī oportēret, reī frūmentāriae prōspiciendum[3] exīstimāvit. Itaque iter ab Helvētiīs āvertit ac Bibracte[4] īre contendit. Hoc oppidum Haeduōrum longē maximum nōn amplius 5 mīlibus passuum XVIII aberat. Ea rēs per fugitīvōs L. Aemilī, decuriōnis[5] equitum Gallōrum, hostibus nūntiātur. Helvētiī, seu quod timōre perterritōs Rōmānōs discēdere ā sē exīstimārent,[6] seu quod rē frūmentāriā interclūdī posse[7] cōnfīderent, mūtātō cōnsiliō atque itinere conversō, nostrōs ab novissimō agmine īnsequī ac lacessere coepērunt. 10 24. Postquam id animadvertit, cōpiās suās Caesar in proximum collem subdūxit equitātumque quī sustinēret hostium impetum mīsit.

---

[1] *Next day;* **eius diēī** *is superfluous.*

[2] From **supersum:** *two days were left before.*

[3] Supply **esse;** impersonal: *he should provide for supplies* (literally, *it should be provided for supplies*). There are constant allusions in Caesar to the problem of feeding his army. He had grain barges on the Saône, but the Helvetians had turned away from that river.

[4] Accusative.   [5] See **274,** II, A, 5.

[6] Subjunctive because Caesar assigns these as the reasons of the Helvetians and not as his own.   [7] Supply **Rōmānōs** as subject.

214

Ipse interim in colle mediō [8] triplicem aciem īnstrūxit legiōnum quattuor veterānārum. In summō iugō duās legiōnēs quās in Galliā citeriōre proximē cōnscrīpserat et omnia auxilia [9] collocāvit. Impedīmenta in ūnum locum cōnferrī, et eum locum ab eīs quī in superiōre aciē cōn- 15 stiterant mūnīrī [10] iussit. Helvētiī cum omnibus suīs carrīs secūtī, impedīmenta in ūnum locum contulērunt; ipsī [11] cōnfertissimā aciē, reiectō nostrō equitātū, sub prīmam nostram aciem successērunt.

25. Caesar prīmum suum,[12] deinde omnium [13] ex cōnspectū remōvit equōs ut, aequātō omnium perīculō, spem fugae tolleret. Cohortātus 20 suōs proelium commīsit. Mīlitēs, ē locō superiōre pīlīs missīs, facile hostēs disiēcērunt et gladiīs in eōs impetum fēcērunt. Gallīs magnō ad pugnam erat impedīmentō quod,[14] plūribus eōrum scūtīs ūnō ictū [15] pīlōrum trānsfīxīs et colligātīs,[16] neque ēvellere neque, sinistrā manū impedītā,[17] satis commodē pugnāre poterant. Itaque multī 25 scūtum manū ēmīsērunt et nūdō [18] corpore pugnāvērunt.

[8] *halfway up the hill.*   [9] Consisting of friendly Gauls and other foreign troops.
[10] With a trench. The claim is made that the course of this trench has actually been discovered in excavations made in recent times.
[11] i.e., the fighting men.   [12] Supply **equum** from **equōs.**
[13] i.e., all the mounted officers, not the cavalry; **omnium** modifies **equōs.**
[14] The clause is subject of **erat.**   [15] *volley.*
[16] The Gauls overlapped their shields, and so two shields were easily pinned together by one spear. Because of the barbed ends and easily bent iron shafts of the spears, it was hard to draw them out. At first it was probably mere chance that this happened, but the Romans were quick to take advantage of the situation and thus to introduce an element of surprise.
[17] By the shield, now pinned to that of another soldier.
[18] *unprotected* by a shield.

A Roman camp. Sentries are on guard on the watchtowers. From the film *Messalina.*
Warner Bros. Pictures Distributing Corp.

QUESTIONS

1. Why did Caesar go to Bibracte?
2. How did Caesar place his troops?
3. What advantages did Caesar have?
4. What disadvantage did the Helvetians have?

314. Grammar Review

Causal clauses with **quod** and **quoniam** (**606,** 16).

315. Translation

1. The enemy advanced crowded together because they did not have their baggage.
2. The Helvetians began to pursue him because (as they thought) he could be cut off.
3. Meanwhile, since Caesar had noticed this, he stationed his cavalry to check [19] them.

316. Vocabulary

aequō, 1, *make equal*

agmen, agminis, n.,
　line of march

animadvertō (animum advertō),
　–ere, –vertī, –versus, *notice*

collocō, 1, *place*

cōnferō, –ferre, contulī, collātus,
　bring together

cōnfertus, –a, –um, *crowded*
　together

cōnfīdō, –ere, cōnfīsus,[20]
　be confident

frūmentārius, –a, –um, *of grain;*
　rēs frūmentāria, *grain supply*

interim, adv., *meanwhile*

pīlum, –ī, n., *spear* (for throwing),
　javelin

sinister, –tra, –trum, *left*

supersum, –esse, –fuī, –futūrus,
　be left (*over*)

317. Word Study

The motto of the state of Maryland is a quotation from the *Psalms:* **scuto bonae voluntatis tuae coronasti nos** (*Thou hast covered us*). The motto of Arkansas is **regnat populus;** of Arizona, **ditat** (*enriches*) **deus.**

From what Latin words are the following derived: **aequō, animadvertō, bīduum, collocō, cōnferō, convertō?**

Explain *collation, collocation, conference, confidence, conversion, equation, prospective, sinister.*

---

[19] Express in three ways.

[20] Semideponent, i.e., active in the present stem, deponent in the perfect stem.

Lesson LVIII

318. THE HELVETIANS SURRENDER

I, 26. Ita diū atque ācriter pugnātum est.[1] Diūtius cum sustinēre nostrōrum impetūs nōn possent, alterī sē in montem recēpērunt, alterī ad impedīmenta et carrōs suōs sē contulērunt. Nam hōc tōtō proeliō, cum [2] ab hōrā septimā ad vesperum pugnātum sit, āversum [3] hostem vidēre nēmō potuit. Ad multam noctem [4] etiam ad impedīmenta 5 pugnātum est, proptereā quod prō vāllō carrōs obiēcerant et ē locō superiōre in nostrōs venientēs tēla coniciēbant, et nōn nūllī inter carrōs trāgulās subiciēbant nostrōsque vulnerābant. Diū cum esset pugnātum, impedīmentīs [5] castrīsque nostrī potītī sunt. Ibi Orgetorīgis fīlia atque ūnus ē fīliīs captus est. Ex eō proeliō circiter hominum mīlia CXXX 10 superfuērunt, eāque tōtā nocte iērunt. In fīnēs Lingonum diē quārtō pervēnērunt, cum [6] et propter vulnera mīlitum et propter sepultūram occīsōrum nostrī eōs sequī nōn potuissent. Caesar ad Lingonas [7] litterās nūntiōsque mīsit nē eōs frūmentō nēve aliā rē iuvārent.[8] Ipse, trīduō intermissō, cum omnibus cōpiīs eōs sequī coepit.   15

27. Helvētiī omnium rērum inopiā adductī lēgātōs dē dēditiōne ad eum mīsērunt. Quī [9] cum eum [10] in itinere convēnissent sēque ad pedēs prōiēcissent flentēsque pācem petīssent,[11] eōs [12] in eō locō quō tum erant suum adventum exspectāre iussit. Eō [13] postquam Caesar pervēnit, obsidēs, arma, servōs quī ad eōs perfūgerant poposcit.   20

Dum ea [14] conquīruntur et cōnferuntur, nocte intermissā, circiter hominum mīlia VI eius pāgī quī Verbigenus appellātur, sīve timōre perterritī,[15] sīve spē salūtis inductī, prīmā nocte [16] ē castrīs Helvētiōrum ēgressī ad Rhēnum fīnēsque Germānōrum contendērunt.

---

[1] *they fought;* what literally?   [2] *although*
[3] i.e., in retreat.   [4] *until late at night.*
[5] Ablative with **potior.**   [6] *since.*
[7] Accusative (Greek form).   [8] A command in indirect discourse (**606,** *Note*).
[9] i.e., the ambassadors.   [10] Object of **convēnissent.**
[11] For **petīvissent.**   [12] i.e., the Helvetians, not the ambassadors.
[13] Adverb.   [14] Neuter plural, referring to **obsidēs, arma, servōs.**
[15] While the grammatical subject is **mīlia,** the logical subject is **hominēs,** with which **perterritī** agrees.   [16] *early in the night.*

1. How long did the battle last?
2. What were Caesar's peace terms?
3. Who refused to accept these terms?
4. How many Helvetians escaped to the Lingones?

319. Grammar Review

Impersonal verbs (193).

320. Translation

1. They were not permitted [17] to keep their arms.
2. They fought [17] six hours before they were compelled to flee.
3. After they arrived [17] in the territory of friends. Caesar ordered them to await his arrival.

321. Vocabulary

conquīrō, –ere, –quīsīvī, –quīsītus,
  seek for

dēditiō, –ōnis, f., *surrender*

nōn nūllī (nōnnūllī), –ae, –a, *some*

obiciō, –ere, obiēcī, obiectus,
  throw against, oppose

trīduum, –ī, n., *three days*

vāllum, –ī, n., *rampart, wall*

322. Word Study

Some Latin-American countries and cities have names ultimately derived from Latin. Ecuador is the Spanish for our word *equator;* both are derived from **aequō,** because the equator divides the earth into *equal* parts. Argentina was so named because it was mistakenly thought to contain *silver* **(argentum);** its capital, Buenos Aires, is Spanish for *good air* (Latin **bonus āer**). Montevideo, the capital of Uruguay, has properly a longer name, ending in pure Latin, de Montevideo, **dē monte videō,** or, possibly, it stands for **monte(m) videō.** The capital of Paraguay, Asunción, is named after the Assumption (from **sūmō**), i.e., the taking into Heaven, of the Virgin. The capital of Bolivia, La Paz, has the name of peace **(pāx).** Rio de Janeiro is from Latin (through Portuguese) **rīvus Ianuārī,** *River of (St.) January.* Honduras is from the Spanish *hondo,* Latin **(pro)fundus,** *deep,* perhaps on account of its deep coastal waters. Costa Rica is *rich coast,* and both Spanish *costa* and English *coast* come from Latin **costa,** *rib* or *side.* Puerto Rico is *rich port,* from **portus.** Salvador is from **salvātor,** the Savior.

---

[17] Use impersonal construction.

Stage of the splendid Roman theater at Sabratha, Libya, in north Africa.

Lesson LIX

323. *THE PRICE OF PEACE*

I, 28. Quod ubi Caesar comperit, hīs quōrum per fīnēs[1] ierant imperāvit utī eōs conquīrerent et redūcerent; eōs reductōs in hostium numerō habuit;[2] reliquōs omnēs, obsidibus, armīs, perfugīs trāditīs, in dēditiōnem accēpit.

Helvētiōs, Tulingōs, Latobrīgōs in fīnēs suōs, unde erant profectī, 5 revertī iussit; et quod, omnibus frūgibus āmissīs, domī nihil erat quō famem sustinērent,[3] Allobrogibus imperāvit ut eīs frūmentī cōpiam facerent; ipsōs oppida vīcōsque, quōs incenderant, restituere iussit. Id eā maximē ratiōne[4] fēcit, quod nōluit eum locum unde Helvētiī discesserant vacāre, nē propter bonitātem agrōrum Germānī, quī trāns 10 Rhēnum incolunt, ē suīs fīnibus in Helvētiōrum fīnēs trānsīrent et fīnitimī Galliae Prōvinciae Allobrogibusque essent. Boiōs,[5] quod ēgregiā virtūte erant, Haeduī in fīnibus suīs collocāre voluērunt; hoc Caesar concessit. Eīs illī agrōs dedērunt, eōsque posteā in parem iūris lībertātisque condiciōnem atque[6] ipsī erant recēpērunt. 15

---

[1] = **per quōrum fīnēs.**

[2] This is just another way of saying that he killed them or sold them into slavery as prisoners of war.   [3] *they might satisfy* (**606,** 10).

[4] *for this reason;* explained by the **quod** clause.

[5] Emphatic; direct object of **collocāre.**

[6] *as;* so regularly with words implying likeness, as **parem** here.

29. In castrīs Helvētiōrum tabulae repertae sunt litterīs Graecīs [7] cōnfectae et ad Caesarem relātae, quibus in tabulīs nōminātim ratiō cōnfecta erat, quī numerus domō exīsset [8] eōrum quī arma ferre possent,[9] et item puerī, senēs mulierēsque. Quārum omnium ratiō-
20 num summa [10] erat Helvētiōrum mīlia CCLXIII, Tulingōrum mīlia XXXVI, Latobrīgōrum XIIII, Rauracōrum XXIII, Boiōrum XXXII; ex hīs quī arma ferre possent, ad mīlia XCII.[11] Summa omnium fuērunt [12] ad mīlia CCCLXVIII. Eōrum quī domum rediērunt, cēnsū habitō, ut Caesar imperāverat, repertus est numerus mīlium C et X.

QUESTIONS

1. Why did Caesar want the Helvetians to restore their former homes?
2. What proportion of the Helvetians and their allies returned home?
3. What did Caesar do to the canton which tried to escape after the surrender?

324. Grammar Review

Volitive clauses (**606, 5**).
Construction with **iubeō** (**606**, 5, *Note a*).

325. Translation

1. Caesar persuaded the neighbors to give the Helvetians food.
2. He ordered [13] them to throw down their arms and return [14] the slaves.
3. He ordered [13] them to return [14] to their own territory and warned them not to flee.

326. Word Study

The original Roman "senate" consisted of **senēs,** *old men,* i.e., men over forty-five, who were considered too old to fight. A "senior" is *older;* he really ought to be addressed as "sir," for "sir" is derived from **senior.**

Explain *circumvallation, exit, famish, incense, restitution, reversion, tabulate.*

---

[7] They learned the Greek alphabet through contact with the Greek colony Massilia (Marseilles) in southern Gaul.

[8] Indirect question implied in the noun **ratiō** and introduced by **quī numerus.**

[9] For the subjunctive see **606,** 10.

[10] *sum total.*

[11] i.e., 25 per cent.

[12] Agrees with the predicate nominative **mīlia.**

[13] Express in two ways.

[14] Distinguish between transitive *return* in the sense of *give back* and intransitive *return* in the sense of *go back.* Two different verbs are used in Latin.

Lesson LX

327. THE GERMAN THREAT

I, 31. Concilium tōtīus Galliae indictum est. Eō conciliō dīmissō, īdem prīncipēs cīvitātum quī ante fuerant [1] ad Caesarem revertērunt petiēruntque utī sibi sēcrētō in occultō dē suā omniumque salūte cum eō agere licēret. Locūtus est prō hīs Dīviciācus Haeduus:

"Galliae tōtīus factiōnēs sunt duae; hārum alterius prīncipātum 5 tenent Haeduī, alterius Arvernī. Hī cum dē prīncipātū inter sē multōs annōs contenderent, factum est [2] utī ab Arvernīs Sēquanīsque Germānī mercēde [3] arcesserentur. Hōrum prīmō circiter mīlia XV Rhēnum trānsiērunt; posteāquam agrōs et cultum et cōpiās [4] Gallōrum hominēs ferī ac barbarī amāre coepērunt, trāductī sunt plūrēs; nunc sunt in 10 Galliā ad centum et XX mīlium numerum.[5] Cum hīs Haeduī eōrumque clientēs semel atque iterum [6] armīs contendērunt; magnam calamitātem pulsī accēpērunt, omnem nōbilitātem, omnem senātum, omnem equitātum āmīsērunt.[7]

"Sed peius [8] victōribus Sēquanīs quam Haeduīs victīs accidit, 15 proptereā quod Ariovistus, rēx Germānōrum, in eōrum fīnibus cōn-sēdit tertiamque partem agrī Sēquanī, quī est optimus tōtīus Galliae, occupāvit, et nunc dē alterā parte tertiā Sēquanōs dēcēdere iubet, proptereā quod, paucīs mēnsibus ante, Harūdum mīlia hominum XXIIII ad eum vēnērunt, quibus locus parātur. Paucīs annīs omnēs 20 Gallī ex Galliae fīnibus pellentur atque omnēs Germānī Rhēnum trānsībunt; neque enim cōnferendus est Gallicus ager cum Germānō-rum agrō, neque haec cōnsuētūdō victūs cum illā.

---

[1] i.e., with Caesar.
[2] *it happened.*
[3] *for pay.* Cf. "mercenary" troops.
[4] *wealth.*
[5] The fighting between Caesar and Ariovistus took place in Alsace, which has been a fertile source for trouble between the Germans and the French, the modern descendants of the Romans, and which has changed hands repeatedly. In 1870 it became part of Germany, in 1918 it passed to France, in 1940 it again passed into German hands, and now it is once more part of France.
[6] *again and again* (literally, *once and again*).
[7] Probably greatly exaggerated.
[8] *a worse thing* (**596**, 2). Appeasement seems to have been worse than military defeat.

"Ariovistus autem, ut [9] semel Gallōrum cōpiās proeliō vīcit, superbē
25 et crūdēliter imperat, obsidēs [10] nōbilissimī cuiusque [11] līberōs poscit,
et in eōs omnia exempla [12] cruciātūsque ēdit, sī qua rēs nōn ad nūtum
aut ad voluntātem eius facta est. Homō est barbarus et īrācundus;
nōn possumus eius imperia diūtius sustinēre. Tū vel auctōritāte tuā
atque exercitūs recentī victōriā vel nōmine populī Rōmānī dēter-
30 rēre [13] potes nē maior multitūdō Germānōrum Rhēnum [14] trādūcātur,
Galliamque omnem ab Ariovistī iniūriā potes dēfendere."

QUESTIONS

1. Which were the leading tribes in the Gallic factions?
2. What steps did one of them take to gain the supremacy?
3. What was the result and what did the Gauls want Caesar to do
   about it?

328. Grammar Review

Perfect and future infinitives in indirect discourse (**613, 5**).

329. Translation

1. They showed that they themselves would endure tortures and
   slavery.
2. They said that certain tribes of the Gauls had sent-for the fierce
   Germans.
3. They stated that the king of the Germans had seized the best
   part of all Gaul.

330. Vocabulary

arcessō, –ere, –īvī, –ītus,
summon
concilium, –lī, n., *council*
factiō, –ōnis, f., *faction*
ferus, –a, –um, *wild*

indīcō, –ere, indīxī, indictus, *call*
occultus, –a, –um, *secret*
prīmō, adv., *at first*
recēns, gen. **recentis,** *recent*
victor, –ōris, m., *victor;* adj., *victorious*

Review **cōnsuētūdō, cruciātus, loquor.**

331. Word Study

From what Latin words are the following derived: **conquīrō, cōnsuētūdō, dēditiō, ēdō, factiō, prīmō, victor, voluntās?**

Explain *deterrent, factional, ferocity, occult, reiterate.*

---

[9] *when.*   [10] In apposition with **līberōs.**
[11] From **quisque:** *of all the nobles.*   [12] *all kinds of cruelties* (with **cruciātūsque**).
[13] *prevent a larger number . . . from being brought over* (**606, 6**).
[14] For the case see **600, 5.**

Summary of Chapter 32. Caesar notices that during all the time that Diviciacus is speaking, the Sequanians remain silent. He asks the reason and is told that the Sequanians are in such fear of the cruelty of Ariovistus that they do not even dare complain or ask aid because they are so completely at the mercy of the Germans, who had occupied their towns.

Although this appears at first sight to be a battle scene, it actually represents a *decursio*, the military parade which took place when an emperor was deified after his death. In this case the emperor was Antoninus Pius (138–161 A.D.). On the relief, a troop of cavalry gallops around two groups of infantrymen, each with its own standard bearers (both at lower left). Note the many details of military dress. Now in one of the gardens of the Vatican.

The Vatican

Remains of a Roman theater at
Vaison, in the land of the Vocontii.

Lesson LXI

332. CAESAR PROMISES TO SUPPORT THE GAULS

I, 33. Hīs rēbus cognitīs, Caesar Gallōrum animōs verbīs cōnfirmāvit, pollicitusque est sibi eam rem cūrae futūram: magnam sē habēre
spem et beneficiō [1] suō et auctōritāte adductum Ariovistum fīnem
iniūriīs factūrum. Hāc ōrātiōne habitā, concilium dīmīsit. Et multae
5 rēs eum hortābantur quārē [2] sibi eam rem cōgitandam et suscipiendam
putāret: in prīmīs quod Haeduōs, frātrēs [3] cōnsanguineōsque populī
Rōmānī saepe ā senātū appellātōs, in servitūte vidēbat Germānōrum
tenērī, eōrumque obsidēs esse apud Ariovistum ac Sēquanōs intellegēbat; quod in [4] tantō imperiō populī Rōmānī turpissimum sibi et
10 reī pūblicae esse arbitrābātur. Paulātim autem Germānōs [5] cōnsuēscere Rhēnum trānsīre et in Galliam magnam eōrum multitūdinem
venīre, populō Rōmānō perīculōsum vidēbat. Hominēs ferōs ac bar-
barōs exīstimābat, omnī Galliā occupātā, in Prōvinciam exitūrōs esse
atque inde in Italiam contentūrōs, praesertim cum Sēquanōs ā prō-

---

[1] Caesar when consul the year before had induced the senate to recognize
Ariovistus by conferring upon him the honorary title **amīcus populī Rōmānī.**
[2] = **ut.**
[3] An honorary title, like that of **amīcus,** conferred upon foreign leaders for
diplomatic reasons. Today decorations are conferred in the same way.
[4] *in view of.*
[5] *for the Germans,* etc. The infinitive clauses **cōnsuēscere . . . venīre** are the
subjects of **esse,** to be supplied with **perīculōsum.**

vinciā nostrā Rhodanus [6] dīvideret; quibus rēbus [7] quam mātūrrimē [8] 15
occurrendum putābat. Ipse autem Ariovistus tantam sibi arrogantiam
sūmpserat ut ferendus [9] nōn vidērētur.

34. Quam ob rem placuit eī ut ad Ariovistum lēgātōs mitteret,
quī ab eō postulārent utī aliquem locum medium [10] utrīusque colloquiō dīligeret: velle [11] sē dē rē pūblicā et summīs utrīusque rēbus 20
cum eō agere. Eī lēgātiōnī Ariovistus respondit:

"Sī quid mihi ā Caesare opus esset, ego ad eum vēnissem; [12] sī quid
ille mē vult,[13] illum ad mē venīre oportet. Praetereā neque sine exercitū in eās partēs Galliae venīre audeō quās Caesar tenet, neque
exercitum sine magnō commeātū atque difficultāte in ūnum locum con- 25
trahere possum. Mihi autem mīrum vidētur quid in meā Galliā, quam
bellō vīcī, aut Caesarī [14] aut omnīnō populō Rōmānō negōtī [15] sit."

QUESTIONS

1. Why did Caesar think he might influence Ariovistus?
2. What reasons led Caesar to promise the Gauls support?
3. What answer did Ariovistus make to Caesar's request for a
conference?

This French stamp shows the Roman arch
in the city of Orange in Provence, southern
France.

333. Grammar Review

Datives of purpose and of reference (**599,** 2–3).

334. Translation

1. He decided to choose a place for a conference.
2. "It will be my concern," he said, "to defend you."
3. He said that the Roman army would be a protection to the
Gauls.

[6] *(only) the Rhone.*
[7] *this situation;* dative with **ocurrendum (esse sibi):** *he ought to meet* (**599,** 7).
[8] Irregular superlative form.   [9] *unbearable* (with **nōn**).
[10] *midway between them* (literally, *both*).
[11] *(stating) that he wished;* indirect statement. The verb of saying is implied in
postulārent.
[12] *if I needed anything from Caesar, I should have come to him.*
[13] *if he wishes anything of me.* **Volō** here is used with two accusatives.
[14] For the case see **599,** 8.
[15] With **quid** (**598,** 3). The answer was not unlike Hitler's indication in 1938
that his demands on Czechoslovakia were his business, not England's.

225

audeō, –ēre, ausus, semideponent, *dare*
cōgitō, 1, *think, consider*
colloquium, –quī, n., *conference*
paulātim, adv., *little by little*

praesertim, adv., *especially*
servitūs, –tūtis, f., *slavery*
turpis, –e, *disgraceful*

Idioms: **opus est, quam ob rem.**
Review **placeō, praetereā, uterque.**

336. Word Study

The original meaning of **commeātus** was *coming and going*. Its use in the sense of *supplies* shows that supply trains for the Roman army must have been on the go all the time and gives an idea of the importance attached to provisioning the soldiers.

From what Latin words are the following derived: **colloquium, praetereā, servitūs?**

Explain *arrogance, cogitate, contract, dividend, turpitude.*

Summary of Chapter 35. After receiving Ariovistus' insolent reply, Caesar sends an ultimatum: first, that Ariovistus is not to bring any more Germans into Gaul; second, that he must return the hostages of the Haeduans; third, that he is not to wage war upon the Haeduans and their allies. If Ariovistus will agree to these demands, there will be peace; otherwise Caesar will protect the interest of the Haeduans.

Arles (ancient Arelate), on the Rhone River in southern France (Provence), has a fine Roman theater and an amphitheater once accommodating over 26,000 spectators.

French Government Tourist Office

The hill of Besançon (ancient Vesontio), a natural fortress, where Caesar placed a guard.

French Government Tourist Office

Lesson LXII

337. ARIOVISTUS' DEFIANT STAND

I, 36. Ad haec Ariovistus respondit:

"Iūs est bellī ut victōrēs victīs quem ad modum velint[1] imperent; item populus Rōmānus victīs nōn ad[2] alterius praescrīptum, sed ad[2] suum arbitrium imperāre cōnsuēvit. Sī ego populō Rōmānō nōn praescrībō quem ad modum suō iūre ūtātur, nōn oportet mē ā populō 5 Rōmānō in meō iūre impedīrī. Haeduī mihi,[3] quoniam bellī fortūnam temptāvērunt et armīs congressī ac superātī sunt, stīpendiāriī sunt factī. Magnam Caesar iniūriam facit quī suō adventū vectīgālia[4] mihi dēteriōra facit. Haeduīs obsidēs nōn reddam, neque hīs neque eōrum sociīs iniūriā[5] bellum īnferam, sī in eō manēbunt[6] quod convēnit stīpen- 10 diumque quotannīs pendent; sī id nōn fēcerint, longē hīs frāternum[7] nōmen populī Rōmānī aberit.[8] Quod[9] mihi Caesar dēnūntiat sē Haeduōrum iniūriās nōn neglēctūrum, nēmō mēcum sine suā perniciē[10] contendit. Cum volet, congrediātur;[11] intelleget quid invictī Germānī, exercitātissimī in armīs, quī inter annōs XIIII tēctum nōn 15 subiērunt, virtūte possint."[12]

---

[1] *as they wish* (**606,** 15); in line 5 **quem ad modum** means *how* (literally, *in what manner*).
[2] *according to.*
[3] Depends on **stīpendiāriī.**
[4] *revenues.*
[5] *unjustly.*
[6] *if they will abide by that* (with **in eō**).
[7] Adj., = **frātrum;** a sneer at the honorary title.
[8] i.e., *will be of little use to them.*
[9] *as to the fact that.*
[10] *destruction.*
[11] *let him come on.*
[12] *can (do).*

Summary of Chapter 37. On hearing of further German outrages Caesar advances rapidly against Ariovistus.

38. Cum trīduī viam prōcessisset, nūntiātum est eī Ariovistum cum suīs omnibus cōpiīs ad occupandum Vesontiōnem,[13] quod est oppidum maximum Sēquanōrum, contendere trīduīque viam ā suīs
20 fīnibus prōcessisse. Hūc Caesar magnīs nocturnīs diurnīsque itineribus contendit occupātōque oppidō, ibi praesidium collocat.

Summary of Chapters 39–41. Exaggerated reports about the Germans throw Caesar's army into a panic, and throughout the camp soldiers may be seen making their wills. The officers even predict mutiny when Caesar gives the order to advance. He restores confidence by recalling how Marius defeated the Germans and by stating that the Helvetians, whom they themselves had just defeated, do not fear the Germans, for they have often beaten them in battle. This speech has a bracing effect and his men clamor for an immediate advance. Caesar marches against Ariovistus.

42. Cognitō Caesaris adventū, Ariovistus lēgātōs ad eum mittit: quod anteā dē colloquiō postulāvisset, id per sē [14] fierī licēre,[15] quoniam propius accessisset, sēque id sine perīculō facere posse exīsti-
25 māret. Nōn respuit condiciōnem Caesar iamque eum ad sānitātem revertī arbitrābātur.

QUESTIONS

1. How did Ariovistus defend his actions?
2. Why did he have such confidence in his Germans?
3. How did he explain his willingness to have a conference?
4. What do you think was the real reason for his changing his mind?

Right: French stamp with Ceres and Mercury, representing Peace and Commerce.
Left: Stamp of Luxembourg with Latin word *caritas,* "charity."

338. Grammar Review

Volitive subjunctive (**606,** 1).
Subjunctive in indirect questions (**606,** 13).

---

[13] Masculine: *Besançon,* one of the strongest natural fortresses in France.
[14] *as far as he was concerned.*
[15] Indirect discourse, dependent on the idea of saying implied in **mittit.**

339. Translation

1. Let us not tempt fortune too often.
2. Let Caesar meet (in battle) with [16] us and learn how Germans conquer.
3. The Germans did not know whether **(utrum)** to kill the prisoner or **(an)** reserve him for **(in)** another time.

340. Vocabulary and Word Study

congredior, congredī, congressus, *meet*   temptō, 1, *test, try*

Idiom: **quem ad modum.**
Review **hūc, pendō, stīpendium, ūtor.**

Explain *convention, covenant, denunciation, deteriorate, journal, journey, pernicious, prescription, sanitation.*

Summary of Chapters 42–54. Caesar grants the request but guards against treachery. In his speech Caesar pleads for peace but insists upon his former demands. Ariovistus is as arrogant as before and demands that Caesar withdraw from *his* Gaul before he drives him out of it. Caesar rejects appeasement and replies that he will not forsake his allies. The conference is brought to a sudden end when the German cavalry attack Caesar's escort. Ariovistus later arrests as spies two Roman envoys whom Caesar sent in response to his request for another conference. Ariovistus then begins actual hostilities by cutting off Caesar's line of communication, but Caesar later reëstablishes it by a skillful maneuver. Learning that the superstitious Germans are waiting for a full moon in order to attack, Caesar, like the good general that he was, takes the initiative and attacks at once. The fighting on both sides is desperate. At the critical moment Crassus sends up the reserves and the Romans win a decisive victory. Ariovistus escapes across the Rhine in a small boat. After establishing his legions in winter quarters at Vesontio, Caesar returns to Cisalpine Gaul.

341. LATĪNUM HODIERNUM

"Nucēs"

In Bellō Magnō Secundō nostrōrum temporum Americānī ā Germānīs in Galliā vincēbantur. Tum dux Germānōrum Americānōs monuit ut sē dēderent. Sed dux Americānus respondisse dīcitur: "Nucēs," et Americānī fortiter pugnantēs Germānōs tandem superā-vērunt. Dux īnfēlix Germānōrum neque vocābulum [17] "nucēs" com- 5 prehendit neque cūr Americānī nōn cēderent. Nunc Dux "Nux" vir īnsignis habētur. Quantum valent parvae nucēs!

---

[16] See **601**, 6, *a.*   [17] *word.*

Everywhere the Romans governed, they established theaters for public entertainment. From the Greek culture, the Romans introduced both comedy and tragedy. Stock masks were used so that the audience could identify various characters at a glance. This Roman theater was constructed in Mérida, Spain, around 18 A.D. In no province did Roman ways take firmer root outside of Italy than in Spain.

Our Heritage

342. THE GALLIC CONQUEST AND ITS EFFECT ON THE WORLD

The immediate result of Caesar's conquest of Gaul was to free Italy for centuries from the fear of another invasion like that of the Gauls who had swept down from the north and sacked Rome in 390 B.C. "Let the Alps sink," Cicero exclaimed; "the gods raised them to shelter Italy from the barbarians; they are now no longer needed."

The Roman conquest of Gaul likewise relieved Italy from the German menace. Two German tribes, the Teutons and Cimbri, had annihilated two Roman armies before Marius and his legions succeeded in stopping their advance in the Alpine passes. Caesar not only drove the Germans out of Gaul but bridged the Rhine and pushed the German tribes back into their own forests. It was Caesar who fixed the frontier of Gaul at the Rhine. Had it not been for Caesar's conquest of Gaul, the country extending from the Rhine to the Pyrenees and from the Alps to the ocean might have become an extension of Germany, embracing the Spanish peninsula as well. The subjugation of Gaul by the Romans gave the Greco-Italic culture time to become thoroughly rooted, not only in Gaul, but also in Spain, before the breakup of the Roman Empire. Belgium, France, Portugal, and Spain became *Latin* instead of *Teutonic*. The language, customs, and arts of Rome were gradually introduced and the "vulgar," or spoken, Latin of Gaul became early French. Thus the whole history of western Europe was profoundly affected by the Roman conquest of Gaul. We should not forget, moreover, that through the Norman-French language our own English speech became predominantly Latin, though Caesar in his two invasions of the island of Britain (England) had merely, according to Tacitus, "revealed Britain to the Romans."

A distinguished historian [1] has said that the French nation is the monument of Caesar's conquest of Gaul.

QUESTIONS

1. Is our English speech the richer because of its Latin elements?
2. What would have been the probable effect upon the history of Europe if the Germans had conquered Gaul?
3. Was Rome, as the possessor of a superior culture, justified in imposing her civilization upon the Gauls?

[1] T. Rice Holmes, *The Roman Republic* (1923), Vol. II, p. 234.

UNIT VI

DĒ BELLŌ GALLICŌ II

The great aqueduct, the Pont du
Gard, near Nîmes, France, is one of
the many Roman monuments in her
provinces. Located in southwestern
France, Nîmes was an important Roman outpost. The Pont du Gard was
built by Agrippa in 19 B.C. It is both
an aqueduct and a bridge.

Erich Lessing/PhotoEdit

In the second century A.D. Hadrian built this wall across northern Britain to keep out invaders from the north.

The National Trust/Art Resource

Lesson LXIII

343. THE BELGIANS UNITE TO WIN INDEPENDENCE

II, 1. Cum esset Caesar in citeriōre Galliā, crēbrī ad eum rūmōrēs afferēbantur,[1] litterīsque item Labiēnī certior fīēbat omnēs Belgās contrā populum Rōmānum coniūrāre obsidēsque inter sē dare.[2] Coniūrandī hae erant causae: prīmum verēbantur nē, omnī pācātā
5 Galliā,[3] ad eōs[4] exercitus noster addūcerētur; deinde ab nōn nūllīs Gallīs sollicitābantur. Multī ex hīs, ut[5] Germānōs diūtius in Galliā versārī nōluerant, ita populī Rōmānī exercitum hiemāre atque manēre in Galliā molestē ferēbant.[6] Aliī mōbilitāte[7] et levitāte animī novīs imperiīs[8] studēbant. Ab nōn nūllīs etiam sollicitābantur, quod in
10 Galliā ā potentiōribus atque eīs quī ad condūcendōs hominēs facultātēs habēbant rēgna occupābantur, quī minus facile eam rem imperiō[9] nostrō cōnsequī poterant.

2. Hīs nūntiīs litterīsque commōtus, Caesar duās legiōnēs in citeriōre Galliā novās cōnscrīpsit et initiō aestātis Q. Pedium[10] lēgātum
15 mīsit quī in ulteriōrem Galliam eās dēdūceret. Ipse, cum[11] prīmum

---

[1] Note the tense.
[2] *were exchanging.*
[3] In the narrow sense; cf. **275,** footnote 8.
[4] Refers to the Belgians.
[5] *as . . . so* (with **ita**).
[6] *were displeased that* ("took it hard").
[7] For the case see **601,** 11.
[8] Dative with **studēbant (599,** 6).
[9] *under our rule;* the ablative here expresses the attendant circumstances.
[10] Caesar's nephew, son of his sister Julia.
[11] With **prīmum:** *as soon as.* The indicative is more common in such clauses.

pābulī cōpia esse inciperet, ad exercitum vēnit. Dat negōtium Senoni-
bus reliquīsque Gallīs quī fīnitimī Belgīs erant, utī ea quae apud eōs
gerantur [12] cognōscant sēque dē hīs rēbus certiōrem faciant. Hī omnēs
nūntiāvērunt manūs cōgī, exercitum in ūnum locum condūcī.[13] Tum
vērō exīstimāvit sē dēbēre ad eōs proficīscī. Rē frūmentāriā prōvīsā, 20
castra movet diēbusque circiter XV ad fīnēs Belgārum pervenit.

3. Eō [14] cum dē imprōvīsō celeriusque omnium opīniōne [15] vēnisset,
Rēmī [16] ad eum lēgātōs Iccium et Andecombogium, prīmōs cīvitātis,
mīsērunt, quī dīcerent:

"Nōs nostraque [17] omnia in fidem atque potestātem populī Rōmānī 25
permittimus; neque cum reliquīs Belgīs cōnsēnsimus neque contrā
populum Rōmānum coniūrāvimus, parātīque sumus et obsidēs dare et
imperāta facere et in oppida vōs recipere et frūmentō cēterīsque rēbus
iuvāre. Reliquī omnēs Belgae in armīs sunt, Germānīque quī citrā
Rhēnum incolunt sēsē cum hīs coniūnxērunt; tantusque est eōrum 30

[12] Subjunctive by attraction. [13] *was being mobilized.*
[14] Adverb.
[15] Ablative of comparison: *sooner than any one expected;* Caesar's usual speed.
[16] Reims, standing on the site of their capital, preserves their name.
[17] *our possessions.*

**Remains of a spectacular
Roman temple at Jerash in
Jordan, between Jerusalem
and Damascus.**

Ace Williams from Shostal

omnium furor ut [18] nē Suessiōnēs [19] quidem, frātrēs cōnsanguineōsque nostrōs, quī eōdem iūre et eīsdem lēgibus ūtuntur, ūnum imperium ūnumque magistrātum nōbīscum habent, coniūrātiōne prohibēre potuerīmus."

QUESTIONS

1. Why did the Belgians plan to revolt against the Romans?
2. What steps did Caesar take when he heard of the Belgian plan?
3. What light does the map (pp. 180–181) throw on the reason for the declaration of loyalty of the Remi?

344. Grammar

Verēbantur nē ad eōs exercitus noster addūcerētur (line 4), *They feared that our army would be led against them.*

Verēmur ut veniat, *We fear that he will not come.*

After verbs meaning *fear* (**timeō, vereor,** etc.), the conjunction **nē** introducing a clause in the subjunctive is to be translated by *that,* **ut** by *that not.*

345. Translation

1. Do you fear that the Remi will not help you with grain?
2. Caesar feared that all Gaul would conspire against the Romans.
3. The Gauls feared that the Roman army would spend-the-winter in Gaul.

346. Vocabulary

dēdūcō, –ere, dēdūxī, dēductus, *lead*
facultās, –tātis, f., *faculty;* pl., *means*
fidēs, –eī, f., *trust, protection*
pācō, 1, *pacify*

prīmum, adv., *first*
rumor, –ōris, m., *rumor*
sollicitō, 1, *stir up*
versō, 1, *turn over;* passive, *live*

Review **coniūrō, cōnsentiō, crēber.**

347. Word Study

In Portuguese the first sentence in the above passage reads:

Como César estivesse na Galia citerior, freqüentes boatos eram levados para êle e igualmente era certificado por uma carta de Labieno que todos os Belgas conspiravam contra o povo romano e davam entre si reféns.

From what Latin words are the following derived: **imperātum, mōbilitās, pācō, partim?**

Explain *bona fide, infuriate, mobility, versatile.*

---

[18] Introduces **potuerīmus** (result).

[19] Accusative; emphatic position between **nē . . . quidem.** Their name survives in Soissons.

These appear to be soldiers of the Praetorian Guard, the troops which guarded the city of Rome itself, in full-dress uniform. Their helmets (*galeae*) have plumes, their breastplates (*loricae*) are very ornate, and their oval shields (*clipei*) seem too fancy for fighting. Notice also that they carry no swords. This relief is now in the Louvre in Paris.

Lesson LXIV

348. CAESAR GETS THE FACTS ABOUT THE BELGIANS

II. 4. Cum ab hīs quaereret quae cīvitātēs quantaeque in armīs essent et quid in bellō possent, sīc reperiēbat:

"Plērīque Belgae sunt ortī ā Germānīs Rhēnumque ōlim trāductī propter locī fertilitātem ibi cōnsēdērunt Gallōsque quī ea loca incolēbant expulērunt; sōlīque sunt quī patrum nostrōrum memoriā, 5 omnī Galliā vexātā, Teutonōs Cimbrōsque intrā suōs fīnēs ingredī [1]

---

[1] Object of **prohibuerint:** *keep the Teutons from entering.*

237

prohibuerint; quā ex rē fit utī eārum rērum memoriā [2] magnam sibi auctōritātem in rē mīlitārī sūmant."

"Plūrimum inter eōs Bellovacī [3] et virtūte et auctōritāte et homi-
10 num numerō valent; hī possunt cōnficere armāta mīlia centum; polli-
citī sunt ex eō numerō mīlia LX tōtīusque bellī imperium sibi postu-
lant. Suessiōnēs nostrī sunt fīnitimī; fīnēs lātissimōs fertilissimōsque
agrōs habent. Apud eōs fuit rēx nostrā etiam memoriā Dīviciācus, [4]
tōtīus Galliae potentissimus, quī cum [5] magnae partis hārum regiōnum,
15 tum etiam Britanniae imperium obtinuit. Nunc est rēx Galba; ad hunc
propter iūstitiam prūdentiamque summa tōtīus bellī omnium voluntāte
dēfertur. Oppida habent numerō XII, pollicentur mīlia armāta L;
totidem Nerviī, quī maximē ferī inter ipsōs habentur longissimēque [6]
absunt; XV mīlia Atrebātēs, [7] Ambiānī [8] X mīlia, Morinī XXV mīlia,
20 Menapiī VIIII mīlia, Caletī X mīlia, Veliocassēs et Viromanduī
totidem, Atuatucī XVIIII mīlia; Condrūsōs, Eburōnēs, Caerōsōs,
Paemānōs, quī ūnō nōmine Germānī appellantur, arbitrāmur ad XL
mīlia posse cōnficere."

QUESTIONS

1. Where was the original home of the Belgians?
2. Which Belgian tribe was the strongest; which was nearest the Remi; which was most remote?

349. Vocabulary

plērīque, plēraeque, plēraque, *most*

potēns, gen. potentis, *powerful*

totidem, indeclinable adj., *the same number*

Review **dēferō, intrā, postulō, propter, reperiō.**

---

[2] Ablative of cause.   [3] The city of Beauvais preserves the name.
[4] Not the Haeduan mentioned in Book I and again in the next chapter.
[5] With **tum:** *not only . . . but also.*
[6] Farthest from where?   [7] They have given their name to the city of Arras.
[8] Hence the name of the city of Amiens.

Swiss stamp issued in 1942 celebrates the two-thousandth anniversary of the first mention of Geneva by Caesar. The bridge that he tells about (p. 199) is shown.

350. Word Study

Translate these Spanish sentences:

En la memoria de nuestros padres solo los belgas han prohibido a los alemanes entrar en su tierra.

Era el rey más poderoso de toda la Galia.

Julius Caesar spent the years from 58–50 B.C. in his military campaigns in the Gallic provinces. This detail of a frieze shows the Roman soldiers fighting the Gauls in battle.

Albert Moldvay

E. Richter, Rome

Stucco relief in an underground building in Rome. Three boys practice with arms.

Lesson LXV

351. CAESAR CROSSES THE AISNE RIVER

II, 5. Caesar Rēmōs cohortātus līberāliterque ōrātiōne prōsecūtus, omnem senātum ad sē addūcī iussit. Quae omnia ab hīs dīligenter ad diem [1] facta sunt. Ipse Dīviciācum Haeduum magnopere cohortātus docet necesse esse manūs hostium distinērī, nē cum tantā multitūdine
5 ūnō tempore cōnflīgendum sit.[2] Id fierī posse, sī suās cōpiās Haeduī in fīnēs Bellovacōrum intrōdūxerint [3] et eōrum agrōs populārī coeperint. Hīs rēbus mandātīs, eum ā sē dīmittit.

Postquam omnēs Belgārum cōpiās in ūnum locum coāctās ad sē venīre neque iam longē abesse ab eīs quōs mīserat explōrātōribus et
10 ab Rēmīs cognōvit, flūmen Axonam,[4] quod est in extrēmīs Rēmōrum fīnibus, exercitum trādūcere mātūrāvit atque ibi castra posuit. Quae rēs [5] et latus [6] ūnum castrōrum rīpīs flūminis mūniēbat et post eum quae erant [7] tūta ab hostibus reddēbat et commeātūs [8] ab Rēmīs reliquīsque cīvitātibus ut sine perīculō ad eum portārī possent efficiēbat.
15 In eō flūmine pōns erat. Ibi praesidium pōnit et in alterā parte flūminis Q. Titūrium Sabīnum lēgātum cum sex cohortibus relinquit; castra in altitūdinem pedum XII vāllō fossāque XVIII pedum mūnīrī iubet.

[1] *on time.* What literally?

[2] Impersonal: *so that the Romans would not have to fight.* Caesar's strategy here, of taking his enemies one at a time, is the same as that attempted by the Germans at the beginning of both World Wars (1914, 1939).

[3] *if the Haeduans should lead,* etc. (**606,** 14). The perfect subjunctive here represents the future perfect indicative of the direct statement.

[4] Now the Aisne. By crossing the river he gained a bridgehead. There was another famous battle of the Aisne in 1914 during World War I. The word is governed by the prefix **trā–** in **trādūcere,** whose direct object is **exercitum.**

[5] *this maneuver.*   [6] Direct object. The preceding **et** means *both.*

[7] For **ea quae post eum erant:** *the rear.*

[8] This and the following words belong in the **ut** clause, which depends on **efficiēbat.**

240

6. Ab hīs castrīs oppidum Rēmōrum nōmine Bibrax [9] aberat mīlia passuum VIII. Id ex itinere [10] magnō impetū Belgae oppugnāre coepērunt. Aegrē eō diē sustentum est.[11] Gallōrum eadem atque [12] 20 Belgārum oppugnātiō est haec: ubi, circumiectā multitūdine hominum, undique in mūrum lapidēs iacī coeptī [13] sunt mūrusque dēfēnsōribus nūdātus est, testūdine [14] factā, propius succēdunt mūrumque subruunt. Quod tum facile fīēbat. Nam cum tanta multitūdō lapidēs ac tēla conicerent,[15] in mūrō cōnsistendī potestās erat nūllī.[16] Cum fīnem 25 oppugnandī nox fēcisset, Iccius Rēmus nūntium [17] ad eum mittit: nisi subsidium sibi submittātur, sēsē diūtius sustinēre nōn posse.

QUESTIONS

1. How did the Belgians attack Bibrax?
2. Where did Caesar station Sabinus?
3. What did Caesar ask the Haeduans to do?
4. On what side of the Aisne did Caesar take his position?

352. Grammar Review

Noun clauses of result (**606, 9**).

353. Translation

1. Caesar will cause the supplies to be brought without delay.
2. By his speed he achieved (the result) that the Belgians could not capture the town.
3. It happened that Caesar's camp was (only) a few miles away from the town of the Remi.

354. Word Study

Distinguish **lātus** (adj.), **lātus** (participle of **ferō**), **latus** (noun). From what Latin words are the following derived: **dēfēnsor, intrōdūcō, oppugnātiō?**

Explain *denudation, intramural, introduction, lapidary, lateral.*

Summary of Chapter 7. Caesar sends help to Bibrax, causing the Belgians to abandon the siege and to proceed towards the Roman army.

[9] *Bī'brax,* now supposed to be Bievre.
[10] *on the march,* i.e., without stopping to make the usual preparations for a siege.
[11] Use the personal construction in translating.
[12] *as.*   [13] For the form see **594.**
[14] A newspaper writer compared the tanks massed close together to defend the evacuation of Dunkirk by the English in 1940 with the locked shields of the **testūdō.**   [15] Why plural (**596, 3,** *Note*)?
[16] Used instead of the dative of **nēmō.**
[17] *message (stating that).*

The Rhone pass at the Swiss border, one of the possible Helvetian routes (see p. 199).

Albert Moldvay

Lesson LXVI

355. FEELING OUT THE ENEMY

II, 8. Caesar prīmō et propter multitūdinem hostium et propter magnam opīniōnem virtūtis proeliō abstinēre statuit. Cotīdiē tamen equestribus proeliīs quid hostis virtūte posset et quid nostrī audērent experiēbātur. Ubi nostrōs nōn esse īnferiōrēs intellēxit, locō [1] prō
5 castrīs ad aciem īnstruendam nātūrā idōneō, ab utrōque latere eius collis in quō castra erant trānsversam fossam dūxit circiter passuum [2] CCCC et ad extrēmās fossās castella cōnstituit ibique tormenta [3] collocāvit. Hoc fēcit nē, cum aciem īnstrūxisset, hostēs ab lateribus [4] pugnantēs [5] suōs circumvenīre possent. Hōc factō, duābus legiōnibus
10 quās proximē cōnscrīpserat in castrīs relīctīs, ut, sī opus esset, subsidiō [6] dūcī possent, reliquās VI legiōnēs prō castrīs in aciē cōnstituit. Hostēs item suās cōpiās ex castrīs ēductās īnstrūxerant.

9. Palūs erat nōn magna inter nostrum atque hostium exercitum. Hanc sī [7] nostrī trānsīrent hostēs exspectābant; nostrī autem, sī ab
15 illīs initium trānseundī fieret,[8] ut [9] impedītōs aggrederentur parātī in armīs erant. Interim proeliō equestrī inter duās aciēs contendēbātur.[10] Ubi neutrī trānseundī initium faciunt, secundiōre [11] equitum proeliō nostrīs, Caesar suōs in castra redūxit. Hostēs prōtinus ex eō locō ad flūmen Axonam contendērunt, quod esse post nostra castra dēmōn-
20 strātum est. Ibi, vadīs repertīs, partem cōpiārum suārum trādūcere

---

[1] Ablative absolute with **idōneō,** or ablative of place.
[2] Depends on **fossam.**
[3] See illustrations on pp. 268, 277.
[4] With **circumvenīre.**
[5] With **suōs,** i.e., Caesar's soldiers.
[6] For the case see **599,** 2.
[7] (*to see*) *whether;* for **trānsīrent** see **606,** 13.
[8] *should be made* (**606,** 15).
[9] A purpose clause, depending on **parātī erant.**
[10] Impersonal.
[11] *the cavalry battle being rather favorable to our men.*

cōnāti sunt, ut,[12] sī possent, castellum cui praeerat Q. Titūrius lēgātus expugnārent pontemque rescinderent; sī minus potuissent,[13] agrōs Rēmōrum vāstārent, quī magnō nōbīs ūsuī ad bellum gerendum erant, commeātūque nostrōs prohibērent.

QUESTIONS

1. Was Caesar's failure to attack at once a sign of fear or prudence? Defend your answer.
2. How did the Belgians plan to defeat Caesar?
3. How did Caesar take precautions to prevent being surrounded?

356. Grammar Review

Ablative of separation (**601, 1**).

357. Translation

1. At first Caesar wanted to refrain from battle.
2. Caesar saw that it was necessary to keep the enemy from the river.
3. He sent the hostages away from the camp on account of the danger.

358. Vocabulary

adeō, adīre, adiī, aditūrus,
  go to, approach
equester, –tris, –tre, (*of*) *cavalry*
experior, experīrī, expertus, *try*

īnferior, –ius, *lower, inferior;*
  superl. **īnfimus** and **īmus,** *lowest*
paulisper, adv., *for a little while*
prōtinus, adv., *immediately*

Idioms: **ex itinere, novissimum agmen.**
Review **collis, cotīdiē, idōneus, moror, palūs, praesum, ūsus.**

359. Word Study

As the firing power of Roman artillery (**399**) was furnished by twisted ropes, the general term for artillery was **tormenta** (from **torqueō,** *twist*); cf. English *torment, torture.*

Secundus is from **sequor,** for what *follows* is "second." A wind is called **secundus** because a *following* wind is a *favorable* one. So too a battle may be **secundum.** We speak of "seconding," i.e., *favoring,* a motion. See also **174.**

From what Latin words are the following derived: **adeō, equester, paulisper?**

Explain *experience, experiment, rescind.*

---

[12] Introduces **expugnārent, rescinderent, vāstārent,** and **prohibērent.**
[13] *if not* (**606,** 15). Represents a future perfect, while **possent** represents a future.

Testudo. At left, on the column of Marcus Aurelius in Rome. The one above is a model (see p. 269).

Anderson

Lesson LXVII

360. THE BELGIANS WITHDRAW

II, 10. Caesar, certior factus ab Titūriō, omnem equitātum et levis armātūrae [1] Numidās, funditōrēs sagittāriōsque pontem trādūcit atque ad eōs contendit. Ācriter in eō locō pugnātum est. Hostēs impedītōs nostrī in flūmine aggressī magnum eōrum numerum occīdērunt. Hostēs
5 ubi et dē expugnandō oppidō et dē flūmine trānseundō spem sē fefellisse [2] intellēxērunt, et nostrōs in locum inīquiōrem nōn prōgredī pugnandī causā vīdērunt, atque ipsōs [3] rēs frūmentāria dēficere coepit, concilium convocāvērunt. Cōnstituērunt optimum esse domum suam quemque [4] revertī ut potius in suīs quam in aliēnīs fīnibus dēcertārent
10 et domesticīs cōpiīs reī frūmentāriae ūterentur. Ad eam sententiam cum reliquīs causīs haec quoque ratiō [5] eōs dēdūxit, quod Dīviciācum atque Haeduōs fīnibus Bellovacōrum appropinquāre cognōverant. Hīs [6] persuādērī ut diūtius morārentur neque [7] suīs auxilium ferrent nōn poterat.
15 11. Eā rē cōnstitūtā, secundā vigiliā magnō cum tumultū castrīs ēgressī, nūllō certō ōrdine [8] neque imperiō, cum sibi quisque prīmum

---

[1] Depends on **Numidās (598, 2).**   [2] *that their hope had failed them.*
[3] Direct object, referring to the enemy.
[4] *(for) each man to return (to) his own home.*   [5] Explained by the **quod** clause.
[6] *the latter could not be persuaded* (**599,** 6, *a*).   [7] *and not.*
[8] Ablative absolute: *there being,* etc.

itineris locum peteret et domum pervenīre properāret, fēcērunt [9] ut
similis fugae profectiō vidērētur. Hāc rē statim Caesar per speculātōrēs
cognitā, īnsidiās veritus, quod quā dē causā discēderent nōndum per-
spexerat, exercitum equitātumque castrīs continuit. Prīmā lūce cōn- 20
firmātā rē ab explōrātōribus, omnem equitātum quī novissimum agmen
morārētur praemīsit eīque Q. Pedium et L. Cottam lēgātōs praefēcit;
T. Labiēnum lēgātum cum legiōnibus tribus subsequī iussit. Hī novis-
simōs adortī et multa mīlia passuum prōsecūtī, magnam multitūdinem
eōrum fugientium concīdērunt. Ita sine ūllō perīculō tantam eōrum 25
multitūdinem nostrī interfēcērunt quantum fuit diēī spatium; [10] sub
occāsum sōlis sequī dēstitērunt sēque in castra, ut erat imperātum,
recēpērunt.

QUESTIONS

1. How did Caesar defeat the plan of the Belgians?
2. What did the Belgians decide to do then? Why?
3. How did Caesar at first interpret the action of the Belgians?

361. Grammar Review

Dative with compound verbs (**599,** 7).

362. Translation

1. Cotta was-in-command-of part of the cavalry.
2. Whom did Caesar put-in-charge-of the other part?

363. Vocabulary

adorior, adorīrī, adortus,
rise up to, attack
audācter, adv., *boldly*
dēcertō, 1, *fight* (*it out*)
perspiciō, –ere, –spexī, –spectus,
see clearly

subsequor, subsequī, subsecūtus,
follow (*closely*)
tumultus, –ūs, m., *uproar*

Review **appropinquō, inīquus, īnsidiae.**

364. Word Study

Adorior comes from **orior,** *rise up to* with hostile intention, i.e.,
attack; cf. **aggredior** (lit., *step up to*) and its English derivative
aggression.

From what Latin words are the following derived: **armātūra,
domesticus, perspiciō, subsequor?**

Explain *insidious, perspicacity, subsequent, tumultuous.*

---

[9] *they made their departure seem,* etc.   [10] *as the length of the day allowed.*

Lesson LXVIII

365. *THE SUESSIONES AND THE BELLOVACI SURRENDER*

II, 12. Postrīdiē eius diēī Caesar, priusquam sē hostēs ex terrōre ac
fugā reciperent,[1] in fīnēs Suessiōnum, quī proximī Rēmīs erant, exercitum dūxit et, magnō itinere cōnfectō, ad oppidum Noviodūnum [2]
contendit. Id ex itinere oppugnāre cōnātus, quod vacuum ab [3] dēfēn-
5 sōribus esse audiēbat, propter lātitūdinem fossae mūrīque altitūdinem,
paucīs [4] dēfendentibus, expugnāre nōn potuit. Castrīs mūnītīs, vīneās
agere quaeque [5] ad oppugnandum ūsuī erant comparāre coepit. Interim
omnis ex fugā Suessiōnum multitūdō in oppidum proximā nocte convēnit. Celeriter vīneīs ad oppidum āctīs, aggere iactō turribusque
10 cōnstitūtīs, magnitūdine [6] operum, quae neque vīderant ante Gallī
neque audierant,[7] et celeritāte Rōmānōrum permōtī, lēgātōs ad
Caesarem dē dēditiōne mittunt et, petentibus Rēmīs ut cōnservārentur,
impetrant.

13. Caesar, obsidibus [8] acceptīs prīmīs cīvitātis atque ipsīus Galbae
15 rēgis duōbus fīliīs, armīsque omnibus ex oppidō trāditīs, in dēditiōnem
Suessiōnēs accēpit exercitumque in Bellovacōs dūcit. Quī cum sē
suaque omnia in oppidum Brātuspantium contulissent, atque ab eō
oppidō Caesar cum exercitū circiter mīlia passuum V abesset, omnēs

---

[1] *before the enemy should recover* (**606,** 12).
[2] Now called Soissons, after the Suessiones. It played an important part in
World War I (1914–18).   [3] *from;* the phrase depends on **vacuum.**
[4] Ablative absolute: *although only,* etc.   [5] i.e., **et quae.**
[6] With **permōtī.**   [7] What form is this? See **595.**
[8] In apposition with **prīmīs** and **fīliīs.**

Battle between Romans and barbarians on an ancient sarcophagus.

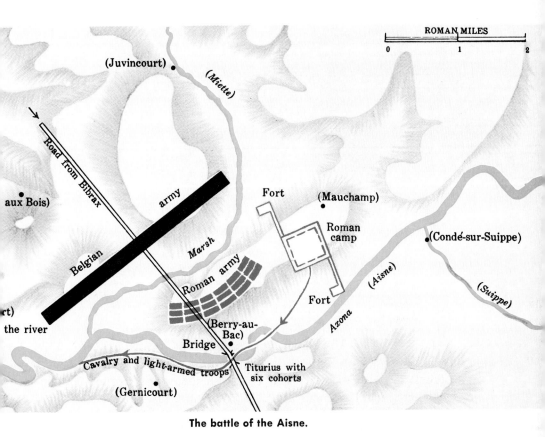

The battle of the Aisne.

maiōrēs nātū [9] ex oppidō ēgressī, manūs ad Caesarem tendere et vōce
significāre [10] coepērunt sēsē in eius fidem ac potestātem venīre neque 20
contrā populum Rōmānum armīs contendere. Item, cum ad oppidum
accessisset castraque ibi pōneret, puerī mulierēsque ex mūrō passīs [11]
manibus suō mōre [12] pācem ab Rōmānīs petīvērunt.

QUESTIONS

1. Trace Caesar's course on the map.
2. What led the Suessiones to surrender?
3. Who of the Bellovaci asked for peace first?

366. Word Study

Explain *conservation, evacuate, insignificant, turret, vacuous,
vacuum.*

---

[9] With **maiōrēs:** *older men;* literally, *older in birth* (**601,** 16).
[10] While they could not speak Latin, they could nevertheless make themselves
understood by signs and cries.   [11] *extended.*   [12] For the case see **601,** 17.

Restoration of Stonehenge, a monument of the early Britons. For a picture of the remains see p. 300.

Taurgo

Lesson LXIX

367. A PLEA FOR MERCY

II, 14. Prō hīs Dīviciācus facit verba:

"Bellovacī omnī tempore in fidē atque amīcitiā cīvitātis Haeduae fuērunt; impulsī ab suīs prīncipibus, quī dīcēbant Haeduōs ā tē in servitūtem redāctōs omnēs indignitātēs contumēliāsque perferre, et ab
5 Haeduīs dēfēcērunt et populō Rōmānō bellum intulērunt. Quī [1] eius cōnsilī prīncipēs fuerant, quod intellegēbant quantam calamitātem cīvitātī intulissent, in Britanniam profūgērunt. Petunt nōn sōlum Bellovacī, sed etiam prō eīs Haeduī, ut tuā [2] clēmentiā in eōs [3] ūtāris. Quod [4] sī fēceris, Haeduōrum auctōritātem apud omnēs Belgās am-
10 plificābis, quōrum auxiliīs atque opibus, sī qua bella incidērunt, sustinēre [5] cōnsuērunt." [6]

15. Caesar, honōris Dīviciācī atque Haeduōrum causā, sēsē eōs in fidem receptūrum et cōnservātūrum dīxit et, quod erat cīvitās magnā inter Belgās auctōritāte atque hominum multitūdine praestābat, DC
15 obsidēs poposcit. Hīs trāditīs omnibusque armīs ex oppidō collātīs, ab eō locō in fīnēs Ambiānōrum pervēnit, quī sē suaque omnia sine morā dēdidērunt. Eōrum fīnēs Nerviī attingēbant; quōrum dē nātūrā mōribusque Caesar cum quaereret, sīc reperiēbat:

Nūllus est aditus ad eōs mercātōribus. Nihil patiuntur vīnī reli-
20 quārumque rērum ad lūxuriam pertinentium īnferrī, quod hīs rēbus

[1] For **eī quī.**
[2] Note the emphatic position before the noun: *your (well-known).*
[3] *toward them.*   [4] Object of **fēceris.**
[5] Used without object: *hold out.*   [6] For **cōnsuēvērunt (595).**

248

relanguēscere animōs virtūtemque remittī exīstimant. Sunt hominēs ferī magnaeque virtūtis; accūsant reliquōs Belgās, quī [7] sē populō Rōmānō dēdiderint patriamque [8] virtūtem prōiēcerint. Cōnfirmant sē neque lēgātōs missūrōs neque ūllam condiciōnem pācis acceptūrōs.

QUESTIONS

1. What did Caesar find out about the Nervii?
2. Who was to blame for the revolt of the Bellovaci?
3. What other tribe surrendered besides the Bellovaci?
4. Why did Diviciacus use the phrase **tuā clēmentiā** (line 8) and why did Caesar quote it?

368. Grammar Review

Ablative with **ūtor** and **potior** (**601,** 10).

369. Translation

1. Their friends begged that Caesar use mercy.
2. He used towers in order to get-possession-of the enemy's town.
3. Upon-being-urged by their leaders, he permitted them to enjoy their liberty and resources.

370. Vocabulary

aditus, –ūs, m., *approach, access*
contumēlia, –ae, f., *insult*
dēdō, dēdere, dēdidī, dēditus,
  surrender

perferō, –ferre, –tulī, –lātus, *endure*
sīc, adv., *so, thus*

Review **causā, ops, poscō, prōiciō.**

371. Word Study

From what Latin words are the following derived: **aditus, amplificō, indignitās, perferō, redigō?**

Explain *amplifier, contumely, languish, opulent, vinous.*

Summary of Chapters 16–19. Caesar learns that the Nervii and their allies have taken a position on the south side of the Sabis (Sambre) River. Deserting Gauls tell the Nervii that the Roman legions are widely separated on the march by baggage trains and that the first could easily be attacked and defeated before the others come up. But when Caesar comes closer to the enemy he places his baggage in the rear. Six legions begin building a camp on a hill sloping down to the river, just opposite a wooded hill where the Nervii are encamped. When the latter see the baggage, supposing that only one legion has arrived, they attack the Roman camp. Then begins the most exciting of Caesar's battles in Gaul.

---

[7] *because they* (**606,** 10, *Note*).   [8] Adjective.

The striking Roman aqueduct at Segovia, in central Spain north of Madrid. There are many Roman monuments in Spain, which became a Roman province at an early date.

Art Resource

Lesson LXX

372. ROMAN SKILL AND EXPERIENCE

II, 20. Caesarī omnia ūnō tempore erant agenda: vēxillum [1] prōpōnendum (quod erat īnsigne [2] cum ad arma concurrī [3] oportēret); ab opere revocandī mīlitēs; quī paulō longius aggeris [4] petendī causā prōcesserant arcessendī; aciēs īnstruenda; mīlitēs cohortandī; signum [5]
5 tubā dandum. Quārum rērum magnam partem temporis brevitās et impetus hostium impediēbat.

Hīs difficultātibus duae rēs erant subsidiō, scientia atque ūsus mīlitum, quod superiōribus proeliīs exercitātī quid [6] fierī oportēret ipsī sibi praescrībere poterant; et quod [7] ab opere singulīsque legiōnibus singu-
10 lōs lēgātōs Caesar discēdere nisi [8] mūnītīs castrīs vetuerat. Hī propter propinquitātem et celeritātem hostium nihil [9] iam Caesaris imperium exspectābant sed per sē quae vidēbantur [10] administrābant.

---

[1] *banner,* a red flag displayed at the general's tent before a battle. Compare the modern practice of "running up the colors."　　[2] Noun.
[3] Impersonal.　　　　　　　　　　　　　　　[4] *material for the rampart.*
[5] To fall in line.
[6] The clause depends on **praescrībere.**
[7] *the fact that;* the second of the **duae rēs.**
[8] With **mūnītīs** (ablative absolute): *unless the camp was fortified.*
[9] = **nōn iam,** but stronger: *not (a moment) longer.*　[10] *seemed best.*

250

21. Caesar, necessāriīs rēbus imperātīs, ad cohortandōs mīlitēs dē-
cucurrit et forte ad legiōnem decimam [11] dēvēnit. Mīlitēs nōn longiōre [12]
ōrātiōne cohortātus est quam utī suae prīstinae virtūtis memoriam 15
retinērent neu perturbārentur animō hostiumque impetum fortiter
sustinērent. Quod nōn longius hostēs aberant quam quō [13] tēlum adigī
posset,[14] proelī committendī signum dedit. Atque in alteram partem
item cohortandī causā profectus, pugnantibus [15] occurrit. Temporis
tanta fuit exiguitās hostiumque tam parātus ad dīmicandum animus ut 20
nōn modo ad īnsignia [16] accommodanda sed etiam ad galeās in-
duendās [17] scūtīsque [18] tegimenta dētrahenda tempus dēfuerit.[19]
Quam [20] quisque ab opere in partem cāsū dēvēnit, quaeque [21] prīma
signa cōnspexit, ad haec cōnstitit, nē in quaerendīs suīs pugnandī
tempus dīmitteret. 25

[11] Caesar's favorite.   [12] *in a speech not longer than* (*this*), *i.e., that they*, etc.
[13] (*the distance*) *to which*.   [14] For the subjunctive see **606**, 10.
[15] See **599**, 7.
[16] The red or black crests or plumes worn on the helmet to show the rank or.
the legion of the wearer.
[17] Like the modern soldier, the Roman soldier ordinarily carried his helmet on
his pack or suspended from his neck while on the march.
[18] For the case see **599**, 4. When not in use the shields were kept in waterproof
cases.   [19] For the sequence see **604,** 5, *Note, b*.
[20] For **quam in partem.**   [21] For **et quae.**

The battle with the Nervii at the Sambre.

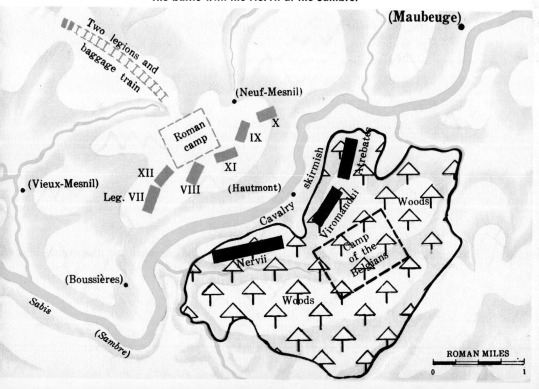

1. What order did Caesar give first?
2. How was the battle line eventually formed?
3. What factors enabled the Romans to meet the emergency?

373. Grammar Review

Future passive participle **(611)**.
Dative of agent (**599,** 9).

374. Translation

1. The time was very short for accomplishing all these things.
2. Caesar had to send certain soldiers for the sake of recalling others.
3. Caesar had to give the signal and recall the soldiers while (**dum** [22]) he drew-up his battle line.

375. Vocabulary

adigō, –ere, adēgī, adāctus,
throw (to)
administrō, 1, *manage, perform*
dēsum, deesse, dēfuī, dēfutūrus,
be lacking

dīmicō, 1, *fight*
necessārius, –a, –um, *necessary*
nēve (neu), conj., *and not, nor*
prīstinus, –a, –um, *former*

Review **cōnspiciō, oportet, perturbō.**

376. Word Study

Distinguish **forte** (noun), **forte** (adjective), and **fortiter** (adverb).

From what Latin words are the following derived: **adigō, dēsum, exercitō, necessārius, scientia, tegimentum?**

What does *per se* mean in English? Explain *administration, perturbation, pristine, propinquity, veto.*

[22] With present indicative (**604,** 2, *a*).

The entrance to the Roman amphitheater at Senlis, north of Paris.

M. Gallois

Evidence of technical progress in Gaul. These water lines, found recently at Ensérune, northeast of Narbonne, may not compare with Roman aqueducts and plumbing, but they show that the Gauls were by no means a primitive and backward people.

Lesson LXXI

377. TENSE MOMENTS

II, 22. Īnstrūctus erat exercitus magis ut locī nātūra et necessitās temporis quam ut reī mīlitāris ratiō atque ōrdō postulābat. Dīversae legiōnēs, aliae [1] aliā in parte, hostibus resistēbant saepibusque [2] dēnsissimīs interiectīs prōspectus impediēbātur. Neque certa subsidia collocārī [3] neque quid in quāque parte opus esset prōvidērī [3] neque ab ūnō omnia imperia administrārī [3] poterant. Itaque in tantā rērum inīquitāte fortūnae [4] quoque ēventūs variī sequēbantur.

Summary of Chapter 23. The ninth and tenth legions, on the left wing, push back the Atrebatians and pursue them across the river. The eighth and eleventh legions also push back the enemy. But the main force of the enemy attacks the exposed front and left sides of the camp.

24. Eōdem tempore equitēs nostrī levisque armātūrae peditēs, quī cùm eīs ūnā [5] fuerant (quōs prīmō hostium impetū pulsōs esse dīxerāmus), cum sē in castra reciperent, adversīs [6] hostibus occurrēbant ac rūrsus aliam in partem fugam petēbant. Cālōnēs,[7] quī ab summō iugō

---

[1] *some in one place, others in another.*
[2] *hedges,* similar to the hedgerows which hampered the invasion of Normandy in 1944.   [3] All the infinitives depend on **poterant.**
[4] Depends on **ēventūs:** *chance results.*   [5] **ūnā cum:** *along with.*
[6] *met the enemy face to face.*   [7] See **274,** I, D, 1.

collis nostrōs victōrēs [8] flūmen trānsīsse cōnspexerant, praedandī causā
ēgressī, cum respexissent et hostēs in nostrīs castrīs versārī vīdissent,
praecipitēs fugae sēsē mandābant. Simul eōrum quī cum impedīmentīs
15 veniēbant clāmor oriēbātur, aliīque aliam in partem perterritī ferē-
bantur.[9] Quibus omnibus rēbus permōtī sunt equitēs Trēverī,[10] quōrum
inter Gallōs virtūtis opīniō est singulāris, quī auxilī causā ā cīvitāte
missī ad Caesarem vēnerant. Cum [11] multitūdine hostium castra nostra
complērī, legiōnēs premī et paene circumventās tenērī, cālōnēs, equitēs,
20 funditōrēs, Numidās dissipātōs in omnēs partēs fugere vīdissent,
dēspērātīs [12] nostrīs rēbus, domum contendērunt. Rōmānōs pulsōs
superātōsque,[13] castrīs [14] impedīmentīsque eōrum hostēs potītōs cīvitātī renūntiāvērunt.

QUESTIONS

1. What did the Treveri do?
2. What did the camp servants do?
3. What happened to the Roman cavalry?
4. What interfered with the Roman view?

378. Grammar Review

Dative with special verbs (**599**, 6).

379. Translation

1. The soldiers were not persuaded to wait.
2. The cavalry could resist no longer and fled to camp.
3. The generals ordered the soldiers not to pursue the enemy.

380. Vocabulary

adversus, –a, –um, *facing, opposite*
dīversus, –a, –um, *different*
magis, adv., *more*

pedes, peditis, m., *foot soldier;*
pl., *infantry*

381. Word Study

From what Latin words are the following derived: **collocō, ēventus, intericiō, necessitās, pedes, praedor, singulāris?**

Explain *adverse, complement, diversity, eventual, singularity.*

---

[8] (*as*) *victors;* i.e., the ninth and tenth legions, mentioned in Chapter 23.

[9] *rushed* (reflexive use of passive, **609**).

[10] Here used as an adjective. Their name survives in that of the city Treves
(Trier).   [11] Introduces **vīdissent.**

[12] *despairing of our success.*   [13] Supply **esse.**

[14] With **potītōs.**

Roman tombs cut out of the rock at Petra, Jordan, like the giant heads in the Black Hills of South Dakota of Washington and other presidents.

Servizio Editorio Fotografico/Art Resource

Lesson LXXII

382. THE CRISIS PASSES

II, 25. Caesar [1] ab decimae legiōnis cohortātiōne ad dextrum cornū profectus est, ubi [2] suōs urgērī, signīsque [3] in ūnum locum collātīs, duodecimae legiōnis cōnfertōs mīlitēs sibi ipsōs ad pugnam esse impedīmentō vīdit. Quārtae cohortis omnēs centuriōnēs occīsī erant, signiferque interfectus, signum āmissum, reliquārum cohortium omnēs 5 ferē centuriōnēs aut vulnerātī aut occīsī. Reliquī erant tardiōrēs et nōn nūllī ab novissimīs [4] dēsertōrēs proeliō excēdēbant ac tēla vītābant. Hostēs neque ā fronte ex īnferiōre locō subeuntēs [5] intermittēbant et ab utrōque latere īnstābant. Caesar rem esse in angustō [6] vīdit neque ūllum esse subsidium quod submittī posset.[7] Scūtō [8] ab novissimīs 10 ūnī mīlitī dētrāctō, quod ipse eō sine scūtō vēnerat, in prīmam aciem prōcessit; centuriōnibusque nōminātim appellātīs,[9] reliquōs cohortātus

[1] This chapter resumes Caesar's account of his own part in the battle, interrupted in Chapter 21.   [2] *where,* introducing **vīdit.**
[3] The **–que** connects the two infinitives, **urgērī** and **esse.**
[4] *in the rear.*   [5] *did not cease coming up.*
[6] *in a tight place.*   [7] For the subjunctive see **606,** 10.
[8] *Seizing a shield from a soldier in the rear ranks.* For **mīlitī** see **599,** 4.
[9] This reveals one secret of Caesar's success as a leader—he knew every non-commisioned officer by name.

mīlitēs signa īnferre et manipulōs laxāre iussit, quō [10] facilius gladiīs
ūtī possent. Cuius adventū spē illātā mīlitibus ac redintegrātō animō,
15 cum [11] prō sē quisque in cōnspectū imperātōris etiam in extrēmīs [12]
suīs rēbus operam nāvāre [13] cuperet, paulum hostium impetus tar-
dātus est.

26. Caesar cum septimam legiōnem, quae iūxtā cōnstiterat, item
urgērī ab hoste vīdisset, tribūnōs mīlitum monuit ut paulātim sē
20 legiōnēs coniungerent et conversa [14] signa in hostēs īnferrent. Quō
factō, cum alius aliī subsidium ferret neque timērent nē āversī [15] ab
hoste circumvenīrentur, audācius resistere ac fortius pugnāre coepērunt. Interim mīlitēs legiōnum duārum quae in novissimō agmine
praesidiō impedīmentīs fuerant, proeliō nūntiātō, cursū incitātō,[16]
25 in summō colle ab hostibus cōnspiciēbantur; et Labiēnus castrīs
hostium potītus et ex locō superiōre quae rēs in nostrīs castrīs gere-
rentur cōnspicātus, decimam legiōnem subsidiō nostrīs mīsit. Quī, cum
ex equitum et cālōnum fugā quō in locō rēs esset quantōque in perīculō
et castra et legiōnēs et imperātor versārētur cognōvissent, nihil ad
30 celeritātem sibi reliquī [17] fēcērunt.

QUESTIONS

1. What did Caesar do?
2. Which legion suffered most?
3. What three things saved the twelfth legion?

383. Vocabulary

centuriō, –ōnis, m., *centurion*
cornū, –ūs, n., *horn, wing* (of an army) [18]

dexter, –tra, –trum, *right*
tardō, 1, *slow up*

Review **opera, vītō.**

384. Word Study

From what Latin words are the following derived: **cohortātiō,
dēsertor, duodecimus, nōminātim, redintegrō, signifer?**

Explain *cornucopia, dexterity, invulnerable, relaxation, retardation,
urgent.*

---

[10] For **ut**; regularly used in a purpose clause containing a comparative.
[11] Causal.   [12] *in the midst of extreme danger to himself.*
[13] With **operam**: *to do his best.*
[14] *face about and advance*, i.e., to meet the attack on the flanks.
[15] *in the rear.*   [16] *advancing double-quick.* Literally?
[17] For the case see **598,** 3; *they came as fast as they could;* literally, *they made
nothing of a remainder* (*in respect*) *to speed.*
[18] The only fourth declension neuter in this book; all the singular forms except
the genitive are identical (see **568**).

The citadel of Namur, where the Atuatuci took refuge.

Lesson LXXIII

385. THE NERVII AND THE ATUATUCI

II, 27. Hōrum adventū tanta rērum commūtātiō est facta ut nostrī, etiam quī vulneribus cōnfectī prōcubuissent [1] scūtīs [2] innīxī proelium redintegrārent, et cālōnēs perterritōs hostēs cōnspicātī etiam inermēs [3] armātīs occurrerent. Equitēs vērō ut turpitūdinem fugae virtūte dēlērent, omnibus in locīs pugnae sē legiōnāriīs mīlitibus praeferēbant.[4] At 5 hostēs etiam in extrēmā spē salūtis tantam virtūtem praestitērunt ut, cum prīmī eōrum cecidissent, proximī iacentibus [5] īnsisterent atque ex eōrum corporibus pugnārent. Hīs dēiectīs et coacervātīs cadāveribus, quī supererant [6] ut ex tumulō [7] tēla in nostrōs coniciēbant pīlaque intercepta remittēbant. Nōn nēquīquam [8] tantae virtūtis hominēs 10 iūdicārī dēbet [9] ausōs esse trānsīre lātissimum flūmen, ascendere altissimās rīpās, subīre inīquissimum locum; quae facilia [10] ex difficillimīs animī magnitūdō redēgerat.

[1] Attracted into the subjunctive. [2] Ablative with **innīxī:** *resting on.*
[3] In agreement with **cālōnēs** (nominative).
[4] *tried to show themselves superior to.* The legionary, or infantry, soldiers formed the real fighting strength of the Roman army.
[5] *the fallen* (from **iaceō**). For the case see **599, 7.**
[6] From **supersum.** [7] *as* (**ut**) *from a mound.*
[8] *not in vain;* with **ausōs.** [9] Literally, *it ought to be judged that.*
[10] Predicate accusative: *had rendered easy instead of* (**ex**).

Summary of Chapter 28. When the noncombatants, who hid in swamps, learn that their army has been almost annihilated, they surrender. Only three out of 600 senators survive, 500 out of 60,000 fighting men. Caesar allows the survivors to return to their homes.

29. Atuatucī, dē quibus suprā dīximus,[11] cum [12] omnibus cōpiīs [13]
15 auxiliō Nerviīs venīrent, hāc pugnā nūntiātā, ex itinere domum revertērunt; omnibus oppidīs castellīsque dēsertīs, sua omnia in ūnum oppidum ēgregiē nātūrā mūnītum contulērunt. Quod cum [14] ex omnibus in circuitū [15] partibus altissimās rūpēs habēret, ūnā ex parte lēniter acclīvis [16] aditus in lātitūdinem nōn amplius [17] pedum CC relinquē-
20 bātur; quem locum duplicī altissimō mūrō mūnierant; [18] tum magnī ponderis saxa et praeacūtās trabēs in mūrō collocābant. Ipsī erant ex Cimbrīs Teutonīsque [19] prōgnātī, quī cum iter in prōvinciam nostram atque Italiam facerent, eīs impedīmentīs [20] quae sēcum agere ac portāre nōn poterant citrā flūmen Rhēnum dēpositīs, custōdiam [21] ex suīs [22]
25 ac praesidium sex mīlia hominum relīquērunt. Hī post eōrum [23] mortem multōs annōs ā fīnitimīs vexātī, cum aliās [24] bellum īnferrent, aliās illātum [25] dēfenderent, cōnsēnsū eōrum omnium pāce factā, hunc sibi domiciliō locum dēlēgērunt.

[11] In Chapter 16.   [12] The conjunction.
[13] Ablative of accompaniment (**601, 6, b**).
[14] *although this* (*town*). This is probably Namur, though some favor a hill near Huy.   [15] *all around.*
[16] *ascending.*   [17] For **amplius quam.**
[18] For the form see **595.**
[19] These two German tribes had been decisively defeated by Marius, Caesar's uncle, in 102 and 101 B.C.
[20] Here *live stock* and *goods,* as shown by **agere** and **portāre.**
[21] (*as*) *a guard.*   [22] **ex suīs** belongs with **sex mīlia.**
[23] The main group.   [24] Adverb: *now . . . now.*   [25] Supply **bellum.**

Ancient statues near the palace of the President of Italy.

Leptis Magna, a Roman city on the coast of Libya, which is east of Tunisia. All northern Africa, from Morocco to Egypt, once belonged to Rome.

Patrick Morin from Monkmeyer

QUESTIONS

1. Trace Caesar's course on the map (pp. 180–181).
2. What did the camp servants of the Romans do?
3. What did the Nervii do when their first line fell?
4. How did the Atuatuci come to make Belgium their home?

386. Grammar Review

Accusative of place to which (**600,** 3).

387. Translation

1. Caesar proceeded to Noviodunum to destroy that town.
2. After the Atuatuci had arrived at that town, they immediately fortified it.
3. Because Caesar admired the courage of the Nervii, he sent home those who survived.

388. Word Study

If John Doe is *otherwise* known as Richard Roe, the latter name is an "alias." The Latin adverb **aliās** became an English noun, just as happened in the case of *item* **(285).** Similarly an "alibi" is claimed when one alleges that he was *elsewhere.*

From what Latin words are the following derived: **commūtātiō, cōnsēnsus, custōdia, domicilium, duplex, inermis, inīquus, legiōnārius, praeferō, turpitūdō?**

Explain *adjacent, cadaver, duplicity, turpitude, vexatious.*

Frankfort High School Chapter, Junior Classical League

Students in Frankfort, Kentucky, made this fine model of a walled town under attack. Can you identify at least five devices used in sieges?

Lesson LXXIV

389. THE ATUATUCI MAKE FUN OF THE ROMAN "TANKS"

II, 30. Ac prīmō adventū exercitūs nostrī crēbrās ex oppidō ēruptiōnēs faciēbant [1] parvulīsque proeliīs cum nostrīs contendēbant; posteā vāllō pedum XII, in circuitū XV mīlium,[2] crēbrīsque castellīs circummūnītī [3] oppidō [4] sē continēbant. Ubi, vīneīs āctīs, aggere 5 exstrūctō, turrim [5] procul cōnstituī vīdērunt, prīmum irrīsērunt ex mūrō quod tanta māchinātiō ā tantō spatiō īnstituerētur: [6] "Quibusnam [7] manibus aut quibus vīribus vōs, praesertim hominēs [8] tantulae statūrae (nam plērumque omnibus Gallīs, prae magnitūdine corporum suōrum, brevitās Rōmānōrum contemptuī est) tantī oneris turrim 10 in mūrō nostrō vōs posse collocāre cōnfīditis?"

31. Ubi vērō movērī [9] et appropinquāre moenibus vīdērunt, novā atque inūsitātā speciē commōtī lēgātōs ad Caesarem dē pāce mīsērunt, quī ad hunc modum locūtī sunt:

[1] Supply **hostēs** as subject.   [2] i.e., **pedum.**
[3] *when hemmed in* (i.e., by Caesar's rampart), agreeing with the subject of **continēbant.**   [4] Ablative of means.
[5] For the form see **567.**   [6] For the mood see **606,** 16.
[7] **–nam** is intensive: *with what hands anyway.*
[8] In apposition with **vōs:** (*being*) *men.*   [9] Supply **turrim** as subject.

"Nōn exīstimāmus vōs sine ope deōrum bellum gerere, quī [10] tantae altitūdinis māchinātiōnēs tantā celeritāte prōmovēre possītis; [15] nōs nostraque omnia vestrae potestātī permittimus. Ūnum petimus et ōrāmus: sī forte prō tuā clēmentiā, quam ab aliīs audīmus, statueris Atuatucōs esse cōnservandōs, nōlī [11] nōs armīs dēspoliāre. Nōbīs omnēs ferē fīnitimī sunt inimīcī ac nostrae virtūtī [12] invident; ā quibus nōs dēfendere, trāditīs armīs, nōn poterimus. Nōbīs praestat, sī in eum [20] cāsum dēdūcāmur,[13] quamvīs [14] fortūnam ā populō Rōmānō patī quam ab eīs per cruciātum interficī inter quōs dominārī cōnsuēvimus."

QUESTIONS

1. Why did the Atuatuci laugh at the Roman preparations?
2. What explanation did their envoys have for Roman ingenuity?
3. What concession did the Atuatuci ask of the Romans?

390. Grammar Review

Conjugation of **volō, nōlō,** and **mālō (592).**
Find five special and compound verbs with the dative (**599,** 6–7) in **385** and **389.**

391. Translation

1. Our neighbors envy us and will want to kill us all if we surrender our arms.
2. When they saw our army approaching the town, they were unwilling to resist us.

392. Vocabulary

ēruptiō, –ōnis, f., *sally*
onus, oneris, n., *weight*
plērumque, adv., *usually*

procul, adv., *far off*
turris, –is, f., *tower*

393. Word Study

The suffix **–lus (–ulus, –ellus)** is a *diminutive,* i.e., it means *little:* **castellum** (from **castra**), **parvulus, tantulus.** In English it often becomes *–le: particle* (from **parti–culum**), *corpuscle* (**corpus–culum**). Sometimes the original form is kept: *formula, gladiolus* (literally, *little sword,* from **gladius,** because of the shape of its leaves).

From what Latin words are the following derived: **brevitās, circummūniō, contemptus, dominor, ēruptiō, statūra?**

Explain *despoil, domination, eruption, exonerate, onerous.*

[10] *since you.* A subjunctive relative clause may express cause.
[11] *do not deprive us of* (**608**).   [12] For the case see **599,** 6.
[13] *we should be brought.*   [14] From **quīvīs:** *any whatever.*

Lesson LXXV

394. SURRENDER, TREACHERY, PUNISHMENT

II, 32. Ad haec Caesar respondit:

"Magis cōnsuētūdine meā quam meritō vestrō cīvitātem cōnservābō, sī, priusquam mūrum ariēs attigerit, vōs dēdideritis; sed dēditiōnis nūlla est condiciō nisi armīs trāditīs. Id quod in [1] Nerviīs fēcī faciam,
5 fīnitimīsque imperābō nē quam dēditīciīs populī Rōmānī iniūriam īnferant." Rē nūntiātā ad suōs, illī sē quae imperārentur facere [2] dīxērunt. Armōrum magnā multitūdine [3] dē mūrō in fossam quae erat ante oppidum iactā, sīc ut prope summam mūrī aggerisque altitūdinem acervī [4] armōrum adaequārent (et tamen circiter parte tertiā, ut
10 posteā perspectum est, cēlātā atque in oppidō retentā), portīs patefactīs, eō diē pāce sunt ūsī.[5]

33. Sub [6] vesperum Caesar portās claudī mīlitēsque ex oppidō exīre iussit, nē quam noctū Atuatucī ā mīlitibus iniūriam acciperent. Illī, ante initō cōnsiliō,[7] quod,[8] dēditiōne factā, nostrōs praesidia
15 dēductūrōs aut dēnique [9] indīligentius servātūrōs crēdiderant, tertiā vigiliā, quā [10] minimē arduus ad nostrās mūnītiōnēs ascēnsus vidēbātur, omnibus cōpiīs repente ex oppidō ēruptiōnem fēcērunt. Celeriter, ut

---

[1] in the case of.   [2] said they were doing.
[3] Translate this and the following ablative absolute as main clauses.
[4] piles.   [5] they observed a truce.   [6] toward.
[7] in accordance with a plan. The adverb **ante** belongs with **initō**, which is from **ineō.**   [8] because.   [9] at least.   [10] where.

ante Caesar imperāverat, ignibus [11] significātiōne factā, ex proximīs castellīs eō concursum est,[12] pugnātumque ab hostibus ita ācriter est ut ā virīs fortibus in extrēmā spē salūtis pugnārī dēbuit, cum in ūnā [13] 20 virtūte omnis spēs cōnsisteret. Occīsīs ad hominum mīlibus IIII, reliquī in oppidum reiectī sunt. Postrīdiē eius diēī frāctīs portīs, cum iam dēfenderet nēmō,[14] atque intrōmissīs mīlitibus nostrīs, sectiōnem [15] eius oppidī ūniversam Caesar vēndidit. Ab eīs quī ēmerant capitum numerus ad eum relātus est mīlium LIII.   25

QUESTIONS

1. Trace Caesar's course on the map, pages 180–181.
2. What happened the night after the surrender?
3. How did Caesar punish the Atuatuci for their treachery?

395. Grammar Review

Find all the examples of the ablative absolute (**601,** 8) in **394.**

---

[11] *fire signals,* in general use among all peoples until more rapid means of communication were invented, such as the telegraph, telephone, and radio. The Indians "telegraphed" news by means of smoke and fire signals.

[12] Translate actively and personally. Do the same with the next two verbs used impersonally, by making **hostibus** and **virīs fortibus** the subjects. The neuter of the perfect participle of intransitive verbs may be used in this construction.

[13] *alone.*   [14] With **iam:** *no one any longer.*

[15] *loot.* Merchants followed Roman armies and purchased the spoils of war. Caesar accepts their count as to the number of slaves they bought. Caesar contrasts the bravery of the Nervii and the treachery of the Atuatuci and his leniency toward the former and severity toward the latter.

The Roman gate, from the Third century A.D., at Trier (Treves), Germany. The city was founded by Augustus and called Augusta Trevirorum.

Servizio Editorio Fotografico/Art Resource

396. Translation

1. If the enemy surrendered [16] their arms, they could not resist the Roman army.
2. After the gates were closed,[16] the enemy concealed [16] their arms and made a sally.
3. Since the enemy had been defeated,[16] Caesar demanded hostages and returned to Italy.

397. Word Study

Why is the constellation Aries so named?

Aries.

From what Latin words are the following derived: **adaequō, concurrō, dēditīcius, intrōmittō, patefaciō?**

Explain *arduous, conceal, vendor, vespers.*

Summary of Chapters 34–35. The coast towns are brought under Roman power by Crassus. The Germans across the Rhine offer to submit. Caesar arranges winter quarters and returns to Italy.

398. LATĪNUM HODIERNUM

Vacca [17] Contenta

Vaccae virtūs est nōbīs lac praebēre ac contenta esse, ut in vāsibus lactis condēnsātī vidērī potest. Fierī quidem saepe potest ut vacca adhūc contenta īram subitō ostendat. Tālis fuit ista quae, lanternā calce [18] ēversā, Chicaginem urbem incendit. Inter fābulās puerīlēs nārrātur dē
5 vaccā quae trāns lūnam trānsiluit. Fuitne īnsāna an cupiditāte altissimē saliendī impulsa est? Dīcī vix potest. Contenta quidem nōn fuit.

Nūper mōs ortus est vaccārum māchinā mulgendārum.[19] Hōc modō plūrimae simul mulgērī possunt. Dum haec rēs geritur, vaccae, sī mūsica dulcis phōnographī praebētur, magis contentae stant. Mūsicam
10 classicam mālunt, hodiernam nōn amant. Quod ad nōs pertinet, plūs lactis bibāmus,[20] quod cibus optimus nōbīs est. Ita nōn modo vaccae sed nōs ipsī magis contentī erimus.

---

[16] Use ablative absolute.
[17] *cow.* Adapted from Norman W. DeWitt in *Classical Journal*, 44 (1948), p. 14.
[18] *heel, kick.*   [19] *milk.*   [20] *let us drink.*

Our Heritage

399. WARFARE IN ANCIENT AND MODERN TIMES

Despite revolutionary changes in warfare, from the introduction of firearms and heavy artillery to the invention of submarines, airplanes, atomic bombs, and guided missiles, there still remain many curious parallels between ancient and modern techniques. The Roman soldier dug trenches in order to fortify his camp; the modern soldier sometimes digs himself in, as he did in Korea, for protection against high-range guns which can drop explosive shells within an enemy's lines from a distance. In Caesar's day the rampart formed by throwing up the earth taken from the trench about the camp gave sufficient protection from the low-range weapons then in use. A Roman army on the march dug itself in in this fashion every night. The use of the spade in modern warfare and the lines of trenches in World War I and the Korean War find their counterpart (on a smaller scale, of course) in Caesar's siege of Alesia, where he constructed ten miles of earthen ramparts and trenches. The Roman trenches were five feet deep and obstructed with wolfholes, sharpened stakes, and brush barricades to guard against attacks from the town (cf. p. 340). Similar devices are used today, especially against tanks.

Like the Romans, modern soldiers are equipped with steel helmets and occasionally steel breastplates and greaves (shin guards) for hazardous work.

Roman soldiers held their spears **(pīla)** until they got within range of the enemy and then hurled them. Before the enemy could recover from this volley, the Romans attacked with their heavy swords **(gladiī)** held close to the body. Today long-range artillery fire prepares the way for a charge, while the hand grenade is used at closer quarters, followed at times by a charge of troops with bayonets fixed. Although artillery and rifle fire have superseded the spear-throwing of the Romans, and the bayonet and the grenade have taken the place of the sword, the principle remains the same. The motor-driven tank has taken the place of the old Roman **turris ambulātōria,** "movable tower," which was pushed forward on rollers toward the besieged town. The closest parallel to the tank, however, was the elephant. First used by Rome's enemies, the elephants terrified the Romans, who had never before seen any. Later the Romans themselves used them. Caesar does not mention them in the *Gallic War,* but a later writer says that Caesar scared the Britons at the Thames River with a single "armored" elephant carrying a tower filled with slingers and bowmen.

The Roman troops often advanced under fire protected by lines of movable sheds **(vīneae)** placed end to end, while occasionally smaller barriers, called **pluteī,** were pushed forward covering the advance of a small party under fire. Similarly, modern infantrymen advance behind the cover of tanks. Smoke screens, now used chiefly by warships, were also used by ancient armies.

In sieges like those at Avaricum and Alesia, Caesar employed the battering-ram **(ariēs)** to break down the enemy's walls. These rams were heavy swinging logs, capped with bronze, which, striking repeated blows at the same spot, would demolish any wall. A ram used by the Romans against Carthage in 148 B.C. was so huge that six thousand men were required to swing it into action. Today tanks and demolition teams are used in this way.

The **onager, ballista,** and **catapulta,** which threw stones or arrows, formed the "heavy" artillery of the Romans and were largely confined to siege operations. The power came from twisted ropes; today boys twist rubber bands in the same way to obtain motive power. For light artillery, the Romans used the **scorpiō,** a large bow mounted on a portable frame. A certain Greek of Alexandria, we are told, invented a **scorpiō** with an arrow magazine which shot arrows in rapid succession, resembling in principle the modern machine gun. From Caesar's account of its use at the siege of Avaricum, we know that this weapon was like a quick-firing gun. The Romans also had their **carroballistae,** or field-pieces, so that the modern gun carriage is nothing new. Incendiary bombs and flame throwers have their parallel in fireballs.

Airplanes are, of course, quite modern, but the first mention of a heavier-than-air flying machine is of one made by a Greek from southern Italy, a friend of Plato, who invented a flying machine resembling a dove **(columba).**

Caesar, in conquering Gallic towns and tribes, regularly demanded a certain number of influential persons to be held by him as hostages **(obsidēs),** or "pledges" that the terms of peace agreed upon would be kept. Unfortunately the word hostage is not yet obsolete.

In recent years much attention has been paid to the construction of military roads for the easy movement of troops. Until very recently, no other nation had built as many miles of paved roadway as had Rome. For durability the Roman roads are still unsurpassed; many miles of their military roads are still in existence after 2000 years.

A Roman bireme (a warship with two banks of oars) filled with soldiers. Decorating the curved prow, which was used to ram the enemy, sits a crocodile.

We have heard much in recent years of "blitzkrieg," or lightning war. Caesar was one of its earliest and most famous exponents. Before the enemy even knew that he was approaching he had already arrived! By use of technical aids he did things faster than his enemies, surprising and terrifying them thereby. It took the Helvetians twenty days to cross the Saône and even then not all of them got over; Caesar built a bridge and crossed in one day. The Remi surrendered because Caesar arrived before he was expected. He crossed the Cévennes mountains in six feet of snow, which the natives considered an impossible feat, and gathered his scattered legions into one place before the Arverni even knew he was there. From Gergovia Caesar marched his legions twenty-five miles, settled the Haeduan revolt, gave his soldiers three hours' rest, and marched back again—fifty miles in less than twenty-four hours.

By comparison with modern fighting, ancient warfare does not seem very deadly. Yet Caesar tells us that one hundred and twenty arrows struck the shield of one of his men at Dyrrachium and that not one of his soldiers was unhurt.

Ancient battles are still studied by military men for the lessons they teach. Generals Douglas MacArthur and George Marshall are examples of soldiers thoroughly familiar with ancient strategy and tactics. General Puller, called the "toughest marine in the corps," carried with him and read the *Gallic War* during World War II because he believed its lessons were still valuable.

There are also striking similarities between the military slang of ancient times and that of today. An ancient writer tells us that the men of the Roman army, many of whom had been brought up on farms in Italy, were fond of calling weapons and things about the camp by the names of animals and objects with which they were familiar as boys. The forked sticks on which Marius' soldiers carried their packs (**sarcinae**) were called "Marius' mules" (**mūlī Mariānī**).[1] A certain kind of **ballista** was named **onager**, "wild ass," from that animal's habit of flinging stones at its pursuers with its hind feet.

Left: Model of a Roman onager. *Right:* A U. S. Army model of a wolf-hole. In Roman times it was called a lily, in Viet Nam a pungee stick. But by whatever name, the simple sharpened stake, set in the ground and camouflaged, has always been a deadly weapon against foot soldiers.

Another type of hurling machine was called **scorpiō,** "scorpion," presumably because it shot arrows which "stung" the enemy. The beam used in battering down the enemy's walls was humorously called **ariēs,** "ram," from that animal's fondness for butting, and, as a matter of fact, it was often capped with a ram's head made of bronze. A defensive formation, when the men stood shoulder to shoulder so that their shields overlapped, while the inner ranks held their shields over their heads, was nicknamed "turtle" **(testūdō).** A large protecting shed, used to shield men while digging toward the walls of a besieged town, was called **mūsculus,** "little mouse," from the burrowing habits of that animal.

The use of animal names by the Roman soldier has its modern parallel in such words as "jeep" (originally the name of a comic-strip animal), "whirlybird" (helicopter), "caterpillar tractor," "weasel" (small caterpillar truck), "duck" (land and water truck), and "grasshoppers" (small planes). Even "scorpion" is used but in a different sense: a tank attachment to explode mines.

Country boys serving in the Roman army probably coined the term **vīneae,** "grape arbors," described above. The term "lilies" **(līlia)** was applied to the conelike holes in the center of which sharpened stakes were set. In World War II the Russians called such devices "asparagus." **Stimulī,** "goads," applied to the barbed pieces of iron set in pieces of wood and implanted in the earth, is another instance of soldier slang. They served the same purpose as the four-pronged iron "crow feet" which the early settlers used to scatter about the frontier forts for prowling Indians to step on. The lead slingstones, or bullets, used by the Romans were called "acorns" **(glandēs);** the French call bullets "chestnuts" or "prunes." "Grenade" came through French from Latin **grānātum,** "pomegranate." "Grapeshot" was the name of one kind of artillery ammunition in earlier years.

QUESTIONS

1. What sort of artillery did the Romans have?
2. How has the introduction of gunpowder affected warfare?
3. What aspects of warfare today are most like and which most unlike those of Caesar's day?

[1] According to some, the soldiers themselves received this name.

UNIT VII

DĒ BELLŌ GALLICŌ III–V

The Forum of Julius Caesar is located a short distance from the Roman Forum. It was begun in 54 B.C., during the period of Caesar's military campaigns. The Forum contained the Temple of Venus Genetrix from whom Caesar claimed descent. In this photo, we can see the shops *(tabernae)* behind the columns of the double colonnade.

Scala/Art Resource

Left: British troops crouch behind concrete tank obstacles. The Romans used ditches, moats, and earthen ramparts against men and machines. *Above:* Model of a battering ram.

Lesson LXXVI

The selections in this and the next lesson are from Book III of Caesar's *Gallic War,* which deals with the campaign against the Veneti. The events described took place in 56 B.C.

Summary of Chapters 1–13. After subduing the Belgians, Caesar decides to make access to their northern country easy and safe for Roman traders by opening a road through the Alps to Italy by way of what we now call the Great St. Bernard Pass. He accordingly sends Servius Galba with a small force to guard this pass and hold the Alpine tribes in check. Galba takes up winter quarters in Octodurus (see map, pp. 180–181). This proves to be a death trap, for the mountaineers, who had pretended to submit, suddenly gather in large numbers on the heights above and attack the Romans before they have completed their fortifications. Galba beats them off, but finding it impossible to get supplies, he burns the village, destroys his camp, and withdraws to the Province.

Caesar had sent Publius Crassus with a legion to establish winter quarters among the coast tribes of what is now Brittany and Normandy. Foremost of these were the Věn'etī. They had pretended to submit and had sent hostages to Crassus but later, in order to force him to restore their hostages, they seize some of the officers sent by him to arrange for supplies. All the northwestern seacoast tribes combine to resist the Romans and send an embassy to Crassus, demanding the hostages. Caesar at once orders ships

272

to be built at the mouth of the Liger (Loire) and oarsmen to be procured from the Province, and hastens north in the early spring. He sends Labienus to the Treveri, near the Rhine, to keep the Belgians under control and to prevent the Germans, whom the Belgians had asked for aid, from crossing the Rhine. Crassus is sent to Aquitania to prevent help from being sent from there into Gaul. Brutus is sent to prevent the coast tribes of the north from aiding the Veneti. Decimus Brutus is put in charge of the fleet which is being obtained from the pacified districts.

The towns of the Veneti are almost inaccessible from the land side because high tide cuts them off, and from the sea because low tide causes ships to be stranded in the shallows. In case of extreme danger the Veneti move from town to town by ship, taking all with them. They have a powerful fleet of seagoing vessels which have every advantage over the Roman galleys, because they have high prows and flat keels and are fitted with sails, being well adapted to fighting in shallow water or to riding out storms at sea.

400. THE FIRST BATTLE ON THE ATLANTIC

III, 14. Complūribus expugnātīs oppidīs, Caesar, ubi intellēxit frūstrā tantum labōrem sūmī, neque hostium fugam, captīs oppidīs, reprimī neque eīs nocērī [1] posse, statuit exspectandam classem.[2] Quae ubi convēnit ac prīmum ab hostibus vīsa est, circiter CCXX nāvēs eōrum parātissimae atque omnī genere armōrum ōrnātissimae ex portū 5 profectae nostrīs adversae cōnstitērunt; neque satis Brūtō,[3] quī classī praeerat, vel tribūnīs mīlitum centuriōnibusque, quibus singulae nāvēs erant attribūtae, cōnstābat quid agerent [4] aut quam ratiōnem pugnae īnsisterent. Rōstrō [5] enim nocērī nōn posse cognōverant; turribus autem excitātīs, tamen [6] hās altitūdō puppium ex [7] barbarīs nāvibus 10 superābat ut neque ex īnferiōre locō satis commodē tēla adigī possent et missa [8] ā Gallīs gravius acciderent. Ūna erat magnō ūsuī rēs praeparāta ab nostrīs—falcēs praeacūtae īnsertae affīxaeque longuriīs [9] nōn absimilī [10] fōrmā mūrālium falcium. Hīs [11] cum [12] fūnēs quī antemnās ad mālōs dēstinābant [13] comprehēnsī adductīque erant, 15 nāvigiō [14] rēmīs incitātō, praerumpēbantur. Quibus abscīsīs, antemnae

---

[1] *that they could not be injured* (**599**, 6, *a*).   [2] i.e., his own.
[3] With **cōnstābat**. This is Decimus Brutus, not the more famous Marcus.
[4] *what they should do.*
[5] *ship's beak.* Ablative, not dative. The ships of the Veneti were made of oak.
[6] What does **tamen** show as to the force of the preceding ablative absolute?
[7] *on.*   [8] *those thrown.*   [9] *long poles.*
[10] *not unlike that of;* **fōrmā** is ablative of description.
[11] Ablative of means, with **comprehēnsī.**
[12] *whenever.*   [13] *bound to the masts.*   [14] i.e., the attacking Roman ship.

necessāriō concidēbant; ut, cum omnis Gallicīs nāvibus [15] spēs in vēlīs armāmentīsque cōnsisteret, hīs ēreptīs, omnis ūsus nāvium ūnō tempore ēriperētur.[16] Reliquum erat certāmen positum in virtūte, quā nostrī
20 mīlitēs facile superābant atque eō magis, quod in cōnspectū Caesaris atque omnis exercitūs rēs gerēbātur, ut nūllum paulō fortius [17] factum latēre posset; omnēs enim collēs ac loca superiōra, unde erat propin-quus dēspectus in mare, ab exercitū tenēbantur.

QUESTIONS

1. Who commanded the Roman fleet?
2. Why were the Romans particularly brave?
3. In what three ways did the Roman and Venetan ships differ?

401. Grammar Review

Purpose and result clauses (606, 2, 3, 4, 8).

402. Translation

1. The ships of the enemy were so high that the Romans could not throw their spears.
2. The soldiers fought with great courage in order not to be beaten in the sight of Caesar.

403. Word Study

Classis orginally meant a calling out of citizens for military service, or draft. Then it came to mean any group, or *class*. One specialized meaning was that of the naval *class,* or *fleet.*

From what Latin words are the following derived: **abscīdō, absimilis, affīgō, attribuō, concidō, praerumpō, reprimō?**

Explain *affix, attribution, insertion, latent, repression.*

---

[15] *in the case of the Gallic ships;* dative of reference.
[16] The Gallic ships, unlike those of the Romans, had no oars.
[17] *a little braver (than usual).*

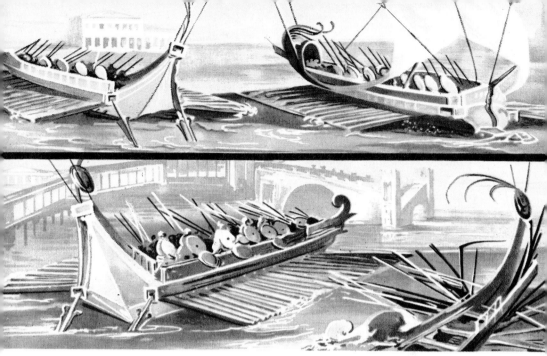

Fortasse trans aquam in Britanniam procedemus. This wall painting from Pompeii shows Roman warships in a battle. The soldiers are visible but the rowers are below deck. In the lower panel one of the ships has been overpowered and beached.

Lesson LXXVII

404. A DECISIVE VICTORY

III, 15. Dēiectīs (ut dīximus) antemnīs, cum[1] singulās[2] bīnae ac ternae nāvēs circumsteterant, mīlitēs summā vī trānscendere in hostium nāvēs contendēbant. Quod postquam barbarī fierī animadvertērunt, expugnātīs complūribus nāvibus, cum eī reī nūllum reperīrētur auxilium, fugā salūtem petere contendērunt. Ac iam conversīs in eam 5 partem nāvibus quō[3] ventus ferēbat,[4] tanta subitō tranquillitās exstitit ut sē ex locō movēre nōn possent. Quae quidem rēs ad negōtium cōnficiendum maximē fuit opportūna; nam singulās nostrī cōnsecūtī expugnāvērunt, ut perpaucae ex omnī numerō noctis interventū ad terram pervenīrent, cum[5] ab hōrā ferē quārtā[6] usque ad sōlis occā- 10 sum pugnārētur.

[1] *whenever.* [2] *each (Gallic vessel).* [3] Adverb. [4] *was blowing.*
[5] Loosely attached to the preceding: *the fighting going on,* etc.
[6] The Roman hour was one-twelfth of daylight and therefore varied from 45 to 75 minutes according to the time of year. Roughly, the fourth hour would be about 10 A.M.

16. Quō proeliō bellum Venetōrum tōtīusque ōrae maritimae cōnfectum est. Nam cum [7] omnis iuventūs, omnēs etiam graviōris [8] aetātis, in quibus aliquid cōnsilī aut dignitātis fuit, eō convēnerant, tum
15 nāvium [9] quod ubīque fuerat [9] in ūnum locum coēgerant; quibus āmissīs reliquī neque quō [10] sē reciperent neque quem ad modum oppida dēfenderent habēbant. Itaque sē suaque omnia Caesarī dēdidērunt. In quōs eō [11] gravius Caesar vindicandum [12] statuit, quō dīligentius in reliquum tempus ā barbarīs iūs lēgātōrum cōnservārētur.
20 Itaque omnī senātū necātō, reliquōs sub corōnā [13] vēndidit.

Summary of Chapters 17–19. Caesar sends Sabinus to subdue the northern allies of the Veneti near Avranches in Normandy. Knowing that he must employ strategy to deal with their overwhelming numbers, Sabinus bribes a Gaul to play the role of a deserter and tell the Gauls that Sabinus is going to Caesar's aid. The ruse works, for the Gauls immediately attack Sabinus in his camp, whereupon, having the advantage of position, he orders his trained soldiers to charge them from the right and left gates and sends them flying. The enemy at once surrenders.

19. Sīc ūnō tempore et dē nāvālī pugnā Sabīnus et dē Sabīnī victōriā Caesar est certior factus, cīvitātēsque omnēs sē statim Titūriō dēdidērunt. Nam ut ad bella suscipienda Gallōrum alacer ac prōmptus est animus, sīc mollis ac minimē resistēns ad calamitātēs ferendās
25 mēns eōrum est.

QUESTIONS

1. What won the sea battle for the Romans?
2. Why did Caesar punish the Veneti more severely than he had punished others?
3. From Caesar's description of the spirit of the Gauls, what do you infer was his idea of Roman spirit?

405. Grammar Review

Conjugation of **ferō** (**590**).
Genitive of the whole (**598**, 3).

---

[7] With **tum:** *not only . . . but also.*
[8] *more advanced.* What literally? Age is thought of as a burden.
[9] Depends on **quod:** *all the ships there were anywhere.*
[10] (*a place*) *where they might take refuge or means whereby.*
[11] *all the more severely,* looking forward to **quō,** for which see **606,** 4.
[12] *that punishment ought to be inflicted.*
[13] "under the crown," i.e., *as slaves.* Prisoners of war were crowned with wreaths when offered for sale.

406. Translation

1. Two of Caesar's ships surrounded one of the enemy's ships.
2. When Caesar had brought together enough ships, he attacked the enemy.

407. Vocabulary

bīnī, –ae, –a, *two at a time*
circumsistō, –ere, –stetī,
——, *surround*
maritimus, –a, –um, *of the sea;*
ōra maritima, *seacoast*

opportūnus, –a, –um, *opportune,*
advantageous
usque, adv., *up to*
ventus, –ī, m., *wind*

Review **alacer, expugnō, necō, statim.**

408. Word Study

From what Latin words are the following derived: **dēiciō, dignitās, interventus, maritimus, nāvālis, perpaucī?**

Explain *alacrity, binary, combine, coronation, dejection, dignitary, intervention, maritime, mollify, ventilate.*

Summary of Chapters 20–29. Crassus, who had been sent by Caesar to subdue Aquitania, is attacked by the Sotiates. He defeats them and captures their city. Advancing farther, Crassus faces a formidable Aquitanian army, which fights according to Roman tactics. Since the enemy's forces are being strengthened daily, Crassus decides to attack their camp at once. Finding that the rear gate is not well guarded, he makes a surprise attack and routs the enemy. The various tribes of Aquitania now surrender and send hostages. In the north, Caesar defeats the Morini and Menapii, who, avoiding a pitched battle, seek refuge in their forests. The Romans pursue and attempt to cut their way after them, but storms prevent. After ravaging the enemy's country, Caesar returns to winter in recently conquered territory.

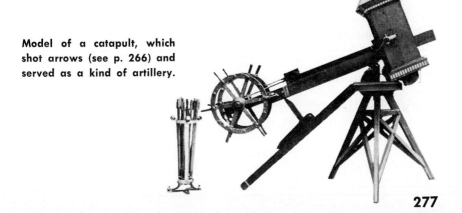

Model of a catapult, which shot arrows (see p. 266) and served as a kind of artillery.

Glans, or bullet (p. 269), with the word
feri, "strike," intended for the enemy. In
World War II the Germans painted the
names of Churchill and others on bombs.

Lesson LXXVIII

In Book IV of the *Gallic War,* represented by Lessons LXXVIII to
LXXXV, Caesar describes his war with the Suebi, a German tribe, and his
first expedition to Britain, made in 55 B.C.

409. DESCRIPTION OF THE SUEBI [1]

IV, 1. Eā quae secūta est hieme, quī [2] fuit annus Cn. Pompeiō [3] M.
Crassō cōnsulibus, Usipetēs Germānī [4] et item Tencterī magnā cum
multitūdine hominum flūmen Rhēnum trānsiērunt, nōn longē ā marī
quō [5] Rhēnus īnfluit. Causa trānseundī fuit quod ab Suēbīs complūrēs
5 annōs exagitātī bellō premēbantur et agrī cultūrā prohibēbantur.

Suēbōrum gēns est longē maxima et bellicōsissima Germānōrum
omnium. Hī centum pāgōs habēre dīcuntur, ex quibus quotannīs
singula [6] mīlia armātōrum bellandī causā suīs ex fīnibus ēdūcunt.
Reliquī, quī domī mānsērunt, sē atque illōs alunt. Hī rūrsus in vicem
10 annō post in armīs sunt, illī domī remanent. Sīc neque agrī cultūra
nec ratiō atque ūsus bellī intermittitur. Sed prīvātī agrī apud eōs nihil
est, neque longius annō [7] remanēre ūnō in locō colendī causā licet.
Neque multum frūmentō, sed maximam partem [8] lacte atque pecore
vīvunt, multumque [9] sunt in vēnātiōnibus; quae rēs [10] et cibī genere
15 et cotīdiānā exercitātiōne et lībertāte vītae, quod ā puerīs [11] nūllō
officiō aut disciplīnā assuēfactī [12] nihil omnīnō contrā voluntātem

---

[1] Ariovistus was a Sueban.

[2] Refers to **hieme** (fem.) but agrees with **annus** (masc.).

[3] Pompey and Crassus had been elected to the consulship for 55 B.C., with
Caesar's political support, on the understanding that they would gain for him
a five-year extension of his term as proconsular governor of Gaul, giving him
the opportunity to complete its conquest.

[4] *the German Usipetes.*   [5] Adverb.

[6] *a thousand each.* What then was their combined military strength?

[7] *than a year* (**601,** 5).   [8] *for the most part.*   [9] *they are much given to.*

[10] *this manner of life,* subject of **alit** and **efficit.**   [11] *from boyhood.*

[12] *accustomed to* (literally, *by*).

faciunt, et vīrēs alit et immānī corporum magnitūdine hominēs efficit. Atque in eam sē cōnsuētūdinem addūxērunt ut locīs [13] frīgidissimīs neque [14] vestītūs praeter pellēs habeant [15] quicquam, quārum propter exiguitātem magna est corporis pars aperta, et laventur in flūminibus. 20

QUESTIONS

1. What were the chief foods of the Suebi?
2. What do you infer was the Romans' chief food?
3. What was the nature of the military system of the Suebi?
4. What modern system of land ownership resembles theirs?
5. Why did the Germans cross the Rhine into Gaul? Where?

410. Word Study

From what Latin words are the following derived: **bellicōsus, exercitātiō, omnīnō, vestītus, voluntās?**

Explain *Frigidaire, lactic acid, lave, pellagra, pelt.*

Summary of Chapters 2–12. The Suebi tolerate the presence of traders solely that they may sell what they take in war. They are teetotalers. They ride bareback, often fighting on foot, making a speedy getaway on horseback if the fighting goes against them. They live in isolation, allowing no one to settle near their borders. They drive out the German Usipetes and Tencteri, who go to the Rhine, where they are held in check by the Menapii, a Gallic tribe, who have settlements on both sides of the river. The Germans, however, make a surprise attack and cross into Gaul. Caesar, knowing the fickle character of the Gauls, fears that they may unite with the Germans against him. He therefore decides to drive out the Germans. When their envoys come to him asking for lands in Gaul, he orders them to leave the country. They plead for delay and gain a truce, but later make a treacherous attack upon the Roman cavalry.

[13] Ablative of place (**601**, 14).   [14] With **et**: *not only not . . . but even.*
[15] When the perfect tense has present perfect force (as **addūxērunt** here), primary sequence may be used.

Model of Caesar's bridge over the Rhine; but the supports were upright piles.

Pontoon bridges, Roman (from a model)
and American. These "boat-bridges" are
suitable for military purposes because they
are easy to construct and destroy.

Lesson LXXIX

411. THE BRIDGING OF THE RHINE

IV, 12. In eō proeliō ex equitibus nostrīs interficiuntur IIII et LXX;
in hīs vir fortissimus, Pīsō Aquītānus, amplissimō genere [1] nātus, cuius
avus in cīvitāte suā rēgnum obtinuerat, amīcus ā senātū nostrō appellātus. Hic cum frātrī interclūsō ab hostibus [2] auxilium ferret, illum ex
5 perīculō ēripuit, ipse equō vulnerātō dēiectus quoad potuit fortissimē
restitit; cum circumventus, multīs vulneribus acceptīs, cecidisset, atque
id frāter, quī iam proeliō excesserat, procul animadvertisset, incitātō
equō, sē hostibus obtulit atque interfectus est.

Summary of Chapters 13–15. After this attack, the Germans send some
of their chiefs to ask for a truce. Caesar seizes them and then, advancing
upon the leaderless force of Germans, annihilates it.

16. Germānicō bellō cōnfectō, multīs dē causīs Caesar statuit sibi
10 Rhēnum esse trānseundum. Quārum illa fuit iūstissima, quod, cum
vidēret Germānōs tam facile impellī ut in Galliam venīrent, suīs

---

[1] Ablative of origin (**601**, 3). 　　　　[2] With **interclūsō.**

quoque rēbus ³ eōs timēre voluit, cum intellegerent et posse et audēre
populī Rōmānī exercitum ⁴ Rhēnum trānsīre.

17. Caesar hīs dē causīs quās commemorāvimus Rhēnum trānsīre
dēcrēverat; sed nāvibus trānsīre neque satis tūtum esse arbitrābātur 15
neque suae neque populī Rōmānī dignitātis ⁵ esse statuēbat. Itaque,
etsī summa difficultās faciendī pontis prōpōnēbātur propter lātitūdinem, rapiditātem, altitūdinemque flūminis, tamen id sibi contenden-
dum ⁶ aut aliter nōn trādūcendum exercitum exīstimābat.

(A technical description of the bridge follows. See illustration.)

QUESTIONS

1. What single reason does Caesar give for crossing the Rhine?
2. What other reasons can you give?
3. What method of crossing did he use?
4. What were his reasons for using this method?

412. Vocabulary

commemorō, 1, *mention*

dēcernō, –ere, dēcrēvī, dēcrētus,
decide

offerō, offerre, obtulī, oblātus, *offer;*

mē offerō, *rush against*

Review **aliter, amplus, eques, nāscor, tūtus.**

413. Word Study

From what Latin words are the following derived: **dēiciō, ēripiō,
interclūdō, trānseō?**

Explain *amplitude, commemorate, proposition, renaissance.*

Summary of Chapters 18–19. Caesar invades Germany and terrifies
the Germans. After eighteen days he returns to Gaul and destroys the
bridge.⁷

---

³ *for their own possessions* (**suīs** is emphatic). Caesar wanted to give them a
taste of their own medicine. Previously they had done their fighting in Gallic
territory.

⁴ Subject of **posse** and **audēre.**

⁵ Predicate genitive of possession: *not in accord with the dignity,* etc. The
building of the bridge, like the use of the atom bomb against Japan, was a
phase of psychological warfare, as it was intended to impress and scare the
Germans, since the Rhine had never before been bridged.

⁶ *he must make the effort.*

⁷ In World War II American troops were able to cross the Rhine by capturing
a bridge at Remagen, about 15 miles north of where Caesar built his bridge.
Near Remagen a Roman milestone of 162 A.D. was found, giving the distance
to Cologne as **m(īlia) p(assuum) XXX.**

Our Heritage

414. CAESAR'S INVASIONS OF BRITAIN

The history and culture of Britain, now called England, may be said to begin with Caesar's two invasions of 55 and 54 B.C., although centuries before that traders had gone there for tin. On August 25, 1946, in recognition of the significance of Caesar's invasion, a tablet "to commemorate the two thousandth anniversary of the landing" was unveiled at Deal (north of Dover), where it is thought Caesar first set foot on British soil.

It is hard for us, in these days of steamships, to imagine what an adventure it was for the Romans to set sail over strange seas from a port in a country that they were just conquering, to an entirely unknown land. Caesar went from Boulogne to Dover. Nowadays the usual Channel crossings are from Calais to Dover and from Boulogne to Folkstone.

Caesar made no attempt at a permanent conquest, perhaps because he saw that it would take too long and he was afraid that the hostile Gallic tribes at his back might cause trouble. He was a long way from home. As the historian Tacitus said a century and a half later, Caesar did not hand Britain over to future generations of Romans but merely revealed it to them. But that in itself was a very important contribution.

Almost exactly a century after Caesar, when all of Gaul, thanks to his efforts, had not only been pacified but Romanized, the Romans began the serious task of conquering Britain. This was under the emperor Claudius in 43 A.D. By the end of the century most of the island had been thoroughly Romanized.

Collingwood, quoting Sir Mortimer Wheeler, writes of Roman London:

Londinium was a civilized city, a comfortable one, with an efficient drainage system and an adequate water-supply. There were probably more buildings of stone and brick than at any subsequent period until after the Great Fire of 1666. There were more adequate and attractive facilities for bathing than ever until the latter part of Queen Victoria's reign.[1]

[1] R. G. Collingwood, *Roman Britain* (London, 1953), p. 58.

282

Lesson LXXX

415. SCARCITY OF INFORMATON ABOUT BRITAIN

IV, 20. Exiguā parte aestātis reliquā,[1] Caesar, etsī in hīs locīs (quod omnis Gallia ad septentriōnēs vergit) mātūrae sunt hiemēs, tamen in Britanniam proficīscī contendit, quod omnibus ferē Gallicīs bellīs [2] hostibus nostrīs inde [3] subministrāta [4] auxilia intellegēbat; et, sī tempus ad bellum gerendum dēficeret, tamen magnō sibi ūsuī fore [5] arbitrā- 5 bātur, sī modo īnsulam adīsset,[6] genus hominum perspexisset, loca, portūs, aditūs cognōvisset, quae omnia ferē Gallīs erant incognita. Neque enim temere [7] praeter mercātōrēs illō [8] adit quisquam, neque

[1] (being) left.
[2] Ablative of time. Note that Caesar feels the need of justifying the invasion of Britain by putting the blame on the enemy.
[3] i.e., ē Britanniā.   [4] Supply esse (see 207).   [5] = futūrum esse.
[6] For adiisset (591).   [7] neque temere, scarcely.   [8] Adverb.

The ruins of a Roman temple of the second century A.D. discovered in the heart of London. This photograph shows the area of the ancient altar.

British Information Services

eīs ipsīs quicquam praeter ōram maritimam atque eās regiōnēs quae
10 sunt contrā Galliam nōtum est. Itaque ēvocātīs [9] ad sē undique
mercātōribus, neque quanta [10] esset īnsulae magnitūdō, neque quae
aut quantae nātiōnēs incolerent, neque quem ūsum bellī habērent
aut quibus īnstitūtīs ūterentur, neque quī essent ad maiōrem nāvium
multitūdinem idōneī portūs reperīre poterat.
15   21. Ad haec cognōscenda priusquam perīculum [11] faceret, idōneum
esse arbitrātus C. Volusēnum [12] cum nāvī longā praemittit. Huic
mandat ut, explōrātīs omnibus rēbus, ad sē quam prīmum revertātur.
Ipse cum omnibus cōpiīs in Morinōs proficīscitur, quod inde erat
brevissimus in Britanniam trāiectus.[13] Hūc [14] nāvēs undique ex fīnitimīs
20 regiōnibus et quam [15] superiōre aestāte ad Veneticum [16] bellum fēcerat
classem iubet convenīre. Interim, cōnsiliō eius cognitō et per mercātōrēs perlātō ad Britannōs, ā complūribus eius īnsulae cīvitātibus ad
eum lēgātī veniunt, quī polliceantur obsidēs dare atque imperiō populī
Rōmānī obtemperāre. Quibus audītīs, līberāliter pollicitus hortātusque
25 ut in eā sententiā permanērent, eōs domum remittit et cum eīs ūnā
Commium, quem ipse, Atrebātibus superātīs, rēgem ibi cōnstituerat,
cuius et virtūtem et cōnsilium probābat, et quem sibi fidēlem [17] esse
arbitrābātur, cuiusque auctōritās in hīs regiōnibus magnī habēbātur,[18]
mittit. Huic imperat quās [19] possit adeat [20] cīvitātēs, hortēturque ut
30 populī Rōmānī fidem sequantur, sēque [21] celeriter eō ventūrum nūntiet.
Volusēnus, perspectīs regiōnibus quantum eī facultātis [22] darī potuit
quī [23] ex nāvī ēgredī ac sē barbarīs committere nōn audēret, quīntō diē
ad Caesarem revertitur quaeque ibi perspexisset renūntiat.

QUESTIONS

1. At what time of year did Caesar go to Britain?
2. What were his reasons for crossing into Britain?
3. How did he try to get information about the island?
4. Why did Caesar and his forces set out for the land of the Morini?

[9] *although he called.*   [10] A series of indirect questions, depending upon **reperīre.**
[11] *the attempt.*   [12] Subject of **esse** and object of **praemittit.**
[13] *passage.*   [14] *to this point* (the modern Boulogne).
[15] The antecedent is **classem.**
[16] *Venetan* (not "Venetian").
[17] But Commius deserted Caesar in 52 B.C.
[18] *was considered great;* literally, *of great* (*value*).
[19] The antecedent is **cīvitātēs.**
[20] Supply **ut** before **adeat, hortētur,** and **nūntiet.**
[21] i.e., Caesar.   [22] With **quantum:** *as far as opportunity,* etc.
[23] The antecedent is **eī:** *to one who.* For the mood see **606,** 10.

British Information Services

The white chalk cliffs of Dover. This one is known as Shakespeare Cliff. Caesar's troops landed several miles farther up the coast.

416. Grammar Review

Volitive clauses (**606,** 5).

417. Translation

1. "Persuade the Britons to send hostages and to refrain from war."
2. He urged his friend to investigate everything and to report as soon as possible.

418. Vocabulary

classis, –is, f., *fleet*	**nātiō, –ōnis,** f., *nation, tribe*
exiguus, –a, –um, *small*	**temere,** adv., *rashly, without reason*

Review **brevis, mātūrus, modo.**

419. Word Study

Motto of the United States Marine Corps: **semper fidelis.**

From what Latin words are the following derived: **ēvocō, fidēlis, incognitus, līberāliter, trāiectus?**

Explain *converge, divergent, fidelity, incognito.*

Summary of Chapter 22. The Morini submit as Caesar prepares to cross the Channel. He gathers together eighty transports for two legions and eighteen for the cavalry, besides several warships for the officers.

Lesson LXXXI

420. MIDNIGHT SAILING

IV, 23. Hīs cōnstitūtīs rēbus, nactus idōneam ad nāvigandum tempestātem tertiā ferē vigiliā nāvēs solvit, equitēsque in ulteriōrem portum prōgredī et nāvēs cōnscendere et sē sequī iussit. Ā quibus cum [1] paulō tardius esset administrātum, ipse hōrā diēī circiter quārtā cum prīmīs
5 nāvibus Britanniam [2] attigit atque ibi in omnibus collibus expositās hostium cōpiās armātās cōnspexit. Hunc ad ēgrediendum nēquāquam idōneum locum arbitrātus, dum reliquae nāvēs eō convenīrent ad hōram nōnam in ancorīs exspectāvit. Interim lēgātīs tribūnīsque mīlitum convocātīs, et quae ex Volusēnō cognōvisset et quae fierī vellet
10 ostendit. Hīs dīmissīs et ventum et aestum ūnō tempore nactus secundum, datō signō et sublātīs ancorīs, circiter mīlia passuum VII ab eō locō prōgressus, apertō ac plānō lītore nāvēs cōnstituit.

24. At barbarī, cōnsiliō Rōmānōrum cognitō, praemissō equitātū et essedāriīs,[3] reliquīs cōpiīs [4] subsecūtī nostrōs nāvibus ēgredī pro-
15 hibēbant.[5] Erat ob hās causās summa difficultās quod nāvēs propter magnitūdinem nisi in altō [6] cōnstituī nōn poterant; mīlitibus [7] autem,

[1] *while they had carried out his order a little too slowly.*
[2] Probably near the steep chalk cliffs of Dover.   [3] *chariot fighters.*
[4] Ablative of accompaniment (**601**, 6, *b*).   [5] Note the imperfect.
[6] *in deep water.*
[7] Dative of agent with **dēsiliendum, cōnsistendum, pugnandum.** Make it the subject in English.

Roman mosaic found at Canterbury, near the site where Caesar defeated the Britons.

ignōtīs locīs, impedītīs manibus, magnō et gravī onere armōrum pressīs, simul et dē nāvibus dēsiliendum et in flūctibus cōnsistendum et cum hostibus erat pugnandum; cum illī [8] aut ex āridō aut paulum in aquam prōgressī, omnibus membrīs expedītīs, nōtissimīs locīs, audācter tēla 20 conicerent et equōs īnsuēfactōs [9] incitārent. Quibus rēbus nostrī perterritī atque huius omnīnō generis [10] pugnae imperītī nōn eādem alacritāte ac studiō quō in pedestribus [11] ūtī proeliīs cōnsuēverant ūtēbantur.

25. Quod ubi Caesar animadvertit, nāvēs [12] longās, quārum speciēs 25 erat barbarīs inūsitātior, paulum removērī ab onerāriīs nāvibus et rēmīs incitārī et ad latus apertum [13] hostium cōnstituī, atque inde fundīs, sagittīs, tormentīs [14] hostēs prōpellī ac submovērī iussit. Quae rēs magnō ūsuī nostrīs fuit. Nam et nāvium figūrā et rēmōrum mōtū et inūsitātō genere tormentōrum permōtī barbarī cōnstitērunt ac paulum 30 pedem rettulērunt. At nostrīs mīlitibus cūnctantibus, maximē propter altitūdinem maris, quī [15] decimae legiōnis aquilam [16] ferēbat obtestātus deōs ut ea rēs legiōnī fēlīciter ēvenīret, "Dēsilīte," inquit, "commīlitōnēs, nisi vultis aquilam hostibus prōdere; ego certē meum reī pūblicae atque imperātōrī officium praestiterō." Hoc cum magnā vōce 35 dīxisset, sē ex nāvī prōiēcit atque in hostēs aquilam ferre coepit. Tum nostrī cohortātī inter sē [17] nē tantum dēdecus admitterētur, ūniversī ex nāvī dēsiluērunt. Hōs item ex proximīs nāvibus [18] cum cōnspexissent, subsecūtī hostibus appropinquāvērunt.

QUESTIONS

1. Why did Caesar not land immediately?
2. What were the difficulties faced by the Romans?
3. With what types of troops did the Britons keep the Romans from landing?
4. What was Caesar's motive in telling the story of the standardbearer?

[8] *while they,* i.e., the Britons. [9] *trained.*
[10] With **imperītī (598, 4)**. [11] i.e., *on land.*
[12] Subject of **removērī, incitārī, cōnstituī.** Note change of subject in **hostēs . . . submovērī.**
[13] Which side—right or left? Why? See pictures of soldiers in this book.
[14] *artillery.* See illustration on p. 272.
[15] Supply the antecedent: *the one who.*
[16] The Roman *eagle* or ensign, like our flag, was regarded with patriotic, almost religious, respect; its loss was considered a great disgrace.
[17] *one another.*
[18] Supply **eī:** *the men on the nearest ships,* used as subject of **cōnspexissent** and **appropinquāvērunt.**

421. Grammar Review

Datives of purpose and reference (**599,** 2–3).

422. Translation

1. Do you think that the ships will be any protection to us?
2. The shields were of no help to the soldiers struggling in the water.

423. Vocabulary

aestus, –ūs, m., *tide*
aquila, –ae, f., *eagle*
expōnō, –ere, exposuī, expositus,
  put out, draw up
mōtus, –ūs, m., *motion*

prōdō, –ere, –didī, –ditus,
  give (forth), betray
sagitta, –ae, f., *arrow*
ūniversus, –a, –um, *all together*

Idioms: **nāvis longa, nāvis onerāria.**

424. Word Study

From what Latin words are the following derived: **alacritās, commīlitō, flūctus, ignōtus, inūsitātus, mōtus, onerārius, praefectus, prōdō?**
Explain *aquiline, arid, dismember, estuary, expository, fluctuate.*

425. LATĪNUM HODIERNUM

Aquila [1]

Mīlitēs Rōmānī aquilam ante legiōnem ferēbant et nummī nostrī imāginem aquilae habent, sed paucī aquilam feram vīdērunt. In hortīs pūblicīs saepe vidērī potest. Ibi in caveā [2] sordidā trīstis sedet, velut rēx in exsiliō. Ō miseram captīvam! [3]

5 Dēmocratica nōn est. Lībertātem amat sed modo suam. Aliās avēs contemnit, etiam aliās aquilās atque pullōs [4] suōs, sī fāma vēra est. In rūpibus excelsīs vel in summīs arboribus ex rāmulīs nīdum [5] turpem aedificat. Ibi, sī Plīniō, auctōrī optimō, crēdimus, usque ad merīdiem sedet. Post merīdiem cibum petit.

10 Ex caelō in terrā serpentem vidēre potest, quod oculōs optimōs habet. Nōn numquam dīcitur in saxum dē caelō testūdinem dēmittere ut frangātur. Quondam aquila in caput calvum [6] poetae clārissimī, ut fāma est, testūdinem dēmīsit. Ō miserum poētam!

---

[1] Adapted from Norman W. DeWitt in *Classical Journal,* 49 (1954), p. 273.
[2] *cage.*   [3] Accusative of exclamation.   [4] *young.*   [5] *nest.*   [6] *bald.*

George Roper

A Roman villa at Chedworth, Gloucestershire, England.

Lesson LXXXII

426. DIFFICULT FIGHTING

IV, 26. Pugnātum est ab utrīsque ācriter. Nostrī tamen, quod neque ōrdinēs servāre neque firmiter īnsistere neque signa subsequī poterant, atque alius [1] aliā ex nāvī quibuscumque signīs occurrerat sē aggregābat, magnopere perturbābantur; hostēs vērō, nōtīs omnibus vadīs, ubi ex lītore aliquōs singulārēs ex nāvī ēgredientēs cōnspexerant, [5] incitātīs equīs, impedītōs adoriēbantur, plūrēs [2] paucōs circumsistēbant, aliī ab latere apertō in ūniversōs tēla coniciēbant. Quod cum animadvertisset Caesar, scaphās [3] longārum nāvium, item speculātōria nāvigia [4] mīlitibus complērī iussit, et quōs labōrantēs cōnspexerat hīs [5] subsidia submittēbat. Nostrī simul [6] in āridō cōnstitērunt, suīs omnibus 10 cōnsecūtīs,[7] in hostēs ·impetum fēcērunt atque eōs in fugam dedērunt; neque longius prōsequī potuērunt, quod equitēs cursum tenēre atque

---

[1] *one from one vessel, another from another would join whatever standard he met.*
[2] *several.*   [3] *boats.*   [4] *scout boats, i.e., patrol craft.*   [5] Antecedent of **quōs.**
[6] *as soon as* (**atque** or **ac** *is understood*).
[7] *and their fellow soldiers caught up with them* (ablative absolute).

īnsulam capere [8] nōn potuerant. Hoc ūnum ad prīstinam fortūnam [9] Caesarī dēfuit.

15   27. Hostēs proeliō superātī, simul [6] atque sē ex fugā recēpērunt, statim ad Caesarem lēgātōs dē pāce mīsērunt. Ūnā cum hīs lēgātīs Commius Atrebās vēnit, quem suprā dēmōnstrāverāmus ā Caesare in Britanniam praemissum. Hunc illī ē nāvī ēgressum, cum [10] ad eōs ōrātōris modō [11] Caesaris mandāta dēferret, comprehenderant atque 20 in vincula coniēcerant. Tum, proeliō factō, remīsērunt [12] et in petendā pāce eius reī culpam in multitūdinem contulērunt, et propter imprū-dentiam ut ignōscerētur [13] petīvērunt. Caesar questus quod,[14] cum ultrō, in continentem lēgātīs missīs, pācem ab sē petīssent, bellum sine causā intulissent, ignōscere [15] imprūdentiae [16] dīxit obsidēsque 25 imperāvit. Quōrum illī partem statim dedērunt, partem ex longin-quiōribus locīs arcessītam paucīs diēbus sēsē datūrōs dīxērunt. Intereā suōs in agrōs remigrāre iussērunt, prīncipēsque undique convenīre et sē cīvitātēsque suās Caesarī commendāre coepērunt.

QUESTIONS

1. What advantage did the Britons have?
2. What caused confusion among the Romans?
3. Why did Caesar have no cavalry to pursue the enemy?
4. How did Caesar come to the aid of those in difficulty?
5. What two things did Caesar complain about to the Britons?

427. Vocabulary

queror, querī, questus, *complain*   **ultrō,** adv., *voluntarily*
quīcumque, quaecumque, quodcumque,
   whoever, whatever

428. Word Study

Distinguish carefully the forms and derivatives of **quaerō** and **queror.** Derivatives of **quaerō** include *conquest, query, quest, question;* of **queror,** *quarrel, querulous.*

From what Latin words are the following derived: **commendō, comprehendō, continēns, imprūdentia, longinquus, mandātum, remi-grō, speculātōrius?**

Explain *aggregation, comprehension, mandate, recommendation.*

---

[8] *reach.* They and their ships were still at the **ulterior portus** (Chapter 23).
[9] Recognized by the Romans as an important factor in a general's success.
[10] *although.*   [11] *as an envoy.* What literally?   [12] Supply **eum.**
[13] Impersonal.   [14] Introduces **intulissent; cum** goes with **petīssent.**
[15] Supply **sē** as subject.   [16] For the case see **599,** 6.

Model of a Roman gate (second century A.D.) at Verulamium (St. Albans), England.

Lesson LXXXIII

429. STORM AND TIDE CAUSE TROUBLE

IV, 28. Hīs rēbus pāce cōnfirmātā, diē quārtō postquam est in Britanniam ventum,[1] nāvēs XVIII dē quibus suprā dēmōnstrātum est, quae equitēs sustulerant, ex superiōre portū lēnī ventō solvērunt. Quae cum appropinquārent Britanniae et ex castrīs vidērentur, tanta tempestās subitō coorta est ut nūlla eārum cursum tenēre posset sed 5 aliae eōdem unde erant profectae referrentur,[2] aliae ad īnferiōrem partem īnsulae, quae est propius sōlis occāsum, magnō suō[3] cum perīculō dēicerentur. Quae[4] tamen, ancorīs iactīs, cum fluctibus complērentur, necessāriō adversā nocte[4] in altum prōvectae continentem petīvērunt. 10

[1] *they came,* literally, *it was come;* see **394,** note 12.
[2] Still part of the **ut** clause.
[3] *to themselves.*
[4] *Nevertheless, when after anchoring they were filling with water, in the face of the night,* etc.

29. Eādem nocte accidit ut esset lūna plēna,[5] quī diēs [6] maritimōs aestūs maximōs in Ōceanō efficere cōnsuēvit, nostrīsque id erat incognitum. Ita ūnō tempore et longās nāvēs, quibus Caesar exercitum [7] trānsportandum cūrāverat quāsque in āridum subdūxerat, aestus complēbat, et onerāriās, quae ad ancorās erant dēligātae, tempestās afflīctābat, neque ūlla nostrīs facultās aut administrandī aut auxiliandī dabātur. Complūribus nāvibus frāctīs, reliquae cum essent ad nāvigandum inūtilēs, magna tōtīus exercitūs perturbātiō facta est. Neque enim nāvēs erant aliae quibus reportārī possent,[8] et omnia deerant quae ad reficiendās nāvēs erant ūsuī; et, quod omnibus cōnstābat hiemārī in Galliā oportēre, frūmentum in hīs locīs [9] in hiemem prōvīsum nōn erat.

30. Quibus rēbus cognitīs, prīncipēs Britanniae, quī post proelium ad ea quae iusserat Caesar facienda convēnerant, inter sē collocūtī, cum et equitēs et nāvēs et frūmentum Rōmānīs deesse intellegerent, et paucitātem mīlitum ex castrōrum exiguitāte cognōscerent—quae hōc [10] erant etiam angustiōra quod sine impedīmentīs Caesar legiōnēs trānsportāverat—optimum esse dūxērunt,[11] rebelliōne factā, frūmentō commeātūque nostrōs prohibēre et rem in hiemem prōdūcere; quod, hīs [12] superātīs aut reditū interclūsīs, nēminem posteā bellī īnferendī causā in Britanniam trānsitūrum cōnfīdēbant. Itaque rūrsus coniūrātiōne factā, paulātim ex castrīs discēdere et suōs clam ex agrīs dēdūcere [13] coepērunt.

QUESTIONS

1. What became of the cavalry?
2. What happened to the main fleet?
3. What three things did the Romans lack?

430. Grammar Review

Ablative of separation (**601,** 1).

431. Translation

1. Caesar was unwilling to depart from Britain until he received hostages.

---

[5] This statement has enabled astronomers to compute the date exactly, August 30 (55 B.C.).   [6] *time.*
[7] Only part of the army had been transported in the warships.
[8] For the subjunctive see **606,** 10.
[9] i.e., in Britain. For **in hiemem** cf. our colloquial use of "against."
[10] *on this account,* explained by the **quod** clause (**601,** 11).
[11] *thought.*   [12] i.e., Caesar's army.
[13] i.e., to mobilize an army.

Mosaic of Spring holding a bird in the hand, from the Roman villa at Chedworth.

2. The Britons thought that they could keep the Romans from their supplies.
3. "Let us cut these Romans off from (the possibility of) return; no one will cross the sea again to attack us."

432. Vocabulary

colloquor, colloquī, collocūtus,
  talk with, confer

cōnstat, *it is evident*
cūrō, 1, *care for, cause (to be done)*

Review **clam, commeātus, compleō, lēnis, prope, subitō.**

433. Word Study

The moon was thought to have an effect not merely on the tide, as Caesar discovered, but also on the human mind: "lunatic" means *moonstruck*.

From what Latin words are the following derived: **auxilior, colloquor, cūrō, exiguitās, inūtilis, perturbātiō, prōvehō, rebelliō, reditus, reportō?**

Explain *colloquy, curative, lunacy, lunar, plenipotentiary.*

Lunatic.

Lesson LXXXIV

434. NEW DIFFICULTIES

IV, 31. At Caesar, etsī nōndum eōrum cōnsilia cognōverat, tamen et ex ēventū [1] nāvium suārum et ex eō [2] quod obsidēs dare intermīserant, fore [3] id quod accidit suspicābātur. Itaque ad omnēs cāsūs subsidia comparābat. Nam et frūmentum ex agrīs cotīdiē in castra
5 cōnferēbat et quae [4] gravissimē afflīctae erant nāvēs, eārum māteriā atque aere ad reliquās reficiendās ūtēbātur, et quae [5] ad eās rēs erant ūsuī ex continentī comportārī iubēbat. Itaque cum summō studiō ā mīlitibus administrārētur,[6] XII nāvibus āmissīs, reliquīs ut nāvigārī satis commodē posset effēcit.[7]

Summary of Chapters 32–33. The Britons attack the seventh legion while it is collecting grain. They use chariots, which give them the mobility of cavalry. Caesar comes to the rescue.

10   34. Quibus rēbus perturbātīs nostrīs [8] tempore opportūnissimō Caesar auxilium tulit. Namque eius adventū hostēs cōnstitērunt, nostrī sē ex timōre recēpērunt. Quō factō, ad lacessendum hostem et committendum proelium aliēnum esse tempus arbitrātus, suō sē locō [9] continuit et, brevī tempore intermissō, in castra legiōnēs redūxit. Dum
15 haec geruntur, nostrīs omnibus occupātīs, quī erant in agrīs reliquī discessērunt.[10] Secūtae sunt continuōs complūrēs diēs tempestātēs quae et nostros in castrīs continērent [11] et hostem ā pugnā prohibērent. Interim barbarī nūntiōs in omnēs partēs dīmīsērunt paucitātemque nostrōrum mīlitum suīs praedicāvērunt, et quanta praedae faciendae

---

[1] *accident to his ships.* What literally?
[2] *from the fact that* (explained by the **quod** clause).
[3] For **futūrum esse.** Its subject is **id.**   [4] Translate as if **eārum nāvium quae.**
[5] Supply **ea.**   [6] Impersonal.
[7] *he made it possible to sail well enough in the others;* **nāvigārī** is used impersonally.
[8] Dative with **auxilium tulit.**   [9] *in a favorable position.* What literally?
[10] i.e., Britons, to join the revolt.   [11] For the mood see **606,** 10.

atque in perpetuum suī līberandī [12] facultās darētur, sī Rōmānōs castrīs 20
expulissent,[13] dēmōnstrāvērunt. Hīs rēbus [14] celeriter magnā multitūdine peditātūs equitātūsque coāctā, ad castra vēnērunt.

36. Lēgātī ab hostibus missī ad Caesarem dē pāce vēnērunt. Hīs [15]
Caesar numerum obsidum quem ante imperāverat duplicāvit, eōsque
in continentem addūcī iussit. Ipse idōneam tempestātem nactus paulō 25
post mediam noctem nāvēs solvit; quae omnēs incolumēs ad continentem pervēnērunt; sed ex eīs onerāriae duae eōsdem portūs quōs [16]
reliquae capere [17] nōn potuērunt et paulō īnfrā [18] dēlātae sunt.

QUESTIONS

1. What led Caesar to expect trouble?
2. What preparations did Caesar make?
3. How did he use the ships that could not be repaired?
4. What postponed the final battle?

435. Grammar Review

Future passive participle and gerund (611–612).

436. Translation

1. The men were sent to fight.
2. There was no chance of attacking.
3. Caesar was occupied in repairing the ships.
4. They went out for the purpose of collecting grain.

437. Vocabulary

continuus, –a, –um, *successive*　　praedicō, 1, *announce*
lacessō, –ere, –īvī, –ītus, *attack*

438. Word Study

From what Latin words are the following derived: **adventus,
complūrēs, cōnferō, ēventus, paucitās?**

Explain *affliction, continuity, perpetuity, propinquity.*

Summary of Chapters 37–38. Three hundred soldiers from the two transports are attacked by the Morini. The Romans fight bravely and are rescued
by reinforcements. Caesar then sends Labienus to pacify the Morini.
Winter quarters are established among the Belgians. The Roman senate
decrees a thanksgiving of twenty days for Caesar's victories.

---

[12] *of freeing themselves forever.*　[13] *if they should drive.*　[14] *by this means.*
[15] *for them.*　[16] We say *as.*　[17] *reach.*
[18] i.e., down the coast.

British Information Services

The Roman lighthouse at Dover, England, 380 feet high, as it appears today. The solidity of its construction (in the first century A.D.) is an indication of the Romans' interest in a permanent conquest and colonization of Britain.

439. AMPHIBIOUS WARFARE—THEN AND NOW

Perhaps no aspect of Caesar's campaigns in Gaul illustrates more strikingly the similarity between the principles of ancient and modern warfare than does his account of the amphibious assault upon the British coast. The means and methods of warfare have changed very greatly in two thousand years, but the principles which underlie them theoretically remain the same. Caesar's neglect or ignorance of several of these principles very nearly brought disaster to the expedition.

296

Amphibious warfare, in which land troops are moved overseas and debark onto hostile territory, has always been one of the most hazardous and difficult operations of war. Its first requirement is that the attacker be able to maintain secure lines of communication from his bases to the area of operations. Since upon his return from Germany Caesar had forced the submission of most of the Morini, who occupied the coast from which he planned to sail, since troops had been dispatched to neutralize the remainder of the neighboring tribes, and finally since a force adequate to hold the harbor was to be left in Gaul, Caesar could be reasonably confident that his ships could move across the Channel unmolested.

The second necessity for a successful amphibious assault is command of the sea (and, today, command of the air) in the combat zone. It would appear that Caesar's defeat in 56 B.C. of the Venetans, the most powerful maritime nation in northern Gaul **(404)**, and the large number of warships and transports which he had constructed for that campaign and which had now assembled for the British expedition **(415)**, assured him that he would receive no serious challenge from hostile naval forces.

Another major consideration in amphibious warfare is the gathering of sufficient intelligence to enable the attacker to do three things: by knowledge of the enemy's location and concealment of his own, to deceive the enemy about the time and place of the intended landing; by assembling information about the enemy's coastline and beaches, to determine which spot is most favorable for landing heavily armed men from boats of shallow draft; and, finally, by having enough information about the tide and weather, to insure that the troops can be landed in calm water and that the invasion fleet will not be wrecked by storms. It was in the area of intelligence that Caesar most seriously failed. He admits that his interrogations of traders were unsatisfactory; instead, the traders themselves gave news of his plans to the Britons **(415)**. The embassy of Commius likewise was unsuccessful, and Volusenus' exploratory survey of the coast could scarcely have revealed much about landing conditions on the coast, since he himself did not dare disembark. The originally intended landfall was but a narrow strip of beach, easily defended from the cliffs behind it, and Caesar was forced to move seven miles up the coast to a smoothly sloping beach free of obstacles **(420)**.

A much more serious predicament arose when Caesar's men were set ashore in water too deep and waves too heavy to allow them to fight. Allied troops had similar difficulties in the landings in North Africa in 1942, although special landing craft had been designed to bring the troops almost up to dry land, and in France in 1944. In the emergency Caesar quickly improvised a method for landing the men from the warships of shallower draft, and rapidly discovered for himself the principle of clearing the beaches by naval shore bombardment. Caesar frankly admits that his legionaries were inexperienced in this type of warfare.

We could not expect Caesar to be familiar with all of the modern methods of weather prediction, but it seems strange that he and his staff were so unaware of the tides and the effect of the full moon upon them that they allowed a great part of the fleet to be swamped or wrecked. Of course, the English Channel is a notoriously treacherous body of water and subject to violent storms, like the one which so imperiled the Allied invasion of Normandy in 1944. So perhaps Caesar's failure to allow for this may be partially excused.

Once the first waves of attacking troops are landed, it is imperative that they advance far enough inland to seize the high ground surrounding the landing area, so that they can control the beachhead until their reinforcements and supplies are unloaded, and until all forces are ready to break out together, converting the action from amphibious to land warfare. It is very dangerous to be pinned down on a narrow beach by enemy infantry and artillery. If this happens, as it did when the Allies were on the Anzio beach in Italy in 1943, the enemy can concentrate all his forces against a very limited area. When Caesar's troops appeared, the Britons, perhaps unwittingly, adopted the proper defensive maneuver: while they could, they engaged the Romans in close combat at the shoreline. Furthermore, when the Britons finally did retire, Caesar was unable to extend his beachhead to any great distance, because his means of pursuit, the cavalry, had not been able to reach the scene of battle in time. Caesar frankly admits his lack of success in this respect **(426).** When the cavalry did arrive four days later, it enabled him to inflict a decisive defeat upon the natives and to prevent their interference with his plans for returning to the continent **(434).**

In the light of modern amphibious warfare, this first expedition to Britain was not an unqualified success. The second expedition in 54 B.C. went better; Caesar had more troops, a larger fleet, and specially designed landing craft. Although he still underestimated the important part played by weather and was seriously hampered by storms before his departure and by the desertion of Dumnorix and the Haeduan cavalry, the whole fleet arrived as a unit at the undefended beach. The convoy was so large that its mere appearance had caused the natives to retreat to higher ground. The landing was unopposed, the movement of the troops inland almost immediate, and the cavalry effective in driving the defenders inland.

The Roman baths at Chedworth, with a double floor for circulation of hot air.

Lesson LXXXV

Book V of the *Gallic War,* from which Lessons LXXXV to LXXXVII are taken, gives an account of Caesar's second invasion of Britain (54 B.C.) and of the Gallic uprisings which he faced upon his return.

Summary of Chapters 1–11. The winter following the first expedition to Britain is spent in preparation for a second invasion. After issuing orders for a large fleet to be ready early the next spring, Caesar sets out for Illyricum because he hears that the Pirustae are raiding the country adjoining his province. After subduing these, he sets out for Gaul, where he finds the ships ready. First, however, he decides to subdue the Treveri, among whom an anti-Roman spirit has developed. Caesar's appearance with an army is sufficient to quell the revolt. He then gives orders for his fleet to assemble at Portus Itius. He decides to take Dumnorix, the crafty and ambitious Haeduan, to Britain, for he fears that in his absence Dumnorix will cause trouble. While the troops are embarking and all is confusion in the Roman camp, Dumnorix escapes. He is soon captured and is killed while resisting arrest.

Caesar, leaving Labienus in charge in Gaul with three legions, takes five legions and 2,000 cavalry with him in more than 800 ships. After some difficulty with the tide, he lands in Britain without opposition. He afterwards learns that the Britons, scared by the number of ships, had taken to the hills. Leaving a force under Quintus Atrius sufficient to guard the ships, Caesar advances inland against the Britons and captures one of their forest strongholds. On the following day, while preparing to pursue them, he learns that a great storm has destroyed about forty ships and damaged many others. These are repaired and beached. The Britons put Cassivellaunus in charge of their army.

299

British Information Services

The early British monument at Stonehenge, probably connected with the worship of the dead (cf. p. 248). Similar stone circles exist at Avebury, Woodhenge, etc.

440. BRITAIN AND ITS PEOPLE

V, 12. Britanniae pars interior ab eīs incolitur quōs nātōs [1] in īnsulā ipsī dīcunt; maritima pars ab eīs quī praedae ac bellī īnferendī causā ex Belgiō trānsiērunt (quī omnēs ferē eīs nōminibus cīvitātum appellantur quibus [2] ortī ex cīvitātibus eō pervēnērunt) et, bellō illātō,
5 ibi remānsērunt atque agrōs colere coepērunt. Hominum est īnfīnīta multitūdō crēberrimaque aedificia ferē Gallicīs cōnsimilia, pecoris magnus numerus. Ūtuntur aut aere aut nummō aureō aut tāleīs [3] ferreīs ad certum pondus exāminātīs prō [4] nummō. Nāscitur ibi plumbum [5] album in mediterrāneīs regiōnibus, in maritimīs ferrum, sed eius
10 exigua est cōpia; aere [6] ūtuntur importātō. Māteria cuiusque generis

---

[1] *originated*, i.e., the natives of the interior claim to be the aboriginal inhabitants of Britain.

[2] *as those from which they originated and from which they migrated to this place.*

[3] *bars.*   [4] *instead of.*

[5] tin (literally, *white lead*). Today "white lead" is a different substance. The mines of Cornwall from early times furnished a large supply of tin, which was carried to all parts of the ancient world.

[6] *bronze,* a composition of copper and tin. Its widespread use at one period of history accounts for the name Bronze Age, immediately preceding the Iron Age. Earliest man belonged to the Stone Age, when all tools were made of stone.

ut in Galliā est praeter fāgum atque abietem.[7] Leporem [8] et gallīnam [9] et ānserem [10] gustāre fās nōn putant; haec tamen alunt animī voluptātisque causā.[11] Loca sunt temperātiōra quam in Galliā, remissiōribus frīgoribus.

13.[12] Īnsula nātūrā triquetra,[13] cuius ūnum latus est contrā Galliam. 15 Huius lateris alter angulus, quī est ad Cantium, quō ferē omnēs ex Galliā nāvēs appelluntur,[14] ad orientem sōlem, īnferior ad merīdiem spectat. Hoc latus pertinet circiter mīlia passuum D. Alterum vergit ad Hispāniam atque occidentem sōlem; quā ex parte est Hibernia, īnsula dīmidiō minor (ut exīstimātur) quam Britannia, sed parī spatiō 20 atque [15] ex Galliā est in Britanniam. In hōc mediō cursū [16] est īnsula quae appellātur Mona; complūrēs praetereā minōrēs obiectae [17] īnsulae exīstimantur; dē quibus īnsulīs nōn nūllī scrīpsērunt diēs continuōs XXX sub brūmam [18] esse noctem. Nōs nihil dē eō reperiēbāmus, nisi

---

[7] *beech and fir.*   [8] *hare.*   [9] *chicken.*

[10] *goose.* The origin of these taboos is uncertain.

[11] *for pastime and pleasure* (as pets).

[12] This chapter, while not geographically accurate, is interesting in that it describes Britain as the Romans imagined it to be, not one of whom at this time had ever sailed around it or explored its interior.

[13] *three-cornered.*   [14] Not from **appellō, –āre.**   [15] *as it is from.*

[16] *in mid-channel.*

[17] Supply **esse:** *are thought to lie off the coast;* literally, *opposite* (*the coast*).

[18] *winter solstice.* Caesar's source was incorrect on this point.

Roman arch in Lincoln, the only one in England under which traffic still flows.

British Information Services

25 certīs ex aquā [19] mēnsūrīs breviōrēs esse quam in continentī noctēs
vidēbāmus. Huius [20] est longitūdō lateris, ut [21] fert illōrum opīniō,
DCC mīlium. Tertium est contrā septentriōnēs, cui partī nūlla est
obiecta terra; sed eius angulus lateris maximē ad Germāniam spectat.
Hoc [22] mīlia passuum DCCC in longitūdinem esse exīstimātur. Ita
30 omnis īnsula est in circuitū vīciēs centum mīlium passuum. [23]

14. Ex hīs omnibus longē sunt hūmānissimī quī Cantium incolunt
(quae regiō est maritima omnis), neque multum ā Gallicā differunt
cōnsuētūdine. Interiōrēs plērīque frūmenta nōn serunt, sed lacte et
carne vīvunt pellibusque sunt vestītī. Omnēs vērō sē Britannī vitrō [24]
35 īnficiunt, quod caeruleum efficit colōrem, atque hōc [25] horridiōrēs
sunt in pugnā aspectū; [25] capillōque [25] sunt prōmissō.

QUESTIONS

1. What was the origin of the Britons?
2. What did the natives do with chickens?
3. What metals were once found in Britain?
4. Draw a map of Britain as described by Caesar.
5. Describe the inhabitants of Britain.

441. Vocabulary

ferrum, –ī, n., *iron*
interior, –ius, *interior*

pecus, pecoris, n., *cattle*

442. Word Study

Believe it or not, *goose* and **ānser** are derived from the same word.
Latin and English and most European languages are descended from a
language called Indo-European, which we know only from the common elements in its descendants. The masculine of goose is *gander*,
which looks a bit more like **ānser.**

Brūma is from **brevima (diēs),** the *shortest day* of the year; **brevima**
is a variant of **brevissima.**

From what Latin words are the following derived: **cōnsimilis, importō, īnfīnītus, mediterrāneus?**

Explain *album, albumen, angular, commensurate, disgust, gustatory, gusto, oriole, plumber, ponderous, voluptuous.*

[19] *with a water* (*glass*), resembling in principle the sand or hour glass.
[20] The side of Britain facing Ireland.   [21] *as their opinion goes.*
[22] Supply **latus.**
[23] Actually it is over twice as great, though the measurement of coast lines is
difficult, and we do not know how Caesar arrived at his estimate. See the map
on pp. 100–101.
[24] *woad* (a plant). Compare the war paint of the American Indians.
[25] Three different ablatives. What are they?

302

Head of Mithras found at Mansion House in the heart of London. Mithras was an oriental god favored by Roman soldiers.

British Information Services

Summary of Chapters 15–43. The Romans on their march are attacked by British charioteers and cavalry, but beat them off. The Britons, by retreating, induce the Roman cavalry to pursue. Then, leaping down from their chariots, they fight on foot, relieving one another at intervals. Later, when Caesar sends out a detachment to forage, the Britons attack his scattered troops and drive them to seek the protection of the legions who are standing guard. The latter charge and drive the Britons off. Caesar leads his army to the Tamesis (Thames) River, which he fords, and again routs the enemy. Cassivellaunus, the British leader, avoiding a general engagement, confines himself to guerrilla tactics. Meanwhile the Trinovantes, the strongest British tribe of that region, surrender and send hostages to Caesar. Other tribes do the same. After an unsuccessful attack on the Roman camp, Cassivellaunus surrenders. Caesar returns to Gaul with his army and prisoners. During the two invasions of Britain not a single ship carrying troops was lost.

Caesar finds it necessary, on account of the scarcity of provisions, to distribute his legions in six divisions among various Gallic tribes. The Gauls seize this opportunity to revolt. The Carnutes kill Tasgetius, whom Caesar had made king over them. Ambiorix, leader of the Eburones, attacks the camp of Sabinus and Cotta. In a conference, Ambiorix, assuming the role of friend, urges Sabinus to leave his camp and join either Cicero or Labienus. Sabinus and Cotta call a council of war. Sabinus favors acting upon the advice given by Ambiorix, but Cotta opposes. In the end Cotta yields. The army then leaves camp, loaded down with baggage, and is ambushed in a valley. Though the Romans fight bravely, they are gradually worn down. After Cotta is wounded, Sabinus has a conference with Ambiorix, at which he is treacherously murdered. The Romans then fight on till they are killed or commit suicide. Only a few escape; not one surrenders. Ambiorix then stirs up the Atuatuci and the Nervii. All proceed to attack Quintus Cicero, brother of the famous orator, in his winter quarters. All the Romans, including the sick and wounded, work day and night on the fortifications. At a conference with Cicero, the Nervii promise to let him and his army withdraw unharmed if Caesar will refrain from quartering his troops in their territory. Cicero is not deceived and refers them to Caesar. The Gauls then begin a siege. They set fire to the Roman camps with fire bombs and burning arrows.

303

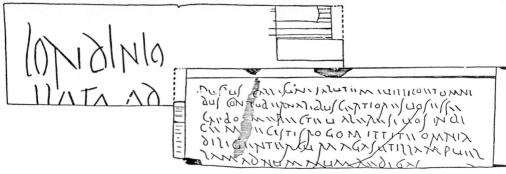

Latin letter on a wax tablet 1900 years old. It begins *Londinio*, "from London," and continues *Rufus Callisuni salutem*, "Rufus (son) of Callisunus greeting."

Lesson LXXXVI

443. TWO RIVAL HEROES

V, 44. Erant in eā legiōne fortissimī virī, centuriōnēs, quī iam prīmīs ōrdinibus appropinquārent, T. Pullō et L. Vorēnus. Hī perpetuās inter sē contrōversiās habēbant uter alterī anteferrētur, omnibusque annīs [1] dē locō contendēbant. Ex hīs Pullō, cum ācerrimē ad mūnī-
5 tiōnēs pugnārētur,

"Quid dubitās," inquit, "Vorēne, aut quem locum probandae virtūtis tuae exspectās? Hic diēs dē nostrīs contrōversiīs iūdicābit."

Haec cum dīxisset, prōcēdit extrā mūnītiōnēs quaeque pars hostium cōnfertissima est vīsa in eam irrumpit. Nē Vorēnus quidem sēsē tum
10 vāllō continet, sed omnium veritus opiniōnem subsequitur. Mediocrī spatiō relīctō, Pullō pīlum in hostēs immittit atque ūnum ex multi-tūdine prōcurrentem trāicit; quō [2] percussō exanimātōque, hunc scūtīs dēfendunt hostēs, in illum ūniversī tēla coniciunt neque dant prōgre-diendī facultātem. Trānsfīgitur scūtum Pullōnī [3] et iaculum in balteō
15 dēfīgitur. Āvertit hic cāsus vāgīnam [4] et gladium ēdūcere cōnantī [5] dextram morātur manum, impedītumque hostēs circumsistunt. Suc-currit inimīcus illī Vorēnus et labōrantī subvenit. Ad hunc sē cōnfestim ā Pullōne omnis multitūdō convertit. Vorēnus gladiō rem gerit atque, ūnō interfectō, reliquōs paulum prōpellit; dum cupidius īnstat, in

[1] *every year.* They were rivals for promotion (**locō**).
[2] The wounded Gaul; ablative absolute. Contrary to rule, **hunc** refers to the same person.
[3] For the case see **599,** 3. In English a genitive is used.
[4] *scabbard.* It was pushed to one side and hard to get at.
[5] Supply **eī:** *when he tried.*

locum dēiectus īnferiōrem concidit. Huic rūrsus circumventō subsidium 20
fert Pullō, atque ambō incolumēs, complūribus interfectīs, summā
cum laude intrā mūnītiōnēs sē recipiunt. Sīc fortūna in certāmine
utrumque versāvit[6] ut alter alterī inimīcus auxiliō salūtīque esset,
neque dīiūdicārī posset uter[7] virtūte anteferendus vidērētur.

45. Erat ūnus in castrīs Nervius nōmine Verticō, locō[8] nātus 25
honestō, quī ad Cicerōnem perfūgerat suamque eī fidem praestiterat.
Hic servō spē lībertātis magnīsque persuādet praemiīs ut litterās ad
Caesarem dēferat. Hās ille in iaculō illigātās[9] effert, et Gallus inter
Gallōs sine ūllā suspīciōne versātus ad Caesarem pervenit. Ab eō dē
perīculīs Cicerōnis legiōnisque cognōscitur.   30

QUESTIONS

1. Who quarreled and why?
2. Which attacked the enemy first?
3. What difficulty did he run into?
4. Which of the two soldiers was the braver?
5. How did Caesar get word of Cicero's situation?

444. Word Study

From what Latin words are the following derived: **anteferō, dēfīgō,
dīiūdicō, honestus, illigō, immittō, irrumpō, succurrō, trāiciō,
trānsfīgō?**

Explain *irruption, laudatory, percussion, succor.*

Summary of Chapters 46–47. Caesar immediately advances with two
legions to relieve Cicero. The Treveri, elated by their recent victory over
Sabinus, now menace Labienus, preventing him from joining Caesar.

---

[6] *dealt with.*   [7] *which seemed superior.*   [8] For the case see **601,** 3.
[9] Perhaps concealed in the shaft, which may have been wrapped as if mended.

Model of a Roman aqueduct at Cherchell, Algeria.

Anderson

Anderson

Roman relief of a ship carrying the still famous Moselle wine. Note the lucky eye.

Lesson LXXXVII

445. A CODED MESSAGE AND A CLEVER TRICK

V, 48. Caesar vēnit magnīs itineribus in Nerviōrum fīnēs. Ibi ex captīvīs cognōscit quae apud Cicerōnem gerantur quantōque in perīculō rēs sit. Tum cuidam ex equitibus Gallīs magnīs praemiīs persuādet utī ad Cicerōnem epistulam dēferat. Hanc Graecīs [1] cōnscrīptam litterīs
5 mittit, nē, interceptā epistulā, nostra ab hostibus cōnsilia cognōscantur. Sī adīre nōn possit, monet ut trāgulam cum epistulā dēligātā intrā mūnītiōnēs castrōrum abiciat. In litterīs scrībit sē cum legiōnibus profectum celeriter adfore; [2] hortātur ut prīstinam virtūtem retineat. Gallus perīculum veritus, ut erat praeceptum, trāgulam mittit. Haec
10 cāsū ad turrim adhaesit, neque ā nostrīs bīduō animadversa, tertiō diē ā quōdam mīlite cōnspicitur; ad Cicerōnem dēfertur. Ille perlēctam [3] in conventū mīlitum recitat maximāque omnēs laetitiā afficit. Tum fūmī incendiōrum [4] procul vidēbantur, quae rēs omnem dubitātiōnem adventūs legiōnum expulit.

---

[1] Probably Latin written in Greek letters. In effect the message was in code.
[2] For **adfutūrum esse.**   [3] *read through (silently)*; supply **epistulam.**
[4] Not of camp fires but of flaming villages fired by the Romans as they advanced.

306

Summary of Chapters 49–51. The Gauls rush to meet Caesar, who is warned by a message from Cicero. By pretending fear, Caesar induces the enemy to attack him on his own ground and defeats them with great loss.

52. Longius prōsequī veritus, quod silvae palūdēsque intercēdē- 15 bant, omnibus suīs incolumibus, eōdem diē ad Cicerōnem pervēnit. Īnstitūtās turrēs, testūdinēs mūnītiōnēsque hostium admīrātur; prō-ductā legiōne, cognōscit nōn decimum quemque [5] esse reliquum mīli-tem sine vulnere. Ex hīs omnibus iūdicat rēbus quantō cum perīculō et quantā virtūte rēs sint administrātae. Cicerōnem prō eius meritō 20 legiōnemque collaudat; centuriōnēs singillātim tribūnōsque mīlitum appellat, quōrum ēgregiam fuisse virtūtem testimōniō Cicerōnis cognōverat.

QUESTIONS

1. How did Cicero get the message from Caesar?
2. What confirmation of the message did he get?
3. What percentage of Cicero's men were wounded?

446. Word Study

From what Latin words are the following derived: **admīror, conventus, dubitātiō, intercēdō, praecipiō, singillātim?**

Explain *adhesive, cohesive, conspicuous, epistolary, indubitable.*

Summary of Chapters 53–58. Despite this victory, the spirit of revolt spreads fast among the Gauls, and Caesar decides to spend the winter with his army. The leader of the Treveri prepares to attack the camp of Labienus, but the latter, feigning fear, lures the enemy to the very walls of his camp; then, by a surprise attack, he routs the Gauls, and the leader is killed. After that Caesar states that he "found Gaul a little more peaceful."

---

[5] *not one soldier in ten.*

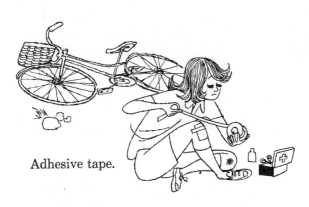

Adhesive tape.

UNIT VIII

DĒ BELLŌ GALLICŌ VI–VII

After spending nine years (58–50 B.C.) conquering and governing Gaul, Julius Caesar crossed the Rubicon River into Italy proper in 49 B.C., precipitating a Civil War. Within three years, he had overpowered his opposition and had become ruler of the Western world. In the next few years, he brought about many reforms in Roman political and economic life. This painting by Pujol (1787–1861) shows Julius Caesar proceeding to the Senate on the Ides of March, 44 B.C., the day he was assassinated.

Giraudon/Art Resource

Lesson LXXXVIII

The readings in Lessons LXXXVIII to XCIV, selected from Book VI of the *Gallic War,* are devoted to Caesar's comparison of the way of life of the Gauls with that of the Germans.

Summary of Chapters 1–10. Caesar, expecting a more serious revolt in Gaul, increases his force by three legions, one of which is supplied by Pompey. Ambiorix and the Treveri are plotting against him. The Nervii, Atuatuci, Menapii, and all the Germans on the Gallic side of the Rhine are in arms against the Romans, and the Senones are conspiring with the Carnutes and other states. Accordingly, before the winter is over, Caesar leads a strong force against the Nervii and compels them to surrender. He next marches against the Senones, and they, as well as the Carnutes, surrender. Caesar, now free to attack Ambiorix, proceeds to cut him off from allied aid. He first crushes the Menapii. Meanwhile, with reinforcements received from Caesar, Labienus defeats the Treveri. Caesar again builds a bridge and crosses the Rhine, partly to prevent the Germans from sending aid to the Treveri, partly to prevent Ambiorix from finding refuge in Germany. He learns that the Suebi have sent aid to the Treveri and are now mobilizing in a large forest.

447. GALLIC LEADERS

VI, 11. Quoniam ad hunc locum [1] perventum est, nōn aliēnum esse vidētur dē Galliae Germāniaeque mōribus et quō [2] differant hae nātiōnēs inter sē prōpōnere. In Galliā nōn sōlum in omnibus cīvitātibus atque in omnibus pāgīs partibusque, sed paene etiam in singulīs
5 domibus factiōnēs sunt, eārumque factiōnum sunt prīncipēs quī summam auctōritātem eōrum [3] iūdiciō habēre exīstimantur, quōrum [4] ad arbitrium iūdiciumque summa omnium rērum cōnsiliōrumque redeat.[5]

12. Cum Caesar in Galliam vēnit, alterius factiōnis prīncipēs erant Haeduī, alterius Sēquanī. Hī cum per sē minus valērent, quod summa
10 auctōritās antīquitus erat in Haeduīs magnaeque eōrum erant clien-

---

[1] i.e., in the story.   [2] *in what respect.*   [3] i.e., the Gauls.
[4] The antecedent is **prīncipēs**, not **eōrum:** *so that to their decision.*
[5] *is referred.* For the mood see **606,** 10.

310

tēlae, Germānōs atque Ariovistum sibi adiūnxerant eōsque ad sē magnīs
iactūrīs pollicitātiōnibusque perdūxerant. Proeliīs vērō complūribus
factīs secundīs atque omnī nōbilitāte Haeduōrum interfectā, tantum
potentiā antecesserant ut magnam partem clientium ab Haeduīs ad sē
trādūcerent obsidēsque [6] ab eīs prīncipum fīliōs acciperent, et pūblicē 15
iūrāre cōgerent nihil sē contrā Sēquanōs cōnsilī [7] initūrōs,[8] et partem
fīnitimī agrī per vim occupātam possidērent [9] Galliaeque tōtīus prīncipātum obtinērent. Quā necessitāte adductus Dīviciācus auxilī petendī
causā Rōmam ad senātum profectus, īnfectā rē, redierat. Adventū
Caesaris factā commūtātiōne rērum, obsidibus Haeduīs redditīs, 20
veteribus clientēlīs restitūtīs, novīs per Caesarem comparātīs, quod eī
quī sē ad eōrum amīcitiam aggregāverant meliōre condiciōne atque
aequiōre imperiō sē ūtī [10] vidēbant, reliquīs rēbus [11] eōrum grātiā
dignitāteque amplificātā, Sēquanī prīncipātum dīmīserant. In eōrum
locum Rēmī successerant; quōs quod adaequāre apud Caesarem grātiā 25
intellegēbātur,[12] eī [13] quī propter veterēs inimīcitiās nūllō modō cum
Haeduīs coniungī poterant, sē Rēmīs in clientēlam dicābant.[14] Hōs illī
dīligenter tuēbantur; ita et novam et repente collēctam auctōritātem
tenēbant. Eō tum statū [15] rēs erat ut longē prīncipēs habērentur Haeduī,
secundum locum dignitātis Rēmī obtinērent.   30

QUESTIONS

1. How were the Gallic leaders chosen?
2. Which tribe had the most power before Caesar came?
3. Which tribe was first after Caesar's arrival? Which was second?

448. Vocabulary

iūrō, 1, *swear*   tueor, tuērī, tūtus, *guard*
repente, adv., *suddenly*   vetus, gen. veteris, *old*

Review colligō, nōn sōlum . . . sed etiam, redeō.

449. Word Study

From what Latin words are the following derived: adaequō, antīquitus, arbitrium, clientēla, commūtātiō, iactūra, īnfectus, iūdicium,
necessitās, pollicitātiō, potentia, status?
Explain *adjunct, dedicate, inveterate, status, tutor, veteran.*

---

[6] *(as) hostages.*   [7] Depends upon nihil.
[8] Supply esse—indirect statement depending upon iūrāre.
[9] *kept;* coördinate with trādūcerent, acciperent, cōgerent, above.
[10] *that they were enjoying.*   [11] *in all other respects.*
[12] Used impersonally: *because it was understood that these* (quōs) *equaled* (*the
    Haeduans*).   [13] *those* (*other tribes*).
[14] With in clientēlam: *they attached themselves.*   [15] *situation.*

Head of Neptune found at
Marseilles, France, in 1947.

Service des Monuments Historiques

Lesson LXXXIX

450. THE DRUIDS

VI, 13. In omnī Galliā eōrum hominum quī aliquō sunt numerō[1]
atque honōre genera sunt duo. Nam plēbēs[2] paene servōrum habētur
locō, quae nihil audet per sē, nūllī adhibētur cōnsiliō. Plērīque, cum
aut aere aliēnō aut magnitūdine tribūtōrum aut iniūriā potentiōrum
5 premuntur, sēsē in servitūtem dant nōbilibus; quibus in hōs[3] eadem
omnia sunt iūra quae[4] dominīs in servōs. Sed dē hīs duōbus generibus
alterum est druidum, alterum equitum. Illī rēbus dīvīnīs intersunt,
sacrificia pūblica ac prīvāta prōcūrant, religiōnēs[5] interpretantur. Ad
hōs magnus adulēscentium numerus disciplīnae causā concurrit,
10 magnōque hī[6] sunt apud eōs[7] honōre. Nam ferē dē omnibus contrōversiīs pūblicīs prīvātīsque cōnstituunt; et, sī quod est facinus admis-
sum, sī caedēs facta, sī dē hērēditāte, dē fīnibus contrōversia est,
īdem[8] dēcernunt; praemia poenāsque cōnstituunt; sī quī aut prīvātus

---

[1] of *some account* (with **aliquō**).
[2] = **plēbs.**
[3] *over them* (the enslaved plebeians).
[4] *as.*
[5] *religious questions.*
[6] The druids.
[7] All the Gauls.
[8] *likewise.*

aut populus eōrum dēcrētō nōn stetit,[9] sacrificiīs prohibent. Haec poena apud eōs est gravissima. Quibus [10] ita est prohibitum, hī numerō 15 impiōrum habentur, hīs [11] omnēs dēcēdunt, aditum eōrum sermōnemque dēfugiunt, nē quid ex contāgiōne incommodī [12] accipiant, neque hīs petentibus iūs redditur neque honōs [13] ūllus commūnicātur. Hīs autem omnibus druidibus praeest ūnus, quī summam inter eōs habet auctōritātem. Hōc mortuō, aut, sī quī [14] ex reliquīs praestat dignitāte, 20 succēdit, aut, sī sunt parēs plūrēs, suffrāgiō druidum dēligitur; nōn numquam etiam armīs dē prīncipātū contendunt. Hī certō annī tempore in fīnibus Carnutum,[15] quae regiō tōtīus Galliae media habētur, cōnsīdunt in locō cōnsecrātō; [16] hūc omnēs undique quī contrōversiās habent conveniunt eōrumque dēcrētīs iūdiciīsque pārent. Disciplīna [17] 25 in Britanniā reperta atque inde in Galliam trānslāta exīstimātur; et nunc quī dīligentius eam rem cognōscere volunt plērumque illō [18] discendī causā proficīscuntur.

QUESTIONS

1. What three classes were there among the Gauls?
2. What were the functions and powers of the druids?
3. What business did the druids transact at their annual meetings?

451. Vocabulary

adhibeō, –ēre, adhibuī, adhibitus,
   hold toward, admit to
commūnicō, 1, *share*
pāreō, –ēre, pāruī, pāritūrus,
   obey (with dative)

religiō, –ōnis, f., *religion,
   superstition*

Review **admittō, adulēscēns, caedēs, hūc, morior.**

452. Word Study

Proxy is shortened from *procuracy* and therefore means *taking care* of something *for* someone.

From what Latin words are the following derived; **adhibeō, commūnicō, cōnsecrātus, dēfugiō, sacrificium, tribūtum?**

Explain *consecration, heredity, interpretation, suffrage.*

---

[9] *did not abide by;* **dēcrētō** is ablative.   [10] Dative. The antecedent is **hī.**
[11] *from these* (**599**, 4).   [12] Genitive.
[13] Old form of **honor.**   [14] For the more usual **quis.**
[15] Chartres preserves the name of the Car'nutēs. Perhaps the annual Council on the Isle of Man is a survival of such meetings.
[16] They met in groves of oak trees, which were sacred, as was the mistletoe which grew on them. Our use of mistletoe at Christmas is an inheritance from the druids.   [17] *system* of druidism.   [18] Adverb.

313

Lesson XC

453. DRUIDS AND KNIGHTS

VI, 14. Druidēs ā bellō abesse [1] cōnsuērunt neque tribūta ūnā cum reliquīs pendunt. Tantīs excitātī praemiīs et suā sponte multī in disciplīnam conveniunt et ā parentibus propinquīsque mittuntur. Magnum ibi numerum versuum ēdiscere [2] dīcuntur. Itaque annōs
5 nōn nūllī vīcēnōs in disciplīnā permanent. Neque fās esse exīstimant ea [3] litterīs mandāre, cum [4] in reliquīs ferē rēbus, pūblicīs prīvātīsque ratiōnibus, Graecīs ūtantur litterīs. Id mihi duābus dē causīs īnstituisse videntur; quod neque in vulgus disciplīnam efferrī velint [5] neque eōs quī discunt litterīs cōnfīsōs minus memoriae studēre [6]—quod ferē
10 plērīsque accidit ut praesidiō litterārum dīligentiam in perdiscendō ac memoriam remittant. In prīmīs hoc volunt persuādēre,[7] nōn interīre animās,[8] sed ab aliīs post mortem trānsīre ad aliōs; atque hōc maximē ad virtūtem excitārī [9] putant, metū mortis neglēctō. Multa praetereā dē sīderibus atque eōrum mōtū, dē mundī ac terrārum magnitūdine,
15 dē rērum nātūrā, dē deōrum immortālium vī ac potestāte disputant et iuventūtī trādunt.

15. Alterum genus est equitum. Hī cum [10] est ūsus [11] atque aliquod bellum incidit (quod [12] ante Caesaris adventum ferē quotannīs accidere solēbat, utī aut ipsī iniūriās īnferrent aut illātās prōpulsārent [13]),
20 omnēs in bellō versantur, atque eōrum ut [14] quisque est genere cōpiīsque amplissimus, ita plūrimōs circum sē ambactōs [15] clientēsque habet. Hanc ūnam grātiam potentiamque nōvērunt.

---

[1] *to be exempt from.*   [2] Note the force of the prefix.

[3] *these principles.*   [4] *although.*

[5] Like the Egyptian priests and their hieroglyphs ("sacred writing").

[6] *pay less attention to the memory.*   [7] *prove.*

[8] *souls;* they believed in reincarnation.

[9] Supply **hominēs** as subject. Some of our Halloween customs are thought to go back to the druids.

[10] *whenever.*   [11] Noun: *need.*

[12] *and this,* explained by the **utī** clauses.

[13] *warded off injuries inflicted (by others).*   [14] *(in proportion) as.*

[15] *retainers* (a Gallic word).

1. What exemptions did the druids have?
2. What were the teaching methods of the druids?
3. What was their belief about the souls of the dead?
4. Why did the druids not put their teachings in writing?

454. Vocabulary

intereō, –īre, –iī, –itūrus, *perish*
metus, –ūs, m., *fear*

vulgus, –ī, n., *common people*

Review **efferō, neglegō, suā sponte.**

455. Word Study

The suffix **–tō (–sō, –itō)** is added to the stems of past participles to form verbs expressing the idea of *keeping on* ("frequentative" verbs): **prōpulsō** (from **prōpulsus**), *keep on warding off.*

From what Latin words are the following derived: **disputō, immortālis?**

Explain *disciple, disputant, divulge, immortality, mundane, sidereal, spontaneity, vulgar, Vulgate.*

Right: Model of a Roman watchtower on the Danube River. *Below:* Model of a tower made at Libbey High School, Toledo, Ohio.

315

The great Gallic Hammer-God. The hammer associates him with both the heavens and the underworld and the rustic panpipe with the woodlands; the Romans appear to have identified him with their own Jupiter, Dispater, and Silvanus. By the Gauls he was variously called Sucellus or Taranis. Around 200 of his images have been found.

Calvet Museum, Avignon

Lesson XCI

456. RELIGION

VI, 16. Nātiō est omnis Gallōrum admodum dēdita religiōnibus; atque ob eam causam quī sunt affectī graviōribus morbīs, quīque in proeliīs perīculīsque versantur, aut prō victimīs hominēs immolant aut sē immolātūrōs vovent, administrīsque[1] ad ea sacrificia druidibus
5 ūtuntur, quod, prō vītā hominis nisi hominis vīta reddātur, nōn posse deōs immortālēs plācārī arbitrantur; pūblicēque eiusdem generis habent īnstitūta sacrificia. Aliī immānī magnitūdine simulācra[2] habent, quōrum contexta vīminibus[3] membra vīvīs hominibus complent; quibus incēnsīs, circumventī flammā exanimantur hominēs. Supplicia
10 eōrum quī in fūrtō aut latrōciniō aut aliquā noxiā sint comprehēnsī grātiōra dīs[4] immortālibus esse arbitrantur; sed, cum eius generis cōpia dēficit, etiam ad innocentium supplicia dēscendunt.

---

[1] (*as*) *ministers.*   [2] *figures* (*of men*).   [3] *twigs.*   [4] = **deīs.**

17. Deōrum maximē Mercurium [5] colunt. Huius sunt plūrima simulācra; hunc omnium inventōrem artium ferunt,[6] hunc viārum atque itinerum ducem, hunc ad quaestūs pecūniae mercātūrāsque 15 habēre vim maximam arbitrantur; post hunc [7] Apollinem et Mārtem et Iovem et Minervam. Dē hīs eandem ferē quam [8] reliquae gentēs habent opīniōnem: Apollinem morbōs dēpellere, Minervam operum atque artificiōrum [9] initia trādere, Iovem imperium deōrum tenēre, Mārtem bella regere. Huic, cum proelium committere cōnstituērunt, ea 20 quae bellō cēperint [10] plērumque dēvovent; [11] cum superāvērunt, animālia capta immolant, reliquās rēs in ūnum locum cōnferunt. Multīs in cīvitātibus hārum rērum exstrūctōs cumulōs locīs cōnsecrātīs cōnspicārī licet.

18. Gallī sē omnēs ab Dīte patre prōgnātōs praedicant idque ab 25 druidibus prōditum dīcunt. Ob eam causam spatia omnis temporis nōn numerō diērum sed noctium [12] fīniunt; diēs nātālēs et mēnsium et annōrum initia sīc observant ut noctem [13] diēs subsequātur.

QUESTIONS

1. Who was chief god of the Gauls?
2. Why did the Gauls sacrifice human beings?
3. Which god did they consider their ancestor?

457. Word Study

From what Latin words are the following derived: **artificium, inventor, noxa, prōgnātus?**

Explain *accumulate, artificial, cumulative, furtive, immolate, implacable, mercantile, morbid, noxious, victimize, votive.*

---

[5] Instead of their Gallic names, Caesar assigns to the deities of the Gauls the names of Roman gods on the basis of supposed resemblances. This was the Roman way of dealing with the Greek gods; with them Zeus was merely the Greek name for Jupiter, Hera for Juno, etc. [6] *they say.* [7] Supply **colunt.**

[8] *as.* [9] *crafts.*

[10] Subjunctive in implied indirect discourse, representing a future perfect.

[11] *they vow.*

[12] Because Dis (Pluto) was god of Hades, i.e., of Darkness. A trace of a similar custom of reckoning time by nights has survived from Anglo-Saxon days in the expression "fortnight" ("fourteen nights").

[13] For holidays beginning in the evening we may compare Christmas Eve. All Jewish holidays begin and end at sunset. The phases of the moon probably had a great deal to do with this, for it is comparatively easy to mark time by full moons, each marking the lapse of a *month* (related to "moon" and Latin **mēnsis**).

From as early as the Fifth century B.C. the Romans had begun worshipping Apollo, the ancient Greek god. Typically he is depicted as a beardless youth with long hair and sometimes wearing a long tunic.

Scala/Art Resource

Lesson XCII

458. MARRIAGES AND FUNERALS; CENSORSHIP

VI, 19. Virī, quantās pecūniās [1] ab uxōribus dōtis nōmine accēpērunt, tantās ex suīs bonīs, aestimātiōne factā, cum dōtibus commūnicant.[2] Huius omnis pecūniae coniūnctim ratiō habētur frūctūsque [3] servantur; uter eōrum vītā superāvit,[4] ad eum pars utrīusque cum
5 frūctibus superiōrum temporum pervenit. Virī in [5] uxōrēs sīcutī in līberōs vītae necisque habent potestātem; et cum pater familiae illūstriōre locō [6] nātus dēcessit, eius propinquī conveniunt et dē morte, sī rēs in suspīciōnem vēnit, dē uxōribus [7] in servīlem modum [8] quaestiōnem habent, et sī [9] compertum est, ignī atque omnibus tormentīs
10 excruciātās interficiunt. Fūnera sunt prō cultū Gallōrum magnifica; omniaque quae vīvīs cāra fuisse arbitrantur in ignem īnferunt, etiam animālia; ac paulō suprā hanc memoriam [10] servī et clientēs quōs ab eīs amātōs esse cōnstābat, iūstīs fūneribus cōnfectīs, ūnā cremābantur.

---

[1] *property,* as the plural shows.   [2] *they combine with.*
[3] *profits, income.*   [4] *survives* (with **vītā**).
[5] *over.* Cf. page 2 for the similar Roman **patria potestās.**
[6] Ablative of origin (**601,** 3).   [7] What does the plural prove?
[8] *as is done in the case of slaves,* i.e., by torture.
[9] *if (their guilt),* etc.   [10] *before our time.*

20. Quae cīvitātēs [11] commodius suam rem pūblicam administrāre exīstimantur habent lēgibus sānctum,[12] sī quis quid [13] dē rē pūblicā 15 ā fīnitimīs rūmōre ac fāmā accēperit, utī ad magistrātum dēferat nēve cum quō [14] aliō commūnicet, quod saepe hominēs temerāriōs [15] atque imperītōs falsīs rūmōribus terrērī et ad facinus impellī et dē summīs rēbus cōnsilium capere cognitum est. Magistrātūs quae vīsa sunt [16] occultant, quaeque esse ex ūsū [17] iūdicāvērunt multitūdinī prōdunt. 20 Dē rē pūblicā nisi per concilium loquī nōn concēditur.

QUESTIONS

1. What rights did the Gallic women have?
2. What power did the husband have over his wife?
3. What was an individual required to do if he got information about public matters?

459. Word Study

From what Latin words are the following derived: **coniūnctim, cultus, dēcēdō, falsus, magnificus, quaestiō, servīlis, temerārius?**

Explain *cremate, crematory, decease, excruciating, funereal, inquest.*

[11] *those states which.*
[12] *have it ordained by law,* explained by the **utī** clauses.
[13] *if anyone has heard anything.*   [14] *anyone.*   [15] *rash.*
[16] *whatever seems best.* This is the practice in totalitarian states today.
[17] *of advantage.*

A reproduction from an excavated villa at Boscoreale, near Pompeii. Boscoreale was known in antiquity for having numerous aristocratic country villas. The villa was discovered in 1900. The panel above the door appears to show a hunting scene.

Erich Lessing/PhotoEdit

Lesson XCIII

460. DESCRIPTION OF THE GERMANS [1]

VI, 21. Germānī multum ab hāc cōnsuētūdine differunt. Nam neque druidēs habent quī rēbus dīvīnīs praesint neque sacrificiīs student. Deōrum numerō eōs sōlōs dūcunt quōs cernunt et quōrum apertē opibus iuvantur, Sōlem et Vulcānum et Lūnam; reliquōs nē fāmā
5 quidem accēpērunt. Vīta omnis in vēnātiōnibus atque in studiīs reī mīlitāris cōnsistit; ā parvīs [2] labōrī ac dūritiae student.

22 Agrī cultūrae nōn student, maiorque pars eōrum vīctūs in lacte, cāseō, carne cōnsistit. Neque quisquam agrī modum certum aut fīnēs habet propriōs; sed magistrātūs ac prīncipēs in annōs singulōs [3]
10 gentibus cognātiōnibusque hominum quantum et quō locō vīsum est agrī [4] attribuunt, atque annō post aliō [5] trānsīre cōgunt. Eius reī multās afferunt causās: nē assiduā cōnsuētūdine captī [6] studium bellī gerendī agrī cultūrā [7] commūtent; nē lātōs fīnēs parāre studeant potentiōrēsque humiliōrēs [8] possessiōnibus expellant; nē accūrātius ad frīgora atque
15 aestūs vītandōs aedificent; nē qua oriātur pecūniae cupiditās, quā ex rē factiōnēs dissēnsiōnēsque nāscuntur; ut animī aequitāte [9] plēbem contineant, cum suās quisque opēs cum potentissimīs aequārī videat.

23. Cīvitātibus maxima laus est quam lātissimē circum sē, vāstātīs fīnibus, sōlitūdinēs habēre.[10] Hoc [11] proprium [12] virtūtis exīstimant,
20 expulsōs agrīs fīnitimōs [13] cēdere neque quemquam prope sē audēre cōnsistere. Simul hōc sē fore tūtiōrēs arbitrantur, repentīnae incursiōnis timōre sublātō. Cum bellum cīvitās aut illātum dēfendit aut īnfert,[14] magistrātūs quī eī bellō praesint et vītae necisque habeant potestātem

---

[1] Compare with description of the Suebi, **409.**   [2] *from childhood.*
[3] *for a single year.*   [4] With **quantum.**   [5] *elsewhere.*
[6] *capitivated by fixed habits (of life).*   [7] *for agriculture.*
[8] Object of **expellant.**   [9] *contentment.*
[10] Similar yet different is Tacitus' remark, put in the mouth of a Briton criticizing the Romans: **ubi sōlitūdinem faciunt pācem appellant.**
[11] explained by **cēdere** and **audēre.**   [12] *a sign of.*
[13] Subject of **cēdere.**
[14] *fights either a defensive or an offensive war.* What literally?

320

dēliguntur. In pāce nūllus est commūnis magistrātus, sed prīncipēs regiōnum atque pāgōrum inter suōs iūs dīcunt[15] contrōversiāsque 25 minuunt. Latrōcinia nūllam habent īnfāmiam quae extrā fīnēs cuiusque cīvitātis fīunt, atque ea[16] iuventūtis exercendae ac dēsidiae[17] minuendae causā fierī praedicant. Hospitem violāre fās nōn putant; quī quācumque dē causā ad eōs vēnērunt ab iniūriā prohibent sānctōsque habent hīsque omnium domūs patent vīctusque commūnicātur.   30

QUESTIONS

1. What were the chief German foods?
2. How did the Gauls and Germans differ?
3. What was the German attitude toward robbery?
4. How did the government differ in war and peace?
5. What advantages were claimed for the German system of public ownership of land?

461. Word Study

Cognātiō is from **co–** and **gnātus,** whose later form was **nātus.** Cf. English *cognate. Cheese* comes from **cāseus,** through the French. When you are "assiduous" you *sit by* (**ad–sedeō**) a job.

Assiduous.

From what Latin words are the following derived: **accūrātus, aequitās, dissēnsiō, dūritia, īnfāmia, possessiō, sōlitūdō, vīctus?**

Explain *casein, diminutive, hospital, hospitality, infamy, inviolate, victuals, volcano, vulcanize.*

Summary of Chapter 24. The Gauls had once been powerful enough to invade and seize the most fertile districts of Germany; but now, as a result of their contact with civilization, they have deteriorated to such an extent that they have grown accustomed to defeat at the hands of the Germans.

---

[15] *pronounce judgment.*
[17] *laziness.*

[16] Accusative; i.e., **latrōcinia.**

Lesson XCIV

462. THE HERCYNIAN FOREST AND ITS ANIMALS

VI, 25. Hercyniae silvae lātitūdō VIIII diērum iter expedītō [1] patet;
nōn enim aliter fīnīrī potest, neque mēnsūrās [2] itinerum nōvērunt.
Multa in eā genera ferārum nāscī cōnstat quae reliquīs in locīs vīsa
nōn sint; ex quibus quae maximē differant ā cēterīs et memoriae
5 prōdenda videantur haec sunt.

26. Est bōs cervī [3] figūrā, cuius ā mediā fronte inter aurēs ūnum [4]
cornū exsistit excelsius magisque dērēctum hīs [5] quae nōbīs nōta sunt
cornibus. Ab eius summō sīcut palmae rāmīque lātē diffunduntur.
Eadem est fēminae marisque nātūra, eadem fōrma magnitūdōque
10 cornuum.

27. Sunt item quae appellantur alcēs.[6] Hārum est cōnsimilis caprīs [7]
figūra et varietās [8] pellium; sed magnitūdine paulō antecēdunt muti-
laeque sunt cornibus et crūra [9] sine articulīs [10] habent; neque quiētis
causā prōcumbunt neque, sī quō afflīctae cāsū concidērunt, ērigere
15 sēsē possunt. Hīs sunt arborēs prō cubīlibus; [11] ad eās sē applicant
atque ita paulum modo reclīnātae quiētem capiunt. Quārum ex
vēstigiīs cum [12] est animadversum ā vēnātōribus [13] quō sē recipere
cōnsuērint, omnēs [14] eō locō aut ab rādīcibus subruunt aut accīdunt
arborēs, tantum ut speciēs eārum [15] stantium relinquātur. Hūc [16] cum
20 sē cōnsuētūdine reclīnāvērunt, īnfirmās arborēs pondere afflīgunt atque
ūnā ipsae concidunt.

---

[1] *for one unencumbered* (with baggage).   [2] i.e., by miles.   [3] *stag.*
[4] Reindeer have two horns, which they shed yearly. Caesar, or his informant,
must have seen one when it had just shed one horn.
[5] *than those horns* (**601**, 5).   [6] *elk.*   [7] *goats.*
[8] *spotted appearance.*   [9] *legs.*
[10] *joints.* Such "nature faking" is known even today; see the "Hodong" story in
465. Did Caesar really believe this tale or was he merely passing on a good
story?   [11] *beds.*
[12] *whenever.*   [13] *hunters.*   [14] Modifies **arborēs.**   [15] i.e., the trees.
[16] *against these.*

28. Tertium est genus eōrum quī ūrī [17] appellantur. Hī sunt magnitūdine paulō īnfrā elephantōs; speciē et colōre et figūrā taurī. Magna vīs eōrum est et magna vēlōcitās; neque hominī neque ferae quam cōnspexērunt parcunt. (Hōs foveīs [18] captōs interficiunt. Hōc sē labōre 25 dūrant adulēscentēs atque hōc genere vēnātiōnis exercent; et quī plūrimōs ex hīs interfēcērunt, relātīs in pūblicum cornibus quae [19] sint testimōniō, magnam ferunt laudem.) Sed assuēscere ad hominēs nē parvulī [20] quidem exceptī possunt. Amplitūdō cornuum et figūra et speciēs multum ā nostrōrum boum [21] cornibus differt. Haec [22] con- 30 quīsīta ab labrīs [23] argentō circumclūdunt atque in amplissimīs epulīs [24] prō pōculīs [25] ūtuntur.

QUESTIONS

1. How was the "urus" trapped?
2. What were its chief characteristics?
3. What was peculiar about the elk described by Caesar?

463. Vocabulary

dērigō (dīrigō), –ere, dērēxī, dērēctus,
  direct; dērēctus, straight
fīniō, –īre, –īvī, –ītus, limit, determine

laus, laudis, f., praise
sīcut (sīcutī), as if, as it were

Review cōnstat, cornū, parcō, quiēs.

464. Word Study

The motto of the state of Maine is **Dirigo.**

To "caper" is to act like a goat **(capra).** The old-fashioned "cab" bounced around like a goat; some taxicabs still do.

From what Latin words are the following derived: **accīdō, amplitūdō, arbor, cōnsimilis, dērigō, diffundō, varietās?**

Explain aural, bovine, Capricorn, eradicate, excelsior, finite, inarticulate, mutilate, radical, ramification, toreador, vestige.

Summary of Chapters 29–44. Caesar, finding it impossible to pursue the Suebi in their forests, decides to return to Gaul. As a constant threat to the Germans, he leaves a large part of the bridge standing, protected by a

---

[17] Some believe that Caesar is here describing the almost extinct aurochs (the European cousin of the American buffalo), now found only in a primeval forest in Poland; others hold that he means the broad-horned "wild ox," the ancestor of our domesticated cattle. These wild cattle became extinct in Europe in 1627.   [18] pits.   [19] to serve as proof.
[20] i.e., ūrī.   [21] Genitive plural of bōs.   [22] Supply cornua.
[23] at the edges.   [24] feasts.   [25] cups.

garrison. Ambiorix is still at large, and Caesar devotes all his energy toward his capture. He divides his army into four divisions to prevent the escape of Ambiorix, but that wily chieftain always eludes capture. At last Caesar gives up the pursuit and, after placing his legions in winter quarters, returns to Italy.

465. LATĪNUM HODIERNUM

Damma Imparicrūs [1]

Virī perītī nōs certiōrēs faciunt omnium animālium ea tantum quae ad loca ubi vīvant aptissima sint perniciem [2] vītāre posse. Aut Nātūra benigna, ut vidētur, aut quaedam fortūna animālia ad loca aptē accommodāvit.

5 Cuius reī exemplum mīrum est quod linguā Americānā *Sidehill Hodong,* Latīnē *damma imparicrūs* appellātur. Gignitur, sī fāmae crēdī potest, in Arizōnā tantum. Cuius cīvitātis lātē patet pars ubi montēs continuī sunt, plānitiēs nūlla, arborēs paucissimae. Quae ad loca hoc animal mīrō modō idōneum est. Nam crūra alterius partis 10 breviōrēs sunt quō celerius loca dēclīvia per trānsversum [3] trānscurrat. Sī in plānum forte venit, in circulōs frūstrā circumcursat. Huius animālis summa fēlīcitās est numquam plānitiem vidēre. Nōnne Nātūra mīrābilis est?

Sī dīcēs illōs quī huic fābulae crēdant stultōs esse equidem hoc 15 nōn negābō.

---

[1] *deer with unequal legs.* Adapted from Norman W. DeWitt in *Classical Journal,* 47 (1952), p. 149.   [2] *annihilation.*   [3] *sideways.*

A rare gold Arvernian coin issued by Vercingetorix, bearing his name and idealized portrait. Note the heavy features and curly hair. Vercingetorix appears on Roman coins also, but as a captive.

Service de Documentation
Photographique de la
Réunion des Musées Nationaux

Lesson XCV

Vercingetorix, the Gallic leader who heads the final desperate revolt against the Romans in 52 B.C., is the dominant figure of Book VII (Lessons XCV to C) of the *Gallic War*.

Summary of Chapters 1–3. The Gauls, learning of political unrest at Rome, feel that the hour for freedom has come. This is the third and greatest of the Gallic revolts (the first was that of the Veneti and their allies; the second, that of Ambiorix). At a secret council a general uprising is planned. The Carnutes strike the first blow by massacring the Romans in Cenabum (Orléans).

466. VERCINGETORIX TAKES CHARGE

VII, 4. Similī ratiōne ibi Vercingetorīx, Celtillī fīlius, Arvernus, summae potentiae adulēscēns, cuius pater prīncipātum tōtīus Galliae obtinuerat et ob eam causam, quod rēgnum appetēbat, ā cīvitāte erat interfectus, convocātīs suīs clientibus, facile incendit.[1] Cognitō eius cōnsiliō, ad arma concurritur. Prohibētur ā patruō[2] suō reliquīsque 5 prīncipibus, quī hanc temptandam fortūnam nōn exīstimābant; expellitur ex oppidō Gergoviā. Nōn dēsistit tamen atque in agrīs habet dīlēctum[3] egentium ac perditōrum.[4] Hāc coāctā manū, quōscumque adit ex cīvitāte, ad suam sententiam perdūcit; hortātur ut commūnis lībertātis causā arma capiant, magnīsque coāctīs cōpiīs, adversāriōs 10 suōs, ā quibus paulō ante erat ēiectus, expellit ex cīvitāte. Rēx ab suīs appellātur. Dīmittit quōqueversus[5] lēgātiōnēs; obtestātur ut in fidē maneant. Celeriter sibi omnēs quī Ōceanum attingunt adiungit; omnium cōnsēnsū ad eum dēfertur imperium. Quā oblātā potestāte, omnibus hīs cīvitātibus obsidēs imperat, certum numerum mīlitum ad 15 sē celeriter addūcī iubet, armōrum quantum quaeque cīvitās domī

---

[1] i.e., the clients. [2] *uncle.* [3] *levy.* [4] *of the needy and desperate.*
[5] *in every direction.*

quodque ante tempus efficiat [6] cōnstituit; in prīmīs equitātuī studet. Summae dīligentiae summam imperī sevēritātem addit; magnitūdine suppliciī dubitantēs cōgit. Nam maiōre commissō dēlīctō, ignī atque
20 omnibus tormentīs necat, leviōre dē causā, auribus dēsectīs aut singulīs effossīs oculīs, domum remittit, ut sint reliquīs documentō et magnitūdine poenae perterreant aliōs.

Summary of Chapters 5–7. The Bituriges join the revolt. Caesar hastens from Italy to Gaul on receipt of the news. He reinforces his troops at Narbo (Narbonne) in the Province, which is threatened with invasion. Caesar's problem is to reach his scattered legions through possibly hostile tribes. As usual, he depends on speed.

8. Etsī mōns Cebenna,[7] quī Arvernōs ab Helviīs disclūdit, dūrissimō tempore annī altissimā nive iter impediēbat, tamen, discussā nive
25 sex in altitūdinem pedum atque ita viīs patefactīs, summō mīlitum labōre ad fīnēs Arvernōrum pervēnit. Quibus oppressīs inopīnantibus, quod sē Cebennā ut mūrō mūnītōs exīstimābant, ac nē singulārī [8] quidem umquam hominī eō tempore annī sēmitae [9] patuerant, equitibus imperat ut quam lātissimē possint vagentur, ut quam maximum
30 hostibus terrōrem īnferant.

QUESTIONS

1. How did Vercingetorix raise an army?
2. How did he become leader of all the Gauls?
3. How did he keep the various tribes faithful?
4. Why did Caesar catch the Arvernians unprepared?

467. Word Study

From what Latin words are the following derived: **adversārius, appetō, cōnsēnsus, disclūdō, documentum?**

Explain *corpus delicti, dissect, document, perdition.*

Summary of Chapters 9–16. Caesar gathers together his scattered troops before the Gauls are aware of what is going on. In rapid succession he captures several towns and then advances against Avaricum (Bourges). This place the Gauls had considered impregnable and had therefore spared, while following a "scorched earth" policy in the rest of the country in their effort to check Caesar's advance by cutting off his supplies. Though harassed in the rear by Vercingetorix, who concentrates on attacking the Romans' foraging parties, Caesar begins the siege of Avaricum.

[6] *how many arms each state should produce and by what time.*   [7] *Cévennes.*
[8] *all alone.* One man had a better chance of getting across than an army. "It can't be done," they said—and so Caesar did it.   [9] *paths.*

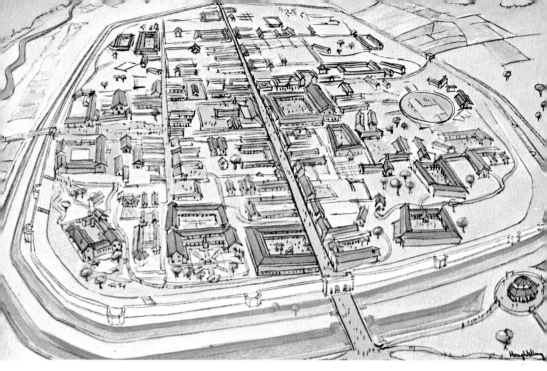

The Roman town of Venta Silurum (now Caerwent) in Wales was built in the first century A.D. By the third century it looked something like this. Like many Roman towns, it preserves something of its original form, that of a Roman military camp. Note the wall and broad main street.

Lesson XCVI

468. ROMAN SPIRIT

VII, 17. Summā difficultāte reī frūmentāriae affectō exercitū, usque eō ut [1] complūrēs diēs frūmentō mīlitēs caruerint,[2] et, pecore ex longinquiōribus vīcīs adāctō, extrēmam famem sustinuerint, nūlla tamen vōx est ab eīs audīta populī Rōmānī maiestāte [3] et superiōribus victōriīs [3] indigna. Quīn etiam Caesar cum in opere singulās legiōnēs 5 appellāret, et, sī [4] acerbius [5] inopiam ferrent, sē dīmissūrum oppugnā-tiōnem dīceret, ūniversī ab eō nē id faceret petēbant sīc sē complūrēs annōs, illō imperante, meruisse [6] ut nūllam ignōminiam acciperent, numquam, īnfectā rē, discēderent; hoc sē ignōminiae locō lātūrōs,[7]

[1] *so much so that.*   [2] *were without,* with ablative (**601,** 1).
[3] Ablative with **indigna,** *unworthy* (**601,** 18).
[4] the clause depends upon **dīmissūrum.**
[5] With **ferrent:** *suffer too severely (from).*
[6] Depends (with **sē** as subject) on the idea of saying in **petēbant.**
[7] *that they would regard as* (literally, *in the place of*).

10 sī inceptam oppugnātiōnem relīquissent; praestāre omnēs perferre acerbitātēs quam nōn cīvēs Rōmānōs quī perfidiā Gallōrum interīssent ulcīscī.

Summary of Chapters 18–56. Vercingetorix tempts Caesar to attack him, but Caesar, finding him too well entrenched, resumes the siege of Avaricum. The Gauls then accuse Vercingetorix of treason because he did not attack the Romans when he was in a position to do so. He successfully defends himself against this charge. The Gauls with renewed determination resolve to hold Avaricum at any cost. Vercingetorix sends a strong reinforcement. The besieged manage to set fire to the Roman siege works and display marked heroism. At length, however, Avaricum falls, and most of the inhabitants are killed. Vercingetorix consoles his troops for the loss of the town by stating that he had from the beginning opposed the defense of the place as untenable. He raises fresh troops. Caesar now marches along the Elaver (Allier) River, passing, no doubt, the site of Vichy (the hot springs of Vichy were known in antiquity). Vercingetorix anticipates Caesar in seizing the hillside near Gergovia, and Caesar can only follow. At this point the Haeduans, who were on their way to join Caesar, mutiny at the instigation of their leader, who had been bribed, but Caesar, making a forced march, meets them and wins them back to his cause. He returns to Gergovia just in time to save his camp from capture by Vercingetorix. Later the Romans attack the town but are badly defeated. In spite of the critical situation, Caesar does not, as his enemies might expect, retreat to the Province, but goes north to protect his supplies at his headquarters on the River Loire.

The Emperor Marcus Aurelius addresses his troops (note the *signa* in the background). The Emperor spent most of his reign campaigning on the borders of the Empire.

Italian stamps in honor of the Emperor Augustus, Caesar's adopted son, showing rostra of a ship (left) and eagles of a legion.

57. Dum haec apud Caesarem geruntur, Labiēnus cum quattuor legiōnibus Luteciam [8] proficīscitur. Id est oppidum Parīsiōrum positum in īnsulā flūminis Sēquanae. Cuius adventū ab hostibus cognitō, 15 magnae ex fīnitimīs cīvitātibus cōpiae convēnērunt. Summa imperī trāditur Camulogenō Aulercō. Is cum animadvertisset perpetuam esse palūdem quae īnflueret in Sēquanam atque illum omnem locum magnopere impedīret, hīc cōnsēdit.

QUESTIONS

1. Whom did Caesar send to Paris?
2. Where was ancient Paris situated?
3. What was the greatest hardship for the Romans?

469. Word Study

A "caret" mark (⌃) indicates that something is *lacking* (caret).
Explain *acerbity, ignominious, influx, perfidious.*

Summary of Chapters 58–68. Labienus retires to Metiosedum (Melun), which he captures. He then again marches toward Lutecia, which he finds in flames. He then learns of Caesar's defeat at Gergovia and receives alarming reports of a general Gallic uprising. Labienus decides to join Caesar and reaches him on the third day. The Haeduans now openly revolt and demand the supreme command, but at a council of the Gauls the command is given to Vercingetorix, who orders the Gauls to furnish hostages and troops, especially cavalry. Caesar sends to Germany for cavalry. The Gallic cavalry attack but are defeated. Vercingetorix heads for Alesia and occupies it. Caesar follows and plans to shut up the Gauls in that town by a series of trenches around it.

[8] The capital of the **Parīsiī** (the original "Parisians"), on the site of modern Paris. The spelling **Lutecia** in place of the more usual **Lutetia** is that of most of the best manuscripts.

329

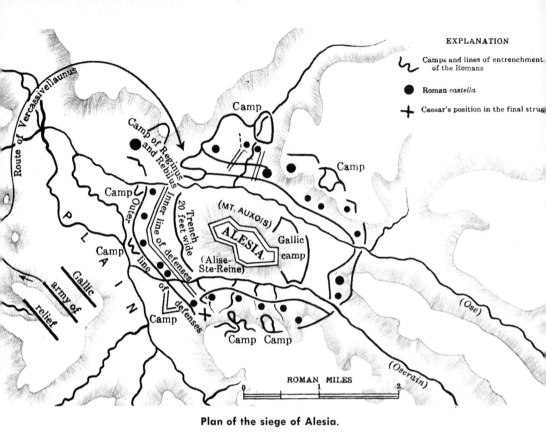

Plan of the siege of Alesia.

Lesson XCVII

470. *THE SIEGE OF ALESIA*

VII, 69. Ipsum erat oppidum in colle summō admodum ēditō locō,
ut nisi obsidiōne expugnārī nōn posse vidērētur. Ante oppidum
plānitiēs circiter mīlia passuum tria in longitūdinem patēbat; reliquīs
ex omnibus partibus collēs, mediocrī interiectō spatiō, oppidum cingē-
5 bant. Sub mūrō, quae pars collis ad orientem sōlem spectābat, hunc
omnem locum [1] cōpiae Gallōrum complēverant fossamque et māce-
riam [2] sex in altitūdinem pedum praedūxerant. Eius mūnītiōnis quae
ab Rōmānīs īnstituēbātur circuitus X mīlia passuum tenēbat.[3] Castra

---

[1] **hunc omnem locum,** i.e., **eam partem (quae . . . spectābat).**
[2] *wall.*   [3] *extended.*

330

opportūnīs locīs erant posita ibique castella [4] XXIII facta, quibus in castellīs interdiū [5] statiōnēs pōnēbantur, nē qua subitō ēruptiō fieret; 10 haec eadem noctū firmīs praesidiīs tenēbantur.

Summary of Chapters 70–75. The Gauls attempt to interfere with Caesar's operations but are repulsed in a great slaughter. Vercingetorix sends his cavalry to get reinforcements. Food runs short and is rationed. Caesar constructs an inner and an outer line of siege works, the former to hem Vercingetorix in Alesia, the latter to defend his own army from attack from without, for Caesar had already learned that the Gauls were raising a great army for the relief of Alesia.

76. Operā Commī fidēlī atque ūtilī superiōribus annīs erat ūsus in Britanniā Caesar; prō quibus meritīs cīvitātem [6] eius immūnem [7] esse iusserat, iūra lēgēsque reddiderat atque ipsī [8] Morinōs attribuerat. Tanta tamen ūniversae Galliae cōnsēnsiō fuit lībertātis vindicandae [9] 15 et prīstinae bellī laudis recuperandae ut neque beneficiīs neque amīcitiae memoriā movērentur,[10] omnēsque et animō et opibus in id bellum incumberent.[11] Coāctīs equitum mīlibus VIII et peditum circiter CCL, haec in Haeduōrum fīnibus recēnsēbantur, et praefectī cōnstituēbantur.[12] Omnēs alacrēs et fīdūciae plēnī ad Alesiam proficīscuntur; 20 neque erat omnium quisquam quī aspectum modo tantae multitūdinis sustinērī posse arbitrārētur, praesertim ancipitī [13] proeliō, cum ex oppidō ēruptiōne pugnārētur, forīs [14] tantae cōpiae equitātūs peditātūsque cernerentur.

QUESTIONS

1. Describe the location of Alesia.
2. What two things led the Gauls to forget Caesar's previous kindnesses?
3. How many Gallic soldiers came to the rescue of Alesia?

---

[4] Eight of these have been found. Alesia is now Mont Auxois, near Dijon. During a recent drought crops were found to be growing at certain places. It was concluded that they were drawing moisture from the walls of the ancient town, which lay underneath.   [5] *in the daytime.*

[6] i.e., the Atrebatians.   [7] *free from tribute.*

[8] Commius, as ruler. In 50 B.C. Commius, who had once been a prisoner in Britain **(415, 426)**, escaped to that island and there became a powerful king.

[9] *agreement to claim.*   [10] Supply **Gallī,** including Commius.   [11] *lent their efforts.*

[12] The representatives of the different states formed a war council, thus producing further division of authority, when what was needed was one commander in chief with supreme power. A similar situation hampered the Allies in the early years of World War I but was largely remedied in World War II.

[13] *on two fronts.*   [14] *outside.*

471. Vocabulary

admodum, adv., *very (much)*
fīdūcia, –ae, f., *confidence*
mediocris, –e, *moderate*

plānitiēs, –ēī, f., *plain*
recuperō, 1, *get back, recover*

Review **ēditus, opportūnus, praesertim, prīstinus.**

472. Word Study

From what Latin words are the following derived: **ēruptiō, fidēlis, interdiū, intericiō, mediocris, plānitiēs?**

Explain *fidelity, fiduciary, immunity, incumbent, infidel, recuperate, replenish, vindication.*

Frankfort High School Chapter, Junior Classical League

A model of a Roman camp made by members of the Junior Classical League in Frankfort, Kentucky. The rectangular area (other camps were square) is surrounded by a broad trench (*fossa*) and an earthen rampart (*agger*) topped by a palisade of sharpened stakes (*vallum*). Each of the four gates is guarded by two towers, and is angled so that no attacker can approach without coming under fire from his unprotected right side and rear. A real camp large enough for two legions would cover about 12 acres of ground and hold upwards of 10,000 men, counting the cavalry, the auxiliaries, and swarms of hangers on. It was marked off by definite streets, and each unit had its own location. In the center was the general's headquarters, the praetorium. One can hardly believe that after a day's marching, one-quarter of the troops could set up such a camp in about two hours' time, even when under attack.

Lesson XCVIII

473. A HORRIBLE SUGGESTION

VII, 77. At eī quī Alesiae obsidēbantur, praeteritā diē quā auxilia suōrum exspectāverant, cōnsūmptō omnī frūmentō, ignōrantēs quid in Haeduīs gererētur, conciliō coāctō, dē exitū suārum fortūnārum cōnsultābant. Apud quōs variīs dictīs sententiīs, quārum pars dēditiōnem, pars, dum vīrēs essent, ēruptiōnem cēnsēbat,[1] nōn praetere- 5 unda [2] vidētur ōrātiō Critognātī propter eius singulārem ac nefāriam crūdēlitātem.

Hic summō in Arvernīs ortus locō et magnae habitus auctōritātis, "Nihil," inquit, "dē eōrum sententiā dictūrus sum quī turpissimam servitūtem dēditiōnis nōmine appellant, neque hōs habendōs cīvium 10 locō neque adhibendōs ad concilium cēnseō. Cum hīs mihi rēs sit [3] quī ēruptiōnem probant; quōrum in cōnsiliō omnium vestrum cōnsēnsū prīstinae residēre virtūtis memoria vidētur. Animī est ista [4] mollitia, nōn virtūs, paulisper inopiam ferre nōn posse. Quī [5] sē ultrō mortī offerant facilius reperiuntur quam quī dolōrem patienter ferant. 15 Atque ego hanc sententiam probārem [6] (tantum apud mē dignitās potest [7]), sī nūllam praeterquam vītae nostrae iactūram fierī vidērem; sed in cōnsiliō capiendō omnem Galliam respiciāmus, quam ad nostrum auxilium concitāvimus. Quid, hominum mīlibus LXXX ūnō locō interfectīs, propinquīs cōnsanguineīsque nostrīs animī [8] fore 20 exīstimātis, sī paene in ipsīs cadāveribus proeliō dēcertāre cōgentur? Nōlīte [9] hōs vestrō auxiliō spoliāre quī vestrae salūtis causā suum perīculum neglēxērunt; nec stultitiā ac temeritāte vestrā aut animī imbēcillitāte omnem Galliam prōsternere et perpetuae servitūtī subicere.

---

[1] *voted for.*   [2] *should not, it seems (to me), be passed over.*
[3] *Let my speech deal with those.*
[4] For **istud;** it is the subject and is explained by **posse.**
[5] *(men) who.*   [6] *I might approve, if I saw.*
[7] *the standing (of its backers) has so much weight with me.*
[8] Depends on **Quid.**
[9] *do not* (literally, *be unwilling to*), the three infinitives depend on it **(608).**

25 "Quid [10] ergō meī cōnsilī est? Facere quod nostrī maiōrēs nēquāquam parī bellō Cimbrōrum Teutonumque fēcērunt; quī in oppida
compulsī ac similī inopiā subāctī, eōrum corporibus quī aetāte ad
bellum inūtilēs vidēbantur vītam sustinuērunt, neque sē hostibus trādi-
dērunt. Cuius reī sī exemplum nōn habērēmus, tamen lībertātis causā
30 īnstituī et posterīs prōdī pulcherrimum iūdicārem.[11] Nam quid illī
simile bellō fuit? Vāstātā Galliā, Cimbrī, magnāque illātā calamitāte,
fīnibus quidem nostrīs aliquandō [12] excessērunt atque aliās terrās
petīvērunt; iūra, lēgēs, agrōs, lībertātem nōbīs relīquērunt. Rōmānī
vērō quid petunt aliud aut quid volunt, nisi invidiā adductī, quōs [13]
35 fāmā nōbilēs potentēsque bellō cognōvērunt, hōrum in agrīs cīvitāti-
busque cōnsīdere atque hīs aeternam iniungere servitūtem? Neque
enim umquam aliā condiciōne bella gessērunt. Quod sī ea quae in
longinquīs nātiōnibus geruntur ignōrātis, respicite fīnitimam Galliam,
quae in prōvinciam redācta, iūre et lēgibus commūtātīs, secūribus [14]
40 subiecta perpetuā premitur servitūte!"

QUESTIONS

1. What three suggestions were made in the council of the Gauls?
2. What was the objection of Critognatus to fighting their way out?
3. In what way, according to Critognatus, were the Romans worse
   than the Cimbri?

474. Word Study

From what Latin words are the following derived: **cōnsultō, ignōrō,
patienter, praetereō, resideō, subiciō, subigō, temeritās?**

Explain *consultative pact, eternity, ignoramus, imbecile, nefarious,
prostrate, residence.*

[10] *What is my plan?* [11] *I should consider.*
[12] *at last.* [13] Supply **esse;** the antecedent is **hōrum.**
[14] Freely, *authority.* The lictors accompanying the consul carried bundles of rods
(**fascēs**) enclosing an ax (**secūris**), the former representing the consul's power
to flog a criminal and the latter, his right to put him to death.

Roman silver vase from Alesia.

This is the Roman Viaduct and Bridge over the Guadiana River at Mérida, in present day southwestern Spain. The Roman province of Spain produced several notable leaders, including the Emperors Hadrian and Trajan. The important capitals were Tarraco (Tarragona), Italica (near Seville), and Emerita (Mérida). Each of these capitals had its own monuments, arena, theater, and hippodrome. Bridges and aqueducts such as this one are found throughout the Roman Empire.

A Gallic baby sleeps peacefully in a cradle. Compare this and the figures on pages 217 and 316 with examples of Roman sculpture. What chief differences in style do you see?

Musée des Beaux-Arts, Beaune

Lesson XCIX

475. INNOCENT VICTIMS OF WAR

VII, 78. Sententiīs dictīs, cōnstituunt ut eī quī valētūdine aut aetāte inūtilēs sint bellō oppidō excēdant, atque omnia prius experiantur quam [1] ad Critognātī sententiam dēscendant; illō tamen potius ūtendum [2] cōnsiliō, sī rēs cōgat atque auxilia morentur, quam aut
5 dēditiōnis aut pācis subeundam condiciōnem. Mandubiī, quī eōs oppidō recēperant, cum līberīs atque uxōribus exīre cōguntur. Hī cum ad mūnītiōnēs Rōmānōrum accessissent, flentēs omnibus precibus ōrābant ut sē in servitūtem receptōs cibō iuvārent. At Caesar, dispositīs in vāllō custōdiīs, recipī [3] prohibēbat.
10 79. Intereā Commius reliquīque ducēs, quibus summa imperī permissa erat, cum omnibus cōpiīs ad Alesiam perveniunt, et, colle exteriōre occupātō, nōn longius mīlle passibus ā nostrīs mūnītiōnibus cōnsīdunt. Posterō diē, equitātū ex castrīs ēductō, omnem eam plānitiem quae in longitūdinem mīlia passuum III patēbat, complent; pedes-
15 trēsque cōpiās paulum ab eō locō abductās in locīs superiōribus cōnstituunt. Erat ex oppidō Alesiā dēspectus [4] in [5] campum. Concurrunt, hīs auxiliīs vīsīs; fit grātulātiō inter eōs atque omnium animī ad laetitiam excitantur. Itaque, prōductīs cōpiīs, ante oppidum cōnsīdunt, sēque ad ēruptiōnem atque omnēs cāsūs comparant.

---

[1] Translate with **prius**: *before*.   [2] *but that plan was to be used.*
[3] Supply **eōs**. These innocent townspeople perished of starvation between the lines. Parallels are not lacking in recent times.
[4] A statue of Vercingetorix was erected by Napoleon III near the spot from which the relief army was seen.   [5] *over.*

Summary of Chapters 80–81. Caesar sends his cavalry out of camp to engage that of the enemy; after a long struggle the enemy is finally defeated. The Gallic relief army, under cover of night, makes a second attack upon the outer works, while Vercingetorix leads an attack upon the inner lines.

82. Dum longius ā mūnītiōne aberant Gallī, plūs multitūdine 20 tēlōrum prōficiēbant; posteāquam propius successērunt, aut sē ipsī stimulīs[6] inopīnantēs induēbant aut in scrobēs[7] dēlātī trānsfodiēbantur aut ex vāllō ac turribus trāiectī pīlīs mūrālibus[8] interībant. Multīs undique vulneribus acceptīs, nūllā mūnītiōne perruptā, cum lūx appeteret, veritī nē ab latere apertō ex superiōribus castrīs ērup- 25 tiōne circumvenīrentur, sē ad suōs recēpērunt. At interiōrēs,[9] dum ea quae ā Vercingetorīge ad ēruptiōnem praeparāta erant prōferunt, priōrēs fossās explent: diūtius in hīs rēbus administrandīs morātī prius suōs discessisse cognōvērunt quam[10] mūnītiōnibus appropinquārent. Ita, rē īnfectā, in oppidum revertērunt. 30

QUESTIONS

1. What plan did the Gauls adopt?
2. What happened to the Mandubii?
3. Why did the night attack of the Gauls fail?

476. Vocabulary

expleō, –ēre, explēvī, explētus, *fill up*
prior, prius, *former, first*

prōficiō, –ere, –fēcī, –fectus, *accomplish*

Review **cibus, fleō, posteāquam, posterus, prex, turris.**

477. Word Study

From what Latin words are the following derived: **appetō, custōdia, dēspectus, dispōnō, grātulātiō, mūrālis, perrumpō?**

Explain *appetite, priority, stimulation, trajectory, translucent.*

Summary of Chapters 83–87. The Gauls send out scouts and find that the Roman camp on the north is in a weak position. So Vercassivellaunus makes a surprise march by night and attacks the camp the next noon. Vercingetorix attacks from Alesia, and the Romans are forced to fight on all sides. Caesar, perceiving that his men are weakening under the attack of Vercassivellaunus, sends Labienus with six cohorts to reinforce them. He then addresses his troops, reminding them that the reward of all their struggles depends upon that day and hour. Vercingetorix attempts a diversion from Alesia. Caesar sends reinforcements and finally goes to the rescue himself.

---

[6] *spurs* (pointed iron stakes). [7] *wolf-holes.* See p. 268. [8] *heavy wall javelins.*
[9] The army within Alesia. [10] With **prius:** *before.*

Lesson C

478. NEAR DISASTER FOLLOWED BY VICTORY

VII, 88. Eius [1] adventū ex colōre [1] vestītūs cognitō, quō īnsignī in proeliīs ūtī cōnsuēverat, turmīsque equitum et cohortibus vīsīs quās sē sequī iusserat, ut dē locīs superiōribus haec dēclīvia cernēbantur, hostēs proelium committunt. Utrimque, clāmōre sublātō, excipit [2]
5 rūrsus ex vāllō atque omnibus mūnītiōnibus clāmor. Nostrī, omissīs pīlīs, gladiīs rem gerunt. Repente post tergum [3] equitātus cernitur; cohortēs aliae appropinquant. Hostēs terga vertunt; fugientibus equitēs occurrunt; fit magna caedēs. Signa mīlitāria LXXIII ad Caesarem referuntur; paucī ex tantō numerō incolumēs sē in castra recipiunt.
10 Cōnspicātī ex oppidō caedem et fugam suōrum, dēspērātā salūte, cōpiās ā mūnītiōnibus redūcunt. Fit prōtinus, hāc rē audītā, ex castrīs Gallōrum fuga. Quod [4] nisi crēbrīs subsidiīs ac tōtīus diēī labōre mīlitēs essent dēfessī, omnēs hostium cōpiae dēlērī potuissent.[5] Dē mediā nocte missus equitātus novissimum agmen cōnsequitur; magnus
15 numerus capitur atque interficitur; reliquī ex fugā in cīvitātēs discēdunt.

89. Posterō diē Vercingetorīx, conciliō convocātō, id bellum sē suscēpisse nōn suārum necessitātum sed commūnis lībertātis causā dēmōnstrat; et quoniam sit fortūnae cēdendum,[6] ad utramque [7] rem sē illīs offerre,[8] seu morte suā Rōmānīs satisfacere seu vīvum trādere
20 velint. Mittuntur dē hīs rēbus ad Caesarem lēgātī. Iubet arma trādī, prīncipēs prōdūcī. Ipse in mūnītiōne prō castrīs cōnsīdit; eō ducēs prōdūcuntur. Vercingetorīx dēditur; arma prōiciuntur. Reservātīs Haeduīs atque Arvernīs, sī per eōs cīvitātēs recuperāre posset, ex reliquīs captīvīs tōtī exercituī capita singula [9] praedae nōmine distribuit.
25 90. Huius annī rēbus ex Caesaris litterīs cognitīs Rōmae diērum vīgintī supplicātiō redditur.

---

[1] Caesar wore a scarlet uniform.
[2] *answers.*
[3] Of the enemy. The cavalry is Roman.
[4] *and.*
[5] *might have been.*
[6] *they must yield to.*
[7] *for either.*
[8] Depends upon **dēmōnstrat.**
[9] *one to each (soldier).*

Scala/Art Resource

According to historians, the Forum of Julius Caesar was paid for by part of the wealth Caesar acquired during the Gallic Wars. Caesar began constructing this forum in 54 B.C. After the Roman Forum, it was the second forum to be built in Rome.

QUESTIONS

1. What led the enemy to begin the attack?
2. What changed the situation and made the enemy flee?
3. What offer did the defeated Vercingetorix make to his soldiers?

479. Developing "Word Sense"

Tollō is a good word to know well, both for its irregular principal parts and for its basic meaning, *raise up or away from a lower position.* Thus, in the proper contexts, **tollō** can mean: *weigh anchor, cheer up a friend, praise someone highly,* or, on the other hand, *plunder booty, get rid of something,* or *"do away" with a man,* i.e., *murder him.*

After the death of the dictator Caesar, his nineteen-year-old adopted son and heir, Octavian (later the Emperor Augustus), began to seize power for himself. The orator Cicero, fearful of what might happen to the Roman Senate, suggested that: **laudandum (esse) adulēscentem, ornandum, tollendum.** Octavian, who had a good sense of humor, was not exactly pleased by the pun.

339

Caesar's siege works at Alesia.

Our Heritage

480. VERCINGETORIX AND ALESIA

In strategic skill, organizing ability, and leadership Vercingetorix was by far the ablest foreign opponent that Caesar faced, but he was unable in a short time to give the Gauls that discipline and military knowledge which the Romans had acquired through centuries of experience. He did succeed for a time in producing Gallic unity, and for that he has been considered the first national hero of France.

After his surrender Vercingetorix was sent to Rome and remained in prison there for six years. In 46 B.C. he was led through the streets before Caesar's chariot in a triumphal procession and then executed as part of the ceremony.

Historians agree that the fall of Alesia constitutes a turning point in the history of northern Europe, for it settled the question of Roman supremacy in Gaul. The striking contrast between Roman efficiency and Gallic inefficiency is here seen most clearly. With all their courage and physical strength, the Gauls were defeated in their own territory by an army scarcely one seventh the size of their own.

The military operations of the two years (51–50 B.C.) following the capture of Alesia were not included by Caesar in his *Commentaries,* but we are indebted to one of his generals, Aulus Hirtius, for a full account, which he added as an eighth book. The military strength of the Gauls had been broken forever, and there remained only the task of subduing certain states that had not yet been fully reduced and of garrisoning the country. Caesar's term as proconsular governor expired in 49 B.C. Thus the conquest of Gaul, with its momentous results, occupied nine years in all.

481. CAESAR DICTĀTOR—A Play in Latin

Persōnae

C. Iūlius Caesar	Senātōrēs I *et* II
Babidus, *scrība senex*	Aedīlis
Frontō, *scrība adulēscēns*	Būbulō, *frāter pistōris* [1] *Caesaris*
M. Terentius Varrō	Syphāx, *margarītārius*
Sōsigenēs, *astronomus*	Calpurnia, *uxor Caesaris*
M. Flāvius, *amīcus Sōsigenis*	Rhoda, *serva*

[The scene is a room in Caesar's house. The time is somewhere between 49 and 44 B.C. The Civil War with Pompey and his followers has ended victoriously for Caesar. Established in Rome as dictator, Caesar is putting into effect his plans for the reorganization of the war-torn state.]

(*Intrant Babidus et Frontō. Tabulās, libellōs, stilōs ferunt.*)

BABIDUS: Dēpōne libellōs, Frontō.

FRONTŌ: Aderuntne hodiē multī salūtātōrēs?

BABIDUS: Multī. Caesarī dictātōrī omnis rēs pūblica cūrae est.

FRONTŌ: Labōrat magis quam servus.   5

BABIDUS: Prō eō saepe timeō. Semper labōrat; cibum nōn capit. Valētūdine minus commodā iam ūtitur. Aliquandō animō quidem linquitur.[2]

FRŌNTŌ: Rūmōrem in urbe audīvī—Caesarem cupere rēgem esse.

BABIDUS: Nūgās![3] Caesar pācem, concordiam, tranquillitātem in 10 urbe et orbe terrārum cōnfirmāre vult.

FRONTŌ: Candidātōs magistrātuum certē ipse nōminat.

BABIDUS: Aliōs nōminat Caesar, aliōs populus. Rēs pūblica antīqua autem mortua est.

FRONTŌ: Suntne libellī bene parātī? Memoriā teneō Caesarem 15 quondam interfēcisse scrībam suum Philēmonem.

BABIDUS: Philēmōn erat nefārius. Servus Caesaris inimīcīs Caesaris prōmīserat sē dominum per venēnum necātūrum esse. Tū es neque nefārius neque servus. Nōlī timēre.

FRONTŌ: Audī! Appropinquat Caesar. (*Intrat C. Iūlius Caesar.*)   20

CAESAR: Salvēte.

BABIDUS ET FRONTŌ: Salvē, imperātor.

CAESAR: Prīmum, acta diurna senātūs populīque. Suntne parāta?

FRONTŌ: Ecce, imperātor. (*Caesarī dat libellum, quem Caesar legit.*)   25

CAESAR: Bene! Bene scrīpta! Nunc ad commentāriōs meōs Dē Bellō Cīvīlī animadvertāmus.

BABIDUS: Ecce, Caesar. (*Caesarī libellum dat.*)

---

[1] *baker.*   [2] *Sometimes he even faints.*   [3] *nonsense!*

CAESAR: Pauca verba addere volō.

30 BABIDUS: Parātus sum. (*Cōnsīdit Babidus; notās*[4] *scrībere parat. Frontō exit.*)

CAESAR (*dictat*): "Caesar, omnibus rēbus relīctīs, persequendum sibi Pompeium exīstimāvit, quāscumque in partēs sē ex fugā recēpisset, nē rūrsus cōpiās comparāre aliās et bellum renovāre posset."

35 BABIDUS: Scrīptum est.

CAESAR: Estne scrīpta epistula mea ad Mārcum Cicerōnem, quam herī dictāvī? (*Intrat Frontō.*)

BABIDUS: Ecce, Caesar. (*Caesarī epistulam dat.*)

CAESAR: Mūtā litterās. Scrībe D prō A, et deinceps.[5]

40 BABIDUS: Intellegō.

FRONTŌ: Adsunt salūtātōrēs, imperātor.

CAESAR: Intret Varrō. (*Exit Frontō, tum intrat cum Varrōne.*) Salvē, Varrō.

VARRŌ: Salvē, imperātor.

45 CAESAR: Varrō, tū es vir doctus. Mihi in animō est maximam bibliothēcam, Graecam Latīnamque, aedificāre. Pūblica erit bibliothēca. Tē bibliothēcae praefectum facere volō.

VARRŌ: Mē?

CAESAR: Tē certē.

50 VARRŌ: Ego autem Pompeiī, inimīcī tuī, eram lēgātus.

CAESAR: Nōlī timēre, Varrō. Dictātor sum—nōn autem tālis dictātor quālis erat Sulla. Prōscrīptiōnēs neque dē capite neque dē bonīs Caesarī placent.

VARRŌ: Imperātor, quō modō tibi grātiam referre possum?

55 CAESAR: Dē grātiā loquī necesse nōn est. Optimus eris bibliothēcae praefectus. Valē, Varrō.

VARRŌ: Dī bene vertant! Valē. (*Exit.*)

CAESAR: Intrent astronomī. (*Exit Frontō. Intrat cum Sōsigene et Flāviō.*) Salvēte, Sōsigenēs et Flāvī.

60 SŌSIGENĒS ET FLĀVIUS: Salvē, imperātor.

CAESAR: Quid effēcistis?

SŌSIGENĒS: Nostrā sententiā, annus ad cursum sōlis accommodandus est. Necesse est annum trecentōrum sexāgintā quīnque diērum esse; necesse est quoque ūnum diem quārtō quōque[6] annō inter-
65 calārī.[7]

---

[4] *shorthand notes.*

[5] *and so on.* Caesar used a simple cipher in writing important letters.

[6] *every.*

[7] *insert.* Caesar had the calendar revised to approximately its present form. The insertion of the leap-year day was a feature of his revision.

342

The Maison Carrée, a perfectly preserved Roman temple at Nîmes, southern France.

CAESAR: Rēctam viam capitis, meā quidem sententiā.

FLĀVIUS: Sī Caesarī placet, mēnsis nātālis Caesaris, nunc Quīnctīlis, nōminētur Iūlius.

CAESAR: Dē hāc rē posteā loquāmur. Intereā, prōcēdite ut incēpistis. Valēte.   70

SŌSIGENĒS ET FLĀVIUS: Valē, imperātor. (*Exeunt.*)

CAESAR: Intrent nunc senātōrēs. (*Exit Frontō. Intrat cum senātōribus.*) Salvēte.

SENĀTŌRĒS: Salvē, Caesar.

CAESAR: Quid est in animō?   75

SENĀTOR I: Nōbīs sunt magnae cūrae, Caesar. Audīvimus tē sine auctōritāte senātūs mīlitēs Rōmānōs ad rēgēs per orbem terrārum submittere ut eīs auxiliō sint; tē pecūniā pūblicā urbēs Asiae, Graeciae, Hispāniae, Galliae operibus ōrnāre.

SENĀTOR II: Tū cīvitātem Rōmānam medicīs et grammaticīs et 80 aliīs dōnāvistī. In senātum Gallōs sēmibarbarōs cōnscrīpsistī. Mīlitēs tuī domōs cīvium ingressī sunt et cibum abstulērunt.[8] Ipse dirēmistī [9] nūptiās cīvium Rōmānōrum.

SENĀTOR I: Rūmōrēs malī per urbem eunt. Quid agis, Caesar?

CAESAR: Dictātor sum. Rem pūblicam, bellō dēiectam, restituō.   85

SENĀTOR II: Rem pūblicam dēlēs, Caesar.

CAESAR: Omnia bene erunt. Nōlīte īram meam concitāre. Valēte, amīcī.

SENĀTŌRĒS: Valē, Caesar. (*Exeunt.*)

---

[8] In an attempt to reduce inflation, Caesar forbade the sale of certain luxurious foods. He sent soldiers to markets and even to private houses to seize such luxuries.   [9] *annul.*

90 CAESAR: Ad rēs fēlīciōrēs animum advertāmus. Intret aedīlis. (*Exit Frontō. Intrat cum aedīle.*) Salvē.

AEDĪLIS: Salvē, imperātor. Omnia parāta sunt, ut imperāvistī—mūnus gladiātōrum, vēnātiō, naumachia, lūdī scaenicī, lūdī circēnsēs.

CAESAR: Bene.

95 AEDĪLIS: Spectācula erunt omnium maxima.

CAESAR: Optimē factum. Tibi grātiās agō.

AEDĪLIS: Mihi est honōrī Caesarem iuvāre. Valē.

CAESAR: Valē. (*Exit aedīlis. Intrat Rhoda. Cibum et epistulās fert. Epistulās Babidō dat.*)

100 RHODA: Domina ōrat ut dominus cibum recipiat.

CAESAR: Abī, abī! (*Rhoda, cibum ferēns, exit.*) Quae sunt illae epistulae?

BABIDUS: Architectus scrīpsit dē Forō Iūliō, dē templō novō, dē statuā equī tuī.[10]

105 CAESAR: Ita, ita.

BABIDUS: Alius scrīpsit dē viā novā mūniendā, dē Isthmō per-fodiendō,[11] dē palūdibus Pomptīnīs siccandīs.

CAESAR: Dā mihi hanc epistulam.

BABIDUS: Veterānus tibi grātiās ēgit prō praedā, servīs, agrīs quōs 110 eī dedistī. Pauper vir Rōmānus tibi grātiās ēgit, aurō et frūmentō receptō.

CAESAR: Illās epistulās iam legam. Quis in vēstibulō manet?

FRONTŌ: Vir magnus—Būbulō. Et margarītārius.

CAESAR: Būbulōne?

115 FRONTŌ: Frāter est pistōris tuī.

CAESAR: Quid petit? Intret. (*Exit Frontō. Intrat cum Būbulōne.*)

BŪBULŌ: Caesar imperātor, tē ōrō, tē ōrō!

CAESAR: Quid petis?

BŪBULŌ: Līberā frātrem meum, pistōrem tuum, in vincula con-120 iectum.

CAESAR: Alium pānem mihi, alium amīcīs meīs in trīclīniō meō· dedit.[12]

BŪBULŌ: Tū autem es Caesar.

CAESAR: Īdem cibus erit mihi et amīcīs meīs. Frāter tuus autem 125 poenās iam solvit. Eum līberābō. (*In tabulā scrībit; tabulam Būbu-lōnī dat.*)

---

[10] Caesar had a horse of which he was very fond; to it he set up a statue in his own Forum.

[11] *digging (a canal through) the Isthmus (of Corinth).* This project was not completed until 1893 and the next one has only recently been finished.

[12] Some rich Romans had special foods served to themselves and less fine foods to their guests. Of this practice Caesar violently disapproved.

344

BŪBULŌ: Ōh, dī tē ament, Caesar! (*Exit. Caesar rīdet.*)

CAESAR: Intret Syphāx margarītārius. (*Exit Frontō. Intrat cum Syphāce.*)

SYPHĀX: Avē, imperātor. Margarītam habeō—maximam. (*Mar-* 130 *garītam Caesarī mōnstrat.*)

CAESAR: Quid dīcis? Haec margarīta nōn est magna. (*Intrat Calpurnia.*) Haec margarīta est parva. Volō rēgīnam margarītārum—prō uxōre meā.

CALPURNIA: Quid audiō? 135

CAESAR: Calpurnia!

CALPURNIA: Mihi margarītam mōnstrā.—Est pulcherrima.

CAESAR: Placetne tibi? Maiōrem tibi dare voluī.

CALPURNIA: Certē placet. Pulchra est—et satis magna.

CAESAR: Tua erit. (*Scrībīs dīcit.*) Cūrāte omnia. 140

SYPHĀX: Tibi grātiās agō, imperātor. (*Exit cum scrībīs.*)

CALPURNIA: Utinam tē aequē ac mē cūrārēs!

CAESAR: Ego valeō.

CALPURNIA: Cibum reicis; nōn satis quiētem capis; etiam per somnum terrērī solēs. 145

CAESAR: Nihil est.

CALPURNIA: Vītam prō rē pūblicā dēdis. Ōmina quoque mala sunt.

CAESAR: Ōmina nōn mē terrent. (*Intrat Babidus. Margarītam Caesarī dat.*) Ecce! Pulcherrimae uxōrī pulcherrimam gemmam dō. Nunc ad prandium eāmus. 150

(*Exeunt Caesar et Calpurnia, tum Babidus.*)

Caesar and his officers, as depicted in the motion picture *Caesar and Cleopatra*.

United Artists

UNIT IX

PLINY'S LETTERS

The ancient Roman city of Pompeii
was destroyed by ash and mud in 79
A.D., when Vesuvius, the volcano we
see here in the distance, erupted.
Due to its complete burial, Pompeii
was well-preserved so that later excavations of the town have given us
one of the most complete pictures of
what life was like in ancient Roman
times.

482. AN ANCIENT LETTER WRITER

Pliny the Younger, who is so called to distinguish him from his uncle and adoptive father, Pliny the Elder, was born at Comum (Como) in northern Italy in 62 A.D. in the reign of Nero. His famous teacher Quintilian filled him with admiration of Cicero, whom he tried to imitate in many ways. Like Cicero he became consul and governor of a province. But his highest ambition was to rival Cicero as an orator; yet only one of his many speeches has survived, and no one reads that.

The fact that many of Cicero's letters were collected and published by his secretary and others gave Pliny the idea of selecting for publication some of his own more polished and less personal letters. These have survived and make fascinating reading for the light they throw on Pliny himself and on life in his day.

Among Pliny's most interesting letters are the two which give a vivid account of the famous eruption of Mt. Vesuvius near Naples in 79 A.D. The author was seventeen years old at the time and was living with his mother and uncle near Naples, at Misenum, where the elder Pliny was stationed as admiral of the fleet. Many years later Pliny wrote the letters describing the eruption.

A general view of Pompeii. The Forum is at the left; unexcavated ruins at rear

Italian Cultural Institute

This great disaster has been a blessing for us, since it preserved as if in a huge plaster cast the towns of Pompeii and Herculaneum. The excavation of these in the last two centuries has made it possible for us to walk into the houses and shops of the people who once lived there and has given us an intimate view of their daily life.

Pliny was a man of fine character, a good representative of the honest and efficient officials who developed and governed the Roman Empire. He was generous and kind. For these reasons we can forgive him his conceit and overseriousness.

483. THE ERUPTION OF VESUVIUS

This letter is a reply to a request by Pliny's great friend, the historian Tacitus, who was gathering eye-witness material for his *Histories*. Though part of this work has survived, the section dealing with the eruption has unfortunately been lost, and we are unable to tell how Tacitus used the information furnished by Pliny.

Petis ut tibi dē avunculī meī morte scrībam ut hoc trādere posterīs possīs. Grātiās agō; nam videō mortī eius immortālem glōriam esse prōpositam. Quamquam ipse opera plūrima et mānsūra scrīpsit, multum tamen eius librōrum aeternitātī [1] tuōrum aeternitās addet. Beātōs eōs putō quibus deōrum mūnere datum est aut facere scrī- 5 benda [2] aut scrībere legenda,[2] beātissimōs vērō eōs quibus utrumque.[3] Hōrum in numerō avunculus meus et suīs librīs [4] et tuīs erit.

Erat Mīsēnī.[5] Hōrā ferē septimā māter mea ostendit eī nūbem inūsitātā magnitūdine et speciē. Ille ascendit locum ex quō optimē mīrāculum illud cōnspicī poterat. Nūbēs ex monte Vesuviō oriēbātur. 10 Fōrmam pīnūs [6] habēbat.

Iubet nāvēs parārī; mihi cōpiam eundī [7] facit. Respondī studēre mē mālle. Tum accipit litterās cuiusdam mulieris perīculō territae. Nāvem ascendit ut nōn illī mulierī modo sed multīs auxilium ferret. Properat illūc unde aliī fugiunt rēctumque cursum in perīculum tenet, tam 15 solūtus timōre ut omnia vīsa ēnotāret.

Iam nāvibus cinis dēnsior incidēbat, iam pūmicēs [8] etiam nigrīque lapidēs. Cum gubernātor monēret ut retrō flecteret, "Fortēs," inquit, "fortūna iuvat." [9] Ubi ad lītus vēnit, amīcum vīdit. Eum territum

---

[1] Dative with **addet;** supply **librōrum** with **tuōrum.**

[2] (*things*) *to be* (i.e., *worthy of being*), etc.

[3] Supply **datum est.**

[4] *because of*, etc. (**601,** 11).

[5] *at Misenum* (near Naples).

[6] (the "umbrella") *pine.*

[7] i.e., with him; gerund of **eō (591).**

[8] *pumice stones.*

[9] A common Roman proverb.

Herculaneum, like Pompeii, was destroyed by the eruption of Vesuvius in 79 A.D.
Less of it has been excavated than of Pompeii because it was covered by liquid
lava, which hardened into rock, unlike Pompeii, which was suffocated by ashes.

20 hortatur. Tum in balneum it et postea ad cenam, aut hilaris aut similis
hilarī.

Interim ē Vesuviō monte lātissimās flammās vīdērunt. Ille, nē
cēterī timērent, dīcēbat ignēs ab agricolīs relīctōs esse. Tum sē quiētī
dedit. Sed nōn multō post servī eum excitāvērunt nē exitus ob cinerem
25 negārētur. Domus crēbrīs tremōribus nunc hūc nunc illūc movērī vidēbātur. Itaque placuit ēgredī in lītus. Cervīcālia [10] capitibus impōnunt.
Sed ille recubāns [11] aquam poposcit et hausit. Tum surrēxit et statim
concidit. Cēterī fugiunt. Posterō diē corpus inventum est integrum.
Similior erat dormientī quam mortuō.
30 Interim Mīsēnī ego et māter—sed nihil ad [12] historiam, nec tū aliud
quam de exitū eius scīre voluistī. Fīnem ergō faciam.

---

[10] *cushions,* used by his slaves as a protection against falling stones.
[11] *lying down.* His death was evidently due to some such cause as heart disease
rather than to the eruption.
[12] (*this has*) *nothing* (*to do*) *with.*

350

484. FLIGHT FROM DISASTER

Taking the hint given in the last sentence in the preceding selection, Tacitus asked about Pliny the Younger's own adventures during the eruption. Pliny replied as follows.

Dīcis tē adductum litterīs quās tibi dē morte avunculī meī scrīpsī cupere cognōscere quōs timōrēs et cāsūs ego pertulerim. "Quamquam animus meminisse horret, incipiam." [1]

Profectō [2] avunculō, ipse reliquum tempus studiīs dedī. Tum balneum, cēna, somnus brevis. Praecesserat per multōs diēs tremor 5 terrae. Illā vērō nocte ita crēvit [3] ut nōn movērī omnia sed vertī [4] vidērentur. Māter et ego in āream domūs iimus et cōnsēdimus. Dubitō utrum [5] cōnstantiam vocāre an imprūdentiam dēbeam (nātus enim eram XVII annōs), sed poscō librum T. Līvī et legō.

Iam hōra diēī prīma erat. Magnus et certus erat ruīnae timor. 10 Tum dēmum [6] excēdere oppidō placuit. Multī nōs sequuntur. Ēgressī cōnsistimus. Multa ibi mīranda, multōs timōrēs patimur. Nam carrī quōs prōdūcī iusserāmus, quamquam in plānissimō campō, in contrāriās partēs agēbantur. Ab alterō latere nūbēs ātra et horrenda appārēbat. Paulō post, illa nūbēs dēscendit in terrās. Tum māter ōrat, 15 hortātur, iubet mē fugere. "Tū potes," inquit; "ego et annīs et corpore gravis bene moriar sī tibi causa mortis nōn erō." Ego vērō dīcō mē nōn incolumem nisi cum eā futūrum esse. Deinde eam prōcēdere cōgō. Pāret aegrē. Iam cinis cadit. Tum nox, nōn quālis sine lūnā est, sed quālis in locīs clausīs, lūmine exstīnctō. Audiuntur ululātūs [7] 20 fēminārum, īnfantium quirītātūs,[8] clāmōrēs virōrum. Aliī parentēs, aliī līberōs, aliī coniugēs vōcibus quaerēbant, vōcibus nōscēbant. Quīdam timōre mortis mortem ōrābant. Multī ad deōs manūs tollēbant, plūrēs nōn iam deōs ūllōs esse aeternamque illam et ultimam noctem dīcēbant. Cinis multus et gravis. Hunc identidem surgentēs excutiēbāmus [9] 25 nē pondus nōbīs nocēret. Possum dīcere mē nōn gemitum in tantīs perīculīs ēdidisse. Tandem nūbēs discessit. Tum diēs vērus. Omnia mūtāta erant altōque cinere tamquam nive tēcta.

---

[1] A quotation from Virgil.   [2] From **proficīscor.**   [3] From **crēscō.**
[4] *to be turning upside down.*   [5] *whether,* introducing **dēbeam.**
[6] *at length.*   [7] *shrieks.*   [8] *wails.*
[9] *shook off.*

351

485. THE SECRET OF SUCCESS

This letter and the next are interesting revelations of the Romans' genius for organization, even of their personal lives.

Mīrāris quō modō tot librōs avunculus meus, homō occupātus, scrībere potuerit. Magis mīrāberis sī scīveris illum causās ēgisse, vīxisse LV annōs, medium [1] tempus impedītum esse officiīs maximīs et amīcitiā prīncipum. Sed erat ācre ingenium, incrēdibile studium. Stu-
5 dēre incipiēbat hieme ab hōrā septimā noctis. Erat somnī [2] parātissimī, nōn numquam [3] etiam inter ipsa studia īnstantis [4] et dēserentis.[4] Ante lūcem ībat ad Vespasiānum imperātōrem (nam ille quoque noctibus ūtēbātur [5]), inde ad officium datum. Reversus domum, reliquum tempus studiīs reddēbat. Post levem cibum saepe aestāte iacēbat in
10 sōle; liber legēbātur,[6] ille ēnotābat. Dīcere solēbat nūllum esse librum tam malum ut nōn aliquā parte ūtilis esset. Post sōlem plērumque frīgidā aquā lavābātur;[7] deinde dormiēbat minimum. Tum quasi aliō diē studēbat in cēnae tempus.

Meminī quendam ex amīcīs, cum lēctor quaedam verba male
15 prōnūntiāvisset, eum revocāvisse et iterum prōnūntiāre coēgisse. Huic avunculus meus dīxit, "Nōnne intellēxerās?" Cum ille nōn negāret, "Cūr revocābās? Decem versūs hōc modō perdidimus."

Etiam dum lavātur audiēbat servum legentem. In itinere, quasi solūtus cēterīs cūrīs, huic ūnī reī vacābat; ad latus servus erat cum
20 librō et tabulīs, cuius manūs hieme manicīs [8] mūniēbantur, nē ūllum tempus studī āmitterētur. Perīre omne tempus nōn studiīs datum arbitrābātur.

---

[1] *time in between.*

[2] *(a man) of.* Napoleon also had the habit of taking short naps at any time or place.   [3] *not never,* i.e., *sometimes.*

[4] Modifies **somnī:** *which came and went.*   [5] The ablative is used with **ūtor.**

[6] i.e., to him by a slave.

[7] *bathed (himself).* The passive is used reflexively.

[8] *gloves.*

Minicia's tombstone. See section 487 and footnote 4, page 353.

486. HOW TO KEEP YOUNG

Spūrinna senex omnia ōrdine agit. Hōrā secundā calceōs poscit, ambulat mīlia passuum tria nec minus animum quam corpus exercet. Sī adsunt amīcī, sermōnēs explicantur; [1] sī nōn, liber legitur dum ambulat. Deinde cōnsīdit et liber rūrsus aut sermō. Tum vehiculum ascendit cum uxōre vel aliquō amīcō. Cōnfectīs septem mīlibus pas- 5 suum iterum ambulat mīlle, iterum cōnsīdit. Ubi hōra balneī nūntiāta est (est autem hieme nōna, aestāte octāva), in sōle ambulat. Deinde pilā [2] lūdit vehementer et diū; nam hōc quoque exercitātiōnis genere pugnat cum senectūte. LXXVII annōs ēgit sed aurium et oculōrum et corporis vigor adhūc est integer. 10

487. THE GOOD DIE YOUNG

In addition to being a touching expression of grief, this letter lists the qualities which the Romans appreciated most in women.

Trīstissimus haec tibi scrībō, Fundānī nostrī fīliā minōre mortuā. Nihil umquam fēstīvius [1] aut amābilius quam illam puellam vīdī. Nōndum annōs XIII complēverat, et iam illī [2] anūs [3] prūdentia, mātrōnae gravitās erat et tamen suāvitās puellae.[4] Ut [5] illa patris cervīcibus [6] haerēbat! Ut nōs, amīcōs patris, et amanter et modestē 5 complectēbātur! [7] Ut magistrōs amābat! Quam studiōsē, quam intel- legenter legēbat! Ut parcē lūdēbat! Quā patientiā, quā etiam cōn- stantiā ultimam valētūdinem tulit! Medicīs pārēbat, sorōrem, patrem adhortābātur, ipsamque sē vīribus animī sustinēbat. Hae vīrēs nec spatiō valētūdinis nec timōre mortis frāctae sunt. Itaque plūrēs 10 graviōrēsque causās dolōris nōbīs relīquit. Iam spōnsa erat ēgregiō iuvenī, iam ēlēctus nūptiārum diēs, iam nōs vocātī.

Nōn possum exprimere verbīs quantum animō vulnus accēperim, cum audīvī Fundānum ipsum imperantem ut illa pecūnia quam in vestēs et gemmās impēnsūrus esset in unguenta et odōrēs impende- 15 rētur.[8] Āmīsit fīliam quae nōn minus mōrēs eius quam vultum referēbat.

---

[1] *take place.*   [2] *ball.*

---

[1] *more charming.*   [2] Dative of possession (**599,** 8).   [3] *of an old woman.*
[4] The urn containing the girl's ashes was actually found in 1881 in the family tomb three miles north of Rome. The inscription on it reads: **d(īs) m(ānibus) Miniciae Mārcellae Fundānī f(īliae). V(īxit) a(nnīs) xii, m(ēnsibus) xi, d(iēbus) vii.** The parts in parentheses complete the abbreviations found in the inscrip- tion. The first two words mean "to the deified shades (of)."
[5] *how.*   [6] *neck.*   [7] *embraced.*
[8] *giving orders that the money which . . . be spent on perfumes* (for the funeral).

The oldest manuscript of Pliny's letters (about 500 A.D.) in existence. It is in the Pierpont Morgan Library, New York.

488. A GHOST STORY

Erat Athēnīs magna domus sed īnfāmis.[1] Per silentium noctis sonus vinculōrum, longius prīmō, deinde ē proximō audiēbātur. Tum appārēbat lārva, senex horrentī capillō. Vincula gerēbat. Deinde malae noctēs erant eīs quī ibi habitābant; mors sequēbātur. Domus dēserta
5 est et illī lārvae relīcta. Prōscrībēbātur [2] tamen, sed nēmō vel emere vel condūcere voluit.

Vēnit Athēnās philosophus Athēnodōrus, lēgit titulum, audītōque pretiō, quaesīvit cūr tam vīlis esset. Omnia cognōscit sed tamen condūcit. Ubi nox vēnit, poposcit tabulās, stilum, lūmen; servōs suōs omnēs
10 dīmīsit, ipse ad scrībendum animum, oculōs, manum intendit nē mēns timōrēs fingeret. Prīmō silentium, deinde vincula audiuntur. Ille nōn tollit oculōs. Tum sonus vinculōrum crēscit, propius venit. Iam in līmine,[3] iam intrā līmen audītur. Ille respicit, videt lārvam. Stābat innuēbatque [4] digitō similis vocantī. Sed philosophus rūrsus studiīs sē
15 dat. Iterum sonus vinculōrum audītur. Ille rūrsus respicit lārvam innuentem. Nōn morātus tollit lūmen et sequitur. Postquam lārva dēflexit in āream domūs, eum dēserit; is signum in locō pōnit. Posterō diē philosophus adit magistrātūs et monet ut illum locum effodī iubeant. Inveniuntur ossa et vincula. Haec collēcta sepeliuntur.[5] In eō aedificiō
20 numquam posteā lārva vīsa est.

489. DON'T BE A HARSH FATHER

Castīgābat quīdam fīlium suum quod paulō sūmptuōsius equōs et canēs emeret. Huic ego: "Heus [1] tū, numquamne fēcistī quod ā patre tuō culpārī posset? Nōn etiam nunc facis quod fīlius tuus, sī pater tuus esset, parī gravitāte culpet?"
5 Haec tibi admonitus magnae sevēritātis exemplō scrīpsī nē tū quoque fīlium acerbius dūriusque tractārēs.[2] Cōgitā et illum puerum esse et tē fuisse atque hominem esse tē et hominis patrem.

---

[1] *with a bad reputation.*   [2] *advertised.* What literally?   [3] *threshold.*
[4] *beckoned.*   [5] *are buried.*

---

[1] *Say!*   [2] *handle.*

490. GRADED FRIENDSHIP IS DEGRADED FRIENDSHIP

Longum est altius repetere [1] quō modō acciderit ut cēnārem apud quendam, ut sibi vidēbātur, lautum et dīligentem, ut mihi, sordidum simul et sūmptuōsum. Nam sibi et paucīs opīma [2] quaedam, cēterīs vīlia pōnēbat. Vīnum etiam parvulīs laguncuĺīs [3] in tria genera dīvīserat, nōn ut potestās ēligendī, sed nē iūs esset recūsandī, aliud sibi 5 et nōbīs, aliud minōribus amīcīs (nam gradātim [4] amīcōs habet), aliud suīs nostrīsque lībertīs. Animadvertit [5] quī mihi proximus accumbēbat et an probārem interrogāvit. Negāvī. "Tū ergō," inquit, "quam cōnsuētūdinem sequeris?" "Eadem omnibus pōnō; ad cēnam enim, nōn ad contumēliam invītō omnibusque rēbus aequō quōs mēnsā aequāvī." 10 "Etiamne lībertōs?" "Etiam: amīcōs enim tum, nōn lībertōs putō." Et ille, "Magnō [6] tibi cōnstat?" "Minimē." "Quō modō fierī potest?" "Quia lībertī meī nōn idem quod ego bibunt, sed idem ego quod lībertī."

491. WANTED, A TEACHER

Note the exquisite courtesy which turns a chore into a pleasure.

Quid ā mē grātius potuistī petere quam ut magistrum frātris tuī līberīs quaererem? Nam beneficiō tuō in scholam redeō et illam dulcissimam aetātem quasi resūmam. Sedeō inter iuvenēs, ut solēbam, atque etiam experior quantum apud illōs auctōritātis ex studiīs meīs habeam. Nam proximē inter sē iocābantur: intrāvī, silentium factum est. Hoc 5 ad illōrum laudem magis quam ad meam pertinet.

Cum omnēs professōrēs audīverō, quid dē quōque sentiam scrībam. Dēbeō enim tibi, dēbeō memoriae frātris tuī hanc fidem, hoc studium, praesertim in tantā rē.

492. A COURAGEOUS WIFE

Pliny gives three examples of Arria's devotion to her husband.

Aeger erat Paetus, marītus Arriae, aeger etiam fīlius. Fīlius dēcessit. Huic illa ita fūnus parāvit ut ignōrāret marītus. Cum [1] cubiculum eius intrāret, vīvere fīlium atque etiam commodiōrem esse dīcēbat, ac saepe marītō interrogantī quid ageret puer respondēbat, "Bene quiētem cēpit et cibum sūmpsit." Deinde, cum lacrimae vincerent, ēgrediēbātur. 5 Tum sē dolōrī dabat. Compositō vultū redībat.

Paetus cum Scrībōniānō arma in Īllyricō contrā Claudium mōverat. Occīsō Scrībōniānō, Rōmam Paetus trahēbātur.[2] Erat ascēnsūrus

---

[1] *go into too deeply.*   [2] *rich (foods).*   [3] *bottles.*
[4] *of different degrees.*   [5] Supply **is.**   [6] *It costs a great deal.*

---

[1] *whenever.*   [2] *i.e., as a prisoner.*

návem; Arria mīlitēs ōrābat ut simul impōnerētur. "Datūrī estis,"
10 inquit, "marītō meō, cōnsulārī virō, servōs aliquōs quōrum ē manū
cibum capiat [3] et vestem et calceōs. Omnia haec ego sōla faciam." Hōc
negātō, illa condūxit parvum nāvigium et magnam nāvem secūta est.

Postquam Rōmam pervēnērunt, illa gladium strīnxit, in corde suō
dēfīxit, extrāxit, marītō dedit, addidit vōcem immortālem ac paene
15 dīvīnam: "Paete, nōn dolet." [4]

493. TWO LOVE LETTERS

Written by Pliny to his third wife, who was much younger than he.

Numquam magis dē occupātiōnibus meīs sum questus,[1] quae mē
nōn sunt passae sequī tē proficīscentem in Campāniam valētūdinis
causā. Nunc enim maximē tēcum esse cupiō ut oculīs meīs videam
quid vīrium cōnsecūta sīs. Et absentia et īnfirmitās tua mē terrent.
5 Vereor omnia, fingō omnia, ea maximē quae maximē timeō. Itaque
rogō ut cotīdiē singulās vel etiam bīnās [2] epistulās scrībās. Sine cūrā
erō dum legō statimque timēbō cum lēgerō. Valē.

Scrībis tē absentiā meā magnopere afficī ūnumque habēre sōlācium,
quod prō mē librōs meōs teneās. Grātum est quod mē requīris. Ego
10 epistulās tuās legō atque identidem in manūs quasi novās sūmō. Tū
quam frequentissimē scrībe. Valē.

494. A FISH STORY

To judge from modern parallels, we consider this story a true one. From
New Zealand comes the report that Opo, a thousand-pound dolphin, or
porpoise, which was a favorite at a beach resort, died in 1956. It would

---

[3] *he may take.*   [4] *it doesn't hurt.* Why did she hand the sword to Paetus?

[1] From **queror,** *complain.*   [2] *two.*

**Ancient statue of a dolphin
and rider; cf. the one on p. 357.**

Modern version of rider and dolphin in Radio City, New York.

frolic with the bathers and permit children to ride on its back. Similar stories come from California and elsewhere.

Est in Āfricā colōnia marī proxima. Hīc omnis aetās [1] piscandī,[2] nāvigandī, atque etiam natandī studiō tenētur, maximē puerī, quī ōtium habent et lūdere cupiunt. Hīs glōria et virtūs est longissimē natāre; victor ille est quī longissimē lītus et aliōs natantēs relīquit. Puer quīdam audācior [3] in ulteriōra tendēbat.[4] Delphīnus occurrit et 5 nunc praecēdit puerum, nunc sequitur, tum subit,[5] dēpōnit, iterum subit territumque puerum perfert prīmum in altum, deinde flectit ad lītus redditque terrae.

Concurrunt omnēs, ipsum puerum tamquam mīrāculum spectant, rogant, audiunt. Posterō diē rūrsus natant puerī, rūrsus delphīnus ad 10 puerum venit. Fugit ille cum cēterīs. Delphīnus, quasi revocāns, exsilit et mergitur.[6] Hoc plūribus diēbus facit. Tandem puerī accēdunt, appellant, tangunt etiam. Crēscit audācia. Maximē puer quī prīmus expertus est natat ad eum, īnsilit tergō, fertur referturque.[7] Amārī sē putat, amat ipse. Neuter timet, neuter timētur. 15

[1] *people of all ages.* What literally? [2] Depends on **studiō.**
[3] i.e., than the rest. [4] *made for.*
[5] *comes up from under,* i.e., takes the boy on its back.
[6] *leaps up and dives.* [7] *is carried (out) and back.*

357

Veniēbant omnēs magistrātūs ad spectāculum, quōrum adventū et morā parva rēs pūblica novīs sūmptibus [8] cōnficitur. Posteā locus ipse quiētem suam āmittēbat. Placuit delphīnum interficī ad quem videndum omnēs veniēbant.

495. ADVICE TO A PROVINCIAL GOVERNOR

This letter indicates not only Pliny's respect for Greek culture, but also his belief that, though man is born free, he must preserve his right to freedom by the way he lives.

Cōgitā tē missum in prōvinciam Achaiam, illam vēram Graeciam, in quā prīmum hūmānitās, litterae, etiam frūgēs inventae esse crēduntur; missum ad hominēs vērē hominēs, ad līberōs [1] vērē līberōs, quī iūs ā nātūrā datum virtūte et meritīs tenuērunt. Reverēre glōriam
5 veterem. Sint antīquitās et magna facta in magnō honōre apud tē. Habē ante oculōs hanc esse terram quae nōbīs mīserit iūra, quae lēgēs nōn victīs sed petentibus dederit, Athēnās esse quās adeās, Lacedaemonem esse quam regās. Plūs potest amor ad obtinendum quod [2] velīs quam timor.

496. A HUMANE MASTER

As slaves were by law merely so much property, they could not legally own money or make wills. But in actual practice most slaves had these and other privileges.

Cōnfēcērunt mē īnfirmitātēs servōrum meōrum, mortēs etiam. Sōlācia duo sunt, nōn paria tantō dolōrī: ūnum, cōpia manūmittendī (videor enim nōn omnīnō perdidisse quōs iam līberōs [1] perdidī); alterum, quod permittō servīs quoque quasi [2] testāmenta facere. Man-
5 dant rogantque in hīs id quod volunt; pāreō ut [3] iussus. Dīvidunt, dōnant, relinquunt, dumtaxat [4] intrā domum; nam servīs rēs pūblica quaedam et quasi cīvitās domus est.

Nōn ignōrō aliōs [5] eius modī cāsūs nihil amplius vocāre quam damnum.[6] Fortasse [7] sunt magnī sapientēsque, ut sibi videntur;
10 hominēs nōn sunt. Homō enim dēbet afficī dolōre.

Dīxī dē hīs plūra fortasse quam dēbuī, sed pauciōra quam voluī. Est enim quaedam etiam dolendī voluptās.

---

[8] *expenses.* The town had to pay for the entertainment of the visiting officials.

---

[1] From **līber,** not **līberī.** He means that true manhood and true freedom had their beginnings in Greece. [2] Supply **id** as antecedent.

---

[1] From **līber.**	[2] *as it were.*	[3] *as.*	[4] *only, however.*
[5] *other men.*	[6] *loss* (of property).	[7] *perhaps.*	

358

497. A BUSY HOLIDAY

Omne hoc tempus inter tabulās ac librōs grātissimā quiēte ēgī. "Quō modō," inquis, "in urbe potuistī?" Circēnsēs lūdī erant, quō genere spectāculī minimē teneor. Nihil novum, nihil varium, nihil quod nōn semel spectāvisse sufficiat. Mīror tot mīlia virōrum tam puerīliter cupere identidem vidēre currentēs equōs, īnsistentēs curribus [1] hominēs. 5 Nōn vēlōcitāte equōrum aut hominum arte trahuntur.[2] Favent pannō,[3] pannum amant. Sī in ipsō cursū hic color illūc, ille hūc trānsferātur,[4] studium favorque trānsferētur,[5] et statim aurīgās illōs, equōs illōs quōs procul nōscunt, quōrum clāmant nōmina, relinquent. Tanta grātia, tanta auctōritās in ūnā vīlissimā tunicā, nōn modo apud vulgus 10 sed apud quōsdam gravēs hominēs. Capiō aliquam voluptātem quod hāc voluptāte nōn capior. Et ōtium meum in litterīs per hōs diēs collocō, quōs aliī perdunt. Valē.

[1] *standing in chariots.*   [2] *they are attracted.*
[3] *the cloth*, referring to the different colors worn by the drivers of the various racing clubs (cf. **tunicā** below); we may compare the colors of college athletic teams and of the professional baseball teams ("Red Sox," "White Sox"). The point is that the spectators are interested, not in the skill of the drivers, but in the side they represent.
[4] *should be transferred.*   [5] Singular because the two subjects represent one idea.

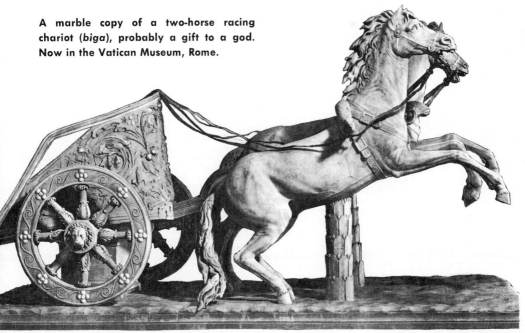

A marble copy of a two-horse racing chariot (*biga*), probably a gift to a god. Now in the Vatican Museum, Rome.

E. Richter, Rome

UNIT X

Marcus Tullius Cicero (106–43 B.C.) was not only the greatest orator of Rome, but also one of its most important statesmen and its greatest prose writer. He lived during a very critical and unsettled time in Roman history. His life spanned almost the same period of time as the life of Julius Caesar. Cicero's influence on later western civilization is immeasurable. It has been said that "Cicero taught Europe how to write."

498. TWO THOUSAND YEARS OF LATIN

Latin literature, as we have it, extends from the third century B.C. to the present time. It contains material of almost every description: fine poetry, absorbing history and biography, amusing stories, moral essays, pithy sayings, passionate oratory, comic and tragic drama, scientific treatises, and much that is pertinent to life today. In this unit you will find a few samples of that literature down to the eighteenth century.

499. ENNIUS

Ennius (239–169 B.C.) has been called the father of Latin poetry. His *Annals,* an epic poem dealing with the history of Rome down to his own time, remained the chief epic of Rome until it was supplanted by Virgil's *Aeneid.* Only fragments of the *Annals* and of his plays have survived, preserved in quotations by later authors. Ennius was a bold experimenter with verse. One of his experiments in alliteration reminds one of "Peter Piper picked a peck of pickled peppers":

> Ō, Tite, tūte,[1] Tatī, tibi tanta,[2] tyranne, tulistī.

This is addressed to Titus Tatius, the Sabine king, by the man who killed him.

Like many other Roman writers, Ennius stressed patriotic and moral qualities:

> Mōribus [3] antīquīs stat rēs [4] Rōmāna virīsque.[3]

500. ROMAN COMEDY

As early as the third century B.C. the Romans had begun to borrow and adapt from the Greeks a type of comedy based on the manners (or bad manners) of middle-class citizens. Its themes were general: thwarted but eventually successful love, paternal strictness versus the

---

[1] = tū.
[2] Neuter plural accusative; i.e., misfortunes.
[3] *because of,* etc.
[4] = rēs pūblica.

frivolity of an ungovernable teen-aged son, the cleverness of a slave who outwits his master to make everything come out right at the end. The plots are complicated, with all sorts of mistaken identities and surprise twists. Much of the humor consists in clever puns, in constant involvement of the characters in embarrassing and humiliating situations, and in the wildest sort of slapstick.

Rome's two masters of comedy were Plautus (ca. 254–184 B.C.), twenty of whose plays survive, and Terence (ca. 190–159 B.C.), who has left us six plays. Terence is much the milder, and, if we consider that originally he was a slave of African birth, the purity of his Latin is truly remarkable. The selection below is taken from the more boisterous Plautus.

501. The Boastful Soldier

The title of the play, *Miles Gloriosus* (*The Boastful Soldier*), describes the subject of the play. The soldier, Pyrgopolinices (whose name means "tower-city-conqueror" in Greek) has a good imagination in recounting his deeds, but his sponging friend Artotrogus ("bread-eater") has an even better one, inventing fantastic tales about his companion.

>   AR. Meminī centum in Cilicā
> et quīnquāgintā, centum in Scytholatrōniā,[1]
> trīgintā Sardōs, sexāgintā Macedonēs—
> sunt hominēs quōs tū—occīdistī ūnō diē.
> PY. Quanta istaec [2] hominum summa est? AR. Septem mīlia.   5
> PY. Tantum esse oportet. Rēctē ratiōnem tenēs.
> AR. Quid in Cappadociā, ubi tū quīngentōs simul,
> nī hebes machaera foret,[3] ūnō ictū [4] occīderās?
> Quid tibi ego dīcam, quod omnēs mortālēs sciunt,
> Pyrgopolinīcem tē ūnum in terrā vīvere   10
> virtūtē et fōrmā et factīs invictissimīs?
> Amant tē omnēs mulierēs neque iniūriā,[5]
> quī sīs tam pulcher; vel [6] illae quae herī palliō
> mē reprehendērunt.[7] PY. Quid eae dīxērunt tibi?
> AR. Rogitābant: "Hicine [8] Achillēs est?"   15
> "Immō [9] eius frāter," inquam, "est."

---

[1] A nonexistent place: "Scythia-robber-land." Cilicia and Cappadocia are in Asia Minor, the Sardinians are west of Italy, and the Macedonians north of Greece.   [2] = **ista.**   [3] *if your sword had not been dull;* **nī** = **nisi.**
[4] *blow.*   [5] *and not without reason;* literally, *not wrongly.*
[6] *for example.*   [7] *caught me by the coat.*
[8] = **hicne.**   [9] *No, but.*

502. LUCRETIUS

Almost nothing certain is known about the life of this great poet, who lived during the first half of the first century B.C. His one poem, the *De Rerum Natura* (*On the Nature of Things*), is a poetic exposition of the theories of the Greek philosopher Epicurus. It is important because it is an attempt to explain the universe in the scientific terms of an atomic theory often surprisingly similar to our own, and to dispel man's superstitious fears about death and terrifying natural phenomena, such as thunder, lightning, and earthquakes, which were commonly attributed to the actions of the gods. It also anticipates modern notions of biological and social evolution.

503. Knowledge Produces a Tranquil Mind

Suāve,[1] marī [2] magnō turbantibus aequora [3] ventīs,
ē terrā magnum alterius spectāre labōrem,
nōn quia vexārī quemquam est iūcunda voluptās,
sed quibus ipse malīs careās [4] quia cernere [5] suāve est.
5 Sed nīl dulcius est, bene quam mūnīta tenēre
ēdita doctrīnā sapientum templa [6] serēnā,
dēspicere unde queās [7] aliōs passimque [8] vidēre
errāre atque viam pālantēs [9] quaerere vītae,
certāre ingeniō, contendere nōbilitāte,
10 noctēs atque diēs nītī [10] praestante labōre
ad summās ēmergere opēs rērumque potīrī.
Ō miserās hominum mentēs,[11] ō pectora caeca! [12]

Italian stamp in honor of the two-thousandth anniversary of Catullus' death. He is one of the world's great lyric poets.

---

[1] Supply **est.**
[2] Ablative of place without a preposition.
[3] *waters.*
[4] *You are free from* (with ablative).
[5] The antecedent of **quibus** (**ea** understood) is the object of **cernere.**
[6] *regions.*   [7] *you can.*   [8] *everywhere.*   [9] *wandering.*
[10] *to strive* (deponent infinitive).   [11] Accusative of exclamation.
[12] *blind.*

Two features of Lucretius' scientific explanation of the universe are that nothing is produced from nothing and that the universe consists only of matter and empty space:

Nīl posse creārī dē nīlō.[13]
Corpora [14] sunt et ināne.

Men are like relay racers; they pass on the torch of life to the next generation:

Sīc rērum summa novātur
semper, et inter sē mortālēs mūtua [15] vīvunt.
Augēscunt aliae gentēs, aliae minuuntur,
inque brevī spatiō mūtantur saecla animantum [16]
et quasi cursōrēs vītāī [17] lampada trādunt.

504. CORNELIUS NEPOS

Nepos wrote biographies of famous Greeks and Romans. He lived in the first century B.C. In this selection he tells about an honest politician who could not be bought.

Phōcion Athēniēnsis saepe exercitibus praefuit summōsque magistrātūs cēpit, sed tamen multō nōtior est ob prīvātam vītam quam ob glōriam reī mīlitāris. Fuit enim semper pauper, quamquam dītissimus esse poterat propter honōrēs dēlātōs potestātēsque summās quae eī ā populō dabantur. Cum magna mūnera pecūniae ā lēgātīs rēgis Philippī 5 dēlāta reiceret, lēgātī dīxērunt: "Sī ipse haec nōn vīs,[1] līberīs tamen tuīs prōspicere tē oportet, quibus difficile erit in summā inopiā tantam patris glōriam servāre." Hīs ille, "Sī meī [2] similēs erunt," inquit, "īdem hic parvus ager illōs alet quī mē ad hanc dignitātem perdūxit; sī dissimilēs sunt futūrī, nōlō meā pecūniā illōrum lūxuriam alī augērīque." 10

505. CATULLUS

Catullus, a younger contemporary of Caesar, Cicero, and Nepos, was Rome's most inspired lyric poet. Many of his poems are addressed to his sweetheart Lesbia. His love affair had its ups and down, but it did not end happily. Other short poems of his are written to friends and enemies, including Caesar, who at different times was friend and foe. Other poems include marriage songs, a short epic, and a lament for his dead brother.

---

[13] From **nīl** (ablative). [14] i.e., of matter. [15] *in turn.*
[16] *of living beings.* [17] = **vītae.**

---

[1] From **volō.** [2] Genitive of **ego,** with **similis:** *like me.*

Passer, deliciae meae puellae. See p. 293.

506. "Poor Little Sparrow"

In this poem Catullus mourns the death of the pet sparrow **(passer)** of his sweetheart Lesbia.

> Lūgēte, ō Venerēs Cupīdinēsque [1]
> et quantum est hominum venustiōrum! [2]
> Passer mortuus est meae puellae,
> passer, dēliciae [3] meae puellae,
> 5   quem plūs illa oculīs [4] suīs amābat;
> nam mellītus [5] erat, suamque nōrat [6]
> ipsam tam bene quam puella mātrem,
> nec sēsē ā gremiō [7] illius movēbat,
> sed circumsiliēns modo [8] hūc modo illūc
> 10 ad sōlam dominam usque pīpiābat.[9]
> Quī nunc it per iter tenebricōsum [10]
> illūc unde negant redīre quemquam.
> At vōbīs male sit, malae tenebrae
> Orcī, quae omnia bella [11] dēvorātis;
> 15 tam bellum mihi passerem abstulistis.
> Ō factum male! Iō miselle [12] passer!
> Tuā nunc operā meae puellae
> flendō turgidulī rubent ocellī.[13]

[1] i.e., all the gods of love and beauty.   [2] *all of the handsome men there are.*

[3] *pet;* nominative.   [4] Ablative of comparison (**601**, 5).

[5] *sweet as honey.*

[6] For **nōverat**. With **suam** supply **dominam** (Lesbia); **ipsam** modifies **mātrem**: *as the girl (knew) her own mother.*

[7] *lap.*   [8] *now . . . now.*

[9] *chirped.* The word imitates the sound ("peep") made by the bird.

[10] *shadowy;* to Hades. See **tenebrae**, *darkness* (line 13).

[11] Adjective, from **bellus**, *beautiful;* cf. English *belle.*

[12] Diminutive of **miser**: *poor little.*

[13] The diminutives (**ocellus** from **oculus**, **turgidulus** from **turgidus**, *swollen*) are used, like **miselle** above, for pathetic effect, as they heighten the tenderness and affection of the expression. **Rubent** means *are red.*

507. Counting Kisses

Vīvāmus, mea Lesbia, atque amēmus,
rūmōrēsque senum sevēriōrum
omnēs ūnius aestimēmus assis.[1]
Sōlēs occidere et redīre possunt;
nōbīs cum semel occidit brevis lūx,[2]   5
nox est perpetua ūna dormienda.
Dā mī [3] bāsia [4] mīlle, deinde centum,
dein mīlle altera, dein secunda centum,
deinde usque altera mīlle, deinde centum.
Dein, cum mīlia multa fēcerīmus,   10
Conturbābimus illa, nē sciāmus
aut nē quis malus invidēre [5] possit,
cum tantum sciat esse bāsiōrum.

508. CICERO

You have already become slightly acquainted with M. Tullius
Cicero (cf. **76, 231**). Now you will get to know him a little better.
If you continue Latin next year, you will become intimately acquainted
with him.

Cicero (106–43 B.C.) was Rome's greatest prose writer. He was
the leading public speaker at a time when the ability to make an
effective speech was even more important than it is today. Many of his
orations still exist, such as those against Catiline and Mark Antony,
and the one for Archias the poet, in which he shows his appreciation
of poetry. He wrote fine essays on moral and philosophical subjects:
on friendship, on old age, on one's duties, etc. He also wrote on the
history and technique of oratory. A large number of his letters, which
he himself had no intention of publishing, have been preserved. Many
are addressed to his intimate friend Atticus. They cover all sorts of
subjects, from bathtubs to politics, from the birth of a son to the
divorce and death of his daughter. He died while vainly attempting to
defend constitutional government against Mark Antony.

509. The Regulation of War

Adapted from Cicero's treatise *De Officiis,* which was written for his son.

In rē pūblicā maximē cōnservanda sunt iūra bellī. Nam sunt duo
genera dēcertandī, ūnum per disputātiōnem, alterum per vim. Illud

---

[1] *at one penny* (genitive of value).   [2] i.e., life.   [3] = **mihi.**
[4] From **bāsium,** *kiss.*   [5] i.e., cast the evil eye.

proprium est hominis, hoc animālium. Itaque nōn fugiendum est[1] ad vim et bellum nisi ūtī nōn licet disputātiōne.[2] Suscipienda quidem 5 bella sunt ut sine iniūriā in pāce vīvāmus; post autem victōriam cōnservandī sunt eī quī nōn crūdēlēs in bellō fuērunt, ut maiōrēs nostrī Tusculānōs, Volscōs, Sabīnōs in cīvitātem etiam accēpērunt. At Carthāginem omnīnō sustulērunt; etiam Corinthum (et hoc vix probō.), sed crēdō eōs hoc fēcisse nē locus[3] ipse ad bellum faciendum 10 hortārī[4] posset. Nam pāx quae nihil habitūra sit īnsidiārum semper est petenda. Sed eī quī, armīs positīs, ad imperātōrum fidem fugiunt recipiendī sunt. In quō, magnopere apud nostrōs iūstitia culta est. Nūllum bellum est iūstum nisi quod[5] aut, rēbus repetītīs, gerātur aut dēnūntiātum ante sit. Bellum autem ita suscipiātur ut nihil nisi pāx 15 quaerī videātur.

510. Good Citizenship

Adapted from various works of Cicero, especially the *De Officiis.*

Nec locus tibi ūllus dulcior esse dēbet patriā.[1]

Omnium societātum[2] nūlla est gravior, nūlla cārior quam ea quae cum rē pūblicā est ūnī cuique[3] nostrum. Cārī sunt parentēs, cārī līberī, propinquī, familiārēs, sed omnēs omnium cāritātēs patria ūna 5 continet, prō quā nēmō bonus dubitet[4] mortem petere. Quō[5] est dētestābilior istōrum immānitās[6] quī lacerāvērunt omnī scelere patriam et in eā dēlendā occupātī et sunt et fuērunt.

Est proprium mūnus[7] magistrātūs intellegere sē gerere persōnam[8] cīvitātis dēbēreque eius dignitātem sustinēre, servāre lēgēs, iūra dī- 10 scrībere,[9] ea[10] fideī suae commissa meminisse. Prīvātum[11] autem oportet aequō et parī iūre cum cīvibus vīvere, atque in rē pūblicā ea velle quae tranquilla et honesta sint: tālem enim solēmus et sentīre bonum cīvem et dīcere.

---

[1] Impersonal; translate: *we must not resort to.*
[2] Ablative with **ūtī.**   [3] *site.*   [4] Supply as object "the inhabitants of Corinth."
[5] *except (one) which.* War should be started only if restitution of stolen property **(rēbus)** is sought or if there is a formal declaration beforehand.

---

[1] Ablative of comparison (**601**, 5).   [2] *associations.*
[3] from **quisque:** *which each one of us has with,* etc. **Nostrum** is from **ego,** not **noster.**   [4] *would hesitate.*   [5] *therefore.*
[6] *ferocity.*   [7] *it is the special duty.*
[8] *represents;* literally, *wears the mask of (plays the part of).*
[9] *administer justice.*
[10] Neuter plural, object of **meminisse.** It is modified by **commissa.**
[11] *a private citizen,* in contrast to **magistrātūs.**

Sī pecūniam aequam omnibus esse nōn placet, sī ingenia omnium paria esse nōn possunt, iūra certē paria dēbent esse eōrum quī sunt 15 cīvēs in eādem rē pūblicā.

Mēns et animus et cōnsilium et sententia cīvitātis posita est in lēgi-bus. Ut corpora nostra sine mente, sīc cīvitās sine lēge suīs partibus ūtī nōn potest.

Fundāmentum iūstitiae est fidēs.   20

511. Quotations from Cicero

1. Aliae nātiōnēs servitūtem patī possunt; populī Rōmānī rēs est propria lībertās.

2. Cavēte, patrēs cōnscrīptī, nē spē praesentis pācis perpetuam pācem āmittātis.

3. Cēdant arma togae.[1]

4. Cōnsuētūdinis magna vīs est.

5. Ō tempora, ō mōrēs!

6. Parēs cum paribus facillimē congregantur.[2]

7. Salūs populī suprēma lēx estō.[3]

512. SALLUST

Sallust (86–34 B.C.) was a politician and officer who held important commands under Caesar during the Civil War. With the fortune he amassed, supposedly from plundering the province of Numidia, he bought a palatial estate in Rome, with magnificent gardens which are still famous. Two of his works which have survived are the *Catiline* and the *Jugurtha,* the former dealing with the conspiracy of Catiline **(231),** the latter with a war against an African king. Sallust claimed impartiality, but he is bitterly critical of the old Roman aristocracy and the decadence for which he thinks they are responsible.

[1] The toga represents *civil life,* as contrasted with *military.* Motto of the state of Wyoming.

[2] *gather.* What is the modern form of this proverb?

[3] *let . . . be.* Motto of the state of Missouri.

Carlsberg   *Carlsberg*

513. The Good Old Days of Early Rome

Igitur domī mīlitiaeque ¹ bonī mōrēs colēbantur; concordia maxima,
minima avāritia erat; iūs bonumque apud eōs nōn lēgibus magis quam
nātūrā valēbat. Iūrgia,² discordiās, simultātēs ³ cum hostibus exercē-
bant, cīvēs cum cīvibus dē virtūte certābant. In suppliciīs deōrum
5 magnificī, domī parcī, in amīcōs fidēlēs erant. Duābus hīs artibus,
audāciā in bellō, ubi pāx ēvēnerat aequitāte, sēque remque pūblicam
cūrābant. Quārum rērum ego maxima documenta haec habeō, quod
in bellō saepius vindicātum est ⁴ in eōs quī contrā imperium in hostem
pugnāverant ⁵ quīque tardius ⁶ revocātī proeliō ⁷ excesserant, quam ⁸
10 quī signa relinquere aut pulsī locō ⁷ cēdere ausī erant; in pāce vērō
quod beneficiīs magis quam metū imperium agitābant et, acceptā
iniūriā, ignōscere quam persequī mālēbant.

514. PUBLILIUS SYRUS AND HIS PROVERBS

Publilius Syrus was a writer of a type of comedy which was very
popular when he wrote, in the time of Caesar. One reason why he won
so much favor was his use of many proverbial expressions. The plays

---

¹ *abroad* (locative). ² *quarrels.* ³ *hatreds.* ⁴ *punishment was inflicted* (*on*).
⁵ Cf. the story of Manlius in **211.** ⁶ *too slowly* (with **excesserant**).
⁷ Ablative (**601, 1**). ⁸ To be taken with **saepius;** supply in **eōs.**

Human nature is remarkably similar throughout the ages, even in its less important aspects. Roman women, too, liked to look different, as shown by these three hairstyles.

Franz Kaufman, Munich

themselves have disappeared, but someone made a collection of the proverbs in them, and these have been preserved. Many are as fresh and applicable today as they were two thousand years ago.

1. Ab aliīs exspectēs [1] alterī [2] quod [3] fēcerīs.
2. Aliēna [4] nōbīs, nostra plūs aliīs placent.
3. Aliēnum aes hominī ingenuō [5] acerba est servitūs.
4. Aut amat aut ōdit mulier; nihil est tertium.
5. Avārus ipse miseriae causa est suae.
6. Avārus, nisi cum moritur, nihil rēctē facit.
7. Bis vincit quī sē vincit in victōriā.
8. Comes fācundus [6] in viā prō vehiculō est.
9. Cui [7] plūs licet quam pār est plūs vult quam licet.
10. Discordiā fit cārior concordia.
11. Effugere cupiditātem rēgnum est vincere.
12. Etiam capillus ūnus habet umbram suam.

---

[1] Subjunctive used in a command.
[2] With **fēcerīs** (perfect subjunctive). What is the modern form of this saying?
[3] Supply **id** as antecedent.   [4] **Aliēna** and **nostra** are used as subjects of **placent.**
[5] *free.*   [6] *eloquent, interesting.*   [7] Supply **is** as antecedent.

13. Inopī bis dat quī cito dat.

14. Male imperandō summum imperium āmittitur.

15. Necesse est minima [8] maximōrum esse initia.

16. Paucōrum improbitās est multōrum calamitās.

17. Perīcula timidus etiam quae nōn sunt videt.

18. Quicquid fit cum virtūte fit cum glōriā.

19. Spīna etiam grāta est ex quā spectātur rosa.

20. Stultī timent fortūnam, sapientēs ferunt.

21. Stultum facit fortūna quem vult perdere.

22. Taciturnitās stultō hominī prō sapientiā est.

515. CATO AND THE WOMEN [1]

Inter bellōrum magnōrum cūrās intercessit rēs parva sed quae [2] in magnum certāmen excesserit.[3] In mediō Pūnicī bellī lēx lāta erat nē qua mulier plūs quam sēmunciam [4] aurī habēret nec veste versi-colōrī ūterētur nec vehiculō in urbe veherētur. Post bellum mulierēs
5 voluērunt hanc lēgem abrogārī. Nec auctōritāte nec imperiō virōrum continērī poterant; omnēs viās urbis obsidēbant; etiam audēbant adīre cōnsulēs. Sed cōnsul, M. Porcius Catō, haec verba fēcit: "Sī in [5] suā quisque uxōre, cīvēs, iūs virī retinēre īnstituisset,[6] minus negōtī cum omnibus fēminīs habērēmus.[7] Quia singulās nōn continuimus, omnēs
10 timēmus. Maiōrēs nostrī voluērunt fēminās agere nūllam rem, nē prīvātam quidem, sine parentibus vel frātribus vel virīs; nōs, sī deīs placet, iam etiam rem pūblicam capere eās patimur. Hāc rē expugnātā, quid nōn temptābunt? Sī eās aequās virīs esse patiēminī, tolerābilēs vōbīs eās futūrās esse crēditis? Simul ac parēs esse coeperint, superiōrēs
15 erunt. Nūlla lēx satis commoda omnibus est; id modo [8] quaeritur, sī maiōrī partī prōsit." [9] Tum ūnus ex tribūnīs contrā lēgem locūtus est, et lēx abrogāta est. Mulierēs vīcerant.

516. HORACE

Horace (65–8 B.C.) was one of the greatest of Roman poets. He was a friend of Augustus and Virgil. His *Odes, Satires,* and *Epistles* are delightful reading. As his poems are not always easy to read, only quotations are given here. They often tell much in very brief but exquisitely phrased language (cf. No. 3 and note 2).

[8] *very little things.*

[1] Adapted from Livy, on whom see **169**.
[2] *(one) which.*
[3] Translate as if indicative: *developed into.*
[4] *half an ounce.*
[5] *in (the case of);* **quisque** is the subject.
[6] *had begun to hold on to the rights of the husband.*
[7] *we should have.*
[8] Adverb: *only.*
[9] *is beneficial;* from **prōsum.**

NON OMNIS MORIAR

Left: Italian stamp with picture of Horace (his name is misspelled!) and a quotation from his poems.
Above: Stamps of Italy and of Réunion Island, Indian Ocean, with quotations from Horace.

1. Aequam mementō[1] rēbus in arduīs servāre mentem.
2. Aurea mediocritās.
3. Carpe diem.[2]
4. Crēscentem sequitur cūra pecūniam.
5. Est modus[3] in rēbus.
6. Levius fit patientiā quicquid[4] corrigere est nefās.
7. Magnās inter opēs inops.
8. Nīl mortālibus arduī[5] est.
9. Nīl sine magnō vīta labōre dedit mortālibus.
10. Permitte dīvīs cētera.
11. Rāra avis.
12. Rīdentem dīcere vērum.
13. Vīxēre[6] fortēs ante Agamemnona.[7]

517. VIRGIL AND OVID

You have already met Virgil (21, 140, 167). You will have a chance to read some selections of his work (558–561). Ovid too is known to you (21, 88). You may read some parts of his poems in 518, 536, 552–556.

---

[1] Imperative: *remember.* **Aequam** modifies **mentem.** In poetry the word order is freer than in prose.
[2] *Seize the (present) day.* It really means: "The day is like a rose that fades fast; pluck it while you may."   [3] In the same sense as **mediocritās** in No. 2.
[4] *whatever.* The clause is the subject of **fit.**
[5] With **nīl:** *nothing hard.*   [6] For **vīxērunt.**
[7] Accusative. Agamemnon led the Greeks in the Trojan War.

518. ROMAN ELEGY

The Greeks had used the elegiac meter for drinking and military songs, for historical and political subjects, for inscriptions on tombstones and laments for the dead, and even for love poetry. It was this last category that the three most famous Roman elegists, Tibullus, Propertius, and Ovid, particularly developed into an extremely personal and sensitive form. Each immortalized the sweetheart to whom he addressed his verse, Tibullus' Delia, Propertius' Cynthia, and Ovid's Corinna. The following selection from Ovid, however, exemplifies elegy's traditional role of mourning for the dead. Ovid here laments the loss of Tibullus, who had joined the earlier elegists in the Elysian Fields.

> Sī tamen ē nōbīs [1] aliquid nisi nōmen et umbra
> restat, in Ēlysiā [2] valle Tibullus erit.
> Obvius huic veniās [3] hederā iuvenālia cīnctus
> tempora [4] cum Calvō, docte Catulle, tuō.
> 5 Hīs comes umbra tua est. Sī qua est modo corporis umbra,
> auxistī numerōs, culte Tibulle, piōs.
> Ossa quiēta, precor,[5] tūtā requiēscite in urnā,[6]
> et sit humus cinerī nōn onerōsa tuō.[7]

519. PHAEDRUS

The fable is a very old type of literature, in which animals generally speak and act like human beings. Usually a moral is attached. The most famous of all fabulists was the Greek writer Aesop, and his stories are still much read in many languages. In Rome during the age of Augustus, Phaedrus put these fables into simple Latin verse. Here are three of them, rewritten in prose.

520. The Wolf and the Lamb

Ad rīvum eundem lupus et agnus vēnerant; superior stābat lupus, longēque īnferior agnus. Tum lupus famē incitātus contrōversiae causam intulit. "Cūr," inquit, "turbulentam fēcistī mihi aquam bibentī?" Agnus timēns respondit: "Quō modō possum hoc facere, lupe? 5 Ā tē dēcurrit aqua ad mē." Repulsus ille vēritātis vīribus: "Ante sex

---

[1] i.e., poets.   [2] The Elysian Fields correspond to our Heaven.
[3] *come to meet him;* **obvius** is an adjective; literally, *in the way.*
[4] *your temples crowned with ivy.* [5] *I pray.*
[6] Bodies were cremated, not buried, in Rome.
A variant of the phrase found on hundreds of Roman tombstones: **sit tibi terra levis.**

Roman dogs in mosaic and stone.

mēnsēs," ait, "male dīxistī [1] mihi." Respondit agnus: "Equidem nātus nōn eram." "Pater certē tuus," ille inquit, "male dīxit mihi." Atque ita raptum lacerat iniūstā nece.

Haec propter illōs scrīpta est hominēs fābula quī fictīs causīs innocentēs opprimant. 10

521. The Greedy Dog

Āmittit meritō [1] suum quī aliēnum appetit. Canis dum per flūmen carnem ferret natāns, in aquā vīdit simulācrum suum, aliamque praedam ab aliō cane ferrī putāns ēripere voluit; sed dēceptus avidus, quem tenēbat ōre dīmīsit cibum nec quem petēbat potuit attingere.

522. Sour Grapes

Famē coācta vulpēs [1] in altā vīneā ūvam [2] petēbat, summīs vīribus saliēns. Quam ubi tangere nōn potuit, discēdēns, "Nōndum mātūra est," inquit; "nōlō acerbam sūmere."

Eī quī verbīs ēlevant [3] quae nōn facere possunt hoc exemplum sibi ascrībere dēbent.

---

[1] With **male**: *swore at.*

---

[1] *deservedly.*

---

[1] *fox.*   [2] *grapes, bunch of grapes.*   [3] *make light of.*

523. *VALERIUS MAXIMUS*

In the first century A.D. Valerius Maximus put together a book of well-known stories from history, both Roman and foreign, to illustrate various human qualities and conditions, such as courage, superstition, cruelty. The purpose of the book was to provide material for a public speaker who wanted to illustrate his points by means of examples from history, just as today many speakers make use of jokebooks.

524. *Damon and Pythias*

Cum Dionȳsius, rēx Syrācūsārum, Pythiam philosophum interficere vellet, hic ā Dionȳsiō petīvit ut sibi licēret domum proficīscī rērum suārum dispōnendārum causā. Amīcus eius Dāmōn erat. Tanta erat amīcitia inter Dāmōnem et Pythiam ut Dāmōn sē vadem [1] prō reditū
5 alterius rēgī dare nōn dubitāret. Appropinquante cōnstitūtō diē nec illō redeunte, ūnus quisque stultitiam Dāmōnis damnāvit. At is nihil sē dē amīcī fidē timēre dīcēbat. Hōrā cōnstitūtā Pythiās vēnit. Admīrātus utrīusque animum Dionȳsius supplicium remīsit et eōs rogāvit ut sē [2] socium amīcitiae reciperent.

525. *A Costly Joke*

P. Scīpiō Nāsīca, cum aedīlitātem [1] adulēscēns peteret, mōre candidātōrum manum cuiusdam agricolae rūsticō opere dūrātam prehendit. Iocī causā rogāvit agricolam num manibus solitus esset ambulāre. Quod [2] dictum ā circumstantibus audītum ad populum allātum est
5 causaque fuit repulsae [3] Scīpiōnís. Nam omnēs agricolae paupertātem suam ab eō rīdērī iūdicantēs īram suam contrā eius iocum ostendērunt.

526. *SENECA*

Seneca, who wrote many books on philosophy, was the tutor and later the adviser of the emperor Nero (54–68 A.D.), who eventually forced him to commit suicide. His books preach Stoic philosophy.

1. Magna rēs est vōcis et silentī tempora nōsse.[1]
2. Maximum remedium īrae mora est.
3. Nōn est in rēbus vitium, sed in ipsō animō.
4. Nōn sum ūnī angulō nātus; patria mea tōtus hic mundus est.
5. Omnis ars imitātiō est nātūrae.

---

[1] (*as*) *bail.* [2] i.e., Dionysius.

---

[1] *aedileship*, a public office. [2] = **Hoc** (**596**, 4, *c*). [3] *defeat.*

---

[1] For **nōvisse.**

6. Optimum est patī quod ēmendāre nōn possīs.[2]
7. Ōtium sine litterīs mors est.
8. Quī beneficium dedit taceat: nārret quī accēpit.
9. Sī vīs amārī, amā.
10. Ubicumque homō est, ibi beneficī locus est.

527. PETRONIUS

Nothing in Latin literature is quite so zany and ludicrous as the *Satiricon* of Petronius. It is a kind of novel, containing a wild medley of prose and poetry, dealing mostly with the escapades of three lower-class rogues who must live by their wits and who are constantly in trouble with the authorities. Best known of their adventures is the account of a fantastic dinner party at the house of an ex-slave named Trimalchio, who was so illiterate that he thought Hannibal took part in the Trojan War and so enormously wealthy that he bought the whole west coast of Italy so that, when he sailed to Sicily, he would not have to sail past anyone else's coastline! The selection below should give you still more indications of the size of Trimalchio's fortune.

Petronius is thought to have lived in the first century A.D. and has been identified with the Petronius who was called the *elegantiae arbiter* of Nero's court because of his exquisite refinement.

In this selection Trimalchio has his own newspaper read aloud to the guests at his dinner party.

[2] Translate as if indicative.

A public eating place from Roman times, in Pompeii. Food was served from the round receptacles in the counter.

Permanent couches built into a dining room in Pompeii. Usually, however, the couches were movable. Covers and many cushions, often brightly colored and made of elegant fabrics, were piled on top of the couches.

Āctuārius [1] tamquam urbis ācta [2] recitāvit: "Hōc diē in praediō Cūmānō [3] quod est Trimalchiōnis, nātī sunt puerī XXX, puellae XL; sublāta in horreum [4] trīticī mīlia modium quīngenta; [5] bovēs domitī [6] quīngentī. Eōdem diē: in arcam [7] relātum est quod collocārī nōn potuit
5 sēstertium centiēs.[8] Eōdem diē: incendium factum est in hortīs Pompeiānīs." "Quid," inquit Trimalchiō, "quandō mihi Pompeiānī hortī ēmptī sunt?" "Annō priōre," inquit āctuārius, "et ideō [9] in ra- tiōnem nōndum vēnērunt." Trimalchiō, "Quīcumque," inquit, "mihi fundī [10] ēmptī fuerint, nisi intrā sextum mēnsem scierō,[11] in ratiōnēs
10 meās īnferrī vetō."

528. QUINTILIAN

Possibly the most famous schoolteacher of all time is Quintilian (ca. 35–96 A.D.), who was appointed the first state-paid professor of rhetoric (oratory) by the emperor Vespasian. After a lifetime of teaching and practice at the bar, at the request of his devoted pupils he put his theories of education into twelve books called the *Institutio*

---

[1] *newsman, secretary.*   [2] *doings, news.*
[3] *the estate at Cumae*—and this was only one of his properties!   [4] *barn.*
[5] *500,000 pecks of wheat*, enough to feed 10,000 people for a year.
[6] *tamed, broken in.*   [7] *vault.*   [8] *10,000,000 sesterces (about $500,000).*
[9] *therefore.*   [10] *estates.*   [11] = **scīverō.**

378

Oratoria (*Introduction to Public Speaking*), which carry the training
of the orator from the cradle to the grave, for he believed in beginning
education when the child was born and continuing it all one's life. So
the nursery school and the kindergarten are not new, nor is adult education. Quintilian's favorite orator was Cicero, although he does not
hestitate to criticize even him. The basic principle of his teaching was
that a man could not be a great orator, whatever his skill, unless he
were first of all a good man.

Ante omnia nē sit vitiōsus sermō nūtrīcibus,[1] quās, sī fierī posset,
sapientēs Chrysippus [2] optāvit, certē quantum rēs paterētur, optimās
ēligī voluit. Et mōrum quidem in hīs haud dubiē [3] prior ratiō est;
rēctē tamen etiam loquantur. Hās prīmum audiet puer, hārum verba
effingere [4] imitandō cōnābitur. Et nātūrā tenācissimī sumus eōrum 5
quae rudibus animīs percēpimus. Et haec ipsa magis pertināciter
haerent quō [5] dēteriōra sunt. Nam bona facile mūtantur in peius; num
quandō [6] in bonum vertēris vitia? Nōn adsuēscat [7] ergō, nē dum īnfans
quidem [8] est, sermōnī quī dēdiscendus sit.[9]

In parentibus vērō quam plūrimum esse ērudītiōnis optāverim,[10] 10
nec dē patribus tantum loquor, nam Gracchōrum ēloquentiae multum
contulisse accēpimus Cornēliam mātrem, cuius doctissimus sermō in
posterōs quoque est epistulīs trāditus; et Laelia C.[11] fīlia reddidisse
in loquendō paternam ēlegantiam dīcitur; et Hortēnsiae Q. fīliae
ōrātiō legitur. Nec tamen iī quibus discere [12] ipsīs nōn contigit 15
minōrem cūram docendī līberōs habeant, sed sint propter hoc ipsum
ad cētera magis dīligentēs.

529. MARTIAL AND HIS WIT

Like Seneca and Quintilian, Martial was born in Spain but moved
to Rome. He is the writer who gave the word epigram its present
meaning. It is generally a short poem which makes fun of someone.
Its clever and often unexpected point is at the end, at times in the
last word.

An Unfair Exchange

1. Cūr nōn mitto meōs tibi, Pontiliāne, libellōs?
   Nē mihi tū mittās, Pontiliāne, tuōs.

---

[1] *nurses.*   [2] A Greek philosopher and teacher.
[3] With **haud:** *undoubtedly.*   [4] *form.*   [5] *according as.*   [6] *at any time.*
[7] *he should not accustom himself.*   [8] With **ne:** *not even.*
[9] *must be unlearned.*   [10] *I could wish.*   [11] **Gāī.**
[12] i.e., to get an education.

A Friend and His Faults

2. Difficilis, facilis, iūcundus, acerbus es īdem.
   Nec tēcum possum vīvere nec sine tē.

"Fifty-Fifty"

3. Nūbere [1] vīs Prīscō: nōn mīror, Paula; sapīstī.[2]
   Dūcere [1] tē nōn vult Prīscus: et [3] ille sapit.

Rich Wives

4. Uxōrem quārē loculpētem [4] dūcere nōlim
   quaeritis? Uxōrī nūbere [5] nōlo meae.
   Īnferior mātrōna suō sit, Prīsce, marītō;
   nōn aliter fīunt fēmina virque parēs.

The Plagiarist

5. Quem recitās meus est, ō Fīdentīne, libellus,
   sed, male cum recitās, incipit esse tuus.

A Good Match

6. Cum sītis similēs parēsque vītā,
   uxor pessima, pessimus marītus,
   mīror nōn bene convenīre [6] vōbīs.

530. TACITUS

Last of the great Roman historians was Cornelius Tacitus (ca. 55–120 A.D.). His two most extensive works are the *Annals* and the *Histories,* which between them originally covered the period of Roman history from the death of Augustus through the reign of Domitian, i.e., from 14 A.D. to 96 A.D. He also wrote monographs on oratory, on Germany, and on the deeds of his father-in-law, Agricola. He was a distinguished orator and public figure, rising to the consulship in 97. His cynical tone, his austerity, and his intense brevity have made him a favorite of students of Latin style, while his bitter senatorial prejudice against the imperial regime has been chiefly responsible for our present impression, largely incorrect, of the corruption and cruelty of Roman emperors. The *Agricola,* from which the following selection is taken, deals largely with Britain, because Tacitus' father-in-law was a successful general there.

---

[1] *marry,* literally, *take the veil for,* used of a woman, whereas the word used of a man is **dūcere (domum).**   [2] For **sapīvistī:** *you are wise.*   [3] *also.*   [4] *rich.*
[5] A man who marries a rich wife becomes the "lady" of the house. See note 1.
[6] Impersonal: *that you are not well suited.*

Agricola's name (GRI only is left) on a stone found in 1955 at Verulamium. Domitian's name was chipped out above GRI by order of his successor Trajan.

Agricola brings Roman culture to Britain.

Iam vērō prīncipum fīliōs līberālibus artibus ērudīre,[1] et ingenia Britannōrum studiīs Gallōrum anteferre,[2] ut quī modo[3] linguam Rōmānam abnuēbant,[4] ēloquentiam concupīscerent.[5] Inde etiam habitūs[6] nostrī honor et frequēns toga. Paulātimque dēscēnsum ad dēlēnīmenta[7] vitiōrum, porticūs et balineās[8] et convīviōrum[9] ēle- 5 gantiam. Idque apud imperītōs hūmānitās vocābātur, cum pars servitūtis esset.

531. JUVENAL

Juvenal was a satirist who lived at the beginning of the second century A.D. He was a contemporary of Pliny the Younger. The vices of his times are the themes of his poems.

1. Probitās laudātur et alget.[1]
2. Pānem et circēnsēs.[2]
3. Nēmō malus fēlīx.
4. Quis custōdiet ipsōs custōdēs?
5. Mēns sāna in corpore sānō.

---

[1] The infinitives are used instead of a past tense of the indicative.
[2] *put ahead of* (with dative).   [3] *recently.*   [4] *were rejecting.*
[5] *were eager for.*   [6] *clothing.*   [7] *enticements.*
[8] = **balnea.** The Roman baths at Bath are still one of the sights of England.
[9] *banquets.*

---

[1] *shivers,* i.e., the honest man is usually too poor to buy warm clothing.
[2] *bread and circus games*—all that the degenerate Romans of his day are interested in, according to Juvenal.

Venatio. From an ancient Roman relief in stone.

532. SUETONIUS

Rome's most important writer of biography was Suetonius, who wrote the lives of the first twelve emperors, down to the end of the first century A.D. Much of the gossip that is still passed around about these emperors comes from his *Lives of the Caesars*. The story of Nero (244) is based on his account.

533. AULUS GELLIUS

The two stories that follow are adapted from Aulus Gellius, a writer of the second century A.D., who tells many curious and interesting anecdotes. His *Noctes Atticae,* or *Attic Nights,* is a sort of literary scrapbook, written during winter evenings in Attica, Greece, to amuse and instruct his children.

534. A Lesson in Voting

Fabricius [1] magnā glōriā vir magnīsque rēbus gestīs fuit. P. Cornēlius Rūfīnus imperātor bonus et fortis et mīlitāris disciplīnae perītus [2] fuit, sed avārus erat. Hunc Fabricius nōn probābat et eī inimīcus ob mōrēs fuit. Sed cum tempore difficillimō reī pūblicae cōnsulēs creandī
5 essent et Rūfīnus peteret cōnsulātum competītōrēsque eius nōn essent bellī perītī, summā ope [3] Fabricius labōrāvit ut Rūfīnō cōnsulātus dēferrētur. Eam rem quibusdam mīrantibus, "Mālō," inquit, "ā cīve spoliārī quam ab hoste venīre." [4] M. Cicerō refert hoc esse dictum,

---

[1] Fabricius was the hero of the war with Pyrrhus, who admired him so much that he offered him part of his kingdom.   [2] With the genitive.   [3] *effort.*
[4] *to be sold* (from **vēneō**).

nōn aliīs, sed ipsī Rūfīnō, cum hic Fabriciō ob opem [5] grātiās ageret.

Hunc Rūfīnum, postquam bis cōnsul et dictātor fuit, cēnsor [6] Fabri- 10 cius ob lūxuriam ē senātū ēiēcit.

535. Androclus [1] and the Lion

In Circō Maximō vēnātiō [2] populō dabātur. Multae ibi ferae erant, sed praeter aliās omnēs ūnus leō magnitūdine corporis animōs oculōs- que omnium in sē converterat.

Inductus erat servus inter complūrēs aliōs ad pugnam ferārum. Eī servō [3] Androclus nōmen fuit. Hunc ille leō ubi vīdit procul, statim 5 quasi admīrāns stetit ac deinde lēniter, quasi cognōscēns ad hominem accēdit. Tum caudam mōre canis movet hominisque manūs linguā lēniter dēmulcet. Androclus, prīmum territus, nunc leōnem spectat. Tum quasi leōne cognitō, homō gaudēre vīsus est.

Eā rē tam mīrā maximī clāmōrēs populī excitātī sunt. Caesar [4] 10 Androclum vocāvit et quaesīvit causam cūr illī ūnī ferōcissimus leō pepercisset. Tum Androclus rem mīrandam nārrat.

"Cum prōvinciae," inquit, "Āfricae dominus meus imperāret, ego iniūstē verberātus fugere coāctus sum. Specum [5] quendam remōtum inveniō et eum ingredior. Neque multō post ad eundem specum venit 15 hic leō, vulnerātō ūnō pede, gemitūs ob dolōrem ēdēns. Prīmō quidem cōnspectū leōnis territus sum. Sed postquam leō ingressus mē vīdit, lēniter accessit et pedem ostendere mihi quasi opis petendae grātiā vīsus est. Ibi ego spīnam magnam, pedī eius haerentem, ēripuī et saniem [6] expressī. Ille tum, pede in manibus meīs positō, quiētem 20 cēpit. Ex eō diē trēs annōs ego et leō in eōdem specū vīximus. Membra ferārum leō mihi ferēbat, quae ego, ignis cōpiam nōn habēns, sōle torrēbam. Sed tandem specum relīquī et ā mīlitibus prehēnsus ad dominum ex Āfricā Rōmam dēductus sum. Is mē statim ad ferās mīsit. Intellegō autem hunc quoque leōnem, posteā captum, grātiam mihi 25 referre."

Haec dīxit Androclus. Omnibus petentibus, dīmissus est et leō eī dōnātus. Posteā Androclus et leō, lōrō [7] ligātus, circum tabernās ībant. Androclus pecūniam accipiēbat, leō flōrēs. Omnēs dīcēbant: "Hic est leō hospes hominis; hic est homō medicus leōnis." 30

---

[5] *help.*
[6] The *censor* had the right to expel senators who committed offenses or whose manner of living was not in accord with the best Roman tradition.

---

[1] Generally called Androcles. [2] *hunt*, i.e., a fight between men and wild beasts.
[3] For the case see **599**, 8. [4] Probably Tiberius. [5] *cave.*
[6] *pus.* [7] *strap.*

536. MISCELLANEOUS QUOTATIONS

No. 1 is from a treatise on farming written by Varro, a contemporary of Cicero. No. 2 is from Sallust. Nos. 3, 4, and 5 are from Ovid. No. 6 is from Livy. No. 7 is attributed to the emperor Tiberius. No. 8 is from Quintilian. No. 9 is from Tacitus. Nos. 10 and 11 are from the poet Claudian (about 400 A.D.). No. 12 is from St. Jerome. No. 13 is from the *Vulgate* (Jerome's translation of the Bible). Nos. 15 and 16 are from the *Corpus Iuris Civilis,* the great law code compiled in the sixth century, the basis of modern law in many countries. No. 17 is from Cassiodorus (sixth century). Nos. 19 and 20 are from Thomas à Kempis, the well-known writer of the Middle Ages. Nos. 21 and 22 are from two modern philosophers, Francis Bacon and Descartes. No. 23 was applied to Benjamin Franklin. Nos. 24, 25, 26 were common proverbs. No. 27 was found in a medieval manuscript.

1. Dīvīna nātūra dedit agrōs, ars hūmāna aedificāvit urbēs.
2. Concordiā parvae rēs[1] crēscunt, discordiā maximae dīlābuntur.[2]
3. Est deus in nōbīs.
4. Fās est et[3] ab hoste docērī.
5. Mediō[4] tūtissimus ībis.
6. Externus[5] timor maximum concordiae vinculum.
7. In cīvitāte līberā linguam mentemque līberās esse (dīcēbat).

[1] Supply **pūblicae.**   [2] *fall.*   [3] *even.*   [4] Supply **itinere.**
[5] *of a foreigner* (literally, *external*).

A mosaic in Sousse, Tunisia, showing Cybele, the Earth Mother, being drawn by tigers. Tamed wild animals symbolize Cybele's supremacy over nature.

8. Damnant quod nōn intellegunt.

9. Omne ignōtum prō magnificō.[6]

10. Ipsa quidem virtūs pretium sibi.

11. Omnia mors aequat.

12. Facis dē necessitāte virtūtem.

13. Magna est vēritās et praevalet.

14. Quī dēsīderat pācem praeparet bellum.

15. Cōgitātiōnis poenam nēmō patitur.

16. Iūris praecepta sunt haec: honestē vīvere, alterum nōn laedere, suum cuique tribuere.

17. Glōriōsa est scientia litterārum, quia, quod prīmum est, in homine mōrēs pūrgat; quod secundum, verbōrum grātiam subministrat.

18. Necessitās nōn habet lēgem.

19. Dē duōbus malīs, minus est semper ēligendum.

20. Ō quam cito trānsit glōria mundī!

21. Ipsa scientia potestās est.

22. Ego cōgitō, ergō sum.

23. Ēripuit[7] caelō fulmen,[8] mox scēptra tyrannīs.

24. Crocodīlī lacrimae.

25. Vestis virum facit.

26. Festīnā lentē.[9]

27. Nōlī dīcere[10] omnia quae scīs; nōlī crēdere omnia quae audīs; nōlī scrībere omnia quae facis; nōlī facere omnia quae potes.

537. TEACHING SCHOOL [1]

Ēgistī[2] ergō mēcum ut mihi persuādērētur Rōmam pergere[3] et potius ibi docēre quod docēbam Carthāginī.[4] Nōn ideō[5] Rōmam pergere[3] voluī, quod maiōrēs quaestūs maiorque mihi dignitās ab amīcīs quī hoc suādēbant prōmittēbātur (quamquam et ista dūcēbant animum tunc meum), sed illa erat causa maxima et paene sōla, quod 5 audiēbam quiētius ibi studēre adulēscentēs et disciplīnā sēdārī, nē in scholam protervē[6] irrumpent. Contrā apud Carthāginem intemperāns est licentia scholasticōrum: irrumpunt impudenter et, perturbant ōrdinem.

---

[6] Supply *is taken for,* i.e., *is regarded as.*
[7] The subject is Benjamin Franklin.   [8] *lightning.*
[9] *make haste slowly.*   [10] *Do not tell.*

---

[1] From the *Confessions* of Augustine (354–430 A.D.). Here he tells why he preferred to teach in a boys' school at Rome rather than in Carthage.
[2] Addressed to God.   [3] *go.*   [4] Locative.
[5] *on this account;* explained by the **quod** clause.   [6] *boldly.*

538. A PALACE FULL OF TRICKS [1]

Est Cōnstantīnopolī domus palātiō proxima, mīrae magnitūdinis et pulchritūdinis. Aerea [2] sed aurō tēcta arbor ante imperātōris solium [3] stābat, cuius rāmōs aereae et aurō tēctae avēs explēbant, quae dīversārum avium vōcēs ēmittēbant. Imperātōris vērō solium huius modī
5 erat arte compositum ut nunc humile, tum excelsius, posteā excelsissimum vidērētur. Leōnēs (incertum est utrum ex aere an lignō [4] factī) aurō tēctī solium custōdiēbant, quī caudā terram percutientēs, apertō ōre, rugītum [5] ēmittēbant.

Ante imperātōris praesentiam sum dēductus. Cum in adventū meō
10 rugītum leōnēs ēmitterent et avēs cantārent, nūllō sum terrōre commōtus, quoniam omnia eī quī bene nōverant mē docuerant. Prōnus imperātōrem adōrāns, caput sustulī, et quem prius moderātā mēnsūrā ā terrā ēlevātum sedēre vīdī, mox aliīs indūtum vestibus ad domūs laquear [6] sedēre prōspexī; quod quō modō fieret cōgitāre nōn potuī,
15 nisi forte sit māchinā hydraulicā sublevātus.

539. THE NORSE DISCOVERY OF AMERICA [1]

Rēx Dāniae [2] īnsulam recitāvit in eō repertam ōceanō [3] quae dīcitur Wīnland quod ibi vītēs [4] sponte nāscantur vīnum optimum ferentēs. Item nōbīs rettulit beātae memoriae pontifex Adalbertus quōsdam nōbilēs virōs in septentriōnēs nāvigāvisse ad ōceanum explōrandum.
5 Relinquentēs Britanniam et glaciālem Īsland [5] subitō in cālīginem [6] cecidērunt quae vix oculīs penetrārī posset. Et iam perīculum cālīginis ēvadentēs appulērunt ad quandam īnsulam altissimīs saxīs mūnītam. Hūc videndōrum grātiā locōrum ēgressī, repperērunt hominēs in

---

[1] From a book of Liutprand, a Lombard of the tenth century, who was sent to Constantinople as ambassador.
[2] *made of bronze.* Tree, birds, and lions were all artificial.
[3] *throne.*   [4] *wood.*   [5] *roar.*   [6] *ceiling.*

---

[1] Adam of Bremen (eleventh century) tells of the supposed discovery of America (Vinland or Winland) by Leif Ericson and his Norsemen. Cape Cod is one of the latest suggestions for the site where they landed. The story is full of possible fact and obvious fiction. [2] *Denmark.* [3] i.e., the Atlantic. [4] *grapevines.*
[5] *icy Iceland.*   [6] *fog.*

antrīs [7] subterrāneīs merīdiē latentēs; prō quōrum iānuis īnfīnīta iacēbat
cōpia vāsōrum aureōrum. Itaque sūmptā parte quam sublevāre pote- 10
rant, laetī ad nāvēs rēmigant, cum subitō venientēs vīdērunt hominēs
mīrae altitūdinis. Ā quibus raptus est ūnus dē sociīs; reliquī vērē
ēvāsērunt perīculum.

540. THIS CRAZY WORLD [1]

Iste mundus
furibundus
falsa praestat gaudia,
quae dēfluunt
et dēcurrunt
ceu [2] campī līlia.

Rēs mundāna,
vīta vāna
vēra tollit praemia:
nam impellit
et submergit
animās in Tartara.

541. SPRING SONG

Ecce grātum
et optātum
vēr [1] redūcit gaudia.
Purpurātum
flōret prātum,[2]

sōl serēnat omnia.
Iam iam cēdant trīstia.
Aestās redit,
nunc recēdit
hiemis saevitia.

542. IN THE TAVERN

1. In tabernā quandō sumus,
   nōn cūrāmus quid sit humus,
   sed ad lūdum [1] properāmus,
   cui semper īnsūdāmus.[2]
   Quid agātur in tabernā,
   ubi nummus est pincerna,[3]
   hoc est opus [4] ut quaerātur,
   sīc quid loquar audiātur.

2. Quīdam lūdunt, quīdam bibunt,
   quīdam indiscrētē vīvunt.
   Sed in lūdō quī morantur
   ex hīs quīdam dēnūdantur;
   quīdam ibi vestiuntur,
   quīdam saccīs [5] induuntur.
   Ibi nūllus timet mortem,
   sed prō Bacchō [6] mittunt
   sortem.[7]

---

[7] *caves.*

---

[1] This and the next two poems are from the *Carmina Burana* (twelfth and
thirteenth centuries), songs of the poor wandering students, or Goliards.
[2] *like.*

---

[1] *spring.*   [2] *meadow.*

---

[1] *game,* i.e., of dice.   [2] *perspire, work hard.*
[3] *waiter,* i.e., money brings service.   [4] *there is need that.*
[5] *sacks,* put on by those who lose their shirts in gambling, contrasted with the
winners of the preceding line.   [6] *wine.*   [7] *cast lots,* i.e., in throwing dice.

543. STĀBAT MĀTER[1]

1. Stābat māter dolōrōsa
iūxtā crucem lacrimōsa
   dum pendēbat fīlius;
cuius animam gementem,
contrīstantem et dolentem
   pertrānsīvit gladius.

3. Quis est homō quī nōn flēret,
mātrem Christī sī vidēret
   in tantō suppliciō?
Quis nōn posset contrīstārī
piam mātrem contemplārī
   dolentem cum fīliō?

5. Pia māter, fōns amōris,
mē sentīre vim dolōris
   fac ut tēcum lūgeam,
fac ut ārdeat cor meum
in amandō Christum Deum,
   ut sibi complaceam.

10. Fac mē cruce custōdīrī,
morte Christī praemūnīrī,
   cōnfovērī grātiā;
quandō corpus moriētur,
fac ut animae donētur
   Paradīsī glōria.

544. DIĒS ĪRAE[1]

1. Diēs īrae, diēs illa
solvet saeclum in favillā,[2]
teste Dāvīd cum Sibyllā.[3]

2. Quantus tremor est futūrus
quandō iūdex est ventūrus,
cūncta strictē [4] discussūrus!

3. Tuba mīrum spargēns sonum
per sepulchra regiōnum
cōget omnēs ante thronum.

4. Mors stupēbit et nātūra
cum resurget creātūra [5]
iūdicantī respōnsūra.

5. Liber scrīptus prōferētur,
in quō tōtum continētur
unde mundus iūdicētur.

11. Iūstae iūdex ultiōnis,[6]
dōnum fac remissiōnis
ante diem ratiōnis.

18. Lacrimōsa diēs illa,
quā resurget ex favillā

19. iūdicandus homō reus,
huic ergō parce, Deus.

20. Pie Iēsū Domine,
dōnā eīs requiem.

---

[1] A famous hymn by Iacopone of Todi (thirteenth century). The Virgin Mary stands by the Cross, mourning over Jesus.

---

[1] Thomas of Celano (thirteenth century) wrote this famous hymn about the Judgment Day.   [2] *ashes.*   [3] i.e., in both Biblical and Roman prophecy.
[4] *completely.*   [5] *(every) creature.*   [6] *vengeance.*

A Greek stamp in honor of NATO (North Atlantic Treaty Organization). It shows an ancient coin issued in 338 B.C. by a somewhat similar ancient organization, the Amphictyonic League.

Above: Tombs found in Pompeii in 1954.
Left: Tombstone of Cominia Tyche, who died just before her twenty-eighth birthday. It is now in the Metropolitan Museum of Art.

545. THE "HANGING TREE" [1]

Homō quīdam flēns dīxit omnibus vīcīnīs suīs: "Heu, heu! [2] Habeō in hortō [3] meō arborem īnfēlīcem, in quā uxor mea prīma sē suspendit, posteā secunda, nunc tertia, et dolōre afficior." Ūnus ex vīcīnīs, "Mīror," inquit, "tē in tantīs successibus lacrimās ēmīsisse. Dā mihi, rogō tē, trēs surculōs [4] illīus arboris, quod volō hōs inter vīcīnōs 5 dīvidere ut habeāmus arborēs ad uxōrēs nostrās suspendendās."

546. PETRARCH AND CICERO [1]

Ab ipsā pueritiā, ubi cēterī Aesōpō sē dant, ego librōs Cicerōnis lēgī. Et illā quidem aetāte nihil intellegere poteram, sōla dulcia quaedam verba mē dētinēbant.

---

[1] Adapted from the *Gesta Romanorum,* a collection of curious stories, some gathered from ancient sources. The collection was probably made about the fourteenth century in England. Most of these stories have fanciful "morals" attached to them. Shakespeare and other modern writers made use of this collection. This story is also told by Cicero.   [2] *alas!*   [3] *garden.*   [4] *sprouts.*

---

[1] Petrarch (1304–1374) has been called the first modern man. He was largely responsible for initiating the movement known as the *Renaissance.* He had an intense interest in the ancient classics, especially in Cicero. This letter tells of his attempts to secure Cicero's works. If it had not been for the activity of Petrarch and some of his followers, many ancient works would have been lost forever.

389

Posteā variās amīcitiās contrāxī, quod concursus ex omnī regiōne
5 factus est in locō in quō eram. Amīcīs abeuntibus et petentibus quid
vellem ē patriā suā mittī, respondēbam nihil praeter librōs Cicerōnis.
Et saepe litterās, saepe pecūniam mīsī, nōn per Italiam modo, ubi eram
nōtior, sed per Galliam atque Germāniam et usque ad Hispāniam
atque Britanniam. Etiam in Graeciam mīsī, et ē locō ē quō Cicerōnem
10 exspectābam habuī Homērum. "Labor omnia vincit," inquit Vergilius.
Multō studiō multāque cūrā multōs librōs collēgī. Sōlus Cicerō mihi [2]
sapiēns erat. Dē quō Quīntiliānus dīxit: "Bene dē sē spēret [3] cui
Cicerō placēbit."

Posteā, cum Leodium [4] pervēnissem, invēnī duās ōrātiōnēs
15 Cicerōnis; ūnam meā manū scrīpsī, alteram amīcus scrīpsit. Et, ut
rīdeās, in tam bonā urbe aliquid ātrāmentī [5] (et id crocō [6] simillimum)
reperīre difficillimum erat.

Et dē librīs quidem *Reī Pūblicae* [7] iam dēspērāns, librum *Dē Cōn-
sōlātiōne* quaesīvī, nec invēnī. Magnum librum epistulārum [8] manū
20 propriā scrīpsī, adversā tum valētūdine; sed valētūdinem magnus amor
operis et gaudium et habendī cupiditās vincēbant. Hunc librum, ut
mihi semper ad manum esset, ad iānuam pōnere solēbam.

[2] *in my eyes* (**599, 3**).   [3] *let him hope.* The subject is the antecedent of **cui**.
[4] *Liège*, in Belgium.   [5] *ink.*   [6] *saffron, yellow.*
[7] Only Book VI has survived complete.   [8] Cicero's letters to his friend Atticus.

Ara Pacis, Altar of Peace, built by Augustus in Rome, reërected a few years ago.

Etruscan vase now in Ferrara,
discovered a few years ago in
a cemetery at Spina, Italy.

Ferrara Museum

547. THE SHREWD PRIEST [1]

Erat quīdam sacerdōs rūsticus admodum dīves. Hic canem sibi
cārum, cum mortuus esset, sepelīvit in coemētēriō. Sēnsit hoc episcopus et in eius pecūniam animum intendēns,[2] sacerdōtem pūniendum
ad sē vocat. Sacerdōs, quī animum episcopī satis nōverat, quīnquāgintā aureōs [3] sēcum dēferēns ad episcopum dēvēnit. Quī sepultūram 5
canis graviter accūsāns iussit ad carcerēs [4] sacerdōtem dūcī. Hic vir
callidus: Ō pater," inquit, "sī nōscerēs quā prūdentiā canis fuit, nōn
mīrārēris [5] sī sepultūram inter hominēs meruit. Fuit enim plūs quam
hūmānus, et in vītā et maximē in morte." "Quidnam hoc est?" ait
episcopus. "Testāmentum," inquit sacerdōs, "in fīne vītae condēns 10
sciēnsque paupertātem tuam tibi quīnquāgintā aureōs ex testāmentō
relīquit, quōs mēcum tulī." Tum episcopus et testāmentum et sepultūram probāns, acceptā pecūniā, sacerdōtem solvit.

548. AN ALARM CLOCK [1]

Hōrologiō [2] ē meā bibliothēcā tibi allātō, ā quō expergēfierī,[3] quā
hōrā volēs, possīs, tē libenter ūtī nōn molestē [4] ferō. Modo tē id nōn
intemperātē [5] ā somnō āvocet. Valētūdinis enim tuae cūram tē habēre
in prīmīs volō. Dē tuōrum studiōrum ratiōne nihil tibi mandō nunc
quidem nisi ūnum: fac ut in tuīs quās ad mē dās litterīs Cicerōnem 5
accūrātius exprimās mōremque illīus scrībendī, verba, numerōs,[6] gravi-
tātem, dīligentius imitēre. Hoc sī fēceris, omnia tē cōnsecūtum putābō.
Magistrō tuō multam salūtem. Valē. MDXLIIII. Rōmā.

---

[1] From the *Facetiae* (joke book) of Poggio, a secretary of the Pope (fifteenth
century). When he and his colleagues had nothing to do they got together and
told stories in what he called a "Lie Factory."   [2] *casting his thoughts towards.*
[3] *gold pieces.*   [4] *prison.*   [5] *if you knew . . . you would not wonder.*

---

[1] Pietro Bembo, an Italian man of letters (1470–1547), wrote this letter to his
young son.   [2] *clock.*   [3] *be awakened.*
[4] With **ferō:** *I don't mind.*   [5] *too early.*   [6] *rhythm.*

391

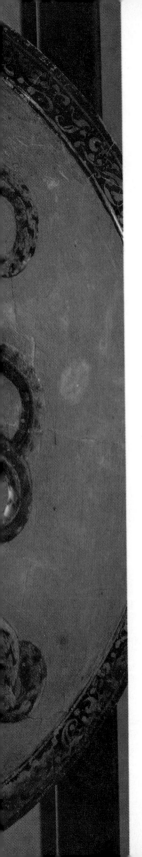

UNIT XI

OVID AND VIRGIL

In Greek mythology, Medusa was the daughter of the sea god Phorcys. She had been beautiful in her youth, but when she bragged of her beauty, the goddess Athena became so jealous that she transformed Medusa into an ugly woman with protruding eyes, and writhing snakes for hair. Medusa was so ugly that anyone who looked at her was turned into stone.

549. OVID'S METAMORPHOSES

Ovid (Publius Ovidius Naso) was born in 43 B.C. Trained for the law and public life, he abandoned his career to devote himself to his great passion, the writing of poetry. In 8 A.D. he incurred the displeasure of the Emperor Augustus and was banished to a little town, Tomi (now Constanza, Romania), on the Black Sea. Here he died in 17 A.D.

Ovid was a very facile poet and left us many poems. The greatest of these is the *Metamor'phoses*. This consists of a series of mythical tales dealing with the transformation (that is what the title means) of men, animals, and things into different forms. The tales are loosely joined together with considerable cleverness and reveal Ovid's great ability as a storyteller. They cover so much of Greek and Roman mythology that they are now our chief source of information about it. The work, from which several selections are given below, has always been a favorite and has left a strong influence on modern literature and art.

550. POETIC WORD ORDER

The word order of Latin poetry is freer than that of prose. Adjectives often are widely separated from their nouns. Words are often taken out of subordinate clauses and precede the introductory words (**quī, ut,** etc.). Subjects often come at or near the end of sentences.

551. READING LATIN VERSE

The rhythm of Latin verse does not depend on word accent as does that of English but on the length of syllables. The rules for determining the length of syllables are:

1. A syllable is *naturally* long if it contains a long vowel or a diphthong.

2 A syllable is long *by position* if it contains a short vowel followed by two or more consonants or the consonant **x** (= **cs**).

A mute (**p, b, t, d, c, g**) followed by a liquid (**l, r**) does not make a syllable long. There are occasional exceptions.

H is disregarded entirely. The combinations **qu** and **gu** (before a vowel) constitute one consonant; the **u** is disregarded.

In poetry a long syllable is treated as twice the length of a short syllable. Since a line of poetry is considered one long word, in a case like **in mē** the first word is a long syllable because the (short) vowel is followed by two consonants (**n, m**).

Orpheus and Eurydice, in a painting by Nicolas Poussin (1594–1665).

Several syllables are combined to form a foot. The dactyl is a foot consisting of a long syllable followed by two short syllables, written − ◡ ◡ .[1] The spondee consists of two long syllables, − −. When a line contains six feet, it is called a hexameter. The *Metamorphoses* and *Aeneid* (see **557**) are written in the dactylic hexameter. A spondee may be substituted for a dactyl in every foot except the fifth. The sixth foot is always a spondee.[2] The beat is on the first syllable of each foot.

If a word ends in a vowel or a vowel plus **m** and the next word begins with a vowel (or **h**), the first vowel disappears entirely (called "elision"; the vowel is said to be "elided"): **mar(e) et,** pronounced **maret; iacer(e) (h)ōs,** pronounced **iacerōs; cūnctant(em) et,** pronounced **cūnctantet.**

---

[1] Do not confuse this marking of syllables with the identical signs used in marking vowels.

[2] The last syllable is often short, but the "rest" at the end of the line fills out the foot.

552. THE FLOOD—DEUCALION AND PYRRHA

Because of the wickedness of human beings, Jupiter sends a flood to destroy the earth. Only Deucā'lion (the Greek Noah) and his wife Pyrrha survive, landing from their boat on Mt. Parnassus (corresponding to Mt. Ararat of the Bible). The first five lines are "scanned" (marked) to show the meter.

The Flood at Its Height—a Topsy-Turvy World

Iamque ma|r(e) et tel|lūs nūl|lum dīs|crīmen ha|bēbant.|

Omnia | pontus e|rant; dee|rant quoque | lītora | pontō.|

Occupat | hic [1] col|lem, cum|bā sedet | alter ad|uncā [2]|

et dū|cit [3] rē|mōs il|līc ubi | nūper a|rārat,|

295 ille [1] su|prā sege|tēs [4] aut | mersae | culmina [5] | vīllae|
nāvigat, hic summā piscem dēprēndit in ulmō.[6]
Fīgitur in viridī,[7] sī fors tulit, ancora prātō
aut subiecta terunt [8] curvae vīnēta carīnae; [9]
et, modo quā [10] gracilēs grāmen carpsēre [11] capellae,[12]
300 nunc ibi dēfōrmēs pōnunt sua corpora phōcae.[13]
Mīrantur sub aquā lūcōs [14] urbēsque domōsque
Nēreidēs, silvāsque tenent delphīnes [15] et altīs
incursant rāmīs agitātaque rōbora [16] pulsant.
Nat [17] lupus inter ovēs,[18] fulvōs [19] vehit unda leōnēs,
305 unda vehit tigrēs.

---

[1] one man. [2] With **cumbā:** *in a curved boat.* [3] *plies.*
[4] *crops.* [5] *top;* poetic plural for singular.
[6] With **summā:** *on top of an elm.* [7] With **prātō:** *green meadow.*
[8] *scrape.* [9] *keels.* i.e., *ships;* subject. [10] = **quā modo.**
[11] = **carpsērunt.** [12] *goats.* [13] *seals.* [14] *groves.*
[15] = **delphīnī** (Greek form). [16] *oaks.* [17] *swims.*
[18] *sheep.* [19] *tawny.*

Stones thrown by Deucalion and Pyrrha grow into people; from an Ovid edition of 1589.

Metropolitan Museum of Art, Whittelsey Fund, 1951

When the waters recede, Deucalion seeks dry land. He laments the fact that Pyrrha and he are the only two people left in the world: **Nōs duo turba sumus,** *We two are a crowd,* he says, for two are a crowd in a world which consists of only two persons. He finds the temple of Themis, goddess of prophecy, and prays for aid and advice.

Deucalion Interprets a Strange Oracle

Mōta dea est sortemque dedit: "Discēdite templō
et vēlāte caput cīnctāsque [20] resolvite vestēs
ossaque post tergum magnae iactāte parentis." [21]
Obstupuēre [22] diū, rumpitque silentia vōce
Pyrrha prior iussīsque deae parēre recūsat,   385
detque [23] sibī veniam pavidō rogat ōre pavetque
laedere iactātīs māternās ossibus umbrās. [24]   387
Inde Promēthīdēs [25] placidīs Epimēthida [26] dictīs   390
mulcet [27] et "aut fallāx," ait, "est sollertia [28] nōbīs [29]
aut pia sunt nūllumque nefās ōrācula suādent.
Magna parēns terra est, lapidēs in corpore terrae
ossa reor [30] dīcī: iacere hōs post terga iubēmur."

The Stones Come to Life

Coniugis auguriō [31] quamquam Tītānia [32] mōta est,   395
spēs tamen in dubiō est; adeō caelestibus ambō
diffīdunt monitīs. [33] Sed quid temptāre nocēbit?
Discēdunt vēlantque caput tunicāsque recingunt
et iussōs lapidēs sua post vēstīgia mittunt.
Saxa (quis hoc crēdat,[34] nisi sit prō teste vetustās?) [35]   400
pōnere [36] dūritiem coepēre [37] suumque rigōrem
mollīrīque morā [38] mollītaque dūcere [39] fōrmam.   402
Inque brevī spatiō superōrum nūmine saxa   411

---

[20] *girt up.* In religious services the head was covered and the tunic allowed to hang down ungirdled.   [21] Modifies **ossa.**   [22] *they were astounded.*

[23] Supply **ut:** *asks that (Themis) grant her pardon.*

[24] *to offend her mother's ghost by throwing her bones.*

[25] *son of Promē′theus,* i.e., Deucalion.

[26] Accusative singular: *daughter of Epimē′theus,* i.e., Pyrrha.

[27] *calms.*   [28] *skill.*   [29] For **mihi;** = **mea.**

[30] *I think that the bones are meant to be.*   [31] *interpretation.*

[32] *the Titan's daughter,* i.e., Pyrrha.   [33] *advice* (**599,** 6).

[34] *would believe* (**607,** 3).

[35] *if antiquity were not a witness.* What do you think of the argument that the age of a story proves it to be true?   [36] For **dēpōnere.**

[37] = **coepērunt.**   [38] *gradually.*   [39] *take on.*

missa virī manibus faciem trāxēre virōrum,
et dē fēmineō reparāta est fēmina iactū.
Inde genus dūrum sumus experiēnsque [40] labōrum
415 et documenta damus quā sīmus orīgine nātī.

(Met. I. 291–415)

553. ECHO AND NARCISSUS

Juno punishes the nymph Echo for her talkativeness by curtailing her power of speech. Thereafter Echo can merely echo what others say. She falls in love with the handsome but cold youth Narcissus.

Echo Falls in Love with Narcissus

Corpus adhūc Ēchō, nōn vōx erat et tamen ūsum
360 garrula nōn alium quam nunc habet ōris [1] habēbat,
361 reddere dē multīs ut verba novissima [2] posset.
370 Ergō ubi Narcissum per dēvia rūra [3] vagantem
vīdit et incaluit,[4] sequitur vēstīgia fūrtim,
372 quōque magis [5] sequitur, flammā propiōre calēscit.
375 Ō quotiēns voluit blandīs accēdere dictīs
et mollēs adhibēre precēs! Nātūra repugnat
nec sinit [6] incipiat; sed, quod [7] sinit, illa parāta est
exspectāre sonōs ad quōs sua verba remittat.

Narcissus Calls to His Companions and Echo Answers

Forte puer comitum sēductus ab agmine fīdō
380 dīxerat "ecquis [8] adest?" et "adest" responderat Ēchō.
Hic stupet, utque aciem [9] partēs dīmittit in omnēs,
vōce "venī!" magnā clāmat; vocat illa vocantem.
Respicit et rūrsus, nūllō veniente, "quid," inquit,
"mē fugis?" et totidem quot dīxit verba recēpit.
385 Perstat et alternae [10] dēceptus imāgine vōcis
"hūc coeāmus," ait, nūllīque [11] libentius umquam
respōnsūra sonō "coeāmus" rettulit Ēchō,

[40] *used to* (with genitive).

---

[1] With **ūsum alium**: *no other use of speech.* She was still a living being.
[2] (*only*) *the last of many* (**598**, 3, *b*).　　　　　　　　[3] *trackless countryside.*
[4] *fell in love.*
[5] *the more . . . the hotter* (literally, *the nearer*) *the flame* (*with which*) *she is inflamed.*　　　　[6] *permits.* Supply **ut** with **incipiat.**
[7] *a thing which.* The main clause is the antecedent.　　　　[8] *is there anyone?*
[9] *glance.*　　　[10] *answering.*　　　　　　　　[11] Modifies **sonō.**

Echo answering a call. A painting by the Swiss artist P. Robert. The poet Milton called Echo a "nymph that liv'st unseen."

Gramstorff Bros.

et verbīs favet [12] ipsa suīs ēgressaque silvā
ībat ut iniceret spērātō bracchia collō.
Ille fugit fugiēnsque "manūs complexibus [13] aufer.   390
Ante," ait, "ēmoriar [14] quam [15] sit tibi cōpia nostrī." [16]
Rettulit illa nihil nisi "sit tibi cōpia nostrī."

Echo Wastes Away to a Mere Voice

Sprēta [17] latet silvīs pudibundaque [18] frondibus ōra
prōtegit et sōlīs ex illō [19] vīvit in antrīs.
Sed tamen haeret amor crēscitque dolōre repulsae,[20]   395
et tenuant vigilēs corpus miserābile cūrae,
addūcitque cutem [21] maciēs et in āera [22] sūcus [23]
corporis omnis abit. Vōx tantum atque ossa supersunt—
vōx manet; ossa ferunt [24] lapidis trāxisse figūram.
Inde latet silvīs nūllōque in monte vidētur,   400
omnibus [25] audītur; sonus est quī vīvit in illā.

                    (Met. III. 359–401)

---

[12] i.e., she suits the action to the words.
[13] *from embraces.*
[14] *may I die.*   [15] With **ante:** *before.*
[16] For **meī:** *a chance at me.*
[17] *spurned.*   [18] *ashamed.*
[19] Supply **tempore.**
[20] *refusal.*   [21] *skin.*
[22] *air* (accusative singular).
[23] *life, strength.*   [24] *they say.*
[25] *by all.*

554. PERSEUS AND ATLAS

Medusa was a maiden with snaky locks, one look at which turned a human being into stone. Perseus, son of Jupiter, is commissioned to bring back her head. With the help of the gods he does this without injury to himself. On his way back he stops at the home of the giant Atlas, in northwest Africa. Atlas is the owner of the famous golden apples. When Atlas refuses hospitality to Perseus, the latter turns Atlas into a mountain of stone by means of Medusa's head.

Themis Predicts the Loss of the Golden Apples

635 Mīlle gregēs [1] illī [2] totidemque armenta [3] per herbās
  errābant, et humum vīcīnia [4] nūlla premēbant.
  Arboreae frondēs aurō radiante nitentēs [5]
  ex aurō rāmōs, ex aurō pōma [6] tegēbant.
  "Hospes," ait Perseus illī, "seu glōria tangit
640 tē generis [7] magnī, generis mihi Iuppiter auctor;
  sīve es mīrātor rērum,[8] mīrābere nostrās.
  Hospitium requiemque petō." Memor ille [9] vetustae
  sortis erat (Themis hanc dederat Parnassia [10] sortem):
  "Tempus, Atlās, veniet tua quō spoliābitur aurō
645 arbor, et hunc praedae titulum [11] Iove nātus [12] habēbit."
  Id metuēns solidīs pōmāria clauserat Atlās
  montibus et vāstō dederat servanda dracōnī
  arcēbatque [13] suīs externōs fīnibus omnēs.
  Huic [14] quoque "vade procul, nē longē glōria rērum
650 quam mentīris," [15] ait, "longē tibi Iuppiter absit." [16]
  Vimque minīs [17] addit manibusque expellere temptat
  cūnctantem et placidīs miscentem fortia dictīs.
  Vīribus īnferior [14] (quis enim pār esset [18] Atlantis
  vīribus?) "at quoniam parvī [19] tibi grātia nostra est,
655 accipe mūnus," ait, laevāque ā parte [20] Medūsae,

---

[1] *flocks.* [2] i.e., Atlas (**599**, 3). [3] *herds.*
[4] *no neighbors hemmed in his land,* i.e., he had vast tracts of land.
[5] *gleaming,* modifying **frondēs.**
[6] *apples of gold;* **ex aurō** modifies **pōma.** These are the golden apples of the Hesperides. It is thought that the mythical apples were really oranges, unknown to Europe in antiquity. [7] i.e., of Perseus.
[8] *deeds,* referring to his defeat of Medusa. Perseus is rather cocky.
[9] i.e., Atlas. [10] With Themis. [11] *the glory for this loot.*
[12] *a son of Jupiter.* Hercules was meant, but when Atlas hears that Perseus is the son of Jupiter, he thinks that he is the one mentioned in the oracle and refuses to admit him. [13] *shut out* (with ablative). [14] i.e., Perseus.
[15] *which you falsely claim.* [16] *be far from you,* i.e., *be of no help to you.*
[17] *threats.* [18] *could be.* [19] *of little value.* [20] *on his left side.*

ipse retrō versus,[21] squālentia prōtulit ōra.
Quantus [22] erat, mōns factus Atlās; nam barba comaeque [23]
in silvās abeunt, iuga sunt umerīque [24] manūsque,
quod caput ante fuit summō est in monte cacūmen.
Ossa lapis fīunt; tum partēs altus in omnēs   660
crēvit in immēnsum [25] (sīc, dī,[26] statuistis), et omne
cum tot sīderibus caelum requiēvit in illō.

(Met. IV. 636–662)

555. ORPHEUS AND EURYDICE

Orpheus was such a fine musician that he could make even the trees and stones listen to and follow him. When his wife Eurydice (Urid'i-sē) died, he followed her to Hades and by his wonderful singing persuaded the king of Hades to let her go back to the land of the living. But there was one condition, that Orpheus should not look back until he had come out of Hades. At the last moment Orpheus looked back to see whether Eurydice was following, and she disappeared forever. There is an opera by Gluck on this theme.

"Omnia dēbēmus vōbīs,[1] paulumque morātī
sērius aut citius sēdem properāmus ad ūnam.
Tendimus hūc omnēs, haec est domus ultima, vōsque
hūmānī generis [2] longissima rēgna tenētis.   35
Haec [3] quoque, cum iūstōs mātūra perēgerit annōs,
iūris erit vestrī; prō mūnere poscimus ūsum.[4]
Quod sī fāta negant veniam [5] prō coniuge, certum est
nōlle [6] redīre mihī; lētō [7] gaudēte duōrum."
Tālia dīcentem [8] nervōsque [9] ad verba moventem   40
exsanguēs flēbant animae.[10]   41

[21] i.e., turning his face away, so as not to look at Medusa's head.
[22] *as huge as he had been* (in life).   [23] *beard and hair.*
[24] *his shoulders become* (**sunt**).
[25] *to an immense size.* Perseus next flies past Ethiopia, where he rescues the beautiful Andromeda from a sea monster and marries her.   [26] = **deī.**

[1] Orpheus is speaking to Pluto and Proserpina, king and queen of Hades.
[2] *over the human race.*   [3] Eurydice.
[4] i.e., not for a permanent gift but as a temporary loan.   [5] *boon,* of longer life.
[6] Supply the subject from **mihī:** *I have resolved that I,* etc. [7] *death* (**601,** 11).
[8] Modifies **eum** understood, object of **flēbant.**   [9] *strings* (of the lyre).
[10] Pluto and Proserpina are so moved that they allow Eurydice to return.

50 Hanc simul et lēgem [11] Rhodopēius [12] accipit Orpheus,
 nē flectat retrō sua lūmina, dōnec [13] Avernās [14]
exierit vallēs; aut irrita [15] dōna futūra.
Carpitur acclīvis per mūta silentia trāmes,[16]
arduus, obscūrus, cālīgine [17] dēnsus opācā.

55 Nec procul āfuerunt tellūris margine summae.
Hic nē dēficeret [18] metuēns avidusque videndī,
flexit amāns oculōs; et prōtinus illa relāpsa est,
bracchiaque intendēns prēndīque et prēndere captāns
nīl nisi cēdentēs īnfēlīx arripit aurās.[19]

(Met. X, 32–59)

556. PYGMALION

The sculptor Pygmalion of Cyprus carved an ivory statue of a woman so beautiful that he fell in love with it. Venus gave it life, and Pygmalion married the girl. George Bernard Shaw borrowed the name for his play in which he has a professor turn an uneducated girl into a fine lady; the musical comedy *My Fair Lady* was based on his play.

[11] *condition;* the **nē** clause is in apposition with **lēgem.**   [12] *Thracian.*
[13] *until.*   [14] Adjective modifying **vallēs:** *of Avernus,* the entrance of Hades.
[15] *void.*   [16] With **acclīvis:** *ascending path* (to the upper world).
[17] *mist.*   [18] The subject is Eurydice.   [19] *breezes.*

Orpheus and Eurydice in a stucco relief in an ancient building beneath the modern railroad tracks of Rome.

E. Richter, Rome

Intereā niveum mīrā fēlīciter arte
sculpsit ebur [1] fōrmamque dedit quā [2] fēmina nāscī
nūlla potest; operisque suī concēpit amōrem.
Virginis est vērae faciēs, quam vīvere crēdās [3]   250
et, sī nōn obstet reverentia, velle movērī;
ars adeō latet arte suā.[4] Mīrātur et haurit
pectore Pygmaliōn simulātī corporis ignēs.[5]
Saepe manūs operī temptantēs admovet an sit
corpus an illud ebur; nec adhūc ebur esse fatētur.[6]   255
Ōscula [7] dat reddīque putat; loquiturque tenetque
et crēdit tactīs digitōs īnsīdere [8] membrīs;
et metuit, pressōs veniat nē līvor [9] in artūs.
Et modo [10] blanditiās adhibet, modo [10] grāta puellīs
mūnera fert illī, conchās teretēsque lapillōs,[11]   260
et parvās volucrēs et flōrēs mīlle colōrum,
līliaque pictāsque [12] pilās et ab arbore lāpsās
Hēliadum lacrimās.[13] Ōrnat quoque vestibus artūs.
Dat digitīs gemmās, dat longa monīlia [14] collō.
Fēsta diēs Veneris tōtā celeberrima Cyprō [15] vēnerat,   270
tūraque [16] fūmābant, cum mūnere fūnctus [17] ad ārās   273
cōnstitit et timidē "sī, dī,[18] dare cūncta potestis,
sit coniūnx, optō," nōn ausus, "eburnea [19] virgō,"
dīcere Pygmaliōn, "similis mea," dīxit, "eburnae."
Ut rediit,[20] simulācra suae petit ille puellae,   280
incumbēnsque torō [21] dedit ōscula. Vīsa tepēre est.
Corpus erat; saliunt temptātae pollice [22] vēnae,   289
                          dataque ōscula virgō   292
sēnsit et ērubuit.

(Met. X. 247–293)

---

[1] *ivory.*   [2] *in which.*   [3] *you could believe.*
[4] Cf. "the art that conceals art."   [5] *the fires (of love).*   [6] *he admits.*
[7] *kisses.*   [8] *sink in, dent.*   [9] *bruise.*
[10] *now.*   [11] *shells and smooth pebbles.*   [12] *colored.*
[13] *tears of the Heliades, fallen from;* the daughters of the Sun, the Heliades, are
    said to have been changed to trees and their tears to amber, which is actually
    the hardened resin of certain trees.   [14] *necklaces.*   [15] *in Cyprus* (feminine).
[16] *incense.*   [17] *having performed* (with ablative).   [18] = **deī.**
[19] *of ivory.*   [20] i.e., home from the altar.   [21] *couch.*
[22] *thumb;* he felt her pulse.

557. VIRGIL'S AENEID

Virgil (Publius Vergilius Maro) was born in 70 B.C. Two thousand years later, in 1930, the entire western world celebrated his birthday, for he is one of the world's greatest and best loved poets. His earlier works were the *Bucolics,* or *Eclogues,* about shepherds, and the *Georgics,* dealing with farming. His chief work, the *Aeneid,* is an epic poem in twelve books which tells of the wanderings of the Trojan Aeneas (Ēnē′as) in his attempt to find a new home after the capture of Troy by the Greeks in the twelfth century B.C., according to tradition. The *Aeneid* also tells of Aeneas' arrival in Italy, where he established his kingdom and where his descendants founded Rome. Thus Virgil gave a background for Roman history and it is no wonder that the Roman people greeted the *Aeneid* as a national poem glorifying Rome and the Roman Empire.

Virgil was planning to spend three years in giving the finishing touches to the *Aeneid* when he died in 19 B.C. He left word to have the poem burned but Augustus insisted that it be published—and the world has been grateful to him ever since.

In one of his *Eclogues* Virgil prophesied the birth of a child. In the Middle Ages this was interpreted as a reference to the birth of Jesus, and Vergilius began to be spelled Virgilius, as if derived from *Virgō,* the Virgin Mary. That is why the traditional English spelling is Virgil. In recent years many have preferred the spelling Vergil, newly formed from the ancient name.

So popular was Virgil in the Middle Ages that he was called a magician, and all sorts of tales were told about his deeds.

558. BOOK I

Juno's anger causes the Trojans under Aeneas to be wrecked off the coast of Africa. They make their way to the place where Dido, a refugee from Tyre in Phoenicia, is building the new city of Carthage. They are cordially welcomed. The poem opens with the poet's statement of his theme.

> Arma virumque canō, Troiae quī prīmus ab ōrīs
> Ītaliam [1] fātō profugus [2] Lāvīniaque [3] vēnit
> lītora,[1] multum ille et terrīs [4] iactātus et altō [4]
> vī superum,[5] saevae memorem Iūnōnis ob īram,
> multa quoque et [6] bellō passus, dum conderet [7] urbem   5
> īnferretque deōs [8] Latiō,[9] genus unde Latīnum
> Albānīque patrēs atque altae moenia Rōmae.

Venus goes to Jupiter to complain that the great destiny of her son Aeneas is not being fulfilled. Jupiter's predictions reassure her.

> "Bellum ingēns geret Ītaliā [10] populōsque ferōcēs   263
> contundet [11] mōrēsque virīs et moenia pōnet.
> At puer Ascanius,[12] cui nunc cognōmen Iūlō [13]   267
> additur,
>   longam multā vī mūniet Albam.[14]
> Rōmulus excipiet gentem et Māvortia [15] condet   276
> moenia Rōmānōsque suō dē nōmine dīcet.
> Hīs ego nec mētās [16] rērum nec tempora pōnō;
> imperium sine fīne dedī. Quīn [17] aspera Iūnō,
> quae mare nunc terrāsque metū [18] caelumque fatīgat,   280
> cōnsilia in melius referet [19] mēcumque fovēbit
> Rōmānōs rērum dominōs gentemque togātam.[20]
> Nāscētur pulchrā Troiānus orīgine Caesar,[21]   286

[1] Poetic usage without **ad** (**600**, 3).   [2] *a fugitive by fate.*
[3] Adj.: *of Lavinium,* a town near Rome.
[4] For the case see **601**, 14; **altō** is used as a noun for **marī.**   [5] = **superōrum.**
[6] *also.*   [7] *until he could found* (**606**, 12).
[8] *his gods,* statues of which he had brought along.
[9] = **in Latium,** *to Lā'shium* (poetic use of dative).   [10] For the case see **601**, 14.
[11] *he* (Aeneas) *will crush.*
[12] Aeneas' son, whose other name (**cognōmen**) was Iulus (Ī-ū'lus).
[13] Attracted into the case of **cui.**   [14] *Alba Longa,* a town southeast of Rome.
[15] *of Mars* (the father of Romulus).   [16] *bounds for their state* (**rērum**).
[17] = **quīn etiam.**   [18] *with her fears.*   [19] *will change for the better.*
[20] *toga-clad;* the toga was the garment of peace.   [21] Augustus.

imperium Ōceanō, fāmam quī terminet [22] astrīs
Iūlius,[21] ā magnō dēmissum nōmen Iūlō.[23]

291 Aspera tum positīs [24] mītēscent saecula [25] bellīs;
cāna [26] Fidēs et Vesta, Remō cum frātre Quirīnus [27]
iūra dabunt; dīrae ferrō et compāgibus artīs [28]
claudentur bellī portae; Furor impius intus [29]
295 saeva sedēns super arma et centum vīnctus aēnīs [30]
post tergum nōdīs fremet [31] horridus ōre cruentō."

559. BOOK IV

Books II and III tell of a banquet Dido gives for Aeneas, at which he
relates his adventures, beginning with the Fall of Troy. The Trojan War
was caused by the elopement of Helen, the wife of the Greek Menelaus,
with the Trojan Paris. As Book IV opens Dido discovers that she is falling
in love with Aeneas.

At rēgīna gravī iam dūdum [1] saucia [2] cūrā
vulnus alit vēnīs et caecō [3] carpitur ignī.
Multa virī virtūs animō multusque recursat
gentis honōs; [4] haerent īnfīxī pectore vultūs [5]
5 verbaque, nec placidam membrīs dat cūra quiētem.
Postera Phoebēā [6] lūstrābat [7] lampade terrās
ūmentemque [8] Aurōra polō [9] dīmōverat umbram,
cum sīc ūnanimam alloquitur male [10] sāna sorōrem:
"Anna soror, quae mē suspēnsam īnsomnia [11] terrent!
10 Quis novus hic nostrīs successit sēdibus hospes,[12]
quem sēsē ōre ferēns,[13] quam fortī pectore [14] et armīs!
Crēdō equidem, nec vāna fidēs, genus esse deōrum.
Dēgenerēs animōs timor arguit.[15] Heu, quibus ille
iactātus fātīs! Quae bella exhausta canēbat!"

[22] *to bound* (**606,** 3).

[23] Virgil emphasizes Augustus' relationship to Julius Caesar and through him to
Iulus, Aeneas' son.   [24] = **dēpositīs.**   [25] *the ages will become gentle.*

[26] *white-haired, venerable.*   [27] = **Rōmulus.**

[28] *tight joints.* The doors of the Temple of Janus were closed in peace by
Augustus for the first time in two hundred years.   [29] *within* (the temple).

[30] With **nōdīs:** *by bronze* (i.e., *hard*) *knots.*   [31] *will rage.*

---

[1] *for a long time.*   [2] *wounded, stricken.*   [3] *blind, unseen.*   [4] = **honor** (nom.).

[5] i.e., *of Aeneas.*   [6] *with Apollo's lamp,* i.e., *the sun.*

[7] *lighted;* the subject is **Aurōra** (*Dawn*).   [8] *damp.*   [9] *from the heavens.*

[10] With **sāna** = *insane.*   [11] *dreams.*   [12] *who* (*is*) *this strange guest* (*who*).

[13] *What a man he shows himself in his looks.*   [14] *For the case see* **601,** 13.

[15] *Fear reveals ignoble souls*—but Aeneas has shown no signs of fear.

Dido Building Carthage. A painting by the English artist Turner.

Dido and Aeneas fall in love, but Jupiter (representing Aeneas' conscience) sends Mercury to remind Aeneas of his duty to establish the Trojans in a new country of their own. Aeneas' reaction is immediate.

At vērō Aenēās aspectū obmūtuit āmēns,[16]
arrēctaeque horrōre comae,[17] et vōx faucibus haesit.   280
Ārdet abīre fugā dulcīsque relinquere terrās,
attonitus [18] tantō monitū imperiōque deōrum.
Heu quid agat? [19] Quō nunc rēgīnam ambīre [20] furentem
audeat affātū? Quae prīma exōrdia [21] sūmat?

Aeneas orders his men to prepare the ships secretly, hoping to sail away without Dido's knowing it.

At rēgīna dolōs (quis fallere possit [22] amantem?)   296
praesēnsit mōtūsque excēpit prīma futūrōs,
omnia tūta [23] timēns; eadem impia Fāma furentī [24]
dētulit armārī classem cursumque parārī.
Tandem hīs Aenēān [25] compellat [26] vōcibus ultrō: 304
"Dissimulāre etiam spērāstī,[27] perfide, tantum   305
posse nefās tacitusque meā dēcēdere terrā?
Nec tē noster amor nec tē data dextera [28] quondam
nec moritūra tenet crūdēlī fūnere Dīdō?"
    At pius Aenēās, quamquam lēnīre dolentem   393

---

[16] confused, he becomes silent.   [17] With **arrēctae:** hair (stood) on end.
[18] astounded.   [19] What should he do?   [20] get around, approach.
[21] beginnings.   [22] would be able.   [23] (even if) safe.   [24] i.e., Dido.
[25] Acc.: Aeneas.   [26] addresses.   [27] See **595.**
[28] = **dextra,** i.e., pledge.

sōlandō [29] cupit et dictīs āvertere cūrās,
395   multa [30] gemēns magnōque animum labefactus [31] amōre,
iussa tamen dīvum exsequitur classemque revīsit.
Tum vērō Teucrī [32] incumbunt [33] et lītore celsās
dēdūcunt tōtō nāvīs.

560. BOOK VI

After consulting the Sibyl at Cumae (near Naples), Aeneas descends to
Hades, where he sees the shades of his father, Dido, and many other famous
persons and learns about the great future of the new country he is about
to establish.

Tālibus ōrābat dictīs ārāsque [1] tenēbat,
125   cum sīc ōrsa [2] loquī vātēs: [3] "Sate [4] sanguine dīvum,
Trōs Anchīsiadē,[5] facilis dēscēnsus Avernō [6]
(noctēs atque diēs patet ātrī iānua Dītis);
sed revocāre gradum superāsque ēvādere ad aurās,[7]
hoc opus, hic labor est. Paucī, quōs aequus amāvit
130   Iuppiter aut ārdēns ēvexit ad aethera [8] virtūs,
dīs genitī [9] potuēre." [10]

Aeneas and the Sibyl come to the entrance of Hades.

Ībant obscūrī [11] sōlā sub nocte per umbram

[29] *by consoling* (*her*).   [30] *much, a great deal.*
[31] *his heart overcome* (literally, *overcome as to his heart*).
[32] *Trojans.*   [33] *get to work* (literally, *bend to*).

---

[1] *altar.*   [2] Supply **est**: *began.*
[3] *prophetess* (referring to the Sibyl).
[4] Voc.: *sprung from.*   [5] Voc.: *Trojan son of Anchises.*
[6] *to Hades;* Lake Avernus was considered the entrance.   [7] *air.*
[8] Acc. sing.: *sky.*   [9] From **gignō**: *descended from the gods.*
[10] *i.e., to do so.*   [11] *in the dark.*

**Dido, Aeneas, and Ascanius go hunting, as shown in a fourth-century floor mosaic
of a Roman bath found in 1945 at Low Ham, Somerset, England.**
C. A. Ralegh Radford

perque domōs Dītis vacuās [12] et inānia rēgna
quāle [13] per incertam lūnam sub lūce malignā [14]   270
est iter in silvīs, ubi caelum condidit umbrā
Iuppiter et rēbus [15] nox abstulit ātra colōrem.
Vēstibulum ante ipsum prīmīsque in faucibus Orcī
Lūctus [16] et ultrīcēs posuēre cubīlia [17] Cūrae
pallentēsque [18] habitant Morbī trīstisque Senectūs   275
et Metus et malesuāda [19] Famēs ac turpis Egestās,[20]
terribilēs vīsū [21] fōrmae, Lētumque [22] Labōsque,[23]
tum cōnsanguineus Lētī Sopor et mala [24] mentis
Gaudia mortiferumque adversō in līmine Bellum
ferreīque Eumenidum thalamī [25] et Discordia dēmēns.   280

Aeneas meets the shade of his father, who points out to him the souls of
various notables.

"Huc geminās [26] nunc flecte aciēs, hanc aspice gentem
Rōmānōsque tuōs; hīc Caesar et omnis Iūlī
prōgeniēs magnum caelī ventūra sub axem.[27]   790
Hic vir, hic est tibi quem prōmittī saepius audīs,
Augustus Caesar, Dīvī [28] genus, aurea condet
saecula quī rūrsus Latiō [29] rēgnāta per arva [30]
Sāturnō [31] quondam; super et Garamantas [32] et Indōs

[12] Because only ghosts lived there.   [13] *just as one goes* (literally, *as is the way*).
[14] *stingy.*   [15] Dative (**599,** 4).
[16] *Grief;* the various feelings and the causes of death are personified.
[17] *couches;* the worries of conscience are there to stay.   [18] *pale.*
[19] *urging to do wrong.*   [20] *Need.*   [21] *to look at.*   [22] *Death.*
[23] = **Labor.**   [24] *wicked.*   [25] *chambers of the Furies.*
[26] With **aciēs:** *both eyes.*   [27] With **sub:** *up to the vault of heaven.*
[28] Julius Caesar, deified after his death. [29] *in Latium.*   [30] *lands.*
[31] *by Saturn* (dat. of agent). Saturn was a god in the mythical "Golden Age,"
when life was peaceful.   [32] *the Garaman'tēs,* an African tribe.

**The Trojan fleet at Carthage as shown in another scene from the Low Ham mosaic.
The entire mosaic is thirteen feet square.**

C. A. Ralegh Radford

795   prōferet imperium (iacet extrā sīdera tellūs,
extrā annī sōlisque viās,[33] ubi caelifer Atlās [34]
axem umerō torquet stēllīs ārdentibus aptum [35])."

Anchises tells Aeneas that the great contribution of the Romans will be good government and peace.

       "Excūdent [36] aliī spīrantia [37] mollius [38] aera
(crēdō equidem), vīvōs dūcent dē marmore vultūs;
ōrābunt causās melius caelīque meātūs [39]
850   dēscrībent radiō [40] et surgentia sīdera dīcent.
Tū regere imperiō populōs, Rōmāne, mementō [41]
(hae tibi erunt artēs) pācīque impōnere mōrem,[42]
parcere subiectīs et dēbellāre superbōs."

Aeneas returns to the upper world through the gate of false dreams.

       Sunt geminae somnī portae; quārum altera fertur
cornea,[43] quā vērīs facilis datur exitus umbrīs,[44]
895   altera candentī [45] perfecta nitēns [46] elephantō,
sed falsa ad caelum mittunt īnsomnia [44] Mānēs.[47]
Hīs [48] ibi tum nātum Anchīsēs ūnāque Sibyllam
prōsequitur dictīs portāque ēmittit eburnā.[49]
Ille viam secat [50] ad nāvīs sociōsque revīsit;
900   tum sē ad Caiētae [51] rēctō [52] fert lītore portum.
Ancora dē prōrā iacitur; stant lītore puppēs.

561. QUOTATIONS FROM VIRGIL

Some of Virgil's famous lines are given in the preceding selections. Here are a few more.

    1. Forsan [1] et [2] haec ōlim meminisse iuvābit.
    2. Hīc domus, haec patria est.

---

[33] i.e., beyond the constellations of the zodiac through which the sun seems to travel in the course of a year.   [34] *heaven-carrying Atlas.*

[35] With **axem:** *the sky studded with.*   [36] *will mold. The Greeks are meant.*

[37] *breathing, lifelike.*   [38] *more delicately.*

[39] *movements* (of the stars).

[40] *with the rod*—with which the movements of the stars were traced in sand.

[41] *remember* (imperative).   [42] i.e., to make peace customary.

[43] (*to be*) *of horn.*   [44] *dreams.*   [45] Abl.: *white.*

[46] *gleaming.*   [47] *the spirits.*

[48] With **dictīs,** referring to Anchises' speech.

[49] *of ivory.*   [50] *makes* (literally, *cuts*).

[51] *Caiē'ta,* a town on the coast near Formiae.   [52] *straight along the shore.*

---

[1] *perhaps.*   [2] *even.* **Haec** refers to the misfortunes of Aeneas.

3. Mēns cōnscia rēctī.[3]
4. Nōn omnia possumus omnēs.
5. Pedibus timor addidit ālās.
6. Quōrum [4] pars magna fuī.
7. Ūna salūs victīs, nūllam spērāre salūtem.
8. Varium et mūtābile [5] semper fēmina.

[3] *right,* with **cōnscia.** This quotation plays a part in a famous story of two rival English shoemakers whose shops adjoined each other. One of them put out a sign with the Virgilian quotation on it. Not to be outdone, his rival, who was innocent of Latin, promptly hung out a sign reading "Mens and Womens Conscia Recti."
[4] Neuter, referring to the destruction of Troy, as seen by Aeneas.
[5] Supply **est.** Used as nouns in the predicate nominative.

Anchises shows the sights of Hades to Aeneas. From a painting by Conca in Sarasota, Florida. Venus, Mercury, and Cupid look on from above.

Ringling Museum of Art

APPENDIX

562. IMPORTANT DATES AND EVENTS

B.C.

753	(Traditional date) Rome founded
753–509	Legendary kings
509	Republic established
496	Battle of Lake Regillus
494	Secession of the plebs
451–450	Laws of the Twelve Tables
390	Gauls capture Rome
343–290	Samnite Wars
280–275	War with Pyrrhus
264–241	First Punic War
218–201	Second Punic War
200–197	War with Philip
171–168	War with Perseus
157?–86	Marius, general
149–146	Third Punic War
146	Capture of Corinth
111–106	War with Jugurtha
106–48	Pompey, general
106–43	Cicero, orator, statesman
102	Marius defeats Cimbri and Teutons
100–44	Caesar, general, statesman
88–63	Mithridatic Wars
86	Sulla captures Athens
80–78	Caesar in Asia
63	Cicero consul. Conspiracy of Catiline
63–A.D. 14	Augustus
62	Caesar praetor (propraetor in Spain in 61)
60	First triumvirate (Caesar, Crassus, Pompey)
59	Caesar consul (proconsul in Gaul and Illyricum, 58–50)
55 and 54	Caesar invades Britain
55 and 53	Caesar invades Germany
52	Fall of Alesia
49	Caesar crosses the Rubicon, thus precipitating civil war
48	Caesar consul. Battle of Pharsalus—Pompey defeated
48–46	Caesar dictator
46	Caesar consul and dictator. Reforms calendar
45	Caesar sole consul
44	Caesar assassinated, March 15
42	Battle of Philippi
31	Battle of Actium
31–A.D. 14	Reign of Augustus

A.D.

9	Defeat of Varus
14–37	Reign of Tiberius
37–41	Reign of Caligula
41–54	Reign of Claudius
54–68	Reign of Nero
68–69	Reigns of Galba, Otho, Vitellius
69–79	Reign of Vespasian
79	Eruption of Mt. Vesuvius
79–81	Reign of Titus
81–96	Reign of Domitian
96–98	Reign of Nerva
98–117	Reign of Trajan
117–138	Reign of Hadrian
138–161	Reign of Antoninus Pius
161–180	Reign of Marcus Aurelius

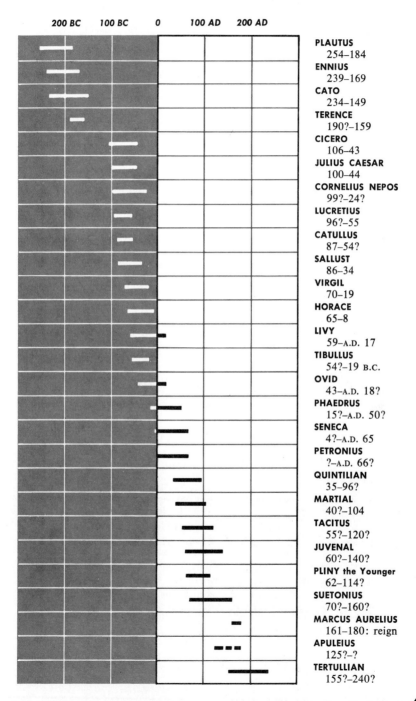

563. LIFE SPANS OF MAJOR LATIN AUTHORS

200 BC	100 BC	0	100 AD	200 AD	
					PLAUTUS 254–184
					ENNIUS 239–169
					CATO 234–149
					TERENCE 190?–159
					CICERO 106–43
					JULIUS CAESAR 100–44
					CORNELIUS NEPOS 99?–24?
					LUCRETIUS 96?–55
					CATULLUS 87–54?
					SALLUST 86–34
					VIRGIL 70–19
					HORACE 65–8
					LIVY 59–A.D. 17
					TIBULLUS 54?–19 B.C.
					OVID 43–A.D. 18?
					PHAEDRUS 15?–A.D. 50?
					SENECA 4?–A.D. 65
					PETRONIUS ?–A.D. 66?
					QUINTILIAN 35–96?
					MARTIAL 40?–104
					TACITUS 55?–120?
					JUVENAL 60?–140?
					PLINY the Younger 62–114?
					SUETONIUS 70?–160?
					MARCUS AURELIUS 161–180: reign
					APULEIUS 125?–?
					TERTULLIAN 155?–240?

BASIC FORMS

Nouns

564.

	First Declension		Second Declension	
	SINGULAR	PLURAL	SINGULAR	PLURAL
NOM.	via	viae	servus	servī
GEN.	viae	viārum	servī	servōrum
DAT.	viae	viīs	servō	servīs
ACC.	viam	viās	servum	servōs
ABL.	viā	viīs	servō	servīs
(VOC.)			(serve)	

Nouns in **–ius** have **–ī** in the genitive and vocative singular: **fīlī, Cornēlī.** The accent does not change.

565.

Second Declension

	SING.	PLUR.	SING.	PLUR.	SING.	PLUR.
NOM.	ager	agrī	puer	puerī	signum	signa
GEN.	agrī	agrōrum	puerī	puerōrum	signī	signōrum
DAT.	agrō	agrīs	puerō	puerīs	signō	signīs
ACC.	agrum	agrōs	puerum	puerōs	signum	signa
ABL.	agrō	agrīs	puerō	puerīs	signō	signīs

Nouns in **–ium** have **–ī** in the genitive singular: **cōnsilī.** The accent does not change.

566.

Third Declension

	SINGULAR	PLURAL	SINGULAR	PLURAL	SINGULAR	PLURAL
NOM.	mīles	mīlitēs	lēx	lēgēs	corpus	corpora
GEN.	mīlitis	mīlitum	lēgis	lēgum	corporis	corporum
DAT.	mīlitī	mīlitibus	lēgī	lēgibus	corporī	corporibus
ACC.	mīlitem	mīlitēs	lēgem	lēgēs	corpus	corpora
ABL.	mīlite	mīlitibus	lēge	lēgibus	corpore	corporibus

567.

Third Declension I-Stems

	SINGULAR	PLURAL	SINGULAR	PLURAL
NOM.	cīvis	cīvēs	mare	maria
GEN.	cīvis	cīvium	maris	marium
DAT.	cīvī	cīvibus	marī	maribus
ACC.	cīvem	cīvēs (–īs)	mare	maria
ABL.	cīve	cīvibus	marī	maribus

Turris and a few proper nouns have **–im** in the accusative singular. **Turris, ignis, nāvis,** and a few proper nouns sometimes have **–ī** in the ablative singular.

(*a*) The classes of masculine and feminine i-stem nouns are:

1. Nouns ending in **–is** and **–ēs** having no more syllables in the genitive than in the nominative: **cīvis, nūbēs.**

2. Nouns of one syllable whose base ends in two consonants: **pars** (gen. **part–is**), **nox** (gen. **noct–is**).
3. Nouns whose base ends in –**nt** or –**rt**: **cliēns** (gen. **client–is**).

   (b) Neuter **i**-stem nouns ending in –**e**, –**al**, –**ar**: **mare, animal, calcar.**

568.

Fourth Declension

	SING.	PLUR.	SING.	PLUR.
NOM.	cāsus	cāsūs	cornū	cornua
GEN.	cāsūs	cāsuum	cornūs	cornuum
DAT.	cāsuī	cāsibus	cornū	cornibus
ACC.	cāsum	cāsūs	cornū	cornua
ABL.	cāsū	cāsibus	cornū	cornibus

569.

Fifth Declension

	SING.	PLUR.	SING.	PLUR.
NOM.	diēs	diēs	rēs	rēs
GEN.	diēī	diērum	reī	rērum
DAT.	diēī	diēbus	reī	rēbus
ACC.	diem	diēs	rem	rēs
ABL.	diē	diēbus	rē	rēbus

570.

Irregular Nouns

	SING.	PLUR.	SING.	SING.	PLUR.
NOM.	vīs	vīrēs	nēmō	domus	domūs
GEN.	——	vīrium	(nūllīus)	domūs (–ī)	domuum (–ōrum)
DAT.	——	vīribus	nēminī	domuī (–ō)	domibus
ACC.	vim	vīrēs (–īs)	nēminem	domum	domōs (–ūs)
ABL.	vī	vīribus	(nūllō)	domō (–ū)	domibus
(LOC.)				(domī)	

Adjectives and Adverbs

571.

First and Second Declensions

	SINGULAR			PLURAL		
	M.	F.	N.	M.	F.	N.
NOM.	magnus	magna	magnum	magnī	magnae	magna
GEN.	magnī	magnae	magnī	magnōrum	magnārum	magnōrum
DAT.	magnō	magnae	magnō	magnīs	magnīs	magnīs
ACC.	magnum	magnam	magnum	magnōs	magnās	magna
ABL.	magnō	magnā	magnō	magnīs	magnīs	magnīs
(VOC.)	(magne)					
NOM.	līber	lībera	līberum	noster	nostra	nostrum
GEN.	līberī	līberae	līberī	nostrī	nostrae	nostrī
DAT.	līberō	līberae	līberō	nostrō	nostrae	nostrō
ACC.	līberum	līberam	līberum	nostrum	nostram	nostrum
ABL.	līberō	līberā	līberō	nostrō	nostrā	nostrō

   Plural, **līberī, līberae, lībera,** etc.   Plural, **nostrī, –ae, –a,** etc.

572. *Third Declension*

(a) THREE ENDINGS

	SINGULAR			PLURAL		
	M.	F.	N.	M.	F.	N.
NOM.	ācer	ācris	ācre	ācrēs	ācrēs	ācria
GEN.	ācris	ācris	ācris	ācrium	ācrium	ācrium
DAT.	ācrī	ācrī	ācrī	ācribus	ācribus	ācribus
ACC.	ācrem	ācrem	ācre	ācrēs (–īs)	ācrēs (–īs)	ācria
ABL.	ācrī	ācrī	ācrī	ācribus	ācribus	ācribus

(b) TWO ENDINGS

	SINGULAR		PLURAL	
	M.F.	N.	M.F.	N.
NOM.	fortis	forte	fortēs	fortia
GEN.	fortis	fortis	fortium	fortium
DAT.	fortī	fortī	fortibus	fortibus
ACC.	fortem	forte	fortēs (–īs)	fortia
ABL.	fortī	fortī	fortibus	fortibus

(c) ONE ENDING [1]

	SINGULAR		PLURAL	
	M.F.	N.	M.F.	N.
NOM.	pār	pār	parēs	paria
GEN.	paris	paris	parium	parium
DAT.	parī	parī	paribus	paribus
ACC.	parem	pār	parēs (–īs)	paria
ABL.	parī	parī	paribus	paribus

573. PRESENT PARTICIPLE

	SINGULAR		PLURAL	
	M.F.	N.	M.F.	N.
NOM.	portāns	portāns	portantēs	portantia
GEN.	portantis	portantis	portantium	portantium
DAT.	portantī	portantī	portantibus	portantibus
ACC.	portantem	portāns	portantēs (–īs)	portantia
ABL.	portante (–ī)	portante (–ī)	portantibus	portantibus

The ablative singular regularly ends in **–e,** but **–ī** is used wherever the participle is used simply as an adjective.

574. IRREGULAR ADJECTIVES AND NUMERALS

	M.	F.	N.	M.F.	N.
NOM.	ūnus	ūna	ūnum	trēs	tria
GEN.	ūnīus	ūnīus	ūnīus	trium	trium
DAT.	ūnī	ūnī	ūnī	tribus	tribus
ACC.	ūnum	ūnam	ūnum	trēs	tria
ABL.	ūnō	ūnā	ūnō	tribus	tribus

	M.	F.	N.	M.F.N. (*adj.*)	N. (*noun*)
NOM.	duo	duae	duo	mīlle	mīlia
GEN.	duōrum	duārum	duōrum	mīlle	mīlium
DAT.	duōbus	duābus	duōbus	mīlle	mīlibus
ACC.	duōs	duās	duo	mīlle	mīlia
ABL.	duōbus	duābus	duōbus	mīlle	mīlibus

[1] **Vetus** has **vetere** in the ablative singular and **veterum** in the genitive plural.

416

Like **ūnus** are **alius, alter, ūllus, nūllus, sōlus, tōtus, uter, neuter, uterque;** plural regular. The nom. and acc. sing. neuter of **alius** is **aliud;** for the genitive sing., **alterius** is generally used. **Ambō** is declined like **duo.**

575. *Comparison of Regular Adjectives and Adverbs*

POSITIVE		COMPARATIVE		SUPERLATIVE	
ADJ.	ADV.	ADJ.	ADV.	ADJ.	ADV.
altus	altē	altior	altius	altissimus	altissimē
fortis	fortiter	fortior	fortius	fortissimus	fortissimē
līber	līberē	līberior	līberius	līberrimus	līberrimē
ācer	ācriter	ācrior	ācrius	ācerrimus	ācerrimē
facilis	facile	facilior	facilius	facillimus	facillimē

Like **facilis** are **difficilis, similis, dissimilis, gracilis, humilis,** but their adverbs (not used in this book) vary in the positive degree. Adjectives in **–er** are like **līber** or **ācer.**

576. *Comparison of Irregular Adjectives*

POSITIVE	COMPARATIVE	SUPERLATIVE
bonus	melior	optimus
malus	peior	pessimus
magnus	maior	maximus
parvus	minor	minimus
multus	——, plūs	plūrimus
īnferus	īnferior	īnfimus *or* īmus
superus	superior	suprēmus *or* summus
——	prior	prīmus
——	propior	proximus
——	ulterior	ultimus

577. *Comparison of Irregular Adverbs*

bene	melius	optimē
male	peius	pessimē
(magnopere)	magis	maximē
——	minus	minimē
multum	plūs	plūrimum
diū	diūtius	diūtissimē
prope	propius	proximē

578. *Declension of Comparatives*

	SINGULAR		PLURAL		SINGULAR	PLURAL	
	M.F.	N.	M.F.	N.	N.	M.F.	N.
NOM.	altior	altius	altiōrēs	altiōra	plūs [1]	plūrēs	plūra
GEN.	altiōris	altiōris	altiōrum	altiōrum	plūris	plūrium	plūrium
DAT.	altiōrī	altiōrī	altiōribus	altiōribus	——	plūribus	plūribus
ACC.	altiōrem	altius	altiōrēs	altiōra	plūs	plūrēs	plūra
ABL.	altiōre	altiōre	altiōribus	altiōribus	plūre	plūribus	plūribus

[1] Masculine and feminine lacking in the singular.

	ROMAN	CARDINAL	ORDINAL
1.	I	ūnus, –a, –um	prīmus, –a, –um
2.	II	duo, duae, duo	secundus (alter)
3.	III	trēs, tria	tertius
4.	IIII *or* IV	quattuor	quārtus
5.	V	quīnque	quīntus
6.	VI	sex	sextus
7.	VII	septem	septimus
8.	VIII	octō	octāvus
9.	VIIII *or* IX	novem	nōnus
10.	X	decem	decimus
11.	XI	ūndecim	ūndecimus
12.	XII	duodecim	duodecimus
13.	XIII	tredecim	tertius decimus
14.	XIIII *or* XIV	quattuordecim	quārtus decimus
15.	XV	quīndecim	quīntus decimus
16.	XVI	sēdecim	sextus decimus
17.	XVII	septendecim	septimus decimus
18.	XVIII	duodēvīgintī	duodēvīcēsimus [1]
19.	XVIIII *or* XIX	ūndēvīgintī	ūndēvīcēsimus
20.	XX	vīgintī	vīcēsimus
21.	XXI	vīgintī ūnus *or* ūnus et vīgintī	vīcēsimus prīmus *or* ūnus et vīcēsimus
30.	XXX	trīgintā	trīcēsimus
40.	XXXX *or* XL	quadrāgintā	quadrāgēsimus
50.	L	quīnquāgintā	quīnquāgēsimus
60.	LX	sexāgintā	sexāgēsimus
70.	LXX	septuāgintā	septuāgēsimus
80.	LXXX	octōgintā	octōgēsimus
90.	LXXXX *or* XC	nōnāgintā	nōnāgēsimus
100.	C	centum	centēsimus
101.	CI	centum (et) ūnus	centēsimus (et) prīmus
200.	CC	ducentī, –ae, –a	ducentēsimus
300.	CCC	trecentī, –ae, –a	trecentēsimus
400.	CCCC	quadringentī, –ae, –a	quadringentēsimus
500.	D	quīngentī, –ae, –a	quīngentēsimus
600.	DC	sescentī, –ae, –a	sescentēsimus
700.	DCC	septingentī, –ae, –a	septingentēsimus
800.	DCCC	octingentī, –ae, –a	octingentēsimus
900.	DCCCC	nōngentī, –ae, –a	nōngentēsimus
1000.	M	mīlle	mīllēsimus
2000.	MM	duo mīlia	bis mīllēsimus

[1] The forms in **–ēsimus** are sometimes spelled **–ēnsimus**.

Pronouns

580.   *Personal*

	SING.	PLUR.		SING.	PLUR.	M.	F.	N.
NOM.	ego	nōs		tū	vōs	is	ea	id
GEN.	meī	nostrum (nostrī)		tuī	vestrum (–trī)	(for declension		
DAT.	mihi	nōbīs		tibi	vōbīs	see 582—		
ACC.	mē	nōs		tē	vōs	demonstrative **is**)		
ABL.	mē	nōbīs		tē	vōbīs			

581.   *Reflexive*

	FIRST PERSON		SECOND PERSON		THIRD PERSON	
	SINGULAR	PLURAL	SINGULAR	PLURAL	SINGULAR	PLURAL
GEN.	meī	nostrī	tuī	vestrī	suī	suī
DAT.	mihi	nōbīs	tibi	vōbīs	sibi	sibi
ACC.	mē	nōs	tē	vōs	sē (sēsē)	sē (sēsē)
ABL.	mē	nōbīs	tē	vōbīs	sē (sēsē)	sē (sēsē)

Not being used in the nominative, reflexives have no nominative form.

582.   *Demonstrative*

	SINGULAR			PLURAL		
	M.	F.	N.	M.	F.	N.
NOM.	hic	haec	hoc	hī	hae	haec
GEN.	huius	huius	huius	hōrum	hārum	hōrum
DAT.	huic	huic	huic	hīs	hīs	hīs
ACC.	hunc	hanc	hoc	hōs	hās	haec
ABL.	hōc	hāc	hōc	hīs	hīs	hīs
NOM.	is	ea	id	eī (iī)	eae	ea
GEN.	eius	eius	eius	eōrum	eārum	eōrum
DAT.	eī	eī	eī	eīs (iīs)	eīs (iīs)	eīs (iīs)
ACC.	eum	eam	id	eōs	eās	ea
ABL.	eō	eā	eō	eīs (iīs)	eīs (iīs)	eīs (iīs)

	SINGULAR			PLURAL		
	M.	F.	N.	M.	F.	N.
NOM.	īdem	eadem	idem	eīdem (īdem)	eaedem	eadem
GEN.	eiusdem	eiusdem	eiusdem	eōrundem	eārundem	eōrundem
DAT.	eīdem	eīdem	eīdem	eīsdem (īsdem)	eīsdem (īsdem)	eīsdem (īsdem)
ACC.	eundem	eandem	idem	eōsdem	eāsdem	eadem
ABL.	eōdem	eādem	eōdem	eīsdem (īsdem)	eīsdem (īsdem)	eīsdem (īsdem)

	SINGULAR			SINGULAR		
	M.	F.	N.	M.	F.	N.
NOM.	ille	illa	illud	ipse	ipsa	ipsum
GEN.	illīus	illīus	illīus	ipsīus	ipsīus	ipsīus
DAT.	illī	illī	illī	ipsī	ipsī	ipsī
ACC.	illum	illam	illud	ipsum	ipsam	ipsum
ABL.	illō	illā	illō	ipsō	ipsā	ipsō

(Plural regular like **magnus**)   (Plural regular)

Iste is declined like **ille.**

583.   *Relative*   *Interrogative*

	SINGULAR			PLURAL			SINGULAR	
	M.	F.	N.	M.	F.	N.	M.F.	N.
NOM.	quī	quae	quod	quī	quae	quae	quis	quid
GEN.	cuius	cuius	cuius	quōrum	quārum	quōrum	cuius	cuius
DAT.	cui	cui	cui	quibus	quibus	quibus	cui	cui
ACC.	quem	quam	quod	quōs	quās	quae	quem	quid
ABL.	quō	quā	quō	quibus	quibus	quibus	quō	quō

Plural of **quis** like **quī.** Interrogative adjective **quī** like relative **quī.**

584.   *Indefinite*

	SINGULAR		PLURAL		
	M.F.	N.	M.	F.	N.
NOM.	aliquis	aliquid	aliquī	aliquae	aliqua
GEN.	alicuius	alicuius	aliquōrum	aliquārum	aliquōrum
DAT.	alicui	alicui	aliquibus	aliquibus	aliquibus
ACC.	aliquem	aliquid	aliquōs	aliquās	aliqua
ABL.	aliquō	aliquō	aliquibus	aliquibus	aliquibus

The adjective form is **aliquī, –qua, –quod,** etc.

	SINGULAR		
	M.	F.	N.
NOM.	quīdam	quaedam	quiddam
GEN.	cuiusdam	cuiusdam	cuiusdam
DAT.	cuidam	cuidam	cuidam
ACC.	quendam	quandam	quiddam
ABL.	quōdam	quādam	quōdam

	PLURAL		
NOM.	quīdam	quaedam	quaedam
GEN.	quōrundam	quārundam	quōrundam
DAT.	quibusdam	quibusdam	quibusdam
ACC.	quōsdam	quāsdam	quaedam
ABL.	quibusdam	quibusdam	quibusdam

The adjective has **quoddam** for **quiddam.**

	SINGULAR			SINGULAR	
	M.F.	N.		M.F.	N.
NOM.	quisquam	quicquam (quidquam)		quisque	quidque
GEN.	cuiusquam	cuiusquam		cuiusque	cuiusque
DAT.	cuiquam	cuiquam		cuique	cuique
ACC.	quemquam	quicquam (quidquam)		quemque	quidque
ABL.	quōquam	quōquam		quōque	quōque

(Plural lacking)   (Plural rare)

The adjective form of **quisque** is **quisque, quaeque, quodque,** etc.

The indefinite pronoun **quis** (declined like the interrogative) and adjective **quī** (declined like the relative, but in the nom. fem. sing. and the nom. and acc. neut. plur. **qua** may be used for **quae**) are used chiefly after **sī, nisi,** and **nē.**

A fanciful Roman scene on modern American wallpaper. One has the feeling of looking out a window to the ruins of an aqueduct and temple.

Albert van Luit

Verbs

585. *First Conjugation*

PRINCIPAL PARTS: **portō, portāre, portāvī, portātus**

ACTIVE   PASSIVE

INDICATIVE

	ACTIVE		PASSIVE	
PRESENT	*I carry*, etc.		*I am carried*, etc.	
	portō	portāmus	portor	portāmur
	portās	portātis	portāris (–re)	portāminī
	portat	portant	portātur	portantur
IMPERFECT	*I was carrying*, etc.		*I was (being) carried*, etc.	
	portābam	portābāmus	portābar	portābāmur
	portābās	portābātis	portābāris (–re)	portābāminī
	portābat	portābant	portābātur	portābantur
FUTURE	*I shall carry*, etc.		*I shall be carried*, etc.	
	portābō	portābimus	portābor	portābimur
	portābis	portābitis	portāberis (–re)	portābiminī
	portābit	portābunt	portābitur	portābuntur

PERFECT	*I carried, have carried*, etc.		*I was carried, have been carried*, etc.	
	portāvī	portāvimus		
	portāvistī	portāvistis	portātus (–a, –um) { sum / es / est }	portātī (–ae, –a) { sumus / estis / sunt }
	portāvit	portāvērunt (–ēre)		
PAST PERFECT	*I had carried*, etc.		*I had been carried*, etc.	
	portāveram	portāverāmus		
	portāverās	portāverātis	portātus (–a, –um) { eram / erās / erat }	portātī (–ae, –a) { erāmus / erātis / erant }
	portāverat	portāverant		
FUTURE PERFECT	*I shall have carried*, etc.		*I shall have been carried*, etc.	
	portāverō	portāverimus		
	portāveris	portāveritis	portātus (–a, –um) { erō / eris / erit }	portātī (–ae, –a) { erimus / eritis / erunt }
	portāverit	portāverint		

SUBJUNCTIVE

PRESENT	portem	portēmus	porter	portēmur
	portēs	portētis	portēris (–re)	portēminī
	portet	portent	portētur	portentur
IMPERFECT	portārem	portārēmus	portārer	portārēmur
	portārēs	portārētis	portārēris (–re)	portārēminī
	portāret	portārent	portārētur	portārentur
PERFECT	portāverim	portāverīmus		
	portāverīs	portāverītis	portātus (–a, –um) { sim / sīs / sit }	portātī (–ae, –a) { sīmus / sītis / sint }
	portāverit	portāverint		
PAST PERFECT	portāvissem	portāvissēmus		
	portāvissēs	portāvissētis	portātus (–a, –um) { essem / essēs / esset }	portātī (–ae, –a) { essēmus / essētis / essent }
	portāvisset	portāvissent		

	ACTIVE	PASSIVE

PRESENT IMPERATIVE

2D SING.	portā, *carry*	portāre, *be carried*
2D PLUR.	portāte, *carry*	portāminī, *be carried*

INFINITIVE

PRESENT	portāre, *to carry*	portārī, *to be carried*
PERFECT	portāvisse, *to have carried*	portātus esse, *to have been carried*
FUTURE	portātūrus esse, *to be going to carry*	

PARTICIPLE

PRESENT	portāns, *carrying*	
PERFECT		portātus, *(having been) carried*
FUTURE	portātūrus, *going to carry*	portandus, *(necessary) to be carried*

GERUND

GEN. portandī   DAT. portandō   ACC. portandum   ABL. portandō, *of carrying*, etc.

586. Second, Third, and Fourth Conjugations

	2d Conj.	3d Conj.	4th Conj.	3d Conj. (–iō)

PRINCIPAL PARTS

	doceō	pōnō	mūniō	capiō
	docēre	pōnere	mūnīre	capere
	docuī	posuī	mūnīvī	cēpī
	doctus	positus	mūnītus	captus

INDICATIVE ACTIVE

PRESENT	doceō	pōnō	mūniō	capiō
	docēs	pōnis	mūnīs	capis
	docet	pōnit	mūnit	capit
	docēmus	pōnimus	mūnīmus	capimus
	docētis	pōnitis	mūnītis	capitis
	docent	ponunt	mūniunt	capiunt
IMPERFECT	docēbam	pōnēbam	mūniēbam	capiēbam
	docēbās	pōnēbās	mūniēbās	capiēbās
	docēbat	pōnēbat	mūniēbat	capiēbat
	docēbāmus	pōnēbāmus	mūniēbāmus	capiēbāmus
	docēbātis	pōnēbātis	mūniēbātis	capiēbātis
	docēbant	pōnēbant	mūniēbant	capiēbant
FUTURE	docēbō	pōnam	mūniam	capiam
	docēbis	pōnēs	mūniēs	capiēs
	docēbit	pōnet	mūniet	capiet
	docēbimus	pōnēmus	mūniēmus	capiēmus
	docēbitis	pōnētis	mūniētis	capiētis
	docēbunt	pōnent	mūnient	capient

	2d Conj.	3d Conj.	4th Conj.	3d Conj. (–iō)
PERFECT	docuī	posuī	mūnīvī	cēpī
	docuistī	posuistī	mūnīvistī	cēpistī
	docuit	posuit	mūnīvit	cēpit
	docuimus	posuimus	mūnīvimus	cēpimus
	docuistis	posuistis	mūnīvistis	cēpistis
	docuērunt	posuērunt	mūnīvērunt	cēpērunt
	(–ēre)	(–ēre)	(–ēre)	(–ēre)
PAST PERFECT	docueram	posueram	mūnīveram	cēperam
	docuerās	posuerās	mūnīverās	cēperās
	docuerat	posuerat	mūnīverat	cēperat
	docuerāmus	posuerāmus	mūnīverāmus	cēperāmus
	docuerātis	posuerātis	mūnīverātis	cēperātis
	docuerant	posuerant	mūnīverant	cēperant
FUTURE PERFECT	docuerō	posuerō	mūnīverō	cēperō
	docueris	posueris	mūnīveris	cēperis
	docuerit	posuerit	mūnīverit	cēperit
	docuerimus	posuerimus	mūnīverimus	cēperimus
	docueritis	posueritis	mūnīverītis	cēperitis
	docuerint	posuerint	mūnīverint	cēperint

Subjunctive Active

	2d Conj.	3d Conj.	4th Conj.	3d Conj. (–iō)
PRESENT	doceam	pōnam	mūniam	capiam
	doceās	pōnās	mūniās	capiās
	doceat	pōnat	mūniat	capiat
	doceāmus	pōnāmus	mūniāmus	capiāmus
	doceātis	pōnātis	mūniātis	capiātis
	doceant	pōnant	mūniant	capiant
IMPERFECT	docērem	pōnerem	mūnīrem	caperem
	docērēs	pōnerēs	mūnīrēs	caperēs
	docēret	pōneret	mūnīret	caperet
	docērēmus	pōnerēmus	mūnīrēmus	caperēmus
	docērētis	pōnerētis	mūnīrētis	caperētis
	docērent	pōnerent	mūnīrent	caperent
PERFECT	docuerim	posuerim	mūnīverim	cēperim
	docuerīs	posuerīs	mūnīverīs	cēperīs
	docuerit	posuerit	mūnīverit	cēperit
	docuerīmus	posuerīmus	mūnīverīmus	cēperīmus
	docuerītis	posuerītis	mūnīverītis	cēperītis
	docuerint	posuerint	mūnīverint	cēperint
PAST PERFECT	docuissem	posuissem	mūnīvissem	cēpissem
	docuissēs	posuissēs	mūnīvissēs	cēpissēs
	docuisset	posuisset	mūnīvisset	cēpisset

	2d Conj.	3d Conj.	4th Conj.	3d Conj. (–iō)
	docuissēmus	posuissēmus	mūnīvissēmus	cēpissēmus
	docuissētis	posuissētis	mūnīvissētis	cēpissētis
	docuissent	posuissent	mūnīvissent	cēpissent

PRESENT IMPERATIVE ACTIVE

	2d Conj.	3d Conj.	4th Conj.	3d Conj. (–iō)
2D SING.	docē	pōne [1]	mūnī	cape [1]
2D PLUR.	docēte	pōnite	mūnīte	capite

INFINITIVE ACTIVE

	2d Conj.	3d Conj.	4th Conj.	3d Conj. (–iō)
PRESENT	docēre	pōnere	mūnīre	capere
PERFECT	docuisse	posuisse	mūnīvisse	cēpisse
FUTURE	doctūrus esse	positūrus esse	mūnītūrus esse	captūrus esse

PARTICIPLE ACTIVE

	2d Conj.	3d Conj.	4th Conj.	3d Conj. (–iō)
PRESENT	docēns	pōnēns	mūniēns	capiēns
FUTURE	doctūrus	positūrus	mūnītūrus	captūrus

GERUND

	2d Conj.	3d Conj.	4th Conj.	3d Conj. (–iō)
GEN.	docendī	pōnendī	mūniendī	capiendī
DAT.	docendō	pōnendō	mūniendō	capiendō
ACC.	docendum	pōnendum	mūniendum	capiendum
ABL.	docendō	pōnendō	mūniendō	capiendō

INDICATIVE PASSIVE

	2d Conj.	3d Conj.	4th Conj.	3d Conj. (–iō)
PRESENT	doceor	pōnor	mūnior	capior
	docēris (–re)	pōneris (–re)	mūnīris (–re)	caperis (–re)
	docētur	pōnitur	mūnītur	capitur
	docēmur	pōnimur	mūnīmur	capimur
	docēminī	pōniminī	mūnīminī	capiminī
	docentur	pōnuntur	mūniuntur	capiuntur
IMPERFECT	docēbar	pōnēbar	mūniēbar	capiēbar
	docēbāris (–re)	pōnēbāris (–re)	mūniēbāris (–re)	capiēbāris (–re)
	docēbātur	pōnēbātur	mūniēbātur	capiēbātur
	docēbāmur	pōnēbāmur	mūniēbāmur	capiēbāmur
	docēbāminī	pōnēbāminī	mūniēbāminī	capiēbāminī
	docēbantur	pōnēbantur	mūniēbantur	capiēbantur

[1] **Dīcō, dūcō,** and **faciō** have **dīc, dūc, fac** in the imperative singular.

Roman toys in the Toronto Museum.

	2d Conj.	3d Conj.	4th Conj.	3d Conj. (–iō)
FUTURE	docēbor	pōnar	mūniar	capiar
	docēberis (–re)	pōnēris (–re)	mūniēris (–re)	capiēris (–re)
	docēbitur	pōnētur	mūniētur	capiētur
	docēbimur	pōnēmur	mūniēmur	capiēmur
	docēbiminī	pōnēminī	mūniēminī	capiēminī
	docēbuntur	pōnentur	mūnientur	capientur
PERFECT	doctus sum	positus sum	mūnītus sum	captus sum
	doctus es	positus es	mūnītus es	captus es
	doctus est	positus est	mūnītus est	captus est
	doctī sumus	positī sumus	mūnītī sumus	captī sumus
	doctī estis	positī estis	mūnītī estis	captī estis
	doctī sunt	positī sunt	mūnītī sunt	captī sunt
PAST PERFECT	doctus eram	positus eram	mūnītus eram	captus eram
	doctus erās	positus erās	mūnītus erās	captus erās
	doctus erat	positus erat	mūnītus erat	captus erat
	doctī erāmus	positī erāmus	mūnītī erāmus	captī erāmus
	doctī erātis	positī erātis	mūnītī erātis	captī erātis
	doctī erant	positī erant	mūnītī erant	captī erant
FUTURE PERFECT	doctus erō	positus erō	mūnītus erō	captus erō
	doctus eris	positus eris	mūnītus eris	captus eris
	doctus erit	positus erit	mūnītus erit	captus erit
	doctī erimus	positī erimus	mūnītī erimus	captī erimus
	doctī eritis	positī eritis	mūnītī eritis	captī eritis
	doctī erunt	positī erunt	mūnītī erunt	captī erunt

SUBJUNCTIVE PASSIVE

	2d Conj.	3d Conj.	4th Conj.	3d Conj. (–iō)
PRESENT	docear	pōnar	mūniar	capiar
	doceāris (–re)	pōnāris (–re)	mūniāris (–re)	capiāris (–re)
	doceātur	pōnātur	mūniātur	capiātur
	doceāmur	pōnāmur	mūniāmur	capiāmur
	doceāminī	pōnāminī	mūniāminī	capiāminī
	doceantur	pōnantur	mūniantur	capiantur
IMPERFECT	docērer	pōnerer	mūnīrer	caperer
	docērēris (–re)	pōnerēris (–re)	mūnīrēris (–re)	caperēris (–re)
	docērētur	pōnerētur	mūnīrētur	caperētur
	docērēmur	pōnerēmur	mūnīrēmur	caperēmur
	docērēminī	pōnerēminī	mūnīrēminī	caperēminī
	docērentur	pōnerentur	mūnīrentur	caperentur
PERFECT	doctus sim	positus sim	mūnītus sim	captus sim
	doctus sīs	positus sīs	mūnītus sīs	captus sīs
	doctus sit	positus sit	mūnītus sit	captus sit

	2d Conj.	3d Conj.	4th Conj	3d Conj. (–iō)
	doctī sīmus	positī sīmus	mūnītī sīmus	captī sīmus
	doctī sītis	positī sītis	mūnītī sītis	captī sītis
	doctī sint	positī sint	mūnītī sint	captī sint
PAST PERFECT	doctus essem	positus essem	mūnītus essem	captus essem
	doctus essēs	positus essēs	mūnītus essēs	captus essēs
	doctus esset	positus esset	mūnītus esset	captus esset
	doctī essēmus	positī essēmus	mūnītī essēmus	captī essēmus
	doctī essētis	positī essētis	mūnītī essētis	captī essētis
	doctī essent	positī essent	mūnītī essent	captī essent

Present Imperative Passive

	2d Conj.	3d Conj.	4th Conj	3d Conj. (–iō)
2D SING.	docēre	pōnere	mūnīre	capere
2D PLUR.	docēminī	pōniminī	mūnīminī	capiminī

Infinitive Passive

	2d Conj.	3d Conj.	4th Conj	3d Conj. (–iō)
PRESENT	docērī	pōnī	mūnīrī	capī
PERFECT	doctus esse	positus esse	mūnītus esse	captus esse

Participle Passive

	2d Conj.	3d Conj.	4th Conj	3d Conj. (–iō)
PERFECT	doctus	positus	mūnītus	captus
FUTURE	docendus	pōnendus	mūniendus	capiendus

This lifelike marble group, representing a stag attacked by dogs, was found in an ancient Roman house at Herculaneum.

Deponent Verbs [1]

	1st Conj.	2d Conj.	3d Conj.	4th Conj.	3d Conj. (–iō)

PRINCIPAL PARTS

	arbitror	vereor	loquor	orior	gradior
	arbitrārī	verērī	loquī	orīrī	gradī
	arbitrātus	veritus	locūtus	ortus	gressus

INDICATIVE

	1st Conj.	2d Conj.	3d Conj.	4th Conj.	3d Conj. (–iō)
PRESENT	arbitror, *I think*	vereor, *I fear*	loquor, *I talk*	orior, *I rise*	gradior, *I walk*
IMPERFECT	arbitrābar	verēbar	loquēbar	oriēbar	gradiēbar
FUTURE	arbitrābor	verēbor	loquar	oriar	gradiar
PERFECT	arbitrātus sum	veritus sum	locūtus sum	ortus sum	gressus sum
PAST PERF.	arbitrātus eram	veritus eram	locūtus eram	ortus eram	gressus eram
FUT. PERF.	arbitrātus erō	veritus erō	locūtus erō	ortus erō	gressus erō

SUBJUNCTIVE

PRESENT	arbitrer	verear	loquar	oriar	gradiar
IMPERFECT	arbitrārer	verērer	loquerer	orīrer	graderer
PERFECT	arbitrātus sim	veritus sim	locūtus sim	ortus sim	gressus sim
PAST PERF.	arbitrātus essem	veritus essem	locūtus essem	ortus essem	gressus essem

PRESENT IMPERATIVE

2D SING.	arbitrāre	verēre	loquere	orīre	gradere
2D PLUR.	arbitrāminī	verēminī	loquiminī	orīminī	gradiminī

INFINITIVE

PRESENT	arbitrārī	verērī	loquī	orīrī	gradī
PERFECT	arbitrātus esse	veritus esse	locūtus esse	ortus esse	gressus esse
FUTURE	arbitrātūrus esse	veritūrus esse	locūtūrus esse	ortūrus esse	gressūrus esse

[1] See **108.**

PARTICIPLE

PRESENT	arbitrāns	verēns	loquēns	oriēns	gradiēns
PERFECT	arbitrātus	veritus	locūtus	ortus	gressus
FUT. ACT.	arbitrātūrus	veritūrus	locūtūrus	ortūrus	gressūrus
FUT. PASS.	arbitrandus	verendus	loquendus	oriendus	gradiendus

GERUND

GEN.	arbitrandī, etc.	verendī, etc.	loquendī, etc.	oriendī, etc.	gradiendī, etc.

A few verbs (called "semideponent") are active in the present system and deponent in the perfect system, as **audeō, audēre, ausus.**

Irregular Verbs

588.   PRINCIPAL PARTS: **sum, esse, fuī, futūrus**

INDICATIVE			SUBJUNCTIVE		
PRESENT	sum, *I am*	sumus, *we are*	PRESENT	sim	sīmus
	es, *you are*	estis, *you are*		sīs	sītis
	est, *he is*	sunt, *they are*		sit	sint
IMPERFECT	*I was,* etc.				
	eram	erāmus	IMPERFECT	essem	essēmus
	erās	erātis		essēs	essētis
	erat	erant		esset	essent
FUTURE	*I shall be,* etc.				
	erō	erimus			
	eris	eritis			
	erit	erunt			
PERFECT	*I was,* etc.				
	fuī	fuimus	PERFECT	fuerim	fuerīmus
	fuistī	fuistis		fuerīs	fuerītis
	fuit	fuērunt (–ēre)		fuerit	fuerint
PAST PERFECT	*I had been,* etc.				
	fueram	fuerāmus	PAST PERFECT	fuissem	fuissēmus
	fuerās	fuerātis		fuissēs	fuissētis
	fuerat	fuerant		fuisset	fuissent
FUTURE PERFECT	*I shall have been,* etc.				
	fuerō	fuerimus			
	fueris	fueritis			
	fuerit	fuerint			

INFINITIVE		IMPERATIVE	
PRESENT	esse, *to be*	2D SING. es, *be*	2D PLUR. este, *be*
PERFECT	fuisse, *to have been*		
FUTURE	futūrus esse, *to be going to be*	PARTICIPLE	
		FUTURE futūrus, *going to be*	

429

589.   Principal Parts **possum, posse, potuī, ——**

	INDICATIVE			SUBJUNCTIVE	
PRESENT	*I am able, I can,* etc.				
	possum	possumus	PRESENT	possim	possīmus
	potes	potestis		possīs	possītis
	potest	possunt		possit	possint

IMPERFECT *I was able, I could,* etc.
poteram, etc.   IMPERFECT possem, etc.

FUTURE   *I shall be able,* etc.
poterō, etc.

PERFECT   *I was able, I could,* etc.
potuī, etc.   PERFECT   potuerim, etc.

PAST
PERFECT   *I had been able,* etc.
potueram, etc.   PAST PERF. potuissem, etc.

FUTURE
PERFECT   *I shall have been able,* etc.
potuerō, etc.

	INFINITIVE		PARTICIPLE	
PRESENT	posse, *to be able*	PRESENT	potēns *(adj.), powerful*	
PERFECT	potuisse, *to have been able*			

590.   Principal Parts: **ferō, ferre, tulī, lātus**

ACTIVE   PASSIVE

INDICATIVE

	ACTIVE		PASSIVE	
PRESENT	ferō	ferimus	feror	ferimur
	fers	fertis	ferris (–re)	feriminī
	fert	ferunt	fertur	feruntur
IMPERFECT	ferēbam, etc.		ferēbar, etc.	
FUTURE	feram, ferēs, etc.		ferar, ferēris, etc.	
PERFECT	tulī, etc.		lātus sum, etc.	
PAST PERF.	tuleram, etc.		lātus eram, etc.	
FUT. PERF.	tulerō, etc.		lātus erō, etc.	

SUBJUNCTIVE

	ACTIVE	PASSIVE
PRESENT	feram, ferās, etc.	ferar, ferāris, etc.
IMPERFECT	ferrem, etc.	ferrer, etc.
PERFECT	tulerim, etc.	lātus sim, etc.
PAST PERF.	tulissem, etc.	lātus essem, etc.

430

PRESENT IMPERATIVE

2D PERS.	fer	ferte	ferre	feriminī

INFINITIVE

PRESENT	ferre	ferrī
PERFECT	tulisse	lātus esse
FUTURE	lātūrus esse	

PARTICIPLE

PRESENT	ferēns	
PERFECT		lātus
FUTURE	lātūrus	ferendus

GERUND

GEN. ferendī	DAT. ferendō	ACC. ferendum	ABL. ferendō

591.

PRINCIPAL PARTS: eō, īre, iī, itūrus

	INDICATIVE		SUBJUNCTIVE	INFINITIVE
PRESENT	eō	īmus	eam, etc.	īre
	īs	ītis		
	it	eunt		
IMPERFECT	ībam, etc.		īrem, etc.	
FUTURE	ībō	ībimus		itūrus esse
	ībis	ībitis		
	ībit	ībunt		
PERFECT	iī	iimus	ierim, etc.	īsse
	īstī	īstis		
	iit	iērunt (–ēre)		
PAST PERF.	ieram, etc.		īssem, etc.	
FUT. PERF.	ierō, etc.			

	PARTICIPLE	IMPERATIVE	GERUND
PRESENT	iēns, GEN. euntis	ī īte	GEN. eundī
			DAT. eundō
FUTURE	itūrus (PASSIVE		ACC. eundum
	eundus)		ABL. eundō

Greek air-mail stamp showing the Temple of Apollo at Corinth (cf. p. 144).

592.

volō	nōlō	mālō
velle	nōlle	mālle
voluī	nōluī	māluī

INDICATIVE

PRESENT	volō	volumus	nōlō	nōlumus	mālō	mālumus
	vīs	vultis	nōn vīs	nōn vultis	māvīs	māvultis
	vult	volunt	nōn vult	nōlunt	māvult	mālunt

IMPERFECT	volēbam, etc.	nōlēbam, etc.	mālēbam, etc.
FUTURE	volam, volēs, etc.	nōlam, nōlēs, etc.	mālam, mālēs, etc.
PERFECT	voluī, etc.	nōluī, etc.	māluī, etc.
PAST PERF.	volueram, etc.	nōlueram, etc.	mālueram, etc.
FUT. PERF.	voluerō, etc.	nōluerō, etc.	māluerō, etc.

SUBJUNCTIVE

PRESENT	velim	velīmus	nōlim	nōlīmus	mālim	mālīmus
	velīs	velītis	nōlīs	nōlītis	mālīs	mālītis
	velit	velint	nōlit	nōlint	mālit	mālint

IMPERFECT	vellem, etc.	nōllem, etc.	māllem, etc.
PERFECT	voluerim, etc.	nōluerim, etc.	māluerim, etc.
PAST PERF.	voluissem, etc.	nōluissem, etc.	māluissem, etc.

PRESENT IMPERATIVE

2D PERS.	—— ——	nōlī	nōlīte	—— ——

INFINITIVE

PRESENT	velle	nōlle	mālle
PERFECT	voluisse	nōluisse	māluisse

PARTICIPLE

PRESENT	volēns	nōlēns	—— ——

593. PRINCIPAL PARTS: **fīō, fierī, (factus)**

	INDICATIVE	SUBJUNCTIVE	IMPERATIVE	INFINITIVE
PRESENT	fīō ——	fīam, etc.		fierī
	—— ——		fī fīte	
	fit fīunt			
IMPERFECT	fīēbam, etc.	fierem, etc.		
FUTURE	fīam, fīēs, etc.			

594.
Defective Verbs

Coepī is used only in the perfect system. For the present system **incipiō** is used. With a passive infinitive the passive of **coepī** is used: **Lapidēs iacī coeptī sunt,** *Stones began to be thrown.* **Meminī** and **ōdī** likewise are used only in the perfect system, but with present meaning. The former has an imperative **mementō, mementōte.**

595.
Contracted Forms

Verbs having perfect stems ending in **–āv–** or **–ēv–** are sometimes contracted by dropping **–ve–** before **–r–** and **–vi–** before **–s–: amārunt, cōnsuēsse.** Verbs having perfect stems ending in **–īv–** drop **–vi–** before **–s–** but only **–v–** before **–r–: audīsset, audierat.**

The Roman baths at Nîmes, in the Roman Province of Gaul.

BASIC SYNTAX [1]

596. Agreement

1. *Adjectives*. Adjectives and participles agree in number, gender, and case with the nouns which they modify.

2. *Adjectives as Nouns*. Sometimes adjectives are used as nouns: **nostrī,** *our* (*men*); **malum,** *evil*.

3. *Verbs*. Verbs agree in person and number with their subjects. When two subjects are connected by **aut, aut . . . aut, neque . . . neque,** the verb agrees with the nearer subject.

Note. A plural verb may be used with a singular subject which is plural in thought (**192,** footnote 8).

4. *Relative Pronoun*. The relative pronoun agrees in gender and number with its antecedent but its case depends upon its use in its own clause.

Note. *a*. The antecedent of the relative is often omitted.

b. Sometimes the antecedent is represented by an entire clause, in which case the pronoun is best translated *a thing which*.

c. In Latin a relative pronoun is often used at the beginning of a sentence to refer to the thought of the preceding sentence. The English idiom calls for a demonstrative or personal pronoun.

> **quā dē causā,** *for this reason.*

5. *Appositives*. Appositives agree in case.

Note. It is often best to supply *as* in translating the appositive.

> **eōdem homine magistrō ūtī,** *to use the same man as teacher.*

Noun Syntax

597. Nominative

1. *Subject*. The subject of a finite verb is in the nominative case.

2. *Predicate*. *a*. A noun or adjective used in the predicate with a linking verb (*is, are, seem,* etc.) is in the nominative.

> **Īnsula est magna,** *The island is large.*
> **Sicilia est īnsula,** *Sicily is an island.*

b. Predicate nouns and adjectives are used not only with **sum** but also with **fīō** and the passive voice of verbs meaning *call, choose, appoint, elect,* and the like.

---

[1] In this summary only those constructions are included which are relatively more important and which recur repeatedly in the text, or are referred to in the book.

Tombs resembling large toy houses in a Roman cemetery near Ostia.

Caesar dux factus est, *Caesar was made leader.*
Cicerō Pater Patriae appellātus est, *Cicero was called the Father of his Country.*

Note. With the active voice of these verbs two accusatives are used.

598. Genitive

1. *Possession.* Possession is expressed by the genitive.

viae īnsulae, *the roads of the island.*

2. *Description.* The genitive, if modified by an adjective, may be used to describe a person or thing.

virī magnae virtūtis, *men of great courage.*

Note. The descriptive genitive is largely confined to permanent qualities such as measure and number.

spatium decem pedum, *a space of ten feet.*

3. *Of the Whole.* The genitive of the whole (also called partitive genitive) represents the whole to which the part belongs.

hōrum omnium fortissimī, *the bravest of all these.*
nihil praesidī, *no guard.*

Note. a. This is similar to the English idiom except when the genitive is used with such words as **nihil, satis, quid.**

b. Instead of the genitive of the whole, the ablative with **ex** or **dē** is regularly used with cardinal numerals (except **mīlia**) and **quīdam,** often also with other words, such as **paucī** and **complūrēs.**

quīnque ex nostrīs, *five of our men.*
quīdam ex mīlitibus, *certain of the soldiers.*

435

4. *With Adjectives.* The genitive is used with certain adjectives. In many cases the English idiom is the same; in others, it is not.

> **bellandī cupidus,** *desirous of waging war.*
> **reī mīlitāris perītus,** *skilled in warfare.*

599. Dative

1. *Indirect Object.* The indirect object of a verb is in the dative. It is used with verbs of *giving, reporting, telling,* etc.

> **Nautae pecūniam dōnō,** *I give money to the sailor.*

2. *Purpose.* The dative is sometimes used to express purpose.

> **Locum castrīs dēlēgit,** *He chose a place for a camp.*

3. *Reference.* The dative of reference shows the person concerned or referred to.

> **sī mihi dignī esse vultis,** *if you wish to be worthy in my sight* (lit., *for me*).

Note. The dative of reference is often used with the dative of purpose to show the person or thing affected ("double" dative).

> **Haec castra erunt praesidiō oppidō,** *This camp will be (for) a protection to the town.*

4. *Separation.* The dative of separation (really reference) is usually confined to persons and occurs chiefly with verbs compounded with **ab, dē,** and **ex.**

> **scūtō ūnī mīlitī dētrāctō,** *having seized a shield from a soldier.*

5. *With Adjectives.* The dative is used with certain adjectives, as **amīcus, idōneus, pār, proximus, similis, ūtilis,** and their opposites. In many cases the English idiom is the same.

> **Hic liber est similis illī,** *This book is similar to that.*

6. *With Special Verbs.* The dative is used with a few intransitive verbs, such as **cōnfīdō, crēdō, dēsum, faveō, ignōscō, imperō, invideō, noceō, parcō, pāreō, persuādeō, placeō, praestō, resistō,** and **studeō.**

> **Tibi pāret sed mihi resistit,** *He obeys you but resists me.*

a. Some of these verbs become impersonal in the passive and the dative is retained. The perfect passive participle of such verbs is used only in the neuter.

> **Eī persuāsum est,** *He was persuaded.*

b. A neuter pronoun or adjective or an **ut** clause may be used as a direct object with **imperō** and **persuādeō.**

> **Hoc mihi persuāsit,** *He persuaded me of this.*

7. *With Compounds.* The dative is often used with certain compound verbs, especially when the noun goes closely with the prefix of the verb. No general rule can be given. Sometimes both an accusative and a dative are used when the main part of the verb is transitive.

Gallīs bellum intulit, *He made war against the Gauls.*

8. *Possession.* The possessor may be expressed by the dative with **sum.**

Liber mihi est, *I have a book.*

9. *Agent.* The dative of agent is used with the future passive participle to indicate the person upon whom the obligation rests **(611).**

Hoc opus vōbīs faciendum est, *This work is to be done by you,* i.e., *This work must be done by you.*

600. *Accusative*

1. *Direct Object.* The direct object of a transitive verb is in the accusative.

Viam parāmus, *We are preparing a way.*

2. *Extent.* Extent of time or space is expressed by the accusative.

Duōs annōs remānsit, *He remained two years.*
Flūmen decem pedēs altum est, *The river is ten feet deep.*

3. *Place to Which.* The accusative with **ad** (*to*) or **in** (*into*) expresses "place to which." These prepositions, however, are omitted before **domum** and names of towns and cities.

Lēgātōs ad eum mittunt, *They send envoys to him.*
Rōmam eunt, *They go to Rome.*

Note. When the preposition **ad** is used with names of towns it means *to the vicinity of.*

4. *Subject of Infinitive.* The subject of an infinitive is in the accusative.

Puerōs esse bonōs volumus, *We want the boys to be good.*

5. *Two Accusatives.* With **trādūcō** and **trānsportō** two accusatives are used. In the passive the word closely connected with the prefix remains in the accusative.

Cōpiās *Rhēnum* trādūcit, *He leads his forces across the Rhine.*
Cōpiae *Rhēnum* trādūcuntur, *The forces are led across the Rhine.*

Note. For two accusatives with verbs meaning *call, choose,* etc., see **597,** 2, *b, Note.*

6. *With Prepositions.* The accusative is used with prepositions (except those listed in **601,** 19). When **in** and **sub** show the direction toward which a thing moves, the accusative is used.

601. Ablative

Summary. The uses of the ablative may be grouped under three heads:

I. The *true* or *"from"* ablative (**ab**, *from,* and **lātus**, *carried*), used with the prepositions **ab, dē,** and **ex**—if any preposition is used.

II. The *associative* or *"with"* ablative, used with the preposition **cum**—if any preposition is used.

III. The *place* or *"in"* ablative, used with the prepositions **in** and **sub**—if any preposition is used.

1. *Separation.* Separation may be expressed by the ablative without a preposition, always so with **careō** and **līberō,** often also with **abstineō, dēsistō, excēdō,** and other verbs.

Note. a. Caesar uses **prohibeō,** *keep from,* usually without a preposition, but occasionally with it.

> **Suīs fīnibus eōs prohibent,** *They keep them from their own territory.*

b. Other verbs expressing separation regularly require the prepositions **ab, dē,** or **ex.**

2. *Place from Which.* The ablative with **ab, dē,** or **ex** expresses "place from which."

> **ex agrīs,** *out of the fields.*

Note. The preposition is regularly omitted before **domō** as well as before names of towns and cities. When it is used with such names, it means *from the vicinity of.*

3. *Origin.* The ablative without or with a preposition (**ab, dē, ex**) expresses origin.

> **amplissimō genere nātus,** *born of most illustrious family.*

4. *Agent.* The ablative with **ā** or **ab** is used with a passive verb to show the person (or animal) by whom something is done.

> **Amāmur ab amīcīs,** *We are loved by our friends.*

5. *Comparison.* After a comparative the ablative is used when **quam** (*than*) is omitted.

> **amplius pedibus decem,** *more than ten feet.*
> **Nec locus tibi ūllus dulcior esse dēbet patriā,** *No spot ought to be dearer to you than your native land.*

6. *Accompaniment.* The ablative with **cum** expresses accompaniment.

> **Cum servō venit,** *He is coming with the slave.*

a. When **cum** is used with a personal, reflexive, or relative pronoun, it is attached to it as an enclitic: **vōbīscum,** *with you;* **sēcum,** *with himself;* **quibuscum,** *with whom.*

b. **Cum** may be omitted in military phrases indicating accompaniment, if modified by an adjective other than a numeral.

> **omnibus suīs cōpiīs,** *with all his forces.*
> **cum tribus legiōnibus,** *with three legions.*

7. *Manner.* The ablative of manner with **cum** describes how something is done. **Cum** is sometimes omitted if an adjective modifies the noun.

> **(Cum) magnō studiō labōrat,** *He labors with great eagerness (very eagerly).*

8. *Absolute.* A noun in the ablative used with a participle, adjective, or other noun and having no grammatical connection with any other word in its clause is called an ablative absolute.

In translating, an ablative absolute should, as a rule, be changed to a clause expressing *time, cause, condition, means,* or *concession,* according to the context. At times it may best be rendered by a coördinate clause.

> **Servō accūsātō, dominus discessit,** *After accusing the slave* (lit., *the slave having been accused), the master departed.*
> **Oppidīs nostrīs captīs, bellum gerēmus,** *If our towns are captured* (lit., *our towns captured), we shall wage war.*

9. *Means.* The means by which a thing is done is expressed by the ablative without a preposition.

> **Ratibus trānsībant,** *They were trying to cross by means of rafts.*

10. *With Special Verbs.* The ablative is used with a few verbs, notably **potior** and **ūtor,** whose English equivalents govern a direct object.

> **Castrīs potītī sunt,** *They got possession of the camp.*

11. *Cause.* The ablative of cause is used chiefly with verbs and adjectives expressing feeling.

> **labōrāre iniūriā,** *to suffer because of the wrong.*
> **vīribus cōnfīsī,** *relying on their strength.*

12. *Measure of Difference.* The ablative without a preposition expresses the measure of difference.

> **tribus annīs ante,** *three years ago* (lit., *before by three years).*
> **multō maior,** *much larger* (lit., *larger by much).*

13. *Description.* The ablative, like the genitive, is used with an adjective to describe a noun. It is regularly used of temporary qualities, such as personal appearance.

> **hominēs inimīcā faciē,** *men with an unfriendly appearance.*

14. *Place Where.* The ablative with **in** or **sub** expresses "place where." The preposition may be omitted, however, with certain words like **locō, locīs,** and **parte,** also in certain fixed expressions like **tōtō orbe terrārum,**

in the whole world. In poetry the omission of the preposition is more frequent. See also Locative.

15. *Time When.* "Time when" or "within which" is expressed by the ablative without a preposition.

> **aestāte,** *in summer;* **paucīs diēbus,** *within a few days.*

16. *Respect.* The ablative tells in what respect the statement applies.

> **Nōs superant numerō,** *They surpass us in number.*

17. *Accordance.* The ablative is used with a few words to express the idea *in accordance with*.

> **mōre suō,** *in accordance with his custom.*

18. *With Dignus.* The ablative is used with **dignus** and **indignus.**

> **dignus patre,** *worthy of his father.*

19. *With Prepositions.* The ablative is used with the prepositions **ab, cum, dē, ex, prae, prō, sine;** sometimes with **in** and **sub** (see 14).

602. Locative

Domus and the names of towns and cities require a separate case, called the locative, to express "place where." The locative has the same ending as the genitive in the singular of nouns of the first and second declensions; it has the same ending as the ablative in the plural of these declensions and in the third declension, singular and plural.

> **domī,** *at home;* **Rōmae,** *at Rome;* **Athēnīs,** *at Athens.*

603. Vocative

The vocative is used in addressing a person. Unless emphatic it never stands first.

> **Quid facis, amīce?** *What are you doing, my friend?*

Verb Syntax

604. Tenses

The tenses of the indicative in Latin are in general used like those in English, but the following points are to be noted.

1. *Present.* The Latin present has the force of the English simple present and of the progressive present.

> **Vocat,** *He calls,* or *He is calling.*

2. *Historical Present.* The historical present is used for vivid effect instead of a past tense in Latin as in English.

> **Rōmam proficīscuntur,** *They depart(ed) for Rome.*

440

a. In clauses introduced by **dum** meaning *while,* the historical present is always used. In translating use the English past. For **dum** meaning *as long as* or *until* see **605**, 2; **606**, 12.

> **dum haec geruntur,** *while these things were going on.*

3. *Imperfect.* The Latin imperfect expresses repeated, customary, or continuous action in the past and is usually best translated by the English progressive past, sometimes by the auxiliary *would,* or by a phrase, such as *used to* or *kept on.*

> **Pugnābant,** *They were fighting.*

4. *Perfect.* The Latin perfect is generally equivalent to the English past, occasionally to the present perfect.

> **Vīcī,** *I conquered,* or *I have conquered.*

5. *Sequence of Tenses.* The subjunctive mood is used chiefly in subordinate clauses, in which its tenses are determined by the principle of "sequence of tenses," as shown in the following summary and examples:

a. PRIMARY TENSES   (referring to the present or future)
   Indicative: present, future, future perfect.
   Subjunctive: present, perfect.

1. **Venit ut mē videat,** *He is coming to see me* (*that he may see me*).
2. **Veniet ut mē videat,** *He will come to see me* (*that he may see me*).
3. **Excesserō priusquam veniat,** *I shall have departed before he comes.*
4. **Rogō quid crās faciās** (or **factūrus sīs**), *I ask what you will do tomorrow.*
5. **Rogō quid herī fēcerīs,** *I ask what you did yesterday.*

b. SECONDARY TENSES   (referring to the past)
   Indicative: imperfect, perfect, past perfect.
   Subjunctive: imperfect, past perfect.

1. **Vēnit ut mē vidēret,** *He came to see me* (*that he might see me*).
2. **Rogābam quid facerēs,** *I kept asking what you were doing.*
3. **Rogābam quid anteā fēcissēs,** *I kept asking what you had done before.*
4. **Excesseram priusquam venīret,** *I had departed before he came.*

Primary indicative tenses are followed by primary subjunctive tenses, secondary by secondary.

Note. a. The "historical" present (**604**, 2), used for vivid effect in describing a past action, is often followed by a secondary tense.

b. In result clauses, the perfect subjunctive sometimes follows a secondary tense.

605. Indicative Mood

The indicative mood is generally used in Latin as in English. The following points are to be noted.

1. *Relative Clauses.* Most relative clauses are in the indicative, as in English. But see **606,** 3, 10, 14.

2. *Adverbial Clauses.* Clauses introduced by **postquam, posteāquam** (*after*), **ubi, ut** (*when*), **cum prīmum, simul ac** (*as soon as*), **dum** (*while, as long as*), **quamquam, etsī** (*although*) are in the indicative.

> **Postquam id cōnspexit, signum dedit,** *After he noticed this, he gave the signal.*

3. *Noun Clauses.* A clause introduced by **quod** (*the fact that, that*) is in the indicative and may be used as subject or object of the main verb or in apposition with a demonstrative.

> **Grātum est quod mē requīris,** *It is gratifying that you miss me.*

606. Subjunctive Mood

1. *Volitive.* The volitive **(volō)** subjunctive represents an act as *willed* and is translated by *let.* The negative is **nē.**

> **Patriam dēfendāmus,** *Let us defend our country.*
> **Nē id videat,** *Let him not see it.*

2. *Purpose Clauses.* The subjunctive is used in a subordinate clause with **ut** or **utī** (negative **nē**) to express the purpose of the act expressed by the principal clause.

> **Venīmus ut videāmus,** *We come that we may see,* or *We come to see.*
> **Fugit nē videātur,** *He flees that he may not be seen.*

3. *Relative Purpose Clauses.* If the principal clause contains (or implies) a definite antecedent, the purpose clause may be introduced by the relative pronoun **quī** (= **ut is** or **ut eī**) instead of **ut.**

> **Mīlitēs mīsit quī hostem impedīrent,** *He sent soldiers to hinder the enemy.*

4. *Quō Purpose Clauses.* If the purpose clause contains an adjective or adverb in the comparative degree, **quō** is generally used instead of **ut.**

> **Accēdit quō facilius audiat,** *He approaches in order that he may hear more easily.*

(For other ways to express purpose see Dative, Future Passive Participle, Gerund.)

5. *Volitive Noun Clauses.* Clauses in the subjunctive with **ut** (negative **nē**) are used as the objects of such verbs as **moneō, rogō, petō, hortor, persuādeō,** and **imperō.**

442

Mīlitēs hortātus est ut fortēs essent, *He urged the soldiers to be brave.*
Helvētiīs persuāsit ut exīrent, *He persuaded the Helvetians to leave.*

Note. a. With **iubeō** (*order*), unlike **imperō,** the infinitive is used. The subject of the infinitive is in the accusative.

Iussit eōs venīre, *He ordered them to come.*
Imperāvit eīs ut venīrent, *He ordered them to come.*

b. **Vetō** (*forbid*) and **cupiō** (*desire*) are used like **iubeō.**

6. *Clauses with Verbs of Hindering.* With verbs of hindering and preventing, as **impediō** and **dēterreō,** the subjunctive introduced by **nē** or **quō minus** is used if the main clause is affirmative, by **quīn** if negative.

Tū dēterrēre potes nē maior multitūdō trādūcātur, *You can prevent a greater number from being brought over.*

Note. The infinitive is often used with **prohibeō** (*prevent*).

Caesar prohibuit eōs trānsīre, *Caesar prevented them from crossing.*

7. *Clauses of Fear.* With verbs of fearing, clauses in the subjunctive introduced by **nē** (*that*) and **ut** (*that not*) are used.

Verēbātur nē tū aeger essēs, *He feared that you were sick.*
Timuī ut venīrent, *I was afraid that they would not come.*

8. *Result Clauses.* The result of the action or state of the principal verb is expressed by a subordinate clause with **ut (utī),** negative **ut nōn (utī nōn),** and the subjunctive.

Tantum est perīculum ut paucī veniant, *So great is the danger that few are coming.*
Ita bene erant castra mūnīta ut nōn capī possent, *So well had the camp been fortified that it could not be taken.*

Note. Result clauses are usually anticipated by some word in the main clause meaning *so* or *such* (**ita, tantus, tot, tam,** etc.).

9. *Noun Clauses of Result.* Verbs meaning *to happen* (**accidō**) or *to cause* or *effect* (**efficiō**) require clauses of result in the subjunctive with **ut (utī)** or **ut (utī) nōn,** used as subject or object of the main verb:

Accidit ut mē nōn vidēret, *It happened that he did not see me.*
Efficiam ut veniat, *I shall cause him to come.*

10. *Descriptive Relative Clauses.* A relative clause with the subjunctive may be used to describe an indefinite antecedent. Such clauses are called relative clauses of description (characteristic) and are especially common after such expressions as **ūnus** and **sōlus, sunt quī** (*there are those who*), and **nēmō est quī** (*there is no one who*).

Note. Sometimes a descriptive clause expresses cause.

11. *Cum Clauses.* In secondary sequence **cum** (*when*) is used with the imperfect or the past perfect subjunctive to describe the circumstances under which the action of the main verb occurred.

Cum mīlitēs redīssent, Caesar ōrātiōnem habuit, *When the soldiers returned, Caesar made a speech.*

a. In some clauses **cum** with the subjunctive is best translated *since*.

Quae cum ita sint, nōn ībō, *Since this is so, I shall not go* (literally, *When this is so*).

b. In some clauses **cum** with the subjunctive is best translated *although*.

Cum ea ita sint, tamen nōn ībō, *Although this is so, yet I shall not go* (literally, *When*, etc.).

When **ut** means *although, granted that,* its clause is in the subjunctive.

12. *Anticipatory Clauses.* **Dum** (*until*), **antequam**, and **priusquam** (*before*) introduce clauses (*a*) in the indicative to indicate *an actual fact*, (*b*) in the subjunctive to indicate an act *as anticipated*.

Silentium fuit dum tū vēnistī, *There was silence until you came.*
Caesar exspectāvit dum nāvēs convenīrent, *Caesar waited until the ships should assemble.*
Priusquam tēlum adigī posset, omnēs fūgērunt, *Before a weapon could be thrown, all fled.*

13. *Indirect Questions.* In a question indirectly quoted or expressed after some introductory verb such as *ask, doubt, learn, know, tell, hear,* etc., the verb is in the subjunctive.

Rogant quis sit, *They ask who he is.*

Note. The first member of a double indirect question is introduced by **utrum** or **–ne**, the second by **an.**

Quaerō utrum vērum an falsum sit, *I ask whether it is true or false.*

14. *Subordinate Clauses in Indirect Discourse.* An indicative in a subordinate clause becomes subjunctive in indirect discourse. If the clause is not regarded as an essential part of the quotation but is merely explanatory or parenthetical, its verb may be in the indicative.

Dīxit sē pecūniam invēnisse quam āmīsisset, *He said that he found the money which he had lost.*

15. *Attraction.* A verb in a clause dependent upon a subjunctive or an infinitive, is frequently "attracted" to the subjunctive, especially if its clause is an essential part of the statement.

Dat negōtium hīs utī ea quae apud Belgās gerantur cognōscant, *He directs them to learn what is going on among the Belgians.*

444

16. *Quod Causal Clauses.* Causal clauses introduced by **quod** (or **proptereā quod**) and **quoniam** (*since, because*) are in the indicative when they give the writer's or speaker's reason, the subjunctive when the reason is presented as that of another person.

> **Amīcō grātiās ēgī quod mihi pecūniam dederat,** *I thanked my friend because he had given me money.*
>
> **Rōmānīs bellum intulit quod agrōs suōs vāstāvissent,** *He made war against the Romans because (as he alleged) they had laid waste his lands.*

607. Outline of Conditions

a. Subordinate clause ("condition") introduced by **sī, nisi,** or **sī nōn.**
b. Principal clause ("conclusion").

1. *Simple* (nothing implied as to truth). Any possible combination of tenses of the indicative, as in English.

> **Sī mē laudat, laetus sum,** *If he praises me, I am glad.*

2. *Contrary to Fact.*

a. Present: imperfect subjunctive in both clauses.

> **Sī mē laudāret, laetus essem,** *If he were praising me* (but he isn't), *I should be glad* (now).

b. Past: past perfect subjunctive in both clauses.

> **Sī mē laudāvisset, laetus fuissem,** *If he had praised me* (but he didn't), *I should have been glad* (then).

c. Mixed: past condition and present conclusion.

> **Sī mē laudāvisset, laetus essem,** *if he had praised me* (but he didn't), *I should be glad* (now).

3. *Future Less Vivid* ("should," "would"). Present subjunctive in both clauses.

> **Sī mē laudet, laetus sim,** *If he should praise me, I should be glad.*

608. Imperative Mood

Affirmative commands are expressed by the imperative; negative commands by the present imperative of **nōlō (nōlī, nōlīte)** and the infinitive. The imperative with **nē** is used in poetry.

> **Amā inimīcōs tuōs,** *Love your enemies.*
> **Nōlīte īre,** *Do not go* (lit., *Be unwilling to go*).

Note. Exhortations (volitive subjunctive, **606,** 1) and commands, though main clauses, become subjunctive in indirect discourse.

> (Direct) **Īte!** *Go!*
> (Indirect) **Dīxit īrent,** *He said that they should go.*

609. Reflexive Use of the Passive

Occasionally the passive form of a verb or participle is used in a reflexive sense: **armārī,** *to arm themselves.*

610. Participle

1. The tenses of the participle (present, perfect, future) indicate time *present, past,* or *future* from the standpoint of the main verb.

2. *a.* Perfect participles are often used simply as adjectives: **nōtus,** *known.*

b. Participles, like adjectives, may be used as nouns: **factum,** "having been done," *deed.*

3. The Latin participle is often a *one-word substitute* for a subordinate clause in English introduced by *who* or *which, when* or *after, since* or *because, although,* and *if.*

611. Future Passive Participle

The future passive participle (gerundive) is a verbal adjective, having thirty forms. It has two distinct uses:

1. As a predicate adjective with forms of **sum,**[1] when it naturally indicates, as in English, *what must be done.* The person upon whom the obligation rests is in the dative (**599,** 9).

> **Caesarī omnia erant agenda,** *Caesar had to do all things* (lit., *all things were to be done by Caesar*).

2. As modifier of a noun or pronoun in various constructions, with no idea of obligation:

> **dē Rōmā cōnstituendā,** *about founding Rome* (lit. *about Rome to be founded*).

Note. With phrases introduced by **ad** and the accusative or by **causā** (or **grātiā**) and the genitive it expresses purpose. **Causā** and **grātiā** are always placed after the participle.

> **Ad eās rēs cōnficiendās Mārcus dēligitur,** *Marcus is chosen to accomplish these things* (lit., *for these things to be accomplished*).
> **Caesaris videndī causā** (or **grātiā**) **vēnit,** *He came for the sake of seeing Caesar* (lit., *for the sake of Caesar to be seen*).

612. Gerund

The gerund is a verbal noun of the second declension with only four forms—genitive, dative, accusative, and ablative singular.

---

[1] The so-called passive periphrastic, a term not used in this book. The term should be avoided because it is not only useless but troublesome.

The uses of the gerund are similar to some of those of the future passive participle:

> **cupidus bellandī,** *desirous of waging war.*
> **Ad discendum vēnī,** *I came for learning* (i.e., *to learn*).
> **Discendī causā** (or **grātiā**) **vēnī,** *I came for the sake of learning.*

Note. The gerund usually does not have an object. Instead, the future passive participle is used, modifying the noun.

613. Infinitive

1. The infinitive is an indeclinable neuter verbal noun, and as such it may be used as the subject of a verb.

> **Errāre hūmānum est,** *To err is human.*
> **Vidēre est crēdere,** *To see is to believe.*

2. With many verbs the infinitive, like other nouns, may be used as a direct object. (Sometimes called the complementary infinitive.)

> **Cōpiās movēre parat,** *He prepares to move the troops.*

3. The infinitive object of some verbs, such as **iubeō, volō, nōlō,** and **doceō,** often has a noun or pronoun subject in the accusative.

4. Statements that give indirectly the thoughts or words of another, used as the objects of verbs of *saying, thinking, knowing, hearing, perceiving,* etc., have verbs in the infinitive with their subjects in the accusative.

> (Direct) **Dīcit, "Puerī veniunt,"** *He says, "The boys are coming."*
> (Indirect) **Dīcit puerōs venīre,** *He says that the boys are coming.*

Note. With the passive third singular (impersonal) of these verbs the infinitive is the subject.

> **Caesarī nūntiātur eōs trānsīre,** *It is reported to Caesar that they are crossing.*

5. *a.* The present infinitive represents time or action as *going on,* from the standpoint of the introductory verb:

> **Dīcit** ⎱ **eōs pugnāre,** *He* {*says* / *said*} (that) they {*are* / *were*} *fighting.*
> **Dīxit** ⎰

b. The future infinitive represents time or actions as *subsequent to* that of the introductory verb:

> **Dīcit** ⎱ **eōs pugnātūrōs esse,** *He* {*says* / *said*} (that) they {*will* / *would*} *fight.*
> **Dīxit** ⎰

c. The perfect infinitive represents time or action as *completed before* that of the introductory verb:

> **Dīcit** ⎱ **eōs pugnāvisse,** *He* {*says* / *said*} (that) they {*have* / *had*} *fought.*
> **Dīxit** ⎰

447

SUMMARY OF PREFIXES AND SUFFIXES

614. Prefixes

A great many Latin words are formed by joining prefixes (**prae,** *in front;* **fīxus,** *attached*) to *root* words. These same prefixes, most of which are prepositions, are those chiefly used in English, and by their use many new words are continually being formed.

Some prefixes change their final consonants to make them like the initial consonants of the words to which they are attached. This change is called assimilation (**ad,** *to;* **similis,** *like*).

Many prefixes in Latin and English may have intensive force, especially **con–, ex–, ob–, per–.** They are then best translated either by an English intensive, as *up* or *out,* or by an adverb, as *completely, thoroughly, deeply.* Thus **commoveō** means *move greatly,* **permagnus,** *very great,* **obtineō,** *hold on to,* **concitō,** *rouse up,* **excipiō,** *catch, receive.*

1. **ab (abs, ā),** *from:* **abs-tineō;** *ab-undance, abs-tain, a-vocation.*
2. **ad,** *to, toward:* **ad-iciō;** *ac-curate, an-nounce, ap-paratus, ad-vocate.*
3. **ante,** *before:* **ante-cēdō;** *ante-cedent.*
4. **bene,** *well:* **bene-dīcō;** *bene-factor.*
5. **bi–, bis–,** *twice, two:* **bi-ennium;** *bi-ennial.*
6. **circum,** *around:* **circum-eō;** *circum-ference.*
7. **con–,** *with, together:* **con-vocō;** *con-voke, col-lect, com-motion, cor-rect.*
8. **contrā,** *against:* **contra-dict.**
9. **dē,** *from, down from, not:* **dē-ferō;** *de-ter.*
10. **dis–,** *apart, not:* **dis-cēdō;** *dis-locate, dif-fuse, di-vert.*
11. **ex (ē),** *out of, from:* **ex-eō;** *ex-port, e-dit, ef-fect.*
12. **extrā,** *outside:* **extra-legal.**
13. **in,** *in, into, against:* **in-dūcō;** *in-habit, im-migrant, il-lusion, en-chant.*
14. **in–,** *not, un–:* **im-mēnsus;** *il-legal, im-moral, ir-regular.*
15. **inter,** *between, among:* **inter-clūdō;** *inter-class.*
16. **intrā,** *within, inside:* **intra-collegiate.**
17. **intrō–,** *within:* **intro-duce.**
18. **male,** *ill:* **male-factor, mal-formation.**
19. **multi–,** *much, many:* **multi-graph.**
20. **nōn,** *not:* **non-sense.**
21. **ob,** *against, toward:* **ob-tineō;** *oc-cur, of-fer, o-mit, op-pose, ob-tain.*
22. **per,** *through, thoroughly:* **per-moveō;** *per-fect.*
23. **post,** *after:* **post-pone.**
24. **prae,** *before, in front of:* **prae-ficiō;** *pre-cede.*
25. **prō,** *for, forward:* **prō-dūcō;** *pro-mote.*
26. **re– (red–),** *back, again:* **re-dūcō, red-igō;** *re-fer.*
27. **sē–,** *apart from:* **sē-cēdō;** *se-parate.*
28. **sēmi–,** *half, partly:* **sēmi-barbarus;** *semi-annual.*
29. **sub,** *under, up from under:* **suc-cēdō;** *suf-fer, sug-gest, sup-port, sub-let*
30. **super (sur–),** *over, above:* **super-sum;** *super-fluous, sur-mount.*
31. **trāns (trā–),** *through, across:* **trā-dūcō;** *trans-fer.*
32. **ultrā,** *extremely:* **ultra-fashionable.**
33. **ūn– (ūni–),** *one:* **uni-form.**

615. Suffixes

Particles which are attached to the ends of words are called suffixes (**sub,** *under, after;* **fīxus,** *attached*). Like the Latin prefixes, the Latin suffixes play a very important part in the formation of English words.

The meaning of suffixes is often far less definite than that of prefixes. In many cases they merely indicate the part of speech.

Suffixes are often added to words which already have suffixes. So *functionalistically* has six suffixes, all of Latin or Greco-Latin origin except the last. A suffix often combines with a preceding letter or letters to form a new suffix. This is especially true of suffixes added to perfect participles whose base ends in **–s–** or **–t–**. In the following list no account is taken of such English suffixes as *–ant,* derived from the ending of the Latin present participle.

1. **–ālis** (*–al*), *pertaining to:* **līber-ālis;** *annu-al.*
2. **–ānus** (*–an, –ane, –ain*), *pertaining to:* **Rōm-ānus;** *capt-ain, hum-ane.*
3. **–āris** (*–ar*), *pertaining to:* **famili-āris;** *singul-ar.*
4. **–ārium** (*–arium, –ary*), *place where:* **aqu-arium,** *gran-ary.*
5. **–ārius** (*–ary*), *pertaining to:* **frūment-ārius;** *ordin-ary.*
6. **–āticum** (*–age*): *bagg-age.*
7. **–āx** (*–ac–ious*), *tending to:* **aud-āx;** *rap-acious.*
8. **–faciō, –ficō** (*–fy*), *make:* **cōn-ficiō;** *satis-fy.*
9. **–ia** (*–y*), **–cia, –tia** (*–ce*), **–antia** (*–ance, –ancy*), **–entia** (*–ence, –ency*), *condition of:* **memor-ia, grā-tia, cōnst-antia, sent-entia;** *memor-y, provin-ce, gra-ce, const-ancy, sent-ence.*
10. **–icus** (*–ic*), *pertaining to:* **pūbl-icus;** *civ-ic.*
11. **–idus** (*–id*), *having the quality of:* **rap-idus;** *flu-id.*
12. **–ilis** (*–ile, –il*), **–bilis** (*–ble, –able, –ible*), *able to be:* **fac-ilis, laudā-bilis;** *fert-ile, no-ble, compar-able, terr-ible.*
13. **–īlis** (*–ile, –il*), *pertaining to:* **cīv-īlis;** *serv-ile.*
14. **–īnus** (*–ine*), *pertaining to:* **mar-īnus;** *div-ine.*
15. **–iō** (*–ion*), **–siō** (*–sion*), **–tiō** (*–tion*), *act* or *state of:* **reg-iō, mān-siō, ōrā-tiō;** *commun-ion, ten-sion, rela-tion.*
16. **–ium** (*–y*), **–cium, –tium** (*–ce*): **remed-ium, sōlā-cium, pre-tium;** *stud-y, edifi-ce.*
17. **–īvus** (*–ive*), *pertaining to:* **capt-īvus;** *nat-ive.*
18. **–lus, –ellus, –ulus** (*–lus, –le*) *little* ("diminutive"): **parvu-lus, castel-lum;** *gladio-lus, parti-cle.*
19. **–men** (*–men, –min, –me*): **lū-men;** *cri-min-al, cri-me.*
20. **–mentum** (*–ment*), *means of:* **im-pedī-mentum;** *comple-ment.*
21. **–or** (*–or*), *state of:* **tim-or;** *terr-or.*
22. **–or, –sor, –tor** (*–sor, –tor*), *one who:* **scrīp-tor;** *inven-tor.*
23. **–ōrium** (*–orium, –ory, –or*), *place where:* **audit-orium,** *fact-ory, mirr-or.*
24. **–ōsus** (*–ous, –ose*), *full of:* **ōti-ōsus;** *copi-ous.*
25. **–tās** (*–ty*), *state of:* **līber-tās;** *integri-ty.*
26. **–tō, –sō, –itō,** *keep on* ("frequentative"): **dic-tō, prēn-sō, vent-itō.**
27. **–tūdō** (*–tude*), *state of:* **magni-tūdō;** *multi-tude.*
28. **–tūs** (*–tue*), *state of:* **vir-tūs;** *vir-tue.*
29. **–ūra, –sūra, –tūra** (*–ure, –sure, –ture*): **fig-ūra, mēn-sūra, agricul-tūra;** *proced-ure, pres-sure, na-ture.*

The Etruscans are said to represent the first advanced civilization in Italy. They were conquered by the Romans in 396 B.C. However, because the Romans prized Etruscan art, much of it survived. The vase is from the Seventh century B.C. The object is an ivory comb.

The Arch of Titus, in the Roman Forum, was erected by Domitian in 81 A.D. in memory of eastern military conquests by his brother Titus. It is one of the finest examples of a triumphal arch. In ancient times, there was a statue of Titus and his father Vespasian in a four-horse chariot on top of the arch.

Fototeca

A striking contrast: The ancient Claudian aqueduct behind modern buildings in Rome.

The Roman bridge at Alcántara, Spain.

Spanish State Tourist Office

VOCABULARY

LATIN–ENGLISH

Verbs of the first conjugation whose parts are regular (i.e., like **portō, 585**) are indicated by the figure 1. Proper names are not included unless they are spelled differently in English or are difficult to pronounce in English. Their English pronunciation is indicated by a simple system. The vowels are as follows: ā as in *hate*, ă as in *hat*, ē as in *feed*, ĕ as in *fed*, ī as in *bite*, ĭ as in *bit*, ō as in *hope*, ŏ as in *hop*, ū as in *cute*, ŭ as in *cut*. In the ending *ēs* the *s* is soft as in *rose*. When the accented syllable ends in a consonant, the vowel is short; otherwise it is long.

A

A., *abbreviation for* **Aulus, –ī,** *m.,* Aulus

ā, ab, abs, *prep. w. abl.,* from, by

abdō, –ere, abdidī, abditus, put away, hide

abdūcō, –ere, abdūxī, abductus, lead *or* take away

abeō, abīre, abiī, abitūrus, go away, depart; change (into)

abiciō, –ere, abiēcī, abiectus, throw away

abrogō, 1, repeal

abscīdō, –ere, –cīdī, –cīsus, cut away

absēns, *gen.* **absentis,** absent

absentia, –ae, *f.,* absence

abstineō, –ēre, –tinuī, –tentus, hold away; refrain

abstulī, *see* **auferō**

absum, abesse, āfuī, āfutūrus, be away, be absent

abundō, 1, be well supplied

ac, *see* **atque**

accēdō, –ere, accessī, accessūrus, come to, approach, be added

accidō, –ere, accidī, —, fall, happen

accīdō, –ere, accīdī, accīsus, cut into

accipiō, –ere, accēpī, acceptus, receive, accept, be told

accommodō, 1, fit (on)

accumbō, –ere, accubuī, accubitūrus, recline (at table)

accūrātē, *adv.,* carefully

accurrō, –ere, accurrī, accursūrus, run

accūsō, 1, blame, criticize

ācer, ācris, ācre, sharp, keen, fierce

acerbē, *adv.,* severely

acerbitās, –tātis, *f.,* bitterness; suffering

acerbus, –a, –um, sour, bitter

Achaia, –ae, *f.,* Achaia (Akā′ya), Greece

aciēs, aciēī, *f.,* battle line

ācriter, *adv.,* fiercely; *comp.* **ācrius;** *superl.* **ācerrimē**

Actium, –tī, *n.,* Actium (Ak′shĭum), *a promontory in Epirus*

acūtus, –a, –um, sharp

ad, *prep. w. acc.,* to, toward, for, near, at, until; *adv., w. numbers,* about

adāctus, *part. of* **adigō**

adaequō, 1, equal

addō, –ere, addidī, additus, add

addūcō, –ere, addūxī, adductus, lead (to), pull in, bring, influence; contract

adeō, adīre, adiī, aditūrus, go to, approach

adeō, *adv.,* so, so much

adfore, *fut. inf. of* **adsum**

adhaereō, –ēre, adhaesī, adhaesus, stick (to)

adhibeō, –ēre, adhibuī, adhibitus, hold toward; admit, use

adhūc, *adv.,* up to this time, still

adiciō, –ere, adiēcī, adiectus, add

adigō, –ere, adēgī, adāctus, bring (to), bring near, throw (to)

aditus, –ūs, *m.,* approach, access

adiungō, –ere, adiūnxī, adiūnctus, join to

administrō, 1, manage, perform

admīrātiō, –ōnis, *f.,* admiration

admīror, 1, wonder (at), admire

admittō, –ere, admīsī, admissus, let to, commit

admodum, *adv.,* very (much)

admoneō, –ēre, admonuī, admonitus, remind, advise

admoveō, –ēre, admōvī, admōtus, move (to)

adoptiō, –ōnis, f., adoption

adoptō, 1, adopt

adorior, adorīrī, adortus, rise up to, attack

adōrō, 1, worship

adsum, adesse, adfuī, adfutūrus, be near, be present, come

adulēscēns, –entis, m., young man

adulēscentia, –ae, f., youth

adveniō, –īre, advēnī, adventūrus, approach

adventus, –ūs, m., arrival, approach

adversārius, –rī, m., opponent

adversus, –a, –um, facing, opposite, unfavorable

aedificium, –cī, n., building

aedificō, 1, build

aedīlis, –is, m., aedile (an official)

aeger, aegra, aegrum, sick

aegrē, adv., with difficulty, reluctantly; w. ferre, be indignant (at)

Aegyptus, –ī, f., Egypt

Aequī, –ōrum, m., the Aequians (E'quians), a people of Italy

aequitās, –tātis, f., fairness

aequō, 1, make equal

aequus, –a, –um, equal, fair, calm

aes, aeris, n., bronze, money, bronze statue; aes aliēnum, (another's money), debt

Aesculāpius, –pī, m., Aesculapius (Esculā'pius), god of healing

Aesōpus, –ī, m., Aesop (E'sop), writer of fables

aestās, –tātis, f., summer

aestimātiō, –ōnis, f., estimate

aestimō, 1, estimate

aestus, –ūs, m., heat; tide

aetās, –tātis, f., age, time of life

aeternitās, –tātis, f., immortality

aeternus, –a, –um, eternal

Aethiopēs, –um, m. pl., the Ethiopians, a people of Africa

affātus, –ūs, m., speech

afferō, afferre, attulī, allātus, bring (to), assign, report

afficiō, –ere, affēcī, affectus, affect, afflict, visit, fill (with joy, etc.)

affīgō, –ere, affīxī, affīxus, fasten to

afflictō, 1, wreck

afflīgō, –ere, afflīxī, afflictus, throw _ down, afflict, damage

Afrī, –ōrum, m. pl., the Africans, Carthaginians; Africānus, –a, –um, African; as noun, m., an African; Africā'nus, an honorary name of Scipio

ager, agrī, m., field, land, farm, country

agger, aggeris, m., mound, rampart

aggredior, aggredī, aggressus, attack

aggregō, 1. attach

agitō, 1, carry on; shake

agmen, agminis, n., line of march, column; novissimum agmen, rear; prīmum agmen, front

agnōscō, –ere, agnōvī, agnitus, recognize

agnus, –ī, m., lamb

agō, –ere, ēgī, āctus, drive, move forward; live or spend (of time); do, perform; discuss, plead; carry on; grātiās agō, thank; quid agit, how is he

agricola, –ae, m., farmer

ait, (he) says

ala, –ae, f., wing

alacer, –cris, –cre, eager

alacritās, –tātis, f., eagerness

Albānus, –a, –um, Alban; as noun, m., an Alban

Alesia, –ae, f., Alē'sia, now Alise-Sainte-Reine

Alexander, –drī, m., Alexander

Alexandrīa, –ae, f., Alexandria, a city in Egypt

aliēnus, –a, –um, another's, unfavorable, out of place

aliquis, aliquid, some one, some, any, something, anything

aliter, adv., otherwise

alius, alia, aliud, other, another; alius . . . alius, one . . . another; aliī . . . aliī, some . . . others; quid aliud, what else.

allātus, part. of afferō

Allobrogēs, –um, m. pl., the Allobroges (Allŏb'rojēs)

alloquor, alloquī, allocūtus, address

alō, –ere, aluī, alitus, feed, nourish, support, raise

Alpēs, –ium, f. pl., the Alps

altē, adv., high, deeply

alter, altera, alterum, the other (of two), another, the second; alter . . . alter, the one . . . the other

altitūdō, –dinis, f., height, depth
altus, –a, –um, high, deep, tall
amābilis, –e, lovely
amanter, adv., lovingly
ambō, –ae, –ō, both
ambulō, 1, walk
amīcitia, –ae, f., friendship
amīcus, –a, –um, friendly; amīcus, –ī, m., friend; amīca, ae, f., (girl) friend
āmittō, –ere, āmīsī, āmissus, let go, lose
amō, 1, love, like
amor, –ōris, m., love, affection
amphitheātrum, –ī, n., amphitheater
amplē, adv., fully; comp. amplius, more
amplificō, 1, increase
amplitūdō, –dinis, f., size
amplius, see amplē
amplus, –a, –um, great; distinguished, magnificent
an, conj., or, introducing the second part of a double question
ancīle, –is, n., shield
ancora, –ae, f., anchor
angulus, –ī, m., corner, little place
angustiae, –ārum, f. pl., narrowness, narrow pass
angustus, –a, –um, narrow, small
anima, –ae, f., soul, spirit
animadvertō, –ere, –vertī, –versus, turn attention, notice
animal, –ālis, n., animal
animus, –ī, m., mind, spirit, courage, feeling; in animō est, intend
Aniō, Aniēnis, m., the Ăn'io river
annus, –ī, m., year
ante, adv. and prep. w. acc., before (of time and space); see antequam
anteā, adv., before
antecēdō, –ere, –cessī, –cessūrus, go before; surpass
anteferō, –ferre, –tulī, –lātus, prefer
antemna, ae, f., yard (of a ship; a spar to which sails are fastened)
antequam (ante . . . quam), conj., before
antīquitās, –tātis, f., antiquity
antīquitus, adv., long ago
antīquus, –a, –um, ancient
Antōnius, –nī, m., Antony
antrum, –ī, n., cave
ānxius, –a, –um, troubled

aperiō, –īre, aperuī, apertus, open, reveal; apertus, open, exposed
apertē, adv., openly, manifestly
Apollō, –inis, m., Apŏl'lo, god of music, prophecy, and medicine
appāreō, –ēre, appāruī, appāritūrus, appear
appellō, 1, call, call upon, speak to
appellō, –ere, appulī, appulsus, drive to, bring up
appetō, –ere, appetīvī, appetītus, seek; approach
Appius, –a, –um, of Ăp'pius, Ăp'pian; as noun, m., Ăp'pius
applicō, 1, apply (to); lean against
appōnō, –ere, apposuī, appositus, set before, serve
appropinquō, 1, come near to, approach
aptus, –a, –um, suited; aptē, adv., suitably
apud, prep. w. acc., among, at the house of, near, with
aqua, –ae, f., water
aquaeductus, –ūs, m., aqueduct
aquila, –ae, f., eagle
Aquileia, –ae, f., Aquilē'ia, a town of Cisalpine Gaul
Aquītānia, –ae, f., Aquitā'nia; Aquītānus, –a, –um, Aquitā'nian
āra, –ae, f., altar
Arar, –aris, acc. –im, abl. –ī, m., the Arar river, now the Saône
arbitrium, –trī, n., decision, judgment
arbitror, 1, think
arbor, –oris, f., tree
arboreus, –a, –um, of a tree
arcessō, –ere, –īvī, –ītus, summon
architectus, –ī, m., architect
ārdeō, –ēre, ārsī, ārsūrus, burn, be eager
arduus, –a, –um, steep, hard
ārea, –ae, f., courtyard
arēna, –ae, f., sand, arena
argentum, –ī, n., silver
āridum, –ī, n., dry land
ariēs, –ietis, m., ram, battering-ram
Aristotelēs, –is, m., Ăr'istŏtle, a Greek philosopher
arma, –ōrum, n. pl., arms, armor
armāmenta, –ōrum, n. pl., equipment
armātūra, –ae, f., armor; levis armātūrae, light-armed
armō, 1, arm, equip

arō, 1, plow
arripiō, –ere, arripuī, arreptus, seize
arrogantia, –ae, f., insolence
ars, artis, f., skill, art
artus, –ūs, m., limb
Arvernus, –ī, m., an Arver'nian
arx, arcis, f., citadel
ascendō, –ere, ascendī, ascēnsus, climb (up); embark
ascēnsus, –ūs, m., ascent
ascrībō, –ere, ascrīpsī, ascrīptus, add to (in writing), apply
aspectus, –ūs, m., appearance, sight
asper, –era, –erum, harsh
aspiciō, –ere, aspexī, aspectus, look on or at
assistō, –ere, astitī, —, stand
assuēscō, –ere, assuēvī, assuētus, become accustomed
astronomus, –ī, m., astronomer
astrum, –ī, n., star
at, conj., but
āter, ātra, ātrum, black, gloomy
Athēna, –ae, f., Athena, Greek goddess of wisdom, the Roman Minerva
Athēnae, –ārum, f. pl., Athens
Athēniēnsis, –is, adj. and n., Athenian
atomus, –ī, f., atom
atque (ac), conj., and, as, than
Atrebās, –ātis, m., an Atrebatian (Atrebā'shian)
ātrium, ātrī, n., atrium, hall
attingō, –ere, attigī, attāctus, touch, reach, border
attribuō, –ere, attribuī, attribūtus, assign
auctor, –ōris, m., author, founder
auctōritās, –tātis, f., authority, influence
audācia, –ae, f., daring, boldness
audācter, adv., boldly
audāx, gen. audācis, daring, bold
audeō, –ēre, ausus, semideponent, dare
audiō, –īre, –īvī, –ītus, hear, hear of
auferō, auferre, abstulī, ablātus, take away
augeō, –ēre, auxī, auctus, increase
augēscō, –ere, —, —, increase
augustus, –a, –um, magnificent; (cap.), of Augustus; August; as noun, m., Augus'tus, the emperor
Aulercus, –ī, m., an Auler'can
aureus, –a, –um, of gold, golden
aurīga, –ae, m., charioteer
auris, –is, f., ear

aurum, –ī, n., gold
auspicium, –cī, n., auspices
aut, or; aut . . . aut, either . . . or
autem, conj. (never first word), however, but, moreover
auxilior, 1, help
auxilium, –lī, n., help, aid; pl. auxiliary troops, reserves
avāritia, –ae, f., greed
avārus, –a, –um, avaricious
Aventīnus (mōns), –ī, m., the Av'entīne Hill
āvertō, –ere, āvertī, āversus, turn away, turn aside
avidus, –a, –um, desirous, greedy
avis, –is, f., bird
āvocō, 1, call away
avunculus, ī, m., uncle
avus, –ī, m., grandfather
Axona, –ae, m., the Axona river, now the Aisne

B

balneum, –ī, n., bath
balteus, –ī, m., belt
barbarus, –a, –um, foreign, barbarous; as noun, m., barbarian
beātus, –a, –um, happy
Belgae, –ārum, m. pl., the Belgians
bellicōsus, –a, –um, warlike
bellicus, –a, –um, of war
bellō, 1, carry on war
bellum, –ī, n., war
bene, adv., well, good; comp. melius, better; superl. optimē, best
beneficium, –cī, n., kindness
benignus, –a, –um, kindly
bibliothēca, –ae, f., library
bibō, –ere, bibī, —, drink
Bibracte, –actis, n., Bibrăc'te, now Mont Beauvray near Autun
bīduum, –ī, n., two days
biennium, –nī, n., two years
bīnī, –ae, –a, two at a time
bis, adv., twice
blanditia, –ae, f., caress
blandus, –a, –um, caressing
bonitās, –tātis, f., goodness
bonus, –a, –um, good; comp. melior, melius, better; superl. optimus, –a, –um, best; bona, –ōrum, n., possessions
bōs, bovis, m., ox, bull
bracchium, bracchī, n., arm
brevis, –e, short

brevitās, –tātis, f., shortness
Britannia, –ae, f., Britain
Britannus, –ī, m., a Briton
Brundisium, –sī, n., Brundisium (Brundizh'ium), a town in Italy, now Brindisi
bulla, –ae, f., bulla, an ornament worn on the neck by children

C

C., abbreviation for Gāius
cacūmen, –minis, n., peak
cadāver, –eris, n., corpse
cadō, –ere, cecidī, cāsūrus, fall
Caecilius, –a, –um, Caecilian (Sēsil'ian); Caecilius, –lī, m., Caecilius; Caecilia, –ae, f., Caecilia
caedēs, –is, f., slaughter, murder
caedō, –ere, cecīdī, caesus, cut (down), beat, kill
caelestis, –e, heavenly
Caelius (mōns), –ī, m., the Caelian (Sē'lian) Hill
caelum, –ī, n., sky
caeruleus, –a, –um, blue
Caesar, –aris, m., Caesar
calamitās, –tātis, f., disaster
calceus, –ī, m., shoe
calidus, –a, –um, hot
callidus, –a, –um, clever
cālō, –ōnis, m., camp servant
campus, –ī, m., plain, field; campus Mārtius, campī Mārtiī, m., Campus Martius (Mar'shius), a park in Rome
candidātus, –ī, m., candidate
canis, –is, m., dog
Cannae, –ārum, f. pl., Cannae (Can'ē), a town in Italy
canō, –ere, cecinī, cantus, sing, tell (about)
Cantium, –tī, n., Kent, a district in Britain
cantō, 1, sing
Capēna (porta), porta Capena (Capē'na), a gate in the wall of Rome
capillus, –ī, m., hair
capiō, –ere, cēpī, captus, take, seize, capture, hold, receive; captivate; adopt
Capitōlium, –lī, n., the Capitol, temple of Jupiter at Rome; the Capitoline Hill
captīva, –ae, f., (female) prisoner; captīvus, –ī, m., prisoner

captō, 1, strive
caput, capitis, n., head, person
cāritās, –tātis, f., affection
carmen, –minis, n., song, poem
Carneadēs, –is, m., Carnē'adēs, a Greek philosopher
carō, carnis, f., meat
carpō, –ere, carpsī, carptus, pick; take; consume
carrus, –ī, m., cart, wagon
Carthāginiēnsēs, –ium, m. pl., the Carthaginians (Carthajin'ians)
Carthāgō, –ginis, f., Carthage, a city i northern Africa
cārus, –a, –um, dear, expensi esteemed
cāseus, –ī, m., cheese
Castalius, –a, –um, Castā'lian
castellum, –ī, n., fort
castīgō, 1, punish
castra, –ōrum, n. pl., camp
cāsus, –ūs, m., chance, accident, misfortune, fate, emergency
Catilīna, –ae, m., Căt'ilīne
cauda, –ae, f., tail
causa, –ae, f., cause, reason; case; causā, for the sake of (w. gen. preceding)
caveō, –ēre, cāvī, cautūrus, beware (of)
cecīdī, see caedō
cēdō, –ere, cessī, cessūrus, move, retreat, yield
celeber, –bris, –bre, celebrated
celer, celeris, celere, swift
celeritās, –tātis, f., swiftness, speed
celeriter, swiftly, quickly
cēlō, 1, hide
celsus, –a, –um, high
cēna, –ae, f., dinner
cēnō, 1, dine
cēnseō, –ēre, cēnsuī, cēnsus, think
cēnsus, –ūs, m., census
centum, indeclinable adj., hundred
centuriō, –ōnis, m., centurion
Cerēs, Cereris, f., Ceres (Sē'rēs), goddess of agriculture
cernō, –ere, crēvī, crētus, separate, see
certāmen, –minis, n., contest, struggle
certē, adv., certainly, at least
certō, 1, strive
certus, –a, –um, fixed, certain, sure; certiōrem eum faciō dē, inform him about; certior fīō, be informed
cēterī, –ae, –a, the other(s), the rest

Christus, –ī, m., Christ
cibus, –ī, m., food
cingō, –ere, cīnxī, cīnctus, surround
cinis, cineris, m., ashes
circēnsis, –e, of the circus
circiter, adv., about
circuitus, –ūs, m., distance around
circulus, –ī, m., circle
circum, prep. w. acc., around
circumclūdō, –ere, –clūsī, –clūsus, surround
circumcursō, 1, run around
circumdō, –dare, –dedī, –datus, put around, surround
circumiciō, –ere, –iēcī, –iectus, throw around
circumsiliō, –īre, –siluī, —, hop around
circumsistō, –ere, –stetī, —, surround
circumstō, –āre, –stetī, —, stand around
circumveniō, –īre, –vēnī, –ventus, surround; cheat
circus, –ī, m., circle; circus; Circus Maximus, the Circus Maximus, at Rome
citerior, –ius, nearer
cito, adv., quickly; comp. citius, sooner
citrā, prep. w. acc., on this side of
cīvīlis, –e, civil
cīvis, –is, m., citizen
cīvitās, –tātis, f., citizenship, state
clam, adv., secretly
clāmō, 1, cry (out), shout, declare
clāmor, –ōris, m., shout
clārus, –a, –um, clear, loud; famous
classis, –is, f., fleet
claudō, –ere, clausī, clausus, close
clēmentia, –ae, f., clemency
cliēns, –entis, m., client
clientēla, –ae, f., clientship
Cn., abbreviation for Gnaeus, –ī, m., Gnaeus (Nē′us)
Cnidiī, –ōrum, m. pl., the Cnidians (Nĭd′ians)
coacervō, 1, pile up
coctus, –a, –um, cooked
coemētērium, –rī, n., cemetery
coeō, coīre, coiī, coitūrus, meet
coepī, coeptus (perf. tenses only), began, have begun
cōgitātiō, –ōnis, f., thought
cōgitō, 1, think, consider
cognātiō, –ōnis, f., related group
cognōmen, –minis, n., cognomen, surname

cognōscō, –ere, –nōvī, –nitus, become acquainted with, learn, recognize; perf., have learned, know
cōgō, –ere, coēgī, coāctus, drive together, collect, compel
cohors, cohortis, f., cohort
cohortātiō, –ōnis, f., encouragement
cohortor, 1, encourage
Colchī, –ōrum, m. pl., the Colchians (Kol′kians)
colligō, 1, fasten together
colligō, –ere, –lēgī, –lēctus, collect, acquire
collis, –is, m., hill
collocō, 1, place, invest
colloquium, –quī, n., conference
colloquor, colloquī, collocūtus, talk with, confer
collum, –ī, n., neck
colō, –ere, coluī, cultus, cultivate, inhabit, worship
colōnia, –ae, f., colony
color, –ōris, m., color
columna, –ae, f., column
combūrō, –ere, –ussī, –ustus, burn up
comes, –itis, m. and f., companion
Comitium, –tī, n., Comitium (Comish′-ium), the assembly place of the Romans; comitia, –ōrum, n. pl., assemblies, election
commeātus, –ūs, m., (going to and fro), supplies
commemorō, 1, mention
commendō, 1, entrust
commentārius, –rī, m., commentary, notes
commīlitō, –ōnis, m., fellow soldier
committō, –ere, –mīsī, –missus, commit, do, entrust; proelium committō, begin battle
commodē, adv., well, suitably, effectively
commodus, –a, –um, suitable, convenient, well
commoveō, –ēre, –mōvī, –mōtus, move (away), disturb, stir up; influence
commūnicō, 1, share
commūniō, –īre, –īvī, –ītus, fortify on all sides
commūnis, –e, common
commūtātiō, –ōnis, f., change
commūtō, 1, change wholly, exchange
comparō, 1, prepare; procure
compellō, –ere, –pulī, –pulsus, drive (together), collect

comperiō, –īre, –perī, –pertus, find out
competītor, –ōris, m., competitor
complaceō = placeō
compleō, –ēre, –ēvī, –ētus, fill, complete
complūrēs, –a or –ia, several, many
compōnō, –ere, –posuī, –positus, put together, compose
comportō, 1, collect
comprehendō, –ere, –hendī, –hēnsus, seize, grasp, catch, understand
cōnātus, –ūs, m., attempt
concēdō, –ere, –cessī, –cessūrus, yield, withdraw, grant, permit
concidō, –ere, –cidī, —, fall down, collapse
concīdō, –ere, –cīdī, –cīsus, cut up, kill
concilium, –lī, n., meeting, council
concipiō, –ere, –cēpī, –ceptus, conceive
concitō, 1, rouse
concordia, –ae, f., harmony
concurrō, –ere, –currī, –cursūrus, run or dash together, rush, flock
concursus, –ūs, m., running together, gathering, onset
condēnsātus, –a, –um, condensed
condiciō, –ōnis, f.. condition, terms
condīmentum, –ī, n., seasoning
condō, –ere, –didī, –ditus, found, establish, make; conceal
condūcō, –ere, –dūxī, –ductus, bring together; hire, rent
cōnferō, cōnferre, contulī, collātus, bring together, compare; give, place; mē cōnferō, proceed
cōnfertus, –a, –um, crowded together, dense
cōnfestim, adv., at once
cōnficiō, –ere, –fēcī, –fectus, complete; do up, exhaust; make, furnish
cōnfīdō, –ere, cōnfīsus, semideponent, have confidence (in), rely on, be confident
cōnfirmō, 1, encourage, strengthen, establish, assert
cōnfīsus, part. of cōnfīdō
cōnflīgō, –ere, –flīxī, –flictus, dash together
cōnfoveō = foveō
cōnfundō, –ere, –fūdī, –fūsus, confuse
congredior, congredī, congressus, meet
coniciō, –ere, –iēcī, –iectus, throw, conjecture
coniūnctim, adv., jointly

coniungō, –ere, –iūnxī, –iūnctus, join (with), unite
coniūnx, –iugis, m. and f., husband, wife
coniūrātiō, –ōnis, f., conspiracy
coniūrō, 1, swear together, conspire
cōnor, 1, try
conquīrō, –ere, –quīsīvī, –quīsītus, seek for
cōnsanguineus, –ī, m., (blood) relative
cōnscendō, –ere, –scendī, –scēnsus, climb (in); embark in
cōnscius, –a, –um, conscious
cōnscrībō, –ere, –scrīpsī, –scrīptus, write, enlist; patrēs cōnscrīptī, senators
cōnsecrātus, –a, –um, sacred
cōnsecūtus, part. of cōnsequor
cōnsēnsiō, –ōnis, f., agreement
cōnsēnsus, –ūs, m., agreement
cōnsentiō, –īre, –sēnsī, –sēnsus, agree, conspire
cōnsequor, cōnsequī, cōnsecūtus, follow, reach, attain
cōnservō, 1, save, preserve, spare
cōnsīdō, –ere, –sēdī, –sessūrus, sit down, encamp, settle
cōnsilium, –lī, n., plan, policy; prudence; advice, counsel; council
cōnsimilis, –e, very similar
cōnsistō, –ere, –stitī, –stitūrus, stand still, stand, stop, take one's place, settle; consist in; depend on
cōnsōlātiō, –ōnis, f., consolation
cōnspectus, –ūs, m., sight
cōnspiciō, –ere, –spexī, –spectus, catch sight of, see
cōnspicor, 1, catch sight of, see
cōnstantia, –ae, f., steadfastness
cōnstitī, see cōnsistō
cōnstituō, –ere, –stituī, –stitūtus, set up, establish, found; appoint, determine, decide; station
cōnstō, –āre, –stitī, –stātūrus, stand together; cōnstat, it is evident, certain
cōnsuēscō, –ere, –suēvī, –suētus, become accustomed; perf., be accustomed
cōnsuētūdō, –dinis, f., custom, habit
cōnsul, –ulis, m., consul
cōnsulāris, –e, of consular rank
cōnsulātus, –ūs, m., consulship
cōnsulō, –ere, –suluī, –sultus, consult (for)

cōnsultō, 1, consult
cōnsūmō, –ere, –sūmpsī, –sūmptus, use up, spend
contāgiō, –ōnis, f., contact
contemnō, –ere, –tempsī, –temptus, despise
contemplor, 1, look at
contemptus, –ūs, m., contempt
contendō, –ere, –tendī, –tentūrus, struggle, hasten, contend
contentus, –a, –um, contented
contexō, –ere, –texuī, –textus, weave (together)
continēns, –entis, f., mainland
contineō, –ēre, –tinuī, –tentus, contain, keep; hem in, bound; restrain
contingō, –ere, –tigī, –tāctus, touch; happen
continuus, –a, –um, successive, continuous
contrā, prep. w. acc., against, contrary to, opposite; adv., on the other hand
contrahō, –ere, –trāxī, –trāctus, draw or bring together, contract
contrārius, –a, –um, opposite
contrīstō, 1, sadden
contrōversia, –ae, f., dispute
contumēlia, –ae, f., insult
conturbō, 1, confuse, mix up
conveniō, –īre, –vēnī, –ventūrus, come together, assemble, meet; convenit, it is agreed upon
conventus, –ūs, m., meeting
convertō, –ere, –vertī, –versus, turn
convocō, 1, call together, summon
coorior, coorīrī, coortus, arise
cōpia, –ae, f., supply, abundance, opportunity; pl., forces, troops; resources
cor, cordis, n., heart
Corinthus, –ī, f., Corinth, a Greek city
cornū, –ūs, n., horn; wing (of an army)
corōna, –ae, f., crown, wreath
corpus, corporis, n., body
corrigō, –ere, –rēxī, –rēctus, correct
cotīdiānus, –a, –um, daily
cotīdiē, adv., daily
crās, adv., tomorrow
crēber, –bra, –brum, frequent, numerous
crēditor, –ōris, m., creditor
crēdō, –ere, crēdidī, crēditus, believe
cremō, 1, burn
creō, 1, elect, appoint

crēscō, –ere, crēvī, crētus, grow, increase
crocodīlus, –ī, m., crocodile
cruciātus, –ūs, m., torture
crūdēlis, –e, cruel
crūdēlitās, –tātis, f., cruelty
crūdēliter, adv., cruelly
cruentus, –a, –um, bloody
crūs, crūris, n., leg
crux, crucis, f., cross
cubiculum, –ī, n., bedroom
culmen, –minis, n., top, roof
culpa, –ae, f., blame, fault
culpō, 1, blame
cultūra, –ae, f., cultivation
cultus, –a, –um, cultured
cultus, –ūs, m., way of living, civilization
cum, prep. w. abl., with
cum, conj., when, whenever, since, although; cum prīmum, as soon as; cum . . . tum, not only . . . but also
cumulus, –ī, m., heap
cūnctor, 1, hesitate
cūnctus, –a, –um, all
cupidē, adv., eagerly
cupiditās, –tātis, f., desire
cupīdō, –dinis, m., desire; Cupid, god of love
cupidus, –a, –um, eager, desirous
cupiō, –ere, –īvī, –ītus, desire
cūr, adv., why
cūra, –ae, f., care, anxiety, love
cūria, –ae, f., senate house; Cūria Iūlia, a senate house named for Julius Caesar
cūriōsitās, –tātis, f., curiosity
cūrō, 1, care (for), cause (to be done)
currō, –ere, cucurrī, cursūrus, run
currus, –ūs, m., chariot
cursor, –ōris, m., runner
cursus, –ūs, m., running, speed, race, course; cursus honōrum, course of offices, career
curvus, –a, –um, curved
custōdia, –ae, f., guard
custōdiō, –īre, –īvī, –ītus, guard
custōs, –ōdis, m., guard

D

damnō, 1, condemn
dē, prep. w. abl., from, down from, concerning, about, during
dea, –ae, f., goddess

dēbellō, 1, crush (*in war*)
dēbeō, –ēre, dēbuī, dēbitus, owe, ought
dēbitum, –ī, *n.,* debt
dēcēdō, –ere, dēcessī, dēcessūrus, depart, go away, die
decem, ten
decemvirī, –ōrum, *m. pl.,* decemvirs (*a board of ten men*)
dēcernō, –ere, dēcrēvī, dēcrētus, decide, vote
dēcertō, 1, fight (it out), contend
decimus, –a, –um, tenth
dēcipiō, –ere, dēcēpī, dēceptus, deceive
dēclīvis, –e, sloping (downward); *as noun, n. pl.,* slopes
dēcrētum, –ī, *n.,* decree, decision
dēcrētus, *part. of* **dēcernō**
dēcurrō, –ere, dēcucurrī, dēcursūrus, run down *or* off
dēdecus, –coris, *n.,* disgrace
dēdicō, 1, dedicate
dēditīcius, –cī, *m.,* prisoner
dēditiō, –ōnis, *f.,* surrender
dēdō, dēdere, dēdidī, dēditus, surrender, devote
dēdūcō, –ere, dēdūxī, dēductus, lead, withdraw, bring, launch
dēfendō, –ere, dēfendī, dēfēnsus, defend, repel
dēfēnsor, –ōris, *m.,* defender
dēferō, dēferre, dētulī, dēlātus, carry, bestow, offer, enroll, report; *passive,* fall
dēfessus, –a, –um, tired
dēficiō, –ere, dēfēcī, dēfectus, fail, revolt
dēfīgō, –ere, dēfīxī, dēfīxus, drive in
dēflectō, –ere, dēflexī, dēflexus, turn aside
dēfluō, –ere, dēflūxī, dēflūxus, flow away
dēfōrmis, –e, unshapely
dēfugiō, –ere, dēfūgī, dēfugitūrus, avoid
dēiciō, –ere, dēiēcī, dēiectus, throw (down), dislodge, drive
dein, deinde, *adv.,* then
dēlātus, *part. of* **dēferō**
dēlēctus, *part. of* **dēligō**
dēleō, –ēre, –ēvī, –ētus, destroy, wipe out
dēlīberō, 1, consider
dēlīctum, –ī, *n.,* crime

dēligō, 1, fasten
dēligō, –ere, dēlēgī, dēlēctus, select
Delphī, –ōrum, *m. pl.,* Delphi
delphīnus, –ī, *m.,* dolphin, porpoise
dēmēns, *gen.* **dēmentis,** mad
dēmittō, –ere, dēmīsī, dēmissus, let *or* drop down, send down, derive
dēmocraticus, –a, –um, democratic
dēmōnstrō, 1, point out, show, mention
Dēmosthenēs, –is, *m.,* Dēmŏs'thenēs, *a Greek orator*
dēmulceō, –ēre, dēmulsī, dēmulctus, lick
dēns, dentis, *m.,* tooth
dēnsus, –a, –um, thick
dēnūdō, 1, strip
dēnūntiō, 1, declare
dēpellō, –ere, dēpulī, dēpulsus, drive away
dēpōnō, –ere, dēposuī, dēpositus, put *or* lay aside, put down, leave with
dēprēndō, –ere, dēprēndī, dēprēnsus, catch
dērigō (dīrigō), –ere, dērēxī, dērēctus, direct; **dērēctus,** straight
dēscendō, –ere, dēscendī, dēscēnsus, descend, resort
dēscēnsus, –ūs, *m.,* descent
dēscrībō, –ere, dēscrīpsī, dēscrīptus, write down, copy, describe
dēsecō, –āre, dēsecuī, dēsectus, cut off
dēserō, –ere, dēseruī, dēsertus, desert
dēsertor, –ōris, *m.,* deserter
dēsīderō, 1, long for
dēsiliō, –īre, dēsiluī, dēsultūrus, jump down
dēsistō, –ere, dēstitī, dēstitūrus, (stand away), cease
dēspectus, –ūs, *m.,* view
dēspērō, 1, despair (of)
dēspiciō, –ere, dēspexī, dēspectus, look down
dēstitī, *see* **dēsistō**
dēsum, deesse, dēfuī, dēfutūrus, be lacking
dēsuper, *adv.,* from above
dēterior, –ius, poorer, less, worse
dētestābilis, –e, detestable
dētineō, –ēre, dētinuī, dētentus, detain
dētrahō, –ere, dētrāxī, dētrāctus, draw off, take (off)
dētrīmentum, –ī, *n.,* loss
deus, –ī, *m.,* god
dēveniō, –īre, dēvēnī, dēventūrus, come

461

dēvorō, 1, devour

dexter, –tra, –trum, right (hand)

dī = deī

dīcō, –ere, dīxī, dictus, say, tell, speak, name; **salūtem dīcō,** pay respects; **causam dīcō,** plead a case

dictātor, –ōris, *m.,* dictator

dictō, 1, dictate

dictum, –ī, *n.,* word, remark

didicī, *see* **discō**

diēs, diēī, *m. and f.,* day

differō, differre, distulī, dīlātus, spread; differ

difficilis, –e, difficult

difficultās, –tātis, *f.,* difficulty

diffīdō, –ere, diffīsus, *semi-deponent,* distrust

diffundō, –ere, –fūdī, –fūsus, spread out

digitus, –ī, *m.,* finger

dignitās, –tātis, *f.,* worth, rank, position

dignus, –a, –um, worthy

diiūdicō, 1, determine

dīligēns, *gen.* **dīligentis,** careful, diligent

dīligenter, *adv.,* carefully

dīligentia, –ae, *f.,* care, diligence

dīmicō, 1, fight

dīmidium, –dī, *n.,* half

dīmittō, –ere, dīmīsī, dīmissus, let go, lose, abandon, send (away), dismiss

dīmoveō, –ēre, dīmōvī, dīmōtus, move away

dīrigō, *see* **dērigō**

dīripiō, –ere, dīripuī, dīreptus, plunder

dīrus, –a, –um, horrible

Dīs, Dītis, *m.,* Pluto, *god of Hades*

discēdō, –ere, –cessī, –cessūrus, go away, depart, draw back

disciplīna, –ae, *f.,* discipline, training, instruction, system

discipulus, –ī, *m.,* pupil

disclūdō, –ere, –clūsī, –clūsus, separate

discō, –ere, didicī, —, learn

discordia, –ae, *f.,* discord

discrīmen, –minis, *n.,* difference

discutiō, –ere, –cussī, –cussus, push aside, destroy

disiciō, –ere, –iēcī, –iectus, scatter

dispergō, –ere, dispersī, dispersus, scatter

dispōnō, –ere, –posuī, –positus, put here and there, arrange

disputātiō, –ōnis, *f.,* discussion

disputō, 1, discuss

dissēnsiō, –ōnis, *f.,* dissension

dissimilis, –e, unlike

dissimulō, 1, conceal

dissipō, 1, scatter

distineō, –ēre, –tinuī, –tentus, keep apart

distribuō, –ere, –tribuī, –tribūtus, distribute, divide, assign

dītissimus, *see* **dīves**

diū, *adv.,* (for) a long time, long; *comp.* **diūtius;** *superl.* **diūtissimē**

diurnus, –a, –um, (by) day; **acta diurna,** journal, newspaper

dīversus, –a, –um, different

dīves, *gen.* **dīvitis,** rich; *comp.* **dītior;** *superl.* **dītissimus**

Dīviciācus, –ī, *m.,* Diviciacus (Divi-shiā'cus)

dīvidō, –ere, dīvīsī, dīvīsus, divide, separate

dīvīnus, –a, –um, divine

dīvitiae, –ārum, *f. pl.,* riches

dīvus, –ī (*gen. pl.* **dīvum**), *m.,* god

dō, dare, dedī, datus, give; **poenam dō,** pay the penalty; **in fugam dō,** put to flight

doceō –ēre, docuī, doctus, teach, explain; **doctus,** skilled

doctrīna, –ae, *f.,* teaching

documentum, –ī, *n.,* proof, warning

doleō, –ēre, doluī, dolitūrus, grieve, be sorry

dolor, –ōris, *m.,* grief, pain suffering

dolōrōsus, –a, –um, grieving

dolus, –ī, *m.,* deceit, trick

domesticus, –a, –um, one's own

domicilium, –lī, *n.,* home

domina, –ae, *f.,* mistress

dominor, 1, be master

dominus, –ī, *m.,* master

domus, –ūs, *f.,* house, home

dōnō, 1, give

dōnum, –ī, *n.,* gift

dormiō, –īre, –īvī, –ītus, sleep

dōs, dōtis, *f.,* dowry

dracō, –ōnis, *m.,* dragon

druidēs, –um, *m. pl.,* druids

dubitātiō, –ōnis, *f.,* doubt

dubitō, 1, hesitate, doubt

dubium, –bī, *n.,* doubt

dūcō, –ere, dūxī, ductus, lead, draw, construct, consider, influence dulcis, –e, sweet, agreeable; *as noun, n. pl.,* cakes

dum, *conj.,* while, until, as long as

duo, –ae, –o, two

duodecim, twelve; duodecimus, –a, –um, twelfth

duplex, *gen.* duplicis, double

duplicō, 1, double

dūrē, *adv.,* harshly

dūritia, –ae, *f.,* hardship

dūritiēs, –ēī, *f.,* hardness

dūrō, 1, harden

dūrus, –a, –um, hard, harsh, cruel

dux, ducis, *m.,* leader, guide, general

Dyrrachium, –chī, *n.,* Dyrrachium, *now* Durazzo, *a city on the east coast of the Adriatic*

E

ē, *see* ex

ecce! *interj.,* look!

ēdīcō, –ere, ēdīxī, ēdictus, appoint

ēdiscō, ēdiscere, ēdidicī, —, learn by heart

ēditus, –a, –um, elevated

ēdō, ēdere, ēdidī, ēditus, give out, publish, inflict, utter

ēducō, 1, bring up

ēdūcō, –ere, ēdūxī, ēductus, lead out; draw

effēminō, 1, weaken

efferō, efferre, extulī, ēlātus, carry out, make known

efficiō, –ere, effēcī, effectus, make, bring about, accomplish, complete, produce

effodiō, –ere, effōdī, effossus, dig up

effugiō, –ere, effūgī, effugitūrus, escape

ego, meī, I

ēgredior, ēgredī, ēgressus, go *or* march out, leave, land

ēgregiē, *adv.,* excellently

ēgregius, –a, –um, distinguished, excellent, outstanding

ēheu! *interj.,* alas!

ēiciō, –ere, ēiēcī, ēiectus, throw (out), stick out, expel

ēlegantia, –ae, *f.,* elegance, style

elephantus, –ī. *m.,* elephant, ivory

Eleusis, –is, *f.,* Eleu'sis, *a Greek city*

ēlevō, 1, raise

ēligō, –ere, ēlēgī, ēlēctus, pick out

ēloquentia, –ae, *f.,* eloquence, rhetoric

ēmendō, 1, correct

ēmergō, –ere, ēmersī, ēmersus, emerge

ēmittō, –ere, ēmīsī, ēmissus, let drop, let *or* send out, shed

emō, –ere, ēmī, ēmptus, take, buy

enim, *conj. (never first word),* for

ēnotō, 1, take notes (on)

ēnūntiō, 1, announce, report

eō, īre, iī, itūrus, go

eō, *adv.,* there

eōdem, *adv.,* to the same place

Ēpīrus, –ī, *f.,* Epī'rus, *a province in northern Greece*

episcopus, –ī, *m.,* bishop

epistula, –ae, *f.,* letter

eques, equitis, *m.,* horseman, knight; *pl.,* cavalry

equester, –tris, –tre, (of) cavalry

equidem, *adv.,* to be sure

equitātus, –ūs, *m.,* cavalry

equus, –ī, *m.,* horse

ergō, *adv.,* therefore

ērigō, –ere, ērēxī, ērēctus, raise up

ēripiō, –ere, ēripuī, ēreptus, snatch away, remove, save

errō, 1, wander; be mistaken

ērubēscō, –ere, ērubuī, —, blush

ērudiō, –īre, –īvī, –ītus, instruct

ērudītiō, –ōnis, *f.,* learning

ēruptiō, –ōnis, *f.,* sally

Ēsquiliae, –ārum, *f. pl.,* Ēsquilīnus (mōns), the Es'quiline Hill

et, *conj.,* and, even; et . . . et, both . . . and

etiam, *adv.,* also, even

Etrūscī, –ōrum, *m. pl.,* the Etruscans, the people of Etruria

etsī, *conj.,* although

ēvādō, –ere, ēvāsī, ēvāsūrus, go out, escape

ēvehō, –ere, ēvexī, ēvectus, carry up

ēvellō, –ere, ēvellī, ēvulsus, pull out

ēveniō, –īre, ēvēnī, ēventūrus, turn out, happen

ēventus, –ūs, *m.,* outcome, result

ēvertō, –ere, ēvertī, ēversus, overturn

ēvocō, 1, call out, summon

ex (ē), *prep. w. abl.,* from, out of, of, as a result of, in accordance with

exāctus, *part. of* exigō

exagitō, 1, drive about, harass

exāminō, 1, weigh

exanimō, 1, exhaust, kill

excēdō, –ere, excessī, excessūrus, go away, depart, withdraw

excelsus, –a, –um, high

excipiō, –ere, excēpī, exceptus, receive, capture, sense

excitō, 1, arouse, erect

excruciō, 1, torture

exemplum, –ī, *n.,* example, sample, precedent

exeō, exīre, exiī, exitūrus, go out (from)

exerceō, –ēre, exercuī, exercitus, train, exercise, make use of

exercitātiō, –ōnis, *f.,* exercise

exercitātus, –a, –um, trained

exercitus, –ūs, *m.,* (trained) army

exhauriō, –īre, exhausī, exhaustus, draw out, endure

exigō, –ere, exēgī, exāctus, drive out, demand

exiguē, *adv.,* scarcely

exiguitās, –tātis, *f.,* scantiness, shortness, smallness

exiguus, –a, –um, small

exīstimō, 1, think

exitus, –ūs, *m.,* outlet, outcome, departure, death

expediō, –īre, –īvī, –ītus, set free, prepare; **expedītus,** unencumbered; free, easy

expellō, –ere, expulī, expulsus, drive out, banish

experior, experīrī, expertus, try; **expertus,** experienced

expleō, –ēre, explēvī, explētus, fill up

explicō, 1, unroll, develop, explain

explōrātor, –ōris, *m.,* scout

explōrō, 1, investigate, explore; **explōrātus,** assured

expōnō, –ere, exposuī, expositus, put out, draw up, expose

exprimō, –ere, expressī, expressus, press out, express, portray, imitate

expugnō, 1, capture, gain

exsanguis, –e, bloodless

exsequor, exsequī, exsecūtus, follow up, enforce

exsiliō, –īre, exsiluī, —, leap up *or* out

exsilium, –lī, *n.,* exile

exsistō, –ere, exstitī, —, stand out, arise

exspectō, 1, expect, wait, await

exspīrō, 1, breathe out, expire

exstinguō, –ere, exstīnxī, exstīnctus, put out, kill

exstruō, –ere, exstrūxī, exstrūctus, pile up, build

exterior, –ius, outer

externus, –ī, *m.,* stranger

extrā, *prep. w. acc.,* out of, outside of, beyond

extrahō, –ere, extrāxī, extrāctus, draw out

extraōrdinārius, –a, –um, (out of order), extraordinary

extrēmus, –a, –um, farthest, last, extreme, end of

F

fābula, –ae, *f.,* story, play

faciēs, –ēī, *f.,* face, appearance

facile, *adv.,* easily

facilis, –e, easy

facinus, facinoris, *n.,* crime

faciō, –ere, fēcī, factus, do, make, act; **verba faciō,** speak, make a speech; **certiōrem eum faciō dē,** inform him about; **iter faciō,** march, travel

factiō, –ōnis, *f.,* faction

factum, –ī, *n.,* deed, act

facultās, –tātis, *f.,* faculty, opportunity; *pl.,* means

fallāx, *gen.* **–ācis,** false

fallō, –ere, fefellī, falsus, deceive

falsus, –a, –um, false; **falsō,** *adv.,* falsely

falx, falcis, *f.,* hook

fāma, –ae, *f.,* report, fame

famēs, –is, *abl.* **famē,** *f.,* hunger

familia, –ae, *f.,* household, family

familiāris, –e, (of the family), friendly; *as noun, m.,* friend

fās, *indeclinable, n.,* right

fatīgō, 1, weary, wear out

fātum, –ī, *n.,* fate

faucēs, –ium, *f. pl.,* throat, jaws

faveō, –ēre, fāvī, fautūrus, be favorable to, favor

favor, –ōris, *m.,* favor

fefellī, *see* **fallō**

fēlīcitās, –tātis, *f.,* happiness

fēlīciter, *adv.,* fortunately, successfully; good luck!

fēlīx, *gen.* **fēlīcis,** happy, fortunate, successful

fēmina, –ae, *f.,* woman, female

fēmineus, –a, –um, of a woman

fera, –ae, *f.,* wild beast

ferē, *adv.,* almost, about, generally

fēriae, –ārum, *f. pl.,* holidays; **fēriae Latīnae,** *festival of the allied Latins.*

ferō, ferre, tulī, lātus, bear, carry, bring, receive, report, propose (*of a law*)

ferōx, *gen.* **ferōcis,** bold, fierce
ferreus, –a, –um, iron
ferrum, –ī, *n.,* iron
fertilis, –e, fertile
fertilitās, –tātis, *f.,* fertility
ferus, –a, –um, wild, fierce
fēstus, –a, –um, festal
fidēlis, –e, faithful
fidēs, –eī, *f.,* trust, protection; word, loyalty
fidūcia, –ae, *f.,* confidence
fīdus, –a, –um, faithful
fīgō, –ere, fīxī, fīxus, fix
figūra, –ae, *f.,* figure, shape
fīlia, –ae, *f.,* daughter
fīlius, –lī, *m.,* son
fingō, –ere, fīnxī, fictus, form, invent, imagine
fīniō, –īre, –īvī, –ītus, limit, determine
fīnis, fīnis, *m. or f.,* end; *pl.,* borders, territory
fīnitimus, –a, –um, neighboring; *as noun,* neighbor
fīō, fierī, (factus), become, be made, be done, happen
firmiter, *adv.,* firmly
firmus, –a, –um, strong, firm
fissus, –a, –um, split
flamma, –ae, *f.,* flame
flectō, –ere, flexī, flexus, bend, turn
fleō, flēre, flēvī, flētus, weep (for)
flōreō, –ēre, flōruī, —, bloom
flōs, flōris, *m.,* flower
flūctus, –ūs, *m.,* wave
flūmen, flūminis, *n.,* river
fluō, –ere, flūxī, flūxus, flow
fōns, fontis, *m.,* spring
fore = **futūrum esse,** *from* **sum**
fōrma, –ae, *f.,* shape, form, beauty
fors, fortis, *f.,* chance
fortasse, *adv.,* perhaps
fortis, –e, brave
fortiter, *adv.,* bravely
fortūna, –ae, *f.,* fortune, fate; *pl.,* property
forum, –ī, *n.,* market place; Forum (*at Rome*)
fossa, –ae, *f.,* trench
foveō, –ēre, fōvī, fōtus, cherish
frangō, –ere, frēgī, frāctus, break, wreck
frāter, frātris, *m.,* brother
fraus, fraudis, *f.,* fraud, wrong
frequēns, *gen.* **frequentis,** frequent, numerous

frequenter, *adv.,* often
frīgidus, –a, –um, cold
frīgus, frīgoris, *n.,* cold
frōns, frondis, *f.,* leaf
frōns, frontis, *f.,* forehead, front
frūctus, –ūs, *m.,* fruit
frūgēs, –um, *f. pl.,* crops
frūmentārius, –a, –um, of grain; fertile; **rēs frūmentāria,** grain supply
frūmentum, –ī, *n.,* grain; *pl.,* ears of grain, crops
frūstrā, *adv.,* in vain
fuga, –ae, *f.,* flight
fugiō, –ere, fūgī, fugitūrus, flee, avoid
fugitīvus, –ī, *m.,* deserter
fūmō, 1, smoke
fūmus, –ī, *m.,* smoke
funda, –ae, *f.,* sling, slingshot
fundāmentum, –ī, *n.,* foundation
funditor, –ōris, *m.,* slinger
fundō, –ere, fūdī, fūsus, pour, shed
fūnis, –is, *m.,* rope
fūnus, fūneris, *n.,* funeral
Furiae, –ārum, *f. pl.,* the Furies, *avenging and tormenting spirits*
furibundus, –a, –um, mad
furō, –ere, —, —, rage
furor, –ōris, *m.,* madness
fūrtim, *adv.,* secretly
furtum, –ī, *n.,* theft
futūrus, *fut. part. of* **sum**

G

galea, –ae, *f.,* helmet
Gallia, –ae, *f.,* Gaul, *ancient France*
Gallicus, –a, –um, Gallic
Gallus, –a, –um, Gallic; *as noun, m.,* a Gaul
garrulus, –a, –um, talkative
gaudeō, –ēre, gāvīsus, *semideponent,* rejoice
gaudium, –dī, *n.,* joy
gāvīsus, *part. of* **gaudeō**
geminus, –a, –um, twin
gemitus, –ūs, *m.,* groan
gemma, –ae, *f.,* precious stone
gemō, –ere, gemuī, —, groan
Genava, *see* **Genua**
gēns, gentis, *f.,* family, people, nation, tribe
Genua, –ae, *f.,* Geneva
genus, generis, *n.,* birth, family, race; kind, class
Germānia, –ae, *f.,* Germany
Germānicus, –a, –um, German

Germānus, –a, –um, German; *as noun, m.,* a German

gerō, –ere, gessī, gestus, carry on, manage, do, hold; wear; *passive,* go on; **mē gerō,** act; **rēs gestae,** deeds

gignō, –ere, genuī, genitus, produce; *passive,* be born

gladiātor, –ōris, *m.,* gladiator

gladius, –dī, *m.,* sword

glōria, –ae, *f.,* glory

glōriōsus, –a, –um, glorious

gracilis, –e, slender

gradior, gradī, gressus, walk

gradus, –ūs, *m.,* step

Graecia, –ae, *f.,* Greece

Graecus, –a, –um, Greek; *as noun, m.,* a Greek

grāmen, grāminis, *n.,* grass

grammaticus, –ī, *m.,* grammarian, teacher of literature

grātia, –ae, *f.,* gratitude, grace, favor, influence; **grātiās agō,** thank; **grātiā,** for the sake of (*w. gen. preceding*)

grātulātiō, –ōnis, *f.,* congratulation

grātus, –a, –um, pleasing, grateful

gravis, –e, heavy, serious, severe, important

gravitās, –tātis, *f.,* weight, dignity, seriousness

graviter, *adv.,* heavily, seriously, severely, decisively

gubernātor, –ōris, *m.,* pilot

gustō, 1, taste

gustus, –ūs, *m.,* taste

H

ha! *interj.,* ha!

habeō, –ēre, habuī, habitus, have, hold, consider; **ōrātiōnem habeō,** deliver a speech

habitō, 1, live

Haeduus, –a, –um, Haeduan (Hĕd'uan); *as noun, m.,* a Haeduan

haereō, –ēre, haesī, haesus, stick, cling

Hamburgiēnsis, –e, of Hamburg

Harpyiae, –ārum, *f. pl.,* the Harpies

haud, *adv.,* by no means

hauriō, –īre, hausī, haustus, drain, drink

Helvētius, –a, –um, Helvetian (Helvē'-shian); *as noun, m. pl.,* the Helvetians

herba, –ae, *f.,* grass, plant, herb

Herculēs, –is, *m.,* Her'culēs

hērēditās, –tātis, *f.,* inheritance

herī, *adv.,* yesterday

heu! *interj.,* alas!

hīberna, –ōrum (*i.e.,* **castra**), *n. pl.,* winter quarters

Hibernia, –ae, *f.,* Ireland

hic, haec, hoc, this, the latter; *as pron.,* he, she, it

hīc, *adv.,* here

hiemō, 1, spend the winter

hiems, hiemis, *f.,* winter

hilaris, –e, gay, cheerful

Hispānia, –ae, *f.,* Spain

Hispānus, –a, –um, Spanish

historia, –ae, *f.,* history

hodiē, *adv.,* today

hodiernus, –a, –um, of today

Homērus, –ī, *m.,* Homer, *a Greek poet*

homō, hominis, *m.,* man, human being; *pl.,* people

honestē, *adv.,* honorably

honestus, –a, –um, honorable

honor, –ōris, *m.,* honor, office

hōra, –ae, *f.,* hour

Horātius, –tī, *m.,* Horace, *a Roman poet;* Horatius (Horā'shius) Cocles

horrēns, *gen.* **horrentis,** shaggy

horreō, –ēre, horruī, —, shudder, dread

horribilis, –e, horrible

horridus, –a, –um, frightful

horror, –ōris, *m.,* horror

hortor, 1, urge, encourage

hortus, –ī, *m.,* garden, park

hospes, hospitis, *m.,* guest, guest-friend, host

hospitium, –tī, *n.,* hospitality

hostis, –is, *m.,* enemy (*usually pl.*)

hūc, *adv.,* to this side, here

hūmānitās, –tātis, *f.,* culture

hūmānus, –a, –um, human, civilized

humilis, –e, low, humble

humus, –ī, *f.,* ground, earth

hydraulicus, –a, –um, hydraulic

I

iaceō, –ēre, iacuī, —, lie

iaciō, –ere, iēcī, iactus, throw, build

iactō, 1, throw, toss

iactūra, –ae, *f.,* (throwing), loss, expense

iactus, –ūs, *m.,* throw

iaculum, –ī, *n.,* javelin, dart

iam, *adv.*, already, by this time, at last, (*w. fut.*) soon; **nōn iam,** no longer
iānua, **-ae,** *f.,* door
ibi, *adv.*, there
īdem, eadem, idem, same, likewise
identidem, *adv.,* again and again
idōneus, **-a, -um,** suitable
igitur, *adv.,* therefore
ignis, **-is,** *m.,* fire
ignōminia, **-ae,** *f.,* disgrace
ignōrō, 1, not know
ignōscō, **-ere, ignōvī, ignōtus,** pardon
ignōtus, **-a, -um,** unknown, strange
illātus, *part. of* īnferō
ille, illa, illud, that, the former; *as pron.,* he, she, it
illigō, 1, tie to
illō, *adv.,* there, to that place
illūc, *adv.,* to that place *or* side
illūstris, **-e,** noble
Illyricum, **-ī,** *n.,* Illȳr'icum, *a region along the east coast of the Adriatic*
imāgō, imāginis, *f.,* statue, likeness, echo
imbecillitās, **-tātis,** *f.,* weakness
imitātiō, **-ōnis,** *f.,* imitation
imitor, 1, imitate
immānis, **-e,** huge, savage
immittō, **-ere, immīsī, immissus,** let go, throw
immolō, 1, sacrifice
immortālis, **-e,** undying, immortal
impār, *gen.* imparis, unequal
impedīmentum, **-ī,** *n.,* hindrance; *pl.,* baggage
impediō, **-īre, -īvī, -ītus,** hinder, obstruct; **impedītus,** burdened
impellō, **-ere, impulī, impulsus,** drive on, influence, incite
impendeō, **-ēre, —, —,** hang over
impendō, **-ere, impendī, impēnsus,** spend
imperātor, **-ōris,** *m.,* commander, general, emperor
imperātum, **-ī,** *n.,* order
imperītus, **-a, -um,** inexperienced, ignorant
imperium, **-rī,** *n.,* command, control, military power; empire, government; **nova imperia,** revolution
imperō, 1, command, rule, demand
impetrō, 1, gain (a request)
impetus, **-ūs,** *m.,* attack, fury
impius, **-a, -um,** impious

impleō, **-ēre, implēvī, implētus,** fill
impōnō, **-ere, imposuī, impositus,** put on, impose
importō, 1, bring in, import
improbitās, **-tātis,** *f.,* dishonesty
imprōvīsus, **-a, -um,** unforeseen; **dē imprōvīsō,** suddenly
imprūdentia, **-ae,** *f.,* poor sense
impudenter, *adv.,* impudently
impulsus, *part. of* impellō
īmus, *see* īnferior
in, *prep. w. acc.,* into, to, towards, against, on; *w. abl.,* in, on, among, at
inānis, **-e,** empty
incēdō, **-ere, incessī, incessus,** enter
incendium, **-dī,** *n.,* fire, burning
incendō, **-ere, incendī, incēnsus,** set on fire, burn; rouse
incertus, **-a, -um,** uncertain
incidō, **-ere, incidī, —,** fall (into *or* upon), happen
incipiō, **-ere, incēpī, inceptus,** take to, begin
incitō, 1, urge on, arouse
inclūdō, **-ere, inclūsī, inclūsus,** shut up
incognitus, **-a, -um,** unknown
incolō, **-ere, incoluī, —** inhabit, live
incolumis, **-e,** unharmed, safe
incommodum, **-ī,** *n.,* harm
incrēdibilis, **-e,** unbelievable
incumbō, **-ere, incubuī, incubitūrus,** lean over
incursiō, **-ōnis,** *f.,* raid
incursō, 1, run against
inde, *adv.,* then, from there, thereafter, therefore
Indī, **-ōrum,** *m. pl.,* the Indians, inhabitants of India
indīcō, **-ere, indīxī, indictus,** call
indignitās, **-tātis,** *f.,* outrage
indīligenter, *adv.,* carelessly
indiscrētē, *adv.,* indiscreetly
indoctus, **-a, -um,** untrained
indūcō, **-ere, indūxī, inductus,** lead in, bring in; influence
induō, **-ere, induī, indūtus,** put on, dress, impale
ineō, inīre, iniī, initus, enter upon; **cōnsilium ineō,** form a plan
inermis, **-e,** unarmed
īnfāmia, **-ae,** *f.,* dishonor
īnfāmis, **-e,** notorious
īnfāns, **-fantis,** *m.,* infant
īnfectus, **-a, -um,** not done

īnfēlīx, *gen.* īnfēlīcis, unlucky, unhappy

inferior, –ius, lower, inferior; *superl.* īmus, īnfimus, lowest

īnferō, īnferre, intulī, illātus, bring in, to, *or* against, place upon, inflict, enter; **signa īnferō,** charge

īnficiō, –ere, īnfēcī, īnfectus, stain, infect

īnfimus, *see* īnferior

īnfīnītus, –a, –um, endless, countless

īnfirmitās, –tātis, *f.,* illness

īnfirmus, –a, –um, weak

īnfīxus, –a, –um, fixed

īnfluō, –ere, īnflūxī, īnflūxus, flow (in)

īnfrā, *adv.,* below, farther on; *prep. w. acc.,* below

īnfundō, –ere, īnfūdī, īnfūsus, pour in

ingenium, –nī, *n.,* ability

ingēns, *gen.* ingentis, huge

ingredior, ingredī, ingressus, step into, enter

iniciō, –ere, iniēcī, iniectus, throw *or* thrust into

inimīcitia, –ae, *f.,* enmity, feud

inimīcus, –a, –um, unfriendly, hostile; *as noun, m.,* enemy

inīquitās, –tātis, *f.,* unfavorableness

inīquus, –a, –um, uneven, unfavorable, unjust

initium, –tī, *n.,* beginning

iniungō, –ere, iniūnxī, iniūnctus, join to, impose on

iniūria, –ae, *f.,* wrong, injustice, injury

iniūstē, *adv.,* unjustly

iniūstus, –a, –um, unjust

innocēns, *gen.* innocentis, innocent

inopia, –ae, *f.,* lack, scarcity, poverty

inopīnāns, *gen.* inopīnantis, unsuspecting

inops, *gen.* inopis, poor, helpless

inquit, said, said he (*after one or more words of a direct quotation*); **inquis,** you say

īnsānia, –ae, *f.,* madness

īnsānus, –a, –um, mad

īnsciēns, *gen.* īnscientis, not knowing

īnscrībō, –ere, īnscrīpsī, īnscrīptus, inscribe

īnsequor, īnsequī, īnsecūtus, follow up, pursue

īnserō, –ere, īnseruī, īnsertus, insert

īnsidiae, –ārum, *f. pl.,* plot, ambush, treachery

īnsignis, –e, remarkable, noted, conspicuous; *as noun,* īnsigne, –is, *n.,* ornament, signal

īnsiliō, –īre, īnsiluī, —, leap upon

īnsistō, –ere, īnstitī, —, stand (on), adopt

īnstituō, –ere, īnstituī, īnstitūtus, establish, decide upon; begin, train; build, provide

īnstitūtum, –ī, *n.,* custom

īnstō, –āre, īnstitī, —, press on

īnstrūmentum, –ī, *n.,* instrument

īnstruō, –ere, īnstrūxī, īnstrūctus, draw up, provide

īnsula, –ae, *f.,* island

integer, –gra, –grum, untouched, fresh, unharmed

intellegenter, *adv.,* intelligently

intellegō, –ere, –lēxī, –lēctus, realize, understand

intemperāns, *gen.* –antis, intemperate

intendō, –ere, intendī, intentus, stretch out, direct

inter, *prep. w. acc.,* between, for, among; **inter sē,** with each other

intercēdō, –ere, –cessī, –cessūrus, go between, intervene

intercipiō, –ere, –cēpī, –ceptus, intercept

interclūdō, –ere, –clūsī, –clūsus, shut off, cut off

intereā, *adv.,* meanwhile

intereō, –īre, –iī, –itūrus, perish

interest, *see* intersum

interficiō, –ere, –fēcī, –fectus, kill

intericiō, –ere, –iēcī, –iectus, throw between, intervene

interim, *adv.,* meanwhile

interior, –ius, interior; **interiōrēs,** those in the interior

intermittō, –ere, –mīsī, –missus, let go, stop, interrupt, intervene

interpōnō, –ere, –posuī, –positus, present

interpretor, 1, explain

interrogō, 1, ask, question

intersum, –esse, –fuī, –futūrus, be between, take part (in); **interest,** it makes a difference

intervāllum, –ī, *n.,* interval, distance

interventus, –ūs, *m.,* coming on

intrā, *prep. w. acc.,* within

intrō, 1, enter

intrōmittō, –ere, –mīsī, –missus, let in

intueor, intuērī, intuitus, look at
inūsitātus,. –a, –um, unusual, strange
inūtilis, –e, useless
inveniō, –īre, invēnī, inventus, come upon, find
inventor –ōris, m., discoverer
invictus, –a, –um, unconquered
invideō, –ēre, invīdī, invīsus, envy
invidia, –ae, f., envy
invītō, 1, invite
invītus, –a, –um, unwilling
iō! interj., oh! ah! hurrah!
iocor, 1, joke
iocus, –ī, m., joke
Iovis, see **Iuppiter**
ipse, ipsa, ipsum, -self, very
īra, –ae, f., anger, wrath
īrācundus, –a, –um, quick-tempered
īrātus –a, –um, angry
irrīdeō, –ēre, irrīsī, irrīsus, laugh at, jeer
irrumpō, –ere, irrūpī, irruptus, break in, rush in
is, ea, id, this, that; as pron., he, she, it
iste, ista, istud, that
ita, adv., so, in such a way, thus, yes; **ita ut(ī),** just as
Italia, –ae, f., Italy
itaque, adv., and so, therefore
item, adv., also, likewise
iter, itineris, n., journey, road, march, way; **iter faciō,** march, travel
iterum, adv., again
iubeō, –ēre, iussī, iussus, order
iūcundus, –a, –um, pleasant
iūdex, iūdicis, m., judge
iūdicium, –cī, n., trial, judgment
iūdicō, 1, judge, decide
iugum, –ī, n., yoke, ridge
Iūlius, –a, –um, of Julius; as noun, f., m., Julia, Julius; July
iungō, –ere, iūnxī, iūnctus, join, harness
iūnior, –ius (comp. of **iuvenis**), younger
Iūnō, –ōnis, f., Juno, a goddess, wife of Jupiter
Iuppiter, Iovis, m., Jupiter, king of the gods
Iūra, –ae, m., Jura, a mountain range
iūrō, 1, swear
iūs, iūris, n., right, justice, law; **iūs iūrandum, iūris iūrandī,** n., oath
iussum, –ī, n., order

iūstitia, –ae, f., justice
iūstus, –a, –um, just, proper, regular
iuvenālis, –e, youthful
iuvenis, –is, m., young man
iuventūs, –tūtis, f., youth, young people
iuvō, –āre, iūvī, iūtus, help, aid, please
iūxtā, adv., close by

L

L., abbreviation for **Lūcius, Lūcī,** m., Lucius (Lū'shius)
labor, –ōris, m., work, task, trouble, hardship
labōrō, 1, work, be hard pressed
lac, lactis, n., milk
Lacedaemon, –onis, f., Sparta, a region in Greece
lacerō, 1, tear to pieces
lacessō, –ere, –īvī, –ītus, attack
lacrima, –ae, f., tear
lacrimōsus, –a, –um, tearful
lacus, –ūs, m., lake
laetitia, –ae, f., joy
laetus, –a, –um, joyful
lampas, –adis, f., lamp, torch
lanterna, –ae, f., lantern
lapis, lapidis, m., stone
Lār, Laris, m., Lar (pl. Lā'rēs), a household god
lārva, –ae, f., ghost
lassitūdō, –dinis, f., weariness
lātē, adv., widely
lateō, latēre, latuī, —, hide, escape notice
Latīnus, –a, –um, Latin; as noun, m., a Latin
lātitūdō, –dinis, f., width
latrō, –ōnis, m., robber, bandit
latrōcinium, –nī, n., robbery
latus, lateris, n., side, flank
lātus, –a, –um, wide, broad
lātus, see **ferō**
laudō, 1, praise
laus, laudis, f., praise
lautus, –a, –um, magnificent
lavō, –āre, lāvī, lautus wash, bathe
laxō, 1, open out
lēctor, –ōris, m., reader
lēgātiō, –ōnis, f., embassy
lēgātus, –ī, m., envoy; general, staff officer; governor
legiō, –ōnis, f., legion
legiōnārius, –a, –um, legionary

legō, –ere, lēgī, lēctus choose, read
Lemannus, –ī, *m., w.* **lacus,** Lake Geneva
lēniō, –īre, –īvī, –ītus, soothe
lēnis, –e, gentle
lēniter, *adv.,* gently
leō, –ōnis, *m.,* lion
Leōnidās, –ae, *m.,* Leŏn'idas
levis, –e, light
levitās, –tātis, *f.,* lightness, inconstancy
lēx, lēgis, *f.,* law
libellus, –ī, *m.,* little book
libenter, *adv.,* willingly, gladly
liber, librī, *m.,* book
līber, –era, –erum, free
līberālis, –e, liberal
līberāliter, *adv.,* liberally, courteously
līberātor, –ōris, *m.,* liberator
līberī, –ōrum, *m. pl.,* children
līberō, 1, free, set free
lībertās, –tātis, *f.,* freedom
lībertus, –ī, *m.,* freedman
librārius, –rī, *m.,* bookseller
licentia, –ae, *f.,* license
licet, –ēre, licuit *or* **licitum est,** it is permitted, one may
ligō, 1, tie, bind
lilium, līlī, *n.,* lily
līmen, līminis, *n.,* threshold
lingua, –ae, *f.,* tongue, language
liquidus, –a, –um, liquid
littera, –ae, *f.,* letter (*of the alphabet*); *pl.,* letter (*epistle*), letters (*if modified by an adjective such as* **multae**), literature
lītus, lītoris, *n.,* shore
Līvius, –vī, *m.,* Livy, *a Roman historian*
locō, 1, place
locus, –ī, *m.* (*pl.* **loca, locōrum,** *n.*), place, country; rank, situation; opportunity
longē, *adv.,* far away, far, by far; **longē lātēque,** far and wide
longinquus, –a, –um, distant
longitūdō, –dinis, *f.,* length
longus, –a, –um, long
loquor, loquī, locūtus, talk, speak
lūdificō, 1, make sport of
lūdō, –ere, lūsī, lūsus, play
lūdus, –ī, *m.,* game, play, school
lūgeō, –ēre, lūxī, lūctus, mourn for
lūmen, lūminis, *n.,* light, lamp; eye
lūna, –ae, *f.,* moon
lupus, –ī, *m.,* wolf

lūx, lūcis, *f.,* light; **prīmā** *or* **ortā lūce,** at dawn
lūxuria, –ae, *f.,* luxury
Lycurgus, –ī, *m.,* Lŷcur'gus

M

M., *abbreviation for* **Mārcus**
Macedonia, –ae, *f.,* Macedonia, *a country northeast of Greece;* **Macedonicus, –a, –um,** Macedonian
māchina, –ae, *f.,* machine
māchinātiō, –ōnis, *f.,* engine
maciēs, –ēī, *f.,* thinness
magicus, –a, –um, magic
magis, *adv.,* more, rather; *superl.* **maximē,** most, very, very greatly, especially, very hard
magister, –trī, *m.,* teacher
magistrātus, –ūs, *m.,* official, office
magnificus, –a, –um, magnificent, generous
magnitūdō, –dinis, *f.,* greatness, size
magnopere, *adv.,* greatly
magnus, –a, –um, large, great, much, loud; *w.* **iter,** forced; *comp.* **maior, maius,** larger, greater; **maiōrēs,** older men, ancestors; *superl.* **maximus, –a, –um,** greatest, very great
maiestās, –tātis, *f.,* dignity, honor
maior, *see* **magnus**
male, *adv.,* badly
mālō, mālle, māluī, —, prefer
malus, –a, –um, bad; *comp.* **peior, peius,** worse; *superl.* **pessimus, –a, –um,** very bad, worst; **malum, –ī,** *n.,* trouble
mandātum, –ī, *n.,* order
mandō, 1, commit, entrust, give, command; **fugae mē mandō,** take to flight
maneō, –ēre, mānsī, mānsūrus, remain, endure
manifēstus, –a, –um, obvious
manipulus, –ī, *m.,* maniple
manūmittō, –ere, –mīsī, –missus, make free
manus, –ūs, *f.,* hand, force
mare, maris, *n.,* sea
margarīta, –ae, *f.,* pearl
margarītārius, –rī, *m.,* pearl dealer
margō, marginis, *m.,* edge
maris, *see* **mare** *and* **mās**
maritimus, –a, –um, of the sea, near the sea; **ōra maritima,** seacoast
marītus, –ī, *m.,* husband

marmor, –oris, *n.*, marble
marmoreus, –a, –um, of marble
Mārs, Mārtis, *m.*, Mars, *god of war*
Mārtius, –a, –um, of Mars; of March; *as noun, m.*, Martius (Mar′shius)
mās, maris, *m.*, male
māter, mātris, *f.*, mother
māteria, –ae, *f.*, timber, wood
mātrimōnium, –nī, *n.*, marriage; in mātrimōnium dō, give in marriage; in mātrimōnium dūcō, marry
mātrōna, –ae, *f.*, wife, married woman
mātūrē, *adv.*, soon, quickly
mātūrō, 1, hasten
mātūrus, –a, –um, ripe, early, mature
maximē, *see* magis; maximus, *see* magnus
mēcum = cum mē
medicīna, –ae, *f.*, medicine
medicus, –ī, *m.*, doctor
mediocris, –e, moderate
mediocritās, –tātis, *f.*, mean
mediterrāneus, –a, –um, inland
medius, –a, –um, middle (of), midst of
mel, mellis, *n.*, honey
melior, *see* bonus; melius, *see* bene
membrum, –ī, *n.*, member, part of the body, limb
meminī (*perf. translated as pres.*), remember
memor, *gen.* memoris, mindful, unforgetting
memoria, –ae, *f.*, memory; memoriā teneō, remember
mēns, mentis, *f.*, mind
mēnsa, –ae, *f.*, table
mēnsis, –is, *m.*, month
mēnsūra, –ae, *f.*, measurement
mentiō, –ōnis, *f.*, mention
mercātor, –ōris, *m.*, trader, merchant
mercātūra, –ae, *f.*, trade
Mercurius, –rī, *m.*, Mercury, *god of trade and gain and messenger of the gods*
mereō, –ēre, meruī, meritus, deserve, earn
merīdiēs, –ēī, *m.*, midday, noon; south
meritum, –ī, *n.*, merit, service
mersus, –a, –um, submerged
mētior, mētīrī, mēnsus, measure (out)
metuō, –ere, –uī, —, fear
metus, –ūs, *m.*, fear
meus, –a, –um, my, mine
migrō, 1, move, depart

mīles, mīlitis, *m.*, soldier
mīlitāris, –e, military
mīlitia, –ae, *f.*, military service
mīlle, *pl.* mīlia, thousand
Minerva, –ae, *f.*, Minerva, *goddess of wisdom*
minimē, *see* minus
minimus, *see* parvus
minor, *see* parvus
minuō, –ere, minuī, minūtus, lessen, settle
minus, *adv.*, less; *superl.* minimē, least, by no means
mīrābilis, –e, wonderful
mīrāculum, –ī, *n.*, wonderful thing
mīrātor, –ōris, *m.*, admirer
mīror, 1, wonder, wonder at, admire
mīrus, –a, –um, wonderful, strange
misceō, –ēre, –uī, mixtus, mix
miser, –era, –erum, unhappy, poor
miserābilis, –e, wretched
miseria, –ae, *f.*, wretchedness
mittō, –ere, mīsī, missus, let go, send, throw
mixta, *see* misceō
mōbilis, –e, moving
mōbilitās, –tātis, *f.*, changeableness
moderātus, –a, –um, moderate
modernus, –a, –um, modern
modestē, *adv.*, modestly
modo, *adv.*, only, merely, even; nōn modo . . . sed etiam, not only . . . but also
modus, –ī, *m.*, measure, manner, kind, plan, way; quem ad modum, how
moenia, –ium, *n. pl.*, (city) walls
molestia, –ae, *f.*, annoyance
molliō, –īre, –īvī, –ītus, soften
mollis, –e, tender
mollitia, –ae, *f.*, weakness
Mona, –ae, *f.*, the Isle of Man, *between England and Ireland*
moneō, –ēre, monuī, monitus, remind, advise, warn
monitus, –ūs, *m.*, warning
mōns, montis, *m.*, mountain, hill, mount
mōnstrō, 1, point out, show
mōnstrum, –ī, *n.*, monster
monumentum, –ī, *n.*, monument
mora, –ae, *f.*, delay, stay
morbus, –ī, *m.*, disease
morior, morī, mortuus, die; mortuus, dead; moritūrus, about to die
moror, 1, delay, stay

mors, mortis, *f.,* death
mortālis, –e, mortal
mortifer, –fera, –ferum, deadly
mortuus, *see* **morior**
mōs, mōris, *m.,* custom; *pl.* character
mōtus, –ūs, *m.,* motion, movement
moveō, –ēre, mōvī, mōtus, move, stir (up)
mox, *adv.,* soon
mūla, –ae, *f.,* mule
mulier, mulieris, *f.,* woman
multitūdō, –dinis, *f.,* multitude, (great) number
multō, *adv.,* much
multum, *adv.,* much, great; *comp.* **plūs,** more; *superl.* **plūrimum,** most, very much
multus, –a, –um, much; *pl.,* many; *comp.* **plūrēs, plūra,** more, several; *superl.* **plūrimus, –a, –um,** most, very many
mundānus, –a, –um, of the world
mundus, –ī, *m.,* world, universe
mūniō, –īre, –īvī, –ītus, fortify, protect; **viam mūniō,** build a road
mūnītiō, –ōnis, *f.,* fortification
mūnus, mūneris, *n.,* duty, gift; *pl.* shows (of gladiators), games
mūrālis, –e, wall
mūrus, –ī, *m.,* wall
Mūsae, –ārum, *f. pl.,* the Muses
mūtābilis, –e, changeable, fickle
mutilus, –a, –um, broken
mūtō, 1, change
mūtus, –a, –um, mute

N

nactus, *part. of* **nancīscor**
nam, namque, *conj.,* for
nancīscor, nancīscī, nactus, gain, obtain, find
nārrō, 1, tell, relate
nāscor, nāscī, nātus, be born, be found; **duōs annōs nātus,** two years old; **nātus, –ī,** *m.,* son
nātālis, –e, of birth; **diēs nātālis,** birthday
nātiō, –ōnis, *f.,* nation, tribe
natō, 1, swim, float
nātūra, –ae *f.,* nature
nātus, *part. of* **nāscor**
naumachia, –ae, *f.,* sea fight
nauta, –ae, *m.,* sailor
nāvālis, –e, naval

nāvigium, –gī, *n.,* boat
nāvigō, 1, sail
nāvis, nāvis, *f.,* ship; **nāvis longa,** warship; **nāvis onerāria,** transport
–ne, *introduces questions; in indirect questions,* whether
nē, *conj.,* not, (so) that . . . not, in order that . . . not, that; *adv.,* not; **nē . . . quidem** (*emphatic word between*), not even
nec, *see* **neque**
necessāriō, *adv.,* necessarily
necessārius, –a, –um, necessary
necesse, *indeclinable adj.,* necessary
necessitās, –tātis, *f.,* necessity
necō, 1, kill
nefārius, –a, –um, unspeakable
nefās, *n., indeclinable,* sin, wrong
neglegō, –ere, –lēxī, –lēctus, disregard, neglect
negō, 1, say no, deny, say . . . not
negōtium, –tī, *n.,* business, trouble, task, job
nēmō, *dat.* **nēminī,** *acc.* **nēminem** (*no other forms*), no one
nepōs, nepōtis, *m.,* grandson
nēquāquam, *adv.,* by no means
neque (*or* **nec**), and not, nor; **neque . . . neque,** neither . . . nor
nesciō, nescīre, nescīvī, —, not know
neu, *see* **nēve**
neuter, –tra, –trum, neither (*of two*)
nēve (neu), *conj.,* and not, nor
nex, necis, *f.,* death
niger, –gra, –grum, black
nihil, nīl, nothing, not
nimis, too much
nisi, *conj.,* unless, except
niveus, –a, –um, snow-white
nix, nivis, *f.,* snow
nōbilis, –e, distinguished, noble
nōbilitās, –tātis, *f.,* nobility
nōbīscum = cum nōbīs
noceō, –ēre, nocuī, nocitūrus, do harm to, injure (*w. dat.*)
noctū, *adv.,* by night
nocturnus, –a, –um, of night, night
nōlō, nōlle, nōluī, —, not want, not wish, be unwilling
nōmen, nōminis, *n.,* name
nōminātim, *adv.,* by name
nōminō, 1, name
nōn, *adv.,* not; **nōn iam,** no longer; **nōn nūllī (nōnnūllī), –ae, –a,** some; **nōn numquam,** sometimes

nōndum, *adv.,* not yet

nōnus, –a, –um, ninth

Nōreia, –ae, *f.,* Norē'ia, *a city of the Norici*

Nōricus, –a, –um, Norican, of the Norici

nōs, we, *pl. of* **ego**

nōscō, –ere, nōvī, nōtus, learn, recognize; *perf.,* have learned, know

noster, –tra, –trum, our, ours

nōtus, –a, –um, known, familiar, well-known

novem, nine

novō, 1, renew

novus, –a, –um, new, strange; **novissimum agmen** *or* **novissimī,** the rear; *w.* **rēs** *or* **imperia,** revolution

nox, noctis, *f.,* night

noxia, –ae, *f.,* crime

nūbēs, –is, *f.,* cloud

nūdō, 1, strip, expose

nūgae, –ārum, *f.,* nonsense

nūllus, –a, –um, no, none; *as noun, m.,* no one; **nōn nūllī,** some

num, *adv., introduces questions expecting negative answer; conj.,* whether

nūmen, nūminis, *n.,* divinity, will

numerus, –ī, *m.,* number

Numidae, –ārum, *m. pl.,* the Numidians

nummus, –ī, *m.,* coin

numquam, *adv.,* never

nunc, *adv.,* now

nūntiō, 1, report, announce

nūntius, –tī, *m.,* messenger; message, news

nūper, *adv.,* recently

nūptiae, –ārum, *f. pl.,* wedding

nūtriō, –īre, –īvī, –ītus, nourish, foster

nūtus, –ūs, *m.,* nod

nux, nucis, *f.,* nut

nympha, –ae, *f.,* nymph

O

ō! *interj.,* O!

ob, *prep. w. acc.,* on account of, for

obiciō, –ere, obiēcī, obiectus, throw to *or* against, put in the way

oblinō, –ere, oblēvī, oblitus, smear

obscūrus, –a, –um, dark

observō, 1, observe, watch

obses, obsidis, *m.,* hostage

obsideō, –ēre, obsēdī, obsessus, besiege, blockade

obsidiō, –ōnis, *f.,* siege

obstō, –āre, obstitī, obstātūrus, prevent

obtemperō, 1, submit to

obtestor, 1, entreat

obtineō, –ēre, obtinuī, obtentus, hold, obtain

occāsiō, –ōnis, *f.,* opportunity

occāsus, –ūs, *m.,* setting; **occāsus sōlis,** sunset, west

occidō, –ere, occidī, occāsūrus, set

occīdō, –ere, occīdī, occīsus, kill

occultō, 1, conceal

occultus, –a, –um, secret

occupātiō, –ōnis, *f.,* business

occupō, 1, seize, occupy; **occupātus,** busy

occurrō, –ere, occurrī, occursūrus, run against, meet, occur

Ōceanus, –ī, *m.,* ocean (*esp. the Atlantic Ocean*)

Octāviānus, –ī, *m.,* Octā'vian, *the emperor Augustus*

octāvus, –a, –um, eighth

octō, eight

oculus, –ī, *m.,* eye

ōdī, ōsūrus (*perf. translated as pres.*), hate

offerō, offerre, obtulī, oblātus, offer; **mē offerō,** rush against

officium, –cī, *n.,* duty

ōh! *interj.,* oh!

ōlim, *adv.,* once, formerly, sometime

Olympia, –ae, *f.,* Olympia, *a Greek city;* **Olympicus, –a, –um,** Olympic

Olympīeum, –ī, *n.,* Olympīe'um, *temple of the Olympian Jupiter*

ōmen, ōminis, *n.,* omen, sign

omittō, –ere, omīsī, omissus, let go, drop, disregard

omnīnō, *adv.,* altogether, at all

omnis, omne, all, every, whole

onerārius, –a, –um, for freight; **nāvis onerāria,** transport

onerōsus, –a, –um, heavy

onus, oneris, *n.,* weight

opācus, –a, –um, gloomy

opera, –ae, *f.,* work, effort

opīniō, –ōnis, *f.,* opinion, expectation; reputation

oportet, –ēre, oportuit, it is necessary, ought

oppidum, –ī, *n.,* town

opportūnus, –a, –um, opportune, advantageous

opprimō, –ere, oppressī, oppressus; overcome, surprise, crush, oppress oppugnātiō, –ōnis, f., siege, method of attack

oppugnō, 1, attack, besiege

ops, opis, f., aid; pl., wealth, resources

optimē, see bene

optimus, see bonus

optō, 1, desire

opus, operis, n., work

opus, n., indeclinable, need; necessary

ōra, –ae, f., coast, edge

ōrāculum, –ī, n., oracle

ōrātiō, –ōnis, f., speech

ōrātor, –ōris, m., speaker, orator

orbis, –is, m., circle; esp. w. terrārum, the world (i.e., the circle of lands around the Mediterranean)

Orcus, –ī, m., Orcus, god of Hades; Hades

ōrdō, ōrdinis, m., order, rank

orīgō, orīginis, f., origin

orior, orīrī, ortus, rise, arise, begin, be descended from

ōrnō, 1, adorn; ōrnātus, fitted out

ōrō, 1, beg, ask, pray (for), plead

Orpheus, –ī, m., Orpheus (Or'fūs), a famous musician

ōs, ōris, n., mouth, face, expression

os, ossis, n., bone

ōsculum –ī, n., kiss

ostendō, –ere, ostendī, ostentus, (stretch out), show, display

ōtium, ōtī, n., leisure, quiet

Ovidius, –dī, m., Ovid

ōvum, –ī, n., egg

P

P., abbreviation for Pūblius

pābulor, 1, forage

pābulum, –ī, n., food (for cattle), fodder

pācō, 1, pacify, subdue

paene, adv., almost

Paestum, –ī, n., Paestum (Pěs'tum), a town in southern Italy

pāgus, –ī, m., district, canton

Palātīnus (mōns), –ī, m., Palātium, –tī, n., the Palatine Hill; palace

palma, –ae, f., hand

palūs, palūdis, f., marsh

pānis, –is, m., bread

pār, gen. paris, equal, fair; as noun, n., pair

parcē, adv., sparingly

parcō, –ere, pepercī, parsūrus, spare, save

parcus, –a, –um, sparing, economical

parēns, –entis, m. and f., parent

pāreō, –ēre, pāruī, pāritūrus, (appear), obey

pariō, –ere, peperī, partus, gain

Parnassius, –a, –um, Parnassian

parō, 1, get, get ready (for), prepare; parātus, prepared, ready

pars, partis, f., part, side, direction

parvulus, –a, –um, very small, little

parvus, –a, –um, small, low; comp. minor, minus, smaller, less, lesser, younger; superl. minimus, –a, –um, smallest, least, very little, youngest

passus, –ūs, m., step, pace (about five feet); mīlle passūs, mile

passus, part. of patior

pāstor, –ōris, m., shepherd

patefaciō, –ere, –fēcī, –factus, open

patēns, gen. patentis, open

pateō, –ēre, patuī, ——, stand open, extend

pater, patris, m., father, senator; patrēs cōnscrīptī, senators

paternus, –a, –um, of the father

patienter, adv., patiently

patientia, –ae, f., patience

patior, patī, passus, suffer, permit

patria, –ae, f., fatherland, country

patrius, –a, –um, of a father, ancestral

paucī, –ae, –a, few, only a few

paucitās, –tātis, f., small number

paulātim, adv., little by little; a few at a time

paulisper, adv., for a little while

paulō and paulum, adv., shortly, a little

pauper, gen. pauperis, poor

paupertās, –tātis, f., poverty

paveō, –ēre, pāvī, ——, fear

pavidus, –a, –um, trembling

pāx, pācis, f., peace

pectus, pectoris, n., breast, heart

pecūnia, –ae, f., money

pecus, pecoris, n., cattle

pedes, peditis, m., foot soldier; pl., infantry

pedester, –tris, –tre, (of) infantry; on foot

peditātus, –ūs, m., infantry

peior, see malus

pellis, –is, f., skin

pellō, –ere, pepulī, pulsus, drive, defeat

pendeō, –ēre, pependī, ——, hang

pendō, –ere, pependī, pēnsus, hang, weigh, pay

penetrō, 1, penetrate

per, *prep. w. acc.,* through, by, during, along

peragō, –ere, –ēgī, –āctus, complete

percipiō, –ere, –cēpī, –ceptus, feel, learn

percutiō, –ere, –cussī, –cussus, strike

perdiscō, –ere, –didicī, —, learn thoroughly

perdō, –ere, –didī, –ditus, lose, destroy, waste

perdūcō, –ere, –dūxī, –ductus, lead *or* bring through, extend, win over

pereō, –īre, –iī, –itūrus, perish, be lost

perferō, perferre, pertulī, perlātus, carry (through), report, endure

perficiō, –ere, –fēcī, –fectus, make of, bring about, finish

perfidia, –ae, *f.,* faithlessness, treachery

perfidus, –a, –um, treacherous

perfuga, –ae, *m.,* deserter

perfugiō, –ere, –fūgī, —, flee

perīculōsus, –a, –um, dangerous

perīculum, –ī, *n.,* trial, danger

perītus, –a, –um, skilled, experienced

perlegō, –ere, –lēgī, –lēctus, read through

permaneō, –ēre, –mānsī, –mānsūrus, remain

permittō, –ere, –mīsī, –missus, let go through, leave, allow, grant, entrust

permoveō, –ēre, –mōvī, –mōtus, move deeply, induce, alarm

perpaucī, –ae, –a, very few

perpetuus, –a, –um, constant, lasting

perrumpō, –ere, –rūpī, –ruptus, break through

Persae, –ārum, *m. pl.,* the Persians

persequor, –sequī, –secūtus, pursue, punish

perspiciō, –ere, –spexī, –spectus, see (clearly), examine

perstō, –āre, –stitī, –stātūrus, persist

persuādeō, –ēre, –suāsī, –suāsūrus, persuade

perterreō, –ēre, –terruī, –territus, scare thoroughly, alarm

pertināciter, *adv.,* persistently

pertineō, –ēre, –tinuī, –tentūrus, extend (to), pertain to

pertrānseō, –īre, –īvī, –itūrus, pass through

perturbātiō, –ōnis, *f.,* confusion

perturbō, 1, disturb, throw into confusion

perveniō, –īre, –vēnī, –ventūrus, come (through), arrive (at)

pēs, pedis, *m.,* foot; **pedibus,** on foot

pessimus, *see* **malus**

petō, –ere, petīvī, petītus, seek, ask; attack

Pharsālus, –ī, *f.,* Pharsā′lus, *a town in Thessaly*

Philippī, –ōrum, *m. pl.,* Philippi (Filĭp′ī), *a city in Macedonia*

Philippus, –ī, *m.,* Philip

philosophus, –ī, *m.,* philosopher

pictūra, –ae, *f.,* picture

pila, –ae, *f.,* ball

pilula, –ae, *f.,* pill

pīlum, –ī, *n.,* spear (*for throwing*), javelin

piscis, –is, *m.,* fish

piscor, 1, fish

pius, –a, –um, dutiful, righteous, pious

placeō, –ēre, placuī, placitūrus, be pleasing to, please; **placet,** it pleases (him), *i.e.,* (he) decides

placidus, –a, –um, gentle

plācō, 1, appease

plānitiēs, –ēī, *f.,* plain

plānus, –a, –um, level

Platō, –ōnis, *m.,* Plā′tō, *a Greek philosopher*

plēbs, plēbis, *f.,* common people

plēnus, –a, –um, full

plērīque, –aeque, –aque, most

plērumque, *adv.,* usually

plūrēs, *see* **multus**

plūrimum, *see* **multum**

plūrimus, *see* **multus**

plūs, *see* **multum, multus**

poena, –ae, *f.,* penalty, punishment

Poenī, –ōrum, *m. pl.,* the Carthaginians

poēta, –ae, *m.,* poet

polliceor, pollicērī, pollicitus, promise

pollicitātiō, –ōnis, *f.,* promise

pōmārium, –rī, *n.,* orchard

pompa, –ae, *f.,* parade, procession

Pompeiānus, –a, –um, at Pompeii

Pompeius, –peī, *m.,* Pompey

Pomptīnae palūdēs, the Pŏn′tīne Marshes, *south of Rome*

pondus, ponderis, *n.,* weight

pōnō, –ere, posuī, positus, put, place, serve, lay down; *passive,* be situated, depend upon; *w.* **castra,** pitch

pōns, pontis, *m.,* bridge
pontifex, pontificis, *m.,* priest
pontus, –ī, *m.,* sea
poposcī, *see* **poscō**
populor, 1, destroy
populus, –ī, *m.,* people; *pl.,* peoples
porta, –ae, *f.,* gate, door
porticus, –ūs, *f.,* colonnade
portō, 1, carry
portus, –ūs, *m.,* harbor, port
poscō, –ere, poposcī, —, demand, call for
possessiō, –ōnis, *f.,* possession
possum, posse, potuī, —, can, can do, be able; **multum (plūs, plūrimum) possum,** be very powerful
post, *adv. and prep. w. acc.,* behind; after, later
posteā, *adv.,* afterwards; **posteāquam,** *conj.,* after
posterus, –a, –um, following, next; *as noun, m. pl.,* posterity, descendants
postquam, *conj.,* after
postrēmō, *adv.,* finally
postrīdiē, *adv.,* on the next day
postulō, 1, demand
potēns, *gen.* **potentis,** powerful
potentia, –ae, *f.,* power
potestās, –tātis, *f.,* power
potior, potīrī, potītus, get possession of (*w. gen. or abl.*)
potius, *adv.,* rather
prae, *prep. w. abl.,* before; in comparison with
praeacūtus, –a, –um, pointed
praebeō, –ēre, –uī, –itus, hold forth, furnish, present, show
praecēdō, –ere, –cessī, –cessūrus, go before, precede
praeceps, *gen.* **praecipitis,** headlong
praeceptum, –ī, *n.,* rule, instruction
praecipiō, –ere, –cēpī, –ceptus, instruct
praeda, –ae, *f.,* loot
praedicō, 1, announce, declare
praedīcō, –ere, –dīxī, –dictus, predict
praedor, 1, loot
praedūcō, –ere, –dūxī, –ductus, extend
praefectus, –ī, *m.,* commander, prefect
praeficiō, –ere, –fēcī, –fectus, put in charge of
praemittō, –ere, –mīsī, –missus, send ahead
praemium, –mī, *n.,* reward
praemūniō = **mūniō**

praenōscō, –ere, –nōvī, –nōtus, learn beforehand
praeparō, 1, prepare
praerumpō, –ere, –rūpī, –ruptus, break off
praescrībō, –ere, –scrīpsī, –scrīptus, direct
praescrīptum, –ī, *n.,* order
praesēns, *gen.* **praesentis,** present
praesentiō, –īre, –sēnsī, –sēnsus, foresee
praesertim, *adv.,* especially
praesidium, –dī, *n.,* garrison, guard, protection, aid
praestāns, *gen.* **praestantis,** outstanding
praestō, –āre, –stitī, –stitūrus, stand before, excel; offer, perform, show; **praestat,** it is better
praesum, –esse, –fuī, –futūrus, be in charge of
praeter, *prep. w. acc.,* besides, except, beyond
praetereā, *adv.,* besides
praetereō, –īre, –iī, –itus, go by, pass
praeterquam, *adv.,* other than
praetor, –ōris, *m.,* praetor (*an official*), judge
praevaleō, –ēre, –valuī, –valitūrus, prevail
prandium, –dī, *n.,* lunch
prātum, –ī, *n.,* meadow
prehendō, –ere, –hendī, –hēnsus, grasp, seize, catch
premō, –ere, pressī, pressus, press, press hard, oppress, crowd
prēndō = **prehendō**
pretium, –tī, *n.,* price; reward
prex, precis, *f.,* prayer, entreaty
prīdiē, *adv.,* on the day before
prīmō, *adv.,* at first
prīmum, *adv.,* first, at first, for the first time; **quam prīmum,** as soon as possible
prīmus, –a, –um, first; **in prīmīs,** especially
prīnceps, prīncipis, *adj. and noun, m.,* chief, first (man), leader, emperor
prīncipātus, –ūs, *m.,* first place, leadership
prior, prius, former, first
prīstinus, –a, –um, former
prius, *adv.,* before, first; **priusquam (prius . . . quam),** *conj.,* before
prīvātus, –a, –um, private; *as noun, m.,* private citizen

476

prō, *prep. w. abl.,* in front of, before, for, instead of, as, in accordance with, in proportion to

probitās, –tātis, *f.,* honesty

probō, 1, prove, approve

prōcēdō, –ere, –cessī, –cessūrus, go forward, advance, proceed

procul, *adv.,* at a distance, far off

prōcumbō, –ere, –cubuī, –cubitūrus, lie down, sink down

prōcūrō, 1, take care of

prōcurrō, –ere, –currī, –cursūrus, run forward

prōdō, –ere, –didī, –ditus, give out, hand down, betray

prōdūcō, –ere, –dūxī, –ductus, lead *or* bring out, prolong

proelium, –lī, *n.,* battle

profectiō, –ōnis, *f.,* departure

prōferō, prōferre, prōtulī, prōlātus, bring out, extend

professor, –ōris, *m.,* professor

prōficiō, –ere, –fēcī, –fectus, accomplish

proficīscor, proficīscī, profectus, set out, start

profugiō, –ere, –fūgī, –fugitūrus, flee

prōgeniēs, –iēī, *f.,* descendants

prōgnātus, –a, –um, descended

prōgredior, prōgredī, prōgressus, step forward, advance

prohibeō, –ēre, –hibuī, –hibitus, prevent, keep from, cut off

prōiciō, –ere, –iēcī, –iectus, throw *or* thrust (forward), abandon

prōlabor, –ī, prōlāpsus, slip

prōmittō, –ere, –mīsī, –missus, let go; promise; **prōmissus,** long

prōmoveō, –ēre, –mōvī, –mōtus, move forward

prōmptus, –a, –um, ready

prōnūntiō, 1, announce, recite

prōnus, –a, –um, flat

prope, *adv.,* almost; *prep. w. acc.,* near

prōpellō, –ere, –pulī, –pulsus, drive away, dislodge

properō, 1, hasten, hurry

propinquitās, –tātis, *f.,* nearness

propinquus, –a, –um, near; *as noun, m.,* relative

propitius, –a, –um, favorable

prōpōnō, –ere, –posuī, –positus, explain, present, offer, raise, propose

proprius, –a, –um, (one's) own, characteristic of

propter, *prep. w. acc.,* on account of

proptereā, *adv.,* on this account; **proptereā quod,** because

prōpugnō, 1, fight on the offensive

prōra, –ae, *f.,* prow

prōscrīptiō, –ōnis, *f.,* proscription, list of condemned

prōsequor, prōsequī, prōsecūtus, pursue, address

prōspectus, –ūs, *m.,* view

prōspiciō, –ere, –spexī, –spectus, look out for, see

prōsternō, –ere, –strāvī, –strātus, overthrow

prōsum, prōdesse, prōfuī, —, benefit, help

prōtegō, –ere, –tēxī, –tēctus, cover

prōtinus, *adv.,* immediately

prōvehō, –ere, –vexī, –vectus, carry forward

prōvideō, –ēre, –vīdī, –vīsus, provide, look out for

prōvincia, –ae, *f.,* province

proximē, *adv.,* recently

proximus, –a, –um, nearest, last, next, very near

prūdēns, *gen.* **prūdentis,** sensible

prūdentia, –ae, *f.,* foresight, good sense

pūblicē, *adv.,* publicly

pūblicus, –a, –um, public

Pūblius, Pūblī, *m.,* Pub'lius

puella, –ae, *f.,* girl

puer, puerī, *m.,* boy, child

puerīlis, –e, boyish, childish

puerīliter, *adv.,* childishly

pueritia, –ae, *f.,* boyhood

pugna, –ae, *f.,* fight, battle

pugnō, 1, fight

pulcher, –chra, –chrum, beautiful

pulchritūdō, –dinis, *f.,* beauty

pulsō, 1, dash against

pulsus, *part. of* **pellō**

Pūnicus, –a, –um, Punic, Carthaginian

pūniō, –īre, –īvī, –ītus, punish

puppis, –is, *f.,* stern

pūrgō, 1, cleanse

purpurātus, –a, –um, purple

putō, 1, think, consider

Pȳrēnaeī montēs, the Pyrenees Mountains

Q

Q., *abbreviation for* **Quīntus**

quā, *adv.,* where

quadringentī, −ae, −a, four hundred

quaerō, −ere, quaesīvī, quaesītus, seek, inquire

quaestiō, −ōnis, f., investigation

quaestor, −ōris, m., quaestor (a Roman official)

quaestus, −ūs, m., gain

quālis, −e, what kind of, what, such as

quam, adv. and conj., how, as; w. comp., than; w. superl., as . . . as possible; quam prīmum, as soon as possible

quamquam, conj., although

quandō, conj., when

quantus, −a, −um, how great, how much, what, as (great or much as)

quārē, why

quārtus, −a, −um, fourth; quārtus decimus, fourteenth

quasi, adv. and conj., as if, like, as it were

quattuor, four

−que, conj. (added to second word), and

queror, querī, questus, complain

quī, quae, quod, rel. pron., who, which, what, that; interrog. adj., what; quī, qua, quod, indef. adj., any

quia, conj., because

quīcumque, quaecumque, quodcumque, whoever, whatever

quid, adv., why

quīdam, quaedam, quiddam and (adj.) quoddam, a certain one or thing; adj., certain, some, a, one

quidem, adv. (follows emphasized word), at least, to be sure; nē . . . quidem, not even

quidnam, what in the world

quiēs, quiētis, f., rest, sleep, quiet

quiētus, −a, −um, quiet; quiētē, adv., quietly

quīn, conj., that; quīn etiam, moreover

Quīnctīlis, −e, (of) July

quīngentī, −ae, −a, five hundred

quīnquāgintā, fifty

quīnque, five

Quīntiliānus, −ī, m., Quintil'ian

quīntus, −a, −um, fifth

Quirīnālis (mōns), −is, m., the Quir'-inal Hill

quis, quid, interrog. pron., who, what; indef. pron., anyone, anything

quisquam, quicquam, anyone, anything, any

quisque, quidque, each one, each thing

quō, adv., where, to which

quō, conj., in order that; quō minus (quōminus), that not

quoad, conj., as long as

quod, conj., because, that; quod sī, but if

quondam, adv., once (upon a time)

quoniam, conj., since, because

quoque, adv. (follows emphasized word), too

quot, indeclinable adj., how many; as (many as)

quotannīs, adv., every year

quotiēns, adv., as often as, how often

R

radiō, 1, shine

rādīx, −īcis, f., root

raeda, −ae, f., carriage, bus

rāmulus, −ī, m., branch

rāmus, −ī, m., branch

rapiditās, −tātis, f., swiftness

rapiō, −ere, rapuī, raptus, seize, carry off

rārus, −a, −um, rare

ratiō, −ōnis, f., account, plan, manner, reason, consideration, method, theory, system, judgment

ratis, −is, f., raft

rebelliō, −ōnis, f., rebellion

recēdō, −ere, recessī, recessūrus, withdraw

recēns, gen. recentis, new, recent

recēnseō, −ēre, recēnsuī, recēnsus, count again, review

recingō, −ere, recīnxī, recīnctus, loosen

recipiō, −ere, recēpī, receptus, take (back), receive, recover; mē recipiō, withdraw, recover

recitō, 1, recite, read aloud

reclīnō, 1, bend back; passive, lean

rēctē, adv., rightly

rēctus, see regō

recuperō, 1, get back, recover

recursō, 1, run back and forth

recūsō, 1, refuse

reddō, −ere, reddidī, redditus, give (back), render, return, restore, reflect

redeō, −īre, rediī, reditūrus, go back, return

redigō, −ere, redēgī, redāctus, bring (back), drive back, reduce

redimō, –ere, redēmī, redēmptus, buy back, ransom
redintegrō, 1, renew
reditus, –ūs, _m._, return
redūcō, –ere, redūxī, reductus, lead back, bring back
referō, referre, rettulī, relātus, bring _or_ carry (back), report, reproduce; **pedem referō,** withdraw; **grātiam referō,** show gratitude
reficiō, –ere, refēcī, refectus, repair, refresh, restore
rēgia, –ae, _f._, palace
rēgīna, –ae, _f._, queen
regiō, –ōnis, _f._, district, region
rēgnō, 1, reign, rule
rēgnum, –ī, _n._, royal power, kingdom, rule
regō, –ere, rēxī, rēctus, rule, direct; **rēctus,** straight
reiciō, –ere, reiēcī, reiectus, drive back, reject
relābor, relābī, relāpsus, slip back
relanguēscō, –ere, –languī, —, become weak
religiō, –ōnis, _f._, religion, superstition
relinquō, –ere, relīquī, relīctus, leave (behind), abandon
reliquus, –a, –um, remaining, rest (of), left; _w._ **tempus,** the future
remaneō, –ēre, remānsī, remānsūrus, remain
remedium, –dī, _n._, remedy
rēmigō, –āre, —, —, row
remigrō, 1, go back
remissiō, –ōnis, _f._, forgiveness
remittō, –ere, remīsī, remissus, send _or_ throw back, remit, relax; **remissus,** mild
removeō, –ēre, remōvī, remōtus, move back, remove; **remōtus,** remote
rēmus, –ī, _m._, oar
Rēmus, –ī, _m._, a Rē′man
renūntiō, 1, report
reparō, 1, restore
repellō, –ere, reppulī, repulsus, drive back, repulse
repente, _adv._, suddenly
repentīnus, –a, –um, sudden
reperiō, –īre, repperī, repertus, find
repetō, –ere, –īvī, –ītus, seek back
reportō, 1, carry _or_ bring back
reprimō, –ere, repressī, repressus, stop
repudiō, 1, divorce
repugnō, 1, oppose

requiēs, –ētis, _f._, rest
requiēscō, –ere, –ēvī, –ētus, rest
requīrō, –ere, requīsīvī, requīsītus, miss
rēs, reī, _f._, thing, matter, affair; **rēs frūmentāria,** grain supply; **rēs mīlitāris,** military affairs, art of war; **rēs pūblica,** public affairs, government, state; **rēs gestae,** deeds
rescindō, –ere, rescidī, rescissus, cut down
reservō, 1, reserve
resideō, –ēre, resēdī, —, remain
resistō, –ere, restitī, —, stand against; resist
resolvō, –ere, resolvī, resolūtus, loosen
respiciō, –ere, respexī, respectus, look back, consider
respondeō, –ēre, respondī, respōnsus, reply, answer; **respōnsum, –ī, _n._,** answer
respuō, –ere, respuī, —, reject
restituō, –ere, restituī, restitūtus, restore
restō, –āre, restitī, —, remain
resūmō, –ere, resūmpsī, resūmptus, take up again, resume
resurgō = surgō
retineō, –ēre, retinuī, retentus, hold back, restrain, keep
retrahō, –ere, retrāxī, retrāctus, drag back
retrō, _adv._, back
rettulī, _see_ **referō**
reus, –ī, _m._, defendant
revereor, reverērī, reveritus, respect
revertō, –ere, revertī, reversus, turn back, return (_sometimes deponent_)
revīsō, –ere, —, —, revisit
revocō, 1, recall, call back
rēx, rēgis, _m._, king
Rhēnus, –ī, _m._, the Rhine river
rhētor, –ōris, _m._, rhetorician
Rhodanus, –ī, _m._, the Rhone river
rīdeō, –ēre, rīsī, rīsus, laugh (at)
rigor, –ōris, _m._, stiffness
rīpa, –ae, _f._, bank (_of a river_)
rōborō, 1, strengthen
rogitō, 1, keep on asking
rogō, 1, ask
Rōma, –ae, _f._, Rome
Rōmānus, –a, –um, Roman; _as noun,_ a Roman
rosa, –ae, _f._, rose
rotundus, –a, –um, round
rudis, –e, untrained, ignorant

ruīna, −ae, f., ruin, destruction
rūmor, −ōris, m., rumor
rumpō, −ere, rūpī, ruptus, break
rūpēs, −is, f., cliff, rock
rūrsus, adv., again
rūsticus, −a, −um, rustic

S

Sabīnus, −a, −um, Sā′bīne: as noun, f., a Sabine woman; pl., the Sā′bīnes, a people of Italy
sacer, sacra, sacrum, sacred
sacerdōs, −dōtis, m., priest
sacrificium, −cī, n., sacrifice
sacrificō, 1, sacrifice
saeculum (saeclum), −ī, n., age
saepe, adv., often
saevitia, −ae, f., fierceness
saevus, −a, −um, cruel
sagitta, −ae, f., arrow
sagittārius, −rī, m., bowman
Saliī, −ōrum, m., pl., the Sā′liī or "Jumpers" (priests of Mars)
saliō, −īre, saluī, saltūrus, jump, beat
saltō, 1, dance
salūs, −ūtis, f., health, safety, greeting
salūtātor, −ōris, m., greeter, visitor
salvē, salvēte, be well, greetings, hail
sānctus, −a, −um, sacred
sanguis, sanguinis, m., blood
sānitās, −tātis, f., sanity
sānus, −a, −um, sound
sapiēns, gen. sapientis, wise
sapientia, −ae, f., wisdom
satis, adv. and indeclinable adj., enough, rather
satisfaciō, −ere, −fēcī, −factus, satisfy
saxum, −ī, n., rock, stone
scaena, −ae, f., stage
scaenicus, −a, −um, of the theater; w. lūdī, stage plays
scelus, sceleris, n., crime
scēptrum, −ī, n., scepter
schola, −ae, f., school
scholasticus, −a, −um, scholastic; as noun, m., student
scientia, −ae, f., knowledge
sciō, scīre, scīvī, scītus, know, know how
scrība, −ae, m., secretary
scrībō, −ere, scrīpsī, scrīptus, write
sculpō, −ere, sculpsī, sculptus, carve
scūtum, −ī, n., shield

Scythae, −ārum, m. pl., the Scythians (Sĭth′ians), people beyond the Black Sea
sē, acc. and abl. of suī
sēcēdō, −ere, sēcessī, sēcessūrus, secede, withdraw
sēcrētō, adv., in private, secretly
sēcum = cum sē
secundus, −a, −um, second, favorable
sed, conj., but
sedeō, −ēre, sēdī, sessūrus, sit
sēdēs, −is, f., abode
sēdō, 1, quiet
sēductus, −a, −um, separated
semel, adv., once
sēmibarbarus, −a, −um, half-barbarian
semper, adv., always
senātor, −ōris, m., senator
senātus, −ūs, m., senate
senectūs, −tūtis, f., old age
senex, senis, m., old man; adj., old; comp. senior
sententia, −ae, f., feeling, opinion
sentiō, −īre, sēnsī, sēnsus, feel, think, realize, vote
sepeliō, −īre, −īvī, sepultus, bury
septem, seven
septentriōnēs, −um, m. pl., seven plow-oxen (the seven stars of the constellation Great Bear or Big Dipper), north
septimus, −a, −um, seventh
sepulchrum, −ī, n., tomb
sepultūra, −ae, f., burial
Sēquana, −ae, m., the Seine river
Sēquanus, −a, −um, Sequā′nian; as noun, m. pl., the Sequanians
sequor, sequī, secūtus, follow, pursue, seek
serēnō, 1, clear up
serēnus, −a, −um, quiet
sērius, comp. adv., later
sermō, −ōnis, m., conversation, talk
serō, −ere, sēvī, satus, plant, sow
serpēns, −entis, f., snake
serva, −ae, f., slave
servīlis, −e, of a slave
servitūs, −tūtis, f., slavery
servō, 1, save, preserve, guard
servus, −ī, m., slave
sēsē, acc. and abl. of suī
seu, see sīve
sevērē, adv., severely
sevēritās, −tātis, f., severity

severus, –a, –um, stern
sex, six; sexāgintā, sixty
Sextīlis, –e, August
sextus, –a, –um, sixth
sī, *conj.,* if
Sibylla, –ae, *f.,* the Sibyl, *a prophetess*
sīc, *adv.,* so, thus
siccō, 1, dry up
Sicilia, –ae, *f.,* Sicily (Sis'ily)
sīcut (sīcutī), *adv.,* just as, as if
sīdus, sīderis, *n.,* star
signifer, –ferī, *m.,* standard bearer
significātiō, –ōnis, *f.,* signal
significō, 1, indicate, mean
signum, –ī, *n.,* sign, signal, standard
silentium, –tī, *n.,* silence
silva, –ae, *f.,* forest, woods
similis, –e, like, similar
simul, *adv.,* at the same time; simul atque (ac), as soon as
simulācrum, –ī, *n.,* image, figure
simulō, 1, pretend
sine, *prep. w. abl.,* without
singillātim, *adv.,* one by one
singulāris, –e, one by one, remarkable
singulī, –ae, –a, *pl. only,* one at a time; one each, single
sinister, –tra, –trum, left
sinō, –ere, sīvī, situs, allow
sīve (seu), *conj.,* or if; sīve (seu) . . . sīve (seu), whether . . . or, either . . . or
socius, –cī, *m.,* comrade, ally
sōl, sōlis, *m.,* sun
sōlācium, –cī, *n.,* comfort
solea, –ae, *f.,* sandal, shoe
soleō, –ēre, solitus, *semideponent,* be used to, be accustomed
solidus, –a, –um, solid
sōlitūdō, –dinis, *f.,* wilderness
sollicitō, 1, stir up
sōlum, *adv.,* only
sōlus, –a, –um, alone, only, lonely
solvō, –ere, solvī, solūtus, loosen, break, free; set sail; *w.* poenam, pay
somnus, –ī, *m.,* sleep
sonus, –ī, *m.,* sound
sopor, –ōris, *m.,* sleep
sordidus, –a, –um, dirty, mean
soror, –ōris, *f.,* sister
sors, sortis, *f.,* lot, prophecy
spargō, –ere, sparsī, sparsus, scatter, sprinkle
Sparta, –ae, *f.,* Sparta, *a Greek city*

Spartacus, –ī, *m.,* Spartacus, *leader in a revolt of gladiators*
Spartānus, –ī, *m.,* a Spartan
spatium, –tī, *n.,* space, distance; time, period
speciēs, speciēī, *f.,* appearance, sight
spectāculum, –ī, *n.,* spectacle, show
spectō, 1, look at *or* on, face
speculātor, –ōris, *m.,* spy
spērō, 1, hope (for)
spēs, speī, *f.,* hope
spīna, –ae, *f.,* thorn
spoliō, 1, rob
spondeō, –ēre, spopondī, spōnsus, promise, engage
spōnsus, –ī, *m.,* betrothed
sponte, *w.* suā, of his (their) own accord, by his (their) own influence
squālēns, *gen.* squālentis, foul
st! *interj.,* hush!
stabulum, –ī, *n.,* stable
statim, *adv.,* at once, immediately
statiō, –ōnis, *f.,* outpost, guard, picket
statua, –ae, *f.,* statue
statuō, –ere, statuī, statūtus, decide, determine
statūra, –ae, *f.,* stature
stēlla, –ae, *f.,* star
stetī, *see* stō
stilus, –ī, *m.,* stylus (*instrument used in writing on wax tablets*)
stīpendiārius, –a, –um, tributary
stīpendium, –dī, *n.,* pay, tribute
stō, stāre, stetī, statūrus, stand, stop
stringō, –ere, strīnxī, strictus, draw
studeō, –ēre, studuī, —, be eager (for), study
studiōsē, *adv.,* eagerly
studium, –dī, *n.,* eagerness, interest, enthusiasm; study, pursuit
stultitia, –ae, *f.,* stupidity, folly
stultus, –a, –um, foolish
stupeō, –ēre, –uī, —, be amazed
suādeō, –ēre, suāsī, suāsūrus, urge
suāvis, –e, sweet
suāvitās, –tātis, *f.,* sweetness
sub, *prep.,* under, close to, at the foot of, just before (*w. acc. after verbs of motion; w. abl. after verbs of rest or position*)
subdūcō, –ere, –dūxī, –ductus, lead up; draw up
subeō, –īre, –iī, –itūrus, go under, enter, come up, undergo

subiciō, –ere, –iēcī, –iectus, throw from below, subject, conquer; subiectus, lying beneath

subigō, –ere, –ēgī, –āctus, force, subdue

subitō, adv., suddenly

sublātus, part. of tollō

sublevō, 1, lighten, raise; w. reflex., rise

submergō, –ere, –mersī, –mersus, plunge

subministrō, 1, furnish

submittō, –ere, –mīsī, –missus, send

submoveō, –ēre, –mōvī, –mōtus, drive back

subruō, –ere, –ruī, –rutus, undermine

subsequor, subsequī, subsecūtus, follow (closely)

subsidium, –dī, n., aid, reserve

subterrāneus, –a, –um, subterranean

subveniō, –īre, –vēnī, –ventūrus, come to help

succēdō, –ere, –cessī, –cessūrus, come up, succeed (w. dat.)

successus, –ūs, m., success

succurrō, –ere, –currī, –cursūrus, run to help

Suēbī, –ōrum, m. pl., the Suē'bans, or Suē'bī

sufficiō, –ere, –fēcī, –fectus, suffice

suffrāgium, –gī, n., vote

suī, of himself, herself, itself, themselves

sum, esse, fuī, futūrus, be

summa, –ae, f., sum; leadership; summa imperī, supreme command

summus, –a, –um, highest, most important, greatest; top of, surface of; summum, –ī, n., top

sūmō, –ere, sūmpsī, sūmptus, take, assume

sūmptuōsē, adv., extravagantly

sūmptuōsus, –a, –um, extravagant

super, prep. w. acc., over, upon

superbē, adv., arrogantly

superbus, –a, –um, haughty

superior, –ius, higher, upper, superior; previous

superō, 1, overcome, conquer; surpass

supersum, –esse, –fuī, –futūrus, be left over, remain, survive

superus, –a, –um, upper; as noun, m. pl., gods (above)

supplex, gen. supplicis, begging

supplicātiō, –ōnis, f., thanksgiving

supplicium, –cī, n., thanksgiving; punishment

suprā, adv. and prep. w. acc., above

suprēmus, –a, –um, highest, last

surgō, –ere, surrēxī, surrēctūrus, rise

suscipiō, –ere, –cēpī, –ceptus, undertake, incur

suspendō, –ere, –pendī, –pēnsus, hang; suspēnsus, in suspense

suspīciō, –ōnis, f., suspicion

suspicor, 1, suspect

sustineō, –ēre, –tinuī, –tentus, hold up, keep up or back; endure, withstand, hold out

sustulī, see tollō

suus, –a, –um, his, her, its, their; his own, her own, etc.

Syrācūsae, –ārum, f. pl., Syracuse, a city in Sicily

T

T., abbreviation for Titus

taberna, –ae, f., shop, tavern

tabula, –ae, f., table (of the law); writing tablet

taceō, –ēre, tacuī, tacitus, be silent; tacitus, silent

taciturnitās, –tātis, f., silence

tālis, –e, such

tam, adv., so (with adjectives and adverbs)

tamen, adv., still, nevertheless; however

tamquam, adv., as if

tandem, adv., at last, finally

tangō, –ere, tetigī, tāctus, touch

tantulus, –a, –um, so small

tantum, adv., only

tantus, –a, –um, so great, so large, so much, such

tardē, slowly

tardō, 1, slow up

tardus, –a, –um, slow, late

Tarquinius, –nī, m., Tarquin'ius, Tarquin

Tartarus, –ī, m., Hades

taurus, –ī, m., bull

tēctum, –ī, n., roof, house

tegimentum, –ī, n., cover

tegō, –ere, tēxī, tēctus, cover

tellus, –ūris, f., earth

tēlum, –ī, n., weapon, missile

temere, adv., rashly, without reason

temeritās, –tātis, f., rashness

temperātus, –a, –um, temperate
tempestās, –tātis, *f.,* weather, storm
templum, –ī, *n.,* temple
temptō, 1, test, try, attempt
tempus, temporis, *n.,* time
tenāx, *gen.* **tenācis,** tenacious
tendō, –ere, tetendī, tentus, stretch, go
tenebrae, –ārum, *f. pl.,* darkness
teneō, –ēre, tenuī, tentus, hold, keep, possess; **memoriā teneō,** remember
tenuō, 1, make thin
tepeō, –ēre, —, —, be warm
ter, *adv.,* three times
tergum, –ī, *n.,* back
ternī, –ae, –a, three at a time
terra, –ae, *f.,* land, earth
terreō, –ēre, terruī, territus, scare
terribilis, –e, frightful
terror, –ōris, *m.,* terror
tertius, –a, –um, third
testāmentum, –ī, *n.,* will
testimōnium, –nī, *n.,* testimony, proof
testis, –is, *m.,* witness
testūdō, –dinis, *f.,* turtle, testudo, shed
Teutonī, –ōrum, *m. pl.,* the Teutons
theātrum, –ī, *n.,* theater
Thēbae, –ārum, *f. pl.,* Thebes, *a Greek city*
Thessalia, –ae, *f.,* Thessaly, *part of Greece*
Thrācia, –ae, *f.,* Thrace, *a country north of Greece*
Thrāx, –ācis, *m.,* a Thracian
thronus, –ī, *m.,* throne
Tiberis, –is, *m.,* the Tī′ber river
Tigurīnus, –ī, *m.,* Tĭgurī′nus, *a Helvetian canton; pl.,* the Tĭgurī′nī
timeō, –ēre, timuī, —, fear, be afraid
timidus, –a, –um, timid; **timidē,** *adv.,* timidly
timor, –ōris, *m.,* fear
titulus, –ī, *m.,* title, sign
toga, –ae, *f.,* toga (*cloak*)
tolerābilis, –e, endurable
tollō, –ere, sustulī, sublātus, raise, carry, remove, destroy
tormentum, –ī, *n.,* torture; artillery
torqueō, –ēre, torsī, tortus, twist, turn, torture
torreō, –ēre, torruī, tostus, roast, scorch
tot, *indeclinable adj.,* so many
totidem, *indeclinable adj.,* just as many
tōtus, –a, –um, whole, entire

trabs, trabis, *f.,* beam
trādō, –ere, –didī, –ditus, give *or* hand over, transmit, relate
trādūcō, –ere, –dūxī, –ductus, lead across, win over
trāgula, –ae, *f.,* javelin
trahō, –ere, trāxī, trāctus, draw, drag; take on
trāiciō, –ere, –iēcī, –iectus, strike through
trānō, 1, swim across
tranquillitās, –tātis, *f.,* calm
tranquillus, –a, –um, peaceful
trāns, *prep. w. acc.,* across
trānscendō, –ere, –scendī, —, climb over
trānscurrō, –ere, –currī, –cursūrus, traverse
trānseō, –īre, –iī, –itūrus, cross, pass, go
trānsferō, trānsferre, trānstulī, trānslātus, carry over
trānsfīgō, –ere, –fīxī, –fīxus, pierce through
trānsfodiō, –ere, –fōdī, –fossus, pierce through
trānsiliō, –īre, –siluī, —, jump across
trānsportō, 1, carry over, transport
trānsversus, –a, –um, cross
trecentī, –ae, –a, three hundred
tremor, –ōris, *m.,* shaking
trēs, tria, three
tribūnus, –ī, *m.,* tribune
tribuō, –ere, tribuī, tribūtus, bestow, grant, assign
tribūtum, –ī, *n.,* tax, tribute
trīclīnium, –nī, *n.,* dining room
trīduum, –ī, *n.,* three days
trīgintā, thirty
triplex, *gen.* **triplicis,** threefold, triple
trīstis, –e, sad, severe
trīstitia, –ae, *f.,* sadness
Troia, –ae, *f.,* Troy, *a city in Asia Minor*
Troiānus, –a, –um, Trojan; *as noun, m. pl.,* the Trojans
tū, tuī, you
tuba, –ae, *f.,* trumpet
tueor, tuērī, tūtus, look, guard
tulī, *see* **ferō**
tum, *adv.,* then
tumultus, –ūs, *m.,* uproar
tunc, *adv.,* then
tunica, –ae, *f.,* tunic

turbō, 1, roughen
turbulentus, –a, –um, muddy
turma, –ae, f., troop (of cavalry)
turpis, –e, disgraceful, ugly
turpitūdō, –dinis, f., disgrace
turris, –is, f., tower
Tusculānī, –ōrum, m. pl., the Tus'-
culans, people of Tusculum, a town
in Italy
tūtus, –a, –um, safe
tuus, –a, –um, your, yours (referring
to one person)
tyrannus, –ī, m., tyrant

U

ubi, adv., where; when
ubicumque, adv., wherever
ulcīscor, ulcīscī, ultus, avenge
ūllus, –a, –um, any, anyone
ulterior, –ius, farther
ultimus, –a, –um, last, farthest
ultrīx, gen. ultrīcis, avenging
ultrō, adv., voluntarily, actually
ultus, part. of ulcīscor
umbra, –ae, f., shade, shadow
umquam, adv., ever, at any time
ūnā, adv., at the same time, along
ūnanimus, –a, –um, of one mind, sym-
pathetic
unda, –ae, f., wave
unde, adv., from which (place), by
which
undique, adv., from or on all sides
ūniversus, –a, –um, all (together)
ūnus, –a, –um, one, alone
urbs, urbis, f., city
urgeō, urgēre, ursī, —, press hard
urna, –ae, f., urn
ūrō, –ere, ussī, ustus, burn
usque, adv., up to, continuously, still
ūsus, –ūs, m., use, practice, experience
ut, conj., in order that, that, to, so that;
as, when
uter, utra, utrum, which (of two);
whichever
uterque, utraque, utrumque, each (of
two), both
utī = ut
ūtilis, –e, useful
ūtilitās, –tātis, f., usefulness
ūtor, ūtī, ūsus, use, make use of (w.
abl.)
utrimque, adv., on both sides
uxor, –ōris, f., wife

V

vacō, 1, be uninhabited, have leisure
vacuus, –a, –um, empty, free
vādō, –ere, —, —, go
vadum, –ī, n., ford, shallow place
vagor, 1, wander
valeō, –ēre, valuī, valitūrus, be strong,
be well, be powerful, prevail; imper.,
valē, valēte, farewell
valētūdō, –dinis, f., health; illness
vallēs, –is, f., valley
vāllum, –ī, n., rampart, wall
vānus, –a, –um, empty, false
varius, –a, –um, changing, varying,
various
vās, vāsis, n., vessel, pot
vāstō, 1, destroy, ruin
vāstus, –a, –um, huge
vehemēns, gen. vehementis, vigorous
vehiculum, –ī, n., carriage
vehō, –ere, vexī, vectus, carry; passive,
sail, ride
Veiī, –ōrum, m. pl., Vē′iī, a town in
Italy
vel, conj., or; vel . . . vel, either . . . or
vellus, –eris, n., fleece
vēlō, 1, cover
vēlōcitās, –tātis, f., swiftness
vēlum, –ī, n., sail
velut, velutī, adv., just as, as
vēna, –ae, f., vein
vēnātiō, –ōnis, f., hunting, hunt
vēndō, –ere, –didī, –ditus, sell
venēnum, –ī, n., poison
Venetī, –ōrum, m. pl., the Věn′etī
veniō, –īre, vēnī, ventūrus, come
ventus, –ī, m., wind
Venus, –eris, f., Vēnus, goddess of love
and beauty
verberō, 1, beat, strike
verbum, –ī, n., word; verba faciō,
speak, make a speech
Vercingetorīx, –īgis, m., Vercingetorix
(Versinjet′orix)
vērē, adv., truly
vereor, verērī, veritus, fear, respect
Vergilius, Vergilī, m., Virgil
vergō, –ere, —, —, slope, lie
vēritās, –tātis, f., truth
vērō, adv., in truth, but, however
versicolor, gen. –ōris, of various colors
versor, 1, move about, be engaged, live,
be
versus, –ūs, m., line, verse

vertō, –ere, vertī, versus, turn; *passive,* turn (oneself); *sometimes deponent*

vērus, –a, –um, true

Vespasiānus, –ī, *m.,* Vespasian (Vespā'zhian), *the emperor*

vesper, –erī, *m.,* evening; **vesperī,** in the evening

Vesta, –ae, *f.,* Vesta, *goddess of the hearth*

Vestālis, –e, Vestal, of Vesta

vester, –tra, –trum, your, yours (*referring to two or more persons*)

vēstibulum, –ī, *n.,* entrance

vēstīgium, –gī, *n.,* footprint, foot

vestiō, –īre, –īvī, –ītus, clothe

vestis, –is, *f.,* clothing, clothes, garment

vestītus, –ūs, *m.,* clothing

veterānus, –a, –um, veteran, experienced

vetō, –āre, vetuī, vetitus, forbid

vetus, *gen.* **veteris,** old

vetustus, –a, –um, old, ancient

vexō, 1, disturb

via, –ae, *f.,* way, road, street; journey

viātor, –ōris, *m.,* traveler

vīcēnī, –ae, –a, twenty (each)

vīciēs, *adv.,* twenty times

vīcīnus, –a, –um, neighboring; *as noun, m.,* neighbor

vicis, –is, *f.,* change; **in vicem,** in turn

victima, –ae, *f.,* victim

victor, –ōris, *m.,* victor; *adj.,* victorious

victōria, –ae, *f.,* victory

vīctus, –ūs, *m.,* living, food

vīcus, –ī, *m.,* village

videō, –ēre, vīdī, vīsus, see; *passive,* be seen, seem, seem best

vigil, *gen.* **vigilis,** wakeful

vigilia, –ae, *f.,* watchman, watch (*a fourth part of the night*)

vīgintī, *indeclinable,* twenty

vigor, –ōris, *m.,* vigor

vīlis, –e, cheap, worthless

vīlla, –ae, *f.,* farmhouse, villa

Vīminālis (mōns), –is, *m.,* the Vīm'inal Hill

vincō, –ere, vīcī, victus, conquer, defeat, overcome, win

vinculum, –ī, *n.,* bond, chain

vīnea, –ae, *f.,* grape arbor, shed

vīnētum, –ī, *n.,* vineyard

vīnum, –ī, *n.,* wine

violō, 1, injure

vir, virī, *m.,* man, husband

virgō, –ginis, *f.,* virgin, maiden

virtūs, –tūtis, *f.,* manliness, courage, virtue

vīs, —, *f.,* force, power, violence; *pl.,* **vīrēs, –ium,** strength

vīta, –ae, *f.,* life

vitiōsus, –a, –um, full of faults

vitium, –tī, *n.,* fault

vītō, 1, avoid

vīvō, –ere, vīxī, victus, live

vīvus, –a, –um, alive, living

vix, *adv.,* scarcely, with difficulty

vōbīscum = cum vōbīs

vocō, 1, call, summon, invite, invoke

volō, 1, fly

volō, velle, voluī, —, want, wish, be willing

Volscī, –ōrum, *m. pl.,* the Volscians (Vŏl'shians)

volucris, –cris, *f.,* bird

voluntās, –tātis, *f.,* wish, consent

voluptās, –tātis, *f.,* pleasure

volvō, –ere, volvī, volūtus, roll (up); turn over; *passive,* toss about

vōs, you, *pl. of* **tū**

voveō, –ēre, vōvī, vōtus, vow, promise

vōx, vōcis, *f.,* voice, word, remark, talk

Vulcānus, –ī, *m.,* Vulcan, *god of fire*

vulgus, –ī, *n.,* common people

vulnerō, 1, wound

vulnus, vulneris, *n.,* wound

vultus, –ūs, *m.,* expression, features

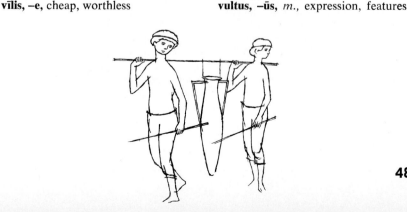

For proper nouns and proper adjectives not given in this vocabulary see the Latin-English Vocabulary or the text.

Verbs of the first conjugation whose parts are regular are indicated by the figure 1.

A

able (be), possum, posse, potuī, —
about, dē, *w. abl.*
accomplice, socius, –cī, *m.*
accomplish, cōnficiō, –ere, –fēcī, –fectus
account (on), *see* on
accustomed (be), cōnsuēscō, –ere, –suēvī, –suētus
achieve, efficiō, –ere, effēcī, effectus
across, trāns, *w. acc.*
add, adiciō, –ere, adiēcī, adiectus
admire, admīror, 1
adopt, adoptō, 1
adorn, ōrnō, 1
after (*conj.*), postquam; *use abl. abs.*
again, iterum
against, contrā, *w. acc.*
agree, cōnsentiō, –īre, –sēnsī, –sēnsus
aid, auxilium, –lī, *n.*
all, omnis, –e; tōtus, –a, –um; **all other,** cēterī, –ae, –a·
allow, licet, –ēre, licuit *or* licitum est
almost, paene
alone, sōlus, –a, –um
already, iam
also, etiam
although, cum; quamquam; *use participle or abl. abs.*
always, semper
among, inter, *w. acc.*
and, et; –que
another, alius, alia, aliud
any(one), ūllus, –a, –um; quis, quid (*after* sī)
appear, appāreō, –ēre, appāruī, appāritūrus
approach (*noun*), adventus, –ūs, *m.;* (*verb*), accēdō, –ere, accessī, accessūrus (*w.* ad); adeō, adīre, adiī, aditūrus; appropinquō, 1 (*w. dat.*)
arena, arēna, –ae, *f.*
arise, orior, orīrī, ortus
arm, armō, 1
arms, arma, –ōrum, *n. pl.*
army, exercitus, –ūs, *m.*
arrival, adventus, –ūs, *m.*
arrive, perveniō, –īre, –vēnī, –ventūrus

art, ars, artis, *f.*
as . . . as possible, quam, *w. superl.;* **as soon as possible,** quam prīmum; **as to,** ut
ask, rogō, 1
at (near), ad, *w. acc.; abl. of time or place*
Athens, Athēnae, –ārum, *f. pl.*
attack, oppugnō, 1; aggredior, aggredī, aggressus
author, auctor, –ōris, *m.*
await, exspectō, 1
away (be), absum, –esse, āfuī, āfutūrus·

B

bad, malus, –a, –um
baggage, impedīmenta, –ōrum, *n. pl.*
bandit, latrō, –ōnis, *m.*
banish, expellō –ere, expulī, expulsus
battle line, aciēs, aciēī, *f.*
be, sum, esse, fuī, futūrus
bear, ferō, ferre, tulī, lātus
beat, superō, 1
beautiful, pulcher, –chra, –chrum
because, *use participle or abl. abs.;* quod, quoniam
become, fīō, fierī, (factus)
before (*adv. and prep.*), ante, *w. acc.*
beg, ōrō, 1; petō, –ere, petīvī, petītus
begin, incipiō, –ere, incēpī, inceptus; **began,** coepī, coeptus
believe, crēdō, –ere, crēdidī, crēditus (*w. dat.*)
besiege, obsideō, –ēre, obsēdī, obsessus
best, optimus, –a, –um
better, melior, melius
between, inter, *w. acc.*
blame, accūsō, 1
book, liber, librī, *m.*
boy, puer, puerī, *m.*
brave, fortis, –e; **bravely,** fortiter
bridge, pōns, pontis, *m.*
bring, ferō, ferre, tulī, lātus; īnferō; **bring together,** condūcō, –ere, –dūxī, –ductus
Britons, Britannī, –ōrum, *m. pl.*
build, exstruō, –ere, exstrūxī, exstrūctus; aedificō, 1

building, aedificium, –cī, *n.*
burn, incendō, –ere, incendī, incēnsus
business, negōtium, –tī, *n.*
but, sed
buy, emō, –ere, ēmī, ēmptus
by, ā, ab, *w. abl.; sometimes abl. alone*

C

call, appellō
camp, castra, –ōrum, *n. pl.*
capture, expugnō, 1; capiō, –ere, cēpī, captus
carry, portō, 1; ferō, ferre, tulī, lātus; **carry on war,** bellum gerō; **carry back,** referō, referre, rettulī, relātus
cause, efficiō, –ere, effēcī, effectus (*w.* ut *and subjunct.*)
cavalry, equitātus, –ūs, *m.;* equitēs, –um, *m. pl.*
certain, a certain (one), quīdam, quaedam, quiddam; **certainly,** certē
chain, vinculum, –ī, *n.*
chance, cōpia, –ae, *f.*
check, sustineō, –ēre, –tinuī, –tentus
children, līberī, –ōrum, *m. pl.*
choose, ēligō, –ere, ēlēgī, ēlēctus; dēligō
circumstance, rēs, reī, *f.*
citadel, arx, arcis, *f.*
citizen, cīvis, cīvis, *m.*
city, urbs, urbis, *f.*
civil, cīvīlis, –e
client, cliēns, –entis, *m.*
close, claudō, –ere, clausī, clausus
collect, cōnferō, cōnferre, contulī, collātus
come, veniō, venīre, vēnī, ventūrus
command (be in), praesum, –esse, –fuī, –futūrus (*w. dat.*)
common people, plēbs, plēbis, *f.*
complete, cōnficiō, –ere, –fēcī, –fectus
conceal, cēlō, 1
concern, cūra, –ae, *f.*
condemn, damnō, 1
condition, condiciō, –ōnis, *f.*
conference, colloquium, –quī, *n.*
conquer, vincō, –ere, vīcī, victus; superō, 1
conspire, coniūrō, 1
consul, cōnsul, –ulis, *m.*
consult, cōnsulō, –ere, –suluī, –sultus
country, patria, –ae, *f.*
courage, virtūs, –tūtis, *f.*
cover, tegō, –ere, tēxī, tēctus
creditor, crēditor, –ōris, *m.*

criticize, accūsō, 1
cross, trānseō, –īre, –iī, –itūrus
crowded together, cōnfertus, –a, –um
cruel, crūdēlis, –e
cruelty, crūdēlitās, –tātis, *f.*
custom, mōs, mōris, *m.*
cut off, interclūdō, –ere, –clūsī, –clūsus

D

daughter, fīlia, –ae, *f.*
day, diēs, diēī, *m.*
dear, cārus, –a, –um
decided (be), placet, –ēre, placuit
decorated, adōrnātus, –a, –um
deed, factum, –ī, *n.*
defeat (*noun*), calamitās, –tātis, *f.;* (*verb*), superō, 1; pellō, –ere, pepulī, pulsus; vincō, –ere, vīcī, victus
defend, dēfendō, –ere, dēfendī, dēfēnsus
defenses, mūnītiō, –ōnis, *f.*
delay, mora, –ae, *f.*
demand, postulō, 1
depart, excēdō, –ere, excessī, excessūrus
departure, exitus, –ūs, *m.;* profectiō, –ōnis, *f.*
desire, cupiō, –ere, cupīvī, cupītus
despair of, dēspērō, 1
destroy, dēleō, –ēre, –ēvī, –ētus
determine, cōnstituō, –ere, –stituī, –stitūtus
die, morior, morī, mortuus
differ, differō, differre, distulī, dīlātus
difficult, difficilis, –e
dinner, cēna, –ae, *f.*
divide, dīvidō, –ere, dīvīsī, dīvīsus
do, faciō, –ere, fēcī, factus; agō, –ere, ēgī, āctus
draw up, īnstruō, –ere, īnstrūxī, īnstrūctus
drive from, expellō, –ere, expulī, expulsus
during, per, *w. acc.*
dutiful, pius, –a, –um
duty, officium, –cī, *n.*

E

each one, quisque, quidque
eager for (be), studeō, –ēre, studuī, — (*w. dat.*)
eagerness, studium, –dī, *n.*
earn, mereō, –ēre, meruī, meritus
earth, terra, –ae, *f.*

easy, facilis, –e; **easily,** facile
elect, creō, 1
elevated, ēditus, –a, –um
embassy, lēgātiō, –ōnis, *f.*
empire, imperium, –rī, *n.*
encourage, cōnfirmō, 1
endure, ferō, ferre, tulī, lātus
enemy (*personal*), inimīcus, –ī, *m.;* (*national*), hostis, –is, *m.*
enjoy, ūtor, ūtī, ūsus (*w. abl.*)
enter, ingredior, ingredī, ingressus
entire, tōtus, –a, –um
entrust, mandō, 1
envoy, lēgātus, –ī, *m.*
envy, invideō, –ēre, invīdī, invīsus (*w. dat.*)
erect, exstruō, –ere, exstrūxī, exstrūctus
escape, fugiō, –ere, fūgī, fugitūrus
establish, cōnstituō, –ere, –stituī, –stitūtus
everything, omne *or* omnia
example, exemplum, –ī, *n.*
excel, praestō, –āre, –stitī, –stitūrus (*w. dat.*)
exclaim, (ex)clāmō, 1

F

fame, fāma, –ae, *f.*
family, familia, –ae, *f.*
famous, clārus, –a, –um
farm, ager, agrī, *m.*
farmer, agricola, –ae, *m.*
farthest, extrēmus, –a, –um; ultimus, –a, –um
father, pater, patris, *m.*
fear, timeō, –ēre, timuī, —; vereor, verērī, veritus
feel, sentiō, –īre, sēnsī, sēnsus
few, paucī, –ae, –a
fierce, ferus, –a, –um
fight, pugnō, 1
find, inveniō, –īre, invēnī, inventus
first, prīmum; **at first,** prīmō
flame, flamma, –ae, *f.*
flee, fugiō, –ere, fūgī, fugitūrus
food, cibus, –ī, *m.*
for (*conj.*), nam; (*prep.*), ad, ob, *w. acc.;* prō, *w. abl.;* **for the purpose** *or* **sake of,** causā *or* grātiā (*preceded by gen.*); *sometimes not expressed*
forest, silva, –ae, *f.*
former (the), ille; **the former . . . the latter,** ille . . . hic
fortify, mūniō, –īre, –īvī, –ītus

fortune, fortūna, –ae, *f.*
free (*adj.*), līber, –era, –erum; (*verb*), līberō, 1
fresh, integer, –gra, –grum
friend, amīcus, –ī; *m.;* **(girl) friend,** amīca, –ae, *f.*
friendly, amīcus, –a, –um
frighten, terreō, –ēre, terruī, territus
frog, rāna, –ae, *f.*
from, ē, ex, ā, ab, dē, *w. abl.;* **from one another,** inter sē
furnish, praebeō, –ēre, –uī, –itus

G

gate, porta, –ae, *f.*
Gaul, Gallia, –ae, *f.;* **Gauls,** Gallī, –ōrum, *m. pl.*
general, dux, ducis, *m.;* lēgātus, –ī, *m.*
get, parō, 1; **get (possession of),** potior, potīrī, potītus (*w. abl.*)
girl, puella, –ae, *f.*
give, dō, dare, dedī, datus
gladiator, gladiātor, –ōris, *m.;* **gladiatorial,** gladiātōrius, –a, –um
go, eō, īre, iī, itūrus; **go out,** ēgredior, ēgredī, ēgressus; exeō
god, deus, –ī, *m.;* **goddess,** dea, –ae, *f.*
gold, aurum, –ī, *n.*
good, bonus, –a, –um
grain, frūmentum, –ī, *n.*
great, magnus, –a, –um; **greater,** maior, maius; **greatest,** maximus, –a, –um; summus, –a, –um; **great deal,** plūrimum; **so great,** tantus, –a, –um
Greece, Graecia, –ae, *f.*
Greek, Graecus, –a, –um
guard, praesidium, –dī, *n.*
guest-friend, hospes, –itis, *m.*

H

happen, accidō, –ere, accidī, —
harbor, portus, –ūs, *m.*
hardly, vix
harsh, dūrus, –a, –um
hasten, properō, 1; contendō, –ere, –tendī, –tentūrus
have, habeō, –ēre, habuī, habitus; **have to,** *use fut. pass. part.*
he, is; hic; ille; *often not expressed*
head, caput, capitis, *n.*
hear, audiō, –īre, –īvī, –ītus
help, auxilium, –lī
her (*poss.*), eius; (*reflex.*), suus, –a, –um; **herself** (*reflex.*), suī

high, altus, −a, −um

hill, mōns, montis, *m.;* collis, −is, *m.*

himself (*reflex.*), suī; (*intens.*), ipse

hinder, impediō, −īre, −īvī, −ītus

his (*poss.*), eius; **his own** (*reflex.*), suus, −a, −um

home, domus, −ūs, *f.*

Horace, Horātius, −tī, *m.*

horse, equus, −ī, *m.*

horseman, eques, equitis, *m.*

hostage, obses, obsidis, *m.*

hour, hōra, −ae, *f.*

house, domus, −ūs, *f.*

how, quō modō; **how much,** quantus, −a, −um

however, autem (*never first word*)

humble, humilis, −e

hurry (on), properō, 1

I

I, ego, meī; *often not expressed*

if, sī

immediately, statim

impel, impellō, −ere, impulī, impulsus

in, in, *w. abl.;* **in order to** *or* **that,** ut (*w. subjunctive*); **in order not to,** nē

influence (*verb*) addūcō, −ere, addūxī, adductus; (*noun*), auctōritās, −tātis, *f.*

inform, (eum) certiōrem faciō, −ere, fēcī, factus; *passive,* certior fīō, fierī

inhabit, incolō, −ere, incoluī, —

inspire, iniciō, −ere, iniēcī, iniectus

into, in, *w. acc.*

investigate, explōrō, 1

invite, vocō, 1

it, is, ea, id; hic, haec, hoc; ille, illa, illud; *often not expressed*

J

journey, iter, itineris, *n.*

K

keep, retineō, −ēre, retinuī, retentus; **keep from,** prohibeō, −ēre, −hibuī, −hibitus

kill, interficiō, −ere, −fēcī, −fectus; caedō, −ere, cecīdī, caesus; occīdō, −ere, occīdī, occīsus

kind, genus, generis, *n.*

kindness, beneficium, −cī, *n.*

king, rēx, rēgis, *m.*

know, sciō, scīre, scīvī, scītus; *perf. of* nōscō, −ere, nōvī, nōtus, *or of* cognōscō, −ere, −nōvī, −nitus

L

large, magnus, −a, −um; **so large,** tantus, −a, −um

later, posteā, post

latter, hic

law, lēx, lēgis, *f.*

lay aside, dēpōnō, −ere, dēposuī, dēpositus

lead, dūcō, −ere, dūxī, ductus; **lead a life,** vītam agō

leader, dux, ducis, *m.;* prīnceps, prīncipis, *m.*

learn, cognōscō, −ere, −nōvī, −nitus

leave (behind), relinquō, −ere, relīquī, relīctus

legion, legiō, −ōnis, *f.*

letter (*epistle*), litterae, −ārum, *f.*

liberty, lībertās, −tātis, *f.*

life, vīta, −ae, *f.*

like, amō, 1

little later, paulō post

live (a life), agō, −ere, ēgī, āctus; (*dwell*), habitō, 1

long, longus, −a, −um; **long** (*adv.*), **(for) a long time,** diū

look at *or* **on,** spectō, 1

lose, āmittō, −ere, āmīsī, āmissus; perdō, −ere, −didī, −ditus

loss, dētrīmentum, −ī, *n.*

love, amor, amōris, *m.*

luxury, lūxuria, −ae, *f.*

M

make, faciō, −ere, fēcī, factus; **make war upon,** bellum īnferō (*w. dat.*)

man, vir, virī, *m.;* homō, hominis, *m.*

many, multī, −ae, −a; **so many,** tot; **very many,** plūrimī, −ae, −a

march, iter, itineris, *n.*

master, dominus, −ī, *m.*

matter, rēs, reī, *f.*

meanwhile, intereā, interim

meet (in battle), congredior, congredī, congressus

mercy, clēmentia, −ae, *f.*

messenger, nūntius, −tī, *m.*

mile, mīlle passūs; *pl.* mīlia passuum

molest, noceō, −ēre, nocuī, nocitūrus (*w. dat.*)

money, pecūnia, −ae, *f.*

month, mēnsis, −is, *m.*

monument, monumentum, −ī, *n.*

more, magis, amplius; *use comparative*

mother, māter, mātris, *f.*

move, moveō, –ēre, mōvī, mōtus; afficiō, –ere, affēcī, affectus
much, multus, –a, –um
must, *use fut. pass. part.*
my, meus, –a, –um

N

name, nōmen, nōminis, *n.*
nature, nātūra, –ae, *f.*
near, ad *w. acc.; (adj.),* propinquus, –a, –um
necessary (it is), oportet, –ēre, oportuit; necesse est
neglect, neglegō, –ere, –lēxī, –lēctus
neighbors, fīnitimī, –ōrum, *m.*
nevertheless, tamen
new, novus, –a, –um
next, proximus, –a, –um
night, nox, noctis, *f.*
no, nūllus, –a, –um; **no longer,** nōn iam
not, nōn, nē (*w. negative volitive and purpose clauses*)
noted, īnsignis, –e; nōtus, –a, –um
nothing, nihil
notice, animadvertō, ere, –vertī, –versus
number, numerus, –ī, *m.*

O

obey, pāreō, –ēre, pāruī, pāritūrus (*w. dat.*)
obstruct, impediō, –īre, –īvī, –ītus
obtain one's request, impetrō, 1
occur, intercēdō, –ere, –cessī, –cessus
often, saepe
old man, senex, senis, *m.*
omen, ōmen, ōminis, *n.*
on, in, *w. abl.;* **on account of,** ob *or* propter, *w. acc.*
one, ūnus, –a, –um
opinion, sententia, –ae, *f.*
oppress, opprimō, –ere, oppressī, oppressus
or, vel
oracle, ōrāculum, –ī, *n.*
order (*noun*), imperium, –rī, *n.;* (*verb*), iubeō, –ēre, iussī, iussus; imperō, 1, *w. dat.;* **in order to** *or* **that,** ut; **in order not to** *or* **that,** nē
other, alius, alia, aliud; **the other,** alter, –a,– um; **others,** *see* **some; all other,** *see* **all**

ought, dēbeō, –ēre, dēbuī, dēbitus; oportet, –ēre, oportuit; *use fut. pass. part.*
our, noster, –tra, –trum
overcome, superō, 1; vincō, –ere, vīcī, victus

P

part, pars, partis, *f.*
pay, pendō, –ere, pependī, pēnsus; **pay the penalty,** poenam dō
peace, pāx, pācis, *f.*
people, populus, –ī, *m.*
permit, licet, –ēre, licuit *or* licitum est; permittō, –ere, –mīsī, –missus
persuade, persuādeō, –ēre, –suāsī, –suāsūrus (*w. dat.*)
place (*noun*), locus, –ī, *m.; pl.* loca, –ōrum, *n.;* (*verb*), pōnō, –ere, posuī, positus; **place in charge,** praeficiō, –ere, –fēcī, –fectus
plan (*noun*), cōnsilium, –lī, *n.;* (*verb*), in animō habeō
please, be pleasing to, placeō, –ēre, placuī, placitūrus (*w. dat.*)
poem, carmen, carminis, *n.*
poet, poēta, –ae, *m.*
Pompey, Pompeius, –peī, *m.*
power, potestās, –tātis, *f.;* imperium, –rī, *n.*
praetor, praetor, –ōris, *m.*
praise, laudō, 1
prefer, mālō, mālle, māluī, ——
prepare, parō, 1
prevent, prohibeō, –ēre, –hibuī, –hibitus
prisoner, captīvus, –ī, *m.*
proceed, prōcēdō, –ere, –cessī, –cessūrus
procession, pompa, –ae, *f.*
promise, polliceor, pollicērī, pollicitus
protection, praesidium, –dī, *n.*
pursue, īnsequor, īnsequī, īnsecūtus
put in charge of, praeficiō, –ere, –fēcī, –fectus

Q

queen, rēgīna, –ae, *f.*
quickly, celeriter

R

read, legō, –ere, lēgī, lēctus
ready, parātus, –a, –um
recall, revocō, 1

receive, accipiō, –ere, accēpī, acceptus; excipiō

recite, recitō, 1

reconnoiter, explōrō, 1

refrain, abstineō, –ēre, –tinuī, –tentus

region, regiō, –ōnis, *f.*

remain, maneō, –ēre, mānsī, mānsūrus

remember, memoriā teneō

repair, reficiō, –ere, refēcī, refectus

reply, respondeō, –ēre, respondī, respōnsus

report (*noun*), nūntius, –tī, *m.;* (*verb*), nūntiō, 1

reserve, reservō, 1

resist, resistō, –ere, restitī, —— (*w. dat.*)

resources, opēs, –um, *f. pl.*

rest (of), reliquus, –a, –um; cēterī, –ae, –a

retire, mē recipiō

return (*verb*), redeō, –īre, rediī, reditūrus; (*noun*), reditus, –ūs, *m.*

revolution, novae rēs, novārum rērum, *f. pl.*

river, flūmen, flūminis, *n.*

road, via, –ae, *f.;* iter, itineris, *n.*

Roman, Rōmānus, –a, –um

rule, regō, –ere, rēxī, rēctus; imperō, 1 (*w. dat.*)

S

safety, salūs, –ūtis, *f.*

sail, nāvigō, 1

sailor, nauta, –ae, *m.*

sake of (for the), causā *or* grātiā (*w. gen. preceding*)

sally, ēruptiō, –ōnis, *f.*

same, īdem, eadem, idem

save, servō, 1

say, dīcō, –ere, dīxī, dictus; inquit (*w. direct quotations*)

scare, terreō, –ēre, terruī, territus

school, lūdus, –ī, *m.*

scout, explōrātor, –ōris, *m.*

sea, mare, maris, *n.*

see, videō, –ēre, vīdī, vīsus

seek, petō, –ere, petīvī, petītus

seem, videor, vidērī, vīsus

seize, capiō, –ere, cēpī, captus; occupō, 1; comprehendō, –ere, –hendī, –hēnsus

select, legō, –ere, lēgī, lēctus; dēligō

senate, senātus, –ūs, *m.*

senator, senātor, –ōris, *m.*

send, mittō, –ere, mīsī, missus; **send out,** dīmittō; **send ahead,** praemittō; **send for,** arcessō, –ere, –īvī, –ītus

set out, proficīscor, proficīscī, profectus; **set on fire,** incendō, –ere, incendī, incēnsus

she, ea; haec; illa; *often not expressed*

shield, scūtum, –ī, *n.*

ship, nāvis, nāvis, *f.*

short, brevis, –e

show (*noun*), mūnus, –eris, *n.;* (*verb*), ostendō, –ere, ostendī, ostentus; dēmōnstrō, 1

sign, signal, signum, –ī, *n.*

sight, cōnspectus, –ūs, *m.*

since, quod, cum, quoniam; *use abl. abs.*

sing, cantō, 1

single one (not a), neque quisquam

sister, soror, –ōris, *f.*

six, sex; **sixty,** sexāgintā

size, magnitūdō, –dinis, *f.*

slave, servus, –ī, *m.*

slavery, servitūs, servitūtis, *f.*

small, parvus, –a, –um

so, ita, tam; **so great** *or* **so large,** tantus, –a, –um; **so that,** ut; **so as not to, so that not,** nē

soldier, mīles, mīlitis, *m.*

some, nōn nūllī, –ae, –a; quīdam, quaedam, quiddam; **some . . . others,** aliī . . . aliī; **some (one),** aliquis

son, fīlius, –lī, *m.*

soon as possible, quam prīmum

speak, dīcō, –ere, dīxī, dictus; loquor, loquī, locūtus; verba faciō

spear, pīlum, –ī, *n.*

spectacle, spectāculum, –ī, *n.*

spend, cōnsūmō, –ere, –sūmpsī, –sūmptus; (*of time*), agō, –ere, ēgī, āctus; **spend the winter,** hiemō, 1

stand, stō, stāre, stetī, stātūrus

start, proficīscor, proficīscī, profectus

state (*noun*), cīvitās, –tātis, *f.;* (*verb*), dīcō, –ere, dīxī, dictus

station, collocō, 1

stop, cōnsistō, –ere, –stitī, –stitūrus

storm, tempestās, –tātis, *f.*

story, fābula, –ae, *f.*

strange, novus, –a, –um

strive, contendō, –ere, –tendī, –tentūrus

struggle, labōrō, 1

succeed, succēdō, –ere, –cessī, –cessus

such great, tantus, –a, –um
summon, vocō, 1; convocō, 1
supplies, commeātus, –ūs, m.
surpass, superō, 1
surrender, trādō, –ere, –didī, –ditus
surround, circumsistō, –ere, –stetī, —
survive, supersum, –esse, –fuī, –futūrus
suspect, suspicor, 1
swiftly, celeriter

T

tablet (of the law), tabula, –ae, f.
talk, loquor, loquī, locūtus
teach, doceō, –ēre, docuī, doctus
teacher, magister, –trī, m.
tell, dīcō, –ere, dīxī, dictus
temple, templum, –ī, n.
tempt, temptō, 1
terrify, terreō, –ēre, terruī, territus
territory, fīnēs, –ium, m. pl.
terror, terror, –ōris, m.
than, quam
that (dem. pron.), ille, illa, illud; is, ea, id
that, in order that, so that (conj.), ut(ī); that . . . not (purpose), nē; (result), ut . . . nōn
their (poss.), eōrum, eārum, eōrum; (reflex.), suus, –a, –um
themselves (reflex.), suī; (intens.), ipsī, –ae, –a
then, tum
they, eī, eae, ea; illī, illae, illa; often not expressed
thing, rēs, reī, f.; often not expressed
think, putō, 1; exīstimō, 1; arbitror, 1
third, tertius, –a, –um
this, hic, haec, hoc; is, ea, id
thousand, mīlle; pl. mīlia
throw, iaciō, –ere, iēcī, iactus; coniciō, –ere, –iēcī, –iectus; throw down, dēiciō, proiciō
time, tempus, temporis, n.
to, ad, in, w. acc.; (purpose), ut
too, quoque; use comparative
top (of), summus, –a, –um
torture, cruciātus, –ūs, m.
toward, ad, w. acc.
tower, turris, –is, f.
town, oppidum, –ī, n.
train, īnstituō, –ere, īnstituī, īnstitūtus
travel, iter faciō
traveler, viātor, –ōris, m.

tribe, gēns, gentis, f.
troops, cōpiae, –ārum, f. pl.
try, cōnor, 1
twenty, vīgintī
two, duo, duae, duo

U

under, sub, w. abl.; under the direction of, dux or prīnceps in abl. abs.
unfriendly, inimīcus, –a, –um
unharmed, incolumis, –e
unless, nisi
unlike, dissimilis, –e
until, dum
unwilling (be), nōlō, nōlle, nōluī, —
urge, hortor, 1; impellō, –ere, impulī, impulsus
use, ūtor, ūtī, ūsus (w. abl.)

V

very, use superlative; very many, plūrimī, –ae, –a
victory, victōria, –ae, f.
villa, vīlla, –ae, f.
village, vīcus, –ī, m.
Virgil, Vergilius, –lī, m.

W

wage war, bellum gerō
wait, exspectō, 1
war, bellum, –ī, n.
warn, moneō, –ēre, monuī, monitus
waste, cōnsūmō, –ere, –sūmpsī, –sūmptus
water, aqua, –ae, f.
wave, unda, –ae, f.
we, nōs; often not expressed
weapons, tēla, –ōrum, n. pl.
wedding, nūptiae, –ārum, f. pl.
weep, fleō, –ēre, flēvī, flētus
well, bene
what (pron.), quis, quid; (adj.), quī, quae, quod
when, ubi; cum; expressed by participle or abl. abs.
which (rel. pron.), quī, quae, quod; which (of two), uter, utra, utrum
who (rel. pron.), quī, quae, quod; (interrog. pron.), quis, quid
whole, tōtus, –a, –um
wholesome, salūbris, –e
why, cūr
willing (be), volō, velle, voluī, —; not be willing, nōlō, nōlle, nōluī, —

win, mereō, –ēre, meruī, meritus
winter, hiems, hiemis, *f.*
wisely, sapienter
wish, cupiō, –ere, –īvī, –ītus; volō, velle, voluī, —; **wish not,** nōlō, nōlle, nōluī, —
with, cum, *w. abl.; sometimes abl. alone*
withdraw, concēdō, –ere, –cessī, –cessūrus; discēdō
without, sine, *w. abl.*
woman, mulier, –eris, *f.;* fēmina, –ae, *f.*
wonder, mīror, 1
word, verbum, –ī, *n.*

worship, colō, –ere, coluī, cultus
worthy, dignus, –a, –um
write, scrībō, –ere, scrīpsī, scrīptus

Y

year, annus, –ī, *m.*
yield, cēdō, –ere, cessī, cessūrus; concēdō
you, tū (*sing.*); vōs (*pl.*); *often not expressed*
young man, iuvenis, –is, *m.*
your, tuus, –a, –um; **yourself** (*reflex.*), tuī
youth, adulēscēns, –entis, *m.*

Bronze statue of a fisherman now in the Naples Museum. He seems to have a bite. Perhaps used as a fountain figure.

493

Roman soldiers in a Roman home. From the motion picture *The Robe*.

Striking picture of the top of the ancient Temple of Bacchus in Baalbek, Syria.

INDEX

Numbers in roman type refer to sections; those in *italic* type to pages containing illustrations.

Pericles, *77*
periphrastic, passive, see **future passive participle**
peristyle, *3, 130*
Perseus and Atlas, 554
personal pronouns, 580
Petra, *255*
Petrarch, 546
Petronius, 527
Phaedrus, 519–522
Philip, 224
Philippides, 135
Phineus, 257
Phocion, 504
Pictūrae Mōbilēs, 198
Pierpont Morgan Library, *354*
place from which, 601, 2
place to which, 219; 600, 3
place where, 601, 14
Plautus, 500
plays, see **Latin plays**
plebeians, 192
Pliny, Younger, 482 ff.; manuscript of, *354;* Elder, 250, 483, 484
Pluto, *45*
Poggio, 547
Pollux, 44
Pompeii, *3, 96, 105, 160, 239, 275, 347, 348, 377, 378, 389*
Pompey, 76, 231
Pont du Gard, *232*
Porsena, 187
Porta Capena, 64
portraits, see **paintings, statues**
Portuguese, 322, 347
possession, dative of, 599, 8; genitive of, 598, 1
possum, conjugation of, 589; idiomatic use, 299; present subjunctive, 90
postquam, with indicative, 97; 605, 2
potior, with ablative, 601, 10
praetorium, *207*
predicate nouns and adjectives, 148; 597, 2
prefixes, see **word studies**
prepositions, ablative wtih, 601, 19; accusative with, 600, 6
present tense, 604, 1–2
procession, *63*
pronouns, declension of, 580 ff.; summary of, 249
Propertius, 518
Propylaea, 101; *57, 58, 60*
Proserpina, *45*
Publilius Syrus, 514
Punic Wars, 217
purpose
    dative of, 159; 599, 2
    with *ad, causā,* or *grātiā,* 142; 611, 2, *Note;* 612

with *quī,* 245; 606, 3
with *quō,* 606, 4
with *ut* (*nē*) and subjunctive, 65, 84; 606, 2
Pygmalion, 556
Pyrrha, *396*

quamquam, with indicative, 605, 2
quantity of syllables, 551
Quem numerum vocas, *146*
quī, declension of, 583
quīdam, 121, 213, 584
quidem, 242
Quintilian, 528, 536
quis (indefinite), 121, 213, 584; (interrogative), declension of, 583
quisque and quisquam, 226, 584
quō, in purpose clauses, 606, 4
quod causal clauses, 606, 16
quoque, 242

ram, *177*
reading in the Latin word order, 7, 14
reading Latin verse, 551
reference, books for, 616
reference, dative of, 159, 591, 3
reflexive pronouns, 581
reflexive use of passive, 609
Regulus, 217
relative pronoun, 583; agreement of, 596, 4; as connective, 218; 596, 4, *c*
relative purpose clauses, 245; 606, 3; with *quō,* 606, 4
religion, 15, 44, 120; *23, 28, 38, 45, 63, 248, 300, 303, 316;* see also **gods, temples**
respect, ablative of, 601, 16
result, subjunctive clauses of, 83, 84; 606, 8; *51;* used as nouns, 136; 606, 9
Réunion Island, *373*
review of syntax, 164
Rhine River, *279*
Rhone River, *198, 201, 202, 226, 242*
Riez, *308*
roads and streets, *39, 40, 212*
Robert, P., *399*
rolls, *14, 104*
Roman Empire, extent of, 250; *32, 33, 37, 56, 62, 89, 92, 100, 106, 121, 142, 151, 159, 176, 182, 183, 193, 195, 207, 212, 219, 224, 225, 230, 232, 233, 234, 235, 250, 252, 255, 259, 263, 283, 286, 289, 291, 293, 296, 301, 303, 304, 308, 309, 312, 315, 327, 334, 335, 343, 384, 408, 409, 433, 452, 494*
Roman Republic, history of, *104, 117, 120, 150, 191, 246, 345*
Romans and Greeks, 152, 167, 495

Rome, the city of, *14, 21, 28, 39, 40, 45, 93, 98, 99, 110, 126, 132, 156, 157, 240, 258, 270, 318, 319, 360, 390, 402, 452; see also* **Forum**
Romulus, 170
rostra, *136, 329*

Sabines, *126*
Sabratha, *219*
Saintes, *204*
St. Peter's, *45, 318, 319*
Salii, 38
Sallust, 512, 536
Sambre, *251*
Sarasota, Fla., *411*
sarcophagus, *68, 69, 246*
Saturn, Temple of, *12, 13, 136*
Scaevola, 187
schools, 82, 95, 491, 537
scribes, *361*
sculpture, *8, 23, 29, 33, 37, 44, 67, 68, 69, 74, 103, 113, 118, 124, 125, 126, 131, 134, 140, 154, 166, 169, 175, 183, 191, 214, 223, 237, 239, 240, 246, 267, 271, 306, 309, 316, 328, 334, 336, 339, 347, 359, 360, 361, 389, 392, 402, 493; see also* **statues**
second conjugation, 586
second declension, adjectives, 571; nouns, 564, 565
Segovia, *250*
semideponent, 587
Senate, Roman, 32; *19, 20*
senators, *369*
Seneca, 526
Senlis, *252*
sentence structure, Latin, 188
separation, ablative of, 232; 601, 1; dative of, 599, 4
Septimius Severus, *371;* Arch of, *12, 13, 19, 339*
sequence of tenses, 71–72, 103, 115; 604, 5; *70*
Servius Tullius, 175
seven wise men, 126
ships, *166, 167, 267, 275, 306, 347, 351, 409*
shrines, *3*
silver, *105, 334*
simul ac, with indicative, 605, 2
Siphnian Treasury, *74*
skeleton, *79*
slaves, 496; *485*
Socrates, 140
soldiers, *20, 123, 139, 150, 183, 188, 191, 215, 223, 232, 237, 239, 246, 260, 267, 325, 328, 339, 345, 494*
Sosii, bookshop of, 21
Sousse, *384*

Spain, *230, 250, 452*
Spanish, 68, 132, 230, 280, 322, 350
Sparta, 127
special verbs, with ablative, 601, 10; with dative, 158; 599, 6
specification (respect), ablative of, 601, 16
spelling helps, see **word studies**
Sphinx of the Naxians, *74*
spina, *391*
Split, *151*
Spurinna, 486
Stābat Māter, 543
stadium, 101; *62, 66, 82, 83*
stamps, *9, 39, 44, 63, 66, 88, 128, 132, 167, 176, 196, 205, 225, 228, 238, 329, 364, 373, 388, 431*
standards, *223, 328, 329*
statues, *viii, 1, 8, 17, 25, 33, 38, 85, 87, 90, 113, 123, 137, 183, 258, 303, 309, 312, 356, 357, 370, 371, 375, 392, 427, 493; see also* **sculpture**
Steuben glass, *393*
Stoa of Attalus, *33, 81*
Stonehenge, *248, 300*
subject, 597, 1; of infinitive, 600, 4
subjunctive endings, *36*
subjunctive mood, 58
  anticipatory clauses, 606, 12
  attraction, 606, 15
  conditions, 607
  cum adversative and causal clauses, 201; 606, 11, *a, b*
  cum clauses, 97; 207; 606, 11
  descriptive relative clauses, 606, 10
  doubting, with verbs of, 258 (n. 1)
  fearing, with verbs of, 344; 606, 7
  hindering, with verbs of, 606, 6
  imperfect, 70
  indirect questions, 115; 606, 13
  noun clauses, 136; 606, 5; 606, 9
  past perfect, 96, 102
  perfect, 102
  present, of first conjugation, 78; of other conjugations, 59; *36;* of *sum* and *possum,* 90
  purpose with *ut* (*utī*) and *nē,* 65; 606, 2; with *quī,* 245; 606, 3; with *quō,* 606, 4
  quod causal clauses, 606, 16
  result and purpose compared, 84
  result with *ut* and *ut nōn,* 83; 606, 8–9
  subordinate clauses in indirect discourse, 606, 14
  substantive clauses, 136; 606, 5; 606, 9
  volitive, 60; 606, 1
  volitive noun clauses, 136; 606, 5
subordinate clauses, in indirect discourse, 606, 14

503